Another Innovative Product from the Wiley CPA Examination Review

The Definitive Resource in Preparation for the CPA Exam:

WILEY CPA EXAMINATION REVIEW

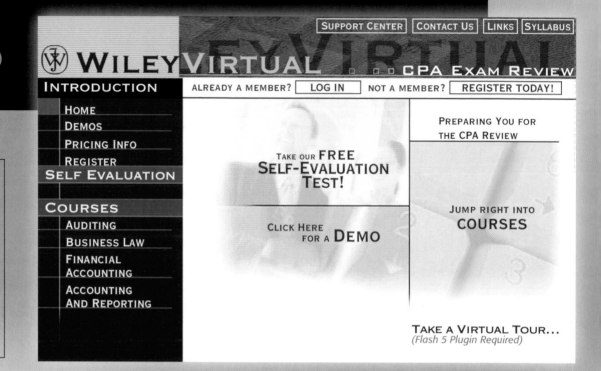

The **Wiley Virtual CPA Examination Review** (www.wileyvirtual.com) is an exciting, new multimedia, fully online interactive CPA Review course that combines first-rate CPA review material with unmatched teaching technology. All subscribers to **Wiley Virtual CPA Examination Review** enjoy:

- Convenience, flexibility, and freedom to study anywhere, any time
- Full control of learning and study pace
- Top-quality material based on the respected Wiley CPA Review Books

- Unlimited access 24 hours a day, 7 days a week
- High-quality product at a very affordable price

- A time-tested plan for organizing study and taking the exam
- State-of-the-art learning technology
- Unlimited practice on a wide variety of problems and question types

Wiley Virtual Benefits include:

- Over 3,900 interactive practice questions including multiple choice, essays, and OOAFs
- Diagnostic exam so that you assess your strengths and weaknesses
- Fully interactive practice exams with full correct and incorrect answer explanations
- Simulates a real exam from start to finish
- State-of-the-art video lectures
- Glossary of terms and key ratios

- Weekly newsletter chock full of helpful hints and study tips
- Course syllabus to help you organize your study attack plan
- Expert-monitored discussion forum
- Tips and techniques for passing the CPA exam
- A motivational video on passing the CPA exam, including study strategies and approaches

- Tools for gauging progress and learning
- Improved learning through video, audio, and visual aids
- User-friendly features like hot links to related and relevant Web sites, a built-in calculator, and printing function
- High-quality audio in a Web-based multimedia format, as well as on-screen graphics such as charts, graphs, and slides of bulleted text for ease of learning

For more information, call 1-877-762-2974 or Visit our Web site at www.wileyvirtual.com

The Next Generation of CPA Review for the Net Generation!

WILEY
CPA
Examination Review

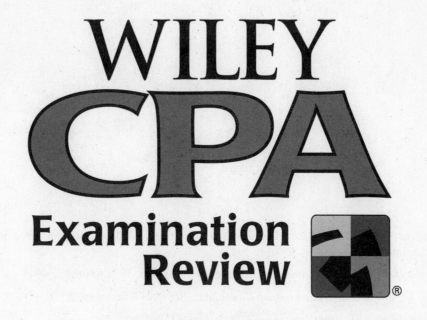

2003

Business Law and Professional Responsibilities

O. Ray Whittington, CPA, PhD   **Patrick R. Delaney,** CPA, PhD

John Wiley & Sons, Inc.

CONTENTS

Regulation

+ federal taxation
for (i) individual
(ii) transactions in Property
(iii) Partnership
(iv) Corporate
(v) Gift and Estates

[1] As explained in Chapter 1, this book is organized into 15 modules (manageable study units). The numbering of the modules commences with number 7 to correspond with the numbering system used in our two-volume set.

PREFACE

Passing the CPA exam upon your first attempt is possible! The *Wiley CPA Examination Review* preparation materials provide you with the necessary materials (visit our website at www.wiley.com/cpa for more information). It's up to you to add the hard work and commitment. Together we can beat the first-time pass rate of less than 20%. All Wiley CPA products are continuously updated to provide you with the most comprehensive and complete knowledge base. Choose your products from the Wiley preparation materials and you can proceed confidently. You can select support materials that are exam-based and user-friendly. You can select products that will help you pass!

Remaining current is one of the keys to examination success. Here is a list of what's new in this edition of the *Wiley CPA Examination Review Business Law and Professional Responsibilities* **text.**

- The latest AICPA Content Specification Outline for Business Law and Professional Responsibilities
- Discussion of the newly designed Objective Answer Sheet with complete instructions on how to complete
- Coverage of new legislation, including the Sarbanes-Oxley Act of 2002
- Revisions to the AICPA Code of Professional Conduct and Interpretations, especially in the areas of

    - CPA Independence
    - Integrity and Objectivity
    - Contingent Fees
    - Acts Discreditable
    - Form of Organization and Name

The objective of this work is to provide you with the knowledge to pass the Business Law and Professional Responsibilities portion of the Uniform Certified Public Accounting (CPA) Exam. The text is divided up into fifteen areas of study called modules. Each module contains written text with discussion, examples, and demonstrations of the key exam concepts. Following each text area, actual American Institute of Certified Public Accountants (AICPA) unofficial questions and answers are presented to test your knowledge. We are indebted to the AICPA for permission to reproduce and adapt examination materials from past examinations. Author constructed questions are provided for new areas or areas that require updating. All author constructed questions are modeled after AICPA question formats. The multiple-choice questions are grouped into topical areas, giving candidates a chance to assess their areas of strength and weakness. Selection and inclusion of topical content is based upon current AICPA Content Specification Outlines. Only testable topics are presented. If the CPA exam does not test it, this text does not present it.

The CPA exam is one of the toughest exams you will ever take. It will not be easy. But if you follow our guidelines and focus on your goal, you will be thrilled with what you can accomplish.

Ray Whittington
November 2002

**Don't forget to visit our website at www.wiley.com/cpa
for supplements and updates.**

ABOUT THE AUTHORS

Patrick R. Delaney was the Arthur Andersen LLP Alumni Professor of Accountancy and Department Chair at Northern Illinois University. He received his PhD in Accountancy from the University of Illinois. He had public accounting experience with Arthur Andersen LLP and was coauthor of *GAAP: Interpretation and Application*, also published by John Wiley & Sons, Inc. He served as Vice President and a member of the Illinois CPA Society's Board of Directors, and was Chairman of its Accounting Principles Committee; was a past president of the Rockford Chapter, Institute of Management Accountants; and had served on numerous other professional committees. He was a member of the American Accounting Association, American Institute of Certified Public Accountants, and Institute of Management Accountants. Professor Delaney was published in *The Accounting Review* and was a recipient of the Illinois CPA Society's Outstanding Educator Award, NIU's Excellence in Teaching Award, and Lewis University's Distinguished Alumnus Award. He was involved in NIU's CPA Review Course as director and instructor.

Ray Whittington, PhD, CPA, CMA, CIA, is the Ledger & Quill Director of the School of Accountancy at DePaul University. Prior to joining the faculty at DePaul, Professor Whittington was the Director of Accountancy at San Diego State University. From 1989 through 1991, he was the Director of Auditing Research for the American Institute of Certified Public Accountants (AICPA), and he previously was on the audit staff of KPMG. He previously served as a member of the Auditing Standards Board of the AICPA and as a member of the Accounting and Review Services Committee and the Board of Regents of the Institute of Internal Auditors. Professor Whittington has published numerous textbooks, articles, monographs, and continuing education courses.

ABOUT THE CONTRIBUTORS

Duane R. Lambert, JD, MBA, CPA, is a Professor of Business Administration at California State University, Hayward, where he teaches courses in Business Law and Accounting. He also has been, on different occasions, a Visiting Lecturer and Visiting Professor at the University of California, Berkeley. Professor Lambert has "Big Five" experience and also has several years experience teaching CPA review courses and helping examinees prepare successfully for the CPA examination. He wrote and revised the Business Law Modules. He also prepared answer explanations for the multiple-choice questions and other objective questions.

Susan Smith, MA, CAS (English), CPA, Garvey International, Inc. Ms. Smith taught rhetoric and technical writing at Northern Illinois University. Ms. Smith prepared material for "Improving Your Writing" in Chapter 3.

1 BEGINNING YOUR CPA REVIEW PROGRAM

To maximize the efficiency of your review program, begin by studying (not merely reading) this chapter and the next three chapters of this volume. They have been carefully organized and written to provide you with important information to assist you in successfully completing the Business Law and Professional Responsibilities section of the CPA exam. Beyond providing a comprehensive outline to help you organize the material tested on the Business Law and Professional Responsibilities exam, Chapter 1 will assist you in organizing a study program to prepare for the Business Law and Professional Responsibilities exam. Self-discipline throughout your study program is essential.

GENERAL COMMENTS ON THE EXAMINATION

Successful completion of the Business Law and Professional Responsibilities section of the CPA Examination is an attainable goal. Keep this point foremost in your mind as you study the first four chapters in this volume and develop your study plan.

Purpose of the Examination[1]

The CPA examination is designed to measure the wide range of knowledge and skills that entry-level CPAs are expected to possess. The examination assesses candidates' knowledge and skills at three different levels of increasing difficulty.

1. Understanding--The ability to recognize or recall learned materials and grasp the meaning.
2. Application--The ability to use learned materials in new situations.
3. Evaluation--The ability to draw conclusions, make decisions, and communicate judgments.

Presently, at least 60% of each examination section assesses candidates' knowledge and skills at the application and evaluation levels. As the majority of the exam is testing at these higher levels of comprehension, **it is crucial that candidates know the material rather than merely being familiar with the material**.

The CPA examination is one of many screening devices to assure the competence of those licensed to perform the attest function and to render professional accounting services. Other screening devices include educational requirements, ethics examinations, and work experience.

---

[1] The following general comments are largely adapted from ***Information for Uniform CPA Examination Candidates,*** *published by the American Institute of Certified Public Accountants.* ***Information for Uniform CPA Examination Candidates*** *is usually sent to CPA candidates by their State Board of Accountancy as they apply to sit for the CPA examination. If you will not be immediately applying to your State Board of Accountancy to sit for the exam, you may purchase the latest edition by contacting the AICPA order department at 888-777-7077. You can find some of the information on the web at www.aicpa.org/edu/index.htm.*

The examination appears to test the material covered in accounting programs of the better business schools. It also appears to be based upon the body of knowledge essential for the practice of public accounting and the audit of a medium-sized client. Since the examination is primarily a textbook or academic examination, you should plan on taking it as soon as possible after completing your undergraduate accounting education.

Examination Content

Guidance concerning topical content of the CPA examination in Business Law and Professional Responsibilities can be found in a document prepared by the Board of Examiners of the AICPA entitled *Content Specification Outlines for the Uniform Certified Public Accountant Examination*. We have included the content outline for Business Law and Professional Responsibilities at the beginning of Chapter 5. Although the exam is now nondisclosed, the outline should be used as an indication of the topics' relative importance on past exams.

The Board's objective in preparing this detailed listing of topics tested on the exam is to help "in assuring the continuing validity and reliability of the Uniform CPA Examination." These outlines are an excellent source of guidance concerning the areas and the emphasis to be given each area on future exams.

The AICPA Board of Examiners issued revised Business Law and Professional Responsibilities Content Specification Outlines in May 2000. These are provided to each candidate in *Information for Uniform CPA Examination Candidates* along with the examination application, or may be purchased by contacting the AICPA order department at 888-777-7077.

New accounting and auditing pronouncements, including those in the governmental and not-for-profit areas, are tested six months after the pronouncement's *effective* date. If early application is permitted, a pronouncement is tested six months after the *issuance* date; candidates are responsible for the old pronouncement also until it is superseded. The exam covers the Internal Revenue Code and federal tax regulations in effect six months before the date of the exam. For the Business Law and Professional Responsibilities section, federal laws are tested six months following their *effective* date and of uniform acts one year after their adoption by a simple majority of jurisdictions. This section deals with federal and widely adopted uniform laws. If there is no federal or uniform law on a topic, the questions are intended to test knowledge of the law of the majority of jurisdictions. Professional ethics questions are based on the AICPA *Code of Professional Conduct* because it is national in its application, whereas codes of other organizations and jurisdictions may be limited in their application. The AICPA posts content changes regularly on its Internet site. The address is www.aicpa.org.

Nondisclosure of Examination Questions and Answers

As of May 1996, the Uniform CPA Examination became nondisclosed. For each exam section, candidates are required to sign a *Statement of Confidentiality*, which states that they will not divulge the nature and content of any exam question. Candidates no longer retain or receive their question booklets after the exam. Complete examination questions and answers are no longer published. The AICPA does however, periodically release selected questions and answers. The released questions are no longer used on actual exams, but they are representative of questions appearing on future exams.

Schedule of Examinations

The 2-day Uniform Certified Public Accountant Examination is given twice a year, usually on the first consecutive Wednesday-Thursday in May and November. The subject and time schedules are

CPA EXAM SCHEDULE AND FORMAT

SECTION	TIME PERIOD		FORMAT MC	OOAF	FRE/P
Business Law and Professional Responsibilities	Wed.	9:00 - Noon	50-60%	20-30%	20-30%
Auditing	Wed.	1:30 - 6:00	50-60%	20-30%	20-30%
Accounting and Reporting (Taxation; Managerial; and Governmental and Not-for-Profit Organizations)	Thurs.	8:30 - Noon	50-60%	40-50%	--
Financial Accounting and Reporting (Business Enterprises)	Thurs.	1:30 - 6:00	50-60%	20-30%	20-30%
	TOTAL	15.5 Hours			
MC = Multiple-Choice; OOAF = Other Objective Answer Formats; FRE/P = Free Response Essay/Problem					

The above schedule presents three basic questions formats.

1. Multiple-Choice
2. Other Objective Answer Formats
3. Free Response Essay/Problem

See the beginning of Chapter 5 for a table of contents of question formats by module and topic. The exact number of multiple-choice, other objective answer format, and essay questions that appear on the exam is unknown. Approximately 10 to 15% of the multiple-choice questions are considered to be "pretest" questions. Pretesting means that some questions are not counted in the tabulation of the candidate's final grade. The pretest questions are used to help the AICPA develop future examination test question databases.

The AICPA no longer lists suggested time limits. In order to avoid the possibility of running out of time, it is imperative that today's candidate utilize some form of time management. See Chapter 4, Allocation of Time, for suggested time management techniques.

The following chart lists upcoming examination administrations and the corresponding uniform mailing dates (dates grades will be mailed by the state boards).

Examination Administration	*Uniform Mailing Date*
May 7 and 8, 2003	August 4, 2003
November 5 and 6, 2003	February 2, 2004

In 2004, the AICPA plans to begin using a computerized Uniform CPA Examination. As of the publication date of this text, very little information has been released. We will post more detailed information as it becomes available on the CPA Examination Review Wiley website at www.wiley.com/cpa.

State Boards of Accountancy

The right to practice public accounting as a CPA is governed by individual state statutes. While some rules regarding the practice of public accounting vary from state to state, all State Boards of Accountancy use the Uniform CPA Examination and AICPA advisory grading service as one of the requirements to practice public accounting. Every candidate should contact the applicable State Board of Accountancy to determine the requirements to sit for the exam (e.g., education, filing dates, references, and fees). A frequent problem candidates encounter is failure to apply by the deadline. **Apply to sit for the examination early. Also, you should use extreme care in filling out the application and mailing the required materials to your State Board of Accountancy.** If possible, have a friend review your completed application before mailing with check, photo, etc. Candidates can be turned down for a particular CPA examination simply because of minor technical details that were overlooked (check not signed, photo not enclosed, question not answered on application, etc.). **Because of the very high volume of applications received in the more populous states, the administrative staff does not have time to call or write to correct minor details and will simply reject your application.** This can be extremely disappointing particularly after spending many hours preparing to sit for a particular exam.

The various state boards, their addresses, and telephone numbers are listed on the following page. Be sure to inquire of your state board for specific and current requirements.

It is possible for candidates to sit for the examination in another state as an out-of-state candidate. Candidates desiring to do so should contact the State Board of Accountancy in their home state.

ATTRIBUTES OF EXAMINATION SUCCESS

Your primary objective in preparing for the Business Law and Professional Responsibilities section is to pass. Other objectives such as learning new and reviewing old material should be considered secondary. The six attributes of examination success discussed below are **essential**. You should study the attributes and work toward achieving/developing each of them **before** taking the examination.

1. **Knowledge of Material**

Two points are relevant to "knowledge of material" as an attribute of examination success. **First,** there is a distinct difference between being familiar with material and knowing the material. Frequently candidates confuse familiarity with knowledge. Can you remember when you just could not answer an examination question or did poorly on an examination, but maintained to yourself or your instructor that you knew the material? You probably were only familiar with the material. On the CPA examination, familiarity is insufficient; you must know the material. Knowledgeable discussion of the material is required on the CPA examination. This text contains outlines of the topical areas in business law. Return to the original material (e.g., your business law textbook, UCC Code Sections, etc.) only if the outlines do

STATE BOARD ADDRESS

	State Board Address	Telephone #
AK	Dept. of Comm. and Econ. Dev. Div. of Occ. Licensing • P.O. Box 110806 • Juneau, AK • 99811-0806	(907) 465-3811
AL	P.O. Box 300375 • Montgomery, AL • 36130-0375	(334) 242-5700
AR	101 E. Capitol • STE 430 • Little Rock, AR • 72201	(501) 682-1520
AZ	3877 N. 7th St. • STE 106 • Phoenix, AZ • 85014	(602) 255-3648
CA	2000 Evergreen St. • STE 250 • Sacramento, CA • 95815-3832	(916) 263-3680
CO	1560 Broadway • STE 1340 • Denver, CO • 80202	(303) 894-7800
CT	Secretary of State • 30 Trinity Street • PO Box 150470 • Hartford, CT • 06115	(860) 509-6179
DC	Dept. of Consumer & Reg. Aff., Rm. 7200 • 941 North Capital St., NE, 7th Fl. • Washington, DC • 20002	(202) 442-4461
DE	Cannon Bldg. • STE 203 • 861 Silver Lake Blvd. • Dover, DE • 19904	(302) 739-4522
FL	240 NW 76 Drive • STE A • Gainesville, FL • 32607	(352) 333-2500
GA	237 Coliseum Drive • Macon, GA • 31217-3858	(478) 207-1400
GU	GCIC Building • 414 W. Soledad Ave. • STE 508 • Hagatua, Guam • 96910-5014	(671) 477-1050
HI	Dept. of Commerce & Consumer Affairs • P.O. Box 3469 • Honolulu, HI • 96801-3469	(808) 586-2696
IA	1918 S.E. Hulsizer Ave. • Ankeny, IA • 50021-3941	(515) 281-4126
ID	P.O. Box 83720 • Boise, ID • 83720-0002	(208) 334-2490
IL	505 E. Green St. • Room 216 • Champaign, IL • 61820-5723	(217) 333-1565
IN	Indiana Prof. Licensing Agc., Indiana Gov. Ctr. S. • 302 W. Washington St. Rm E034 • Indianapolis, IN • 46204-2246	(317) 232-5987
KS	Landon State Office Building • 900 S.W. Jackson Street • STE 556 • Topeka, KS • 66612-1239	(785) 296-2162
KY	332 W. Broadway • STE 310 • Louisville, KY • 40202-2115	(502) 595-3037
LA	601 Poydras St. • STE 1770 • New Orleans, LA • 70139	(504) 566-1244
MA	239 Causeway St. • STE 450 • Boston, MA • 02114	(617) 727-1806
MD	500 N. Calvert St. • Room 308 • Baltimore, MD • 21202-3651	(410) 333-6322
ME	Dept. of Prof. & Fin. Reg. Div. of Lic. & Reg. • #35 State House Station • Augusta, ME • 04333-0035	(207) 624-8603
MI	Dept. of Consumer & Industry Services • P.O. Box 30018 • Lansing, MI • 48909-7518	(517) 241-9249
MN	85 E. 7th Pl. • STE 125 • St. Paul, MN • 55101	(651) 296-7938
MO	P.O. Box 613 • Jefferson City, MO • 65102-0613	(573) 751-0012
MS	653 N. State St. • Jackson, MS • 39202-3304	(601) 354-7320
MT	301 S. Park • P.O. Box 200513 • Helena, MT • 59620-0513	(406) 841-2389
NC	1101 Oberlin Rd. • STE 104 • P.O. Box 12827 • Raleigh, NC • 27605-2827	(919) 733-4222
ND	2701 S. Columbia Rd. • Grand Forks, ND • 58201-6029	(701) 775-7100
NE	P.O. Box 94725 • Lincoln, NE • 68509-4725	(402) 471-3595
NH	6 Chenell Drive • STE 220 • Concord, NH • 03301	(603) 271-3286
NJ	124 Halsey St., 6th floor • P.O. Box 45000 • Newark, NJ • 07101	(973) 504-6380
NM	1650 University N.E. • STE 400A • Albuquerque, NM • 87102	(505) 841-9108
NV	200 S. Virginia St. • STE 670 • Reno, NV • 89501-2408	(775) 786-0231
NY	State Education Dept. Div. of Professional Licensing Services • 89 Washington Ave • Albany, NY • 12234-1000	(518) 474-3817 ext. 160
OH	77 S. High St. • 18th Flr. • Columbus, OH • 43266-0301	(614) 466-4135
OK	4545 Lincoln Blvd. • STE 165 • Oklahoma City, OK • 73105-3413	(405) 521-2397
OR	3218 Pringle Rd SE #110 • Salem, OR • 97302-6307	(503) 378-4181
PA	124 Pine St., 1st Fl. • Harrisburg, PA • 17101-2649	(717) 783-1404
PR	Box 3271 • Old San Juan Station • San Juan, Puerto Rico • 00904-3271	(787) 722-4816
RI	233 Richmond St. • STE 236 • Providence, RI • 02903-4236	(401) 222-3185
SC	110 Centerview Drive – Kingstree Building • P.O. Box 11329 • Columbia, SC • 29211-1329	(803) 896-4492
SD	301 E. 14th St. • STE 200 • Sioux Falls, SD • 57104-5022	(605) 367-5770
TN	500 James Robertson Prkwy. • 2nd Flr. • Nashville, TN • 37243-1141	(615) 741-2550
TX	333 Guadalupe • Tower 3 • STE 900 • Austin, TX • 78701-3900	(512) 305-7800
UT	P.O. Box 146741 • Salt Lake City, UT • 84114-6741	(801) 530-6720
VA	3600 West Broad Street • Richmond, VA • 23230-4917	(804) 367-8507
VI	Dept. of Licensing & Consumer Affairs • Office of Boards and Commissions Golden Rock Shopping Center • Christiansted • St. Croix, VI • 00822	(340) 773-4305
VT	Office of Professional Regulation • 26 Terrace Street, Drawer 09 • Montpelier, VT • 05609-1106	(802) 828-2191
WA	P.O. Box 9131 • Olympia, WA • 98507-9131	(360) 753-2585
WI	1400 E. Washington Ave. • P.O. Box 8935 • Madison, WI • 53708-8935	(608) 266-5511
WV	200 L & S Bldg • 812 Quarrier St. • Charleston, WV • 25301-2695	(304) 558-3557
WY	2020 Carey Ave. • Cheyenne, WY • 82002-0610	(307) 777-7551

NOTE: The publisher does not assume responsibility for errors in the above information. You should request information concerning requirements in your state at least six months in advance of the exam dates.

not reinforce material you already know. **Second,** the Business Law and Professional Responsibilities exam tests a literally overwhelming amount of material at a rigorous level. **Furthermore,** as noted earlier, the CPA exam will test new material, sometimes as early as six months after issuance. In other words, you are not only responsible for material you learned in your business law course(s), but also for all new developments in business law.

2. **Commitment to Exam Preparation**

    Your preparation for the CPA exam should begin at least four months prior to your scheduled exam date. Over the course of your preparation, you will experience many peaks and valleys. There will be days when you feel completely prepared and there will also be days when you feel totally overwhelmed. This is not unusual and, in fact, should be expected.

    The CPA exam is a very difficult and challenging exam. How many times in your college career did you study months for an exam? Probably not too many. Therefore, candidates need to remain focused on the objective--succeeding on the CPA exam.

    Develop a personal study plan so that you are reviewing material daily. Of course, you should schedule an occasional study break to help you relax, but don't schedule too many breaks. Candidates who dedicate themselves to studying have a much greater chance of going through this process one time. On the other hand, a lack of focus and piecemeal preparation will only extend the process over several exams.

3. **Solutions Approach**

    The solutions approach is a systematic approach to solving the questions found on the CPA examination. Many candidates know the material fairly well when they sit for the CPA exam, but they do not know how to take the examination. Candidates generally neither work nor answer questions efficiently in terms of time or grades. The solutions approach permits you to avoid drawing "blanks" on CPA exam questions; using the solutions approach coupled with grader orientation (see below) allows you to pick up a sizable number of points on questions testing material with which you are not familiar. Chapter 3 outlines the solutions approach for multiple-choice, other objective format and essay questions. Example questions are worked as well as explained.

4. **Grader Orientation**

    Your score on each section of the exam is determined by the sum of points assigned to individual questions. Thus, you must attempt to maximize your points on each individual question. The name of the game is to satisfy the grader, as s/he is the one who awards you points. Your answer and the grading guide (which conforms closely to the unofficial answer) are the basis for the assignment of points.

    This text helps you develop grader orientation by analyzing AICPA grading procedures and grading guides (this is explained further in Chapter 2). The authors believe that the solutions approach and grader orientation, properly developed, are worth at least 10 to 15 points on each section to most candidates.

5. **Examination Strategy**

    Prior to sitting for the examination, it is important to develop an examination strategy, i.e., a preliminary inventory of the questions, the order in which to work questions, etc. Your ability to cope successfully with 3 hours of examination can be improved by

    a. Recognizing the importance and usefulness of an examination strategy
    b. Using Chapter 4 "Taking the Examination" and previous examination experience to develop a "personal strategy" for the exam
    c. Testing your "personal strategy" on previous CPA questions under examination conditions (using no reference material and with a time limit)

6. **Examination Confidence**

    You need confidence to endure the physical and mental demands of 3 hours of test-taking under tremendous pressure. Examination confidence results from proper preparation for the exam which includes mastering the first four attributes of examination success. Examination confidence is necessary to enable you to overcome the initial frustration with questions for which you may not be specifically prepared.

    This study manual, when properly used, contributes to your examination confidence. Build confidence by completing the questions contained herein.

Common Candidate Mistakes

The CPA Exam is a formidable hurdle in your accounting career. With a first-time pass rate of less than 20%, the level of difficulty is obvious. The good news, though, is that about 20% of all candidates (first-time and re-exam) sitting for each examination eventually pass. The authors believe that the first-time pass rate could be higher if candidates would be more careful. Seven common mistakes that many candidates make are

1. Failure to understand the exam question requirements
2. Misunderstanding the supporting text of the problem
3. Lack of knowledge of material tested, especially recently issued pronouncements
4. Inability to apply the solutions approach
5. Lack of an exam strategy (e.g., allocation of time)
6. Sloppiness and computational errors
7. Failure to proofread and edit

These mistakes are not mutually exclusive. Candidates may commit one or more of the above items. Remind yourself that when you decrease the number of common mistakes, you increase your chances of successfully becoming a CPA. Take the time to read carefully the exam question requirements. Don't jump into a quick start, only to later find out that you didn't understand what information the examiners were asking for. Read slowly and carefully. Take time to recall your knowledge. Respond to the question asked. Apply an exam strategy such as allocating your time among all question formats. Don't spend too much time on the multiple-choice questions, leaving no time to spend on preparing your essay responses. Write neatly and label all answer sections. Upon completion of the essays, proofread and edit your answer. Answer questions quickly but precisely, avoid common mistakes, and increase your score.

PURPOSE AND ORGANIZATION OF THIS REVIEW TEXTBOOK

This book is designed to help you prepare adequately for the Business Law and Professional Responsibilities examination. There is no easy way to prepare for the successful completion of the CPA Examination; however, through the use of this manual, your approach will be systematic and logical.

The objective of this book is to provide study materials supportive to CPA candidates. While no guarantees are made concerning the success of those using this text, this book promotes efficient preparation by

1. Explaining how to "**satisfy the grader**" through analysis of examination grading and illustration of the solutions approach
2. **Defining areas tested** through the use of the content specification outlines described. Note that predictions of future exams are not made. You should prepare yourself for all possible topics rather than gambling on the appearance of certain questions.
3. **Organizing your study program** by comprehensively outlining all of the subject matter tested on the examination in 15 easy-to-use study modules. Each study module is a manageable task which facilitates your exam preparation. Turn to Chapter 5 and peruse the contents to get a feel for the organization of this book.
4. **Providing CPA candidates with previous examination questions** organized by topic (e.g., contracts, commercial paper, etc.) Questions have also been developed for new areas.
5. **Explaining the AICPA unofficial answers** to the examination questions included in this text. The AICPA publishes unofficial answers for all questions from exams administered prior to 1996 and for any released questions from exams administered on or after May 1996. However, no explanation is made of the approach that should have been applied to the examination questions to obtain these unofficial answers. Relatedly, the AICPA unofficial answers to multiple-choice questions provide no justification and/or explanation.

As you read the next few paragraphs which describe the contents of this book, flip through the chapters to gain a general familiarity with the book's organization and contents. Chapters 2, 3, and 4 are to help you "satisfy the grader."

Chapter 2   Examination Grading and Grader Orientation
Chapter 3   The Solutions Approach
Chapter 4   Taking the Examination

Chapters 2, 3, and 4 contain material that should be kept in mind throughout your study program. Refer back to them frequently. Reread them for a final time just before you sit for the exam.

Chapter 5 (Business Law and Professional Responsibilities Modules) contains

1. AICPA Content Specification Outlines of material tested on the Business Law and Professional Responsibilities examination

2. Multiple-choice questions
3. Other objective questions
4. Essay questions
5. AICPA unofficial answers with the author's explanations for the multiple-choice questions
6. AICPA unofficial answers with the author's explanations for the other objective questions
7. AICPA unofficial answers prefaced by the author's answer outlines for the essay questions

Also included at the end of this text is a complete Sample Business Law and Professional Responsibilities Examination. The selection of multiple-choice, other objective format, and essays was based on a statistical analysis of recent exams. The sample exam is included to enable candidates to gain experience in taking a "realistic" exam. While studying the modules, the candidate can become accustomed to concentrating on fairly narrow topics. By working through the sample examination near the end of their study programs, candidates will be better prepared for taking the actual examination.

Other Textbooks

This text is a comprehensive compilation of study guides and outlines; it should not be necessary to supplement them with accounting textbooks and other materials for most topics. You probably already have a business law textbook. In such a case, you must make the decision whether to replace it and trade familiarity (including notes therein, etc.), with the cost and inconvenience of obtaining the newer text containing a more updated presentation.

Before spending time and money acquiring a new book, begin your study program with *CPA EXAMINATION REVIEW: BUSINESS LAW and PROFESSIONAL RESPONSIBILITIES* to determine your need for a supplemental text.

Ordering Other Textual Materials

If you want to order AICPA materials, locate an AICPA educator member to order your materials, since educator members are entitled to a 30% discount and may place telephone orders. The backlog at the order department is substantial; telephone orders decrease delivery time.

AICPA
   Telephone: 888-777-7077

Address: Order Department
American Institute of Certified
Public Accountants
P.O. Box 2209
Jersey City, NJ 07303-2209

A variety of supplemental CPA products are available from John Wiley & Sons, Inc. By using a variety of learning techniques, such as software, computer-based learning, and audio CDs, the candidate is more likely to remain focused during the study process and to retain information for a longer period of time. Visit our website at **www.wiley.com/cpa** for other products, supplements, and updates.

Working CPA Questions

The AICPA content outlines, study outlines, etc., will be used to acquire and assimilate the knowledge tested on the examination. This, however, should be only **one-half** of your preparation program. The other half should be spent practicing how to work questions. Some candidates probably spend over 90% of their time reviewing material tested on the CPA exam. Much more time should be allocated to working previous examination questions **under exam conditions**. Working previous examination questions serves two functions. First, it helps you develop a solutions approach as well as solutions that will satisfy the grader. Second, it provides the best test of your knowledge of the material.

The multiple-choice questions and answer explanations can be used in many ways. First, they may be used as a diagnostic evaluation of your knowledge. For example, before beginning to review commercial paper you may wish to answer 10 to 15 multiple-choice questions to determine your ability to answer CPA examination questions on commercial paper. The apparent difficulty of the questions and the correctness of your answers will allow you to determine the necessary breadth and depth of your review. Additionally, exposure to examination questions prior to review and study of the material should provide motivation. You will develop a feel for your level of proficiency and an understanding of the scope and difficulty of past examination questions. Moreover, your review materials will explain concepts encountered in the diagnostic multiple-choice questions.

Second, the multiple-choice questions can be used as a poststudy or postreview evaluation. You should attempt to understand all concepts mentioned (even in incorrect answers) as you answer the questions. Refer to the explanation of the answer for discussion of the alternatives even though you selected the correct response. Thus, you should read the explanation of the unofficial answer unless you completely understand the question and all of the alternative answers.

Third, you may wish to use the multiple-choice questions as a primary study vehicle. This is probably the quickest but least thorough approach in preparing for the exam. Make a sincere effort to understand the question and to select the correct response before referring to the unofficial answer and explanation. In many cases, the explanations will appear inadequate because of your lack of familiarity with the topic. Always refer back to an appropriate study source, such as the outlines and text in this volume, your business law textbook, UCC Code Sections, etc.

The multiple-choice questions outnumber the essay questions by greater than 10 to 1 in this book. This is similar to recent CPA exams. The numbers are somewhat misleading in that many essay questions contain multiple (and often unrelated) parts. One problem with so many multiple-choice questions is that you may overemphasize them. Candidates generally prefer to work multiple-choice questions because they are

1. Shorter and less time-consuming
2. Solvable with less effort
3. Less frustrating than essay questions

Another problem with the large number of multiple-choice questions is that you may tend to become overly familiar with the questions. The result may be that you begin reading the facts and assumptions of previously studied questions into the questions on your examination. Guard against this potential problem by reading each multiple-choice question with **extra** care.

Beginning with the May 1992 examination, the AICPA began testing with other objective formats. The other objective format questions that were given on previous exams and others prepared by the author are incorporated in the modules to which they pertain (see the listing of question material at the beginning of Chapter 5). Essay questions require the ability to organize and compose a solution, as well as knowledge of the subject matter. Remember, working essay questions is just as important as, if not more important than, working multiple-choice questions. The essay questions and unofficial answers may also be used for study purposes without preparation of answers. Before turning to the unofficial answers, study the question and outline the solution (either mentally or in the margin of the book). Look at our answer outline preceding the unofficial answer for each question and compare it to your own. Next, read the unofficial answer, underlining keywords and phrases. The underlining should reinforce your study of the answer's content and also assist you in learning how to structure your solutions. Answer outlines, representing the major concepts found in the unofficial answer, are provided for each Business Law and Professional Responsibilities question. These will facilitate your study of essay questions.

Remember! The AICPA does **not** accept solutions in outline form. **The AICPA expects the grading concepts to be explained in clear, concise, well-organized sentences**. However, you may prepare answers in list form as long as the listed items complete a sentence that begins with a lead-in phrase.

The questions and solutions in this volume provide you with an opportunity to diagnose and correct any exam-taking weaknesses prior to sitting for the examination. Continually analyze your incorrect solutions to determine the cause of the error(s) during your preparation for the exam. Treat each incorrect solution as a mistake that will not be repeated (especially on the examination). Also attempt to generalize your weaknesses so that you may change, reinforce, or develop new approaches to exam preparation and exam taking.

After you have reviewed for the Business Law and Professional Responsibilities part of the exam, work the complete Business Law and Professional Responsibilities Sample Exam provided in Appendix A.

SELF-STUDY PROGRAM

CPA candidates generally find it difficult to organize and complete their own self-study programs. A major problem is determining **what** and **how** to study. Another major problem is developing the self-discipline to stick to a study program. Relatedly, it is often difficult for CPA candidates to determine how much to study (i.e., determining when they are sufficiently prepared.) The following suggestions will assist you in developing a **systematic**, **comprehensive**, and **successful** self-study program to help you complete the Business Law and Professional Responsibilities exam.

Remember that these are only suggestions. You should modify them to suit your personality, available study time, and other constraints. Some of the suggestions may appear trivial, but CPA candidates generally need all the assistance they can get to systemize their study programs.

Study Facilities and Available Time

Locate study facilities that will be conducive to concentrated study. Factors that you should consider include

1. Noise distraction
2. Interruptions
3. Lighting
4. Availability (e.g., a local library is not available at 5:00 A.M.)
5. Accessibility (e.g., your kitchen table vs. your local library)
6. Desk or table space

You will probably find different study facilities optimal for different times (e.g., your kitchen table during early morning hours and local libraries during early evening hours.)

Next review your personal and professional commitments from now until the exam to determine regularly available study time. Formalize a schedule to which you can reasonably commit yourself. At the end of this chapter, you will find a detailed approach to managing your time available for the exam preparation program.

Self-Evaluation

The *CPA EXAMINATION REVIEW: BUSINESS LAW and PROFESSIONAL RESPONSIBILITIES* self-study program is partitioned into 15 topics or modules. Since each module is clearly defined and should be studied separately, you have the task of preparing for the CPA Business Law and Professional Responsibilities exam by tackling 15 manageable tasks. Partitioning the overall project into 15 modules makes preparation psychologically easier, since you sense yourself completing one small step at a time rather than seemingly never completing one or a few large steps.

By completing the following "Preliminary Estimate of Your Present Knowledge of Subject" inventory below, organized by the 15 modules in this program, you will tabulate your strong and weak areas at the beginning of your study program. This will help you budget your limited study time. Note that you should begin studying the material in each module by answering up to 1/4 of the total multiple-choice questions covering that module's topics (see instruction 4.A. in the next section). This "mini-exam" should constitute a diagnostic evaluation as to the amount of review and study you need.

PRELIMINARY ESTIMATE OF YOUR PRESENT KNOWLEDGE OF SUBJECT*

No.	Module	Proficient	Fairly Proficient	Generally Familiar	Not Familiar
7	Contracts				
8	Sales				
9	Commercial Paper				
10	Secured Transactions				
11	Bankruptcy				
12	Debtor-Creditor Relationships				
13	Agency				
14	Partnerships and Joint Ventures				
15	Corporations				
16	Federal Securities Acts				
17	Professional Responsibilities				
18	Regulation of Employment and Environment				
19	Property				
20	Insurance				
21	Trusts and Estates				

* *NOTE: The numbering of modules in this text commences with number 7 to correspond with the numbering system used in our two-volume set.*

Time Allocation

The study program below entails an average of 75 hours (Step 5. below) of study time. The breakdown of total hours is indicated in the left margin.

[2 1/2 hrs.]   1. Study Chapters 2-4 in this volume. These chapters are essential to your efficient preparation program. (Time estimate includes candidate's review of the examples of the solutions approach in Chapters 2 and 3.)

[1/2 hr.]   2. Begin by studying the introductory material at the beginning of Chapter 5.

               3. Study one module at a time. The modules are listed above in the self-evaluation section.

               4. For each module

[6 hrs.]   A. Work 1/4 of the multiple-choice questions (e.g., if there are 40 multiple-choice questions in a module, you should work every 4th question). Score yourself.
                       This diagnostic routine will provide you with an index of your proficiency and familiarity with the type and difficulty of questions.
                       Time estimate: 3 minutes each, not to exceed 1 hour total.

[20 hrs.]   B. Study the outlines and illustrations. Where necessary, refer to your business law textbook and original authoritative pronouncements (e.g., UCC code sections). (This will occur more frequently for topics in which you have a weak background.)
                       Time estimate: 1 hour minimum per module with more time devoted to topics less familiar to you.

[15 hrs.]   C. Work the remaining multiple-choice questions. Study the explanations of the multiple-choice questions you missed or had trouble answering.
                       Time estimate: 3 minutes to answer each question and 2 minutes to study the answer explanation of each question missed.

[3 hrs.]   D. Work the other objective format questions.
                       Time estimate: 20 minutes for each other objective question and 10 minutes to study the answer explanations for each item missed.

[12 hrs.]   E. Under exam conditions, work at least 2 essay questions. Work additional questions as time permits.
                       Time estimate: 20 minutes for each essay question and 10 minutes to review the answer outline and unofficial answer for each question worked.

[4 hrs.]   F. Work through the sample CPA examination presented at the end of this text. Each exam should be taken in one sitting.
                       Take the examination under simulated exam conditions (i.e., in a strange place with other people present [your local municipal library]). Apply your solutions approach to each question and your exam strategy to the overall exam.
                       You should limit yourself to the time you will have when taking the actual CPA exam section (3 hours for the Business Law and Professional Responsibilities section).
                       Spend time afterwards grading your work and reviewing your effort. It might be helpful to do this with other CPA candidates. Another person looking over your exam might be more objective and notice things such as clarity of essays, etc.
                       Time estimate: To take the exam and review it later, approximately 4 hours.

               5. The total suggested time of 63 hours is only an average. Allocation of time will vary candidate by candidate. Time requirements vary due to the diverse backgrounds and abilities of CPA candidates. Allocate your time so you gain the most proficiency in the least time. Remember that while 63 hours will be required, you should break the overall project down into 15 more manageable tasks. Do not study more than one module during each study session.

Using Notecards

Below are one candidate's notecards on business law topics which illustrate how key definitions, lists, etc., can be summarized on index cards for quick review. Since candidates can take these anywhere they go, they are a very efficient review tool.

1) *Consideration of Land (i.e., mortgages, leases)*
2) *Agreements > 1 year (From "date" of agreement)*
3) *. Answer for Debt of another*
4) *Consideration of Marriage*
5) *Sale of goods > $500*
   NOTE: a) Any form will do
        b) Can be in more than one document
        c) Writing need not occur at time of contract

Commercial Paper → Requirement of Negotiability
1) *Must be in writing (written)*
2) *Must be signed by person who is ordering payment (signed)*
3) *Promise (note) or order (draft) to pay (promise or order)*
4) *Must be unconditional*
5) *State a specific amount of money (sum certain)*
6) *Contain no other promises or orders*
7) *Be payable on demand or at a definite time*
8) *Be payable "To Order" or "Bearer"*

Prepared by Maureen McBeth, Northern Illinois University CPA Law Faculty member

Level of Proficiency Required

What level of proficiency must you develop with respect to each of the topics to pass the exam? You should work toward a minimum correct rate on the multiple-choice questions of 80%. As explained in Chapter 2, recent exams in Business Law and Professional Responsibilities have been graded by adding "difficulty points" to the candidates' raw scores. Working toward a correct rate of 80% or higher will give you a margin.

Warning: Disproportional study time devoted to multiple-choice and other objective questions (relative to essay questions) can be disastrous on the exam. You should work a substantial number of essay questions under exam conditions, even though multiple-choice questions are easier to work and are used to gauge your proficiency. The authors believe that practicing essay questions will also improve your proficiency on the multiple-choice questions.

Multiple-Choice Feedback

One of the benefits of working through previous exam questions is that it helps you to identify your weak areas. Once you have graded your answers, your strong areas and weak areas should be clearly evident. Yet, the important point here is that you should not stop at a simple percentage evaluation. The percentage only provides general feedback about your knowledge of the material contained within that particular module. The percentage **does not** give you any specific feedback regarding the concepts which were tested. In order to get this feedback, you should look at the questions missed on an individual basis because this will help you gain a better understanding of **why** you missed the question.

This feedback process has been facilitated by the fact that within each module where the multiple-choice answer key appears, two blank lines have been inserted next to the multiple-choice answers. As you grade the multiple-choice questions, mark those questions which you have missed. However, instead of just marking the questions right and wrong, you should now focus on marking the questions in a manner which identifies **why** you missed the question. As an example, a candidate could mark the questions in the following manner: ✓ for math mistakes, x for conceptual mistakes, and ? for areas which the candidate was unfamiliar with. The candidate should then correct these mistakes by reworking through the marked questions.

The objective of this marking technique is to help you identify your weak areas and thus, the concepts which you should be focusing on. While it is still important for you to get between 75% and 80% correct when working multiple-choice questions, it is more important for you to understand the concepts. This understanding applies to both the questions answered correctly and those answered incorrectly. Remember, questions on the CPA exam will be different from the questions in the book; however, the concepts will be the same. Therefore, your preparation should focus on understanding concepts, not just getting the correct answer.

Conditional Candidates

If you have received conditional status on the examination, you must concentrate on the remaining part(s). Unfortunately, many candidates do not study after conditioning the exam, relying on luck to get them through the remaining part(s). Conditional candidates will find that material contained in Chapters 1-4 and the information contained in the appropriate modules will benefit them in preparing for the remaining part(s) of the examination.

PLANNING FOR THE EXAMINATION

Overall Strategy

An overriding concern should be an orderly, systematic approach toward both your preparation program and your examination strategy. A major objective should be to avoid any surprises or anything else that would rattle you during the examination. In other words, you want to be in complete control as much as possible. Control is of paramount importance from both positive and negative viewpoints. The presence of control on your part will add to your confidence and your ability to prepare for and take the exam. Moreover, the presence of control will make your preparation program more enjoyable (or at least less distasteful). On the other hand, a lack of organization will result in inefficiency in preparing for and taking the examination, with a highly predictable outcome. Likewise, distractions during the examination (e.g., inadequate lodging, long drive) are generally disastrous.

In summary, establishing a systematic, orderly approach to taking the examination is of paramount importance.

1. Develop an overall strategy at the beginning of your preparation program (see below)
2. Supplement your overall strategy with outlines of material tested on the Business Law and Professional Responsibilities exam
3. Supplement your overall strategy with an explicitly stated set of question-solving procedures--the solutions approach
4. Supplement your overall strategy with an explicitly stated approach to each examination session (See Chapter 4)
5. Evaluate your preparation progress on a regular basis and prepare lists of things "to do." (See Weekly Review of Preparation Program Progress on following page.)
6. RELAX: You can pass the exam. About 10,000 candidates successfully complete the exam each sitting. You will be one of them if you complete an efficient preparation program and execute well (i.e., solutions approach and exam strategy) while writing the exam.

The following outline is designed to provide you with a general framework of the tasks before you. You should tailor the outline to your needs by adding specific items and comments.

A. Preparation Program (refer to Self-Study Program discussed previously)

1. Obtain and organize study materials
2. Locate facilities conducive for studying and block out study time
3. Develop your solutions approach (including solving essay questions as well as multiple-choice and other objective questions)
4. Prepare an examination strategy
5. Study the material tested recently and prepare answers to actual exam questions on these topics under examination conditions
6. Periodically evaluate your progress

B. Physical Arrangements

1. Apply to and obtain acceptance from your State Board
2. Reserve lodging for examination night(s)

C. Taking the Examination (covered in detail in Chapter 4)

1. Become familiar with exam facilities and procedures
2. Implement examination strategies and the solutions approach

Weekly Review of Preparation Program Progress

The following pages contain a hypothetical weekly review of program progress. You should prepare a similar progress chart. This procedure, taking only 5 minutes per week, will help you proceed through a more efficient, complete preparation program.

Make notes of materials and topics

1. That you have studied
2. That you have completed
3. That need additional study

Weeks to go		Comments on progress, "to do" items, etc.
08	1)	Read CONT and SALES → made notecards
	2)	Worked some MC, Other Objective, and Essay questions in these areas
07	1)	Read CPAP and SECU → made notecards
	2)	Worked some MC, Other Objective, and Essay questions in these areas
	3)	Reviewed remedies for breach
06	1)	Read BANK, DBCR, AGEN → made notecards
	2)	Worked some MC, Other Objective, and Essay questions in these areas
	3)	Reviewed firm offer examples and battle of forms
05	1)	Read PTJV, CORP, FEDE, RESP → made notecards
	2)	Worked some MC, Other Objective, and Essay questions in these areas
	3)	Requirements of negotiability needs work
04	1)	Reviewed requirements of negotiability → made notecards
	2)	Worked Essays from various mods
03	1)	Read EMEN, PROP, INSU, TRUS → made notecards
	2)	Worked some MC, Other Objective, and Essay questions in these areas
	3)	Still need work on CORP, AGEN, FEDE
02	1)	Reviewed strong areas → CONT, CPAP, SECU, etc.
	2)	Worked through Essays in strong areas
	3)	Worked MC in strong areas
	4)	Worked Other Objective questions in strong areas
01	1)	Reviewed weak areas → CORP, TRUSTS and Estates, Federal Securities Acts
	2)	Worked through Essays in weak areas
	3)	Worked MC in weak areas
	4)	Worked Other Objective questions in weak areas
00	1)	Took sample exam in Bus. Law and Prof. Resp.
	2)	Reviewed exam policies and procedures
	3)	Reviewed notecards
	4)	Reviewed mini outlines

Time Management of Your Preparation

As you begin your CPA exam preparation, you obviously realize that there is a large amount of material to cover over the course of the next 3 to 4 months. Therefore, it is very important for you to organize your calendar, and maybe even your daily routine, so that you can allocate sufficient time to studying. An organized approach to your preparation is much more effective than a last week cram session. An organized approach also builds up the confidence necessary to succeed on the CPA exam.

An approach which we have already suggested, is to develop weekly "to do" lists. This technique helps you to establish intermediate objectives and goals as you progress through your study plan. You can then focus your efforts on small tasks and not feel overwhelmed by the entire process. And as you accomplish these tasks you will see yourself moving one step closer to realizing the overall goal, succeeding on the CPA exam.

Note, however, that the underlying assumption of this approach is that you have found the time during the week to study and thus accomplish the different tasks. Although this is an obvious step, it is still a very important step. Your exam preparation should be of a continuous nature and not one that jumps around the calendar. Therefore, you should strive to find available study time within your daily schedule, which can be utilized on a consistent basis. For example, everyone has certain hours of the day which are already committed for activities such as jobs, classes, and, of course, sleep. There is also going to be the time you spend relaxing because CPA candidates should try to maintain some balance in their lives. Sometimes too much studying can be counterproductive. But there will be some time available to you for studying and working through the questions. Block off this available time and use it only for exam prep. Use the time to accomplish your weekly tasks and to keep yourself committed to the process. After awhile your preparation will develop into a habit and the preparation will not seem as overwhelming as it once did.

**NOW IS THE TIME
TO MAKE YOUR COMMITMENT**

2 EXAMINATION GRADING AND GRADER ORIENTATION

All State Boards of Accountancy use the AICPA advisory grading service. As your grade is to be determined by this process, it is very important that you understand the AICPA grading process and its **implications for your preparation program and for the solutions techniques you will use during the examination.**

The AICPA has a full-time staff of CPA examination personnel whose responsibilities include

1. Preparing questions for the examination
2. Working with outside consultants who prepare questions
3. Preparing grading guides and unofficial answers
4. Supervising and reviewing the work of examination graders

The AICPA examination staff is under the supervision of the AICPA Board of Examiners, which has responsibility for the CPA examination.

This chapter contains a description of the AICPA grading process including a determination of the passing standard and a description of AICPA grading in *Information for Uniform CPA Examination Candidates*.

Setting the Passing Standard of the Uniform CPA Examination

Until May 1997, the passing standard for the CPA examination was based on the policy that all candidates who achieved a raw score of 75% on each section would pass; however, if nationally fewer than 30% of the candidates achieved this standard, candidates' raw scores were bumped up to 75 or higher; this policy passed the top 30% on each section for every examination administration. Consequently, if a group of candidates were particularly well prepared or not, the top 30% would pass, regardless.

Today, the 30% criterion no longer exists, since neither the Board of Examiners (BOE) nor the state boards were comfortable with it. The passing standard for each section of the Uniform CPA Examination is currently based on the Angoff passing standard studies which were held during 1996. The procedure, known as a modified Angoff standard-setting method, generally involves convening a panel of judges familiar with the work of entry-level professionals who evaluate each question of each section of an examination. Each panelist's task is to estimate the probability that a "borderline" or "minimally qualified" professional would answer each question correctly. For the May 1996 exam, the panelists were given the questions and official answers for the specific sections they were assigned. They were instructed to read each question and assign a minimum pass level (MPL). The individual MPLs were tallied and the panelists were provided with a summary of the range of MPLs they had assigned. Then the panelists were given the statistics on actual candidate performance. They were then instructed to rate each question again. The second set of MPLs for all questions were tallied to arrive at the "initial passing score" that, in the judgment of the panelists, was needed for the minimally qualified candidate to pass that section of the examination.

The BOE uses a method called "equating" to determine if one examination is more or less difficult than another examination and to test for evidence that the candidate pools are significantly different. Examinations are "equated" by imbedding questions from earlier examinations into later ones. If the candidate pools are equal in ability, they should perform equally well on the equating questions. If the candidates perform significantly better or worse on the equating questions, it is assumed the candidate pools were different.

Grading the Examination

The AICPA exercises very tight control over all of the examination papers during the grading process and prior to their return to the individual State Boards of Accountancy.

Multiple-choice and other objective questions are graded electronically. Only the candidates' responses are graded. No consideration is given to any comments or explanations. **The AICPA has begun to pretest** multiple-choice questions on the exam; approximately 10-15% of the questions in each section of the exam are pretest questions that are not included in the candidate's grade. Different versions of each exam section contain different pretest questions. Essay and problem answers are graded individually on the basis of grading guides. Grading guides consist of **grading concepts,** which are ideas, constructs, principles, etc., that can be clearly defined.

While tentative grading guides (answers) are prepared prior to the examination, the final grading guides are based upon a test grading of samples of actual examinations. Objective questions are analyzed to determine whether a significant number of candidates selected an answer other than the one identified as the best answer by the AICPA. If an alternative answer is determined to be valid, the Grading Subcommittee may accept both answers. Other acceptable concepts may be added to the grading guide as a result of the test grading process. Additionally, alternative interpretations and approaches to essay and problem solutions may result in changes in the grading guides. Once grading guides are fully developed, "production graders" perform the first grading of the examination. The "production graders" are practicing CPAs, university professors, attorneys, etc., commissioned by the AICPA on a per diem basis to grade the examination. These graders specialize in a single essay or problem answer and grade answers to that question for about 6 weeks.

In this process examination papers move from grader to grader. Attached to each essay/problem is a grading guide similar to the "Hypothetical Grading Guide" on page 18. The objective at this stage is to separate candidates' papers into three categories: obvious pass, marginal, and obvious failure.

A **first review** is performed by highly experienced graders. Essays or problem answers that receive this review fall in the 65-79 range. Quality control is obtained in this process because the reviewer examines the work of individual graders to make sure that the grading guides are being applied correctly. Grading errors are corrected in this process.

Upon completion of the first review for all sections of the exam, a **second review** is done. To qualify for a second review, the candidates' papers must earn grades from 72 through 74 on the section of the exam failed. According to the *Information for Uniform CPA Examination Candidates*, as amended, the second review consists of

1. Manual verification of the accuracy of the objective answer grade
2. Independent verification of the accuracy of the essay and problem grading by a reviewer who did not perform the first review

Based on this review, candidate grades are adjusted to reflect any scoring inconsistencies. Second reviews are also given to failing papers of candidates who need to meet a minimum grade requirement in their state in order to condition the exam.

The examination grades are returned to the individual state boards several weeks prior to the official grade release date. The grade release date is usually at the beginning of February for the November exam and at the beginning of August for the May exam.

Multiple-Choice Grading

In the past, each correct response on the Business Law and Professional Responsibilities section of the examination was assigned one point. Since your grade is based on an overall curve for the Business Law and Professional Responsibilities section of the exam, you should do your best regardless of the difficulty of the questions. Perfect and use the "multiple-choice question solutions approach" discussed in Chapter 3. If you are unsure about a particular question, you should make an educated guess (i.e., pick the "best" answer). Your grade will be based on your total correct answers since no penalty exists for incorrect answers. The grading procedure for multiple-choice questions is explained in the instructions at the beginning of each section of the exam. As mentioned earlier, 10-15% of the multiple-choice questions are pretest items that are not included in the candidate's grade. The importance of carefully reading and following these and all other instructions cannot be overemphasized.

Other Objective Question Grading

These questions are also graded electronically. The weight for each item will depend on the points assigned to the question. For example, if a question that has been assigned 10 points contains 13 items, each correct response would be worth .77 (10/13) of a point. Again, do not be discouraged by your performance; the Business Law and Professional Responsibilities section is curved on an overall basis.

Essay Grading

To illustrate the grading of essay questions, we have included an essay question from the Business Law Examination in this section. Following the question are the AICPA Unofficial Answer and a hypothetical grading guide.

ESSAY QUESTION

On June 1, Classic Corp., a manufacturer of desk chairs, orally agreed to sell 100 leather desk chairs to Rand Stores, a chain of retail furniture stores, for $50,000. The parties agreed that delivery would be completed by September 1, and the shipping terms were "FOB seller's loading dock." On June 5, Classic sent Rand a signed memorandum of agreement containing the terms orally agreed to. Rand received the memorandum on June 7 and made no response.

On July 31, Classic identified the chairs to be shipped to Rand and placed them on its loading dock to be picked up by the common carrier the next day. That night, a fire on the loading dock destroyed 50 of the chairs. On August 1, the remaining 50 chairs were delivered to the common carrier together with 50 vinyl chairs. The truck carrying the chairs was involved in an accident, resulting in extensive damage to 10 of the leather chairs and 25 of the vinyl chairs.

On August 10, the chairs were delivered to Rand. On August 12, Rand notified Classic that Rand was accepting 40 of the leather chairs and 10 of the vinyl chairs, but the rest of the shipment was being rejected. Rand also informed Classic that, due to Classic's failure to perform under the terms of the contract, Rand would seek all remedies available under the Sales Article of the UCC.

Classic contended that it has no liability to Rand and that the shipment was strictly an accommodation to Rand because Rand failed to sign the memorandum of agreement, thus preventing a contract from being formed.

The above parties and transactions are governed by the provisions of the Sales Article of the UCC.

Required:

a. Determine whether Classic's contention is correct and give the reasons for your conclusion.

b. Assuming that a valid contract exists between Classic and Rand, answer the following questions and give the reasons for your conclusions. Do not consider any possible liability owed by the common carrier.

1. Who bears the risk of loss for the 50 destroyed leather chairs?

2. Who bears the risk of loss for the 25 damaged vinyl chairs?

3. What is the earliest date that title to any of the chairs would pass to Rand?

c. With what UCC requirements must Rand comply to be entitled to recover damages from Classic?

d. Assuming that a valid contract exists between Classic and Rand, state the applicable remedies to which Rand would be entitled. Do not consider any possible liability owed by the common carrier.

UNOFFICIAL ANSWER

a. Classic's contention is incorrect. Under the provisions of the Sales Article of the UCC, a written memorandum stating an agreement between merchants does not have to be signed by both parties. The contract is enforceable against Classic because Classic signed the memorandum and against Rand because Rand did not object to the memorandum within 10 days of receiving it.

b. 1. Classic bears the risk of loss for the 50 leather chairs destroyed in the fire. Even though the goods were identified to the contract and placed on the loading dock, the risk of loss remains with Classic. The shipping terms "FOB seller's loading dock" provide that risk of loss remains with the seller until the goods are delivered to the common carrier. The 50 leather chairs destroyed in the fire had not yet been delivered to the carrier.

2. Classic bears the risk of loss for the damaged vinyl chairs. Even though these goods were delivered to the common carrier, the risk of loss did not pass to Rand because the vinyl chairs were nonconforming goods.

3. August 1 was the earliest date that title to any of the chairs passed to Rand. Title passed when goods identified to the contract were delivered to the carrier.

c. Under the Sales Article of the UCC, for Rand to be entitled to damages from Classic, Rand must comply with the following requirements:

• Rand has to notify Classic of the rejection of the goods within a reasonable time.

• Rand must act in good faith with respect to the rejected goods by following any reasonable instructions from Classic.

• Rand must give Classic the opportunity to cure until the contract time of performance expires.

d. Rand would be entitled to the following remedies:

• The right to cancel the contract
• The right of cover
• The right to recover monetary damages for nondelivery

Essay questions are generally graded based on the number of **grading concepts** in the candidate's solution. The grading guide is a list of the grading concepts and raw point(s) assigned to each concept. It is necessary for candidates to identify all concepts listed in the AICPA Unofficial Answer in order to receive all available points. A hypothetical grading guide for the preceding Business Law essay question appears below.

In the grading guide which follows, note that each grading concept is summarized by several **keywords**. Graders undoubtedly scan for these **keywords** during the first grading. Note that if one of the writing samples, worth 2 points, were taken from the above essay, then each concept would be worth 1/2 point (8 ÷ 16). However, the number of points allocated to writing skills will not be specified in the candidate's grade.

To assure full credit, however, candidates should be very careful to organize their answers to meet the question requirements; you should answer requirement **a.** in answer **a.**, answer requirement **b.** in answer **b.**, etc. Additionally, the efficient use of time is of the utmost importance. If you have included grading concepts in one part of a question that are applicable to another part of the same question, **do not repeat them**. Simply refer the grader to your previous answer.

Two common misconceptions about the AICPA grading of essay questions have cost candidates points in recent years. First, answers should **not** consist of a listing (or outline) of **keywords**. Answers should be set forth in short, concise sentences, organized per the requirements of the question. However, it is acceptable to prepare answers in list form so long as the listed items are in sentence form (i.e., the listed items complete an introductory phrase). Second, a candidate should **not** answer only one or two parts of a question very thoroughly and leave the remaining parts blank. Maximize your points by attempting all question requirements.

The examiners grade two samples from essay questions (e.g., requirement "c." from one essay and requirement "b." from another essay) in the Business Law and Professional Responsibilities exam for writing skills. Five percent of the points available on each of these sections are allocated to writing skills. The samples are graded according to the following characteristics:

1. Coherent organization
2. Conciseness
3. Clarity

4. Use of standard English
5. Responsiveness to the requirements of the question
6. Appropriateness for the reader

The "holistic" grading process will provide for the same graders who grade for content to assign 0-5 points based on their overall evaluation of the six characteristics as follows:

0	1	2	3	4	5
	Less than competent		Competent	More than competent	

Prior to the actual grading, writing consultants will grade a sample of papers and assign points as shown above. The content graders then use the consultant's evaluations as a guide.

HYPOTHETICAL GRADING GUIDE[1]

Grading Concepts	*Grading Concepts Mentioned*
a. Classic's contention is incorrect	○
Written memorandum is enforceable against both parties	○
Against Classic because Classic signed it	
Against Rand because contract was between merchants	
and Rand did not object to it within 10 days after receiving it	○
b. 1. Classic has risk of loss for the 50 leather chairs destroyed by fire	○
"FOB seller's loading dock" means risk of loss remains with the seller	
until goods are delivered to carrier	○
2. Classic has risk of loss for the vinyl chairs	○
Because sent nonconforming goods	○
3. August 1 was earliest date that title of chairs passed to Rand	○
This is when goods identified to contract were delivered to carrier	○
c. To be entitled to damages, Rand must	
Notify Classic of rejection of goods within reasonable time	○
Follow any reasonable instructions of Classic	○
Give Classic opportunity to cure until contract time of performance expires	○
d. Rand's remedies include rights	
To cancel contract	○
Of cover	○
To recover monetary damages for nondelivery	○
Grading Concepts Mentioned	═

---

[1] *The AICPA Board of Examiners does not release the grading guides used for scoring essay questions. The grading guide above was prepared by the authors to illustrate to candidates the manner in which points are allocated to grading concepts.*

The conversion scale below converts the number of concepts mentioned to the grade earned on the question.

CONVERSION SCALE

Concepts Mentioned	16	15	14	13	12	11	10	9	8	7	6	5	4	3	2	1	0
Grade	10	9.375	8.75	8.125	7.5	6.875	6.25	5.625	5	4.375	3.75	3.125	2.5	1.875	1.25	0.625	0

The grading guide might be thought of as a brief outline of the unofficial answer. Note the similarities between the grading guide and the unofficial answer shown with question Number 1. In the above grading guide, note that each grading concept is summarized by several keywords. Graders undoubtedly scan for **keywords** during the first grading. Note that if one of the writing samples, worth 2 points, were taken from the above essay then each concept would be worth 1/2 point [(10 total points – 2 writing points) ÷ 16 concepts mentioned.] If the candidate received a 4 (out of 5 available writing points) on the writing sample from this question, 1.6 (4/5 x 2) points would be added to the points received for the concepts portion of the question.

Overall Grade

A hypothetical example appears below to indicate how a candidate's grade is determined for the Business Law and Professional Responsibilities section of the exam. The example presents one possibility for the format and point distribution on this section of the exam. Candidates should remember that the point assignment on the Law exam could consist of 50-60% multiple-choice, 20-30% other objective answer format, and 20-30% essay.

Type Question	Question number	Points allocated	Points
Multiple-choice	1	60*	47.0*
Other Objective Answer Format	2	10	6.5
	3	10	5.8
Essay	4	10	8.9**
	5	10	5.4**
Raw points earned		100	73.6
Rounding adjustment***			.4
			74.0
Angoff adjustment			4.0
Grade reported to candidate			78.0

   * *Excluding pretested questions.*
  ** *Including writing skill points.*
 *** *If less than .5, rounding adjustment would be negative.*

Allocation of Points to Questions

Candidates should be concerned with point allocations for the purpose of allocating their time on the exam. When answering each question, candidates should allocate the total examination time in proportion to the question's point value. For more information, see "Allocation of Time" in Chapter 4.

Grading Implications for CPA Candidates

Analysis of the grading process helps you understand what graders are looking for and how you can present solutions to "satisfy the grader." Before turning to Chapter 3 for a discussion of how to prepare solutions, consider the following conclusions derived from the foregoing grading analysis.

1. Present solutions in a neat and organized manner to maximize points earned
2. Allocate your time based on point value
3. Do your best on every question, no matter how difficult

   a. Remember that the test is graded on a relative basis
   b. If a question is difficult for you, it probably is difficult for others also
   c. Develop a "solutions approach" to assist you

4. No supporting notes or computations are required for the multiple-choice questions. Use the margins of the Examination Booklet for related notes. The multiple-choice answers are machine-graded and any related work on the Examination Booklet is ignored.
5. Essay solutions should be numbered and organized according to the problem requirements (e.g., a., b.1., b.2., c.1., c.2., c.3.)

   a. Start your solution to each question at the top of a new page b.　Emphasize keywords

    c.　Separate grading concepts into individual sentences or short paragraphs

        (1)　Do not bury grading concepts in lengthy paragraphs that might be missed by the grader. Include as many **sensible** grading concepts as possible.

        (2)　Use short, uncomplicated sentence structure

        (3)　**Do not present your answer in outline format**

    d.　Do not omit any requirements

In summary, **satisfy the grader**. You need neat, readable solutions organized according to the requirements, which will also be the organization of the grading guides. Remember that a legible, well-organized, grammatically correct answer gives a professional appearance. Additionally, recognize the plight of the grader having to decipher one mess after another, day after day. Give him/her a break with a neat, orderly solution. The "halo" effect will be rewarded by additional consideration (and hopefully points!).

Candidate Diagnostic Report

State Boards may include a "Candidate Diagnostic Report" along with the candidates' scores. A sample Business Law and Professional Responsibilities report appears below. The report provides useful information to candidates who must repeat a section. In those areas where the percentage of points is low (10% or less), be cautious as the results are based on very few questions.

JURISDICTION ILLINOIS			CANDIDATE NUMBER 1-09-000426		EXAMINATION DATE MAY 2000					
SECTION	GRADE		CONTENT AREAS AND PERCENT COVERAGE		PERCENTAGE OF AREA EARNED					
					≤50	51-60	61-70	71-80	81-90	>90
LPR	83	I	Professional and Legal Responsibilities	15%				*		
		II	Business Organizations	20%					*	
		III	Contracts	10%					*	
		IV	Debtor-Creditor Relationships	10%	*					
		V	Government Regulation of Business	15%					*	
		VI	Uniform Commercial Code	20%			*			
		VII	Property	10%						*
				100%						

3 THE SOLUTIONS APPROACH

The solutions approach is a systematic problem-solving methodology. The purpose is to assure efficient, complete solutions to CPA exam problems, some of which are complex and confusing relative to most undergraduate accounting problems. Unfortunately, there appears to be a widespread lack of emphasis on problem-solving techniques in accounting courses. Most accounting books and courses merely provide solutions to specific types of problems. Memorization of these solutions for examinations and preparation of homework problems from examples is "cookbooking." "Cookbooking" is perhaps a necessary step in the learning process, but it is certainly not sufficient training for the complexities of the business world. Professional accountants need to be adaptive to a rapidly changing complex environment. For example, CPAs have been called on to interpret and issue reports on new concepts such as price controls, energy allocations, and new taxes. These CPAs rely on their problem-solving expertise to understand these problems and to formulate solutions to them.

The steps outlined below are only one of many possible series of solution steps. Admittedly, the procedures suggested are **very** structured; thus, you should adapt the suggestions to your needs. You may find that some steps are occasionally unnecessary, or that certain additional procedures increase your own problem-solving efficiency. Whatever the case, substantial time should be allocated to developing an efficient solutions approach before taking the examination. You should develop your solutions approach by working questions and problems.

Note that the steps below relate to any specific question or problem; overall examination or section strategies are discussed in Chapter 4.

Multiple-Choice Question Solutions Approach Algorithm

1. **Work individual questions in order.**

   a. If a question appears lengthy or difficult, skip it until you can determine that extra time is available. Put a big question mark in the margin to remind you to return to questions you have skipped or need to review.

2. **Cover the choices before reading each question.**

   a. The answers are sometimes misleading and may cause you to misread or misinterpret the question.

3. **Read each question *carefully* to determine the topical area.**

   a. Study the requirements **first** so you know which data are important.
   b. Underline keywords and important data.
   c. Identify pertinent information with notations in the margin of the exam.
   d. Be especially careful to note when the requirement is an **exception**, for example, "Which of the following is **not** an effective disclaimer of the implied warranty of merchantability?"
   e. If a set of data is the basis for two or more questions, read the requirements of each of the questions first before beginning to work the first question (sometimes it is more efficient to work the questions out of order or simultaneously).
   f. Be alert to read questions as they are, not as you would like them to be. You may encounter a familiar looking item; don't jump to the conclusion that you know what the answer is without reading the question completely.

4. **Anticipate the answer before looking at the alternative answers.**

    a. Recall the applicable principle (e.g., offer and acceptance, requisites of negotiability, etc.) and the respective applications thereof.
    b. If a question deals with a complex area, it may be very useful to set up a timeline or diagram using abbreviations.

5. **Read the answers and select the *best* alternative.**
6. **Mark the correct answer (or your educated guess) on the examination booklet itself.**
7. **After completing all of the individual questions in an overall question, transfer the answers to the machine gradable answer sheet with extreme care.**

    a. Be very careful not to fall out of sequence with the answer sheet. A mistake would cause most of your answers to be wrong. **Since the AICPA uses answer sheets with varying formats, it would be very easy to go across the sheet instead of down or vice versa.** Note the format of your answer sheet carefully!
    b. Review to check that you have transferred the answers correctly.
    c. Do not leave this step until the end of the exam as you may find yourself with too little time to transfer your answers to the answer sheet. **The exam proctors are not permitted to give you extra time to transfer your answers.**

    EXAMPLE: *The following is an example of the manner in which the answer sheet should be marked for a multiple-choice question. A No. 2 pencil should be used to blacken the appropriate oval(s) on the Objective Answer Sheet to indicate the answer.*

Item	Select One
19	Ⓐ ⬤ Ⓒ Ⓓ
20	Ⓐ Ⓑ Ⓒ ⬤

Multiple-Choice Question Solutions Approach Example

A good example of the multiple-choice solutions approach follows, using an actual multiple-choice question from the previous Examination in Business Law and Professional Responsibilities.

Step 3:

Topical area? Contracts—Revocation and Attempted Acceptance

Step 4:

Principle? An offer may be revoked at any time prior to acceptance and is effective when received by offeree

Step 5:

a. Incorrect—Mason's acceptance was ineffective because the offer had been revoked prior to Mason's acceptance.
b. Incorrect—Same as a.
c. **Correct**—Peters' offer was effectively revoked when Mason learned that the lawn mower had been sold to Bronson.
d. Incorrect—Peters' was not obligated to keep the offer open because no consideration had been paid by Mason. Note that if consideration had been given, an option contract would have been formed and the offer would have been irrevocable before June 20.

13. On June 15, Peters orally offered to sell a used lawn mower to Mason for $125. Peters specified that Mason had until June 20 to accept the offer. On June 16, Peters received an offer to purchase the lawn mower for $150 from Bronson, Mason's neighbor. Peters accepted Bronson's offer. On June 17, Mason saw Bronson using the lawn mower and was told the mower had been sold to Bronson. Mason immediately wrote to Peters to accept the June 15 offer. Which of the following statements is correct?

a. Mason's acceptance would be effective when received by Peters.
b. Mason's acceptance would be effective when mailed.
c. Peters' offer had been revoked and Mason's acceptance was ineffective.
d. Peters was obligated to keep the June 15 offer open until June 20.

Currently, all multiple-choice questions are scored based on the number correct (i.e., there is no penalty for guessing). The rationale is that a "good guess" indicates knowledge. Thus, you should answer all multiple-choice questions.

Other Objective Questions Solutions Approach Algorithm

The following three types of other objective questions have been tested previously on the Business Law and Professional Responsibilities Section:

   a) Matching
   b) Yes/no or true/false
   c) Numerical computations

The following solutions approach is suggested for answering other objective questions:

1. **Glance over the entire problem.** Scan the problem to get a feel for the topical area and related concepts that are being tested. Even though the format of the question may vary, the exam continues to test your understanding of applicable principles or concepts. Relax, take a deep breath, and determine your strategy for conquering the problem.

2. **Identify the requirements of the problem.** This step will help you focus in more quickly on the solution(s) without wasting time reading irrelevant material.

3. **Study the items to be answered.** As you do this and become familiar with the topical area being tested, you should review the concepts of that area. This will help you organize your thoughts so that you can relate logically the requirements of the question with the applicable concepts.

4. **Answer each item one at a time.** The type of OOAF question determines how the candidate should accomplish this step. For instance, when the answer choices are presented in a matching question, the candidate must first understand how the answer choices apply to the question items. The candidate will then be able to differentiate among the answer choices in order to select the appropriate answer for each question. You may want to work backwards from the answers to the questions. Don't be afraid to answer questions out of order. Just be careful to place your selected answer next to the appropriate item number in your question booklet.

5. **Use time lines, etc., as appropriate.** The use of these items helps to lay out the information in a logical manner to avoid silly mistakes.

6. **Mark your selected answer on the examination booklet itself.** Once the candidate has selected an answer it should be clearly marked on the examination booklet before moving on to the next question.

7. **After completing all of the items, carefully transfer the answers to the answer sheet.** It is very important that all items be recorded on the objective answer sheet, as they cannot be graded if they are not.

Other Objective Questions Solutions Approach Example

Problem 1   (15 to 20 minutes)[1]

On June 10, 2000, Bond sold real property to Edwards for $100,000. Edwards assumed the $80,000 recorded mortgage Bond had previously given to Fair Bank and gave a $20,000 purchase money mortgage to Heath Finance. Heath did not record this mortgage. On December 15, 2001, Edwards sold the property to Ivor for $115,000. Ivor bought the property subject to the Fair mortgage but did not know about the Heath mortgage. Ivor borrowed $50,000 from Knox Bank and gave Knox a mortgage on the property. Knox knew of the unrecorded Heath mortgage when its mortgage was recorded. Ivor, Edwards, and Bond defaulted on the mortgages. Fair, Heath, and Knox foreclosed and the property was sold at a judicial foreclosure sale for $60,000. At the time of the sale, the outstanding balance of principal and accrued interest on the Fair mortgage was $75,000. The Heath mortgage balance was $18,000 and the Knox mortgage was $47,500.

Fair, Heath, and Knox all claim that their mortgages have priority and should be satisfied first from the sale proceeds. Bond, Edwards, and Ivor all claim that they are not liable for any deficiency resulting from the sale.

The above transactions took place in a jurisdiction that has a notice-race recording statute and allows foreclosure deficiency judgments.

Matching Question Example

Required:

Step 2:

a.   Items 101 through 103. For each mortgage, select from List A the priority of that mortgage and blacken the corresponding oval on the Objective Answer Sheet. A priority should be selected only once.

---

[1]   *Estimated time is no longer provided on the Uniform CPA Examination. See "Allocation of Time" in Chapter 4.*

Step 6:   *List A*

101. Knox Bank. *Knew of Heath - C*   A. First Priority.
102. Heath Finance.   *- B*   B. Second Priority.
103. Fair Bank.   *first recorded - A*   C. Third Priority.

b.   Items 104 through 106. For each mortgage, select from List B <u>the reason for its priority</u> and blacken the corresponding oval on the Objective Answer Sheet. A reason <u>may be selected once, more than once, or not at all</u>.

Step 6:   *List B*   *Step 3: True or False?*

104. Knox Bank. *Knew of Heath - D*   A. An unrecorded mortgage has priority over any subse-
105. Heath Finance.   *- D*   quently recorded mortgage. *False*
106. Fair Bank.   *first recorded - C*   B. A recorded mortgage has priority over any unrecorded
                                                 mortgage. *False*
                                             C. The first recorded mortgage has priority over all sub-
                                                 sequent mortgages. *True.*
                                             D. An unrecorded mortgage has priority over a subse-
                                                 quently recorded mortgage if the subsequent mortgage
                                                 knew of the unrecorded mortgage. *True*
                                             B. A purchase money mortgage has priority over a previ-
                                                 ously recorded mortgage. *False*

c.   Items 107 through 109. Determine whether each party would be liable to pay a mortgage foreclosure deficiency judgment on the Fair Bank mortgage. If the party would be held liable, select from List D the reason for that party's liability and blacken the corresponding oval on the Objective Answer Sheet. If you determine there is **no** liability, blacken Ⓓ on the Objective Answer Sheet. A reason may be selected once, more than once, or not at all.

Step 6   *List D*

107. Edwards. *Assumed mortgage - B*   A. Original mortgagor.
108. Bond. *Liable as orig. mortgage - A*   B. Assumed the mortgage.
109. Ivor. *Not liable because took subject to mortgage - D*   C. Took subject to the mortgage.
                                                  D. Not liable.

OTHER OBJECTIVE ANSWERS AND ANSWER EXPLANATIONS

Problem 1

Part a.

101.(C) **102.**(B) **103.**(A) Under a notice-race recording statute, a subsequent mortgagee (lender) who loans money without notice of the previous mortgagee and records the mortgage first has priority over that previous mortgagee. Once a mortgagee records, this gives constructive notice to any subsequent parties who then cannot obtain priority over the one who recorded. In this fact pattern, Fair Bank was the first mortgagee. Since Fair Bank also recorded this mortgage first, Fair Bank has the first priority over the subsequent mortgagees. Therefore, the answer to number 103 is (A). Of the two remaining mortgagees, Heath Finance was next in time but did not record the mortgage. Knox Bank was third in time and did record. However, Knox is unable to gain priority over Heath because Knox, when it recorded, knew of the Heath mortgage. Therefore, Knox does not meet all of the rules necessary to have priority over Heath. Thus Heath has the second priority after Fair Bank and Knox has the third priority. Therefore, the answer to number 102 is (B) and number 101 is (C).

Part b.

104.(D) **105.**(D) **106.**(C) This part covers the reason for the priority that applies to each of the mortgagees. Reason (A) states that "an unrecorded mortgage has priority over any subsequently recorded mortgage." This is incorrect for all mortgagees and goes against the policy behind the recording statutes to encourage recording to warn subsequent parties of the previous mortgages. Reason (B) is not a correct statement. It states that "A recorded mortgage has priority over any unrecorded mortgage." In this fact pattern, Knox recorded but Heath did not; however, Knox still has a lower priority because Knox knew of the Heath mortgage when its mortgage was recorded. Reason (C) is the correct answer for Fair Bank. It states that "the first recorded mortgage has priority over all subsequent mortgages." This is true because once Fair Bank recorded, subsequent mortgagees had constructive notice of the Fair Bank mortgage and thus could not obtain priority. The correct answer to number 106 is therefore (C). Reason (D) states that "An unrecorded mortgage has priority over a subsequently recorded mortgage if the subsequent mortgagee knew of the unrecorded mortgage." In this fact pattern, the Heath mortgage was the unrecorded mortgage that still had a higher priority than the recorded Knox mortgage because Knox Bank knew of the Heath mortgage when its mortgage was recorded. Thus Knox never fulfilled the rule which would allow it as the subsequent mortgagee, to gain a higher priority. Therefore, reason (D) is the correct answer for both Knox Bank, number 104, and Heath Finance, number 105, because the same rule determines the relative priority of these two parties. Note that reason (E) is not a correct statement for any of the mortgagees because there is no rule that gives purchase money mortgages priority over previously recorded mortgages.

Part c.

107.(B) 108.(A) 109.(D) When a foreclosure sale does not provide enough money to pay off the mortgages, the mortgagee, in states that allow foreclosure deficiency judgments, will attempt to collect any deficiency from the parties involved. In this fact pattern, Bond is liable because s/he was the original mortgagor on the property and as such agreed to pay the mortgage. Thus, (A) is the correct answer for number 108. When Edwards later bought the property from Bond, s/he assumed the Fair Bank mortgage. Edwards, thus, became personally liable on the mortgage even though the seller, Bond, also remained liable. Therefore, (B) is the correct answer for number 107. When Ivor subsequently purchased the property from Edwards, Ivor purchased the property subject to the Fair Bank mortgage. In so doing, s/he did not accept any liability on the mortgage. Note that although reason (C) states "Took subject to the mortgage," the correct answer for number 109 is (D) "Not liable." This is true because the directions to part d. indicate that reasons (A), (B), or (C) are to be chosen as reasons **for liability** and (D) is to be chosen if the party is **not** liable.

Yes/No and Numerical Computations Example

Problem 1   (15 to 25 minutes)[2]

On April 15, 2001, Wren Corp., an appliance wholesaler, was petitioned involuntarily into bankruptcy under the liquidation provisions of Chapter 7 of the Federal Bankruptcy Code.

When the petition was filed, Wren's creditors included

Secured creditors	*Amount owed*
Fifth Bank—1st mortgage on warehouse owned by Wren	$50,000
Hart Manufacturing Corp.—perfected purchase money security interest in inventory	30,000
TVN Computers, Inc.—perfected security interest in office computers	15,000

Unsecured creditors	*Amount owed*
IRS—1998 federal income taxes	$20,000
Acme Office Cleaners—services for January, February, and March 2001	750
Ted Smith (employee)—February and March 2001 wages	4,700
Joan Sims (employee)—March 2001 commissions	3,000
Power Electric Co.—electricity charges for January, February, and March 2001	600
Soft Office Supplies—supplies purchased in 2000	2,000

The following transactions occurred before the bankruptcy petition was filed:

- On December 31, 2000, Wren paid off a $5,000 loan from Mary Lake, the sister of one of Wren's directors.
- On January 30, 2001, Wren donated $2,000 to Universal Charities.
- On February 1, 2001, Wren gave Young Finance Co. a security agreement covering Wren'ts office fixtures to secure a loan previously made by Young.
- On March 1, 2001, Wren made the final $1,000 monthly payment to Integral Applicance Corp. on a 2-year note.
- On April 1, 2001, Wren purchased from Safety Co., a new burglar alarm system for its factory, for $5,000 cash.

contemporaneous   *exchange*

All of Wren's assets were liquidated. The warehouse was sold for $75,000, the computers were sold for $12,000, and the inventory was sold for $25,000. After paying the bankruptcy administration expenses of $8,000, secured creditors, and priority general creditors, there was enough cash to pay each nonpriority general creditor 50 cents on the dollar.

Required:

a. **Items 101 through 105** represent the transactions that occurred before the filing of the bankruptcy petition. For each transaction, determine if the transaction would be set aside as a preferential transfer by the bankruptcy court. On the Objective Answer Sheet, blacken (Y) if the transaction would be set aside or (N) if the transaction would **not** be set aside.

101. Payment to Mary Lake

102. Donation to Universal Charities

103. Security agreement to Young Finance Co.

104. Payment to Integral Appliance Corp.

105. Purchase from Safety Co.

---

[2] *Estimated time is no longer provided on the Uniform CPA Examination. See "Allocation of Time" in Chapter 4.*

b.   Items 106 through 110 represent creditor claims against the bankruptcy estate. Select from List I e<u>ach creditor's</u> <u>order of payment in relation to the other creditors named in items 106 through 110</u> and blacken the corresponding oval on the Objective Answer Sheet.

		List I
106.	Bankruptcy administration expense	A. First
107.	Acme Office Cleaners	B. Second
		C. Third
108.	Fifth Bank	D. Fourth
109.	IRS	E. Fifth
110.	Joan Sims	

c.   Items 111 through 115 also represent creditor claims against the bankruptcy estate. For each of the creditors listed in Items 111 through 115, <u>select from List II the amount that creditor will receive</u> and blacken the corresponding oval on the Objective Answer Sheet.

		List II	
111.	TVN Computers, Inc.	A. $0	H. $ 4,700
112.	Hart Manufacturing Corp.	B. $ 300	I. $12,000
		C. $ 600	J. $13,500
113.	Ted Smith	D. $ 1,000	K. $15,000
		E. $ 1,200	L. $25,000
114.	Power Electric Co.	F. $ 4,300	M. $27,500
115.	Soft Office Supplies	G. $ 4,500	N. $30,000

OTHER OBJECTIVE ANSWERS AND ANSWER EXPLANATIONS

Problem 1

Part a.

The trustee in bankruptcy may set aside preferential transfers of nonexempt property made to a creditor within the 90 days prior to the filing of the bankruptcy petition while the debtor was insolvent. Preferential transfers are those made for antecedent debts which enable the creditor to receive more than s/he would otherwise be entitled to under a Chapter 7 liquidation proceeding. Preferential transfers made to insiders within the previous 12 months may also be set aside.

101.   (Y)   This payment may be set aside because Mary Lake is an insider since she is the sister of one of Wren's directors. The preferential transfer to her on December 31, 2000, falls within the 12 months prior to the filing of the bankruptcy petition on April 15, 2001.

102.   (N)   This transaction represents a donation rather than payment on an antecedent debt, therefore it would not be set aside as a preferential transfer.

103.   (Y)   The transaction would be set aside as a preferential transfer. On February 1, 2001, Wren gave Young Finance Co. a security agreement to secure a loan previously made by Young. Preferential transfers include the granting of a security interest by the debtor to secure an antecedent debt.

104.   (N)   Transfers in the ordinary course of business are not voidable preferences.

105.   (N)   In this case Wren purchased a new burglar alarm system for its factory for $5,000 cash. A contemporaneous exchange between a creditor and debtor whereby the debtor receives new value is not a preferential transfer.

Part b.

106.   (B)   Following satisfaction of the secured debts, bankruptcy administration expenses have the highest priority. Therefore, the administrative expenses will have second priority.

107.   (E)   Acme Office Cleaners is a general creditor and therefore receives the lowest priority for services performed before the bankruptcy petition was filed.

108.   (A)   The claim of Fifth Bank will be the first claim satisfied because it had a 1st mortgage on the warehouse owned by Wren. This warehouse was sold for $75,000 which more than satisfies the $50,000 owed to Fifth Bank.

109.   (D)   The IRS has priority for taxes due just before the priority of general creditors, therefore the IRS has fourth priority.

110.   (C)   Joan Sims, the employee, will have third priority because the bankrupt's employees have highest priority for wages and commission accrued within 3 months before the filing of the bankruptcy petition (up to a maximum of $4,300 each) after the administration costs have been satisfied.

Part c.

The fact pattern states that after paying the secured creditors, the bankruptcy administration expenses, and the priority general creditors, each nonpriority general creditor receives 50 cents on the dollar.

111.   **(J)**   TVN will receive $13,500. This is true because TVN's collateral sold for $12,000. TVN receives all of this $12,000 as a secured creditor owed $15,000. TVN becomes a general creditor for the remaining debt of $3,000 and receives 50 cents on the dollar for this which amounts to $1,500. TVN, therefore, receives $13,500 in total.

112.   **(M)**   Hart's collateral was sold for $25,000. The remaining $5,000 of the debt owed to Hart is paid at 50 cents on the dollar which amounts to $2,500. Hart, therefore, receives a total of $27,500.

113.   **(G)**   Ted Smith receives $4,300 as a priority for wages earned within the previous 3 months. Any wages in excess of the $4,300 are treated as a general claim, therefore he receives 50 cents on the dollar for the remaining $400 owed to him for a total of $4,500.

114.   **(B)**   Power Electric Co., as a general creditor, receives half of the $600 of charges which amounts to $300.

115.   **(D)**   Soft Office Supplies is a general creditor and thus receives 50 cents on the dollar for the $2,000 debt owed for a total of $1,000.

Essay Question Solutions Approach Algorithm

1. **Glance over the question.** Scan the question to get a feel for the topical area addressed. Do not read it. Until you understand the requirements, you cannot discriminate important data from irrelevant data.
2. **Study the requirements.** "Study" as differentiated from "read." Candidates continually lose points due to misunderstanding the requirements. Underline key phrases and words.
2a. **Visualize the solution format.** Determine the expected format of the required solution. As you would expect, the usual format for the solution to essay questions will be the paragraph format. However, there will be occasions where the requirements of the question may be answered by a list of items. Also, a single question may contain two or more requirements. Explicitly recognize multiple requirements (e.g., a, b, c) by numbering or lettering them on your examination booklet, expanding on the letters already assigned to the question (e.g., a.1, a.2, a.3, b.1, b.2,...).
3. **Outline the required procedures mentally.** Interrelate the background data given in the question to the expected solution format, mentally formulating a "to do" list. Determine what it is you are going to do before you begin doing it. You should work through the requirements in order but be alert for questions with interrelated requirements.
3a. **Review applicable principles, knowledge.** Before immersing yourself in the details of the essay, quickly (30-60 seconds) review and organize your knowledge of the principles applicable to the question. Jot down any acronyms, formulas, or other memory aids relevant to the topics of the question. Otherwise, the details of the question may confuse and overshadow your previous knowledge of the applicable principles.
4. **Study the text of the question.** Read the question carefully. With the requirements in mind, you can now begin to discriminate relevant from irrelevant data. Underline and circle important data. The data necessary for answering each requirement may be scattered throughout the question. List the requirements in the margin alongside the data to which they pertain. Remember—this is your exam and you should use whatever technique you find effective to highlight important data and concepts.
4a. **Write down keywords (concepts).** Jot down a list of keywords (grading concepts) in the margin of the examination booklet. Some candidates may want to organize the list of keywords into a solutions outline.
5. **Prepare the solution.** You are now in a position to write a neat, complete, and organized solution. Remember that 5% of your score on each section comes from the grading of your writing skills. Therefore, it is very important that you write something for each requirement of the question and take the time to develop a clear and organized essay for the reader/grader.
6. **Proofread and edit.** Do not underestimate the benefits of this step. Just recall all of the "silly" mistakes you made on undergraduate exams. Corrections of errors and completion of oversights during this step can easily be the difference between passing and failing.
7. **Review the requirements.** Assure yourself that you have answered them all.

Essay Question Solutions Approach Example

To illustrate the use of the solutions approach in answering essay questions, we have included Question 1 from the May 1998 Examination in Business Law & Professional Responsibilities section. The illustration appears on the following pages.

Highlights of the Solutions Approach to Essay Questions

After studying the requirements and visualizing the format of the unofficial answer, study the text of the question, making notes and also preparing a **keyword** outline. After the keyword outline has been prepared, a basic distinction must be made as to the type of essay question presented. The first type of essay question contains one fact situation from which two or more requirements cover the **same** or similar auditing topics, points of law, or accounting rules. The proper method of answering this type of question is to handle the requirements simultaneously. In other words, apply each step in the solutions approach to all of the requirements before moving on to the next step.

The second type of essay question contains one fact situation from which two or more requirements cover **different** topics or rules. The proper method of answering this type of question is to handle the requirements independently, following each step of the solutions approach separately for each requirement. Thus, after the first requirement is completed, repeat the solutions approach for each remaining requirement. The benefit to handling the requirements independently is to keep the different topics or rules separate in your mind. This allows you to complete one requirement before moving on to another requirement and mentally "changing gears."

When you have identified the type of question involved, reorganize the keyword outline for the entire answer. Make sure that you have answered each requirement (and only that requirement) completely. Be careful not to preempt an answer to another requirement. The **keyword** outline for the example question should be similar to the grading guide in Chapter 2. Next, write up your solution and edit as needed. Use only 3/4 of each page to write up your solution. The remaining 1/4 can then be used to add material and to make revisions which can be keyed to the text with asterisks. The solution will thus be easier for the grader to read, and also easier for you to proofread and edit. Remember, there is no limit on the amount of lined paper you may use. If you have time later, review your solution again.

Problem 1

On June 1, Classic Corp., a manufacturer of desk chairs, orally agreed to sell 100 leather desk chairs to Rand Stores, a chain of retail furniture stores, for $50,000. The parties agreed that delivery would be completed by September 1, and the shipping terms were "FOB seller's loading dock." On June 5, Classic sent Rand a signed memorandum of agreement containing the terms orally agreed to. Rand received the memorandum on June 7 and made no response.

On July 31, Classic identified the chairs to be shipped to Rand and placed them on its loading dock to be picked up by the common carrier the next day. That night, a fire on the loading dock destroyed 50 of the chairs. On August 1, the remaining 50 chairs were delivered to the common carrier together with 50 vinyl chairs. The truck carrying the chairs was involved in an accident, resulting in extensive damage to 10 of the leather chairs and 25 of the vinyl chairs.

On August 10, the chairs were delivered to Rand. On August 12, Rand notified Classic that Rand was accepting 40 of the leather chairs and 10 of the vinyl chairs, but the rest of the shipment was being rejected. Rand also informed Classic that, due to Classic's failure to perform under the terms of the contract, Rand would seek all remedies available under the Sales Article of the UCC.

Classic contended that it has no liability to Rand and that the shipment was strictly an accommodation to Rand because Rand failed to sign the memorandum of agreement, thus preventing a contract from being formed.

The above parties and transactions are governed by the provisions of the Sales Article of the UCC.

Required:

a. Determine whether Classic's contention is correct and give the reasons for your conclusion.

b. Assuming that a valid contract exists between Classic and Rand, answer the following questions and give the reasons for your conclusions. Do **not** consider any possible liability owed by the common carrier.

1. Who bears the risk of loss for the 50 destroyed leather chairs?

2. Who bears the risk of loss for the 25 damaged vinyl chairs?

3. What is the earliest date that title to any of the chairs would pass to Rand?

c. With what UCC requirements must Rand comply to be entitled to recover damages from Classic?

d. Assuming that a valid contract exists between Classic and Rand, state the applicable remedies to which Rand would be entitled. Do **not** consider any possible liability owed by the common carrier.

Keyword Outline

Governed by Sales Article of UCC

Both parties are merchants

General rule: Sale of goods > $500--must be in writing (Statute of Frauds)

Exception: Oral agreement followed by confirmation forms enforceable agreement for merchants if nonsigning party does not object within 10 days

FOB Seller's loading dock--FOB shipping
*   --seller has risk of loss until delivered to common carrier*

Vinyl chairs--nonconforming goods
*   --buyer has no risk of loss for nonconforming goods*

FOB shipping--Buyer has title once delivered to common carrier - Aug 1

To receive damages
*   --notify of rejection*
*   --follow reasonable instructions (ship chairs, sell chairs)*
*   --give until Sept 1 to cure*

Remedies for buyer

*   --cancel contract*

*   --cover*

*   --recover monetary damages*

Step 1:

Glance over quickly

Step 2:

Study requirements

Step 2A:

Visualize solution format

1. The solution will be in paragraph form
2. For requirement a., one may expect the solution to discuss the Statute of Frauds, and any exceptions to the Statute of Frauds under the UCC.
3. For requirement b., one may expect the solution to discuss shipment terms and risk of loss and title under the UCC.
4. For requirement c., one may expect the solution to discuss UCC requirements for recovering damages.
5. For requirement d., one may expect the solution to discuss a buyer's remedies available under the UCC.

For steps 3 - 7, each requirement should be addressed and fully answered **before** the next requirement is addressed.

For requirement a.

Step 3:

Outline required procedures mentally. The approach will be to carefully read the question and determine the facts related to the formation of the contract and whether or not the requirements for meeting the Statute of Frauds were met.

Step 3A:

Review applicable principles with regard to the Statute of Frauds under the UCC.

a. Agreement for sale of goods for $500 or more is required to be in writing under the UCC.
b. When a writing is required, it must indicate in writing that a contract for sale has been made, be signed by party to be charged, and specify quantity of goods sold.
c. Exception to signature requirement exists under UCC when both parties are merchants. One party may send written confirmation stating terms of oral agreement to other party within reasonable time, then nonsigning party must object within 10 days or the contract is enforceable against him/her.

Step 4:

Study the text

Step 4A:

Keyword outline (see previous page containing the question)

*Step 5:

Prepare solution

*Step 6:

Proofread and edit

*Step 7:

Review
* See Unofficial Answer in Chapter 2

For requirement b.

Step 3:

Outline required procedures mentally. The approach will be to consider the shipping terms, "FOB seller's loading dock" and how the shipping terms affect risk of loss and title under the UCC.

Step 3A:

Review applicable principles with regard to FOB shipping point and risk of loss and title.

a. FOB shipping point—buyer obtains risk of loss and title and bears shipping costs once goods are delivered to carrier.
b. If seller breaches (sends nonconforming goods), risk of loss remains with seller until cure by seller or acceptance by buyer.
c. If seller breaches, title passes under original terms despite delivery of nonconforming goods.

Step 4:

Study the text

Step 4A:

Keyword outline (see previous page containing the question)

*Step 5:

Prepare solution

*Step 6:

Proofread and edit

*Step 7:

Review
*See Unofficial Answer in Chapter 2

For requirement c.

Step 3:

Outline required procedures mentally. The approach will be to carefully read the question and determine the facts related to the breach of contract and what UCC requirements would be applicable for Rand to comply with in order to recover damages.

Step 3A:

Review applicable principles with regard to a buyer receiving nonconforming goods (the seller's breach of contract) and what UCC requirement the buyer must comply with in order to recover damages.

a. Buyer may reject nonconforming goods, either in entirety or any commercial unit.

b. If buyer rejects nonconforming goods, s/he must do so in reasonable time and give notice to seller.

c. If buyer is a merchant, s/he must follow reasonable instructions of seller (e.g., ship, sell)

d. Buyer must allow seller to cure nonconformity within original time of contract.

Step 4:

Study the text

Step 4A:

Keyword outline (see previous page containing the question)

*Step 5:

Prepare solution

*Step 6:

Proofread and edit

*Step 7:

Review
* See Unofficial Answer in Chapter 2

For requirement d.

Step 3:

Outline required procedures mentally. The approach will be to consider applicable remedies to which Rand (the buyer) would be entitled, based on Classic's breach of contract.

Step 3A:

Review applicable principles with regard to a buyer's remedies based on a seller's breach of contract (delivery of nonconforming goods).

a. The most common remedy under contract law is monetary damages.

b. If seller does not notify buyer of his intention to cure, buyer has right to cancel contract.

c. Buyer has the right of cover and will still have the right to damages.

d. Punitive damages are not allowed for a breach of contract.

e. Specific performance is used only when money damages will not suffice. (When subject matter is unique or rare)

Step 4:

Study the text

Step 4A:

Keyword outline (see previous page containing the question)

*Step 5:

Prepare solution

*Step 6:

Proofread and edit

*Step 7:

Review
* See Unofficial Answer in Chapter 2

NOTE: You **must** write out the answers to the essay questions. **Keyword** outlines are not sufficient. The AICPA requires you to show an understanding of the grading concepts, not merely a listing of grading concepts. However, you may prepare answers in list form so long as the listed items are in sentence format. Prepare brief paragraphs consisting of several concise sentences about each grading concept. The paragraphs may be numbered in an outline format similar to that of the unofficial answers.

The examiners grade candidates on their writing skills. Samples will be taken from each section of the exam (e.g., requirement **c.** from one essay and requirement **b.** from another essay). Candidates will not be told which responses will be evaluated. Writing skills will be assessed by the same individuals who grade the essay responses for technical content. The grading will be done using a holistic approach. Holistic grading attempts to measure the effectiveness with which you communicate your knowledge and ideas; thus, the graders judge your work by how easily they understand the ideas which you are attempting to present. Five percent of the total points available on the Business Law and Professional Responsibilities section will be based on writing skills. However, candidates' scores with respect to writing skills will not be disclosed separately in the candidate diagnostic report.

Candidates' writing skills will be graded according to the following six characteristics:

1. **Coherent organization**

   Candidates should organize their responses in a manner that is logical and easy to follow. Jumbled paragraphs and disorderly sentences will only confuse the grader and make his/her job more difficult. The following techniques will help improve written coherence.[3]

   • Use short paragraphs composed of short sentences
   • Indent paragraphs to set off lists, equations, key ideas, etc. when appropriate
   • Maintain coherence **within** paragraphs

---

[3] *Adapted from **Writing for Accountants** by Aletha S. Hendrickson (Cincinnati, OH: Southwestern Publishing Co., 1993) pp. 128-209.*

- Use a topic sentence at the beginning of each paragraph
- Develop and support this topic throughout the rest of the paragraph
- Present old or given information before discussing new information
- Discuss ideas in chronological order
- Use parallel grammatical structure
- Be consistent in person, verb tense, and number
- Substitute pronouns or synonyms for previously used keywords
- Use transitions (e.g., therefore, finally)

- Maintain coherence **between** paragraphs
    - Repeat keywords from previous paragraph
    - Use transitions

As discussed above, candidates are strongly advised to keyword outline their responses **before** writing their essays. This technique helps the candidate to focus on the flow of ideas s/he wants to convey before starting the actual writing task.

2. Conciseness

Candidates should express themselves in as few words as possible. Complex, wordy sentences are hard to understand. Conciseness can be improved using the following guidelines.

- Write in short sentences
- Use a simple word instead of a long word if it serves the same purpose
- Avoid passive constructions (e.g., **was** evaluat**ed**)
- Use words instead of phrases
- Combine sentences, if possible
- Avoid empty fillers (e.g., **it is** apparent; **there seems to be**)
- Avoid multiple negatives (e.g., **no** reason for **not** using)

3. Clarity

Written responses should leave no doubt in the reader's mind as to the meaning intended. Clarity can be improved as follows:

- Do **not** use abbreviations
- Use correct terminology
- Use words with specific and precise meanings
- Write in short, well-constructed sentences
- Make sure subjects and verbs agree in number
- Make sure pronouns and their antecedents agree in number (e.g., the partnership must decide how **it** (not **they**) wants to split profits.)
- Avoid unclear reference to a pronoun's antecedent (e.g., A should inform B that **he** must perform on the contract by January 1.—To whom does "he" refer?)

4. Use of standard English

Spelling, punctuation, and word usage should follow the norm used in most books, newspapers, and magazines. Note the following common mistakes:

- Confusion of its/it's
    *The firm issued **its** stock.*
    ***It's** (it is) the stock of that firm.*

- Confusion of there/their/they're
    ***There** will be a contract.*
    ***Their** contract was signed last week.*
    ***They're** (they are) signing the contract.*

- Spelling errors
    *Separate **not** seperate*
    *Receivable **not** recievable*

5. Responsiveness to the question's requirements

Candidates should respond directly to the question being asked. No more information should be given than necessary. Broad expositions on the general topic demonstrate an inability to focus and organize writing to fulfill a specific purpose. Avoid irrelevance by following your keyword outline.

6. **Appropriateness for the reader**

Essay questions may ask the candidate to prepare a document for a certain reader (e.g., a memorandum for a client). Writing that is appropriate for the reader will take into account the reader's background, knowledge of the subject, interests, and concerns. (When the intended reader is not specified, the candidate should write for a knowledgeable CPA.)

Intended readers may include those who are unfamiliar with most terms and concepts, and who seek financial information because of self-interest (i.e., clients, stockholders). Try the following techniques for these readers:

- Avoid jargon, if possible (i.e., HDC, etc.)
- Use parenthetical definitions

    - *limited partner (liable only to the extent of contributed capital)*
    - *marketable equity securities (short-term investments in stock)*

- Set off definitions as appositives

    A note, a two-party negotiable instrument, is one type of commercial paper.

- Incorporate a "you" attitude

The requirement of a question may also specify that the response should be directed to professionals who are knowledgeable of most terms and concepts. Employ the following techniques with these readers:

- Use jargon
- Refer to authoritative sources (i.e., Article 3 of the UCC)
- Incorporate a "we" attitude

Again, preparing a keyword outline will assist you in meeting many of these requirements. You should also reread each written answer in its entirety. **Writing errors are common during the exam, so take time to proofread and edit your answers.**

Methods for Improving Your Writing Skills

1. **Organization**

In preparing to answer a CPA exam essay, read the question carefully, determining the exact requirements of the question. Reread the question, underlining main points and noting them in the margin of your exam booklet. (This is the keyword approach.) Once you have identified the keywords, take a few minutes to organize these ideas in a logical manner.

For example, if the question requires a discussion of Chapter 7 bankruptcy and Chapter 11 reorganization, you might consider these main points: the goal of the proceedings, eligibility requirements, appointment of a trustee, and the right to retain assets. This question lends itself to comparison/contrast type development. Thus you would arrange your keywords to reflect that type of organization. Your first body paragraph(s) might discuss the goal of Chapter 7, detailing the liquidation provisions, exemptions, and who may initiate the proceedings. Your next paragraph(s) would discuss the above points as they relate to Chapter 11.

Sometimes, a long narrative is provided prior to the actual questions. This narrative exists to facilitate your answer; it provides data to work with so that you do not have to make up all your own examples. If this type of narrative exists, read through it, searching for legal issues and examples; these will come in handy when actually writing your response.

2. **Development**

Frequently, the CPA exam essays merely require you to recite a list of main points in an essay format. The graders are looking more for how many points you have covered than the depth with which you covered any one of them. Unfortunately, putting together a number of semirelated facts into a coherent essay may prove to be a more difficult task than coming up with the facts to begin with.

In this situation, try to see if you can group your points into categories. These categories may be thematic, chronological, or descriptive. If you are able to group the points, then each category can be discussed in one paragraph. If not, you may have to unify your answer with a topic sentence that indicates the many facets of the problem about which you are writing. This type of sentence sets up your essay for listing these facets.

Regardless of how you begin, do not simply list your points—this becomes monotonous. Rather, list, explain, and provide an example. Move from general to specific: provide the general concept, explain it in more specific terms, and provide a very pointed example. In addition, do not forget to use sequential connectors such as "first," "second," "next," etc.

3. **Syntax, grammar, and style**

By the time you sit for the CPA exam, you have at your disposal various grammatical constructs from which you may form sentences. Believe it or not, you know quite a bit of English grammar; if you did not, you would never have made it this far in your studies. So in terms of your grammar, relax! You already know it.

A frequent problem with writing occurs with the syntactic structure of sentences. Although the Board of Examiners does not expect the rhetoric of Cicero, it does expect to read and understand your answer. The way in which the graders will assess writing skills further indicates that they are looking more for writing skills at the micro level (sentence level) than at the macro level (organizational level).

a. Basic syntactic structure (transitive and intransitive action verbs)

Most English sentences are based on this simple dynamic: that someone or something (the subject) does some action (the predicate). These sentences involve action verbs and are grouped in the following categories:

(1) Subject-Verb

The OFFEROR WAITED for 3 weeks to get an acceptance.

(2) Subject-Verb-Direct Object (The object receives the action of the verb.)

The OFFEREE SIGNED the CONTRACT.

(3) Subject-Verb-Indirect Object-Direct Object (The direct object receives the action of the verb, but the indirect object is also affected by this action, though not in the same way as the direct object.)

Our MERCHANT GAVE US an EXPRESS WARRANTY well beyond our expectations.

b. Syntactic structure (linking verbs)

Linking verbs are verbs which, rather than expressing action, say something about the subject's state of being. In sentences with linking verbs, the subject is linked to a word which describes it or renames it.

(1) Subject-Linking Verb-Nominative (The nominative renames the subject.)

In the field of Accounting, the FASB IS the standard-setting BOARD.

(2) Subject-Linking Verb-Adjective (The adjective describes the subject.)

Evidence of SCIENTER IS always HELPFUL in proving fraud.

c. Subordinate clauses

(1) Adverbial clauses (subordinating connector + sentence). These clauses modify the action of the main clause.

When ordinary duress occurs, a voidable agreement is created.

(2) Noun clauses (nominal connectors + sentence). These clauses function as nouns in the main sentence.

In sales of goods for $500 or more, we know that a writing is required under the UCC.

(3) Adjective clauses [relative pronoun + verb + (object/nominative/adjective)]. These clauses function as noun modifiers.

The security interest which has the greatest priority is the one that was perfected or filed first.

d. The above are patterns which form basic clauses (both dependent and independent). In addition, numerous phrases may function as modifiers of the basic sentence elements.

(1) Prepositional (a preposition + an object)

    of the FASB
    on the data
    about a holder in due course

(2) Verbal

    (a) Verb + ing + a modifier (noun, verb, adverb, prepositional phrase)

        i] Used as an adjective

           the sales agreement requiring a writing
           the option minimizing damages from breach of contract

        ii] Used as a noun (gerund)

           Performing all of the duties required by a contract is necessary to avoid breach.

    (b) Verb + ed + modifier (noun, adverb, prepositional phrase)

        i] Used as an adjective

           The remedy used when money damages will not suffice is specific performance.

    (c) Infinitive (to + verb + object)

        i] Used as a noun

           The company needs to perfect that security interest by filing a financing statement.

4. **Sentence clarity**

    a. When constructing your sentences, do not separate basic sentence elements with too many phrases.

        The liability for partnership losses exceeding capital contributions is another characteristic of a general partnership.

    Better: *One characteristic of a general partnership is the liability for partnership losses which exceed capital contributions.*

    b. Refrain from lumping prepositional and infinitive phrases together.

        The delegation of authority by a corporate director of day-to-day or routine matters to officers and agents of that corporation is a power and a duty of the director.

    Better: *Delegating authority for routine matters to officers and agents is a power and a duty of a corporation's directors.*

    c. Make sure that your pronouns have a clear and obvious referent.

        When an accountant contracts with a client for the primary benefit of a third party, they are in privity of contract.

    Better: *When known to be a primary beneficiary of an accountant-client contract, a third party is in privity of contract with the accountant.*

    d. Make sure that any adjectival verbal phrase clearly modifies a noun stated in the sentence.

        To avoid breaching the contract, each obligation was performed exactly as agreed.

    Better: *To avoid breaching the contract, we performed each obligation exactly as agreed.*

Time Requirements for the Solutions Approach

Many candidates bypass the solutions approach because they feel it is too time-consuming. Actually, the solutions approach is a time-saver and, more importantly, it helps you prepare better solutions to all essays.

Without committing yourself to using the solutions approach, try it step-by-step on several essay questions. After you conscientiously go through the step-by-step routine a few times, you will begin to adopt and modify aspects of the technique which will benefit you. Subsequent usage will become subconscious and painless. The important point is that you must try the solutions approach several times to accrue any benefits.

Efficiency of the Solutions Approach

The mark of an inefficient solution is one wherein the candidate immediately begins to write an essay solution. Remember, the final solution is one of the last steps in the solutions approach. You should have the solution under complete control (with the **keyword** outline) before you begin your final solution.

While the large amount of intermediary work in the solutions approach may appear burdensome and time-consuming, this technique results in more complete solutions in less time than do haphazard approaches. Moreover, the solutions approach really allows you to work out essays that you feel unfamiliar with at first reading. The solutions approach, however, must be mastered prior to sitting for the CPA examination. In other words, the candidate must be willing to invest a reasonable amount of time into perfecting his/her own solutions approach.

In summary, the solutions approach may appear foreign and somewhat cumbersome. At the same time, if you have worked through the material in this chapter, you should have some appreciation for it. Develop the solutions approach by writing down the steps in the solutions approach algorithm at the beginning of this chapter, and keep them before you as you work previous CPA exam questions. Remember that even though the suggested procedures appear **very structured** and **time-consuming,** integration of these procedures into your own style of problem solving will help improve **your** solutions approach. The next chapter discusses strategies for the overall examination.

**NOW IS THE TIME
TO MAKE YOUR COMMITMENT**

4 TAKING THE EXAMINATION

This chapter is concerned with developing an examination strategy (e.g., how to cope with the environment at the examination site, the order in which to work questions, etc.).

EXAMINATION STRATEGIES

Your performance during the 2-day examination is final and not subject to revision. While you may sit for the examination again if you are unsuccessful, the majority of your preparation will have to be repeated, requiring substantial, additional amounts of time. Thus, examination strategies (discussed in this chapter) which maximize your exam-taking efficiency are very important.

Getting "Psyched Up"

The CPA exam is quite challenging and worthy of your best effort. Explicitly develop your own psychological strategy to get yourself "up" for the exam. Pace your study program such that you will be able to operate at peak performance when you are actually taking the exam. Many candidates give up because they have a bad day or encounter a rough problem. Do the best you can; the other candidates are probably no better prepared than you.

Examination Supplies

The AICPA recommends that candidates prepare their solutions in pencil. As you practice your solutions approach, experiment with pencils, lead types, erasers, etc., that are comfortable to use and that also result in good copy for the grader.

In addition to an adequate supply of pencils and erasers, it is very important to take a watch to the examination. Also, take refreshments (as permitted), which are conducive to your exam efficiency. Finally, dress to assure your comfort during the exam. Layered clothing is recommended for possible variations in temperature at the examination site.

Do **not** take study materials to the examination room. You will not be able to use them. They will only muddle your mind and get you "uptight." Finally, **do not** carry notes or crib sheets upon your person—this can only result in the gravest of problems. Do not risk being expelled from the exam.

Lodging, Meals, Exercise

Make advance reservations for comfortable lodging convenient to the examination facilities. Do not stay with friends, relatives, etc. Both uninterrupted sleep and total concentration on the exam are a must. Consider the following in making your lodging plans:

1. Proximity to exam facilities
2. Lodging and exam parking facilities
3. Availability of meals and snacks
4. Recreational facilities

Plan your meal schedule to provide maximum energy and alertness during the day and maximum rest at night. Do not experiment with new foods, drinks, etc., during the examination time period. Within reasonable limits, observe your normal eating and drinking habits. Recognize the overconsumption of coffee during the exam could lead to a hyperactive state and disaster. Likewise, overindulgence in alcohol to overcome nervousness and to induce sleep the night before might contribute to other difficulties the following morning.

Tenseness should be expected before and during the examination. Rely on a regular exercise program to unwind at the end of the day. As you select your lodging for the examination, try to accommodate your exercise pleasure (e.g., running, swimming, etc.). Continue to indulge in your exercise program on the days of the examination.

To relieve tension or stress while studying, try breathing or stretching exercises. Use these exercises before and during the examination to start and to keep your adrenaline flowing. Do not hesitate to attract attention by doing pushups, jumping jacks, etc., in a lobby outside of the examination room if it will improve your exam efficiency. Remain determined not to go through another examination to obtain your certificate.

A problem you will probably experience during the exam related to general fatigue and tenseness is writer's cramp. Experiment with alternate methods of holding your pencil, rubbing your hand, etc., during your preparation program.

In summary, the examination is likely to be both rigorous and fatiguing. Expect it and prepare for it by getting in shape, planning methods of relaxation during the exam and exam evenings, and finally, building the confidence and competence to complete the exam (successfully).

Examination Facilities and Procedures

Visit the examination facilities at least the evening before the examination to assure knowledge of the location. Remember: no surprises. Having a general familiarity with the facilities will lessen anxiety prior to the examination.

Talking to a recent veteran of the examination will give you background for the general examination procedures, such as

1. Procedures for distributing exam booklets, papers, etc.
2. Accessibility of restrooms
3. Availability of beverages and snacks at exam location
4. Admissibility of beverages and snacks in the exam room
5. Peculiar problems of exam facilities (e.g., noise, lighting, temperature, etc.)
6. Permissibility of early departure from the exam
7. Experience in taking the exam
8. Other important information

As you can see, it is important to talk with someone who recently sat for the examination at the same location where you intend to sit. The objective is to reduce your anxiety just prior to the examination and to minimize any possible distractions. Finally, if you have any remaining questions regarding examination procedure, call or write your state board.

On a related point, do not be distracted by other candidates who show up at the examination completely relaxed and greet others with confidence. These are most likely candidates who have been there before. Probably the only thing they are confident of is a few days' vacation from work. Also, do not become distracted when candidates leave early. A candidate's early departure may mean s/he is giving up.

Arrive at the Examination Early

On the day of the exam, be sure to get to the examination site at least 30 minutes early to reduce tension and to get yourself situated. Most states have assigned seating. If this is the case, you will be seated by your candidate ID number. However, if you have a choice, it is probably wise to sit away from the door and the administration table to avoid being distracted by candidates who arrive late, leave early, ask questions, etc., and by proctors who occasionally converse. **Avoid all possible distractions. Stay away from friends.** Find a seat that will be comfortable; consider sunlight, interior lighting, heating/air conditioning, pedestrian traffic, etc.

Usually the proctors open the sealed boxes of exams and distribute the Examination Booklets to candidates ten minutes before the scheduled beginning of the examination. Shown below are the cover sheets for the Examination Question Booklet and the Examination Answer Booklet from the November 1995 Business Law and Professional Responsibilities exam, the latest disclosed exam. Now, candidates receive only one booklet that contains both the questions and the answer sheets. Record your 7-digit candidate number in the boxes provided at the upper right-hand corner of the front cover of the Examination Question Booklet. You are not permitted to open the booklet until the starting signal is given, but you should study the instructions printed on the front cover. The instructions generally explain

1. How to turn in examination papers
2. Handling of Examination Question and Answer Booklet

3. Examiners' consideration of the candidate's ability to express him/herself in acceptable written language

The Examination Answer Booklet is divided into four sections:

1. An Attendance Record and Statement of Confidentiality
2. Examination Questions
3. An Objective Answer Sheet
4. Essay/Problem Answer Ruled/Columnar Paper

Prior to the start of the exam, you will be instructed to complete and detach the Attendance Record and to sign a Statement of Confidentiality, which will be retained by the State Boards of Accountancy. You should record your 7-digit candidate number on this record and on all other papers you submit. You will also be permitted to record your 7-digit candidate number in the upper right-hand corner and blacken the corresponding oval below each box on the front and back covers of your booklet.

The Objective Answer Sheet contained in the booklet will be used to record answers to both the multiple-choice section of the exam and the other objective format questions. In some states, you will be asked to detach the Objective Answer Sheet and turn it in separately; however, in other states the Objective Answer Sheet is to remain attached to the booklet. Follow the instructions of your state board. Also, record your candidate number where indicated.

The AICPA is now using a "generic" two-sided objective answer sheet (shown below). The multiple-choice answers should be entered on side 1, and the other objective answers should be entered on side 2. The information and numbering for each side is as follows:

- **Side 1:**   **Multiple-choice** answers contain spaces to answer question numbers **1 to 100,** with letter **choices "a" through "d**." Use only what you need. For example, the Law exam usually contains 60 multiple-choice questions (excluding pretest). In this case, the remaining numbers up to 100 will be left blank. The Auditing exam might contain 90 multiple-choice questions (excluding pretest). Again, use only what you need. **Then, turn over the answer sheet to side 2 to use for the other objective questions.**
- **Side 2:**   **Other objective** answers contain spaces to answer question numbers **101 to 165,** with letter **choices "a" through "z."** Again, use only what you need. For example, if the other objective questions end at number 150, leave numbers 151 through 165 blank.

It is very important to turn the answer sheet over and always begin the other objective answers with question number 101. Take your time, darkening an oval for each answer, one question at a time.

Two different versions of the Objective Answer Sheet from the November 1995 Business Law and Professional Responsibilities exam are shown below. **Candidates should be aware that different versions of the answer sheet have different arrangements for the multiple-choice questions. The answer sheet may be organized vertically, horizontally, or a combination of the two. The candidate, therefore, must be sure to correctly transfer all answers to the answer sheet.**

The essay answer ruled paper will be used for answering the essay questions. Record your candidate number on the ruled paper where indicated. As you proceed through the exam, you will write in the upper left-hand corner the essay question number which is being answered. Always begin the answer to a question on top of a new page. Additional ruled paper is available if needed and should be enclosed in the booklet when turning it in. If you do not want the grader to grade a particular page, place a large "X" over the page.

Inventory of the Examination Content

When you receive your booklet, carefully read the instructions. The objective is to review the standard instructions, to note any new or special items, and to comply with examination procedures. After reviewing the instructions on the front of your booklet, make note of the number of questions and the point value of each. Immediately after receiving permission to open the booklet, glance over each of the questions sufficiently and jot down the topics on the front of the booklet. This will give you an overview of the ensuing 3 hours of work. **Before** you forget them, you may find it to your advantage to write down keywords, acronyms, etc. on the front of the booklet, **after** you have been told to begin the examination.

Allocation of Time

Budget your time. Time should be carefully allocated in an attempt to maximize points per minute. While you must develop your own strategy with respect to time allocation, some suggestions may be useful. Allocate 5 minutes to reading the instructions and to taking an inventory, jotting down the topics tested by question on

EXAMINATION QUESTIONS

UNIFORM CERTIFIED PUBLIC ACCOUNTANT EXAMINATION
Business Law & Professional Responsibilities

LPR

November 1, 1995; 9:00 A.M. to 12:00 NOON

The point values for each question, and estimated time allotments based primarily on point value, are as follows:

	Point Value	Estimated Minutes Minimum	Maximum
No. 1	60	90	100
No. 2	10	10	15
No. 3	10	10	15
No. 4	10	15	25
No. 5	10	15	25
Totals	100	140	180

INSTRUCTIONS TO CANDIDATES
Failure to follow these instructions may have an adverse effect on your Examination grade.

1. Do not break the seal around *Examination Questions* (pages 3 through 18) until you are told to do so.

2. Question Numbers 1, 2, and 3 should be answered on the *Objective Answer Sheet*, which is pages 27 and 28. You should attempt to answer all objective items. Since there is no penalty for incorrect responses, the objective items are computer-graded, your comments and calculations associated with them are not considered. Be certain that you have entered your answers on the *Objective Answer Sheet* before the examination time is up. The objective portion of your examination will not be graded if you fail to record your answers on the *Objective Answer Sheet*. You will not be given additional time to record your answers.

3. Question Numbers 4 and 5 should be answered beginning on page 19. If you have not completed answering a question on a page, fill in the appropriate spaces in the wording on the bottom of the page "QUESTION NUMBER ___ CONTINUES ON PAGE ___." If you have completed answering a question, fill in the appropriate space in the wording on the bottom of the page "QUESTION NUMBER ___ ENDS ON THIS PAGE." Always

4. Although the primary purpose of the examination is to test your knowledge and application of the subject matter, selected essay responses will be graded for writing skills.

5. You are required to turn in by the end of each session:
   a. Attendance Record Form, page 1;
   b. *Examination Questions*, pages 3 through 18;
   c. *Essay Ruled Paper*, pages 19 through 26;
   d. *Objective Answer Sheet*, pages 27 and 28; and
   e. All unused examination materials.

   Your examination will not be graded unless the above listed items are handed in before leaving the examination room.

6. Unless otherwise instructed, if you want your *Examination Questions* mailed to you, write your name and address in both places indicated on page 18 and place 55 cents postage in the space provided. *Examination Questions* will be distributed no sooner than the day following the administration of this examination.

Examination Questions Booklet No.

2 03909 Q

over

3

EXAMINATION QUESTION AND ANSWER BOOKLET

ATTENDANCE RECORD
(To Be Retained by State Board)

Name _____
(please print)

Home Address _____

City _____ State _____ Zip Code _____

Signature _____ Date _____

LPR
VERSION 3

UNIFORM CERTIFIED PUBLIC ACCOUNTANT EXAMINATION
Business Law & Professional Responsibilities

November 1, 1995; 9:00 A.M. to 12:00 NOON

INSTRUCTIONS TO CANDIDATES

(This *Examination Question and Answer Booklet* contains an *Attendance Record, Examination Questions, Essay Ruled Paper,* and *Objective Answer Sheet*)

1. Do not begin writing on this *Booklet* until you are told to do so.

2. Complete the *Attendance Record* and your 7-digit candidate number above. Detach the page at the perforation so it can be collected and retained by the State Board.

3. Turn the *Booklet* over and record your 7-digit candidate number and state on the *Objective Answer Sheet*.

4. The *Objective Answer Sheet* is on pages 27 and 28. The objective portion of your examination will not be graded if you fail to record your answers on the *Objective Answer Sheet*.

5. See instructions 3 and 4 on page 3 for instructions on how to record your answers to Question Numbers 4 and 5.

6. In order to grade your *Objective Answer Sheet* and essay answers, the Booklet No. above must be identical to the Booklet Nos. on pages 3, 19, and 28.

over

1

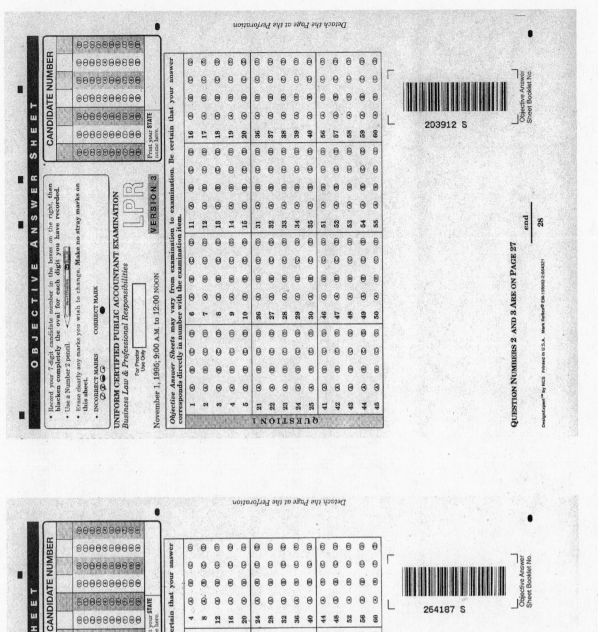

Detach the Page at the Perforation

OBJECTIVE ANSWER SHEET

CANDIDATE NUMBER

- Record your 7-digit candidate number in the boxes on the right, then blacken completely the oval for each digit you have recorded.
- Use a Number 2 pencil.
- Erase clearly any marks you wish to change. Make no stray marks on this sheet.

INCORRECT MARKS   CORRECT MARK

UNIFORM CERTIFIED PUBLIC ACCOUNTANT EXAMINATION
Business Law & Professional Responsibilities

LPR

For Proctor Use Only

Print your STATE name here.

VERSION 3

November 1, 1995; 9:00 A.M. to 12:00 NOON

Objective Answer Sheets may vary from examination to examination. Be certain that your answer corresponds directly in number with the examination item.

QUESTION I

Objective Answer Sheet Booklet No.

QUESTION NUMBERS 2 AND 3 ARE ON PAGE 27

end

28

DesignExpert™ by NCS Printed in U.S.A. Mark Reflex® EM-159592-2:654321

Detach the Page at the Perforation

OBJECTIVE ANSWER SHEET

CANDIDATE NUMBER

- Record your 7-digit candidate number in the boxes on the right, then blacken completely the oval for each digit you have recorded.
- Use a Number 2 pencil.
- Erase clearly any marks you wish to change. Make no stray marks on this sheet.

INCORRECT MARKS   CORRECT MARK

UNIFORM CERTIFIED PUBLIC ACCOUNTANT EXAMINATION
Business Law & Professional Responsibilities

LPR

For Proctor Use Only

Print your STATE name here.

VERSION 2

November 1, 1995; 9:00 A.M. to 12:00 NOON

Objective Answer Sheets may vary from examination to examination. Be certain that your answer corresponds directly in number with the examination item.

QUESTION I

Objective Answer Sheet Booklet No.

QUESTION NUMBERS 2 AND 3 ARE ON PAGE 27

end

28

DesignExpert™ by NCS Printed in U.S.A. Mark Reflex® EM-159590-2:654321

101	Ⓐ Ⓑ	Ⓒ Ⓓ	Ⓔ Ⓕ	Ⓖ Ⓗ	Ⓘ Ⓙ	Ⓚ Ⓛ	Ⓜ Ⓝ	Ⓞ Ⓟ	Ⓠ Ⓡ	Ⓢ Ⓣ	Ⓤ Ⓥ	Ⓦ Ⓧ	Ⓨ Ⓩ
102	Ⓐ Ⓑ	Ⓒ Ⓓ	Ⓔ Ⓕ	Ⓖ Ⓗ	Ⓘ Ⓙ	Ⓚ Ⓛ	Ⓜ Ⓝ	Ⓞ Ⓟ	Ⓠ Ⓡ	Ⓢ Ⓣ	Ⓤ Ⓥ	Ⓦ Ⓧ	Ⓨ Ⓩ
103	Ⓐ Ⓑ	Ⓒ Ⓓ	Ⓔ Ⓕ	Ⓖ Ⓗ	Ⓘ Ⓙ	Ⓚ Ⓛ	Ⓜ Ⓝ	Ⓞ Ⓟ	Ⓠ Ⓡ	Ⓢ Ⓣ	Ⓤ Ⓥ	Ⓦ Ⓧ	Ⓨ Ⓩ
104	Ⓐ Ⓑ	Ⓒ Ⓓ	Ⓔ Ⓕ	Ⓖ Ⓗ	Ⓘ Ⓙ	Ⓚ Ⓛ	Ⓜ Ⓝ	Ⓞ Ⓟ	Ⓠ Ⓡ	Ⓢ Ⓣ	Ⓤ Ⓥ	Ⓦ Ⓧ	Ⓨ Ⓩ
105	Ⓐ Ⓑ	Ⓒ Ⓓ	Ⓔ Ⓕ	Ⓖ Ⓗ	Ⓘ Ⓙ	Ⓚ Ⓛ	Ⓜ Ⓝ	Ⓞ Ⓟ	Ⓠ Ⓡ	Ⓢ Ⓣ	Ⓤ Ⓥ	Ⓦ Ⓧ	Ⓨ Ⓩ
106	Ⓐ Ⓑ	Ⓒ Ⓓ	Ⓔ Ⓕ	Ⓖ Ⓗ	Ⓘ Ⓙ	Ⓚ Ⓛ	Ⓜ Ⓝ	Ⓞ Ⓟ	Ⓠ Ⓡ	Ⓢ Ⓣ	Ⓤ Ⓥ	Ⓦ Ⓧ	Ⓨ Ⓩ
107	Ⓐ Ⓑ	Ⓒ Ⓓ	Ⓔ Ⓕ	Ⓖ Ⓗ	Ⓘ Ⓙ	Ⓚ Ⓛ	Ⓜ Ⓝ	Ⓞ Ⓟ	Ⓠ Ⓡ	Ⓢ Ⓣ	Ⓤ Ⓥ	Ⓦ Ⓧ	Ⓨ Ⓩ
108	Ⓐ Ⓑ	Ⓒ Ⓓ	Ⓔ Ⓕ	Ⓖ Ⓗ	Ⓘ Ⓙ	Ⓚ Ⓛ	Ⓜ Ⓝ	Ⓞ Ⓟ	Ⓠ Ⓡ	Ⓢ Ⓣ	Ⓤ Ⓥ	Ⓦ Ⓧ	Ⓨ Ⓩ
109	Ⓐ Ⓑ	Ⓒ Ⓓ	Ⓔ Ⓕ	Ⓖ Ⓗ	Ⓘ Ⓙ	Ⓚ Ⓛ	Ⓜ Ⓝ	Ⓞ Ⓟ	Ⓠ Ⓡ	Ⓢ Ⓣ	Ⓤ Ⓥ	Ⓦ Ⓧ	Ⓨ Ⓩ
110	Ⓐ Ⓑ	Ⓒ Ⓓ	Ⓔ Ⓕ	Ⓖ Ⓗ	Ⓘ Ⓙ	Ⓚ Ⓛ	Ⓜ Ⓝ	Ⓞ Ⓟ	Ⓠ Ⓡ	Ⓢ Ⓣ	Ⓤ Ⓥ	Ⓦ Ⓧ	Ⓨ Ⓩ
111	Ⓐ Ⓑ	Ⓒ Ⓓ	Ⓔ Ⓕ	Ⓖ Ⓗ	Ⓘ Ⓙ	Ⓚ Ⓛ	Ⓜ Ⓝ	Ⓞ Ⓟ	Ⓠ Ⓡ	Ⓢ Ⓣ	Ⓤ Ⓥ	Ⓦ Ⓧ	Ⓨ Ⓩ
112	Ⓐ Ⓑ	Ⓒ Ⓓ	Ⓔ Ⓕ	Ⓖ Ⓗ	Ⓘ Ⓙ	Ⓚ Ⓛ	Ⓜ Ⓝ	Ⓞ Ⓟ	Ⓠ Ⓡ	Ⓢ Ⓣ	Ⓤ Ⓥ	Ⓦ Ⓧ	Ⓨ Ⓩ
113	Ⓐ Ⓑ	Ⓒ Ⓓ	Ⓔ Ⓕ	Ⓖ Ⓗ	Ⓘ Ⓙ	Ⓚ Ⓛ	Ⓜ Ⓝ	Ⓞ Ⓟ	Ⓠ Ⓡ	Ⓢ Ⓣ	Ⓤ Ⓥ	Ⓦ Ⓧ	Ⓨ Ⓩ
114	Ⓐ Ⓑ	Ⓒ Ⓓ	Ⓔ Ⓕ	Ⓖ Ⓗ	Ⓘ Ⓙ	Ⓚ Ⓛ	Ⓜ Ⓝ	Ⓞ Ⓟ	Ⓠ Ⓡ	Ⓢ Ⓣ	Ⓤ Ⓥ	Ⓦ Ⓧ	Ⓨ Ⓩ
115	Ⓐ Ⓑ	Ⓒ Ⓓ	Ⓔ Ⓕ	Ⓖ Ⓗ	Ⓘ Ⓙ	Ⓚ Ⓛ	Ⓜ Ⓝ	Ⓞ Ⓟ	Ⓠ Ⓡ	Ⓢ Ⓣ	Ⓤ Ⓥ	Ⓦ Ⓧ	Ⓨ Ⓩ
116	Ⓐ Ⓑ	Ⓒ Ⓓ	Ⓔ Ⓕ	Ⓖ Ⓗ	Ⓘ Ⓙ	Ⓚ Ⓛ	Ⓜ Ⓝ	Ⓞ Ⓟ	Ⓠ Ⓡ	Ⓢ Ⓣ	Ⓤ Ⓥ	Ⓦ Ⓧ	Ⓨ Ⓩ
117	Ⓐ Ⓑ	Ⓒ Ⓓ	Ⓔ Ⓕ	Ⓖ Ⓗ	Ⓘ Ⓙ	Ⓚ Ⓛ	Ⓜ Ⓝ	Ⓞ Ⓟ	Ⓠ Ⓡ	Ⓢ Ⓣ	Ⓤ Ⓥ	Ⓦ Ⓧ	Ⓨ Ⓩ
118	Ⓐ Ⓑ	Ⓒ Ⓓ	Ⓔ Ⓕ	Ⓖ Ⓗ	Ⓘ Ⓙ	Ⓚ Ⓛ	Ⓜ Ⓝ	Ⓞ Ⓟ	Ⓠ Ⓡ	Ⓢ Ⓣ	Ⓤ Ⓥ	Ⓦ Ⓧ	Ⓨ Ⓩ
119	Ⓐ Ⓑ	Ⓒ Ⓓ	Ⓔ Ⓕ	Ⓖ Ⓗ	Ⓘ Ⓙ	Ⓚ Ⓛ	Ⓜ Ⓝ	Ⓞ Ⓟ	Ⓠ Ⓡ	Ⓢ Ⓣ	Ⓤ Ⓥ	Ⓦ Ⓧ	Ⓨ Ⓩ
120	Ⓐ Ⓑ	Ⓒ Ⓓ	Ⓔ Ⓕ	Ⓖ Ⓗ	Ⓘ Ⓙ	Ⓚ Ⓛ	Ⓜ Ⓝ	Ⓞ Ⓟ	Ⓠ Ⓡ	Ⓢ Ⓣ	Ⓤ Ⓥ	Ⓦ Ⓧ	Ⓨ Ⓩ
121	Ⓐ Ⓑ	Ⓒ Ⓓ	Ⓔ Ⓕ	Ⓖ Ⓗ	Ⓘ Ⓙ	Ⓚ Ⓛ	Ⓜ Ⓝ	Ⓞ Ⓟ	Ⓠ Ⓡ	Ⓢ Ⓣ	Ⓤ Ⓥ	Ⓦ Ⓧ	Ⓨ Ⓩ
122	Ⓐ Ⓑ	Ⓒ Ⓓ	Ⓔ Ⓕ	Ⓖ Ⓗ	Ⓘ Ⓙ	Ⓚ Ⓛ	Ⓜ Ⓝ	Ⓞ Ⓟ	Ⓠ Ⓡ	Ⓢ Ⓣ	Ⓤ Ⓥ	Ⓦ Ⓧ	Ⓨ Ⓩ
123	Ⓐ Ⓑ	Ⓒ Ⓓ	Ⓔ Ⓕ	Ⓖ Ⓗ	Ⓘ Ⓙ	Ⓚ Ⓛ	Ⓜ Ⓝ	Ⓞ Ⓟ	Ⓠ Ⓡ	Ⓢ Ⓣ	Ⓤ Ⓥ	Ⓦ Ⓧ	Ⓨ Ⓩ
124	Ⓐ Ⓑ	Ⓒ Ⓓ	Ⓔ Ⓕ	Ⓖ Ⓗ	Ⓘ Ⓙ	Ⓚ Ⓛ	Ⓜ Ⓝ	Ⓞ Ⓟ	Ⓠ Ⓡ	Ⓢ Ⓣ	Ⓤ Ⓥ	Ⓦ Ⓧ	Ⓨ Ⓩ
125	Ⓐ Ⓑ	Ⓒ Ⓓ	Ⓔ Ⓕ	Ⓖ Ⓗ	Ⓘ Ⓙ	Ⓚ Ⓛ	Ⓜ Ⓝ	Ⓞ Ⓟ	Ⓠ Ⓡ	Ⓢ Ⓣ	Ⓤ Ⓥ	Ⓦ Ⓧ	Ⓨ Ⓩ
126	Ⓐ Ⓑ	Ⓒ Ⓓ	Ⓔ Ⓕ	Ⓖ Ⓗ	Ⓘ Ⓙ	Ⓚ Ⓛ	Ⓜ Ⓝ	Ⓞ Ⓟ	Ⓠ Ⓡ	Ⓢ Ⓣ	Ⓤ Ⓥ	Ⓦ Ⓧ	Ⓨ Ⓩ
127	Ⓐ Ⓑ	Ⓒ Ⓓ	Ⓔ Ⓕ	Ⓖ Ⓗ	Ⓘ Ⓙ	Ⓚ Ⓛ	Ⓜ Ⓝ	Ⓞ Ⓟ	Ⓠ Ⓡ	Ⓢ Ⓣ	Ⓤ Ⓥ	Ⓦ Ⓧ	Ⓨ Ⓩ
128	Ⓐ Ⓑ	Ⓒ Ⓓ	Ⓔ Ⓕ	Ⓖ Ⓗ	Ⓘ Ⓙ	Ⓚ Ⓛ	Ⓜ Ⓝ	Ⓞ Ⓟ	Ⓠ Ⓡ	Ⓢ Ⓣ	Ⓤ Ⓥ	Ⓦ Ⓧ	Ⓨ Ⓩ
129	Ⓐ Ⓑ	Ⓒ Ⓓ	Ⓔ Ⓕ	Ⓖ Ⓗ	Ⓘ Ⓙ	Ⓚ Ⓛ	Ⓜ Ⓝ	Ⓞ Ⓟ	Ⓠ Ⓡ	Ⓢ Ⓣ	Ⓤ Ⓥ	Ⓦ Ⓧ	Ⓨ Ⓩ
130	Ⓐ Ⓑ	Ⓒ Ⓓ	Ⓔ Ⓕ	Ⓖ Ⓗ	Ⓘ Ⓙ	Ⓚ Ⓛ	Ⓜ Ⓝ	Ⓞ Ⓟ	Ⓠ Ⓡ	Ⓢ Ⓣ	Ⓤ Ⓥ	Ⓦ Ⓧ	Ⓨ Ⓩ
131	Ⓐ Ⓑ	Ⓒ Ⓓ	Ⓔ Ⓕ	Ⓖ Ⓗ	Ⓘ Ⓙ	Ⓚ Ⓛ	Ⓜ Ⓝ	Ⓞ Ⓟ	Ⓠ Ⓡ	Ⓢ Ⓣ	Ⓤ Ⓥ	Ⓦ Ⓧ	Ⓨ Ⓩ
132	Ⓐ Ⓑ	Ⓒ Ⓓ	Ⓔ Ⓕ	Ⓖ Ⓗ	Ⓘ Ⓙ	Ⓚ Ⓛ	Ⓜ Ⓝ	Ⓞ Ⓟ	Ⓠ Ⓡ	Ⓢ Ⓣ	Ⓤ Ⓥ	Ⓦ Ⓧ	Ⓨ Ⓩ
133	Ⓐ Ⓑ	Ⓒ Ⓓ	Ⓔ Ⓕ	Ⓖ Ⓗ	Ⓘ Ⓙ	Ⓚ Ⓛ	Ⓜ Ⓝ	Ⓞ Ⓟ	Ⓠ Ⓡ	Ⓢ Ⓣ	Ⓤ Ⓥ	Ⓦ Ⓧ	Ⓨ Ⓩ
134	Ⓐ Ⓑ	Ⓒ Ⓓ	Ⓔ Ⓕ	Ⓖ Ⓗ	Ⓘ Ⓙ	Ⓚ Ⓛ	Ⓜ Ⓝ	Ⓞ Ⓟ	Ⓠ Ⓡ	Ⓢ Ⓣ	Ⓤ Ⓥ	Ⓦ Ⓧ	Ⓨ Ⓩ
135	Ⓐ Ⓑ	Ⓒ Ⓓ	Ⓔ Ⓕ	Ⓖ Ⓗ	Ⓘ Ⓙ	Ⓚ Ⓛ	Ⓜ Ⓝ	Ⓞ Ⓟ	Ⓠ Ⓡ	Ⓢ Ⓣ	Ⓤ Ⓥ	Ⓦ Ⓧ	Ⓨ Ⓩ
136	Ⓐ Ⓑ	Ⓒ Ⓓ	Ⓔ Ⓕ	Ⓖ Ⓗ	Ⓘ Ⓙ	Ⓚ Ⓛ	Ⓜ Ⓝ	Ⓞ Ⓟ	Ⓠ Ⓡ	Ⓢ Ⓣ	Ⓤ Ⓥ	Ⓦ Ⓧ	Ⓨ Ⓩ
137	Ⓐ Ⓑ	Ⓒ Ⓓ	Ⓔ Ⓕ	Ⓖ Ⓗ	Ⓘ Ⓙ	Ⓚ Ⓛ	Ⓜ Ⓝ	Ⓞ Ⓟ	Ⓠ Ⓡ	Ⓢ Ⓣ	Ⓤ Ⓥ	Ⓦ Ⓧ	Ⓨ Ⓩ
138	Ⓐ Ⓑ	Ⓒ Ⓓ	Ⓔ Ⓕ	Ⓖ Ⓗ	Ⓘ Ⓙ	Ⓚ Ⓛ	Ⓜ Ⓝ	Ⓞ Ⓟ	Ⓠ Ⓡ	Ⓢ Ⓣ	Ⓤ Ⓥ	Ⓦ Ⓧ	Ⓨ Ⓩ
139	Ⓐ Ⓑ	Ⓒ Ⓓ	Ⓔ Ⓕ	Ⓖ Ⓗ	Ⓘ Ⓙ	Ⓚ Ⓛ	Ⓜ Ⓝ	Ⓞ Ⓟ	Ⓠ Ⓡ	Ⓢ Ⓣ	Ⓤ Ⓥ	Ⓦ Ⓧ	Ⓨ Ⓩ
140	Ⓐ Ⓑ	Ⓒ Ⓓ	Ⓔ Ⓕ	Ⓖ Ⓗ	Ⓘ Ⓙ	Ⓚ Ⓛ	Ⓜ Ⓝ	Ⓞ Ⓟ	Ⓠ Ⓡ	Ⓢ Ⓣ	Ⓤ Ⓥ	Ⓦ Ⓧ	Ⓨ Ⓩ
141	Ⓐ Ⓑ	Ⓒ Ⓓ	Ⓔ Ⓕ	Ⓖ Ⓗ	Ⓘ Ⓙ	Ⓚ Ⓛ	Ⓜ Ⓝ	Ⓞ Ⓟ	Ⓠ Ⓡ	Ⓢ Ⓣ	Ⓤ Ⓥ	Ⓦ Ⓧ	Ⓨ Ⓩ
142	Ⓐ Ⓑ	Ⓒ Ⓓ	Ⓔ Ⓕ	Ⓖ Ⓗ	Ⓘ Ⓙ	Ⓚ Ⓛ	Ⓜ Ⓝ	Ⓞ Ⓟ	Ⓠ Ⓡ	Ⓢ Ⓣ	Ⓤ Ⓥ	Ⓦ Ⓧ	Ⓨ Ⓩ
143	Ⓐ Ⓑ	Ⓒ Ⓓ	Ⓔ Ⓕ	Ⓖ Ⓗ	Ⓘ Ⓙ	Ⓚ Ⓛ	Ⓜ Ⓝ	Ⓞ Ⓟ	Ⓠ Ⓡ	Ⓢ Ⓣ	Ⓤ Ⓥ	Ⓦ Ⓧ	Ⓨ Ⓩ
144	Ⓐ Ⓑ	Ⓒ Ⓓ	Ⓔ Ⓕ	Ⓖ Ⓗ	Ⓘ Ⓙ	Ⓚ Ⓛ	Ⓜ Ⓝ	Ⓞ Ⓟ	Ⓠ Ⓡ	Ⓢ Ⓣ	Ⓤ Ⓥ	Ⓦ Ⓧ	Ⓨ Ⓩ
145	Ⓐ Ⓑ	Ⓒ Ⓓ	Ⓔ Ⓕ	Ⓖ Ⓗ	Ⓘ Ⓙ	Ⓚ Ⓛ	Ⓜ Ⓝ	Ⓞ Ⓟ	Ⓠ Ⓡ	Ⓢ Ⓣ	Ⓤ Ⓥ	Ⓦ Ⓧ	Ⓨ Ⓩ
146	Ⓐ Ⓑ	Ⓒ Ⓓ	Ⓔ Ⓕ	Ⓖ Ⓗ	Ⓘ Ⓙ	Ⓚ Ⓛ	Ⓜ Ⓝ	Ⓞ Ⓟ	Ⓠ Ⓡ	Ⓢ Ⓣ	Ⓤ Ⓥ	Ⓦ Ⓧ	Ⓨ Ⓩ
147	Ⓐ Ⓑ	Ⓒ Ⓓ	Ⓔ Ⓕ	Ⓖ Ⓗ	Ⓘ Ⓙ	Ⓚ Ⓛ	Ⓜ Ⓝ	Ⓞ Ⓟ	Ⓠ Ⓡ	Ⓢ Ⓣ	Ⓤ Ⓥ	Ⓦ Ⓧ	Ⓨ Ⓩ
148	Ⓐ Ⓑ	Ⓒ Ⓓ	Ⓔ Ⓕ	Ⓖ Ⓗ	Ⓘ Ⓙ	Ⓚ Ⓛ	Ⓜ Ⓝ	Ⓞ Ⓟ	Ⓠ Ⓡ	Ⓢ Ⓣ	Ⓤ Ⓥ	Ⓦ Ⓧ	Ⓨ Ⓩ
149	Ⓐ Ⓑ	Ⓒ Ⓓ	Ⓔ Ⓕ	Ⓖ Ⓗ	Ⓘ Ⓙ	Ⓚ Ⓛ	Ⓜ Ⓝ	Ⓞ Ⓟ	Ⓠ Ⓡ	Ⓢ Ⓣ	Ⓤ Ⓥ	Ⓦ Ⓧ	Ⓨ Ⓩ
150	Ⓐ Ⓑ	Ⓒ Ⓓ	Ⓔ Ⓕ	Ⓖ Ⓗ	Ⓘ Ⓙ	Ⓚ Ⓛ	Ⓜ Ⓝ	Ⓞ Ⓟ	Ⓠ Ⓡ	Ⓢ Ⓣ	Ⓤ Ⓥ	Ⓦ Ⓧ	Ⓨ Ⓩ
151	Ⓐ Ⓑ	Ⓒ Ⓓ	Ⓔ Ⓕ	Ⓖ Ⓗ	Ⓘ Ⓙ	Ⓚ Ⓛ	Ⓜ Ⓝ	Ⓞ Ⓟ	Ⓠ Ⓡ	Ⓢ Ⓣ	Ⓤ Ⓥ	Ⓦ Ⓧ	Ⓨ Ⓩ
152	Ⓐ Ⓑ	Ⓒ Ⓓ	Ⓔ Ⓕ	Ⓖ Ⓗ	Ⓘ Ⓙ	Ⓚ Ⓛ	Ⓜ Ⓝ	Ⓞ Ⓟ	Ⓠ Ⓡ	Ⓢ Ⓣ	Ⓤ Ⓥ	Ⓦ Ⓧ	Ⓨ Ⓩ
153	Ⓐ Ⓑ	Ⓒ Ⓓ	Ⓔ Ⓕ	Ⓖ Ⓗ	Ⓘ Ⓙ	Ⓚ Ⓛ	Ⓜ Ⓝ	Ⓞ Ⓟ	Ⓠ Ⓡ	Ⓢ Ⓣ	Ⓤ Ⓥ	Ⓦ Ⓧ	Ⓨ Ⓩ
154	Ⓐ Ⓑ	Ⓒ Ⓓ	Ⓔ Ⓕ	Ⓖ Ⓗ	Ⓘ Ⓙ	Ⓚ Ⓛ	Ⓜ Ⓝ	Ⓞ Ⓟ	Ⓠ Ⓡ	Ⓢ Ⓣ	Ⓤ Ⓥ	Ⓦ Ⓧ	Ⓨ Ⓩ
155	Ⓐ Ⓑ	Ⓒ Ⓓ	Ⓔ Ⓕ	Ⓖ Ⓗ	Ⓘ Ⓙ	Ⓚ Ⓛ	Ⓜ Ⓝ	Ⓞ Ⓟ	Ⓠ Ⓡ	Ⓢ Ⓣ	Ⓤ Ⓥ	Ⓦ Ⓧ	Ⓨ Ⓩ
156	Ⓐ Ⓑ	Ⓒ Ⓓ	Ⓔ Ⓕ	Ⓖ Ⓗ	Ⓘ Ⓙ	Ⓚ Ⓛ	Ⓜ Ⓝ	Ⓞ Ⓟ	Ⓠ Ⓡ	Ⓢ Ⓣ	Ⓤ Ⓥ	Ⓦ Ⓧ	Ⓨ Ⓩ
157	Ⓐ Ⓑ	Ⓒ Ⓓ	Ⓔ Ⓕ	Ⓖ Ⓗ	Ⓘ Ⓙ	Ⓚ Ⓛ	Ⓜ Ⓝ	Ⓞ Ⓟ	Ⓠ Ⓡ	Ⓢ Ⓣ	Ⓤ Ⓥ	Ⓦ Ⓧ	Ⓨ Ⓩ
158	Ⓐ Ⓑ	Ⓒ Ⓓ	Ⓔ Ⓕ	Ⓖ Ⓗ	Ⓘ Ⓙ	Ⓚ Ⓛ	Ⓜ Ⓝ	Ⓞ Ⓟ	Ⓠ Ⓡ	Ⓢ Ⓣ	Ⓤ Ⓥ	Ⓦ Ⓧ	Ⓨ Ⓩ
159	Ⓐ Ⓑ	Ⓒ Ⓓ	Ⓔ Ⓕ	Ⓖ Ⓗ	Ⓘ Ⓙ	Ⓚ Ⓛ	Ⓜ Ⓝ	Ⓞ Ⓟ	Ⓠ Ⓡ	Ⓢ Ⓣ	Ⓤ Ⓥ	Ⓦ Ⓧ	Ⓨ Ⓩ
160	Ⓐ Ⓑ	Ⓒ Ⓓ	Ⓔ Ⓕ	Ⓖ Ⓗ	Ⓘ Ⓙ	Ⓚ Ⓛ	Ⓜ Ⓝ	Ⓞ Ⓟ	Ⓠ Ⓡ	Ⓢ Ⓣ	Ⓤ Ⓥ	Ⓦ Ⓧ	Ⓨ Ⓩ
161	Ⓐ Ⓑ	Ⓒ Ⓓ	Ⓔ Ⓕ	Ⓖ Ⓗ	Ⓘ Ⓙ	Ⓚ Ⓛ	Ⓜ Ⓝ	Ⓞ Ⓟ	Ⓠ Ⓡ	Ⓢ Ⓣ	Ⓤ Ⓥ	Ⓦ Ⓧ	Ⓨ Ⓩ
162	Ⓐ Ⓑ	Ⓒ Ⓓ	Ⓔ Ⓕ	Ⓖ Ⓗ	Ⓘ Ⓙ	Ⓚ Ⓛ	Ⓜ Ⓝ	Ⓞ Ⓟ	Ⓠ Ⓡ	Ⓢ Ⓣ	Ⓤ Ⓥ	Ⓦ Ⓧ	Ⓨ Ⓩ
163	Ⓐ Ⓑ	Ⓒ Ⓓ	Ⓔ Ⓕ	Ⓖ Ⓗ	Ⓘ Ⓙ	Ⓚ Ⓛ	Ⓜ Ⓝ	Ⓞ Ⓟ	Ⓠ Ⓡ	Ⓢ Ⓣ	Ⓤ Ⓥ	Ⓦ Ⓧ	Ⓨ Ⓩ
164	Ⓐ Ⓑ	Ⓒ Ⓓ	Ⓔ Ⓕ	Ⓖ Ⓗ	Ⓘ Ⓙ	Ⓚ Ⓛ	Ⓜ Ⓝ	Ⓞ Ⓟ	Ⓠ Ⓡ	Ⓢ Ⓣ	Ⓤ Ⓥ	Ⓦ Ⓧ	Ⓨ Ⓩ
165	Ⓐ Ⓑ	Ⓒ Ⓓ	Ⓔ Ⓕ	Ⓖ Ⓗ	Ⓘ Ⓙ	Ⓚ Ⓛ	Ⓜ Ⓝ	Ⓞ Ⓟ	Ⓠ Ⓡ	Ⓢ Ⓣ	Ⓤ Ⓥ	Ⓦ Ⓧ	Ⓨ Ⓩ

the front cover. Assuming 60 individual multiple-choice (excluding pretest questions) and 4 essay/other objective questions, you should spend about 5 minutes **keyword** outlining each of the 2 or 3 essay questions. Budget your time based on the points allocated to each question. The Law exam is a 3-hour (180 minutes) exam which could have points allocated as follows:

Hypothetical Time Budget
(3-hour exam)

Question	Type	Point value	Calculated maximum time
No. 1	Multiple-choice	60	60/100 x 180 min = 108 min
No. 2	OOAF	10	10/100 x 180 min = 18 min
No. 3	OOAF	10	10/100 x 180 min = 18 min
No. 4	Essay	10	10/100 x 180 min = 18 min
No. 5	Essay	10	10/100 x 180 min = 18 min
Total		100	180 min

Note that this budget can be done easily without a calculator which is not provided for the Business Law exam. It is your responsibility to be ready at the start of the session and to stop writing when told to do so. Therefore, take control of the exam from the very start. Plan on spending about 1 1/2 minutes working each of the individual multiple-choice questions. Next, work the other objective answer format questions. (Do not prepare the final solution to the essay questions until you work all of the multiple-choice questions. Frequently, multiple-choice questions will jog your memory of additional grading concepts for the essays.) Then complete the objective question answer sheet by **carefully** transferring your answers to the machine-gradable form one question at a time. The answers must be transferred before the exam session ends. **The proctors are not allowed to give you extra time to transfer answers.**

After completing these tasks, you now have spent 2 1/4 hours and have substantially completed both the objective questions and essay questions. Revise the **keyword** outline and prepare the final solutions of the essay questions one at a time. Allocate about 15 minutes to each solution. Recognize that you can write all the grader will care to read in 15 minutes from a well-developed outline. This time should also include proofreading and editing. Remember that this is a hypothetical time allocation for illustrative purposes only.

Techniques for Time Management
The law exam has historically had 60 multiple-choice questions (excluding pretest questions). Referring to the above hypothetical time budget, note that the maximum time you should take to complete a group of 20 questions is 30 minutes per group. Remember that you alone control watching your progress towards successfully completing this exam.

One possible way of monitoring your progress is to write check times throughout the exam. For example, if you begin the multiple-choice at 9:00 a.m. go to question number 20 and write 9:30. By question number 40, write 10:00, and by question number 60, write 10:30. Now you have benchmarks to check your time against as you proceed through the exam. If you complete the multiple-choice questions by 10:20 a.m., you have successfully banked 10 minutes to use when answering the other objective and essay questions.

Order of Working Questions
Select the question that you are going to work first from the notes you made on the front of your examination. Some will select the question that appears easiest to get started and build confidence. Others will begin with the question they feel is most difficult to get it out of the way. Objective questions generally should not be worked first on the Business Law and Professional Responsibilities exam, since each question may contain 4 or 5 grading concepts (for possible inclusion in your essay solutions) as alternate answers. You should therefore work through the objective questions only after you have **keyword** outlined all of the essay questions (but before you write your final solution). This way, when doing the objective questions, you may pick up a grading concept or keyword which you had not included in your initial keyword outline.

Once you select a question, you should apply the solutions approach. Essay questions should be worked only through the **keyword** outline prior to moving on to the next question. Recall that essay questions are generally graded with an open-ended grading guide. Thus, you want to include as many grading concepts as possible in your solution. Waiting to write your essay solution until after all other questions have been dealt with will force you to take a fresh look at the question. As a result, additional grading concepts are often found. As you recognize grading concepts applicable to other questions, turn to the respective question and jot down the **keywords** (remember that the **keyword** outlines should be prepared in the margin of your exam booklet).

Candidates should allocate more time to the questions which are troublesome. The natural tendency is to write on and on for questions with which you are conversant. Remember to do the opposite—spend more time where more points are available (i.e., you may already have earned the maximum allowable on the question familiar to you).

Never, but never, leave a question blank, as this almost certainly precludes a passing grade on that section. Some candidates talk about "giving certain types of questions to the AICPA" (i.e., no answer). The only thing being given to the AICPA is grading time since the grader will not have to read a solution. Expect a couple of "far out" or seemingly insurmountable questions. Apply the solutions approach—imagine yourself having to make a similar decision, explanation, etc., in an actual situation and come up with as much as possible to answer the question.

Postmortem of Your Performance

Don't do it and especially don't do it until Thursday evening. Do not speak to other candidates about the exam after completing sections on Wednesday noon, Wednesday evening and Thursday noon. Exam postmortem will only upset, confuse, and frustrate you. Besides, the other candidates probably will not be as well prepared as you, and they certainly cannot influence your grade. Often, those candidates who seem very confident have overlooked an important requirement(s) or fact(s). As you leave the exam room after each session, think only ahead to achieve the best possible performance on each of the remaining sections.

AICPA GENERAL RULES
GOVERNING EXAMINATION*

Rules for Examination Day

The examination is a closed-book examination and no reference materials are permitted to be taken to an examination site. Candidates are not permitted to bring calculators, computers, other electronic data storage, or communication devices into the examination room.

At the examination site, candidates are provided with an Examination Question and Answer Booklet for each section they are taking. In addition, for the Accounting and Reporting-taxation, managerial, and governmental and not-for-profit organizations and Financial Accounting and Reporting sections, candidates are provided with official AICPA calculators. Candidates should bring adequate supplies of Number 2 pencils and erasers. Rulers are not allowed.

The general candidate instructions are as follows:

1. Prior to the start of the examination, you will be required to sign a *Statement of Confidentiality* which states:

   I hereby attest that I will not divulge the nature or content of any question or answer to any individual or entity, and I will report to the board of accountancy any solicitations and disclosures of which I become aware. I will not remove, or attempt to remove, any Uniform CPA Examination materials, notes, or other unauthorized materials from the examination room. I understand that failure to comply with this attestation may result in invalidation of my grades, disqualification from future examinations, and possible civil and criminal penalties.

2. The only aids you are allowed to take to the examination tables are pens, No. 2 pencils, and erasers.

3. You will receive a prenumbered identification card (or admission notice) with your 7-digit candidate number on it. The prenumbered identification card must be available for inspection by the proctors throughout the examination.

4. Any reference during the examination to books or other materials or the exchange of information with other persons shall be considered misconduct sufficient to bar you from further participation in the examination.

   Penalties will be imposed on any candidate who is caught cheating before, during, or after the examination. These penalties may include expulsion from the examination, denial of applications for future examinations, and civil or criminal penalties.

5. You must observe the fixed time for each session. It is your responsibility to be ready at the start of the session and to stop writing when told to do so.

6. The following is an example of point values for each question as they might appear in the *Examination Questions* portion of the *Examination Question and Answer Booklet* (*Booklet*).

	Point value
No. 1	60
No. 2	10
No. 3	10
No. 4	10
No. 5	10
Total	100

When answering each question, you should allocate the total examination time in proportion to the question's point value.

---

* *Information for Uniform CPA Examination Candidates*, Sixteenth Edition, AICPA, 2000, p. 44.

7. The *Booklet* will be distributed shortly before each session begins. Do not break the seal around the *Examination Questions* portion of the *Booklet* until you are told to do so.

   Prior to the start of the examination, you are permitted to complete page 1 of the *Booklet* by recording your 7-digit candidate number in the boxes provided in the upper right-hand corner of the page and by filling out and signing the *Attendance Record*. You are also permitted to turn the *Booklet* over and record your 7-digit candidate number and State on the *Objective Answer Sheet* portion of the *Booklet*.

   You must also check the booklet numbers on the *Attendance Record*, *Examination Questions*, *Objective Answer Sheet*, and *Essay Paper*. Notify the proctor if any of these numbers do not match.

   You must also review the *Examination Questions* (after you are told to break the seal), *Objective Answer Sheet*, and *Essay Paper* for any possible defects, such as missing pages, blurred printing, or stray marks (*Objective Answer Sheet* only). If any defects are found, request an entirely new *Booklet* from a proctor before you answer any questions.

8. For the Business Law and Professional Responsibilities (LPR), Auditing (AUDIT), and Financial Accounting and Reporting (FARE) sections, your answers to the essay questions or problems must be written on the paper provided in the *Essay Paper* portion of the *Booklet*. After the start of the examination, you should record your 7-digit candidate number, State, and question number on the first page of the *Essay Paper* portion of the *Booklet* and on the other pages where indicated.

9. For the ARE and FARE examination sections, you will be given a calculator. You should test the calculator in accordance with the instructions on the cover page of the *Booklet*. Inform your proctor if your calculator is defective. Calculators will not be provided for the LPR and AUDIT examination sections because the number of questions requiring calculations is minimal and the calculations are simple.

10. All amounts are to be considered material unless otherwise stated.

11. Answer all objective items on the *Objective Answer Sheet* provided. Use a No. 2 pencil only. You should attempt to answer all objective items, as there is no penalty for incorrect responses. Since the objective items are scanned optically, your comments and calculations associated with them are not considered. You should blacken the ovals as darkly as possible and erase clearly any marks you wish to change. You should make no stray marks.

    Approximately 10-15% of the multiple-choice items are included for pretesting only and are not included in your final grade.

12. It is important to pay strict attention to the manner in which your *Objective Answer Sheet* is structured. As you proceed with the examination, be certain that you blacken the oval that corresponds exactly with the item number in the *Examination Questions* portion of your *Booklet*. If you mark your answers in the *Examination Questions* portion of your *Booklet*, be certain that you transfer them to the *Objective Answer Sheet* before the session ends. Your examination paper will not be graded if you fail to record your answers on the *Objective Answer Sheet*. You will not be given additional time to record your answers.

13. Answer all essay questions and problems on the *Essay Paper* provided. Always begin your answer to a question on the top of a new page (which may be the reverse side of a sheet of paper). Cross out anything that you do not want graded.

14. Selected essay responses will be graded for writing skills.

15. Include all computations to the problems in the FARE section. This may assist the graders in understanding your answers.

16. You may not leave the examination room with any examination materials, nor may you take notes about the examination with you from the examination room. You are required to turn in by the end of each session:

    a. *Attendance Record* and *Statement of Confidentiality*
    b. *Examination Questions*
    c. *Essay Paper* (for LPR, AUDIT, and FARE). Do not remove unused pages.
    d. *Objective Answer Sheet*
    e. Calculator (for ARE and FARE)
    f. All unused examination materials
    g. Prenumbered Identification Card (or Admission Notice) at the last examination section for which you sit (if required by your examining jurisdiction)

    Your examination will not be graded unless you hand in these items before you leave the examination room.

17. If you believe one or more questions contain errors and want your concerns evaluated, you must fax your comments to the AICPA (201-938-3443). The fax should include the precise nature of any error; your rationale; and, if possible, references. The fax should include your 7-digit candidate identification number and must be received by the AICPA within 4 days of the completion of the examination administration. This will ensure that all comments are reviewed before the grading bases for the Uniform CPA Examination are confirmed. Although the AICPA cannot respond directly to each fax, it will investigate all comments received within the 4-day period.

18. Contact your board of accountancy for information regarding any other applicable rules.

In addition to the above general rules, oral instructions will be given by the examination supervisor shortly before the start of each session. They should include the location and/or rules concerning

- a. Storage of briefcases, handbags, books, personal belongings, etc.
- b. Food and beverages
- c. Smoking (usually not permitted)
- d. Rest rooms
- e. Telephone calls and messages
- f. Requirements (if any) that candidates must take all parts not previously passed each time they sit for the examination. Minimum grades (if any) needed on parts failed to get credit on parts passed.
- g. Official clock, if any
- h. Additional supplies
- i. Assembly, turn-in, inspection, and stapling of solutions

The next section provides a detailed listing (mind-jogger) of things to do for your last-minute preparation. It also contains a list of strategies for the exam.

CPA EXAM CHECKLIST

One week before exam

___ 1. Review law notecards, **mini outlines,** and other law notes for important terms, lists, and key phrases.

___ 2. If time permits, work through a few questions in your weakest areas so that applicable law principles and concepts are fresh in your mind.

___ 3. Assemble materials listed under 1. above into a "last review" notebook to be taken with you to the exam.

What to bring

___ 1. *Registration material*—for the CPA exam. You will save time at the examination site by filling out ahead of time the survey that you received with your registration materials.

___ 2. *Hotel confirmation.*

___ 3. *Cash*—payment for anything by personal check is rarely accepted.

___ 4. *Major credit card*—American Express, Master Card, Visa, etc.

___ 5. *Alarm clock*—this is too important an event to trust to a hotel wake-up call that might be overlooked.

___ 6. *Food*—candidates should carefully review the instructions provided by their own State Board of Examiners regarding policies about food at the exam.

___ 7. *Clothing*—should be comfortable and layered to suit the temperature range over the 2-day period and the examination room conditions.

___ 8. *Watch*—it is imperative that you be aware of the time remaining for each session.

___ 9. *Earplugs*—even though an examination is being given, there is constant activity in the examination room (e.g., people walking around, rustling of paper, people coughing, etc.). The use of earplugs would block out this distraction and help you concentrate to your fullest extent.

___ 10. *Other*—"last review" materials, pencils, erasers, leads, sharpeners, pens, etc.

While waiting for the exam to begin

1. Put your ID card on the table for ready reference to your number. The front page of your Examination Booklet contains an Attendance Record and Statement of Confidentiality. When told to do so, complete this information so the proctor can collect it prior to the start of the exam.

2. Realize that proctors will be constantly circulating throughout each exam session. You need only raise your hand to receive more paper at any time.

3. Take a few deep breaths and compose yourself. Resolve to do your very best and to go after every point you can get!

Before leaving for exam each day

1. Put your ID card in your wallet, purse, or on your person for entry to take the exam. This is your official entrance permit that allows you to participate in all sections of the exam.

2. Remember your hotel room key.

3. Pack snack items and lunch (optional).

4. Limit consumption of liquids.

5. Realize that on Thursday morning you must check out and arrange for storage of your luggage (most hotels have such a service) **prior to** departing for the exam in order to prevent late charges on your hotel bill.

Evenings before exams

1. Reviewing the evenings before the exams could earn you the extra points needed to pass a section. Just keep this last-minute effort in perspective and do **not** panic yourself into staying up all night trying to cover every possible point. This could lead to disaster by sap-

ping your body of the endurance needed to attack questions creatively during the next 7 to 8-hour day.

2. Reread key outlines or notecards for law on Tuesday evening, reviewing important terms, key phrases, and lists (i.e., essential elements for a contract, requirements for a holder in due course, etc.) so that they will be fresh in your mind Wednesday morning.

3. Go over mnemonics and acronyms you have developed as study aids. Test yourself by writing out the letters on paper while verbally giving a brief explanation of what the letters stand for.

4. Avoid postmortems during the examination period. Nothing you can do will affect your grade on sections of the exam you have already completed. Concentrate only on the work ahead in remaining sections.

5. **Set your alarm and get a good night's rest!** Being well rested will permit you to meet each day's challenge with a fresh burst of creative energy.

Exam-taking strategy

1. Check the exam booklet for completeness as you note the number of objective questions (you can expect at least 60) and read "required" sections of essay/objective format questions.

2. Reconcile the question numbers with the questions listed on the front of the Examination Booklet and check consecutive page numbers in your booklet. Allocate the 180 minutes to each question based on the AICPA points shown on the front of the booklet.

3. You will need the maximum time available for the law essay questions because they usually consist of unrelated yet involved fact situations that you **must** address. **Thus, you must use the minimum time allotted in answering the law objective questions.**

4. The crucial technique to use for business law objective questions is to read through each fact situation **carefully,** underlining keywords such as "oral," "without disclosing," "subject to mortgage," etc. Then **read each choice** carefully before you start eliminating inappropriate answers. In business law, often the first or second answer may sound correct, but a later answer **may be more correct**. Be discriminating! Reread the question and choose the right response.

5. Law essay fact situations are often lengthy and involved. Read carefully and decide which areas of law apply.

6. The most important technique to use for ALL essay questions is to constantly remind yourself that the grader assumes you know nothing (s/he cannot read your mind) and you, as a candidate for a professional designation, must convince him/her of your knowledge of the subject matter under question. **Never omit the obvious!** Explain each answer as if you were explaining the concept to a beginning business student.

7. Tell the grader that you are applying the UCC or Common Law, or the Act of 1933 or 1934, etc.

8. State the issue involved or the requirements that you are testing for (i.e., all 6 elements of a contract are present).

9. State the rule of law that applies to the issue.

10. Tell the grader how this affects the parties involved.

11. Limit discussion to relevant issues. Too often, candidates spend more time than allotted on a question they are sure of, only to sacrifice points on another question where those extra minutes are crucial.

12. Remember that on the law section you have a maximum of about 10 minutes per fact situation. Constantly compare your progress with the time remaining. **Never** spend more than the maximum allotted time on any question until **all** questions are answered and time remains.

13. If you draw a blank as to a conclusion, telling the grader all the points of law that you know about the fact situation may salvage the question.

14. As each question is completed, quickly reread the "required" section to make sure you have responded to each requirement.

15. Double check to make certain you have answered ALL parts of EVERY question to the best of your ability.

16. Transfer objective question answers to the form provided. Be especially careful to follow the numbers exactly, because number patterns differ on each answer form! Don't leave this until it's too late. **The proctors are not authorized to give you extra time for this.**

17. Remember: A legible, well-organized, grammatically correct answer gives a professional appearance. Avoid the use of abbreviations.

18. Take your Examination Booklet and additional pages to the front of the exam room and staple them together.

**HAVE YOU MADE YOUR
COMMITMENT?**

5 BUSINESS LAW AND PROFESSIONAL RESPONSIBILITIES

Introduction

Module 7/Contracts (CONT)

Module 8/Sales (SALE)

Module 9/Commercial Paper (CPAP)

	No. of	*Page no.*	
	minutes	*Problem*	*Answer*
50 Multiple-Choice		141	151
2 Other Objective		147	156
2 Essay Questions:			
1. Fictitious Payee; Drawee Bank's Acceptance of Check with Forgery of Drawer's Signature	15-25	150	158
2. Requisites for Negotiability; Transfer and Negotiation; Holders and Holders in Due Course; Liabilities and Rights	15-20	150	158

Module 10/Secured Transactions (SECU)

	Page no.			*Page no.*
Overview	160	D.	Other Issues under Secured Transactions	163
A. Scope of Secured Transactions	160		tions	163
B. Attachment of Security Interests	160	E.	Priorities	164
C. Perfecting a Security Interest	161	F.	Rights of Parties upon Default	165

	No. of	*Page no.*	
	minutes	*Problem*	*Answer*
30 Multiple-Choice		167	172
1 Other Objective		170	175
2 Essay Questions:			
1. Purchase Money Security Interest; Priority of Bankruptcy Trustee; Purchase Money Secured Party in Equipment and Buyer in Ordinary Course of Business	15-20	171	176
2. Risk of Loss; Rights under Entrusting of Possession of Goods; Attachment of Security Interest; Perfection of Security Interests	15-20	171	176

Module 11/Bankruptcy (BANK)

	Page no.			*Page no.*
Overview	178	E.	Chapter 7 Bankruptcy Proceedings	180
A. Alternatives to Bankruptcy Proceedings	178	F.	Claims	183
		G.	Discharge of a Bankrupt	185
B. Bankruptcy in General	178	H.	Debts Not Discharged by Bankruptcy	185
C. Chapter 7 Voluntary Bankruptcy Petitions	178	I.	Revocation of Discharge	186
		J.	Reaffirmation	186
		K.	Business Reorganization Chapter 11	186
D. Chapter 7 Involuntary Bankruptcy Petitions	178	L.	Debts Adjustment Plans Chapter 13	187

	No. of	*Page no.*	
	minutes	*Problem*	*Answer*
29 Multiple-Choice		189	197
3 Other Objective		193	200
2 Essay Questions:			
1. Dischargeability of Debts in Bankruptcy; Preferential Transfers	15-20	196	202
2. Requirements for Involuntary Bankruptcy; Claims and Preferences—Secured Creditor; Preferential Transfer	15-20	196	202

Module 12/Debtor-Creditor Relationships (DBCR)

	Page no.			*Page no.*
Overview	204	D.	Surety's and Guarantor's Rights and Remedies	209
A. Rights and Duties of Debtors and Creditors	204	E.	Surety's and Guarantor's Defenses	209
B. Nature of Suretyship and Guaranty	206	F.	Cosureties	212
C. Creditor's Rights and Remedies	208	G.	Surety Bonds	213

	No. of	*Page no.*	
	minutes	*Problem*	*Answer*
27 Multiple-Choice		214	219
1 Other Objective		217	222
1 Essay Question:			
1. Minority; Reasonable Covenant Not to Compete; Surety's Defenses	15-20	218	223

INTRODUCTION

The Business Law and Professional Responsibilities Section of the CPA examination tests the candidate's

1. Ability to recognize legal problems
2. Knowledge of legal principles with respect to the topics listed above
3. Ability to apply the legal principles to the problem situation in order to derive the textbook solution

Refer to "Self-Study Program" in Chapter 1 for detailed suggestions on how to study the Business Law and Professional Responsibilities outlines and questions. The basic procedure for each of the fifteen Business Law and Professional Responsibilities Modules is

1. Work 1/4 of the multiple-choice questions to indicate your proficiency and familiarity with the type and difficulty of questions.
2. Study the outlines in this volume.
3. Work the remaining multiple-choice questions. Study the answer explanations of those you missed or had trouble with.
4. Work the other objective questions.
5. Work the essay questions.

Answering Business Law and Professional Responsibilities Questions

Law essay questions frequently require a conclusion, for example,

Is the instrument in question negotiable commercial paper?
Assuming the instrument is negotiable, does Meglo qualify as a holder in due course entitled to collect the full $3,000?

In many cases, you will be asked to begin your answer with an unequivocal yes or no followed by a period. Recognize that you are not used to this type of situation. Follow the solutions approach for essay questions as outlined in Chapter 3.

Virtually all of these questions requiring conclusions also require the reasons for the conclusions. Clearly, an unsupported yes or no will be worth little more than a blank answer. Always explain the legal principle(s) involved, and justify your application of the principle(s). Do not wander into other areas or deal with legal principles not specifically required by the question. Try to predict what will appear on the unofficial solution.

AICPA Content Specification Outline

The AICPA Content Specification Outline of the coverage of Business Law and Professional Responsibilities appears below. This outline was issued by the AICPA, effective as of November 2000.

AICPA CONTENT SPECIFICATION OUTLINE: BUSINESS LAW AND PROFESSIONAL RESPONSIBILITIES

I. Professional and Legal Responsibilities (**15%**)

  A. Code of Professional Conduct
  B. Proficiency, Independence, and Due Care
  C. Responsibilities in Other Professional Services
  D. Disciplinary Systems Imposed by the Profession and State Regulatory Bodies
  E. Common Law Liability to Clients and Third Parties
  F. Federal Statutory Liability
  G. Privileged Communications and Confidentiality
  H. Responsibilities of CPAs in Business and Industry, and in the Public Sector

II. Business Organizations (**20%**)

  A. Agency

   1. Formation and Termination
   2. Duties of Agents and Principals
   3. Liabilities and Authority of Agents and Principals

  B. Partnership, Joint Ventures, and Other Unincorporated Associations

   1. Formation, Operation, and Termination

   2. Liabilities and Authority of Partners and Owners

  C. Corporations

   1. Formation and Operation
   2. Stockholders, Directors, and Officers
   3. Financial Structure, Capital, and Distributions
   4. Reorganization and Dissolution

  D. Estates and Trusts

   1. Formation, Operation, and Termination
   2. Allocation between Principal and Income
   3. Fiduciary Responsibilities
   4. Distributions

III. Contracts (**10%**)

  A. Formation
  B. Performance
  C. Third-Party Assignments
  D. Discharge, Breach, and Remedies

IV. Debtor-Creditor Relationships (**10%**)

  A. Rights, Duties, and Liabilities of Debtors and Creditors

B. Rights, Duties, and Liabilities of Guarantors

C. Bankruptcy

V. Government Regulation of Business **(15%)**

   A. Federal Securities Acts

   B. Employment Regulation

   C. Environmental Regulation

VI. Uniform Commercial Code **(20%)**

A. Negotiable Instruments

B. Sales

C. Secured Transactions

D. Documents of Title

VII. Property **(10%)**

   A. Real Property Including Insurance

   B. Personal Property Including Bailments and Computer Technology Rights

Sources of the Law

Law comes from both statutes and common law. Common law has evolved through court decisions. Decisions of higher courts are binding on lower courts in the same jurisdiction. Statutory law has priority over common law; therefore, common law applies when no statute covers the issue in question. Court cases can also be used to interpret the meaning of statutes.

Some of the law tested on the CPA exam comes from federal statutory law. Examples of this are the Security Act of 1933 and the Securities Exchange Act of 1934. Other law affected heavily by federal statutes include bankruptcy law, a good portion of employment law, and parts of accountants' legal liability as provided in the securities laws. The AICPA has published the guideline that "federal laws are tested six months following their effective date. . . ."

Most of business law is regulated by the individual states and therefore may differ from state to state. However, several uniform laws have been adopted by many states. One example is the Uniform Commercial Code (UCC) which has been adopted by all states (sometimes with changes) except Louisiana, and also is the law in the District of Columbia. This uniform law and others are not federal laws but are laws that each jurisdiction may choose to adopt by statute. Often these uniform laws are amended. For example, the Uniform Commercial Code has been amended a few times. The AICPA has published the guideline that the "uniform acts [are tested] one year after their adoption by a simple majority of jurisdictions." This is also interpreted to mean that as these uniform laws are amended, the amended version is tested one year after a simple majority of jurisdictions have adopted it.

When the states have not adopted uniform laws, general rules of law can still be stated by examining how the majority of states settle an area of law either with their own common law or their own statutes. These are called the majority rule when it can be shown that a majority of jurisdictions have settled the legal issue the same way. The CPA exam generally tests the majority rules; however, it tests some minority rules that are considered very significant. For example, the CPA exam has tested in the accountants' legal liability area, both the majority rule and a minority rule known as the Ultramares decision, as discussed in Module 17. The AICPA has generally not published guidelines on when such minority rules are tested or when new majority rules would be tested.

Mini Outlines/Final Review

We have provided Mini Outlines of the Business Law Modules at the end of this chapter. These outlines are to be used as a final review tool and not as a primary study source.

CONTRACTS

Overview

The area of contracts is very heavily tested on the CPA examination. A large portion of the contract rules serves as a basis for many other law topics; consequently, a good understanding of the material in this module will aid you in comprehending the material in other modules.

It is important that you realize that there are two sets of contract rules to learn. The first is the group of common law contract rules that, in general, apply to contracts that are not a sale of goods. Examples of contracts that come under common law are those that involve real estate, insurance, employment, and professional services. The second set is the contract rules contained in Article Two of the Uniform Commercial Code (UCC). The UCC governs transactions involving the sale of goods (i.e., tangible personal property). Hence, if the contract is for the sale or purchase of tangible personal property, the provisions of the UCC will apply, and not the common law. For every contract question, it is important that you determine which set of rules to apply. Fortunately many of the rules under the two sets are the same. The best way for you to master this area is to first study the common law rules for a topic. Then review the rules that are different under the UCC. Since the common law and the UCC rules have much in common, you will be learning contract law in the most understandable and efficient manner.

Contract law is tested by both essay and multiple-choice questions. You need to know the essential elements of a contract because the CPA examination tests heavily on offer and acceptance. Also, understand that an option is an offer supported by consideration. Distinguish between an option and a firm offer and understand how these are affected by revocations and rejections. You need to comprehend what consideration is and that it must be bargained for to be valid. The exam also requires that you understand that "past consideration" and moral obligations are not really consideration at all. You should have a solid understanding of the Statute of Frauds.

Once a contract is formed, third parties can obtain rights in the contract. An assignment is one important way this can happen.

If a contract is not performed, one of the parties may be held in breach of contract. Note that the possible remedies include monetary damages, specific performance, liquidated damages, and anticipatory repudiation.

A. Essential Elements of a Contract

1. Offer
2. Acceptance

   a. When offer and acceptance have occurred, an agreement is said to have been made

3. Consideration
4. Legal capacity
5. Legality (legal purpose)
6. Reality of consent

   a. Technically not a true element, but important to consider because may be necessary for enforceability of contract

7. Statute of Frauds

   a. Not a true element, but each factual situation should be examined to determine whether it applies because certain contracts must be in writing as explained later

B. Types of Contracts

1. Express contract—terms are actually stated orally or in writing
2. Implied contract—terms of contract not specifically given but some or all of terms are inferred from conduct of parties and circumstances
3. Executed contract—one that has been fully performed
4. Executory contract—one that has not been fully performed by both parties
5. Quasi contract—not a real contract but public policy creates legal obligation in certain circumstances
6. Unilateral contract—one party gives promise for completion of requested act

   EXAMPLE: *A promises to pay B $1,000 to cross the Golden Gate Bridge on foot within one week. This is a unilateral offer. Once B does the act it is a unilateral contract.*

7. Bilateral contract—each party exchanges promises

   EXAMPLE: *A promises to deliver 100 widgets to B for $1,000 and B promises to buy and pay for them.*

8. Voidable contract—one that is enforceable unless party that has right pulls out of contract

C. Discussion of Essential Elements of a Contract

   1. Offer

      a. May be either written or oral (or sometimes by actions)

        EXAMPLE: Offeror takes can of soup to check out stand and pays for it without saying anything.

      b. Based on intent of offeror

        (1) Courts use objective test to determine intent

           (a) That is, would reasonable person think that offer had been intended

        (2) Subjective intent (what offeror actually intended or meant) is not considered

        (3) Promises made in apparent jest are not offers

           (a) Promises that objectively appear real are offers

             EXAMPLE: S says, "I offer to sell to you, B, my car for $5,000." This is an offer, even though S may be actually joking, as long as given the way it was said, a reasonable person would think that S did intend to make the offer to sell his/her car.

        (4) Statements of opinion or of intent are not offers

           EXAMPLE: A doctor tells a patient that he will fully recover in a couple of days, but it actually takes two weeks. This is a statement of opinion, not an offer.

           EXAMPLE: "I am going to sell my car for $400." This is a statement of intent, not an offer.

        (5) Invitations to negotiate (preliminary negotiations) are not offers (e.g., price tags or lists, auctions, inquiries, general advertisements)

           EXAMPLE: A says: "What would you think your car is worth?" B says: "About $5,000." A says: "I accept your offer so I'll buy it for $5,000." B never gave an offer. However, when A said that he would accept, this is actually an offer that B may then accept if she wishes.

      c. Offer must be definite and certain as to what will be agreed upon in contract under common law

        (1) Courts allow some reasonable terms to be left open if customary to do so

           EXAMPLE: C calls P, a plumber, to come and fix a clogged drain. No price is mentioned. However, upon P's completion of the work, he has the right to collect customary fee from C.

        (2) Under UCC, output or requirements contracts are considered reasonably definite because output is based upon actual output that does occur in good faith and requirements are actual good-faith requirements

      d. Must be communicated to offeree by offeror or his/her agent

        (1) Offeree may learn of a public offer (e.g., reward) in any way; s/he merely needs knowledge of it

      e. Unilateral offer is one that expects acceptance by action rather than with promise

        EXAMPLE: M says he will pay J $5 if she will mow his lawn. M has made a unilateral offer that is accepted when J mows the lawn. If J never mows the lawn, there is no contract and therefore no breach of contract.

        (1) Unilateral contract contains one promise (offer by offeror) and acceptance by action

      f. Bilateral offer is one that expects acceptance by a promise from offeree

        (1) Bilateral contract is formed when offeree accepts with a promise

           EXAMPLE: R says to E, "Will you agree to work for me for three months at $5,000 per month?" This is a bilateral offer.

        (2) Bilateral contract contains two promises

      g. Mistakes in transmission of offer are deemed to be offeror's risk because s/he chose method of communication; therefore, offer is effective as transmitted

      h. Termination of offer

(1) Rejection by offeree

    (a) Must be communicated to offeror to be effective

    (b) Rejection is effective when received by offeror

(2) Revocation by offeror

    (a) Generally, offeror may revoke offer at any time prior to acceptance by offeree

        1] Revocation is effective when received by offeree

        EXAMPLE: X offers to sell his car to Y stating that the offer will remain open for ten days. However, on the fifth day Y receives a revocation of the offer from X. The offer would be terminated on the fifth day even though X stated that it would remain open for ten days.

    (b) If offeree learns by reliable means that offeror has already sold subject of offer, it is revoked

    (c) Public offers must be revoked by same amount of publicity used in making offer

    EXAMPLE: Offer of reward for apprehension of arsonist in a newspaper makes headlines. It cannot be revoked by a small notice in the back of the newspaper.

    (d) An **option** is an offer that is supported by consideration and cannot be revoked before stated time

        1] Option is actually a separate contract to keep offer open

            a] Also called an option contract

            EXAMPLE: O offers to sell her car to P and states that she will keep the offer open for ten days if P will pay her $50. P pays the $50 and six days later O attempts to revoke the offer. P then accepts the offer by the seventh day. An agreement has been formed because the offer was an option and could not be revoked before the ten days. Note that there were actually two contracts between O and P. The first one was the option to keep the offer open. The second was the actual sale of the car.

            EXAMPLE: Same example as above except that O asked P to promise to pay $50 within ten days to keep the offer open. The result is the same because a promise to pay money is also consideration.

        2] Also, rejection does not terminate option

        3] Note differences between option and firm offer by merchants concerning sale of goods under UCC as discussed later

(3) Counteroffer is a rejection coupled with offeree making new offer

    EXAMPLE: An offer is made to sell a car for $3,000 and a counteroffer is, "I'll give you $2,500."

    (a) Mere inquiry or request for additional or different terms is not a counteroffer and does not terminate offer

    EXAMPLE: An offer is made to sell a car for $3,000 and an inquiry is, "Will you sell for $2,500?"

(4) Lapse of time may terminate offer

    (a) Offeror may specify period of time (e.g., one week)

    (b) If no time is specified, after reasonable time

(5) Death or insanity of offeror terminates ordinary offers

(6) Illegality

    (a) Offer terminates if after making offer and before it is accepted, it becomes illegal

    EXAMPLE: X offers to rent to Y an upstairs floor for a cabaret. Before Y accepts, the city adopts a fire code making use of the premises illegal without substantial rebuilding.

(7) Bankruptcy or insolvency of either offeror or offeree terminates offer

(8) Impossibility

    (a) Offer terminates if after making offer and before it is accepted, performance becomes impossible

    EXAMPLE: X offers his car to Y for $500, but before Y agrees to the purchase, X's car is destroyed by fire.

(9) Destruction of subject matter

2. Acceptance

    a. May be written or oral

    b. Offer may be accepted only by person to whom it was directed

       (1) Use objective test—to whom would a reasonable person believe it to be directed?

       (2) Rewards can usually be accepted by anyone who knows of them

    c. Offeree must have knowledge of offer in order to accept

       EXAMPLE: D advertises a reward of $100 for the return of his pet dog. G, unaware of the offer, returns D's dog. G cannot require that D pay the $100 (if he later hears of the offer) because he was unaware of the offer when he returned the dog. He could not "accept" an offer he did not know existed.

    d. Intent to accept is required

       (1) Courts generally find click-on agreements legally enforceable when the offeree completes the contract on-line by clicking on a button that shows acceptance

          (a) Main issue is that offeree did clearly intend to accept offer by this action

    e. Acceptance must generally be in form specified by offer

    f. Acceptance must be unequivocal and unconditional (mirror image rule) under common law

       (1) An acceptance that attempts to change terms of offer is not acceptance, but is both a rejection and a counteroffer

       EXAMPLE: O offers to sell some real estate for $100,000 cash. E says "I accept. I'll give you $50,000 now and $50,000 plus 13% interest one year from now."

          (a) Mere inquiry or request is not a counteroffer so offer remains in effect

          EXAMPLE: O gives the same offer as above but this time E asks if O would accept $50,000 now and $50,000 plus 13% interest one year from now. The offer is neither accepted nor terminated.

       (2) A condition which does not change or add to terms of contract is not a counteroffer (i.e., a condition that is already part of contract because of law, even though not expressed in previous negotiations)

    g. Silence is not acceptance unless

       (1) Offer indicated silence would constitute acceptance (e.g., offer states "your silence is acceptance," and offeree intended his/her silence as acceptance)

          (a) If offeree does not intend to accept, such language has no effect

             1] Offeree is under no duty to reply

       (2) Offeree has taken benefit of services or goods and exercised control over them when s/he had opportunity to reject them

          (a) However, statutes usually override common law rule by providing that unsolicited merchandise may be treated as a gift

       (3) Through prior dealings, by agreement between parties, or when dictated by custom, silence can be acceptance

    h. Time of acceptance under common law

       (1) If acceptance is made by method specified in offer or by same method used by offeror to communicate the offer, acceptance is effective when sent (e.g., when placed in mail or when telegram is dispatched)

       EXAMPLE: Offeror mails a written offer without stating the mode of acceptance. Offeree mails acceptance. Offeror, before receipt, calls offeree to revoke the offer. The contract exists because acceptance was effective when mailed and revocation of offer came too late.

(a) Exception: If offeree sends rejection and then acceptance, first received is effective even though offeree sent acceptance by same method used by offeror

(2) Other methods of acceptance are considered effective when actually received by offeror
(3) Late acceptance is not valid—it is a counteroffer and a valid contract is formed only if original offeror then accepts
(4) If acceptance is valid when sent, a lost or delayed acceptance does not destroy validity

> EXAMPLE: *R wires an offer to E asking her to accept by mail. The acceptance is correctly mailed but never arrives. There is a valid agreement.*

(5) Offeror can change above rules by stating other rule(s) in offer

> EXAMPLE: *Offeror mails a written offer to offeree stating that acceptance is valid only if **received** by the offeror within ten days. Offeree mails back the acceptance within ten days but it arrives late. Acceptance has not occurred even though the offeree used the same method.*

i. Once there is an offer and acceptance, an agreement is formed

(1) Details can be worked out later
(2) Formalization often occurs later
(3) Attempted revocations or rejections after agreement is formed are of no effect

j. Offers, revocations, rejections, and counteroffers are valid when received (under both common law and UCC)

(1) Compare with rules for acceptances which are sometimes valid when sent and other times are valid when received

> EXAMPLE: *S offers to sell his land to B for $20,000. The offer is mailed to B. Later that same day, S changes his mind and mails B a revocation of this offer. When B receives the offer, she mails her acceptance. B receives the revocation the day after she mailed the acceptance. S and B have a valid contract because the acceptance was valid when sent but the revocation would have been valid when B received it. Once the offer is accepted, any attempted revocation will not be valid.*

> EXAMPLE: *Use the same facts as above except that the offeree uses a different method than the mailed acceptance. If B receives the revocation before S receives the acceptance, there is no contract.*

k. **Uniform Commercial Code rules** (Important differences from common law rules above for offers and acceptances)

(1) The UCC applies to sale of goods, for example, tangible personal property (not real property, services, or insurance contracts)
(2) A **written** and **signed** offer for sale of goods, **by a merchant** (i.e., one who regularly deals goods under contract), giving assurance that it will be held open for specified time is irrevocable for that period

(a) Called firm offer

> EXAMPLE: *Herb, an automobile dealer, offers to sell a car to Ike stating, "I promise to keep this offer open for forty-five days." Since the offer is not written and signed by Herb, the firm offer rule does not apply and Herb may revoke the offer at any time prior to Ike's acceptance.*

> EXAMPLE: *Same facts as above except that the offer is written and signed by Herb. In this case, the firm offer rule applies and Herb cannot revoke the offer for the stated period.*

(b) Unlike an option, no consideration needed
(c) Period of irrevocability may not exceed three months

> EXAMPLE: *A merchant in a signed, written offer agrees to keep the offer open for four months. The firm offer may be revoked or otherwise terminated once three months has passed.*

(d) If no time is specified, reasonable time is inferred, up to three months
(e) If assurance is given on form supplied by offeree, it must be separately signed by offeror
(f) Compare

1] Firm offer rule does not work under common law
2] Options are valid under UCC as well as common law and do not require a merchant seller

        3]   Options are not limited to three months

> *EXAMPLE: C (not a merchant) agrees to sell an automobile to B, with the offer to remain open for four months. This is not a firm offer so C may revoke this offer at any time by communicating the revocation to B.*

> *EXAMPLE: Same facts as above except that B pays C to keep the offer open for four months. C cannot revoke this offer for four months because although it is not a firm offer, it is an option.*

> *EXAMPLE: Same facts as the first example except that C is a merchant and engages in a signed written offer. This is a firm offer that C could not revoke during the first three months, but could revoke the offer during the last month.*

  (3)   Unless otherwise indicated, an offer for sale of goods shall be construed as inviting acceptance in any manner and by any medium reasonable under circumstances

  (4)   Time of acceptance under UCC

     (a)   Acceptance valid when sent if reasonable method used

> *EXAMPLE: A offers to sell her stereo to B. The offer is sent via telegram. B mails back an acceptance. This acceptance is valid when B mails the acceptance even though B used a method different from that used for the offer because it was an offer to sell under the UCC.*

> *EXAMPLE: Same as above except that the offer was to sell land rather than a stereo. The acceptance is valid when received by A because the common law rules apply.*

> *EXAMPLE: A telegraphs an offer to B without specifying when acceptance is valid but does state the offer will remain open for five days. Within the five days, B mails back the acceptance which arrives after that five days. If the subject matter is a sale of goods, there is a contract because the acceptance was good when sent. Under common law, however, the acceptance takes effect under these facts when received, so no contract would result.*

     (b)   Above rule does not apply if another rule is stated in offer

> *EXAMPLE: O faxes an offer to sell his car to B for $17,000. The offer states that O must receive the acceptance in three days. B mails back the acceptance in two days but the letter does not arrive until the fourth day. No contract is formed.*

  (5)   An offer to buy goods may be accepted either by seller's promise to ship the goods or by the actual shipment

     (a)   Blurs distinction between unilateral and bilateral contracts

     (b)   With respect to a unilateral offer, beginning of performance by offeree (i.e., part performance) will bind offeror if followed within a reasonable time by notice of acceptance

  (6)   Unequivocal acceptance of offer for sale of goods is not necessary under UCC (Battle of Forms)

     (a)   An acceptance containing additional terms is valid acceptance (unless acceptance is expressly conditional upon offeror's agreement to additional terms)

        1]   Recall, under common law, this would be a rejection and counteroffer

     (b)   Between nonmerchants, the additional terms are considered proposals to offeror for additions to contract, and unless offeror agrees to the additions, contract is formed on offeror's terms

     (c)   Between merchants, these additional terms become part of contract and contract is formed on offeree's terms unless

        1]   Original offer precludes such additions
        2]   New terms materially alter original offer
        3]   The original offeror gives notice of his/her objection within a reasonable time

> *EXAMPLE: O offers to sell M a group of stereos under certain terms including a three-month warranty. Both parties are merchants. M faxes back that he accepts the offer but that he wants a one-year warranty. O and M have a contract. The three-month warranty is part of the contract because the one-year warranty is a material alteration.*

     (d)   If at least one party is a nonmerchant, use nonmerchant rule

EXAMPLE: O, a merchant, offers by telegram to sell B, a nonmerchant, a truck for $20,000 that B had looked at earlier. B telegraphs back that he accepts the offer and adds an additional term that the seat be re-upholstered. O and B have a contract. The additional term is only a proposal to the contract.

(7) Even if terms are left open, a contract for sale of goods will not fail for indefiniteness if there was intent to contract and a reasonable basis for establishing a remedy is available

    (a) Open price term—construed as reasonable price at time of delivery

        1] Or parties may agree to decide price at future date or can agree to allow third party to set price

        EXAMPLE: B accepts an offer from S to buy 1,000 bushels of pears in one month. No mention is made of the price. The contract is valid and the price will be the market value of the pears at the time of delivery.

        EXAMPLE: Same as above except that B and S agree to let N decide what the price will be for the pears. This is a valid contract.

        EXAMPLE: Un D. Sided and Tube Issy agree on a contract for 1,000 bushels of avocados to be delivered in three months for a price that they will decide in one month. If they fail to agree on the price, the contract will be for the market value at delivery.

    (b) Open place of delivery term—seller's place of business, if any

        1] Otherwise, seller's residence or if identified goods are elsewhere and their location is known to both parties at time of contracting, then at that location

    (c) Open time of shipment or delivery—becomes a reasonable time

    (d) Open time for payment—due at time and place of delivery of goods or at time and place of delivery of documents of title, if any

        1] If on credit, credit period begins running at time of shipment

(8) Even if writings do not establish a contract, conduct by parties recognizing a contract will establish one

    (a) The terms will be those on which writings agree and those provided for in UCC where not agreed on (e.g., reasonable price, place of delivery)

    (b) Often occurs when merchants send preprinted forms to each other with conflicting terms and forms are not read for more than quantity and price

l. Auctions

  (1) Bid is offer

  (2) Bidder may retract bid until auctioneer announces sale completed

  (3) If auction is "with reserve," auctioneer may withdraw goods before s/he announces completion of sale

  (4) If auction "without reserve," goods may not be withdrawn unless no bid made within reasonable time

  (5) Auctions are "with reserve" unless specified otherwise

m. On-line auctions

  (1) Many individuals and businesses are conducting auctions on-line

    (a) Many businesses sell excess inventory or services this way

    (b) Becoming increasingly popular as buyers and sellers rely on fluidity of contract-making abilities

3. Consideration—an act, promise, or forbearance that is offered by one party and accepted by another as inducement to enter into agreement

a. A party binds him/herself to do (or actually does) something s/he is not legally obligated to do, or when s/he surrenders legal right

    EXAMPLE: B pays S $500 for S's stereo that he hands over to B. B's consideration is the $500. S's consideration is the stereo.

EXAMPLE: S gives B a stereo today. B promises to pay S $500 in one week. The promise to pay $500, rather than the $500 itself, is the consideration. Thus, the element of consideration is met today.

EXAMPLE: A hits and injures P with his car. P agrees not to sue A when A agrees to settle out of court for $10,000. A's promise to pay the money is consideration. P's promise to refrain from bringing a lawsuit is consideration on his/her side.

EXAMPLE: Using the fact pattern above, further assume that it is not clear whether A is at fault. The settlement (contract) is still enforceable if made in good faith because of possible liability.

   b.   Legal detriment does not have to be economic (e.g., giving up drinking, smoking, and swearing)

      (1) If party agrees to have something accomplished but has someone else do it, this is consideration

   c.   Consideration must be bargained for (this is essential)

   d.   Preexisting legal duty is not sufficient as consideration because no new legal detriment is suffered by performing prior obligation

      (1) Agreement to accept from debtor a lesser sum than owed is unenforceable if the debt is a liquidated (undisputed) debt

EXAMPLE: C agrees to accept $700 for a $900 debt that D owes C. The amount is not disputed. D still owes C the additional $200.

         (a) But if debtor incurs a detriment in addition to paying, creditor's promise to accept lesser sum will be binding

EXAMPLE: X owes Y $1,000. Y agrees to accept $500 and X will also install Y's new furnace at no additional cost.

         (b) Note that agreement to accept a lesser sum is enforceable if amount of debt is unliquidated (disputed) because both parties give up right to more favorable sum

EXAMPLE: C claims that D owes him $1,000. D claims that the amount owed is $600. If C and D agree to settle this for $700, the agreement is supported by consideration since C gave up right to attempt to collect more than $700 and D gave up right to attempt settlement for a lesser sum.

      (2) Promise to pay someone for refraining from doing something s/he has no right to do is unenforceable

      (3) Promise to pay someone to do something s/he is already obligated to do is not enforceable.

EXAMPLE: Agreement to pay police officer $200 to recover stolen goods is unenforceable.

EXAMPLE: X promises to pay Y, a jockey, $50 to ride as hard as he can in the race. Y already owes his employer, Z, that duty so there is no consideration to enforce the agreement.

         (a) Agreement to pay more to finish a job, such as building a house, is unenforceable unless unforeseen difficulties are encountered (e.g., underground stream or marshy land under a house)

   e.   Past consideration (consideration for a prior act, forbearance, or agreement) is not sufficient for new contract because it is not bargained for

   f.   Moral obligation except in a minority of states is not consideration

      (1) In majority of states these need no consideration

         (a) Promise to pay debt barred by statute of limitations.

         (b) Promise to pay debt barred by bankruptcy. Promise must adhere to strict rules stated in Bankruptcy Reform Act of 1978 concerning reaffirmations of dischargeable debts.

   g.   Consideration must be legally sufficient

      (1) This does not refer to amount of consideration but refers to validity of consideration

EXAMPLE: C does not have a CPA license. For $1,000 he promises not to hire himself out as a CPA. This promise is not supported by legally sufficient consideration because C has no right to hire himself out as a CPA.

   h.   Adequacy of consideration—courts generally do not look into amount of exchange as long as it is legal consideration and **bargained for**

   i.   In majority of states, seals placed on contracts are not substitutes for consideration

j.   Modifying existing contracts

   (1) Modification of contract needs new consideration on both sides to be legally binding

   EXAMPLE: S agrees in a written contract to sell a piece of land to P for $40,000. S later changes his mind and demands $50,000 for the same piece of land. The original contract is enforceable (at $40,000) even if P agrees to the increased price because although P has agreed to give more consideration, S has not given any new consideration.

   (2) Under UCC, a contract for sale of goods may be modified orally or in writing without consideration if in good faith

   EXAMPLE: S agrees to sell P 300 pairs of socks for $1.00 each. Due to rapid price increases in S's costs, he asks P if he will modify the price to $1.20 each. P agrees. The contract as modified is enforceable because it is covered under the UCC and does not need new consideration on both sides.

k.   Requirements contracts

   (1) If one party agrees to supply what other party requires, agreement is supported by consideration

      (a) Reason: supplying party gives up right to sell to another; purchasing party gives up right to buy from another
      (b) Cannot be required to sell amounts unreasonably disproportionate to normal requirements

l.   Output contract

   (1) If one party agrees to sell all his/her output to another, agreement is supported by consideration because s/he gives up right to sell that output to another

      (a) However, illusory contracts are not supported by consideration (e.g., party agrees to sell all s/he wishes)

m.   Promissory estoppel acts as substitute for consideration and renders promise enforceable—promisor is estoppel from asserting lack of consideration

   (1) Elements

      (a) Detrimental reliance on promise
      (b) Reliance is reasonable and foreseeable
      (c) Damage results (injustice) if promise is not enforced

   (2) Usually applied to gratuitous promises but trend is to apply to commercial transactions. At least recovery of expenses is allowed.

   EXAMPLE: A wealthy man in the community promises to pay for a new church if it is built. The church committee reasonably (and in good faith) relies on the promise and incurs the expenses.

n.   Mutuality of obligation—means both parties must be bound or neither is bound

   (1) Both parties must give consideration by paying or promising to pay for the act, promise, or forbearance of the other with something of legal value

o.   Promise to donate to charity is enforceable based on public policy reasons

4. Legal Capacity

   a.   An agreement between parties in which one or both lack the capacity to contract is void or, in some cases, voidable
   b.   Minors (persons under age eighteen or twenty-one)

      (1) A minor may contract, but agreement is voidable by minor

         (a) Adult is held to contract unless minor disaffirms

      (2) If minor has purchased nonnecessaries, when minor disaffirms, s/he is required to give back any part s/he still has

         (a) Minor may recover all of consideration given
         (b) In most courts, minor need not pay for what s/he cannot return

        (c) A few courts require minor to pay for use or depreciation of equipment or machinery

     (3) Minor is liable for reasonable value of necessaries furnished to him/her

        (a) Minor may disaffirm contract if it is executory (i.e., not completed)

        (b) Necessaries include food, clothing, shelter, education, etc., considering his/her age and position in life

     (4) Minor may disaffirm contract at any time until a reasonable time after reaching majority age

        (a) Failure to disaffirm within reasonable time after reaching majority acts as ratification (e.g., one year is too long in the absence of very special circumstances such as being out of the country)

     (5) Minor may choose to ratify within a reasonable time after reaching age of majority

        (a) By words, either orally or in writing but must ratify all, or

        (b) By actions that indicate ratification

        (c) Ratification prior to majority is not effective

     (6) If minor misrepresents his/her age when making contract, courts are split on effect

        (a) Some courts allow minor to disaffirm contract anyway but allow other party to sue for fraud

        (b) Some allow minor to disaffirm if minor returns consideration in similar condition

        (c) Other courts will not allow minor to disaffirm especially if it was a business contract

     (7) A minor usually is liable for own torts (civil wrongs), but this may depend on his/her age (above 14 commonly liable)

        (a) Parents are not liable for torts of minors unless they direct or condone certain conduct or were negligent themselves

  c. Incompetent persons

     (1) Contract by person adjudicated insane is void

        (a) Insane person need not return consideration

     (2) If contract is made before adjudication of insanity, it may be voidable by incompetent person

        (a) Where courts hold such agreements voidable, restitution is condition precedent to disaffirmance

  d. Legal capacity of one intoxicated is determined by his/her ability to understand and by degree of intoxication

     (1) Contracts are enforceable, in general, unless extent of intoxication at time contract made was so great that intoxicated party did not understand terms or nature of contract—then contract voidable at option of one intoxicated if s/he returns items under contract

  e. Corporations contract through agents and are limited by their charters

5. Legality

  a. Agreement is unenforceable if it is illegal or violates public policy

  b. When both parties are guilty, neither will be aided by court (i.e., if one party had already given some consideration, s/he will not get it back)

     (1) But if one party repudiates prior to performance, s/he may recover his/her consideration

        EXAMPLE: X contracts to buy stolen goods from Y. If X pays Y but then repents and refuses to accept the stolen goods, X may recover the money he paid Y.

  c. When one party is innocent, s/he will usually be given relief

     (1) A member of a class of people designed to be protected by statute is considered innocent (e.g., purchaser of stock issued in violation of blue-sky laws)

d. Types of illegal contracts

(1) Agreement to commit crime or tort

(a) If agreement calls for intentional wrongful interference with a valid contractual relationship, it is an illegal agreement

1] However, a sale of a business containing a covenant prohibiting seller from owning or operating similar business as well as the termination of an employee who has agreed not to compete are legal and enforceable provided the agreement

a] Protects legitimate interests of buyer or employer without creating too large a burden on seller or employee (based on ability to find other work)

b] Is reasonable as to length of time under the circumstances to protect those interests

c] Is reasonable as to area to protect interests of same area

d] Same whether employer or employee initiated termination

EXAMPLE: Seller of a small bakery agrees not to compete in Washington, DC, for six months.

(2) An agreement to not press criminal charges for consideration is illegal

EXAMPLE: A has embezzled money from his employer. The employer agrees to not press charges if A pays back all of the money.

(3) Services rendered without a license when statute requires a license

(a) Two types of licensing statutes

1] Regulatory licensing statute—one that seeks to protect public from incapable, unskilled, or dishonest persons

a] Contract is unenforceable by either party

b] Even if work done, other need not pay because not a contract

EXAMPLE: X, falsely claiming to have a CPA license, performs an audit for ABC Company. Upon learning the true facts, ABC may legally refuse to pay X any fees or expenses.

2] Revenue-seeking statute—purpose is to raise revenue for government

a] Contract is enforceable

EXAMPLE: Y, based on a contract, performed extensive yard work for M. M then finds out that Y failed to obtain a license required by the local government to raise revenue. M is obligated to pay Y the agreed-upon amount.

(4) Usury (contract for greater than legal interest rate)

(5) Contracts against public policy

(a) Contracts in restraint of trade such as covenant not to compete after end of an employment contract

1] Courts must balance need of former employer such as protection of trade secrets or customer base with need of employee to practice his/her line of work

2] Typically, contract will restrict employee from competing in named areas for stated period of time

3] Employer must show that covenant not to compete is needed to protect interests of employer and that restraints are reasonable as to geographical area and as to time period

(b) Upon sale of business, seller agrees to not compete with sold type of business in named areas for stated period of time

1] Courts are less restrictive than in employment contract situation but will look at reasonableness as to geographical area, reasonableness as to time, and whether covenant is unduly restrictive for public's need

(c) Exculpatory clauses are clauses found in contracts in which one party tries to avoid liability for own negligence

1] These are generally against public policy and not enforceable unless both parties have relatively equal bargaining power

EXAMPLE: An automobile dealership agrees to fix the engine of a car brought in by a consumer for repair. A clause in the contract provides that the dealer will not be liable for any mistakes it may make during the repair.

6. Reality of Consent—If one of the following concepts is present, a contract may be void (i.e., no contract) or voidable (i.e., enforceable until party having right decides to pull out).

a. Fraud—includes following elements

(1) Misrepresentation of a material fact

(a) Can be falsehood or concealment of physical defect
(b) Silence is not misrepresentation unless there is duty to speak, for example,

1] Fiduciary relationship between parties
2] Seller of property knows there is a dangerous latent (hidden) defect

(c) Must be statement of past or present fact

1] Opinion (e.g., of value) is not fact

a] Experts' opinion does constitute fraud

EXAMPLE: An expert appraiser of jewelry appraises a diamond to be worth $500 when he knows it is actually worth $1,500. This fulfills the "misrepresentation of a material fact" element. If the remaining elements of fraud are met, then there is fraud.

2] Prophecy is not fact (e.g., "Next year you will make twice as much")
3] Puffing or sales talk is not fact

EXAMPLE: A seller claims her necklace is worth $1,000. The buyer pays $1,000 and later finds out that he can buy a very similar necklace from another seller for $700. Even if the other elements of fraud are present, this opinion does not constitute fraud.

4] Presently existing intention in mind of the speaker is fact

(2) Intent to mislead—"scienter"

(a) Need knowledge of falsity with intent to mislead, **or**
(b) Reckless disregard for truth can be substituted

1] If all elements (1) through (4) are present but reckless disregard is proven instead of actual knowledge of falsity, then it is called constructive fraud

(3) Reasonable reliance by injured party

(a) One who knows the truth or might have learned it by a reasonable inquiry may not recover

(4) Resulting in injury to others
(5) Remedies for fraud

(a) Defrauded party may affirm agreement and sue for damages under tort of deceit, or if party is sued on contract, then s/he may set up fraud in reduction of damages, or
(b) Defrauded party may rescind contract and sue for damages that result from the fraud

(6) Fraud may occur

(a) In the inducement

1] The misrepresentation occurs during contract negotiations
2] Creates voidable contract at option of defrauded party

EXAMPLE: A represents to B that A's car has been driven 50,000 miles when in fact it has been driven for 150,000 miles. If B purchases A's car in reliance on this misrepresentation, fraud in the inducement is present, creating a voidable contract at B's option.

    (b) In the execution

        1] Misrepresentation occurs in actual form of agreement
        2] Creates void contract

        EXAMPLE: Larry Lawyer represents to Danny that Danny is signing his will, when in fact he is signing a promissory note payable to Larry. This promissory note is void because fraud in the execution is present.

b. Innocent misrepresentation

  (1) An innocent misstatement made in good faith (i.e., no scienter)
  (2) All other elements same as fraud
  (3) Creates right of rescission (cancellation) in other party—to return both parties to their precontract positions

    (a) All benefits must be returned by both parties
    (b) Does not allow aggrieved party to sue for damages

c. Mistake—an act done under an erroneous conviction

  (1) Mutual mistake (i.e., by both parties) about existence, identity, or important characteristics of subject matter in contract makes contract voidable by either party

  EXAMPLE: S and B make a contract in which B agrees to buy a boat from S. Although neither party knew it at the time, this boat had been destroyed before this contract was made. This is a mutual mistake about the existence of the boat; therefore, either party may void this contract by law. Note that legally either party may pull out although usually only one party may wish to do so.

    (a) Also exists when both parties reasonably attach different meanings to word or phrase
    (b) Also called bilateral mistake
    (c) Mistake about value of subject matter is not grounds for voiding contract

  (2) Unilateral mistake generally does not allow party to void contract

    (a) Major exception for mistakes in computations for bids

        1] Contract based on mistake is voidable by party making mistake if calculation is far enough off so that other party should have known that a mistake was made

d. Duress—a contract entered into because of duress can be voided because of invalid consent

  (1) Any acts or threats of violence or extreme pressure against party or member of party's family, which in fact deprives party of free will and causes him/her to agree, is duress

  EXAMPLE: X threatens to criminally prosecute Y unless he signs contract. This contract is made under duress.

    (a) May involve coercion that is social or economic that leaves him/her with no reasonable alternative

  (2) Physical duress in which party agrees to contract under physical force
  (3) Extreme duress causes agreement to be void
  (4) Ordinary duress creates voidable agreement

e. Undue influence—unfair persuasion of one person over another which prevents understanding or voluntary action

  (1) Usually occurs when very dominant person has extreme influence over weaker person
  (2) Also occurs through abuse of fiduciary relationship (e.g., CPA, attorney, guardian, trustee, etc.)
  (3) Normally causes agreement to be voidable

f. Unconscionable contract—an oppressive contract in which one party has taken severe, unfair advantage of the other, usually because of latter's absence of choice or poor education

  (1) Under these circumstances court may void contract or reform terms so as to be fair to both parties

g. Changes in weather conditions, economic conditions, etc., that cause hardship to one party will not create voidable contracts when conditions are not so extreme that the parties could have contemplated them

EXAMPLE: B had a contract to purchase 50,000 gallons of heating oil from S at specified prices. B refuses to take more than 40,000 gallons because the weather was warmer than normal. B is obligated on all 50,000 gallons because the warmer weather could have been contemplated by the parties.

h. Infancy, incompetency, and noncompliance with Statute of Frauds may also create voidable contract

i. Adhesion contract—offeror is in position to say "take it or leave it" because of superior bargaining power

   (1) Usually occurs when large business entity requires its customers to use their standard form contract without allowing modification

7. Conformity with the Statute of Frauds

   a. Contracts required to be in writing and signed by party to be charged—these are said to be within the Statute

      (1) An agreement to sell land or any interest in land

         (a) Includes buildings, easements, and contracts to sell real estate
         (b) Part performance typically satisfies Statute even though real estate contract was oral, but this requires

            1] Possession of the land
            2] Either part payment or making of improvements on real estate
            3] Many courts require all three

      (2) An agreement that cannot be performed within one year from the making of agreement

         (a) Contract that can be performed in exactly one year or less may be oral

         EXAMPLE: W agrees to hire X for ten months starting in four months. This contract must be in writing because it cannot be performed until fourteen months after the agreement is made.

         (b) Any contract which can conceivably be completed in one year, irrespective of how long the task actually takes, may be oral

         EXAMPLE: A agrees to paint B's portrait for $400. It actually is not completed until over a year later. This contract did not have to be in writing because it was possible to complete it within one year.

         (c) If performance is contingent on something which could take place in less than one year, agreement may be oral

         EXAMPLE: "I will employ you as long as you live." Party could possibly die in less than one year.

         (d) But if its terms call for more than one year, it must be written even if there is possibility of taking place in less than one year

         EXAMPLE: "I will employ you for five years." The employee's death could occur before the end of five years, but the terms call for the writing requirement under the Statute of Frauds.

         (e) Generally, if one side of performance is complete but other side cannot be performed within year, it is not within Statute (i.e., may be oral). Especially true if performance has been accepted and all that remains is the payment of money.

         EXAMPLE: X agrees to pay E $6,000 salary per month and a bonus of $50,000 if he works for at least two years. After two years, X refuses to pay the bonus. The $50,000 is payable and the Statute of Frauds is no defense here.

      (3) An agreement to answer for debt or default of another (contract of guaranty)

         (a) A secondary promise is within this section of the Statute of Frauds (i.e., must be in writing)

         EXAMPLE: "If Jack doesn't pay, I will."

(b) A primary promise is not within this section of the Statute of Frauds because it is in reality the promisor's own contract

> EXAMPLE: *"Let Jack have it, and I will pay."*

(c) Promise for benefit of promisor may be oral

> EXAMPLE: *Promisor agrees to answer for default of X, because X is promisor's supplier and he needs X to stay in business to keep himself in business.*

(d) Promise of indemnity (will pay based on another's fault, for example, insurance) is not within Statute

(e) Assignor's promise to assignee, guaranteeing obligor's performance is not within Statute

(4) Agreement for sale of goods for $500 or more is required to be in writing under UCC

> EXAMPLE: *Oral contract for the sale of fifty calculators for $10 each is not enforceable.*

> EXAMPLE: *Oral contract to perform management consulting services over the next six months for $100,000 is enforceable because the $500 rule does not apply to contracts that come under common law.*

> EXAMPLE: *Same as previous example except that the agreed time was for fourteen months. This one was required to be in writing to be enforceable because of the one-year rule.*

  (a) Exceptions to writing requirement (these are important)

    1] Oral contract involving specially manufactured goods (i.e., not saleable in ordinary course of business) if seller has made substantial start in their manufacture (or even made a contract for necessary raw materials) is enforceable

    2] Oral contract is enforceable against party who admits it in court but not beyond quantity of goods admitted

    3] Goods that have been paid for (if seller accepts payment) or goods which buyer has accepted are part of enforceable contract even if oral

> EXAMPLE: *B orally agrees to purchase 10,000 parts from S for $1 each. B later gives S $6,000 for a portion of the parts. S accepts the money. In absence of a written agreement, B may enforce a contract for 6,000 parts but not for the full 10,000 parts.*

  (b) Modifications of written contracts involve two issues under UCC

    1] New consideration on both sides is not required under UCC although it is required under common law

      a] Under UCC, modification must be done in good faith

    2] Modified contract must be in writing if contract, as modified, is within Statute of Frauds (i.e., sale of goods for $500 or more)

> EXAMPLE: *S agrees orally to sell B 100 widgets for $4.80 each. B later agrees, orally, to pay $5.00 for the 100 widgets due to changed business conditions. The modified contract is not enforceable because it must have been in writing. Therefore, the original contract is enforceable.*

> EXAMPLE: *Same as above except that the modification is in writing. Now the modified contract is enforceable despite the fact that S is giving no new consideration.*

> EXAMPLE: *X and Y have a written contract for the sale of goods for $530. They subsequently both agree orally to a price reduction of $40. The modified contract for $490 is enforceable.*

  (c) Parties may exclude future oral agreements in a signed writing

(5) Agreement for sale of intangibles over $5,000 must be in writing (e.g., patents, copyrights, or contract rights)

(6) Sale of securities must be in writing

  (a) Must include price and quantity

b. When a writing is required and the UCC applies, it must

  (1) Indicate in writing that a contract for sale has been made

  (2) Be signed by party to be charged, and

  (3) Specify quantity of goods sold

(4) However, note the following:

   (a) Any written form will do (e.g., letter, telegram, receipt, fax)
   (b) Need not be single document (e.g., two telegrams)
   (c) Need not be made at same time as contract

       1]   Must be made before suit is brought
       2]   Need not exist at time of suit (i.e., may have been destroyed)

   (d) Signature need not be at end nor be in a special form so long as intent to authenticate existed (e.g., initials, stamp, printed letterhead, etc., of party to be charged)

       1]   Generally, signature sent by fax is enforceable

   (e) May omit material terms (e.g., price, delivery, time for performance) as long as quantity is stated. Reasonable terms will be inferred.
   (f) Exception to signature requirement exists under UCC when both parties are merchants—one party may send signed written confirmation stating terms (especially quantity) of oral agreement to other party within reasonable time, then nonsigning party must object within ten days or the contract is enforceable against him/her

   EXAMPLE: B agreed on January 10 to purchase 100 widgets at $6 each from S. They agreed that delivery would take place on January 31. On January 14, B sent S a letter on B's letterhead that stated: "We no longer need the 100 widgets we ordered on January 10. Don't ship them."
       This contract is enforceable against B even though the writing was later than the original oral agreement.

   EXAMPLE: Note that in the example above, if B and S are both merchants, not only is the contract enforceable against B, but it is also enforceable against S (the nonsigning party) unless S objects in ten days.

   (g) Only a few states allow a seal to substitute for signature when signature required

c. Noncompliance with Statute of Frauds (i.e., failure to make a writing) will make contract unenforceable

   (1) Promissory estoppel when aggrieved party has justifiably relied upon promise and when court rules justice demands it, may be used to defeat defense that contract was required to be in writing under Statute of Frauds

d. Other issues for signed writing

   (1) Parol evidence rule

   (a) Provides that any written agreement intended by parties to be final and complete contract (called an integration) may not be contradicted by previous or contemporaneous (written or oral) evidence

       1]   Applies to such written contracts whether Statute of Frauds required writing or not
       2]   Evidence of integration is often shown by a clause such as "This agreement is the complete agreement between the parties; no other representations have been made."

       EXAMPLE: A and B enter into a home purchase agreement which is intended as a complete contract. B wishes to introduce oral evidence into court that the price of $150,000 that was in the home purchase agreement was put in to get a larger loan from a bank. B claims that they orally agreed the price would be $130,000. The oral evidence is not allowed to contradict the written contract under the parol evidence rule.

   (b) Exceptions (party may present oral proof)

       1]   To show invalidity of contract between parties (e.g., fraud, forgery, duress, mistake, failure of consideration)
       2]   To show terms not inconsistent with writing that parties would not be expected to have included

       EXAMPLE: Builder promises orally to use reasonable care not to damage nearby trees when building a house.

3] To explain intended meaning of an ambiguity (proof cannot contradict terms in contract but can explain them)

4] To show condition precedent—proof can be presented to show a fact or event must occur before agreement is valid

5] Under UCC, written terms may be supplemented or explained by course of dealing, usage of trade, or course of performance

(c) Does not apply to subsequent transactions (e.g., promises made after original agreement, or separate and distinct agreement made at same time as written contract)

EXAMPLE: M and N have a complete written employment contract. Later, M and N orally modify the contract with M agreeing to pay more and N agreeing to take on more duties. The oral evidence is allowed because it arose subsequent to the written contract.

8. Contracting using faxes

a. Legal issues arise with use of faxes

(1) Was an agreement really reached?

(a) Courts examine faxes to see if "meeting of minds" actually took place under common law principles

1] Businesses should retain all faxes concerning contract to preserve paper trail

(2) Validity of signatures sent by faxes

(a) Majority of courts that have examined this issue conclude that signatures sent by fax are valid

9. Contracting on-line

a. When individuals make contracts over the Internet, basic rules of contract law still apply; however, this technology has created and will create more additional legal issues—only some of which have been settled

b. E-SIGN Act—Federal law that makes electronic signatures valid like written ones, also makes electronic documents as valid as ones on paper

(1) Electronic signature is valid only if parties in contract had agreed for it to be

(2) Electronic document is valid only if it is in form that is retainable and is accurately reproduced

(3) Some documents are exempt from E-SIGN Act such as wills, court papers, foreclosures

(4) Act is considered important to promote use of technology

(a) Does not provide standard for authenticating e-signatures

(b) Various states are adopting statutes that provide for procedures to determine validity of e-signatures

(c) Many companies enter into written contracts to accept electronic data and e-signatures between them

(d) Companies and individuals may use exceptions that exist under statute of frauds without need to resort to E-SIGN Act or state statutes

10. Computer shrink-wrap licenses and contracts generally enforceable

a. Sale of shrink-wrap licenses is often conducted over Internet

b. Individual or company often buys these without seeing or reviewing them first (thus the term shrink-wrap)

(1) Court cases have held these shrink-wrap licenses or goods purchased on-line to be enforceable especially if purchaser has time to examine them with right of return

D. Assignment and Delegation

1. Assignment is the transfer of a right under a contract by one person to another
2. Delegation is the transfer of duties under a contract
3. Generally, a party's rights in a contract are assignable and duties are delegable

a. No consideration is needed for valid assignment

(1) Gratuitous assignments are revocable

EXAMPLE: A owes B a debt for services B performed for A, but B has been unable to collect because A has been in financial difficulty. B may gratuitously assign this debt to X if X can collect it. If A's financial position improves, B may revoke the assignment to X and collect the debt himself or assign it to another for consideration.

b.   Rights may be assigned without delegating duties, or duties may be delegated without assigning rights
c.   Partial assignments may be made (e.g., only assign part of one's rights such as right to receive money)
d.   An assignment of a contract is generally taken to mean both assignment of rights and delegation of duties unless language or facts indicate otherwise
e.   Exceptions to ability to make assignments and delegations

 (1)   Contract involving personal services, trust, or confidence (e.g., an artist cannot delegate his/her duty to paint a portrait)

  (a)   With permission, these can be delegated
  (b)   Note that a contractor building a house according to a blueprint can delegate his/her duty to someone qualified

 (2)   Provision of contract or statute prohibits assignment or delegation

  (a)   Trend is to look with disfavor on prohibitions against assignments where only a right to money is concerned
  (b)   The UCC makes prohibition against assignment of monetary rights ineffective

 (3)   If assignment would materially change risk or burden of obligor

  (a)   For example, insurance contracts, requirement and output contracts, and contracts where personal credit is involved

f.   A delegation of duties is not an anticipatory breach

EXAMPLE: X Company contracted to deliver certain goods to Y. If X Company is low on these goods, it may delegate this duty to S Company, its subsidiary. It is not an anticipatory breach because X has not indicated that performance will not occur.

4.   An assignment generally extinguishes any rights of assignor but a delegation does not relieve delegant of his/her duties

a.   The assignee acquires assignor's rights against obligor and has exclusive right to performance
b.   If obligor has notice of assignment, s/he must pay assignee, not assignor

 (1)   If obligor has no notice, s/he may pay assignor and assignee can only recover from assignor

c.   Unless there is a novation, delegating party is still liable if delegatee does not perform

 (1)   Novation occurs when one of original parties to contract is released and new party is substituted in his/her place

  (a)   Requires consent of all three parties

  EXAMPLE: A sells a car to B and accepts payments over time. B sells the car to C who agrees to take over the payments. No novation has occurred unless A agrees to accept C and release B.

5.   Party taking an assignment generally steps into shoes of assignor—s/he gets no better rights than assignor had

a.   Assignee is subject to any defenses obligor could assert against assignor
b.   If assignee releases obligor, then assignor is also released

EXAMPLE: A and B enter into a contract in which B agrees to pay A $300 for a stereo he received. A assigns his right to the $300 to C. C then releases B from the obligation of paying C the $300. This also releases A.

6.   Assignor for value makes implied warranties to assignee that

a.   Assignor will do nothing to impair rights of assignee
b.   Assignor has no knowledge of any fact that would impair value of assignment

7. If assignor makes more than one assignment of same right, there are two rules to be applied depending upon the state

   a. First assignment prevails regardless of notices (majority rules)
   b. First assignee to give notice to obligor prevails (minority rules)

E. Third-Party Beneficiary Contracts

1. Contracting parties enter into agreement intended to benefit third party(ies)

   a. Creditor beneficiary—a debtor contracts with a second party to pay the debt owed to creditor (third-party beneficiary)

   EXAMPLE: X owes C $100. X contracts with Y to paint Y's house if Y will pay C $100. C is a creditor beneficiary.

   EXAMPLE: B buys some real estate from S and agrees to assume S's mortgage that is owed to XYZ bank. XYZ is a creditor beneficiary because B and S made a contract in which B agreed to pay XYZ. If B later defaults, XYZ may recover from either B or S. XYZ may recover from S based on the original contract. XYZ may recover from B because XYZ is a creditor beneficiary.

   EXAMPLE: Buyer purchases some property subject to a mortgage that the seller owes a Bank. The bank is not a third-party beneficiary because buyer did not agree to pay the mortgage. The seller is still the only debtor on the mortgage.

   b. Donee beneficiary—almost the same as creditor beneficiary except promisee's intent is to confer a gift upon third party through promisor's performance

   EXAMPLE: X contracts to buy Y's car if Y will deliver it to D, X's son. D is a donee beneficiary.

   c. Incidental beneficiary—third party who receives an unintended benefit from a contract. S/he obtains **no** rights under the contract

   EXAMPLE: X and Y contract to build an apartment building. A, a nearby store owner, would benefit from increased business and is an incidental beneficiary.

2. Only intended beneficiary (creditor or donee) can maintain an action against contracting parties for nonperformance

   a. Intent of the promisee controls
   b. Creditor beneficiary can proceed against either contracting party

   EXAMPLE: X owes C $100. X contracts with M to paint M's house if M will pay C $100. If X does not paint M's house, C may sue X because X still owes C $100. C may also sue M, because M now owes C $100 under the contract. C is a creditor beneficiary and can sue either party.

   c. Donee beneficiary can proceed against the promisor only

   EXAMPLE: X contracts to buy Y's car if Y will deliver it to D. If Y does not deliver the car, D may sue Y. However, D may not sue X because it was a gift from X, not an obligation.

3. If the third-party beneficiary contract is executory, the parties may rescind and defeat the third party's rights

   EXAMPLE: X owes C $100. X contracts with Y to paint Y's house if Y will pay C $100. X and Y may rescind the contract before Y pays C $100. Then there is no contract for C to enforce; however, C may still sue X for the $100 owed. Or in other words, C has no third-party rights on an executory contract.

4. The promisor can assert any defenses against third-party beneficiary that s/he has against promisee

F. Performance of Contract

1. Duty to perform may depend upon a condition

   a. Condition precedent is condition that must occur before stated promise or duty in contract becomes due

   EXAMPLE: B agrees to plant trees on specified land once C removes an old tennis court from the land.

   b. Condition subsequent is condition that when it occurs it modifies or takes away a duty specified in contract.

   EXAMPLE: M agrees to rent N a certain home until M finds a buyer.

c. Satisfaction as a condition—normally when a contract guarantees satisfaction, this means agreement is performed when a reasonable person would be satisfied. However, if agreement is expressly conditioned upon personal satisfaction of one of contracting parties, then performance does not occur until that party is actually satisfied.

2. Tender of performance is an offer to perform (e.g., offer to pay debt)

EXAMPLE: X has contracted to buy goods from Y with delivery and payment to take place concurrently. X must offer the money to Y before Y has breached the contract for failure to deliver.

3. Under the **doctrine of substantial performance** (very important), performance is satisfied if

a. There has been substantial performance (i.e., **deviations are minor**), and
b. There has been **good-faith** effort to comply with contract
c. Then damages for deviations are deducted from price if above are met
d. This is often used in relation to construction contracts

4. Payment of less than agreed-upon sum does not fulfill obligation unless both parties compromise based on a bona fide dispute as to amount owed
5. Executory contract—has not yet been performed; only promises have been given
6. Standards of interpretation of contracts

a. For ordinary words, courts use normal meaning in dictionary
b. For technical words, courts use technical meaning supplied by expert testimony if necessary
c. Any ambiguity in contract is construed against party who drafted contract.
d. Typed words prevail over preprinted words—handwritten words prevail over both preprinted and typed words
e. When both parties are members of same profession or trade, words are given meaning in that profession or trade unless contact states otherwise.

G. Discharge of Contracts

1. By agreement—new consideration is necessary, but often it is supplied by a promise for a promise (e.g., both parties agreeing to release other party of contractual obligation)

a. Both parties may mutually agree to rescind contract
b. Under UCC, no consideration is needed to modify a contract (for sale of goods) if in good faith
c. A novation is an agreement by three parties whereby a previous agreement is discharged by creation of a new agreement

(1) May involve substitution of creditors, debtors, or of obligations

EXAMPLE: X has agreed to do some accounting work for Y for $2,000. Since X is very busy, X, Y, and Z all agree to let X out of the contract and insert Z in his place. This is a novation. X and Y no longer have any obligations to each other.

EXAMPLE: A party purchases land and assumes a mortgage. The original mortgagor is still liable unless a novation has occurred.

2. By performance becoming objectively impossible

a. But mere fact of performance becoming more costly does not excuse performance

EXAMPLE: A agreed to sell a specified quantity of corn to B at specified prices. He had planned to sell his own corn until his crop was destroyed. Even though he may make less profit or even suffer a loss, he can still fulfill the contract by purchasing the corn from others to resell to B under his contract.

3. By breach of contract
4. Anticipatory breach (repudiation) is renunciation before performance is due

a. May sue at once, or
b. Cancel contract, or
c. Wait until time performance is due or for a reasonable time and then sue
d. If other party has not changed position in reliance upon the repudiation, repudiating party can retract repudiation and perform at appointed time, thereby discharging his/her contractual obligation

EXAMPLE: X agrees to convey and Y agrees to pay for land on April 1. On February 1, Y learns that X has sold the land to Z. Y may sue before April 1, or he may wait and sue on April 1.

EXAMPLE: M agrees to deliver 1,000 widgets to Q by December 1. Three months before that date, M says, he will be unable to deliver on December 1.

H. Remedies

1. Monetary damages

   a. Purpose is to place injured party in as good a position as s/he would have occupied if contract had been performed

   b. Actual or compensatory damages are equal to amount caused by breach

      (1) This is the **most common remedy** under contract law
      (2) Damages must be foreseeable before being recoverable

   c. Punitive damages are generally not allowed in contract law

   d. Liquidated damage clause is a provision agreed to in a contract to set the amount of damages in advance if a breach occurs

      (1) These are used instead of awarding actual compensatory damages
      (2) Not enforceable if punitive; therefore, amount set in advance must be reasonably based on what actual damages are expected to be
      (3) For sales of goods, if contract has no provision for liquidated damages, seller may retain deposit of up to $500 when buyer defaults

   e. Party injured by breach must use reasonable care to minimize loss because s/he cannot recover costs that could have been avoided—called mitigation of damages

   EXAMPLE: One who receives perishables which are not the goods bargained for must take reasonable steps to prevent loss from spoilage.

   EXAMPLE: X contracts to fix Y's car. After X begins work, Y breaches and says "Stop." X cannot continue to work and incur more costs (i.e., put in more parts and labor).

2. Rescission—cancellation of contract whereby parties are placed in position they were in before contract was formed

3. Specific performance—compels performance promised

   a. Used only when money damages will not suffice (e.g., when subject matter is unique, or rare, as in contract for sale of land)

   b. Injured party may seek compensatory damages if s/he chooses

   c. Not available to compel personal services

4. Restitution—return of consideration to injured party

5. Injunction—compels an act or restrains an act

6. Release—one party relieves other party of part of obligations in contract

7. Waiver—one party voluntarily gives up some right in contract either by express agreement or by consistently not enforcing such right in past

8. Arbitration—resolution of dispute, outside of judicial system, agreed to by disputing parties

9. Reformation—if parties have failed to express true intentions in contract, court may reform it to express true intentions of contract

   a. Note—court needs clear proof

I. Statute of Limitations

1. Bars suit if not brought within statutory period

   a. Periods vary for different types of cases
   b. Periods vary from state to state

2. Statute begins to run from time cause of action accrues (e.g., breach)

3. Running of statute may be stopped when defendant is absent from jurisdiction

J. Jurisdiction over Defendant for On-Line Transactions

1. Courts generally grant plaintiffs personal jurisdiction over defendants in foreign state if plaintiff intentionally engaged in commercial activities for use outside of home state
2. Merely transmitting information to defendants of other states does not grant personal jurisdiction in other states
3. Parties to contracts made on-line may agree to use law of given jurisdiction just as in other contracts

   a. Often, websites put forum selection clause at end of home page in case lawsuit is brought against on-line company

      (1) Some courts may not enforce these clauses since they are not negotiable and thus lead to adhesion contracts

         (a) Increasing trend is not to enforce these unless they are fair and reasonable because they are typically in small print at end of home page

MULTIPLE-CHOICE QUESTIONS (1-57)

1. Carson Corp., a retail chain, asked Alto Construction to fix a broken window at one of Carson's stores. Alto offered to make the repairs within three days at a price to be agreed on after the work was completed. A contract based on Alto's offer would fail because of indefiniteness as to the
    a. Price involved.
    b. Nature of the subject matter.
    c. Parties to the contract.
    d. Time for performance.

2. On September 10, Harris, Inc., a new car dealer, placed a newspaper advertisement stating that Harris would sell ten cars at its showroom for a special discount only on September 12, 13, and 14. On September 12, King called Harris and expressed an interest in buying one of the advertised cars. King was told that five of the cars had been sold and to come to the showroom as soon as possible. On September 13, Harris made a televised announcement that the sale would end at 10:00 PM that night. King went to Harris' showroom on September 14 and demanded the right to buy a car at the special discount. Harris had sold the ten cars and refused King's demand. King sued Harris for breach of contract. Harris' best defense to King's suit would be that Harris'
    a. Offer was unenforceable.
    b. Advertisement was **not** an offer.
    c. Television announcement revoked the offer.
    d. Offer had **not** been accepted.

3. On June 15, Peters orally offered to sell a used lawn mower to Mason for $125. Peters specified that Mason had until June 20 to accept the offer. On June 16, Peters received an offer to purchase the lawn mower for $150 from Bronson, Mason's neighbor. Peters accepted Bronson's offer. On June 17, Mason saw Bronson using the lawn mower and was told the mower had been sold to Bronson. Mason immediately wrote to Peters to accept the June 15 offer. Which of the following statements is correct?
    a. Mason's acceptance would be effective when received by Peters.
    b. Mason's acceptance would be effective when mailed.
    c. Peters' offer had been revoked and Mason's acceptance was ineffective.
    d. Peters was obligated to keep the June 15 offer open until June 20.

4. Calistoga offers to sell her home to Drake for $300,000. Drake asks her if she would accept $250,000. Which of the following is true?
    a. Drake's response is mere inquiry; therefore, the $300,000 offer by Calistoga is still in force.
    b. Drake's response is a counteroffer effectively terminating the $300,000 offer and instigating an offer for $250,000.
    c. Drake's response is a rejection of the $300,000 offer, and there is no offer for $250,000 because it is too indefinite to be an offer.
    d. Because of ambiguity, both offers are terminated by operation of law.

5. Opal offered, in writing, to sell Larkin a parcel of land for $300,000. If Opal dies, the offer will

    a. Terminate prior to Larkin's acceptance only if Larkin received notice of Opal's death.
    b. Remain open for a reasonable period of time after Opal's death.
    c. Automatically terminate despite Larkin's prior acceptance.
    d. Automatically terminate prior to Larkin's acceptance.

6. On April 1, Fine Corp. faxed Moss an offer to purchase Moss' warehouse for $500,000. The offer stated that it would remain open only until April 4 and that acceptance must be received to be effective. Moss sent an acceptance on April 4 by overnight mail and Fine received it on April 5. Which of the following statements is correct?
    a. No contract was formed because Moss sent the acceptance by an unauthorized method.
    b. No contract was formed because Fine received Moss' acceptance after April 4.
    c. A contract was formed when Moss sent the acceptance.
    d. A contract was formed when Fine received Moss' acceptance.

7. On February 12, Harris sent Fresno a written offer to purchase Fresno's land. The offer included the following provision: "Acceptance of this offer must be by registered or certified mail, received by Harris no later than February 18 by 5:00 p.m. CST." On February 18, Fresno sent Harris a letter accepting the offer by private overnight delivery service. Harris received the letter on February 19. Which of the following statements is correct?
    a. A contract was formed on February 19.
    b. Fresno's letter constituted a counteroffer.
    c. Fresno's use of the overnight delivery service was an effective form of acceptance.
    d. A contract was formed on February 18 regardless of when Harris actually received Fresno's letter.

8. Kay, an art collector, promised Hammer, an art student, that if Hammer could obtain certain rare artifacts within two weeks, Kay would pay for Hammer's postgraduate education. At considerable effort and expense, Hammer obtained the specified artifacts within the two-week period. When Hammer requested payment, Kay refused. Kay claimed that there was no consideration for the promise. Hammer would prevail against Kay based on
    a. Unilateral contract.
    b. Unjust enrichment.
    c. Public policy.
    d. Quasi contract.

9. On September 27, Summers sent Fox a letter offering to sell Fox a vacation home for $150,000. On October 2, Fox replied by mail agreeing to buy the home for $145,000. Summers did not reply to Fox. Do Fox and Summers have a binding contract?
    a. No, because Fox failed to sign and return Summers' letter.
    b. No, because Fox's letter was a counteroffer.
    c. Yes, because Summers' offer was validly accepted.
    d. Yes, because Summers' silence is an implied acceptance of Fox's letter.

10. Wick Company made a contract in writing to hire Zake for five years for $150,000 per year. After two years, Zake asked Wick for a raise of $20,000 per year. Wick at first refused but agreed after Zake put on some pressure. After the fifth year, Zake left and Wick sued to get back the extra $20,000 per year for the last three years. Who wins?

    a.   Zake, because Wick agreed to the raise.
    b.   Zake, if the raise was agreed to in writing.
    c.   Wick, even though Wick agreed to the raise.
    d.   Wick, because Zake had applied some pressure to get the raise.

11. Grove is seeking to avoid performing a promise to pay Brook $1,500. Grove is relying on lack of consideration on Brook's part. Grove will prevail if he can establish that

    a.   Prior to Grove's promise, Brook had already performed the requested act.
    b.   Brooks' only claim of consideration was the relinquishment of a legal right.
    c.   Brook's asserted consideration is only worth $400.
    d.   The consideration to be performed by Brook will be performed by a third party.

12. Dunne and Cook signed a contract requiring Cook to rebind 500 of Dunne's books at $0.80 per book. Later, Dunne requested, in good faith, that the price be reduced to $.70 per book. Cook agreed orally to reduce the price to $.70. Under the circumstances, the oral agreement is

    a.   Enforceable, but proof of it is inadmissible into evidence.
    b.   Enforceable, and proof of it is admissible into evidence.
    c.   Unenforceable, because Dunne failed to give consideration, but proof of it is otherwise admissible into evidence.
    d.   Unenforceable, due to the statute of frauds, and proof of it is inadmissible into evidence.

13. In which of the following situations does the first promise serve as valid consideration for the second promise?

    a.   A police officer's promise to catch a thief for a victim's promise to pay a reward.
    b.   A builder's promise to complete a contract for a purchaser's promise to extend the time for completion.
    c.   A debtor's promise to pay $500 for a creditor's promise to forgive the balance of a $600 liquidated debt.
    d.   A debtor's promise to pay $500 for a creditor's promise to forgive the balance of a $600 disputed debt.

14. Which of the following will be legally binding despite lack of consideration?

    a.   An employer's promise to make a cash payment to a deceased employee's family in recognition of the employee's many years of service.
    b.   A promise to donate money to a charity on which the charity relied in incurring large expenditures.
    c.   A modification of a signed contract to purchase a parcel of land.
    d.   A merchant's oral promise to keep an offer open for sixty days.

15. Rail, who was sixteen years old, purchased an $800 computer from Elco Electronics. Rail and Elco are located in a state where the age of majority is eighteen. On several occasions Rail returned the computer to Elco for repairs.

Rail was very unhappy with the computer. Two days after reaching the age of eighteen, Rail was still frustrated with the computer's reliability, and returned it to Elco, demanding an $800 refund. Elco refused, claiming that Rail no longer had a right to disaffirm the contract. Elco's refusal is

    a.   Correct, because Rail's multiple requests for service acted as a ratification of the contract.
    b.   Correct, because Rail could have transferred good title to a good-faith purchaser for value.
    c.   Incorrect, because Rail disaffirmed the contract within a reasonable period of time after reaching the age of eighteen.
    d.   Incorrect, because Rail could disaffirm the contract at any time.

16. Green was adjudicated incompetent by a court having proper jurisdiction. Which of the following statements is correct regarding contracts subsequently entered into by Green?

    a.   All contracts are voidable.
    b.   All contracts are valid.
    c.   All contracts are void.
    d.   All contracts are enforceable.

17. All of the following are effective methods of ratifying a contract entered into by a minor **except**

    a.   Expressly ratifying the contract after reaching the age of majority.
    b.   Failing to disaffirm the contract within a reasonable time after reaching the age of majority.
    c.   Ratifying the contract before reaching the age of majority.
    d.   Ratifying the contract by implication after reaching the age of majority.

18. Under a personal services contract, which of the following circumstances will cause the discharge of a party's duties?

    a.   Death of the party who is to receive the services.
    b.   Cost of performing the services has doubled.
    c.   Bankruptcy of the party who is to receive the services.
    d.   Illegality of the services to be performed.

19. Which of the following would be unenforceable because the subject matter is illegal?

    a.   A contingent fee charged by an attorney to represent a plaintiff in a negligence action.
    b.   An arbitration clause in a supply contract.
    c.   A restrictive covenant in an employment contract prohibiting a former employee from using the employer's trade secrets.
    d.   An employer's promise **not** to press embezzlement charges against an employee who agrees to make restitution.

20. Which of the following, if intentionally misstated by a seller to a buyer, would be considered a fraudulent inducement to make a contract?

    a.   Nonexpert opinion.
    b.   Appraised value.
    c.   Prediction.
    d.   Immaterial fact.

21. If a buyer accepts an offer containing an immaterial unilateral mistake, the resulting contract will be

    a.   Void as a matter of law.

b. Void at the election of the buyer.
c. Valid as to both parties.
d. Voidable at the election of the seller.

22. If a person is induced to enter into a contract by another person because of the close relationship between the parties, the contract may be voidable under which of the following defenses?
a. Fraud in the inducement.
b. Unconscionability.
c. Undue influence.
d. Duress.

23. Long purchased a life insurance policy with Tempo Life Insurance Co. The policy named Long's daughter as beneficiary. Six months after the policy was issued, Long died of a heart attack. Long had failed to disclose on the insurance application a known preexisting heart condition that caused the heart attack. Tempo refused to pay the death benefit to Long's daughter. If Long's daughter sues, Tempo will
a. Win, because Long's daughter is an incidental beneficiary.
b. Win, because of Long's failure to disclose the pre-existing heart condition.
c. Lose, because Long's death was from natural causes.
d. Lose, because Long's daughter is a third-party donee beneficiary.

24. Petersen went to Jackson's home to buy a used car advertised in the newspaper. Jackson told Petersen that "it is a great car" and that "the engine had been overhauled a year ago." Shortly after he bought the car, Petersen began experiencing problems with the engine. When Jackson refused to refund his money, Petersen sued for fraud based on it was not a "great car" and also based on the fact, as learned later, the overhaul was done thirteen months ago, not a year. Will Petersen win his case?
a. Yes, Jackson's statement that "it is a great car" is actionable fraud.
b. Yes, Jackson's statement about the overhaul is actionable fraud.
c. Yes, both the statement that "it is a great car" and the statement about the overhaul are actionable fraud.
d. No.

25. A building subcontractor submitted a bid for construction of a portion of a high-rise office building. The bid contained material computational errors. The general contractor accepted the bid with knowledge of the errors. Which of the following statements best represents the subcontractor's liability?
a. Not liable because the contractor knew of the errors.
b. Not liable because the errors were a result of gross negligence.
c. Liable because the errors were unilateral.
d. Liable because the errors were material.

26. Maco, Inc. and Kent contracted for Kent to provide Maco certain consulting services at an hourly rate of $20. Kent's normal hourly rate was $90 per hour, the fair market value of the services. Kent agreed to the $20 rate because Kent was having serious financial problems. At the time the agreement was negotiated, Maco was aware of Kent's finan-

cial condition and refused to pay more than $20 per hour for Kent's services. Kent has now sued to rescind the contract with Maco, claiming duress by Maco during the negotiations. Under the circumstances, Kent will
a. Win, because Maco refused to pay the fair market value of Kent's services.
b. Win, because Maco was aware of Kent's serious financial problems.
c. Lose, because Maco's actions did **not** constitute duress.
d. Lose, because Maco **cannot** prove that Kent, at the time, had **no** other offers to provide consulting services.

27. To prevail in a common law action for fraud in the inducement, a plaintiff must prove that the
a. Defendant was an expert with regard to the misrepresentations.
b. Defendant made the misrepresentations with knowledge of their falsity and with an intention to deceive.
c. Misrepresentations were in writing.
d. Plaintiff was in a fiduciary relationship with the defendant.

28. Under the UCC Sales Article, a plaintiff who proves fraud in the formation of a contract may
a. Elect to rescind the contract and need **not** return the consideration received from the other party.
b. Be entitled to rescind the contract and sue for damages resulting from the fraud.
c. Be entitled to punitive damages provided physical injuries resulted from the fraud.
d. Rescind the contract even if there was **no** reliance on the fraudulent statement.

29. On June 1, 2001, Decker orally guaranteed the payment of a $5,000 note Decker's cousin owed Baker. Decker's agreement with Baker provided that Decker's guaranty would terminate in eighteen months. On June 3, 2001, Baker wrote Decker confirming Decker's guaranty. Decker did not object to the confirmation. On August 23, 2001, Decker's cousin defaulted on the note and Baker demanded that Decker honor the guaranty. Decker refused. Which of the following statements is correct?
a. Decker is liable under the oral guaranty because Decker did **not** object to Baker's June 3 letter.
b. Decker is **not** liable under the oral guaranty because it expired more than one year after June 1.
c. Decker is liable under the oral guaranty because Baker demanded payment within one year of the date the guaranty was given.
d. Decker is **not** liable under the oral guaranty because Decker's promise was **not** in writing.

30. Nolan agreed orally with Train to sell Train a house for $100,000. Train sent Nolan a signed agreement and a downpayment of $10,000. Nolan did not sign the agreement, but allowed Train to move into the house. Before closing, Nolan refused to go through with the sale. Train sued Nolan to compel specific performance. Under the provisions of the Statute of Frauds
a. Train will win because Train signed the agreement and Nolan did **not** object.
b. Train will win because Train made a downpayment and took possession.

    c.   Nolan will win because Nolan did **not** sign the agreement.

    d.   Nolan will win because the house was worth more than $500.

31. Cherry contracted orally to purchase Picks Company for $1,500,000 if it is profitable for one full year after the making of the oral contract. An auditor would be brought in at the end of the year to verify this. Even though the company turns out to be profitable during the upcoming year, Cherry refuses to go through with the contract, claiming that it was unenforceable because it was not in writing. Is Cherry correct?

    a.   Yes, because the contract could not be completed within one year.

    b.   Yes, because the contract was for $500 or more.

    c.   No, because the company was profitable as agreed for one year.

    d.   No, because Picks Company relied on Cherry's promise.

32. Which of the following statements is true with regard to the Statute of Frauds?

    a.   All contracts involving consideration of more than $500 must be in writing.

    b.   The written contract must be signed by all parties.

    c.   The Statute of Frauds applies to contracts that can be fully performed within one year from the date they are made.

    d.   The contract terms may be stated in more than 1 document.

33. Carson agreed orally to repair Ives' rare book for $450. Before the work was started, Ives asked Carson to perform additional repairs to the book and agreed to increase the contract price to $650. After Carson completed the work, Ives refused to pay and Carson sued. Ives' defense was based on the Statute of Frauds. What total amount will Carson recover?

    a. $0

    b. $200

    c. $450

    d. $650

34. Landry Company contracted orally with Newell to pay her $50,000 for the completion of an ethics audit of Landry Company. The report is to span a period of time of at least ten months and is due in fourteen months from now. Newell has agreed orally to perform the ethics audit and says that she will begin within three months, noting that even if she delays the full three months, she will have the report ready within the fourteen-month deadline. Does this contract fall under the Statute of Frauds?

    a.   Yes, because the contract is for $500 or more.

    b.   Yes, because the deadline for the contract is over one year.

    c.   No, despite the due date of fourteen months.

    d.   No, because both parties waived the Statute of Frauds by their oral agreement.

35. Rogers and Lennon entered into a written computer consulting agreement that required Lennon to provide certain weekly reports to Rogers. The agreement also stated that Lennon would provide the computer equipment necessary to perform the services, and that Rogers' computer would not be used. As the parties were executing the agreement, they orally agreed that Lennon could use Rogers' computer. After executing the agreement, Rogers and Lennon orally agreed that Lennon would report on a monthly, rather than weekly, basis. The parties now disagree on Lennon's right to use Rogers' computer and how often Lennon must report to Rogers. In the event of a lawsuit between the parties, the parol evidence rule will

    a.   Not apply to any of the parties' agreements because the consulting agreement did **not** have to be in writing.

    b.   Not prevent Lennon from proving the parties' oral agreement that Lennon could use Rogers' computer.

    c.   Not prevent the admission into evidence of testimony regarding Lennon's right to report on a monthly basis.

    d.   Not apply to the parties' agreement to allow Lennon to use Rogers' computer because it was contemporaneous with the written agreement.

36. Where the parties have entered into a written contract intended as the final expression of their agreement, which of the following agreements will be admitted into evidence because they are **not** prohibited by the parol evidence rule?

	Subsequent oral agreements	Prior written agreements
a.	Yes	Yes
b.	Yes	No
c.	No	Yes
d.	No	No

37. In negotiations with Andrews for the lease of Kemp's warehouse, Kemp orally agreed to pay one-half of the cost of the utilities. The written lease, later prepared by Kemp's attorney, provided that Andrews pay all of the utilities. Andrews failed to carefully read the lease and signed it. When Kemp demanded that Andrews pay all of the utilities, Andrews refused, claiming that the lease did not accurately reflect the oral agreement. Andrews also learned that Kemp intentionally misrepresented the condition of the structure of the warehouse during the negotiations between the parties. Andrews sued to rescind the lease and intends to introduce evidence of the parties' oral agreement about sharing the utilities and the fraudulent statements made by Kemp. The parol evidence rule will prevent the admission of evidence concerning the

	Oral agreement regarding who pays the utilities	Fraudulent statements by Kemp
a.	Yes	Yes
b.	No	Yes
c.	Yes	No
d.	No	No

38. Joan Silver had viewed some land that she wished to purchase. It was offered for sale by Daniel Tweney over the Internet for $200,000. Silver believes this to be a good deal for her and thus wishes to purchase it. Silver and Tweney have communicated on-line and wish to make a contract for the land over the Internet. Which of the following statements is(are) correct?

I. Because this contract is covered by the Statute of Frauds, this contract cannot be accomplished over the Internet.

II. Because of the parol evidence rule, this contract cannot be completed over the Internet.

III. Because this contract is covered by the Uniform Commerical Code, it may not be accomplished over the Internet.

    a. Only I is correct.
    b. I and II only are correct.
    c. I and III only are correct.
    d. Neither I, II, nor III is correct.

39. Generally, which of the following contract rights are assignable?

	Option contract rights	*Malpractice insurance policy rights*
a.	Yes	Yes
b.	Yes	No
c.	No	Yes
d.	No	No

40. One of the criteria for a valid assignment of a sales contract to a third party is that the assignment must

    a. Be supported by adequate consideration from the assignee.
    b. Be in writing and signed by the assignor.
    c. Not materially increase the other party's risk or duty.
    d. Not be revocable by the assignor.

Items 41 and 42 are based on the following:

Egan contracted with Barton to buy Barton's business. The contract provided that Egan would pay the business debts Barton owed Ness and that the balance of the purchase price would be paid to Barton over a ten-year period. The contract also required Egan to take out a decreasing term life insurance policy naming Barton and Ness as beneficiaries to ensure that the amounts owed Barton and Ness would be paid if Egan died.

41. Barton's contract rights were assigned to Vim, and Egan was notified of the assignment. Despite the assignment, Egan continued making payments to Barton. Egan died before completing payment and Vim sued Barton for the insurance proceeds and the other payments on the purchase price received by Barton after the assignment. To which of the following is Vim entitled?

	Payments on purchase price	*Insurance proceeds*
a.	No	Yes
b.	No	No
c.	Yes	Yes
d.	Yes	No

42. Which of the following would describe Ness' status under the contract and insurance policy?

	Contract	*Insurance policy*
a.	Donee beneficiary	Donee beneficiary
b.	Donee beneficiary	Creditor beneficiary
c.	Creditor beneficiary	Donee beneficiary
d.	Creditor beneficiary	Creditor beneficiary

43. Your client, Bugle, owns a parking lot near downtown San Francisco. One day Bugle is excited because he learns that Fargo, who owns a parking lot next door, has made a contract with ABC Company to sell her land. ABC Company can then construct a building that will contain several nice professional offices. Bugle figures that he will charge more for his parking. He later discovers that the contract fell through. He says that when he finds out who breached the contract, he will sue that party for lost profits that he would have earned. Which of the following is correct?

    a. If Fargo was the one who breached the contract, Bugle may sue her if ABC had already made some payments on the contract.
    b. If ABC was the party who breached, ABC is liable to Bugle.
    c. Bugle may sue either party, and the nonbreaching party may then recover from the breaching party.
    d. Bugle has no legal rights against either party.

44. Baxter, Inc. and Globe entered into a contract. After receiving valuable consideration from Clay, Baxter assigned its rights under the contract to Clay. In which of the following circumstances would Baxter **not** be liable to Clay?

    a. Clay released Globe.
    b. Globe paid Baxter.
    c. Baxter released Globe.
    d. Baxter breached the contract.

45. Mackay paid Manus $1,000 to deliver a painting to Mackay's friend Mann. When they met and signed the contract, Mackay said she wanted the painting delivered as soon as possible because it was a gift for Mann's birthday. Several months have passed without the delivery. Mann can maintain lawsuits against which parties to get the painting?

    a. Manus only.
    b. Mackay only.
    c. Manus, but only if he also brings suit against Mackay.
    d. Manus or Mackay at Mann's option.

46. Ferco, Inc. claims to be a creditor beneficiary of a contract between Bell and Allied Industries, Inc. Allied is indebted to Ferco. The contract between Bell and Allied provides that Bell is to purchase certain goods from Allied and pay the purchase price directly to Ferco until Allied's obligation is satisfied. Without justification, Bell failed to pay Ferco and Ferco sued Bell. Ferco will

    a. Not prevail, because Ferco lacked privity of contract with either Bell or Allied.
    b. Not prevail, because Ferco did **not** give any consideration to Bell.
    c. Prevail, because Ferco was an intended beneficiary of the contract between Allied and Bell.
    d. Prevail, provided Ferco was aware of the contract between Bell and Allied at the time the contract was entered into.

47. Parc hired Glaze to remodel and furnish an office suite. Glaze submitted plans that Parc approved. After completing all the necessary construction and painting, Glaze purchased minor accessories that Parc rejected because they did not conform to the plans. Parc refused to allow Glaze to complete the project and refused to pay Glaze any part of the contract price. Glaze sued for the value of the work performed. Which of the following statements is correct?

    a. Glaze will lose because Glaze breached the contract by **not** completing performance.
    b. Glaze will win because Glaze substantially performed and Parc prevented complete performance.
    c. Glaze will lose because Glaze materially breached the contract by buying the accessories.
    d. Glaze will win because Parc committed anticipatory breach.

48. Which of the following types of conditions affecting performance may validly be present in contracts?

	Conditions precedent	Conditions subsequent	Current conditions
a.	Yes	Yes	Yes
b.	Yes	Yes	No
c.	Yes	No	Yes
d.	No	Yes	Yes

49. Which of the following actions if taken by one party to a contract generally will discharge the performance required of the other party to the contract?
a. Material breach of the contract.
b. Delay in performance.
c. Tender.
d. Assignment of rights.

50. Which of the following actions will result in the discharge of a party to a contract?

	Prevention of performance	Accord and satisfaction
a.	Yes	Yes
b.	Yes	No
c.	No	Yes
d.	No	No

51. To cancel a contract and to restore the parties to their original positions before the contract, the parties should execute a
a. Novation
b. Release
c. Rescission
d. Revocation

52. Kaye contracted to sell Hodges a building for $310,000. The contract required Hodges to pay the entire amount at closing. Kaye refused to close the sale of the building. Hodges sued Kaye. To what relief is Hodges entitled?
a. Punitive damages and compensatory damages.
b. Specific performance and compensatory damages.
c. Consequential damages or punitive damages.
d. Compensatory damages or specific performance.

53. Ames Construction Co. contracted to build a warehouse for White Corp. The construction specifications required Ames to use Ace lighting fixtures. Inadvertently, Ames installed Perfection lighting fixtures which are of slightly lesser quality than Ace fixtures, but in all other respects meet White's needs. Which of the following statements is correct?
a. White's recovery will be limited to monetary damages because Ames' breach of the construction contract was **not** material.
b. White will **not** be able to recover any damages from Ames because the breach was inadvertent.
c. Ames did not breach the construction contract because the Perfection fixtures were substantially as good as the Ace fixtures.
d. Ames must install Ace fixtures or White will **not** be obligated to accept the warehouse.

54. Master Mfg., Inc. contracted with Accur Computer Repair Corp. to maintain Master's computer system. Master's manufacturing process depends on its computer system operating properly at all times. A liquidated damages clause in the contract provided that Accur pay $1,000 to Master for each day that Accur was late responding to a service request. On January 12, Accur was notified that Master's computer system failed. Accur did not respond to Master's service request until January 15. If Master sues Accur under the liquidated damage provision of the contract, Master will
a. Win, unless the liquidated damage provision is determined to be a penalty.
b. Win, because under all circumstances liquidated damage provisions are enforceable.
c. Lose, because Accur's breach was **not** material.
d. Lose, because liquidated damage provisions violate public policy.

55. Nagel and Fields entered into a contract in which Nagel was obligated to deliver certain goods to Fields by September 10. On September 3, Nagel told Fields that Nagel had no intention of delivering the goods required by the contract. Prior to September 10, Fields may successfully sue Nagel under the doctrine of
a. Promissory estoppel.
b. Accord and satisfaction.
c. Anticipatory repudiation.
d. Substantial performance.

56. Maco Corp. contracted to sell 1,500 bushels of potatoes to LBC Chips. The contract did not refer to any specific supply source for the potatoes. Maco intended to deliver potatoes grown on its farms. An insect infestation ruined Maco's crop but not the crops of other growers in the area. Maco failed to deliver the potatoes to LBC. LBC sued Maco for breach of contract. Under the circumstances, Maco will
a. Lose, because it could have purchased potatoes from other growers to deliver to LBC.
b. Lose, unless it can show that the purchase of substitute potatoes for delivery to LBC would make the contract unprofitable.
c. Win, because the infestation was an act of nature that could **not** have been anticipated by Maco.
d. Win, because both Maco and LBC are assumed to accept the risk of a crop failure.

57. Ordinarily, in an action for breach of a construction contract, the statute of limitations time period would be computed from the date the
a. Contract is negotiated.
b. Contract is breached.
c. Construction is begun.
d. Contract is signed.

OTHER OBJECTIVE QUESTIONS

Problem 1   (10 to 15 minutes)

Required:

For each of the numbered statements or groups of statements select either A, B, or C.

Questions

1. Party S feels a moral obligation because Party F let S stay in his place for free when S attended college. S now promises to pay F for the past kindness.

2. F agrees to deliver all of the sugar that Company S will need in her business for the following year. S agrees to purchase it at the market price.

3. F does not smoke for one year pursuant to S's agreement to pay F $200 if she does not smoke for one year.

4. F dies leaving a valid will which gives S $100,000.

5. F is an auditor of XYZ Company. S is a potential investor of XYZ and offers to pay F $1,000 if F performs a professional, quality audit of XYZ Company. The $1,000 is in addition to the fee F will get from XYZ. F does perform a professional, quality audit.

6. F had agreed, in writing, to work for S for five years for $100,000 per year. After two years, F asks for a 20% raise. S first agrees then later changes his mind. F, while not agreeing to additional duties or changing his position, wants to enforce the raise in salary.

7. S promised to pay F $1,000 if he crosses the Golden Gate Bridge on his hands and knees. F does so.

8. F promised to pay S $200 for a computer worth $2,000. S agreed to the deal.

9. F agreed to purchase all of the parts from S that S can produce in her business for the next six months. S also agreed.

10. S agreed to accept $1,000 from F for a $1,500 debt that is not disputed. S now wants the additional $500. Focus on the agreement to accept the lesser amount.

11. S agreed to accept $1,000 from F for a debt that S claims is $1,500 but F in good faith claims is $800. F agreed to the $1,000 initially, then decides he will pay only $800. Focus on the enforceability of the agreement for $1,000.

12. S agreed to donate $100 to F, a public charity.

List

A. Both parties have given consideration legally sufficient to support a contract.

B. One of the parties has **not** given consideration legally sufficient to support a contract. The promise, agreement, or transaction is generally **not** enforceable.

C. One of the parties has **not** given consideration legally sufficient to support a contract. However, the promise, agreement, or transaction **is** generally enforceable.

Problem 2   (15 to 25 minutes)

On January 15, East Corp. orally offered to hire Bean, CPA, to perform management consulting services for East and its subsidiaries. The offer provided for a three-year contract at $10,000 per month. On January 20, East sent Bean a signed memorandum stating the terms of the offer. The memorandum also included a payment clause that hadn't been discussed and the provision that Bean's acceptance of the offer would not be effective unless it was received by East on or before January 25. Bean received the memorandum on January 21, signed it, and mailed it back to East the same day. East received it on January 24. On January 23, East wrote to Bean revoking the offer. Bean received the revocation on January 25.

On March 1, East Corp. orally engaged Snow Consultants to install a corporate local area network system (LAN) for East's financial operations. The engagement was to last until the following February 15 and East would pay Snow $5,000 twice a month. On March 15, East offered Snow $1,000 per month to assist in the design of East's Internet home page. Snow accepted East's offer. On April 1, citing excess work, Snow advised East that Snow would not assist with the design of the home page. On April 5, East accepted Snow's withdrawal from the Internet home page design project. On April 15, Snow notified East that Snow had assigned the fees due Snow on the LAN installation engagement to Bank Computer Consultants. On April 30, East notified Snow that the LAN installation agreement was canceled.

Required:

Items 1 through 5 are based on the transaction between East Corp. and Bean. For each item, select the best answer from List I. An answer may be selected once, more than once, or not at all.

1. What was the effect of the event(s) that took place on January 20?

2. What was the effect of the event(s) that took place on January 21?

3. What was the effect of the event(s) that took place on January 23?

4. What was the effect of the event(s) that took place on January 24?

5. What was the effect of the event(s) that took place on January 25?

List I

    A. Acceptance of a counteroffer.
    B. Acceptance of an offer governed by the mailbox rule.
    C. Attempted acceptance of an offer.
    D. Attempted revocation of an offer.
    E. Formation of an enforceable contract.
    F. Formation of a contract enforceable only against East.
    G. Invalid revocation because of prior acceptance of an offer.
    H. Offer revoked by sending a revocation letter.
    I. Submission of a counteroffer.
    J. Submission of a written offer.

Items 6 through 10 are based on the transaction between East Corp. and Snow Consultants. For each item, select the best answer from List II. An answer may be selected once, more than once, or not at all.

6. What was the effect of the event(s) that took place on March 1?

7. What was the effect of the event(s) that took place on March 15?

8. What was the effect of the event(s) that took place on April 5?

9. What was the effect of the event(s) that took place on April 15?

10. What was the effect of the event(s) that took place on April 30?

List II

    A. Breach of contract.
    B. Discharge from performance.
    C. Enforceable oral contract modification.
    D. Formation of a voidable contract.
    E. Formation of an enforceable contract.
    F. Formation of a contract unenforceable under the Statute of Frauds.
    G. Invalid assignment.
    H. Mutual rescission.
    I. Novation.
    J. Unilateral offer.
    K. Valid assignment of rights.
    L. Valid assignment of duties.
    M. Valid assignment of rights and duties.

Problem 3   (10 to 15 minutes)

    On December 15, Blake Corp. telephoned Reach Consultants, Inc. and offered to hire Reach to design a security system for Blake's research department. The work would require two years to complete. Blake offered to pay a fee of $100,000 but stated that the offer must be accepted in writing, and the acceptance received by Blake no later than December 20.

    On December 20, Reach faxed a written acceptance to Blake. Blake's offices were closed on December 20 and Reach's fax was not seen until December 21.

    Reach's acceptance contained the following language:

"We accept your $1,000,000 offer. Weaver has been assigned $5,000 of the fee as payment for sums owed Weaver by Reach. Payment of this amount should be made directly to Weaver."

    On December 22, Blake sent a signed memo to Reach rejecting Reach's December 20 fax but offering to hire Reach for a $75,000 fee. Reach telephoned Blake on December 23 and orally accepted Blake's December 22 offer.

Required:

a.   Items 1 through 7 relate to whether a contractual relationship exists between Blake and Reach. For each item, determine whether the statement is true (T) or false(F).

1. Blake's December 15 offer had to be in writing to be a legitimate offer.

2. Reach's December 20 fax was an improper method of acceptance.

3. Reach's December 20 fax was effective when sent.

4. Reach's acceptance was invalid because it was received after December 20.

5. Blake's receipt of Reach's acceptance created a voidable contract.

6. If Reach had rejected the original offer by telephone on December 17, he could not validly accept the offer later.

7. Reach's December 20 fax was a counteroffer.

b.   Items 8 through 12 relate to the attempted assignment of part of the fee to Weaver. Assume that a valid contract exists between Blake and Reach. For each item, determine whether the statement is true (T) or false(F).

8. Reach is prohibited from making an assignment of any contract right or duty.

9. Reach may validly assign part of the fee to Weaver.

10. Under the terms of Reach's acceptance, Weaver would be considered a third-party creditor beneficiary.

11. In a breach of contract suit by Weaver, against Blake, Weaver would not collect any punitive damages.

12. In a breach of contract suit by Weaver, against Reach, Weaver would be able to collect punitive damages.

c.   Items 13 through 15 relate to Blake's December 22 signed memo. For each item, determine whether the statement is true (T) or false(F).

13. Reach's oral acceptance of Blake's December 22 memo may be enforced by Blake against Reach.

14. Blake's memo is a valid offer even though it contains no date for acceptance.

15. Blake's memo may be enforced against Blake by Reach.

PROBLEMS

Problem 1   (15 to 25 minutes)

Victor Corp. engaged Bell & Co., CPAs, to audit Victor's financial statements for the year ended December 31, 2001. Victor is in the business of buying, selling, and servicing new and used construction equipment. While reviewing Victor's 2001 records, Bell became aware of the following disputed transactions:

- On September 8, Victor sent Ambel Contractors, Inc. a signed purchase order for several pieces of used construction equipment. Victor's purchase order described twelve different pieces of equipment and indicated the price Victor was willing to pay for each item. As a result of a mathematical error in adding up the total of the various prices, the purchase price offered by Victor was $191,000 rather than the correct amount of $119,000. Ambel, on receipt of the purchase order, was surprised by Victor's high price and immediately sent Victor a written acceptance. Ambel was aware that the fair market value of the equipment was approximately $105,000 to $125,000. Victor discovered the mistake in the purchase order and refused to purchase the equipment from Ambel. Ambel claims that Victor is obligated to purchase the equipment at a price of $191,000, as set forth in the purchase order.

- On October 8, a Victor salesperson orally contracted to service a piece of equipment owned by Clark Masons, Inc. The contract provided that for a period of thirty-six months, commencing November 2000, Victor would provide routine service for the equipment at a fixed price of $15,000, payable in three annual installments of $5,000 each. On October 29, Clark's president contacted Victor and stated that Clark did not intend to honor the service agreement because there was no written contract between Victor and Clark.

- On November 3, Victor received by mail a signed offer from GYX Erectors, Inc. The offer provided that Victor would service certain specified equipment owned by GYX for a two-year period for a total price of $81,000. The offer also provided as follows:

    "We need to know soon whether you can agree to the terms of this proposal. You must accept by November 15, or we will assume you can't meet our terms."

On November 12, Victor mailed GYX a signed acceptance of GYX's offer. The acceptance was not received by GYX until November 17, and by then GYX had contracted with another party to provide service for its equipment. Victor has taken the position that GYX is obligated to honor its November 3 offer. GYX claims that no contract was formed because Victor's November 12 acceptance was not received timely by GYX.

- On December 19, Victor contracted in writing with Wells Landscaping Corp. The contract required Victor to deliver certain specified new equipment to Wells by December 31. On December 23, Victor determined that it would not be able to deliver the equipment to Wells by December 31 because of an inventory shortage. Therefore, Victor made a written assignment of the contract to Master Equipment, Inc. When Master attempted to deliver the equipment on December 31, Wells refused to accept it, claiming that Victor could not properly delegate its duties under the December 19 contract to another party without the consent of Wells. The contract is silent with regard to this issue.

Required:

State whether the claims of Ambel, Clark, GYX, and Wells are correct and give the reasons for your conclusions.

Problem 2   (15 to 20 minutes)

In a signed letter dated March 2, 2001, Stake offered to sell Packer a specific vacant parcel of land for $100,000. Stake had inherited the land, along with several apartment buildings in the immediate vicinity. Packer received the offer on March 4. The offer required acceptance by March 10 and required Packer to have the property surveyed by a licensed surveyor so the exact legal description of the property could be determined.

On March 6, Packer sent Stake a counteroffer of $75,000. All other terms and conditions of the offer were unchanged. Stake received Packer's counteroffer on March 8, and, on that day, telephoned Packer and accepted it. On learning that a survey of the vacant parcel would cost about $1,000, Packer telephoned Stake on March 11 requesting that they share the survey cost equally. During this conversation, Stake agreed to Packer's proposal.

During the course of the negotiations leading up to the March communications between Stake and Packer, Stake expressed concern to Packer that a buyer of the land might build apartment units that would compete with those owned by Stake in the immediate vicinity. Packer assured Stake that Packer intended to use the land for a small shopping center. Because of these assurances, Stake was willing to sell the land to Packer. Contrary to what Packer told Stake, Packer had already contracted conditionally with Rolf for Rolf to build a forty-eight-unit apartment development on the vacant land to be purchased from Stake.

During the last week of March, Stake learned that the land to be sold to Packer had a fair market value of $200,000. Also, Stake learned that Packer intended to build apartments on the land. Because of this information, Stake sued Packer to rescind the real estate contract, alleging that

- Packer committed fraud in the formation of the contract, thereby entitling Stake to rescind the contract.
- Stake's innocent mistake as to the fair market value of the land entitles Stake to rescind the contract.
- The contract was not enforceable against Stake because Stake did not sign Packer's March 6 counteroffer.

Required:

State whether Stake's allegations are correct and give the reasons for your conclusions.

Problem 3   (15 to 25 minutes)

On July 5, 2001, Korn sent Wilson a written offer to clear Wilson's parking lot whenever it snowed through December 31, 2001. Korn's offer stated that Wilson had until October 1 to accept.

On September 28, 2001, Wilson mailed Korn an acceptance with a request that the agreement continue through March, 2002. Wilson's acceptance was delayed and didn't reach Korn until October 3.

On September 29, 2001, Korn saw weather reports indicating the snowfall for the season would be much heavier than normal. This would substantially increase Korn's costs to perform under the offer.

On September 30, 2001, Korn phoned Wilson to insist that the terms of the agreement be changed. When Wilson refused, Korn orally withdrew the offer and stated that Korn would not perform.

Required:

a.   State and explain the points of law that Korn would argue to show that there was **no** valid contract.

b.   State and explain the points of law that Wilson would argue to show that there was a valid contract.

c.   Assuming that a valid contract existed:

1.   Determine whether Korn breached the contract and the nature of the breach and

2.   State the common law remedies available to Wilson.

MULTIPLE-CHOICE ANSWERS*

1. a __ __	13. d __ __	25. a __ __	37. c __ __	49. a __ __
2. b __ __	14. b __ __	26. c __ __	38. d __ __	50. a __ __
3. c __ __	15. c __ __	27. b __ __	39. b __ __	51. c __ __
4. a __ __	16. c __ __	28. b __ __	40. c __ __	52. d __ __
5. d __ __	17. c __ __	29. d __ __	41. c __ __	53. a __ __
6. b __ __	18. d __ __	30. b __ __	42. d __ __	54. a __ __
7. b __ __	19. d __ __	31. a __ __	43. d __ __	55. c __ __
8. a __ __	20. b __ __	32. d __ __	44. a __ __	56. a __ __
9. b __ __	21. c __ __	33. d __ __	45. a __ __	57. b __ __
10. c __ __	22. c __ __	34. c __ __	46. c __ __	
11. a __ __	23. b __ __	35. c __ __	47. b __ __	1st: __/57 = __%
12. c __ __	24. d __ __	36. b __ __	48. a __ __	2nd: __/57 = __%

MULTIPLE-CHOICE ANSWER EXPLANATIONS

C.1. Offer

1.   (a)   Under common law, an offer must be definite and certain as to what will be agreed upon in the contract. Essential terms are the parties involved, the price, the time for performance, and the subject matter (quantity and type). The price element of the contract was not present.

2.   (b)   Advertisements in almost all cases are merely invitations for interested parties to make an offer. Thus, Harris has not made an offer, but is seeking offers through the use of the advertisement.

3.   (c)   Generally an offeror may revoke an offer at any time prior to acceptance by the offeree. Revocation is effective when it is received by the offeree. Revocation also occurs if the offeree learns by a reliable means that the offeror has already sold the subject of the offer. In this situation, Peters' offer was effectively revoked when Mason learned that the lawn mower had been sold to Bronson. Therefore, Mason's acceptance was ineffective. Answers (a) and (b) are incorrect because the offer had been revoked prior to Mason's acceptance. Answer (d) is incorrect because Peters was not obligated to keep the offer open. Note that if consideration had been paid by Mason to keep the offer open, an option contract would exist and the offer could not be revoked before the stated time.

4.   (a)   Drake did not intend to reject the $300,000 offer but is simply seeing if Calistoga might consider selling the home for less. Answer (b) is incorrect because a counteroffer takes place when the original offer is rejected and a new offer takes its place. Answer (c) is incorrect because Drake showed no intention of rejecting the offer by his mere inquiry. Answer (d) is incorrect because ambiguity is not one of the grounds to have an offer terminated by operation of law.

5.   (d)   An offer automatically terminates upon the occurrence of any of the following events: (1) the death or insanity of either the offeror or offeree, (2) bankruptcy or insolvency of either the offeror or offeree, or (3) the destruction of the specific, identified subject matter. Thus the offer automatically terminates at the date of Opal's death. It does not matter whether Larkin received notice of the death. If Larkin had accepted the offer prior to Opal's death, a valid contract would have been formed.

C.2. Acceptance

6.   (b)   Under the mailbox rule, an acceptance is ordinarily effective when sent if transmitted by the means authorized by the offeror, or by the same means used to transmit the offer if no means was authorized. However, the offeror may stipulate that acceptance is effective only when received by the offeror. In this situation, no contract was formed because Moss' acceptance was not received by the date specified in Fine's offer. Under common law, a method of acceptance other than the means specified in the offer or the method used to communicate the offer, is considered effective when received by the offeror.

7.   (b)   Fresno's acceptance by overnight delivery was made by a method other than the methods specified by Harris in the written offer. When acceptance is sent by a method other than the method specified in the offer or different than the method used to transmit the offer, acceptance is considered valid only when actually received by the offeror. Late acceptance is not valid, but instead constitutes a counteroffer. A valid contract would be formed only if the original offeror (Harris) then accepts.

8.   (a)   A unilateral offer exists when the offeror expects acceptance of an offer by action of the offeree. A unilateral contract is then formed when the offeree accepts the contract through performance of the offeror's required action. In this case, a valid contract is formed when Hammer accepts Kay's unilateral offer by obtaining the artifacts within a two-week period. Answers (b) and (d) are incorrect because a quasi contract is an implied-in-law rather than express agreement which results when one of the parties has been unjustly enriched at the expense of the other. The law creates such a contract when there is no binding agreement present to keep the unjust enrichment from occurring. Answer (c) is incorrect because public policy causes enforcement of promises despite lack of any other legal enforcement of the contract. For example, public policy would normally allow enforcement of a promise by a debtor to pay a debt barred by the statute of limitations.

9.   (b)   Common law applies to this contract because it involves real estate. In this situation, Fox's reply on October 2 is a counteroffer and terminates Summers' original offer made on September 27. The acceptance of an offer must conform exactly to the terms of the offer under com-

---

* *Explanation of how to use this performance record appears on page 11.*

mon law. By agreeing to purchase the vacation home at a price different from the original offer, Fox is rejecting Summers' offer and is making a counteroffer. Answer (a) is incorrect because the fact that Fox failed to return Summers' letter is irrelevant to the formation of a binding contract. Fox's reply constitutes a counteroffer as Fox did not intend to accept Summers' original offer. Answer (c) is incorrect because Summers' offer was rejected by Fox's counteroffer. Answer (d) is incorrect because with rare exceptions, silence does not constitute acceptance.

C.3. Consideration

10.   (c)   Both Zake and Wick had a contract that was binding for five years. For them to modify this contract, both of them must give new consideration under common law rules which apply to employment contracts such as this one. When Wick agreed to the raise, only Wick gave new consideration in the form of $20,000 additional each year. Zake did not give new consideration because he would perform in the last three years as originally agreed. Answers (a) and (b) are incorrect because Zake did not give new consideration whether or not the raise was in writing. Answer (d) is incorrect because duress needed to make a contract voidable or void requires more than "some pressure."

11.   (a)   Consideration is an act, promise, or forbearance which is offered by one party and accepted by another as inducement to enter into an agreement. A party must bind him/herself to do something s/he is not legally obligated to do. Furthermore, the consideration must be bargained for. Past consideration is not sufficient to serve as consideration for a new contract because it is not bargained for. Answer (b) is incorrect because relinquishment of a legal right constitutes consideration. Answer (c) is incorrect because even though the consideration must be adequate, courts generally do not look into the amount of exchange, as long as it is legal consideration and is bargained for. Answer (d) is incorrect as this performance by a third party is still deemed consideration.

12.   (c)   The rebinding of Dunne's books is considered a service and not a sale of goods, therefore, common law applies. Under common law, modification of an existing contract needs new consideration by both parties to be legally binding. Since Dunne has not given any new consideration for Cook's reduction in price, the contract is unenforceable. Additionally, the parol evidence rule prohibits the presentation of evidence of any prior or contemporaneous oral or written statements for the purpose of modifying or changing a written agreement intended by the payor to be the final and complete expression of their contract. However, it does not bar from evidence any oral or written agreements entered into by the parties subsequent to the written contract. Therefore, the agreement between Dunne and Cook is unenforceable, but evidence of the modification is admissible into evidence. Note that if the contract had been for the sale of goods (UCC), modification of the contract terms would have been enforceable. Under the UCC, a contract for the sale of goods may be modified orally or in writing without new consideration if such modification is done in good faith.

13.   (d)   A preexisting legal duty is not sufficient as consideration because no new legal detriment is suffered by performing the prior obligation. For example, when a creditor agrees to accept as full payment an amount less than the full amount of the undisputed (liquidated) debt, the agreement lacks valid consideration to be enforceable. However, when the amount of an obligation is disputed, the creditor's promise to accept a lesser amount as full payment of the debt is enforceable. Preexisting legal duties are not valid as consideration.

14.   (b)   A promise to donate money to a charity which the charity relied upon in incurring large expenditures is a situation involving promissory estoppel. Promissory estoppel acts as a substitute for consideration and renders the promise enforceable. The elements necessary for promissory estoppel are (1) detrimental reliance on a promise, (2) reliance on the promise is reasonable and foreseeable, and (3) damage results (injustice) if the promise is not enforced. Answer (a) is incorrect because the failure to enforce an employer's promise to make a cash payment to a deceased employee's family will not result in damages, and therefore, promissory estoppel will not apply. Answer (c) is incorrect because the modification of a contract requires consideration, unless the contract involves the sale of goods under the UCC. Answer (d) is incorrect because an irrevocable oral promise by a merchant to keep an offer open for sixty days is an option contract that must be supported by consideration. A firm offer under the UCC requires an offer signed by the merchant.

C.4. Legal Capacity

15.   (c)   A minor may disaffirm a contract at any time during his minority and within a reasonable time after reaching the age of majority. When Rail disaffirmed the contract two days after reaching the age of eighteen, he did so within a reasonable time after reaching majority age. Answer (a) is incorrect because Rail could ratify the contract only after reaching the age of majority. Answer (b) is incorrect because although Rail could have transferred good title to a good-faith purchaser for value, Rail's title was still voidable and subject to disaffirmance. Answer (d) is incorrect because Rail could disaffirm the contract only for a reasonable time after reaching the age of majority. Failure to disaffirm within a reasonable time serves to act as ratification.

16.   (c)   When a person has previously been adjudicated by a court of law to be incompetent, all of the contracts that s/he makes are void. Answer (a) is incorrect because the contracts are only voidable at the option of Green if there was no formal, previous court determination of incompetence for Green. Answer (b) is incorrect because once the court determines that Green is incompetent, all of the contracts that s/he makes are not valid but are void. Answer (d) is incorrect because the contracts cannot be enforced by either Green or the other contracting party.

17.   (c)   Ratification of a contract prior to reaching majority age is not effective. A minor **may** ratify a contract expressly or by actions indicating ratification after reaching the age of majority. Failure to disaffirm within a reasonable time after reaching majority age **does** act as ratification.

C.5. Legality

18.   (d)   An agreement is unenforceable if it is illegal or violates public policy. Therefore, if the personal services of the contract are illegal, the party will not have to perform them. Answer (a) is incorrect because the death of the party who is to **receive** the benefits does not terminate the duties under the contract. His/her heirs can still receive and pay for the personal services. Answer (b) is incorrect because making less profit or losing money are not grounds for getting out of a contract. Answer (c) is incorrect because bankruptcy of the receiver does not discharge the performer from the contract, although it can allow for forgiveness of all or part of the payment.

19. (d) An employer's promise not to press criminal charges against an employee-embezzler who agrees to return the embezzled money is not legally binding. The promise not to press charges is an illegal bargain, and, even if the employee returns the money, the employer is free to cooperate in prosecution of the criminal.

C.6.   Reality of Consent

20. (b) Fraud is the intentional misrepresentation of a material fact upon which a third party reasonably relies to his or her detriment. An intentionally misstated appraised value would be an example of a fraudulent inducement to make a contract. Answers (a) and (c) are incorrect because a third party cannot reasonably rely on a nonexpert opinion or a prediction. Answer (d) is incorrect because by definition, fraud applies to material facts.

21. (c) An immaterial unilateral mistake generally does not allow either party to void the contract.

22. (c) Undue influence is a defense that makes a contract voidable. Classic situations of this concept involve close relationships in which a dominant person has extreme influence over a weaker person. Answer (a) is incorrect because although fraud in the inducement can make a contract voidable, it typically does not occur between parties that have a close relationship. Answer (b) is incorrect because unconscionability involves an oppressive contract in which one party has taken severe, unfair advantage of another which is often based on the latter's absence of choice or poor education rather than the parties' close relationship. Answer (d) is incorrect because duress involves acts or threats of violence or pressure, which need not result from close relationships.

23. (b) An insurance policy is voidable at the option of the insurer if the insured failed to inform the insurer at the time of application of a fact material to the insurer's risk (e.g., failure to disclose a preexisting heart condition on a life insurance application). The insured's concealment causes the policy to be voidable regardless of the type of beneficiary designated or the nature of the insured's death.

24. (d) One of the elements needed to prove fraud is a misrepresentation of a material fact. That statement that "it is a great car" is sales talk or puffing and does not establish this element. The fact that the overhaul was done thirteen months earlier instead of the stated one year is not a misrepresentation of a **material** fact.

25. (a) A mistake is an understanding that is not in agreement with a fact. A unilateral mistake (made by one party) generally does not allow the party to void the contract. However, a mistake unknown to the party making it becomes voidable if the other party recognizes it as a mistake. Particularly, this is the case in bid contract computations. The contract is voidable by the party making the

mistake if the other party knew of the mistake or if the calculation was far enough off that the other party should have known that a mistake was made.

26. (c) Duress is any wrongful threat or act of violence made toward a person (or his family) which forces a person to enter into a contract against his will. For duress to be present, a threat must be made and the threatened party must believe that the other party has the ability to carry out the threat. In this situation, Maco's actions did not constitute duress. Kent's safety and property were in no way threatened by Maco and Kent was able to validly consent to the contract. Answers (a) and (b) are incorrect because regardless of Kent's financial problems and the FMV of Kent's services, duress was not present in that Kent was able to enter into the contract at will. Answer (d) is incorrect because Maco does not need to prove that Kent had no other offers to provide financial services.

27. (b) To establish a common law action for fraud, the following elements must be present: (1) misrepresentation of a material fact, (2) either knowledge of the falsity with intent to mislead or reckless disregard for the truth (scienter), (3) reasonable reliance by third party, and (4) injury resulted from misrepresentation. If the misrepresentation occurs during contract negotiations, fraud in the inducement is present resulting in a contract voidable at the option of the injured party. Answer (a) is incorrect because the defendant need not be an expert with regard to the misrepresentation to establish fraud in the inducement. Answer (c) is incorrect because the misrepresentation may be written or oral. Answer (d) is incorrect because the presence of fraud in the inducement does not require a fiduciary relationship between the parties.

28. (b) There are two remedies for fraud under the UCC Sales Article: (1) the plaintiff may affirm the agreement and sue for damages under the tort of deceit, or (2) the plaintiff may rescind the contract and sue for damages resulting from the fraud. Answer (a) is incorrect because the plaintiff must return any consideration received from the other party when the contract is rescinded. Answer (c) is incorrect because although punitive damages are allowed in fraud actions because they are intentional torts, they do not require physical injuries. Answer (d) is incorrect because without reliance by the plaintiff on the misrepresentation, there is no fraud, and therefore, the plaintiff may not rescind the contract.

C.7.   Conformity with the Statute of Frauds

29. (d) The Statute of Frauds requires that a contract to answer the debt or default of another be in writing and signed by the party to be charged. The guarantee that Decker made was only oral. Answer (b) is incorrect, as the reason Decker is not liable for the oral guaranty is not because it expires more than one year after June 1, but because a contract of guaranty must be in writing. Decker is not liable regardless of Baker's confirmation letter; thus answer (a) is incorrect. Answer (c) is incorrect because Decker's oral guaranty is not enforceable. The time period between the date of the oral guaranty and the date payment is demanded has no bearing in this situation.

30. (b) Any agreement to sell land or any interest in land falls under the requirements of the Statute of Frauds. Agreements within the Statute of Frauds require contracts to be in writing and signed by the party to be charged (the party being sued). An exception to the above rule is "part performance" by the purchaser. Part performance exists when the purchaser of property takes possession of the property with the landowner's consent. Some states also require either partial payment for the property or permanent improvement of the property by the purchaser. Answer (b) is correct because even though Nolan failed to sign a written agreement, the part performance exception has been satisfied. Answer (a) is incorrect because the fact that Nolan simply failed to object to the agreement does not make the contract valid under the Statute of Frauds. Answer (c) is incorrect because the part performance exception has been met and Train will therefore prevail. Answer (d) is incorrect because no such requirement exists to alleviate Nolan's liability. The part performance rule allows Train to prevail. Note that **all** sales of land are covered under the Statute of Frauds, and not just those greater than $500.

31. **(a)** Contracts that cannot be performed within one year must be in writing. In this case Cherry agreed to purchase Picks Company if an audit after one year shows that the company has been profitable. This would take longer than a year to perform. Answer (b) is incorrect because the $500 provision is in the Uniform Commercial Code for a sale of goods. Answer (c) is incorrect because despite the actual profitability, the contract could not be completed within one year of the making of the contract. Answer (d) is incorrect because although promissory estoppel may be used in the absence of a writing, there are not the facts sufficient to show promissory estoppel.

32. **(d)** Contracts which fall within the requirements of the Statute of Frauds are required to be in writing and signed by the party to be charged. It is not required that the contract terms be formalized in a single writing. Two or more documents may be combined to create a writing which satisfies the Statute of Frauds as long as one of the documents refers to the others. Answer (a) is incorrect because the Statute of Frauds requires that agreements for the sale of goods for $500 or more be in writing; however, contracts that come under common law are not included in this requirement. Answer (b) is incorrect because the Statute of Frauds requires that the written contract be signed by the party to be charged, not by all parties to the contract. Answer (c) is incorrect because the Statute of Frauds applies to contracts that **cannot** be performed within one year from the making of the agreement.

33. **(d)** The Statute of Frauds applies to the following types of contracts: (1) an agreement to sell land or any interest in land, (2) an agreement that cannot be performed within one year from the making of the agreement, (3) an agreement to answer for the debt or default of another, and (4) an agreement for the sale of goods for $500 or more. Since the agreement between Carson and Ives meets none of the above requirements, it is an enforceable oral contract under common law. Furthermore, under common law, modification of an existing contract needs new consideration by both parties to be legally binding. Since Ives received the benefit of additional repairs to his book, Carson's increase in the contract price is enforceable. Therefore, Carson will recover $650.

34. **(c)** Under The Statute of Frauds, agreements that can be performed within one year of their making can be

oral. In this case the ethics audit need only span ten months and the completion of the report will take less than one additional month for a total of less than one year. We know that the report can be done in less than a month because Newell points out that even if she delays start for three months, she will still complete the ten-month audit before the fourteen-month deadline. The fact that it might take longer than a year does not require it to be in writing since it **possibly could** be completed within one year. Answer (a) is incorrect because the $500 provision is for sales of goods not services. Answer (b) is incorrect because the contract can be completed within one year. Answer (d) is incorrect because there is no such provision involved here for the Statute of Frauds.

C.7.d.(1) Parol Evidence Rule

35. **(c)** The parol evidence rule provides that a written agreement intended by contracting parties to be a final and complete contract may not be contradicted by previous or contemporaneous oral evidence. The parol evidence rule does not apply to any subsequent oral promises made after the original agreement. Thus, the subsequent oral agreement between Rogers and Lennon regarding Lennon's right to report on a monthly basis will be allowed as evidence in a lawsuit between the parties. Answer (a) is incorrect because the parol evidence rule applies to all written contracts regardless of the applicability of the Statute of Frauds. Answer (b) is incorrect because the parol evidence rule will prevent the admission into evidence of the contemporaneous oral agreement that Lennon could use Rogers' computer. Answer (d) is incorrect because the parol evidence rule does apply to the contemporaneous oral agreement.

36. **(b)** The parol evidence rule provides that any written agreement intended by parties to be final and complete contract may not be contradicted by previous or contemporaneous evidence, written or oral. Thus, previous written agreements are prohibited by the rule. Exceptions to the parol evidence rule include proof to invalidate the contract between the parties, to show terms not inconsistent with writing that parties would not be expected to have included, to explain the intended meaning of an ambiguity, or to show a condition precedent. The parol evidence rule does not apply to subsequent transactions, such as oral promises made after the original agreement.

37. **(c)** The parol evidence rule prohibits the presentation as evidence of any prior or contemporaneous oral statements concerning a written agreement intended by the parties to be the final and complete expression of their contract. Therefore, the evidence related to the oral agreement regarding the payment of utilities would not be allowed. However, the parol evidence rule does **not** bar the admission of evidence which is presented to establish fraud.

C.9. Contracting On-line

38. **(d)** Even though this contract falls under the Statute of Frauds and, therefore, generally must be written and signed, most states have passed laws allowing contracts to be made over the Internet to facilitate commerce. The statutes encourage technology to overcome concerns over authenticity of such contracts. Therefore, answer (a) is incorrect. Answer (b) is incorrect because the parol evidence rule does not specify when a contract must be written and signed.

Answer (c) is incorrect because a sale of land is governed by common law rules and not the UCC.

D. Assignment and Delegation

39. **(b)** Assignment is the transfer of a right under a contract by one person to another. Almost all contract rights are assignable as long as the parties agree to it, but there are some exceptions. Contracts involving personal services, trust or confidence are not assignable. If assignment would materially change the risk or burden of the obligor, it is not allowed. For example, a contract for insurance against certain risks are not assignable because they were made upon the character of the contracting party (the insured). Assigning the rights to another party would alter the risk. Therefore, malpractice insurance policy rights are not assignable. A further exception is that future rights are not assignable, with the exception under the UCC that future rights for the sale of goods are assignable, whether based on an existing or nonexisting contract. As the assignment of option contract rights does not fall under any exception, they would be assignable.

40. **(c)** Assignment is the transfer of a right under a contract by one person to another. No consideration is needed for valid assignment. Normally an assignment is done in writing, but any act, oral or written, is sufficient if it gives clear intent of the assignment. Only situations included under the Statute of Frauds are required to be in writing. When consideration is given in exchange for an assignment, it is irrevocable. Also, as a general rule a gratuitous assignment is revocable unless it is evidenced by a writing signed by the assignor, effected by a delivery of a writing used as evidence of the right (i.e., bill of lading), and the assignment is executed. A contract right cannot be assigned if it would materially change the risk or burden of the obligor.

41. **(c)** Assignment is the transfer of a right under a contract by one person to another. If the obligor has notice of the assignment, s/he must pay the assignee, not the assignor. The contract between Barton and Egan provided for both payments on the purchase price and the insurance policy in case of Egan's death. Because Barton assigned his contract rights to Vim, Vim was then entitled to payments on the purchase price and the insurance proceeds. Since Barton received payments on the purchase price and insurance proceeds after the assignment, Vim is entitled to sue Barton for these amounts.

E. Third-Party Beneficiary Contracts

42. **(d)** When a debtor contracts with a second party to pay the debt owed to a creditor, the creditor becomes a creditor beneficiary. Barton contracted with Egan for Egan to pay Ness the business' debts. The contract also required Egan to provide a life insurance policy to pay Ness if Egan died. In both the contract and the insurance policy, Ness was a creditor beneficiary. Neither the contract nor the insurance policy were entered into to confer a gift to Ness, and therefore he was not a donee beneficiary.

43. **(d)** Bugle would have received an unintended benefit under the contract between Fargo and ABC Company. Therefore, Bugle is an incidental beneficiary, not an intended beneficiary and, thus, has no legal rights against ei-ther Fargo or ABC. No matter who breached the contract, Bugle has no rights against either party.

44. **(a)** In an assignment, the assignee (Clay) acquires the assignor's (Baxter) rights against the obligor (Globe) and has the right to performance. Baxter is still liable to the assignee if Globe does not perform. However, if Clay released Globe from the contract, Baxter would also be released and no longer liable to Clay. Answer (b) is incorrect because if the obligor has no notice of the assignment, s/he may pay the assignor, and the assignee must recover from the assignor. Thus, if Globe was unaware of the assignment and paid Baxter, Clay would have to collect from Baxter. Answers (c) and (d) are incorrect because even if Baxter released Globe or breached the contract, Baxter would still be liable to Clay.

45. **(a)** Mann is a donee beneficiary and, thus, can bring suit against the promissor, Manus, only. He cannot maintain a suit against Mackay, who was just giving a gift. Mann cannot maintain any action against Mackay either alone or in combination with Manus.

46. **(c)** When a debtor contracts with a second party to pay the debt owed to a creditor, the creditor becomes a creditor beneficiary. A creditor beneficiary has the right to enforce the contract which gives him the intended benefits and may commence an action for nonperformance against either of the contracting parties. For this reason, Ferco (creditor beneficiary) will prevail in a lawsuit against Bell because Ferco has an enforceable right to receive payment. Answer (a) is incorrect because Ferco, as a creditor beneficiary, has the right to recover from either Bell or Allied. Answer (b) is incorrect because the creditor beneficiary is not required to give consideration to have an enforceable right. Answer (d) is incorrect because having knowledge of the contract between Bell and Allied at the time the contract was made is not necessary to later enforce this legal action. Ferco must establish that he is a creditor beneficiary to maintain an action for nonperformance.

F. Performance of Contract

47. **(b)** Under the doctrine of substantial performance, a contract obligation may be discharged even though the performance tendered was not in complete conformity with the terms of the agreement. Under this doctrine, if it can be shown that the defect in performance was only minor in nature, that a good-faith effort was made to conform completely with the terms of the agreement, and if the performing party is willing to accept a decrease in compensation equivalent to the amount of the minor defect in performance, the contractual obligation will be discharged. Since the defect in Glaze's performance was only minor in nature, and since Parc refused to allow Glaze to complete the project, Glaze will prevail in its action against Parc. Anticipatory breach applies only to executory bilateral contracts. An executory contract is a contract wherein both parties have yet to perform. In this instance, Glaze has substantially performed its part of the agreement.

48. **(a)** The duty to perform a contract may depend upon a condition. Conditions that could be present include: condition precedent, which is one that must occur before there is duty to perform; condition subsequent, which is one that removes a preexisting duty to perform; or condition concurrent, which is mutually dependent upon performance at nearly the same time.

G. Discharge of Contracts

49.   (a)   Once one party materially breaches the contract, the other party is discharged from performing his or her obligations under the contract. Answer (b) is incorrect because a reasonable delay in the performance of the contract is not a breach unless time was of the essence. Answer (c) is incorrect because tender or offer to pay or perform obligates the other party to do what s/he promised. Answer (d) is incorrect because assignment of rights typically is allowed under contract law.

50.   (a)   The discharge of a contract can come about in several ways. The first is by agreement. Accord and satisfaction involves an agreed substitute for performance under the contract (accord) and the actual performance of that substitute (satisfaction). An agreement can also be entered into by three parties whereby the previous agreement is discharged by the creation of a new agreement (a novation). The second method of discharge is by release of the contract or parties from performance. Another method of discharging a contract is by performance of the specified action becoming impossible, such as destruction of the subject matter, or death of a party where personal service is necessary. Lastly, breach of the contract discharges the injured party.

51.   (c)   Rescission entails canceling a contract and placing the parties in the position they were in before the contract was formed. Answer (a) is incorrect as a novation is an agreement between three parties whereby a previous agreement is discharged by the creation of a new agreement. Answer (b) is incorrect because release is a means of discharging (abandoning) a contract but it does not place the parties in the same position as before the contract. Answer (d) is incorrect because revocation is used by an offeror to terminate an offer.

H. Remedies

52.   (d)   The remedy of specific performance is used when money damages will not sufficiently compensate the afflicted party due to the unique nature of the subject matter of the contract. In a contract for the sale of land, the buyer has the right to enforce the agreement by seeking the remedy of specific performance because real property is considered unique. Another remedy for this breach of contract would be for the buyer to seek compensatory damages. If the buyer desires, s/he may seek this remedy instead of specific performance. However, in this situation, Hodges could only sue for either specific performance or compensatory damages but would not be entitled to both remedies. An injured party is generally not allowed to seek punitive damages. Punitive damages are awarded only when the court is seeking to punish a party for their improper actions and are not usually granted in breach of contract actions.

53.   (a)   Under the doctrine of substantial performance, a contract obligation may be discharged even though the performance tendered was not in complete conformity with the terms of the agreement. If it can be shown that the defect in performance was only minor in nature, that a good-faith effort was made to conform completely with the terms of the agreement, and if the performing party is willing to accept a decrease in compensation equivalent to the amount of the

minor defect in performance, the contractual obligation will be discharged. Because Ames' breach of contract was both inadvertent and not material, the doctrine of substantial performance applies and recovery will be limited to monetary damages. The installation of fixtures other than those specified in the contract constitutes a breach, although the breach is considered immaterial. The doctrine of substantial performance applies in this situation and the contractual obligation will be discharged.

54.   (a)   A liquidated damage clause is a contractual provision which states the amount of damages that will occur if a party breaches the contract. The liquidated damage clause is enforceable if the amount is reasonable in light of the anticipated or actual harm caused by the breach. Excessive liquidated damages will not be enforceable in court even if both parties have agreed in writing. A clause providing for excessive damages is a penalty and the courts will not enforce a penalty. Materiality does not impact the enforceability of liquidated damage provisions.

55.   (c)   The doctrine of anticipatory repudiation allows a party to either sue at once or wait until after performance is due when the other party indicates s/he will not perform. This doctrine is in effect because Nagel told Fields that Nagel had no intention of delivering the goods (i.e., repudiation of the contract) prior to the date of performance. Answer (a) is incorrect because promissory estoppel acts as a substitute for consideration which is an element in the forming of a contract but is not relevant in this fact situation. Answer (b) is incorrect because accord and satisfaction is an agreement wherein a party with an existing duty or performance under a contract promises to do something other than perform the duty originally promised in the contract. Answer (d) is incorrect because the doctrine of substantial performance would allow for a contract obligation to be discharged even though the performance tendered was not in complete conformity with the terms of the agreement. In this case, Fields is suing Nagel for breach of contract.

56.   (a)   Events occurring after a contract is entered into usually do not affect performance. Some exceptions to this rule include subsequent illegality of the performance, death of a party, or destruction of the subject matter, all of which constitute impossibility of performance. In this case, even though Maco's own potatoes were destroyed, it wasn't specified that Maco's own potato crop be used to fulfill the contract. It was not impossible, therefore, for Maco to perform, because he could have purchased potatoes from another grower to deliver to LBC. If there had been a worldwide infestation of the potato crop, Maco would have reason to not perform on the basis of impossibility.

I.   Statute of Limitations

57.   (b)   The statute of limitations bars suit if it is not brought within the statutory period. The period varies for different types of cases and from state to state. The statute begins to run from the time the cause of action accrues (e.g., breach).

OTHER OBJECTIVE ANSWERS AND ANSWER EXPLANATIONS

Problem 1

1.   **(B)** Party F gave S a gift in the past. S's promise to now pay for the usage is not enforceable because F's action is past consideration, and the contract needs consideration on both sides. Furthermore, S's feeling of a moral obligation does not create consideration.

2.   **(A)** This is an example of a requirements contract. F has given consideration because s/he gave up the right to sell that sugar to someone else.

3.   **(A)** F refrained from doing something which she had a right to do. This constitutes consideration.

4.   **(C)** This is not enforceable under contract law because S does not give any consideration in return. It is enforceable, however, as a will which does not require the elements of a contract such as consideration, but does require other formalities.

5.   **(B)** F already had a preexisting legal duty to do a professional, quality audit of XYZ Company.

6.   **(B)** F had a contract to work for S for five years for $100,000 per year. F is not giving any new consideration for the raise since during that five years, he already is obligated to complete the contract.

7.   **(A)** F did something which he did not have to do in exchange for the agreed $1,000. This is a unilateral contract.

8.   **(A)** F agreed to pay $200 and in exchange S agreed to sell the computer. Both have given consideration that is **legally** sufficient. Legally sufficient refers to the validity of the consideration, not the amount. Consideration does not have to be of equal value as long as it is legal consideration and bargained for.

9.   **(A)** Both parties have given consideration for this output contract. F gave up the right to buy these parts elsewhere and S gave up the right to sell her output to someone else.

10.   **(B)** F has a preexisting legal duty to pay the full $1,500. When S agreed to accept less, F gave up nothing. F still owes the remaining $500.

11.   **(A)** In this case, both parties gave consideration. S, in agreeing to accept the $1,000, gave up the right to collect more of the disputed amount. F gave up the right to pay less of the disputed amount.

12.   **(C)** Although the charity gave no consideration in exchange for the promised donation, the promise to donate to a charity is generally enforceable based on public policy reasons.

Problem 2

1.   **(J)** On January 20, East sent Bean a signed memorandum stating the terms of the offer.

2.   **(C)** On January 21, Bean signed the written offer and sent it back. This does not count as an actual acceptance at this point because the offer stated that acceptance would not be effective until it is received by East, the offeror, by January 25.

3.   **(D)** On January 23, East wrote Bean to revoke the offer. A revocation, however, is not effective until received by the offeree.

4.   **(E)** An enforceable contract was formed on January 24 because the offer was still valid. The revocation is not effective until received by the offeree, which took place a day later. Therefore, the acceptance was valid on January 24 when East, the offerer, received it since the offer required its receipt to be effective.

5.   **(G)** Once an offer has been accepted, an attempted revocation is no longer effective. The attempted revocation was not effective on January 23 because a revocation must be received by the offeree to be effective. Furthermore, the attempted revocation is not effective on January 25 because it was too late; the offer had already been accepted the day before.

6.   **(E)** Even though it was done orally, East and Snow formed a contract on March 1. This contract was not required to be in writing under the Statute of Frauds because the contract was to be completed in less than one year. Also, the $500 rule does not apply here because it was a service contract, not a contract for the sale of goods.

7.   **(E)** On March 15, East and Snow agreed to another contract in which Snow was to assist in the design of East's Internet home page.

8.   **(H)** On April 5, East accepted Snow's withdrawal from the second contract. This is a mutual rescission of the contract in which both parties are free from any further obligations under that contract, since both parties agreed to the rescission.

9.   **(K)** On April 15, Snow notified East that Snow assigned his fees under the first contract to another party. This is a valid assignment of the right to receive the fees and it does not require East's approval. Note that Snow assigned only the right to the fees. There was no delegation of Snow's duties under the contract.

10.   **(A)** East breached the contract on April 30, when East notified Snow that the first contract was canceled. This is not a rescission since both parties did not agree to this.

Problem 3

Part a.

1.   (F)   Although the final contract has to be in writing to be enforceable since performance of contract would take longer than a year, the offer itself can be oral.

2.   (F)   The offer specified that the acceptance must be in writing. Since Reach put the acceptance in writing and faxed it to Blake, this was a proper method of acceptance.

3.   (F)   Common law applies to this fact pattern since the contract does not involve a sale of goods. Reach's attempted acceptance stated $1,000,000 instead of $100,000 as contained in the offer. Reach's attempted acceptance thus was instead a counteroffer. Under both common law and the Uniform Commercial Code, offers, revocations, rejections and counteroffers are valid when received.

4.   (F)   Blake's offer specified that the acceptance must be received no later than December 20. Reach's faxed acceptance was received in Blake's office on December 20 on the fax machine. Therefore, Blake did receive the fax on time even though it was not seen until the following day.

5.   (F)   Reach's attempted acceptance stated $1,000,000 instead of $100,000 as contained in the offer. Since the terms did not match, no contract was formed, voidable or otherwise.

6.   (T)   Since there is no firm offer or option contract, the rejection terminates the offer.

7.   (T)   Since the December 20 fax terms did not match the original offer's terms, it serves as a counteroffer which rejects the original offer and creates a new offer.

Part b.

8.   (F)   Parties may typically assign the contract right to receive money to another party.

9.   (T)   When parties have a right to receive money, they may validly assign all or a portion of this right to a third party.

10.   (T)   The terms of Reach's acceptance names Weaver as a third-party beneficiary to receive $5,000. Since the intent was to pay a debt owed by Reach to Weaver, this makes Weaver a creditor beneficiary.

11.   (T)   Punitive damages are not awarded for mere breach of contract cases such as this suit by Weaver against Blake.

12.   (F)   In a suit by Weaver against Reach, no punitive damages will be awarded since this would be only a breach of contract case.

Part c.

13.   (F)   Since the work would require two years to complete, the contract cannot be performed within one year and, therefore, must be in writing to be enforceable. The party to be charged must have signed the contract and Reach did not do this.

14.   (T)   An offer does not need to have a date for acceptance, in which case, the offer remains open for a reasonable time.

15.   (T)   Blake's signed memo sets forth an offer which was later accepted orally by Reach. This can be construed as enough written evidence to satisfy the Statute of Frauds. Because Blake, the party to be charged, signed the memo, it is enforceable against Blake by Reach.

Problem 1   Unilateral Mistake; Statute of Frauds under
                 Service Contract; Effectiveness of Accep-
                 tance; Assignment and Delegation

Ambel's claim is incorrect

  Victor will be granted relief
  Ambel knew the approximate FMV of equipment
  Had reason to know that a mathematical error had been
    made by Victor
  Therefore, the mistaken party will be granted relief from
    the offer

Clark's claim is correct

  Victor can't enforce the oral contract with Clark
  Statute of Frauds requires a written contract if terms can-
    not be performed within one year of its creation
  These terms span over one year

GYX's claim is incorrect

  Victor has a valid contract with GYX
  An acceptance of an offer is effective when dispatched, if
    an appropriate mode of communication is used.
  Since GYX's offer was by mail, Victor's communication
    of acceptance by mail is appropriate and effective on
    November 12, not when GYX received the acceptance
    on November 17.
  The acceptance was effective before the November 15
    deadline

Wells is incorrect

  Victor is entitled to assign the contract.
  Unless assignment is prohibited in the contract, statute, or
    public policy, or the duties are personal in nature, a con-
    tract is assignable.

UNOFFICIAL ANSWER

Problem 1   Unilateral Mistake; Statute of Frauds under
                 Service Contract; Effectiveness of Accep-
                 tance; Assignment and Delegation

   Ambel is incorrect. The general rule is that when a
party knows, or reasonably should know, that a mistake has
been made in the making of an offer, the mistaken party will
be granted relief from the offer. In this case, because Ambel
was aware of the approximate fair market value of the
equipment, it had reason to be aware of the mathematical
error made by Victor and will not be allowed to take advantage of it.

   Clark is correct. A contract that cannot by its terms be
performed within one year from the date it is made must be
evidenced by a writing that satisfies the requirements of the
Statute of Frauds. The contract between Victor and Clark is
not enforceable by Victor against Clark, because the contract
was oral and provided for performance by the parties for
longer than one year from the date the contract was entered
into.

   GYX is incorrect. An acceptance of an offer is effective when dispatched (in this case, when mailed), provided
that the appropriate mode of communication is used. The
general rule is that an offer shall be interpreted as inviting
acceptance in any manner and by any medium reasonable in
the circumstances. In this case, GYX made its offer by mail.
An acceptance by mail, if properly addressed with adequate
postage affixed, would be considered a reasonable manner
and method of acceptance. Therefore, Victor's acceptance

was effective (and a contract was formed) when the acceptance was mailed on November 12 and not when received by
GYX on November 17.

   Wells is incorrect. As a general rule, most contracts are
assignable and delegable unless: prohibited in the contract,
the duties are personal in nature, or the assignment or delegation is prohibited by statute or public policy. Victor was
entitled to assign the contract to Master, because none of
these exceptions apply to the contract.

Problem 2   Fraud; Mistake under a Contract; Statute of
                 Frauds under Real Estate Contract

First allegation is correct—Stake may rescind contract
  Packer committed fraud in formation of contract
  Elements of fraud
    False representation of material fact
    Intent to mislead (scienter)
    Reasonable reliance by injured party
Second allegation is incorrect
  Mistake involving adequacy of consideration generally
    does not allow aggrieved party to rescind contract
Third allegation is correct
  Counteroffer is unenforceable
  Real estate contract must satisfy Statute of Frauds
    Must be in writing
    Must be signed by party to be charged

UNOFFICIAL ANSWER

Problem 2   Fraud; Mistake under a Contract; Statute of
                 Frauds under Real Estate Contract

Stake's first allegation, that Packer committed fraud in the
formation of the contract, is correct and Stake may rescind
the contract. Packer had assured Stake that the vacant parcel
would be used for a shopping center when, in fact, Packer
intended to use the land to construct apartment units that
would be in direct competition with those owned by Stake.
Stake would not have sold the land to Packer had Packer's
real intentions been known. Therefore, the elements of
fraud are present

   •   A false representation;
   •   Of a fact;
   •   That is material;
   •   Made with knowledge of its falsity and intention to
deceive;
   •   That is justifiably relied on.

   Stake's second allegation, that the mistake as to the fair
market value of the land entitles Stake to rescind the contract, is incorrect. Generally, mistakes as to adequacy of
consideration or fairness of a bargain are insufficient
grounds to entitle the aggrieved party to rescind a contract.

   Stake's third allegation, that the contract was not enforceable against Stake because Stake did not sign the
counteroffer, is correct. The contract between Stake and
Packer involves real estate and, therefore, the Statute of
Frauds requirements must be satisfied. The Statute of
Frauds requires that a writing be signed by the party against
whom enforcement is sought. The counteroffer is unenforceable against Stake, because Stake did not sign it. As a
result, Stake is not obligated to sell the land to Packer under
the terms of the counteroffer.

ANSWER OUTLINE

Problem 3   Withdrawal of Offer; Mailbox Rule; Anticipatory Breach

a.   Korn would argue

Offer not accepted before was withdrawn on September 30

Offer can be withdrawn before stated time

Additional terms act as rejection and counteroffer

b.   Wilson would argue

Mailing of offer is acceptance before offer withdrawn

Attempt to extend contract was not counteroffer but mere request

c.   If valid contract, Korn's call is an anticipatory breach of contract

Wilson could either cancel contract or sue for compensatory damages

UNOFFICIAL ANSWER

Problem 3   Withdrawal of Offer; Mailbox Rule; Anticipatory Breach

a.   Korn would argue two points of law to show there was no valid contract. Korn would argue that the July 5 offer was not accepted by Wilson before it was withdrawn on September 30. An offer can be withdrawn at any time before it is accepted even if it states that it will remain open for a definite period of time.

Korn would also argue that Wilson's response of September 28 was not a valid acceptance because Wilson included additional terms and Wilson's attempt to change the terms of the contract was a rejection and a counteroffer.

b.   Wilson would argue two points of law to show there was a valid contract. Wilson would argue that the mailing of the acceptance on September 28 was an effective acceptance under the mailbox rule. There is a valid contract because there was a valid acceptance before the offer was withdrawn.

Wilson would also argue that the attempt to extend the contract was not a condition of acceptance but a requested immaterial modification that did not negate the acceptance.

c.   If a valid contract existed, Korn's September 30 telephone call resulted in Korn's anticipatory breach of the contract because Wilson could no longer rely on Korn performing.

Under common law, Wilson could either cancel the contract or sue to collect compensatory damages for the additional amount it would cost to obtain the services.

Keep practicing! Wiley's CPA Examination Review Software has over 2,800 questions.

Available at www.wiley.com/cpa

SALES

Overview

The law of sales governs contracts for the sale of goods. Since a sale of goods is involved, Article 2 of the Uniform Commercial Code (UCC) applies. A sale of goods under the UCC is the sale of tangible, moveable property.

One of the areas tested in sales is product liability. When studying this area, you should pay particular attention to the different legal theories under which an injured party may recover. Realize that an injured party may recover under the legal theories of breach of warranty, negligence, and strict liability. It is important that you know the circumstances under which these theories may be used. Other areas that are often tested are warranties; disclaimers; risk of loss; and remedies, rights, and duties of the buyer and seller.

You should understand that a binding contract may be present under the UCC if the parties had intended to be bound, even though certain elements of a contract may be missing. These open terms will be filled by specific provisions of the UCC. The parties to a sale need not be merchants for the UCC to apply; however, some rules vary if merchants are involved in the sales contract.

As you study this area, note that it builds on much of the material under contracts in the previous module. Therefore, as you study this area you should review the contract law rules, especially those in the previous module that apply to the UCC.

A. Contracts for Sale of Goods

1. Article 2 of the Uniform Commercial Code, in general, controls contracts for the sale of goods for any dollar amount

   a. "Goods" include tangible personal property (whether specially manufactured or not)

      (1) Do not include sales of investment securities, accounts receivable, contract rights, copyrights, or patents

      EXAMPLE: S sells B a stereo. The UCC applies.

      EXAMPLE: S sells a home to B. The common law rules rather than the UCC rules apply to this contract since it involves the sale of real property.

      EXAMPLE: F sells to M several bushels of wheat. The UCC applies to fungible goods also (i.e., goods in which one unit is considered the equivalent of the other units).

   b. In general, UCC applies to sales and leases of hardware as well as to sales and licensing of software.

      (1) However, if software is heavily customized based on services of consultant, common law applies.

   c. UCC applies whether sale is between merchants or consumers but some rules change if merchant involved

      EXAMPLE: S sells his used refrigerator to B, a neighbor. The UCC applies to this transaction.

   d. Thrust of UCC is to find a contract in cases where it is the intent of the parties to do so, even though some technical element of contract may be missing

   e. Open terms (missing terms) will not cause a contract for sale of goods to fail for indefiniteness if there was intent to contract and a reasonable basis for establishing a remedy is available

      (1) Elements of sales contracts are generally same as common law contracts

2. General concepts

   a. Merchant—one who deals in the kind of goods being sold, or one who holds self out as having superior knowledge and skills as to the goods involved, or one who employs another who qualifies as a merchant

   b. Firm offer—a written, signed offer concerning the sale of goods, by a merchant, giving assurance that it will be held open for a specified time is irrevocable for that period, not to exceed three months

      (1) Note that only offeror need be a merchant under this rule

      (2) If firm offer does not state specific time, it will remain open for reasonable time, not to exceed three months

      (3) Written form may be supplied by either party as long as it is signed by merchant-offeror

EXAMPLE: M, a merchant, agrees in a letter signed by M to sell B 1,000 widgets, with the offer to remain open for five weeks. Even if M tries to revoke this offer before the five-week period, B may still accept.

EXAMPLE: M, a merchant, agrees in signed writing to sell B 1,000 widgets, stating that the offer will remain open for 120 days. B accepts the offer on the 95th day. If nothing has occurred to terminate offer prior to acceptance, offer and acceptance are present. The irrevocable nature of this offer would end after ninety days, but the offer would not automatically terminate. The offer would remain in existence for the stated period (120 days) unless terminated by other means.

EXAMPLE: Same facts as above except that B gives M $100 to keep the offer open for six months. This is an option supported by consideration, so the firm offer restrictions do not apply. That is, the offer remains open for the full six months. (This would be true even if M is not a merchant.)

c.   Battle of forms—between merchants, additional terms included in the acceptance become part of the contract unless

   (1) Original offer precludes such, or
   (2) New terms materially alter the original offer, or
   (3) The original offeror gives notice of his/her objection within a reasonable time

   EXAMPLE: P offers in writing to sell to Q 1,000 type xxx widgets for $10,000. Q replies, "I accept, but I will personally pick these up with my truck." Both P and Q are merchants. They have a contract with the stated delivery terms.

d.   Under the UCC, a contract may be modified without new consideration if done in good faith

   EXAMPLE: B agrees in a contract to buy 300 electrical parts for $1.00 each from S. B later points out to S that he can get the same parts from D for $.90 each and asks for a price reduction. S reduces the price to $.90 each. This new contract is enforceable even though B gave no new consideration. Note that if S had required B to pay the $1.00 as originally agreed, B would be in breach of contract if he failed to go through with the original contract.

   (1) Common law requires new consideration on both sides for any modification

   EXAMPLE: B agreed, in a written contract, to pay $10,000 to S for certain real estate. Later, B said he was having difficulty getting the $10,000 so S agreed to reduce the price to $9,000. S can still enforce the full $10,000 because B gave no new consideration for the modification.

e.   Recall that under UCC version of Statute of Frauds, contracts for sale of goods for $500 or more must be in writing with some exceptions

   (1) Writing must contain quantity and signature of party to be charged

      (a) Need not contain all details required under common law version

   (2) If contract is modified, must be in writing if after modification it is for $500 or more

   EXAMPLE: B agrees in a contract to buy widgets from S for $500. Later, S agrees to a reduction in price to $490. The first contract must be in writing (absent any exceptions), but the modified contract may be oral.

   (3) This $500 rule generally applies only in the US because the United Nations Convention on Contracts for the Sale of Goods (CISG) covers most international transactions for sales of goods

      (a) CISG has no writing requirement

f.   Consignment—arrangement in which agent (consignee) is appointed by consignor to sell goods if all the following conditions are met

   (1) Consignor keeps title to goods,
   (2) Consignee is not obligated to buy or pay for goods,
   (3) Consignee receives a commission upon sale, and
   (4) Consignor receives proceeds of sale

g.   Document of title—any document that in the regular course of business is accepted as adequate evidence that the person in possession of the document is entitled to receive, hold, and dispose of the document and the goods it covers

h.   Bill of lading—a document of title that is issued by a private or common carrier in exchange for goods delivered to it for shipment. It may be negotiable or nonnegotiable.

  i. Warehouse receipt—a document of title issued by a person engaged in the business of storing goods (i.e., a warehouseman). It acknowledges receipt of the goods, describes the goods stored, and contains the terms of the storage contract. It may be negotiable or nonnegotiable.

B. Product Liability—a manufacturer or seller may be responsible when a product is defective and causes injury or damage to a person or property. There are three theories under which manufacturers and sellers may be held liable. (In each fact pattern, consider all three, although proof of any one creates liability.)

 1. Warranty Liability—purchaser of a product may sue based on the warranties made

  a. Warranty of title

   (1) Seller warrants good title, rightful transfer and freedom from any security interest or lien of which the buyer has no knowledge

    EXAMPLE: A seller of stolen goods would be liable to a buyer for damages.

   (2) Merchant warrants goods to be free of rightful claim of infringement (e.g., patent or trademark), unless buyer furnished specifications to seller for manufacture of the goods

   (3) Can only be disclaimed by specific language or circumstances that give buyer reason to know s/he is receiving less than full title

    (a) Cannot be disclaimed by language such as "as is"

  b. Express warranties (may be written or oral)

   (1) Any affirmation of fact or promise made by the seller to the buyer that relates to the goods and becomes part of the basis of the bargain creates an express warranty that the goods shall conform to the affirmation or promise

    (a) Sales talk, puffing, or a statement purporting to be merely the seller's opinion does not create a warranty
    (b) No reliance is necessary on part of buyer
    (c) Must form part of the basis of bargain

     1] Would include advertisements read by buyer
     2] Normally would not include warranties given after the sale or contract was made

    (d) No intent to create warranty is needed on the part of the seller
    (e) Seller or buyer may be merchant or consumer

   (2) Any description of the goods which is made part of the basis of the bargain creates an express warranty that the goods shall conform to the description
   (3) Any sample or model that is made part of the basis of the bargain creates an express warranty that the goods shall conform to the sample or model
   (4) It is not necessary to the creation of an express warranty that the seller use formal words such as "warranty" or "guarantee"

  c. Implied warranties

   (1) Warranty of merchantability—goods are fit for ordinary purpose

    (a) This warranty also guarantees that goods are properly packaged and labeled
    (b) This warranty applies if

     1] Seller is a merchant with respect to goods of the kind being sold, and
     2] Warranty is not modified or excluded
     3] Then if goods not fit for ordinary use, breach of this warranty occurs

   (2) Warranty of fitness for a particular purpose

    (a) Created when the seller knows of the particular use for which the goods are required and further knows that the buyer is relying on skill and judgment of seller to select and furnish suitable goods for this particular use

EXAMPLE: A buyer relies upon a paint salesperson to select a particular exterior house paint that will effectively cover existing siding.

    (b) Buyer must actually rely on seller's skill and judgment
    (c) Product is then warranted for the particular expressed purpose and seller may be liable if the product fails to so perform
    (d) Applicable both to merchants and nonmerchants

  d. UCC, being consumer oriented, allows these warranties to extend to parties other than the purchaser even without privity of contract (contractual connection between parties)

    (1) Extends to a buyer's family and also to guests in the home who may reasonably be expected to use and/or be affected by the goods and who are injured

    EXAMPLE: A dinner guest breaks a tooth on a small piece of metal in the food. Note that in food, the substance causing injury normally must be foreign, not something customarily found in it (bone in fish).

  e. Disclaimers—warranty liability may be escaped or modified by disclaimers (also available at common law without rules defining limits of disclaimers)

    (1) A disclaimer of merchantability can be written or oral but must use the word "merchantability" unless all implied warranties are disclaimed as in (3) below
    (2) To disclaim the implied warranty of fitness for a particular purpose, the disclaimer must be in writing and conspicuous
    (3) Both the warranty of merchantability and fitness for a particular purpose can be disclaimed by oral or written language such as "as is" or "with all faults"
    (4) Written disclaimers must be clear and conspicuous
    (5) If the buyer has had ample opportunity to inspect the goods or sample, there is no implied warranty as to any defects which ought reasonably to have been discovered
    (6) Implied warranties may be excluded or modified by course of dealings, course of performance, or usage of trade
    (7) A disclaimer inconsistent with an express warranty is not effective (i.e., a description of a warranty in a contract cannot be disclaimed)
    (8) Limitations on consequential damages for personal injuries are presumed to be unconscionable if on consumer goods

2. Negligence

  a. Must prove the following elements

    (1) Duty of manufacturer to exercise reasonable (due) care

      (a) Consider likelihood of harm, seriousness of harm, and difficulty of correction
      (b) May be based on violation of statute but this is not necessary
      (c) If accident is type that would not normally happen without negligence, then presumption of negligence exists

    (2) Breach of duty of reasonable care

      (a) Insufficient instructions may cause breach of duty

    (3) Damages or injury
    (4) Cause in fact

      (a) In general, if injury would not have happened without defendant's conduct, there is cause in fact

    (5) Proximate cause

      (a) General standard here is whether the type of injury was foreseeable

  b. Privity of contract is not needed because suit not based on contract

  EXAMPLE: A car manufacturer is negligent in the manufacture and design of brakes and as a result, a driver is severely injured. The driver may sue the manufacturer even if he bought the car from a retailer.

EXAMPLE: In the example above, even a pedestrian injured because of the brake problem may recover from the manufacturer.

    c. Often difficult to prove this type of negligence because facts are frequently controlled by defendant

    d. Defenses to negligence

       (1) Contributory negligence

          (a) That is, plaintiff helped cause accident

          (b) Complete bar to recovery

          (c) Some states instead use comparative negligence in which damages are allocated between plaintiff and defendant based on relative fault

       (2) Assumption of risk

  3. Strict liability

    a. Manufacturers, sellers, and lessors who normally deal in this type of product are liable to users of products without proof of fault or lack of reasonable care if following other elements are proven

       (1) Product was defective when sold

          (a) Based on poor design, inadequate warnings, improper assembly, or unsafe materials

       (2) Defect is unreasonably dangerous to user

          (a) Based on normal expectations

       (3) Product reaches user without significant changes

       (4) Defect caused the injury

    b. Defense of contributory negligence, comparative negligence, disclaimer or lack of privity is unavailable

       (1) Assumption of risk and misuse are defenses

EXAMPLE: Herb is injured while lifting up his power lawnmower to trim his hedges. Manufacturer would not be liable since product was not being used for intended purpose.

C. Transfer of Property Rights

  1. If party having voidable title transfers goods to a good-faith purchaser for value, the latter obtains good title

    a. Examples in which there is voidable title

       (1) Goods paid for with a check subsequently dishonored

       (2) Goods obtained by fraud, mistake, duress, or undue influence

       (3) Goods obtained from minor

       (4) Thief does **not** have voidable title but void title

EXAMPLE: B buys a stereo from S but the check bounces. P, a good-faith purchaser, pays B for the stereo. S cannot get the stereo from P but must recover money from B.

EXAMPLE: Same as above except that B stole the stereo. P does not obtain title of the stereo.

  2. If a person entrusts possession of goods to a merchant who deals in those goods, a good-faith purchaser for value obtains title to these goods, unless s/he knew that this merchant did not own the goods

EXAMPLE: C leaves his watch at a shop for repairs. The shop mistakenly sells the watch to B who is unaware of C's interest. C cannot force B to turn over the watch because B now has title. Of course, C can recover monetary damages from the shop.

  3. Passage of title

    a. Once goods are identified to the contract, the parties may agree as to when title passes

       (1) Sale cannot take place until goods exist and have been identified to the contract

      (a) Identification—occurs when the goods that are going to be used to perform the contract are shipped, marked or otherwise designated as such

      (b) Identification gives buyer

         1] An insurable interest in the goods once they are identified to contract

         2] Right to demand goods upon offering full contract price once other conditions are satisfied

  b. Otherwise, title generally passes when the seller completes his/her performance with respect to physical delivery

    (1) If a destination contract, title passes on tender at destination (i.e., buyer's place of business)

    (2) If a shipping (point) contract, title passes when seller puts goods in the possession of the carrier

  c. If seller has no duty to move the goods

    (1) Title passes upon delivery of documents of title

       EXAMPLE: Delivery of negotiable or nonnegotiable warehouse receipt passes title to buyer.

    (2) If no document of title exists, title passes at the time and place of contracting if the goods are identifiable

    (3) If goods not identified, there is only a contract to sell; no title passes

  d. Rejection (justified or not) of goods or a justified revocation of acceptance by buyer reverts title to seller

  e. Taking a security interest is irrelevant to passage of title

D. Risk of Loss and Title

1. Risk of loss is independent of title under UCC, but rules regarding the transfer of both are similar
2. General rules

  a. Parties may agree as to which party bears risk of loss or has title; otherwise UCC rules below apply

  b. Shipment terms

    (1) FOB destination point—seller retains risk of loss and title and bears costs of transportation until s/he tenders delivery of goods at point of destination

      (a) FOB means "free on board"

    (2) FOB shipping point—buyer obtains risk of loss and title and bears shipping costs once goods are delivered to carrier

      EXAMPLE: Seller is in San Francisco and buyer is in Chicago: FOB San Francisco.

      EXAMPLE: Under FOB shipping point contract, seller delivers perishable goods to a nonrefrigerated carrier. Seller still has risk of loss since carrier was not appropriate type.

    (3) CIF—shipping contract (shipping point contract) in which cost, insurance, and freight are included in price

      (a) Seller puts goods in hands of a carrier and obtains insurance in buyer's name, who then has risk of loss and title

    (4) C & F—shipping contract in which cost and freight are included in price

      (a) Seller need not buy insurance for buyer

      (b) Risk of loss and title pass to buyer upon delivery of goods to carrier

    (5) COD—Collect on delivery

      (a) Carrier not to deliver goods until paid for

      (b) Buyer cannot inspect goods first unless stated in contract

c. In international sales shipment contracts under United Nations Convention for the International Sale of Goods, risk of loss passes to buyer upon delivery to first carrier for transmission to buyer.

    (1) This can be modified by agreement.

d. If no shipping terms are specified, then seller holds conforming goods for buyer and gives buyer notice to allow buyer to take possession of goods

e. Sale on approval—goods may be returned even if they conform to the contract

    (1) Not considered sold until buyer approves or accepts as sale
    (2) Goods bought for trial use
    (3) Seller retains title and risk of loss until buyer accepts goods
    (4) Creditors of buyer cannot reach goods until buyer accepts

f. Sale or return—goods may be returned even if they conform to the contract

    (1) Goods bought for use or resale
    (2) Sale is final if goods not returned during period specified
    (3) Buyer obtains risk of loss and title according to shipping terms in contract

       (a) Both risk of loss and title return to seller if and when goods are returned to seller
       (b) Return of goods is at buyer's expense
       (c) Buyer retains risk of loss during shipment back to seller if returns goods

    (4) Creditors of buyer can reach the goods while in buyer's possession, unless notice of seller's interest is posted or filed as required
    (5) Also termed sale and return

g. Often difficult to distinguish sale on approval vs. sale or return

    (1) Unless buyer and seller agree otherwise

       (a) Transaction is deemed to be sale on approval if goods for buyer's use
       (b) Transaction is presumed to be sale or return if goods are for buyer's resale

h. Effect of breach on risk of loss

    (1) If seller breaches

       (a) Risk of loss remains with seller until cure by seller or acceptance by buyer to extent of buyer's deficiency in insurance coverage
       (b) Title passes under original terms despite delivery of nonconforming goods

    (2) If buyer breaches

       (a) Risk of loss passes to buyer to extent of seller's deficiency in insurance for a commercially reasonable time

i. If goods are held in warehouse and seller has no right to move them, risk of loss passes to buyer

    (1) Upon proper negotiation of a negotiable document of title
    (2) Within a reasonable time after delivery of a nonnegotiable document of title
    (3) Once warehouseman acknowledges buyer's right to goods if no document of title

j. Voidable title

    (1) One who purchases in good faith from another who has voidable title takes good title

       (a) Good faith—purchaser unaware of facts that made previous title voidable
       (b) One may obtain voidable title by purchasing with a check that is later dishonored

         EXAMPLE: A purchases 1,000 widgets from B. B had purchased these from C but B's check had been dishonored by the bank before A purchased the widgets. A was unaware of these facts. B's title was voidable but A takes good title as a good-faith purchaser.

k. In situations not covered above, risk of loss passes to buyer on physical receipt of goods if seller is a merchant. Otherwise, risk passes on tender of delivery.

l.   Risk of loss can be covered by insurance. In general, party has an insurable interest whenever s/he can suffer damage.

(1) Buyer usually allowed an insurable interest when goods are identified to the contract
(2) Seller usually has an insurable interest so long as s/he has title or a security interest

E. Performance and Remedies under Sales Law

1.   In general, either party may, upon breach by other, cancel the contract and terminate executory obligations

a.   Unlike common law rescission, however, cancellation does not discharge a claim for damages

2.   Seller's duty to perform under a contract for sale is excused if performance as agreed has been made impracticable by the occurrence of a contingency, the nonoccurrence of which was a basic assumption on which the contract was made

a.   May sometimes substitute performance if, for example, method of delivery specified in contract is not available so seller chooses another reasonable delivery method

3.   Anticipatory breach (anticipatory repudiation) takes place when party indicates that s/he will not be performing contract and performance is not yet due

a.   Aggrieved party has options

(1) Treat it as a **present** breach of contract and use remedies available for breach of contract

(a) Sue for damages, or
(b) Cancel contract

(2) Aggrieved party may wait for performance for reasonable time hoping party will change his/her mind
(3) Aggrieved party may demand assurance of performance and treat silence as breach of contract under UCC
(4) Punitive damages are not allowed

b.   If aggrieved party is seller of uncompleted goods, then seller may

(1) Complete goods and identify to contract,
(2) Cease and sell for scrap, or
(3) Proceed in other reasonable manner

c.   Any of the above must be done while exercising reasonable commercial judgment
d.   Buyer who breaches is then liable for damages measured by whatever course of action seller takes

4.   Either party may demand adequate assurance of performance when reasonable grounds for insecurity arise with respect to performance of the other party

a.   For example, buyer falls behind in payments or seller delivers defective goods to other buyers
b.   Party may suspend performance while waiting for assurance
c.   Failure to provide assurance within a reasonable time, not to exceed thirty days, is repudiation of the contract
d.   Provision in contract, that seller may accelerate payment when s/he has a good-faith belief that makes him/her insecure, is valid

5.   Seller's remedies

a.   Seller has right to cure nonconformity (i.e., tender conforming goods)

(1) Within original time of contract, or
(2) Within reasonable time if seller thought nonconforming tender would be acceptable
(3) Seller must notify buyer of his intention to cure

b.   Seller may resell goods if buyer breaches before acceptance

(1) May be public or private sale

          (a) If private, must give notice to buyer who breached; otherwise, losses cannot be recovered

          (b) If seller resells in a commercially reasonable manner, s/he may recover any loss on the sale from the buyer who breached, but s/he is not responsible to buyer who breached for profits made on resale

          (c) In any event, good-faith purchasers take free of original buyer's claims

  c. If seller learns that buyer is insolvent and buyer does not have the document of title, seller may stop delivery of goods in carrier's possession unless buyer pays cash

  d. Seller may recover goods received by an insolvent buyer if demand is made within ten days of receipt

      (1) However, if the buyer has made a written misrepresentation of solvency within three months before delivery, this ten-day limitation does not apply

      (2) If buyer is insolvent, seller may demand cash to make delivery

  e. Seller may recover damages

      (1) If buyer repudiates agreement or refuses goods, seller may recover the difference between market price at time of tender and contract price, plus incidental damages, minus expenses saved due to buyer's breach

      (2) If the measure of damages stated above in (1) is inadequate to place the seller in as good a position as performance would have, then the seller can sue for the lost profits, plus incidental damages, less expenses saved due to the buyer's breach

          (a) Loss profits are consequential damages and as such are recoverable when foreseeable by breaching party

      (3) The seller can recover the full contract price when

          (a) The buyer has already accepted the goods

          (b) Conforming goods have been destroyed after the risk of loss had transferred to buyer

          (c) The seller is unable to resell the identified goods

6. Buyer's remedies

  a. Buyer may reject nonconforming goods, either in entirety or any commercial unit (e.g., bale, carload, etc.)

      (1) Buyer has right to inspect goods before acceptance or payment

          (a) Must do so in reasonable time and give notice to seller (failure may operate as acceptance)

          (b) Buyer must have reasonable time to inspect

      (2) Buyer must care for goods until returned

      (3) If buyer is a merchant, s/he must follow reasonable instructions of seller (e.g., ship, sell)

          (a) Right to indemnity for costs

      (4) If goods are perishable or threatened with decline in value, buyer must make reasonable effort to sell

      (5) Buyer has a security interest in any goods in his/her possession to the extent of any payments made to seller and any expenses incurred

          (a) S/he may sell the goods to recover payments

  b. Buyer may accept nonconforming goods

      (1) Buyer must pay at contract price but may still recover damages (i.e., deduct damages from price if s/he gives seller notice)

      (2) Buyer may revoke acceptance in a reasonable time if

          (a) Accepted expecting nonconformity to be cured

          (b) Accepted because of difficulty of discovering defect

          (c) Accepted because seller assured conformity

    c. Buyer may recover damages measured by the difference between the contract price and the market value of the goods at the time buyer learns of the breach, plus any incidental damages and consequential damages

        (1) Consequential damages are damages resulting from buyer's needs that the seller was aware of at the time of contracting

        (2) Consequential damages cannot be recovered if buyer could reasonably have prevented these (mitigation of damages)

    d. Buyer has the right of cover

        (1) Buyer can buy substitute goods from another seller—buyer will still have the right to damages after engaging in "cover"

            (a) Damages are difference between cost of cover and contract price, plus incidental and consequential damages

            (b) Failure to cover does not bar other remedies

    e. Once goods to the contract have been identified, buyer obtains rights in those goods

        (1) Identification occurs when goods under contract are

            (a) Shipped
            (b) Marked as part of the contract, or
            (c) In some way designated as part of contract

        (2) Buyer obtains

            (a) Insurable interest in those goods, and
            (b) Right to obtain goods, called replevin, upon offering contract price

                1] Replevin is not allowed if buyer can cover

    f. Buyer may obtain specific performance if goods are unique or in other proper circumstances even if goods are not identified to the contract

        (1) Proper circumstances may exist when other remedies (such as monetary damages or remedy of cover) are inadequate

            EXAMPLE: S agrees to sell B an antique car of which only one exists. If S later refuses to go through with the contract, B may require S to sell him the unique car under the remedy of specific performance.

  7. Statute of limitations for sale of goods is four years

    a. An action for breach must be commenced within this period
    b. Parties may agree to reduce to not less than one year but may not extend it
    c. Statute of limitations begins running when the contract is breached

F. Leases under UCC

  1. Law governing leases has been slow to develop and has been "tacked on" for various other areas of law such as property law and secured transactions
  2. Now Article 2A of the UCC applies to any transaction creating a lease regardless of form
  3. Article 2A is now law in majority of states
  4. Article 2A is quite lengthy, but for purpose of CPA exam, note that its provisions are similar to Article 2 except that Article 2A applies to leases and Article 2 applies to sales of goods
  5. Note the following provisions where Article 2A is similar to Article 2:

    a. Statute of frauds except that stated minimum is $1,000 instead of $500 that applies to sales of goods
    b. Rules on acceptance, revocation of acceptance, and rejection of goods
    c. Remedies are similar to sellers' and buyers' remedies including the important concept of cure
    d. Principles for performance include anticipatory repudiation or breach, (including use of adequate assurance to avoid a breach), and the concept of impracticability
    e. Use general principles of contract and sales law for these

      (1) Warranties
      (2) Parol evidence
      (3) Firm offers
      (4) Risk of loss rules
      (5) Concept of unconscionable agreements

f.   Leases may be assigned
g. Provision for sublease by lessee
h. Leased goods may become fixtures
i.   Lessor has right to take possession of leased property after default without requirement of court adjudication

MULTIPLE-CHOICE QUESTIONS (1-47)

1. Under the Sales Article of the UCC, when a written offer has been made without specifying a means of acceptance but providing that the offer will only remain open for ten days, which of the following statements represent(s) a valid acceptance of the offer?

I. An acceptance sent by regular mail the day before the ten-day period expires that reaches the offeror on the eleventh day.
II. An acceptance faxed the day before the ten-day period expires that reaches the offeror on the eleventh day, due to a malfunction of the offeror's printer.

   a.   I only.
   b.   II only.
   c.   Both I and II.
   d.   Neither I nor II.

2. Under the Sales Article of the UCC, a firm offer will be created only if the
   a.   Offer states the time period during which it will remain open.
   b.   Offer is made by a merchant in a signed writing.
   c.   Offeree gives some form of consideration.
   d.   Offeree is a merchant.

3. On May 2, Mason orally contracted with Acme Appliances to buy for $480 a washer and dryer for household use. Mason and the Acme salesperson agreed that delivery would be made on July 2. On May 5, Mason telephoned Acme and requested that the delivery date be moved to June 2. The Acme salesperson agreed with this request. On June 2, Acme failed to deliver the washer and dryer to Mason because of an inventory shortage. Acme advised Mason that it would deliver the appliances on July 2 as originally agreed. Mason believes that Acme has breached its agreement with Mason. Acme contends that its agreement to deliver on June 2 was not binding. Acme's contention is
   a.   Correct, because Mason is not a merchant and was buying the appliances for household use.
   b.   Correct, because the agreement to change the delivery date was not in writing.
   c.   Incorrect, because the agreement to change the delivery date was binding.
   d.   Incorrect, because Acme's agreement to change the delivery date is a firm offer that cannot be withdrawn by Acme.

4. Under the Sales Article of the UCC, which of the following statements is correct?
   a.   The obligations of the parties to the contract must be performed in good faith.
   b.   Merchants and nonmerchants are treated alike.
   c.   The contract must involve the sale of goods for a price of more than $500.
   d.   None of the provisions of the UCC may be disclaimed by agreement.

5. Which of the following contracts is handled under common law rules rather than under Article 2 of the Uniform Commercial Code?
   a.   Oral contract to have hair styled in which expensive products will be used on the hair.
   b.   Oral contract to purchase a textbook for $100.
   c.   Written contract to purchase an old handcrafted chair for $600 from a private party.
   d.   Written contract to purchase a heater from a dealer to be installed by the buyer in her home.

6. Cookie Co. offered to sell Distrib Markets 20,000 pounds of cookies at $1.00 per pound, subject to certain specified terms for delivery. Distrib replied in writing as follows:

We accept your offer for 20,000 pounds of cookies at $1.00 per pound, weighing scale to have valid city certificate.

Under the UCC
   a.   A contract was formed between the parties.
   b.   A contract will be formed only if Cookie agrees to the weighing scale requirement.
   c.   No contract was formed because Distrib included the weighing scale requirement in its reply.
   d.   No contract was formed because Distrib's reply was a counteroffer.

7. EG Door Co., a manufacturer of custom exterior doors, verbally contracted with Art Contractors to design and build a $2,000 custom door for a house that Art was restoring. After EG had completed substantial work on the door, Art advised EG that the house had been destroyed by fire and Art was canceling the contract. EG finished the door and shipped it to Art. Art refused to accept delivery. Art contends that the contract cannot be enforced because it violated the Statute of Frauds by not being in writing. Under the Sales Article of the UCC, is Art's contention correct?
   a.   Yes, because the contract was not in writing.
   b.   Yes, because the contract cannot be fully performed due to the fire.
   c.   No, because the goods were specially manufactured for Art and cannot be resold in EG's regular course of business.
   d.   No, because the cancellation of the contract was not made in writing.

8. On May 2, Handy Hardware sent Ram Industries a signed purchase order that stated, in part, as follows:

Ship for May 8 delivery 300 Model A-X socket sets at current dealer price. Terms 2/10/net 30.

Ram received Handy's purchase order on May 4. On May 5, Ram discovered that it had only 200 Model A-X socket sets and 100 Model W-Z socket sets in stock. Ram shipped the Model A-X and Model W-Z sets to Handy without any explanation concerning the shipment. The socket sets were received by Handy on May 8.
   Which of the following statements concerning the shipment is correct?
   a.   Ram's shipment is an acceptance of Handy's offer.
   b.   Ram's shipment is a counteroffer.
   c.   Handy's order must be accepted by Ram in writing before Ram ships the socket sets.
   d.   Handy's order can only be accepted by Ram shipping conforming goods.

9. Under the UCC Sales Article, which of the following conditions will prevent the formation of an enforceable sale of goods contract?
   a.   Open price.
   b.   Open delivery.
   c.   Open quantity.
   d.   Open acceptance.

10. Webstar Corp. orally agreed to sell Northco, Inc. a computer for $20,000. Northco sent a signed purchase order to Webstar confirming the agreement. Webstar received the purchase order and did not respond. Webstar refused to deliver the computer to Northco, claiming that the purchase order did not satisfy the UCC Statute of Frauds because it was not signed by Webstar. Northco sells computers to the general public and Webstar is a computer wholesaler. Under the UCC Sales Article, Webstar's position is

    a. Incorrect because it failed to object to Northco's purchase order.

    b. Incorrect because only the buyer in a sale-of-goods transaction must sign the contract.

    c. Correct because it was the party against whom enforcement of the contract is being sought.

    d. Correct because the purchase price of the computer exceeded $500.

11. Patch, a frequent shopper at Soon-Shop Stores, received a rain check for an advertised sale item after Soon-Shop's supply of the product ran out. The rain check was in writing and stated that the item would be offered to the customer at the advertised sale price for an unspecified period of time. A Soon-Shop employee signed the rain check. When Patch returned to the store one month later to purchase the item, the store refused to honor the rain check. Under the Sales Article of the UCC, will Patch win a suit to enforce the rain check?

    a. No, because one month is too long a period of time for a rain check to be effective.

    b. No, because the rain check did not state the effective time period necessary to keep the offer open.

    c. Yes, because Soon-Shop is required to have sufficient supplies of the sale item to satisfy all customers.

    d. Yes, because the rain check met the requirements of a merchant's firm offer even though no effective time period was stated.

12. A sheep rancher agreed in writing to sell all the wool shorn during the shearing season to a weaver. The contract failed to establish the price and a minimum quantity of wool. After the shearing season, the rancher refused to deliver the wool. The weaver sued the rancher for breach of contract. Under the Sales Article of the UCC, will the weaver win?

    a. Yes, because this was an output contract.

    b. Yes, because both price and quantity terms were omitted.

    c. No, because quantity cannot be omitted for a contract to be enforceable.

    d. No, because the omission of price and quantity terms prevents the formation of a contract.

13. Under the Sales Article of the UCC, the warranty of title

    a. Provides that the seller cannot disclaim the warranty if the sale is made to a bona fide purchaser for value.

    b. Provides that the seller deliver the goods free from any lien of which the buyer lacked knowledge when the contract was made.

    c. Applies only if it is in writing and assigned by the seller.

    d. Applies only if the seller is a merchant.

14. Under the Sales Article of the UCC, most goods sold by merchants are covered by certain warranties. An example of an express warranty would be a warranty of

    a. Usage of trade.

    b. Fitness for a particular purpose.

    c. Merchantability.

    d. Conformity of goods to sample.

15. Under the Sales Article of the UCC, which of the following statements is correct regarding the warranty of merchantability arising when there has been a sale of goods by a merchant seller?

    a. The warranty must be in writing.

    b. The warranty arises when the buyer relies on the seller's skill in selecting the goods purchased.

    c. The warranty cannot be disclaimed.

    d. The warranty arises as a matter of law when the seller ordinarily sells the goods purchased.

16. On May 2, Handy Hardware sent Ram Industries a signed purchase order that stated, in part, as follows:

> Ship for May 8 delivery 300 Model A-X socket sets at current dealer price. Terms 2/10/net 30.

Ram received Handy's purchase order on May 4. On May 5, Ram discovered that it had only 200 Model A-X socket sets and 100 Model W-Z socket sets in stock. Ram shipped the Model A-X and Model W-Z sets to Handy without any explanation concerning the shipment. The socket sets were received by Handy on May 8.

Assuming a contract exists between Handy and Ram, which of the following implied warranties would result?

   I. Implied warranty of merchantability.

  II. Implied warranty of fitness for a particular purpose.

III. Implied warranty of title.

    a. I only.

    b. III only.

    c. I and III only.

    d. I, II, and III.

17. Under the UCC Sales Article, an action for breach of the implied warranty of merchantability by a party who sustains personal injuries may be successful against the seller of the product only when

    a. The seller is a merchant of the product involved.

    b. An action based on negligence can also be successfully maintained.

    c. The injured party is in privity of contract with the seller.

    d. An action based on strict liability in tort can also be successfully maintained.

18. Which of the following conditions must be met for an implied warranty of fitness for a particular purpose to arise in connection with a sale of goods?

   I. The warranty must be in writing.

  II. The seller must know that the buyer was relying on the seller in selecting the goods.

    a. I only.

    b. II only.

    c. Both I and II.

    d. Neither I nor II.

19. Under the UCC Sales Article, the implied warranty of merchantability

a.   May be disclaimed by a seller's oral statement that mentions merchantability.

b.   Arises only in contracts involving a merchant seller and a merchant buyer.

c.   Is breached if the goods are **not** fit for all purposes for which the buyer intends to use the goods.

d.   Must be part of the basis of the bargain to be binding on the seller.

20. Cook Company, a common carrier trucking company, made a contract to transport some video equipment for Jackson Company. Cook is trying to limit its liability in the contract. In which of the following situations can Cook **not avoid** liability?

I.   In transit, the driver of Cook's truck damages the video equipment when the driver causes an accident.

II. An unknown thief steals the video equipment while in transit. Cook committed no negligence in this theft.

III. The video equipment is destroyed when a bridge under the truck collapses because of an earthquake.

a.   I only.
b.   I and II only.
c.   I, II, and III.
d.   I and III only.

21. High sues the manufacturer, wholesaler, and retailer for bodily injuries caused by a power saw High purchased. Which of the following statements is correct under strict liability theory?

a.   Contributory negligence on High's part will always be a bar to recovery.

b.   The manufacturer will avoid liability if it can show it followed the custom of the industry.

c.   Privity will be a bar to recovery insofar as the wholesaler is concerned if the wholesaler did **not** have a reasonable opportunity to inspect.

d.   High may recover even if he **cannot** show any negligence was involved.

22. To establish a cause of action based on strict liability in tort for personal injuries that result from the use of a defective product, one of the elements the injured party must prove is that the seller

a.   Was aware of the defect in the product.
b.   Sold the product to the injured party.
c.   Failed to exercise due care.
d.   Sold the product in a defective condition.

23. A common carrier bailee generally would avoid liability for loss of goods entrusted to its care if the goods are

a.   Stolen by an unknown person.
b.   Negligently destroyed by an employee.
c.   Destroyed by the derailment of the train carrying them due to railroad employee negligence.
d.   Improperly packed by the party shipping them.

24. McGraw purchased an antique rocking chair from Tillis by check. The check was dishonored by the bank due to insufficient funds. In the meantime, McGraw sold the rocking chair to Rio who had no knowledge that McGraw's check had been dishonored. Which of the following is correct?

a.   Tillis may repossess the rocking chair from Rio.
b.   Tillis may recover money damages from Rio.

c.   Tillis may recover money damages from McGraw.
d.   Tillis may recover damages from McGraw based on fraud.

25. Yancie took her bike in to Pete's Bike Sales and Repair to have it repaired. Pete said he would need to have her leave it for two days. The next day, one of Pete's employees sold Yancie's bike to Jake. Jake paid for the bike with a credit card, unaware that Pete did not own the bike. Which of the following is correct?

a.   Yancie can repossess the bike from Jake if she pays Jake. Yancie then recovers the price from Pete.

b.   Pete can repossess the bike from Jake and then return it to Yancie.

c.   Yancie can sue Jake for monetary damages only.

d.   Jake has title to the bike.

26. Under the Sales Article of the UCC, unless a contract provides otherwise, before title to goods can pass from a seller to a buyer, the goods must be

a.   Tendered to the buyer.
b.   Identified to the contract.
c.   Accepted by the buyer.
d.   Paid for.

27. Under the Sales Article of the UCC, in an FOB place of shipment contract, the risk of loss passes to the buyer when the goods

a.   Are identified to the contract.
b.   Are placed on the seller's loading dock.
c.   Are delivered to the carrier.
d.   Reach the buyer's loading dock.

28. On May 2, Lace Corp., an appliance wholesaler, offered to sell appliances worth $3,000 to Parco, Inc., a household appliances retailer. The offer was signed by Lace's president, and provided that it would not be withdrawn before June 1. It also included the shipping terms: "FOB Parco's warehouse." On May 29, Parco mailed an acceptance of Lace's offer. Lace received the acceptance June 2.

If Lace inadvertently ships the wrong appliances to Parco and Parco rejects them two days after receipt, title to the goods will

a.   Pass to Parco when they are identified to the contract.

b.   Pass to Parco when they are shipped.

c.   Remain with Parco until the goods are returned to Lace.

d.   Revert to Lace when they are rejected by Parco.

29. Under the Sales Article of the UCC and the United Nations Convention for the International Sale of Goods (CISG), absent specific terms in an international sales shipment contract, when will risk of loss pass to the buyer?

a.   When the goods are delivered to the first carrier for transmission to the buyer.

b.   When the goods are tendered to the buyer.

c.   At the conclusion of the execution of the contract.

d.   At the time the goods are identified to the contract.

30. Which of the following statements applies to a sale on approval under the UCC Sales Article?

a.   Both the buyer and seller must be merchants.

b.   The buyer must be purchasing the goods for resale.

c.   Risk of loss for the goods passes to the buyer when the goods are accepted after the trial period.

   d.   Title to the goods passes to the buyer on delivery of the goods to the buyer.

31. Under the Sales Article of UCC, which of the following events will result in the risk of loss passing from a merchant seller to a buyer?

	Tender of the goods at the seller's place of business	*Use of the seller's truck to deliver the goods*
a.	Yes	Yes
b.	Yes	No
c.	No	Yes
d.	No	No

32. Cey Corp. entered into a contract to sell parts to Deck, Ltd. The contract provided that the goods would be shipped "FOB Cey's warehouse." Cey shipped parts different from those specified in the contract. Deck rejected the parts. A few hours after Deck informed Cey that the parts were rejected, they were destroyed by fire in Deck's warehouse. Cey believed that the parts were conforming to the contract. Which of the following statements is correct?

   a.   Regardless of whether the parts were conforming, Deck will bear the loss because the contract was a shipment contract.

   b.   If the parts were nonconforming, Deck had the right to reject them, but the risk of loss remains with Deck until Cey takes possession of the parts.

   c.   If the parts were conforming, risk of loss does **not** pass to Deck until a reasonable period of time after they are delivered to Deck.

   d.   If the parts were nonconforming, Cey will bear the risk of loss, even though the contract was a shipment contract.

33. Under the Sales Article of the UCC, which of the following factors is most important in determining who bears the risk of loss in a sale of goods contract?

   a.   The method of shipping the goods.

   b.   The contract's shipping terms.

   c.   Title to the goods.

   d.   How the goods were lost.

34. Bond purchased a painting from Wool, who is not in the business of selling art. Wool tendered delivery of the painting after receiving payment in full from Bond. Bond informed Wool that Bond would be unable to take possession of the painting until later that day. Thieves stole the painting before Bond returned. The risk of loss

   a.   Passed to Bond at Wool's tender of delivery.

   b.   Passed to Bond at the time the contract was formed and payment was made.

   c.   Remained with Wool, because the parties agreed on a later time of delivery.

   d.   Remained with Wool, because Bond had **not** yet received the painting.

35. Funston, a retailer, shipped goods worth $600 to a customer by using a common carrier. The contract used by the common carrier, and agreed to by Funston, limited liability to $100 unless a higher fee is paid. Funston did not pay the higher fee. The goods were shipped FOB destination point and were destroyed in transit due to a flash flood. Which of the following is correct?

   a.   Funston will suffer a loss of $500.

   b.   Funston will suffer a loss of $600.

   c.   Funston's customer will suffer a loss of $500.

   d.   Funston's customer will suffer a loss of $600.

36. Under the Sales Article of the UCC, which of the following statements regarding liquidated damages is(are) correct?

   I.   The injured party may collect any amount of liquidated damages provided for in the contract.

   II.   The seller may retain a deposit of up to $500 when a buyer defaults even if there is no liquidated damages provision in the contract.

   a.   I only.

   b.   II only.

   c.   Both I and II.

   d.   Neither I nor II.

37. Under the Sales Article of the UCC, and unless otherwise agreed to, the seller's obligation to the buyer is to

   a.   Deliver the goods to the buyer's place of business.

   b.   Hold conforming goods and give the buyer whatever notification is reasonably necessary to enable the buyer to take delivery.

   c.   Deliver all goods called for in the contract to a common carrier.

   d.   Set aside conforming goods for inspection by the buyer before delivery.

38. Under the Sales Article of the UCC, which of the following rights is(are) available to a seller when a buyer materially breaches a sales contract?

	Right to cancel the contract	*Right to recover damages*
a.	Yes	Yes
b.	Yes	No
c.	No	Yes
d.	No	No

39. Under the Sales Article of the UCC, the remedies available to a seller when a buyer breaches a contract for the sale of goods may include

	The right to resell goods identified to the contract	*The right to stop a carrier from delivering the goods*
a.	Yes	Yes
b.	Yes	No
c.	No	Yes
d.	No	No

40. Lazur Corp. entered into a contract with Baker Suppliers, Inc. to purchase a used word processor from Baker. Lazur is engaged in the business of selling new and used word processors to the general public. The contract required Baker to ship the goods to Lazur by common carrier pursuant to the following provision in the contract: "FOB Baker Suppliers, Inc. loading dock." Baker also represented in the contract that the word processor had been used for only ten hours by its previous owner. The contract included the provision that the word processor was being sold "as is" and this provision was in a larger and different type style than the remainder of the contract.

    Assume that Lazur refused to accept the word processor even though it was in all respects conforming to the contract and that the contract is otherwise silent. Under the UCC Sales Article,

a. Baker can successfully sue for specific performance and make Lazur accept and pay for the word processor.

b. Baker may resell the word processor to another buyer.

c. Baker must sue for the difference between the market value of the word processor and the contract price plus its incidental damages.

d. Baker cannot successfully sue for consequential damages unless it attempts to resell the word processor.

41. On February 15, Mazur Corp. contracted to sell 1,000 bushels of wheat to Good Bread, Inc. at $6.00 per bushel with delivery to be made on June 23. On June 1, Good advised Mazur that it would not accept or pay for the wheat. On June 2, Mazur sold the wheat to another customer at the market price of $5.00 per bushel. Mazur had advised Good that it intended to resell the wheat. Which of the following statements is correct?

a. Mazur can successfully sue Good for the difference between the resale price and the contract price.

b. Mazur can resell the wheat only after June 23.

c. Good can retract its anticipatory breach at any time before June 23.

d. Good can successfully sue Mazur for specific performance.

42. Pickens agreed to sell Crocket 100 cases of napkins with the name of Crocket's restaurant on the napkins. In the enforceable contract, it was specified that delivery will take place on April 15, 2001, which is one month after Pickens and Crocket signed the contract. Crocket wanted the napkins by April 15 because the grand opening of the restaurant was scheduled for April 17. On April 11, Pickens tells Crocket that he has too many orders and will not be able to deliver the napkins. What options does Crocket have?

I. Treat it as a present breach of contract and cancel the contract.

II. Wait for a reasonable time to see if Pickens will deliver.

a. I only.

b. II only.

c. Either I or II.

d. Neither I nor II.

43. Under the Sales Article of the UCC, which of the following rights is(are) available to the buyer when a seller commits an anticipatory breach of contract?

	Demand assurance of performance	Cancel the contract	Collect punitive damages
a.	Yes	Yes	Yes
b	Yes	Yes	No
c.	Yes	No	Yes
d.	No	Yes	Yes

44. Larch Corp. manufactured and sold Oak a stove. The sale documents included a disclaimer of warranty for personal injury. The stove was defective. It exploded causing serious injuries to Oak's spouse. Larch was notified one week after the explosion. Under the UCC Sales Article, which of the following statements concerning Larch's liability for personal injury to Oak's spouse would be correct?

a. Larch **cannot** be liable because of a lack of privity with Oak's spouse.

b. Larch will **not** be liable because of a failure to give proper notice.

c. Larch will be liable because the disclaimer was **not** a disclaimer of all liability.

d. Larch will be liable because liability for personal injury **cannot** be disclaimed.

45. Under the Sales Article of the UCC, which of the following events will release the buyer from all its obligations under a sales contract?

a. Destruction of the goods after risk of loss passed to the buyer.

b. Impracticability of delivery under the terms of the contract.

c. Anticipatory repudiation by the buyer that is retracted before the seller cancels the contract.

d. Refusal of the seller to give written assurance of performance when reasonably demanded by the buyer.

46. Rowe Corp. purchased goods from Stair Co. that were shipped COD. Under the Sales Article of the UCC, which of the following rights does Rowe have?

a. The right to inspect the goods before paying.

b. The right to possession of the goods before paying.

c. The right to reject nonconforming goods.

d. The right to delay payment for a reasonable period of time.

47. Sklar, CPA, purchased from Wiz Corp. two computers. Sklar discovered material defects in the computers ten months after taking delivery. Three years after discovering the defects, Sklar commenced an action for breach of warranty against Wiz. Wiz has raised the statute of limitations as a defense. The original contract between Wiz and Sklar contained a conspicuous clause providing that the statute of limitations for breach of warranty actions would be limited to eighteen months. Under the circumstances, Sklar will

a. Win because the action was commenced within the four-year period as measured from the date of delivery.

b. Win because the action was commenced within the four-year period as measured from the time he discovered the breach or should have discovered the breach.

c. Lose because the clause providing that the statute of limitations would be limited to eighteen months is enforceable.

d. Lose because the statute of limitations is three years from the date of delivery with respect to written contracts.

OTHER OBJECTIVE QUESTIONS

Problem 1 (15 to 25 minutes)

Angler Corp., a food distributor, is involved in the following disputes:

• On September 8, Angler shipped the wrong grade of tuna to Mason Restaurants, Inc. under a contract that stated as follows: "FOB Angler's loading dock." During shipment, the tuna was destroyed in an accident involving the common carrier's truck. Mason has refused to pay for the tuna, claiming the risk of loss belonged to Angler at the time of the accident.

• On October 3, Angler shipped 100 bushels of peaches to Classic Foods, Inc., a retail grocer. Because of a delay in shipping, the peaches rotted. Classic elected to reject the peaches and notified Angler of this decision. Angler asked Classic to return the peaches at Angler's expense. Classic refused the request, claiming it had no obligation to do so.

• On October 23, Angler orally contracted to sell Regal Fast-Food 1,500 pounds of hamburger meat for $1,500. Delivery was to be made on October 31. On October 29, after Angler had shipped the hamburger meat to Regal, Regal sent Angler the following signed correspondence:

"We are not going to need the 1,500 pounds of meat we ordered on October 23. Don't ship."

Regal rejected the shipment and claimed it is not obligated to purchase the hamburger meat because there is no written contract between Angler and Regal.

Required:

Determine whether each of the numbered legal conclusions is correct or incorrect.

1.   When the accident happened, the risk of loss belonged to Angler.

2.   If Angler had shipped the correct grade of tuna to Mason, the risk of loss would have been Angler's at time of the accident.

3.   The contract between Angler and Mason was an FOB destination point contract.

4.   Angler had title to the tuna at time of the accident since Angler shipped nonconforming goods.

5.   Classic is required to return the peaches at Angler's expense per Angler's instructions.

6.   Classic may throw the peaches away because they were rotted.

7.   Since Classic elected to reject the rotted peaches, Classic may not also sue for damages.

8.   Regal is not obligated to purchase the hamburger meat because there was no written contract between Angler and Regal.

9.   The Uniform Commercial Code applies to the contract between Angler and Regal.

10.   Regal's correspondence to Angler, dated October 29, satisfies the appropriate Statute of Frauds.

11.   Angler should keep the hamburger until Regal finally accepts it and sue Regal for $1,500.

12.   Assuming that all of the original facts are the same except that Regal never sent Angler the correspondence dated October 29, then Angler may hold Regal in breach of contract.

13.   Assuming that all of the original facts are the same except that the contract was for $450, then Angler may hold Regal in breach of contract.

14.   Assume that all of the original facts are the same except that Regal never sent Angler the correspondence and Angler shipped to Regal 800 pounds of the hamburger on October 29. Regal accepted the 800 pounds. Regal, then, on October 31 orally rejected the shipment for the remaining 700 pounds. Under these facts, the contract is enforceable against Regal for the 800 pounds but not the full 1,500 pounds.

15.   Under the same facts found in **14.** above, the contract is enforceable against Regal for the full 1,500 pounds.

Problem 2   (5 to 10 minutes)

On February 1, 2001, Grand Corp., a manufacturer of custom cabinets, contracted in writing with Axle Co., a kitchen contractor, to sell Axle 100 unique, custom-designed, kitchen cabinets for $250,000. Axle had contracted to install the cabinets in a luxury condominium complex. The contract provided that the cabinets were to be ready for delivery by April 15 and were to be shipped FOB seller's loading dock. On April 15, Grand had eighty-five cabinets complete and delivered them, together with fifteen standard cabinets, to the trucking company for delivery to Axle. Grand faxed Axle a copy of the shipping invoice, listing the fifteen standard cabinets. On May 1, before reaching Axle, the truck was involved in a collision and all the cabinets were damaged beyond repair.

Required:

Items 1 through 5 refer to the above fact pattern. For each item, determine whether (A), (B), or (C) is correct.

1. A. The contract between Grand and Axle was a shipment contract.
    B. The contract between Grand and Axle was a destination contract.
    C. The contract between Grand and Axle was a consignment contract.

2. A. The risk of loss for the eighty-five custom cabinets passed to Axle on April 15.
    B. The risk of loss for the 100 cabinets passed to Axle on April 15.
    C. The risk of loss for the 100 cabinets remained with Grand.

3. A. The contract between Grand and Axle was invalid because **no** delivery date was stated.
    B. The contract between Grand and Axle was voidable because Grand shipped only eighty-five custom cabinets.
    C. The contract between Grand and Axle was void because the goods were destroyed.

4. A. Grand's shipment of the standard cabinets was a breach of the contract with Axle.
    B. Grand would **not** be considered to have breached the contract until Axle rejected the standard cabinets.
    C. Grand made a counteroffer by shipping the standard cabinets.

5. A. Axle is entitled to specific performance from Grand because of the unique nature of the goods.
    B. Axle is required to purchase substitute goods (cover) and is entitled to the difference in cost from Grand.
    C. Axle is entitled to punitive damages because of Grand's intentional shipment of nonconforming goods.

PROBLEMS

Problem 1   (15 to 25 minutes)

Debco Electronics, Inc. sells various brands of computer equipment to retail and business customers. An audit of Debco's 2001 financial statements has revealed the following transactions:

• On September 1, 2001, a Debco salesperson orally agreed to sell Rapid Computers, Inc. eight TMI computers for $11,000, to be delivered on October 15, 2001. Rapid sells computers to the general public. The Debco salesperson sent Rapid a signed confirmation of the sales agreement. Rapid received the confirmation on September 3, but did not respond to it. On October 15, 2001, Debco tendered delivery of the computers to Rapid. Rapid refused to accept delivery, claiming it had no obligation to buy the computers because it had not signed a contract with Debco.

• On October 12, 2001, Debco mailed TMI Computers, Inc. a signed purchase order for certain specified computers for delivery by November 30, 2001. The purchase order also stated the following:

> This purchase order will not be withdrawn on or before October 31, 2001. You must accept by that date or we will assume you cannot meet our terms. Ship FOB our loading dock.

TMI received the purchase order on October 15, 2001.

• On October 25, Debco mailed the following signed correspondence to TMI, which TMI received on October 29:

> Cancel our October 12, 2001, purchase order. We have found a better price on the computers.

• On October 31, 2001, TMI mailed the following signed correspondence to Debco, which Debco received on November 3:

> We have set aside the computers you ordered and turned down other offers for them. Therefore, we will ship the computers to you for delivery by November 30, 2001, FOB your loading dock with payment terms 2/10; net 30.

There were no further communications between TMI and Debco.

TMI shipped the computers on November 15, and Debco received them on November 29. Debco refused to accept delivery. In justifying its refusal to accept delivery, Debco claimed the following:

• Its October 25 correspondence prevented the formation of a contract between Debco and TMI;

• TMI's October 31 correspondence was not an effective acceptance because it was not received by Debco until November 3;

• TMI's October 31 correspondence was not an effective acceptance because it added payment terms to Debco's purchase order.

Debco, Rapid, and TMI are located in a jurisdiction that has adopted the UCC.

Required:

a. State whether Rapid's claim is correct and give the reasons for your conclusions.

b. State whether Debco's claims are correct with regard to the transaction involving TMI and give the reasons for your conclusions.

MULTIPLE-CHOICE ANSWERS

1. c ___ ___	11. d ___ ___	21. d ___ ___	31. d ___ ___	41. a ___ ___
2. b ___ ___	12. a ___ ___	22. d ___ ___	32. d ___ ___	42. c ___ ___
3. c ___ ___	13. b ___ ___	23. d ___ ___	33. b ___ ___	43. b ___ ___
4. a ___ ___	14. d ___ ___	24. c ___ ___	34. a ___ ___	44. d ___ ___
5. a ___ ___	15. d ___ ___	25. d ___ ___	35. b ___ ___	45. d ___ ___
6. a ___ ___	16. c ___ ___	26. b ___ ___	36. b ___ ___	46. c ___ ___
7. c ___ ___	17. a ___ ___	27. c ___ ___	37. b ___ ___	47. c ___ ___
8. a ___ ___	18. b ___ ___	28. d ___ ___	38. a ___ ___	
9. d ___ ___	19. a ___ ___	29. a ___ ___	39. a ___ ___	1st: ___/47 = __%
10. a ___ ___	20. b ___ ___	30. c ___ ___	40. b ___ ___	2nd: ___/47 = __%

MULTIPLE-CHOICE ANSWER EXPLANATIONS

A. Contracts for Sale of Goods

1. **(c)** Under the Sales Article of the UCC, acceptance is valid when sent if a reasonable method is used; therefore answer (c) is correct as both acceptances were sent prior to the end of the ten-day period.

2. **(b)** A firm offer is a written, signed offer concerning the sale of goods, by a merchant, giving assurance that it will be held open for a specified time and is irrevocable for that period, not to exceed three months. Answer (a) is incorrect because if the firm offer does not state a period of time, it will remain open for a reasonable period of time, not to exceed three months. Answer (c) is incorrect as consideration is not required for a firm offer, but for an option contract. Answer (d) is incorrect because under the firm offer rule, only the offeror need be a merchant.

3. **(c)** Under the UCC, an oral modification of an existing contract for the sale of goods for a price less than $500 is considered binding. Since the washer and dryer Mason contracted to buy cost less than $500, Acme's oral agreement to change the date of delivery would be enforceable. The fact that Mason is not a merchant won't affect whether or not the oral modification is binding. In order to have a firm offer, the offer must be made by a merchant in a signed writing which gives assurance that the offer will be held open. In this situation, the modification of an offer already accepted is being discussed rather than a firm offer.

4. **(a)** Under the Sales Article of the UCC, both the seller and buyer are obligated to perform a contract in good faith. Answer (b) is incorrect because certain provisions, such as the battle of forms provision, only apply to merchants. Answer (c) is incorrect because the Sales Article of the UCC applies to the sale of goods without regard to the price of goods. Answer (d) is incorrect because certain provisions of the UCC may be disclaimed by written or oral agreement, such as warranty liability.

5. **(a)** Article 2 of the UCC applies to sales of goods. Common law generally applies to contracts for services and real estate. Even though goods are used in this service contract, the predominate feature of this contract is the service. Article 2 of the UCC governs this contract even though it is oral and for a small sum. Even though the chair at one time involved a lot of labor, it is still a sale of goods. Also, whether the parties are merchants or not is not an issue on whether Article 2 applies. The heater which is not yet installed in the home is a sale of goods. Once it is installed in the home, it becomes part of the real estate for any future sale of the home. Common law rules would apply to any such future sale.

6. **(a)** Under common law, an acceptance must be unequivocal and unqualified in agreeing to the precise terms specified by the offer. However, the Uniform Commercial Code alters this general rule as far as the sales of goods is concerned. Under the UCC, an acceptance containing additional terms is a valid acceptance unless the acceptance is expressly conditional upon the offeror's agreement to the additional terms. In this situation, a valid contract has been formed between Cookie Co. and Distrib Markets. Distrib Markets' acceptance was not conditional upon Cookie's agreement to the additional term and, thus, a contract is formed regardless of Cookie's agreement or objection to the additional term. This contract was for the sale of goods and is governed by the UCC rather than by common law. Under common law, Distrib Markets' reply would have been a rejection and counteroffer; but under the UCC, a contract was formed.

7. **(c)** This exception for specially manufactured goods, even if the contract is for over $500, is one of the important exceptions found in the Statute of Fraud provisions of the Uniform Commercial Code. Answer (a) is incorrect because the exception for specially manufactured goods applies to this fact pattern and thus this contract need not be in writing. Answer (b) is incorrect because the fire did not prevent the custom door contract from being performed. Answer (d) is incorrect because the contract was fully enforceable and Art had no legal right to cancel the contract.

8. **(a)** Ram may accept the offer by shipping the goods. Under the UCC, shipping nonconforming goods constitutes an acceptance, also unless the seller notifies the buyer that the shipment is given only as an accommodation to the buyer. Answer (b) is incorrect because this shipment counts as an acceptance, not as a counteroffer. Answer (c) is incorrect because an order to buy goods for prompt shipment allows the seller to accept by either a prompt promise to ship or by the actual prompt shipment itself.

9. **(d)** In order to have a contract, there must be both an offer and an acceptance. Even though an acceptance can occur in different ways, by speech, by writing, or by action, the actual acceptance is a required element of a contract. Under the UCC Sales Article, a binding contract may be present if the parties had intended to form a contract even though certain elements of the contract are missing. These open terms will be filled by specific provisions of the UCC, including provisions for open price, open delivery, or open quantity. Note that in the case of quantity, output contracts, requirements contracts, and exclusive dealing's contracts are enforceable though the actual quantity may not be known in advance.

10.   (a)   The UCC provides that a confirmation satisfies the UCC Statute of Frauds, if an oral contract between merchants is confirmed in writing within a reasonable period of time, and the confirmation is signed by the party sending it and received by the other party. Both parties are bound unless the party receiving the confirmation submits a written objection within ten days of receipt. In this situation, a valid contract has been formed since Webstar did not object to Northco's purchase order. In a sale-of-goods transaction, the contract must be signed by the party to be charged to be enforceable. However, in the case of a written confirmation of an oral agreement between merchants, the confirmation need only be signed by the party sending the confirmation. The use of a signed purchase order satisfies the UCC Statute of Frauds.

11.   (d)   A firm offer is an offer for the sale of goods that is written and signed by a merchant (or employee of the merchant) that agrees to keep the offer open. This offer is valid without consideration for three months since no time was specified in the fact pattern. Patch will win in a suit to enforce the rain check because Patch tried to use it one month later. Answer (a) is incorrect because the UCC specifies a three-month period when no time is detailed in the firm offer. Answer (b) is incorrect because when no time is specified, the UCC gives Patch three months to accept the offer. Answer (c) is incorrect because there was no offer and acceptance when Patch first tried to purchase the advertised item.

12.   (a)   An output contract is enforceable under the UCC even though an actual quantity is not mentioned in the contract. The output contract is supported by consideration because the seller has agreed not to sell that output to any other party. Answer (b) is incorrect because when the price is omitted, the UCC construes it as the reasonable price at the time of delivery. The quantity is construed as the output of the sheep rancher. Answer (c) is incorrect because although quantity is an important term in the contract, the UCC allows the quantity term to be defined by output. Answer (d) is incorrect because the UCC allows price terms to be based on the reasonable price and quantity terms to be defined by output.

B.1.a.   Warranty of Title

13.   (b)   Under the warranty of title, the seller warrants good title, rightful transfer and freedom from any security interest or lien of which the buyer has no knowledge at the time of sale. Answer (a) is incorrect because the warranty of title can be disclaimed by specific language or circumstances which give the buyer reason to know s/he is receiving less than full title. Answer (c) is incorrect because the warranty does not have to be in writing. Answer (d) is incorrect because the seller does not have to be a merchant for the seller to give the warranty of title.

B.1.b.   Express Warranties

14.   (d)   In the Sales Article of the UCC, express warranties include warranties that the goods will conform to any description used or any sample or model shown. Answer (a)

is incorrect because although usage of trade can help interpret terms used in contracts, it is not a warranty. Answers (b) and (c) are incorrect because the warranty of fitness for a particular purpose and the warranty of merchantability are both implied warranties.

B.1.c.   Implied Warranties

15.   (d)   The implied warranty of merchantability, which guarantees that goods are fit for ordinary purposes, arises as a matter of law when the seller is a merchant who ordinarily sells the goods purchased. Answer (a) is incorrect because the warranty is implied, and therefore need not be in writing. Answer (c) is incorrect because the warranty applies unless specifically disclaimed by the merchant.

16.   (c)   The implied warranty of merchantability is always implied if the seller is a merchant with respect to the type of goods being sold. Since Ram is a merchant, this warranty would apply. Also, under the UCC, the seller warrants good title, rightful transfer, and freedom from any security interest or lien of which the buyer has no knowledge when the contract was made. This warranty of title applies unless the merchant specifically disclaims it. In this situation, both the implied warranty of merchantability and the implied warranty of title apply. The implied warranty of fitness for a particular purpose is created only when a seller has reason to know the buyer's particular purpose and knows the buyer is relying on the skill and judgment of the seller selecting the goods.

17.   (a)   The implied warranty of merchantability applies only when the seller is a merchant with respect to the type of goods being sold. The seller must be a merchant in order for the buyer to successfully sue under this warranty. Answer (b) is incorrect because the buyer does not have to prove negligence to be able to recover under this implied warranty. Answer (c) is incorrect because the implied warranty of merchantability extends to parties other than the purchaser even without privity of contract. Answer (d) is incorrect because an action for a breach based on the warranty of merchantability would not depend on the outcome of an action based on strict liability.

18.   (b)   The implied warranty of fitness for a particular purpose is created when a seller (merchant or nonmerchant) has reason to know the buyer's particular purpose and knows the buyer is relying on the skill and judgment of the seller selecting the goods. Since the warranty of fitness for a particular purpose is an implied warranty, there is no requirement that it be made in writing.

19.   (a)   The implied warranty of merchantability may be disclaimed by a seller's oral or written statement. This statement normally must contain some form of the word "merchantability" to be effective. However, goods sold "as is" or "with all faults" are an exception to that rule. Answer (b) is incorrect because the implied warranty of merchantability arises whenever the seller is a merchant with respect to the goods being sold. The status of the buyer is irrelevant. Answer (c) is incorrect because the implied warranty of merchantability guarantees that the goods are of an average fair quality and are fit for ordinary purposes. Under this warranty, the seller does not guarantee that the goods are fit for all purposes for which the buyer intends to use the goods. Answer (d) is incorrect because this warranty is always implied if the seller is a merchant. It does not have to be a part of the basis of the bargain to be binding on the seller.

B.3. Strict Liability

20. (b)   Common carriers' liability is based on strict liability. As such, the common carrier is liable for losses to property whether or not the common carrier was negligent. Common law exceptions to strict liability include natural disasters which are responsible for damages.

21. (d)   Under the theory of strict liability, the plaintiff must establish the following: (1) the seller was engaged in the business of selling the product, (2) the product was defective, (3) the defect was unreasonably dangerous to the plaintiff, and (4) the defect caused injury to the plaintiff. If the plaintiff can prove these elements, then the seller will be liable regardless of whether the seller was negligent or at fault for the defect. Thus, High can recover even if he cannot show any negligence was involved. Answer (a) is incorrect because contributory negligence is not an available defense in a strict liability case. Answer (b) is incorrect because the manufacturer's only defenses are misuse and assumption of risk by the buyer. The fact that the manufacturer followed the custom of the industry is irrelevant under strict liability. Answer (c) is incorrect because privity of contract is not a defense under strict liability since the suit is not based on contract law.

22. (d)   Under the theory of strict liability, the plaintiff must establish the following: (1) the seller was engaged in the business of selling the product, (2) the product was defective when sold, (3) the defect was unreasonably dangerous to the plaintiff, and (4) the defect caused injury to the plaintiff. If the plaintiff can prove these elements, then the seller will be liable regardless of whether the seller was negligent or at fault for the defect.

23. (d)   The standard of care required for a common carrier bailee is based on strict liability rather than reasonable care. Common carrier bailees, however, are not liable for acts of God, acts of the shipper, or acts of a public enemy. In this case, the improper packing was done by the party doing the shipping. Answer (a) is incorrect because acts or theft by other parties make the common carrier liable. Answer (b) is incorrect because acts such as negligence, by others, still leave the common carrier liable. Answer (c) is incorrect because acts of a railroad employee cause the common carrier to be liable.

C. Transfer of Property Rights

24. (c)   Since Rio was a good-faith purchaser, Rio obtains good title to the rocking chair. Therefore, the remedy that Tillis has left is to sue McGraw for money damages. There are insufficient facts to show fraud.

25. (d)   If a person entrusts possession of goods to a merchant who normally deals in that type of goods, a good-faith purchaser obtains title to those goods. Jake purchased the bike as he was unaware that Pete did not own the bike. As a good-faith purchaser, he obtains title to the bike. Answer (a) is incorrect because Yancie cannot repossess the bike from Jake because Jake obtained good title to the bike. Yancie can, however, get the value of the bike from Pete. Answer (b) is incorrect because Jake obtains title to the bike

and, thus, Pete cannot repossess it from him. Answer (c) is incorrect because Yancie can recover the value of the bike from Pete, not Jake.

26. (b)   A requirement needed for the title of goods to pass to the buyer is that the goods must have been identified to the contract. Answers (a) and (c) are incorrect because the seller can keep possession of goods and identify them to the contract and still have title pass to the buyer. Answer (d) is incorrect because title passes to the buyer based upon the terms of the agreement. Payment can take place before or after.

D. Risk of Loss and Title

27. (c)   In an FOB place of shipment contract, the buyer obtains the risk of loss once the goods are delivered to the carrier.

28. (d)   The title of goods generally passes to the buyer when the seller completes performance with respect to the physical delivery of the goods. Because the shipping terms of the contract are FOB Parco's warehouse, the title of goods passes to Parco on tender at the destination. This is true even if the goods are nonconforming. However, Parco's rejection of the appliances will revert the title of the goods back to Lace at the time of the rejection.

29. (a)   Under the Sales Article of the Uniform Commercial Code and the United Nations Convention for the International Sale of Goods, generally the risk of loss of the goods sold will pass to the buyer when the seller delivers goods to the first carrier for transmission to the buyer. Answers (b), (c), and (d) are incorrect because these would result in risk of loss to the buyer only if the contract specifically stated so, thus changing the general rule.

30. (c)   The purchase of goods on a sale on approval allows the buyer to return the goods even if they conform to the contract. Therefore, the seller retains the title and the risk of loss until the buyer accepts the goods.

31. (d)   Risk of loss transfers from a merchant seller to a buyer upon the buyer's physical receipt of goods. Therefore, neither tender of the goods at the seller's place of business, nor use of the seller's truck to deliver the goods are events which transfer risk of loss to the buyer as the merchant seller still retains possession of the goods.

32. (d)   The UCC places risk of loss on the breaching party. Since Cey shipped nonconforming goods, it breached the contract and would have risk of loss until the nonconforming goods were accepted by the buyer or until the goods were cured by Cey. Since Deck rejected the goods and Cey did not cure the goods, risk of loss remained with Cey. Shipping terms have no bearing on risk of loss in this situation because the goods did not conform to the contract. Answer (a) is incorrect because Deck would only bear risk of loss if the goods conformed to the contract. Answer (b) is incorrect because the risk of loss was never transferred to Deck since the goods were nonconforming. Answer (c) is incorrect because if the goods were conforming, risk of loss would pass to Deck at Cey's warehouse based on the shipping terms "FOB Cey's warehouse."

33.   **(b)**   The parties to the contract may agree as to which party bears risk of loss. In the absence of this, under the UCC, the shipping terms determine who bears risk of loss.

34.   **(a)**   In this situation, since Wool is not a merchant seller, the risk of loss passed to Bond on Wool's tender of delivery. If Wool had been a merchant seller, then the risk of loss would not have passed until the buyer received the goods. Answers (c) and (d) are incorrect because the risk of loss passed when the nonmerchant seller (Wool) tendered delivery of the painting. Answer (b) is incorrect because the risk of loss would not pass at the time the contract was formed since the seller still had possession of the painting and had not attempted to deliver it to the buyer.

35.   **(b)**   Common carriers are not liable for losses due to causes deemed acts of God. Although a common carrier may limit its damages to a dollar amount specified in the contract, it is not liable at all in this case. Funston, not the customer, had the risk of loss due to the FOB terms.

E.5. Seller's Remedies

36.   **(b)**   Statement I is incorrect because a liquidated damages provision is enforced if it is not punitive but amounts to a reasonable estimate of what the loss will be in the event of a breach of contract. If a reasonable estimate of the loss from a breach of contract cannot be estimated with a reasonable degree of certainty, the parties can agree on an amount, but still the amount cannot be punitive. Statement II is correct because a seller is allowed to retain a deposit of up to $500 when a buyer defaults even if the parties had not agreed to a liquidated damages clause.

37.   **(b)**   The seller generally discharges his obligation to the buyer by placing conforming goods at the buyer's disposition and giving the buyer reasonable notice to enable the buyer to take delivery.

38.   **(a)**   Under the Sales Article of the UCC, the seller has the following remedies against the buyer upon breach: withhold delivery of the goods; stop delivery of the carrier of the goods; resell the goods; recover compensatory and incidental damages; recover the goods from the buyer upon the buyer's insolvency; cancel the contract. Therefore, answer (a) is correct as the seller has the rights of contract cancellation and damage recovery available to him/her.

39.   **(a)**   The UCC gives the seller a choice of many remedies when the buyer breaches the contract involving a sale of goods. These remedies include allowing the seller to resell the goods identified to the contract and to recover the amount that the seller receives that is less than the contract price. Also, once the buyer breaches, the seller may suspend his/her performance and may prevent the carrier from making the delivery of the goods.

40.   **(b)**   A seller has the right to resell goods to another if the buyer refuses to accept the goods upon delivery. Answer (a) is incorrect because specific performance is not a remedy available to the seller. Baker cannot force Lazur to accept the word processor. Answer (c) is incorrect because Baker has a couple of additional remedies available. Baker can recover the full contract price plus incidental damages if he is unable to resell the identified goods. Alternatively, if the difference between the market value and contract price is inadequate to place Baker in as good a position as perfor-

mance would have, then Baker can sue for lost profits plus incidental damages. Answer (d) is incorrect because Baker could sue for consequential damages that Lazur had reason to know Baker would incur as a result of Lazur's breach.

41.   **(a)**   By advising Mazur on June 1 that it would not accept or pay for the wheat, Good has engaged in anticipatory repudiation. Anticipatory repudiation occurs when a party renounces the duty to perform the contract before the party's obligation to perform arises. Anticipatory repudiation discharges the nonrepudiating party (Mazur) from the contract and allows this party to sue for breach immediately. In this situation, Mazur could successfully sue Good for the difference between the resale price and the contract price on June 2. Answer (b) is incorrect because Mazur was discharged from the contract on June 1 and would not have to wait until after June 23 to resell the wheat. Answer (c) is incorrect because Good would only be allowed to retract its anticipatory breach if Mazur had ignored this breach and awaited performance at the appointed date. Answer (d) is incorrect because specific performance is only allowed for unique goods or for other situations in which monetary damages are not appropriate.

E.6. Buyer's Remedies

42.   **(c)**   Pickens has committed an anticipatory breach of contract. Thus, Crocket, as the aggrieved party, has different options. Crocket may treat it as a present breach of contract with the remedies available for breach of contract. One of these remedies is that the aggrieved party (Crocket) may cancel the contract. Another option is that Crocket may wait for a reasonable time to see if Pickens will change his/her mind and still deliver.

43.   **(b)**   The buyer has the following remedies against the seller: upon receipt of nonconforming goods, the buyer may reject the goods, accept the goods, or accept any unit and reject the remainder; the buyer has the right to cover (purchase goods elsewhere upon the seller's breach); the buyer may recover damages (not punitive) for nondelivery of goods or repudiation of the sales contract by the seller; the buyer may recover damages (not punitive) for breach in regard to accepted goods; the buyer may recover goods identified in the contract in possession of the seller upon the seller's insolvency; the buyer may sue for specific performance when the goods are unique; the buyer has the right of replevin (form of legal action to recover specific goods from the seller which are being withheld from the buyer wrongfully); the buyer can cancel the contract; the buyer has a security interest in the goods after the seller's breach; the buyer can recover liquidated damages.

44.   **(d)**   UCC Section 2-719(3) states that a limitation of damages for personal injury **in the case of consumer goods** is considered to be unconscionable and thus not allowed. Although limitations of damages for personal injury in the case of nonconsumer goods can be allowed, answer (d) is correct since one limits "personal injury" to the stove which was apparently being used for consumer use in this fact pattern. Answer (a) is incorrect because under the UCC, the spouse, being a member of the household expecting to use the stove, may recover for damages. Answer (b) is incorrect because Larch was notified shortly after the explosion. This notice, however, was not required. Answer (c) is incorrect because even though the disclaimer did not disclaim all liability, it did attempt to disclaim personal injury. This disclaimer for personal injuries, however, is not allowed for the reasons mentioned above. Answer (d) is chosen as being more specific than answer (c).

45. (d) Either party in a sales contract under the Sales Article of the UCC may demand adequate assurance of performance when reasonable grounds for insecurity exist with respect to the performance of the other party. Refusal to give written assurance will release the other party from all obligations from the sales contract. Answer (a) is incorrect because the buyer has assumed the risk of loss. Answer (b) is incorrect because a seller may substitute another reasonable delivery method if the method of delivery specified in the contract has been made impracticable. A seller may recover damages based on a buyer's repudiation of the agreement, but here the repudiation has been retracted and the obligations of buyer and seller remain intact.

46. (c) The Sales Article of the UCC provides that a buyer has the right to reject goods which are not in conformity with the terms of contract between seller and buyer. The buyer also has the option to accept nonconforming goods and recover damages resulting from the nonconformity. The UCC allows the buyer to inspect the goods before payment except when they are shipped COD. When goods are shipped COD, the buyer's payment for the goods is required for delivery.

E.7. Statute of Limitations

47. (c) The statute of limitations for the sale of goods is generally four years; however, the parties may agree to reduce the statute to a period of not less than one year. Therefore, Sklar will lose because the clause providing that the statute of limitations would be limited to eighteen months is enforceable, and the action was not brought within the required time period. Answer (b) is incorrect because a breach of warranty occurs upon the tender of delivery, not upon the discovery of the defect, and the statute begins running at the time the breach occurs. Answer (d) is incorrect because the statute is eighteen months as outlined in the contract.

OTHER OBJECTIVE ANSWERS AND ANSWER EXPLANATIONS

Problem 1

1.   (C) Angler breached the contract by shipping nonconforming goods to Mason. Therefore, Angler retains the risk of loss until it cures or until Mason accepts the goods despite the nonconformity.

2.   (I) This was an FOB shipping point contract so that the risk of loss would have passed over to the buyer upon delivery to the carrier.

3.   (I) Because the terms were FOB the seller's loading dock, it was an FOB shipping point contract.

4.   (I) Title and risk of loss do not necessarily pass to a buyer at the same time. In this case, risk of loss remained with the seller because of the shipment of nonconforming goods. However, title passed under the original terms despite the breach of contract.

5.   (C) Classic is obligated to follow any reasonable instructions of the seller as a merchant who rejects goods, even nonconforming, under a contract.

6.   (I) Classic must follow the reasonable instructions given by Angler to return the peaches at Angler's expense.

7.   (I) Classic may also sue for any damages that were caused by the delay in shipping.

8.   (I) Although the contract must be evidenced by a writing because it involved a sale of goods for more than $500, the correspondence that Regal sent to Angler on October 29 satisfies the writing requirement under the UCC Statute of Frauds. It indicated that a contract had been made. It was signed by Regal, the party to be charged, and it stated the quantity. The price was not needed in the correspondence.

9.   (C) The Uniform Commercial Code applies because the contract was for a sale of goods (i.e., hamburger meat).

10.   (C) The correspondence satisfies the UCC Statute of Frauds which does not require that all terms be in writing.

11.   (I) Angler should resort to an appropriate remedy such as reselling the hamburger to someone else in a commercially reasonable fashion. If Angler gets less than the original contract price, it may recover the difference from Regal.

12.   (I) Since there was no writing to evidence the contract for $1,500, it is not enforceable.

13.   (C) The contract need not be in writing because it was for less than $500.

14.   (C) Since Angler shipped and Regal accepted a portion of the goods, the oral contract is enforceable up to the amount shipped and accepted. This is one of the exceptions in the UCC Statute of Frauds.

15.   (I) The exception in the UCC Statute of Frauds allows the oral contract to be enforced up to the amount delivered and accepted or paid for.

Problem 2

1.   (A) The terms of the contract were "FOB seller's loading dock" which is a shipment contract. Answer (B) is incorrect because a destination contract would state terms meaning FOB buyer's location. Answer (C) is incorrect because a consignment is treated as a sale or return. That is, the owner of the goods delivers them to another party to attempt to sell them. If this other party, known as the consignee, does not sell the goods, they are returned. Such is not the case in this fact pattern.

2.   (C) Risk of loss would normally pass to the buyer, Axle Co., under this shipment contract. However, since the seller, Grand, breached the contract, risk of loss remains with Grand. Since the cabinets are "custom designed, kitchen cabinets" for a luxury condominium complex, they would need to match. Therefore, the 100 units could be construed as a commercial unit and the risk of loss for the entire 100 cabinets remained with Grand. Answer (A) is incorrect because the 100 cabinets were a commercial unit and thus the risk of loss of the entire commercial unit remained with Grand. Answer (B) is incorrect because even though the terms were "FOB seller's loading dock," the risk of loss remained with the seller, Grand, because of Grand's breach of contract.

3.   (B) The contract between Grand and Axle was voidable because Axle may at its option choose to accept or reject all or part of the cabinets. Answer (C) is incorrect because if the contract were void, neither party would have the option of remaining in the contract. Answer (A) is incorrect because under the UCC, if the delivery date is not stated, the time becomes within a reasonable time.

4.   (A) Once Grand ships nonconforming goods, a breach of contract has occurred. Answer (B) is incorrect because the breach has occurred even without Axle needing to reject the shipment. Axle then has the right to accept all, part, or none of the shipment. Answer (C) is incorrect because the shipment of nonconforming goods acts as a breach rather than a counteroffer.

5.   (A) Since the cabinets are unique and custom-designed, specific performance is allowed if Axle so chooses. Answer (B) is incorrect because Axle is not required to cover, especially because the cabinets are unique. Answer (C) is incorrect because punitive damages are generally not allowed for a breach of contract even if the breach is intentional.

ANSWER OUTLINE

Problem 1   Statute of Frauds under UCC; Firm Offer;
                Acceptance with Different Terms

a.   Rapid's claim is incorrect

    An oral contract between merchants under the UCC is binding even if the party that receives the confirmation fails to sign it

      Signature is only required of party that sends the confirmation

    Receiving party will not be bound if written objection to confirmation made within ten days of receipt

      Rapid did not make a written objection so will be bound to oral contract

b.   Debco's first claim is incorrect

    Debco's October 12 purchase order is a firm offer under the UCC because:

      • Debco is merchant

      • Purchase order is written and signed

      • Purchase order states it will not be withdrawn for time specified

    A firm offer cannot be revoked

      Debco's October 25 attempt will be ineffective

    Debco's second claim is incorrect

    Acceptance of an offer is effective when sent if using a reasonable method

      TMI's acceptance was effective when mailed on October 31

    Debco's third claim is incorrect

    Acceptance is effective even if terms are different from offer if expression to accept is definite

      TMI's October 31 acceptance was effective despite additional payment terms

UNOFFICIAL ANSWER

Problem 1   Statute of Frauds under UCC; Firm Offer;
                Acceptance with Different Terms

a.   Rapid's claim is incorrect. Both Debco and Rapid are merchants under the UCC because they both deal in the type of goods involved in the transaction (computers).

The UCC provides that a confirmation satisfies the UCC Statute of Frauds, if an oral contract between merchants is

    •   Confirmed in writing within a reasonable period of time, and

    •   The confirmation is signed by the party sending it and received by the other party

Both parties are bound even though the party receiving the confirmation fails to sign it. This is correct unless the party receiving the confirmation submits a written objection within ten days of receipt. Rapid will be bound even though it did not sign the confirmation because no written objection was made.

b.   Debco's first claim, that its October 25 correspondence prevented the formation of a contract, is incorrect. Debco's October 12 purchase order will be regarded as a firm offer under the UCC because:

    •   Debco is a merchant.

    •   The purchase order is in writing and signed.

    •   The purchase order states that it will not be withdrawn for the time specified.

Because Debco's October 12 purchase order is considered a firm offer, Debco cannot revoke it, and its October 25 attempt to do so is ineffective.

Debco's second claim, that TMI's October 31 correspondence is not an effective acceptance because it was not received until November 3, is incorrect. An acceptance of an offer is effective when dispatched (in this case, when mailed), provided that an appropriate mode of communication is used. The UCC provides that an offer shall be construed as inviting acceptance in any manner and by any medium reasonable in the circumstances. In this case, Debco made its offer by mail, which, if adequately addressed with proper postage affixed, would be considered a reasonable manner and medium for acceptance. As a result, TMI's acceptance was effective when mailed on October 31.

Debco's third claim, that TMI's acceptance is not effective because it added payment terms to Debco's offer, is also incorrect. The UCC provides that a definite and timely expression of acceptance of an offer will form a contract, even if the terms of the acceptance are different from those in the offer, unless acceptance is expressly made conditional on accepting the different terms. Therefore, TMI's October 31 correspondence, which expressly stated that TMI would ship the computers ordered by Debco, was an effective acceptance, and a contract was formed despite the fact that TMI added payment terms.

COMMERCIAL PAPER

Overview

Commercial paper is heavily tested on the CPA exam. Coverage includes the types of negotiable instruments, the requirements of negotiability, negotiation, the holder in due course concept, defenses, and the rights of parties to a negotiable instrument. The functions of commercial paper are to provide a medium of exchange that is readily transferable like money and to provide an extension of credit. It is easier to transfer than contract rights and not subject to as many defenses as contracts are. To be negotiable, an instrument must

a. Be written
b. Be signed by the maker or drawer
c. Contain an unconditional promise or order to pay
d. State a fixed amount in money
e. Be payable on demand or at definite time
f. Be payable to order or bearer

These requirements must be present on the face of the instrument. Instruments that do not comply with these provisions are nonnegotiable and are transferable only by assignment. The assignee of a nonnegotiable instrument takes it subject to all defenses.

A central theme of exam questions on negotiable instruments is the liability of the primary parties and of the secondarily liable parties under various fact situations. Similar questions in different form emphasize the rights that a holder of a negotiable instrument has against primary and secondary parties. Your review of this area should emphasize the legal liability arising upon execution of negotiable commercial paper, the legal liability arising upon various types of endorsements, and the warranty liabilities of various parties upon transfer or presentment for payment. A solid understanding of the distinction between real and personal defenses is required. Also tested is the relationship between a bank and its customers.

A. General Concepts of Commercial Paper

1. Commercial paper has two important functions

    a. Used as a substitute for money

        EXAMPLE: *One often pays a bill with a check instead of using cash.*

    b. Used as extension of credit

        EXAMPLE: *X gives a promissory note to Y for $100 that is due one year later.*

2. To encourage commercial paper to be transferred more easily by making it easier to be collected, **negotiable** commercial paper was established

    a. If an instrument is negotiable, favorable laws of Article 3 of UCC apply as discussed in this module

    b. If an instrument is nonnegotiable, laws of ordinary contract law apply (i.e., assignment of contract rights)

        (1) Assignees of contract rights can get only the rights given by the assignor and therefore are burdened by any defenses between prior parties

        EXAMPLE: *C receives a nonnegotiable instrument from B. C now wishes to collect from A, the one who had issued the nonnegotiable note to B when he purchased some goods from B. Assume that A would have owed B only two-thirds of the amount stated on the instrument due to defects in the goods. Since C obtained only the rights that B had under an assignment under contract law, C can only collect two-thirds from A on this nonnegotiable instrument.*

3. It is helpful to get "the big picture" of negotiable instruments (negotiable commercial paper) before covering details

    a. Whether an instrument is negotiable or not is determined by looking at its form and content on the face of the instrument

        (1) This is so that individuals seeing an instrument can determine whether it is negotiable or not

        (2) If a person has a negotiable instrument and also is a holder in due course (discussed later), s/he may collect on instrument despite most defenses that may be raised such as contract defenses

B. Types of Commercial Paper

1. Article 3 of UCC describes two types of negotiable commercial paper

    a. A draft (also called bill of exchange)

(1) Has three parties in which one person or entity (drawer) orders another (drawee) to pay a third party (payee) a sum of money

EXAMPLE:

June 5, 2002

On June 5, 2003, pay to the order of Bob Smith $1,000 plus 10% annual interest from June 5, 2002.

To: ABC Corporation

(Signed) Sue Van Deventer

The above is a draft in which Sue Van Deventer is the drawer, ABC Corporation is the drawee, and Bob Smith is the payee

  (a) A check

    1] Is a special type of draft that is payable on demand (unless postdated) and drawee must be a bank

      a] Definition of bank includes savings and loan associations, credit unions, and trust companies

    2] One writing check is drawer (and customer of drawee bank)

b. A note (also called a promissory note)

  (1) Unlike a draft or check, is a two-party instrument

    (a) One party is called the maker—this party promises to pay a specified sum of money to another party called the payee

EXAMPLE:

July 10, 2002

I promise to pay to the order of Becky Hoger $5,000 plus 10% annual interest on July 10, 2003.

(Signed) Bill Jones

The above is a note in which Bill Jones is the maker and Becky Hoger is the payee.

  (2) May be payable on demand or at a definite time

    (a) Certificate of deposit (CD)

      1] Is an acknowledgment by a financial institution of receipt of money and promise to repay it

        a] Most CDs are commercial paper so that they can be easily transferred

      2] Is actually a special type of note in which financial institution is the maker

C. Requirements of Negotiability

1. All of the following requirements must be on face of instrument for it to be a negotiable instrument (be sure to know these)
2. To be negotiable, the instrument must

  a. Be written
  b. Be signed by maker or drawer
  c. Contain an unconditional promise or order to pay
  d. State a fixed amount in money
  e. Be payable on demand or at a definite time
  f. Be payable to order or to bearer, unless it is a check

3. Details of requirements of negotiability

   a. **Must be in writing**

   (1) Satisfied by printing, typing, handwriting or any other reduction to physical form that is relatively permanent and portable

   b. **Must be signed by maker (of a note or CD) or drawer (of a draft or check)**

   (1) Signature includes any symbol used with intent to authenticate instrument

      (a) Rubber stamp, initials, letterhead satisfy signing requirement
      (b) Assumed name or trade name operates as that party's signature
      (c) Signature may be anywhere on face of instrument

   c. **Must contain an unconditional promise or order to pay**

   (1) If payment depends upon (is subject to) another agreement or event, then it is conditional and therefore destroys negotiability

   EXAMPLE: An instrument that is otherwise negotiable states that it is subject to a particular contract. This condition destroys the negotiability of this instrument.

   EXAMPLE: An instrument states: "I, Janice Jones, promise to pay to the order of Richard Riley, $1,000 if the stereo delivered to me is not defective." This instrument is not negotiable whether the stereo is defective or not because it contains a conditional promise.

      (a) However, the following are permitted and do not destroy negotiability

         1] Instrument may state its purpose

         EXAMPLE: On a check, the drawer writes "for purchase of textbooks."

         2] Instrument may refer to or state that it arises from another agreement
         3] Instrument is permitted to show that it is secured by a mortgage or by collateral
         4] Instrument is permitted to contain promise to provide extra collateral
         5] Instrument is permitted to limit payment out of particular fund

   (2) An IOU is not a promise or order to pay but an acknowledgement of debt, thus, an IOU is not negotiable

   d. **Must state a fixed amount in money—called sum certain under former law**

   (1) Amount of principal but not interest must be determinable from instrument without need to refer to other sources

      (a) Stated interest rates are allowed because amount can be calculated

         EXAMPLE: A negotiable note states that $1,000 is due one year from October 1, 2001 at 14% interest.

         EXAMPLE: A note states that $1,000 is payable on demand and bears interest at 14%. This also is negotiable because once payment is demanded, the amount of interest can be calculated.

         1] Variable interest rates are allowed and do not now destroy negotiability even if formula for interest rate or amount requires reference to information outside of negotiable instrument

         EXAMPLE: The following do not destroy negotiability in an otherwise negotiable instrument: Interest rates tied to some published key interest rate, consumer index market rate, etc.

         2] If interest rate based on legal rate or judgment rate (fixed by statute), then negotiability not destroyed

      (b) Stated different rates of interest before and after default or specified dates are allowed
      (c) Stated discounts or additions if instrument paid before or after payment dates do not destroy negotiability
      (d) Clauses allowing collection costs and attorney's fees upon default are allowed because they reduce the risk of holding instruments and promote transferability
      (e) Must be payable only in money

1] Option to be payable in money or something else destroys negotiability because of possibility that payment will not be in money

EXAMPLE: A note is payable in $1,000 or its equivalent in gold. This note is not negotiable.

2] Foreign currency is acceptable even though reference to exchange rates may be needed due to international trade realities

e. **Must be payable on demand or at a definite time**

(1) On demand includes

(a) Payable on sight
(b) Payable on presentation
(c) No time for payment stated

(2) It is a definite time if payable

(a) On a certain date, or
(b) A fixed period after sight, or
(c) Within a certain time, or
(d) On a certain date subject to acceleration

1] For example, when a payment is missed, total balance may become due at once

(e) On a certain date subject to an extension of time if

1] At option of holder, or
2] At option of maker or drawer only if extension is limited to a definite amount of time

(3) It is not definite if payable on an act or event that is not certain as to time of occurrence

EXAMPLE: An instrument contains a clause stating that it is payable ten days after drawer obtains a bank loan. This destroys negotiability.

f. **Must be payable to order or to bearer unless it is a check (these are magic words of negotiability and are often a central issue on the CPA exam)**

(1) Instrument is payable to order if made payable to the order of

(a) Any person, including the maker, drawer, drawee, or payee
(b) Two persons together or alternatively
(c) Any entity

(2) Instrument is also payable to order if it is payable "to A or order"
(3) Instrument other than a check is not payable to order if it is only payable to a person (e.g., "Pay John Doe")

EXAMPLE: A draft that is otherwise negotiable states: "Pay to XYZ Corporation." This statement destroys negotiability because the draft is not payable "to the order of" XYZ Corporation.

(a) It is not negotiable
(b) "Pay to the order of John Doe" would be negotiable

(4) If a **check** says "pay to A," it is negotiable order paper—this is not true of other instruments
(5) Instrument is payable to bearer if it is payable to

(a) "Bearer"
(b) "Cash"
(c) "A person or bearer" is bearer paper if "bearer" handwritten

1] However, "pay to John Doe, the bearer" is not negotiable because it is not payable to order or to bearer but to a person and simply refers to him as the bearer

(d) "Order of bearer" or "order of cash"
(e) Pay to the order of (payee left blank) is bearer paper unless holder inserts payee's name

(6) Instrument cannot be made payable to persons consecutively (i.e., maker cannot specify subsequent holders)

D. Interpretation of Ambiguities in Negotiable Instruments

1. Contradictory terms

    a. Words control over figures
    b. Handwritten terms control over typewritten and printed (typeset) terms
    c. Typewritten terms control over printed (typeset) terms

2. Omissions

    a. Omission of date does not destroy negotiability unless date necessary to determine when payable

        EXAMPLE: A check is not dated. It is still negotiable because a check is payable on demand.

        EXAMPLE: A draft states that it is payable thirty days after its date. If the date is left off, it is not payable at a definite time and, therefore, it is not negotiable.

    b. Omission of interest rate is allowed because the judgment rate of interest (rate used on a court judgment) is automatically used
    c. Statement of consideration or where instrument is drawn or payable not required

3. Other issues

    a. Instrument may be postdated or antedated and remain negotiable

        (1) A bank may pay postdated check before date on check unless drawer notifies bank to defer payment

    b. Instrument may have a provision that by endorsing or cashing it, the payee acknowledges full satisfaction of debt and remain negotiable
    c. If an instrument is payable to order of more than one person

        (1) Either payee may negotiate or enforce it if payable to him/her in the alternative

            EXAMPLE: "Pay $100 to the order of X or Y." Either X or Y may endorse it.

        (2) All payees must negotiate or enforce it if **not** payable to them in the alternative

    d. If not clear whether instrument is draft or note, holder may treat it as either

E. Negotiation

1. There are two methods of transferring commercial paper

    a. By assignment

        (1) Assignment occurs when transfer does not meet all requirements of negotiation
        (2) Assignee can obtain only same rights that assignor had

    b. By negotiation

        (1) One receiving negotiable instrument by negotiation is called a holder
        (2) If holder further qualifies as a holder in due course (as discussed later) s/he can obtain **more rights** than what transferor had
        (3) There are two methods of negotiation

            (a) Negotiating order paper requires both endorsement by transferor and delivery of instrument

                1] Order paper includes negotiable instruments made payable to the order of X

            (b) Negotiating bearer paper may be accomplished by delivery alone (endorsement not necessary)

                EXAMPLE: A check is made payable to the order of cash.

          1] Subsequent parties may require endorsements (even though UCC does not) for identification

          2] Holder may, in any event, endorse it if s/he chooses to do so

    (4) Endorsement (Indorsement) refers to signature of payee, drawee, accommodation endorser, or holder

2. Types of endorsements

    a. Blank endorsement

        (1) Does not specify any endorsee

           EXAMPLE: A check made to the order of M on the front can be endorsed in blank by M writing only his signature on the back.

        (2) Converts order paper into bearer paper

        (3) Note that bearer paper may be negotiated by mere delivery

           EXAMPLE: B endorses a check in blank that had been made payable to his order. He lost it and C found it who delivered it to D. D is a valid holder since C's endorsement was not required.

    b. Special endorsement

        (1) Indicates specific person to whom endorsee wishes to negotiate instrument

           EXAMPLE: On the back of a check payable to the order of M. Jordan he signs as follows: Pay to L. Smith, (signed) M. Jordan.

          (a) Note that words "pay to the order of" are not required on back as endorsements—instrument need be payable to order or to bearer on front only

          (b) Also, note that if instrument is not payable to order or to bearer on its face, it **cannot** be turned into a negotiable instrument by using these words in an endorsement on the back

             EXAMPLE: A particular instrument would have been negotiable except that on the front it was payable to A. On the back, A signed it. "Pay to the order of B, (signed) A." This does not convert it into a negotiable instrument.

        (2) Bearer paper may be converted into order paper by use of special endorsement

           EXAMPLE: A check made out to cash is delivered to Carp. Carp writes on the back; Pay to Durn, (signed) Carp. It was bearer paper until this special endorsement.

           EXAMPLE: Continuing the previous example, Durn simply endorses it in blank. The check is bearer paper again.

        (3) If last (or only) endorsement on instrument is a blank endorsement, any holder may convert that bearer paper into order paper by writing "Pay to X," etc., above that blank endorsement

    c. Restrictive endorsement

        (1) Requires endorsees to comply with certain conditions

           EXAMPLE: Endorsement reads "For deposit only, (signed) A. Bell."

           EXAMPLE: Another endorsement reads "Pay to X only if X completes work to my satisfaction on my car within three days of the date on this check, (signed) A." Neither X nor any subsequent holder can enforce payment until this condition has been met.

        (2) Note that conditions in restrictive endorsements do not destroy negotiability even though conditions placed on front of instruments do destroy negotiability because they create conditional promises or orders to pay

        (3) Endorsements cannot prohibit subsequent negotiation

           EXAMPLE: Above her endorsement, M wrote: "Pay to N only." This indicates that N is the new endorsee but does not stop further negotiation after N when N endorses.

    d. Qualified endorsement

        (1) Normally, endorser, upon signing, promises automatically to pay holder or any subsequent endorser amount of instrument if it is later dishonored

        (2) Qualified endorsement disclaims this liability

EXAMPLE: Ann Knolls endorses "Without recourse, (signed) Ann Knolls."

 (3) Qualified endorsements, otherwise, have same effects as other endorsements

 (4) Combinations of endorsements occur

  (a) Special qualified endorsement

EXAMPLE: "Pay to Pete Bell without recourse, (signed) Tom Lack." Tom Lack has limited his liability and also Pete Bell's endorsement is needed to negotiate this instrument further.

  (b) Blank qualified endorsement

EXAMPLE: "Without recourse, (signed) D. Hamilton."

  (c) Endorsement that is restrictive, qualified, and blank

EXAMPLE: "For deposit only, without recourse, (signed) Bill Coffey."

  (d) Endorsement that is restrictive, qualified, and special

EXAMPLE: "Pay to X if she completes work today, without recourse, (signed) D. Magee."

3. If payee's name misspelled, s/he may endorse in proper spelling or misspelling or both

 a. But endorsee may require both

4. If an order instrument is transferred for value without endorsement, transferee may require endorsement from transferor

 a. Upon obtaining endorsement, will become a holder

5. Recent federal law standardizes endorsements on checks—now endorser should turn check over (just like before) and sign in the 1 ½ inch portion of check next to short edge

 a. Purpose is to avoid interference with bank's endorsements

 b. Endorsements placed outside this area do not destroy negotiability but may delay clearing process.

6. If check has statement that it is nonnegotiable, not governed by Article 3, etc., check is still negotiable

 a. This is not true of other negotiable instruments whereby such statements destroy negotiability

F. Holder in Due Course

1. Concept of **holder in due course** (also called **HDC**) is very important for CPA exam purposes. A HDC is entitled to payment on negotiable instrument **despite most defenses** that maker or drawer of instrument may have

 a. Recall that an assignee of contract rights receives only rights that assignor had (i.e., assignee takes subject to all defenses that could have been asserted against assignor)

 b. Likewise, an ordinary holder of a negotiable instrument has same rights as assignee

2. To be holder in due course, a taker of instrument must

 a. Be a **holder** of a properly negotiated negotiable instrument

 b. Give **value** for instrument

  (1) Holder gives value if s/he

   (a) Pays or performs agreed consideration

    1] An executory promise (promise to give value in the future) is not value until performed

   (b) Takes as a satisfaction of a previous existing debt

   (c) Gives another negotiable instrument

   (d) Acquires a security interest in the instrument (e.g., the holder takes possession of the instrument as collateral for another debt)

  (2) A bank takes for value to the extent that credit has been given for a deposit and withdrawn

(a) FIFO method is used to determine whether it has been withdrawn (money is considered to be withdrawn from an account in the order in which it was deposited)

(3) Value does not have to be for full amount of instrument;

(a) Purchase at a discount is value for full face amount of instrument provided HDC took in good faith (i.e., as long as not too large a discount)

EXAMPLE: Purchase of a $1,000 instrument in good faith for $950 is considered full value, but purchase of the same instrument for $500 is not considered full value when market conditions show that the discount is excessive.

EXAMPLE: Handy purchases a negotiable note that has a face value of $1,000. She gives $600 in cash now and agrees to pay $350 in one week. Handy has given value only to the extent of $600 and thus can qualify as a HDC for $600. Once she pays the remaining $350, she qualifies as a HDC for the full $1,000. Note that even though she paid only $950, she has HDC status for the entire $1,000 because it was a reasonable discount.

c. Take in **good faith**

(1) Good faith defined as honesty in fact and observance of reasonable commercial standards of fair dealing

d. Take **without notice** that it is overdue, has been dishonored, or that any person has a defense or claim to it

(1) Holder has notice when s/he knows or has reason to know (measured by objective "reasonable person" standard)
(2) Overdue

EXAMPLE: H acquires a note or draft that is three weeks past the due date on the instrument.

(a) Instrument not overdue if default is on payment of interest only
(b) Domestic check, although payable on demand, is overdue ninety days after its date

(3) Defense or claim

(a) Obvious signs of forgery or alteration so as to call into question its authenticity
(b) Incomplete or irregular
(c) If purchaser has notice of any party's claim or that all parties have been discharged

(4) There is no notice of a defense or claim if

(a) It is antedated or postdated
(b) S/he knows that there has been a default in payment of interest

(5) But if one acquires notice **after** becoming a holder and giving value, s/he may still be a HDC

(a) That is, once one is a HDC, acquiring notice does not end HDC status

3. Payee of a negotiable instrument may qualify as a HDC if meets all requirements

G. Rights of a Holder in Due Course (HDC)

1. The general rule is that a transfer of a negotiable instrument to a HDC cuts off all **personal defenses** against a HDC

a. Personal defenses are assertable against ordinary holders and assignees of contract rights to avoid payment

EXAMPLE: Art Dobbs negotiates a note to Mary Price in payment of a stereo. Mary negotiates this note to D. Finch who qualifies as a HDC. When Finch seeks payment, Dobbs points out that Price breached the contract by never delivering the stereo. Finch, as a HDC, still has the right to collect because breach of contract is a personal defense. Dobbs then has to seek recourse directly against Price.

b. EXCEPTION—HDC takes subject to all personal defenses of person with whom HDC directly dealt

2. Some defenses are assertable against any party including a HDC—these defenses are called **real (or universal) defenses**

3. Types of **personal defenses**

    a. Breach of contract

        (1) Includes breach of warranty

    b. Lack or failure of consideration

    c. Prior payment

        EXAMPLE: Maker of a negotiable note pays on the note but does not keep or cancel the note. A subsequent party who qualifies as a HDC seeks to collect on this same note. Maker, having only a personal defense, must pay the HDC even though it was paid previously.

    d. Unauthorized completion

        EXAMPLE: X signs a check leaving the amount blank. He tells Y to fill in the amount necessary to buy a typewriter. Y fills in $22,000 and negotiates the check to a HDC. The HDC may enforce the full amount of the check against X.

    e. Fraud in the inducement

        (1) Occurs when person signs a negotiable instrument and knows what s/he is signing; however, s/he was induced into doing so by intentional misrepresentation

    f. Nondelivery

        (1) Occurs when bearer instrument is lost or stolen

        EXAMPLE: M issues a note that is bearer paper. It is stolen by T who sells it to a HDC. The HDC wins against M.

    g. Ordinary duress or undue influence

        (1) Most types of duress are considered a personal defense unless they become very extreme and thus are considered real defenses

        EXAMPLE: Signing a check based on fear of losing a real estate deal constitutes a personal defense.

    h. Mental incapacity

        (1) Personal defense if state law makes transaction voidable
        (2) Real defense if state law makes transaction void

    i. Illegality

        (1) Personal defense if state law makes transaction voidable
        (2) If state law makes it void, then real defense

    j. Theft by holder or subsequent holder after theft

4. **Real Defenses**

    a. Forgery

        (1) Forgery of maker's or drawer's signature does not act as his/her signature

            (a) Does allow forger to be held liable

            EXAMPLE: X forges M's name on a note and sells it to P. P cannot collect from M whether she is a HDC or not. Her recourse is against X.

    b. Bankruptcy

    c. Fraud in the execution

        (1) Occurs when a party is tricked into signing a negotiable instrument believing it to be something else

            (a) This defense will not apply if signer, based on his/her age, experience, etc., should have known what was happening

        (2) Recall that fraud in the inducement is a personal defense

    d. Minority (or infancy)

(1) When minor may disaffirm contract under state law, then is a real defense for a negotiable instrument

e. Mental incapacity, illegality, or extreme duress

(1) Real defenses if transaction is void under state law

f. Material alteration of instrument

(1) Is actually only partially a real defense

(a) If dollar amount was altered, then HDC can collect according to original terms—a non-HDC collects nothing

(b) If an instrument was incomplete originally and then completed without authorization, HDC can enforce it as completed—a non-HDC collects nothing

(2) Material alteration exists when terms between any two parties are changed in any way including

(a) Changes in amount, rate of interest, or days

1] Considered "material" even if small change such as a penny

EXAMPLE: Janice Parks negotiates a $200 negotiable note to Jim Bivins. Bivins deftly changes the amount to $500 and transfers it to E. Melvin for $500 who qualifies as a HDC. The HDC can collect only the original $200 from Janice Parks.

EXAMPLE: Same facts as before except that the material alteration is poorly done by Jim Bivins so that E. Melvin could not qualify as a holder in due course because the change was obvious. E. Melvin cannot collect even the original $200.

(b) Additions to writing or removal of part of instrument

(c) Completion of instrument without authorization

(d) But not material alteration if done to correct error on address or math computations, or to place marks on instrument for audit purposes

1] Alterations that are not material are neither real nor personal defenses so all non-HDCs as well as HDCs can enforce the instrument

(e) Not a real defense if maker's or drawer's negligence substantially contributed to the alteration—is a personal defense

5. Holder through a holder in due course

a. A party who does not qualify as a HDC but obtains a negotiable instrument from a HDC is called a holder through a holder in due course

b. Obtains all rights of a HDC

(1) Based on fact that is an assignee who gets rights of previous party

(2) Also called shelter provision

c. A HDC "washes" an instrument so that any holder thereafter can be a holder through a holder in due course

EXAMPLE: A HDC transfers a note to H.V. Shelter who knew that the maker of the note has a personal defense. Shelter does not qualify as a HDC but has the same rights because he is a holder through a holder in due course.

EXAMPLE: Extending the example, H.V. Shelter gives the note to B. Evans. B. Evans does not qualify as a HDC (no value given) but is a holder through a holder in due course.

d. Exceptions

(1) If a party reacquires an instrument, his/her status remains what it originally was

EXAMPLE: P acquires a check from the payee. Neither qualifies in this case as a holder in due course. P delivers the check to Q who qualifies as a HDC. If the check is negotiated back to P, his rights remain those of a non-HDC.

(2) One who was involved in fraud or illegality affecting the instrument may not become a holder through a holder in due course

6. FTC holder in due course rule

 a. Applies when seller of consumer goods or services receives a note from a consumer or arranges a loan with a bank, etc., for that consumer
 b. Requires seller or lender to put a notice on these negotiable instruments that all holders take subject to any defenses which debtor could assert against seller
 c. Note that rule does not apply to any nonconsumer transactions and does not apply to any consumer noncredit transactions

 EXAMPLE: Connie Consumer purchases goods for consumer use and writes out a check. Subsequent holders are governed by ordinary HDC law.

H. Liability of Parties—there are two general types of warranties on negotiable instruments: contractual liability and warranty liability

1. Contractual liability

 a. Refers to liability of any party who signs negotiable instrument as a maker, drawer, drawee, or endorser
 b. Maker of a note has **primary liability** that means s/he has absolute liability to pay according to note's terms until it is paid or until statute of limitations (period to sue) has run
 c. No party of a draft (or check) initially has primary liability because drawee has only been ordered to pay by drawer

 (1) Drawee's obligation is to drawer to follow order but has not promised to holder of the draft to pay
 (2) Drawee obtains primary liability if s/he accepts (certifies) draft which means s/he promises to holder to pay it when due

 (a) Often, holder may simply present draft for payment without asking for acceptance
 (b) Some drafts require acceptance before they are paid
 (c) Even if draft does not require it, holder may request acceptance (especially on a time draft before due date)

 d. Drawer has **secondary liability** on draft—s/he is liable only if drawee fails to pay
 e. Endorsers of note or draft have secondary liability—holder can hold endorser liable if primary parties obligated to make payment fail to pay and if following conditions met

 (1) Holder must demand payment or acceptance in a timely manner

 (a) This demand is called presentment
 (b) Presentment for payment must be on or before due date or within reasonable time for demand instruments

 1] For domestic checks, holder must present check for payment within thirty days of its date in order to hold drawer secondarily liable

 (2) Holder must give endorsers timely notice of dishonor (i.e., that note or draft was refused payment or acceptance)

 (a) For domestic checks, holder must present check for payment within thirty days of endorsement to hold endorser secondarily liable

 f. Drawers and endorsers may avoid secondary liability by signing without recourse
 g. Upon certification of check, drawer and all previous endorsers are discharged from liability because bank has accepted check and agreed to pay it

2. Warranty liability—two types under which holder can seek payment from secondary parties are transfer warranties and presentment warranties

 a. Transfer warranties—transferor gives following transfer warranties whenever negotiable instrument is transferred for consideration

 (1) Transferor has good title
 (2) All signatures are genuine or authorized

(3) Instrument has not been materially altered

(4) No defense of any party is good against transferor

(5) Transferor has no notice of insolvency of maker, drawer, or acceptor

b. These warranties generally give loss to parties that dealt face to face with wrongdoer and thus were in best position to prevent or avoid forged, altered, or stolen instruments

(1) Party bearing loss must then seek payment if possible, from one who forged, altered, or stole instrument

c. Note that transferor, if s/he did not endorse, makes all five warranties only to immediate transferee but if transferor did endorse, makes them to all subsequent holders taking in good faith

d. Presentment warranties—holder presenting negotiable instrument for payment or acceptance makes only warranties of title, of no knowledge that drawer's signature is unauthorized, or of no material alteration

(1) HDC does not give these three warranties to bank

e. To recover under warranty liabilities (either transfer or presentment warranties), party does not have to meet conditions of proper presentment, dishonor, or timely notice of dishonor that are required under contractual liability against endorsers

3. Signatures by authorized agents

a. Agent may sign on behalf of another person (principal) and that principal is liable, not agent, if signature indicates the principal is liable

EXAMPLE: A negotiable instrument has the following signature, signed entirely by A. Underwood, the authorized agent: Mary Johnson, by A. Underwood, agent.

EXAMPLE: If A. Underwood had simply signed Mary Johnson as she had authorized, this would also bind Mary Johnson.

EXAMPLE: If A. Underwood had signed his name only, he is liable. The principal is not liable even if agent intended her to be because her name is not on the instrument.

4. Accommodation party is liable on the instrument in the capacity in which s/he has signed even if taker knows of his/her accommodation status

EXAMPLE: Accommodating maker is liable as a maker would be.

EXAMPLE: Accommodating endorser is liable as an endorser would be.

a. Accommodation party is one who signs to lend his/her name to other party

EXAMPLE: Father-in-law endorses a note for son-in-law so creditor will accept it.

(1) Notice of default need not be given to accommodation party

(2) The accommodation party has right of recourse against accommodated party if accommodation party is held liable

5. Holding parties liable

a. If there are multiple endorsers, each is liable in full to subsequent endorsers or holders

(1) That is, liability moves from bottom up

EXAMPLE: A negotiable note has the following endorsements on the back from top to bottom: A, B, C, D, and E. Suppose E has sought payment from the maker but was unsuccessful. E, therefore, can seek payment from any previous endorser. Assume he collects from C. C then seeks payment from B. (He may seek from B or A but not D.)

EXAMPLE: Note that in the previous example, if A eventually pays, he may try to collect from the maker. If unsuccessful, A may not try to collect from any endorser up the line from him.

6. Discharge of parties

a. Once primary party pays, all endorsers are discharged from liability

b. Cancellation of prior party's endorsement discharges that party from liability

(1) Oral renunciation or oral attempt to discharge a party is not effective

    c.   Intentional destruction of instrument by holder discharges prior parties to instrument

7.   Liability on instruments with forged signatures

    a.   Person whose signature was forged on instrument is not liable on that instrument

        (1) Unless later ratifies it

    b.   Forged signature operates as signature of forger

    c.   Therefore, if signature of **maker or drawer** is forged, instrument can still be negotiated between parties and thus a holder can acquire good title

        (1) Recall that forgery is a real defense so that innocent maker or drawer cannot be required to pay even a HDC—forger can be required to pay if found

    d.   However, a **forged endorsement** does **not** transfer title; thus, persons receiving it after forgery cannot collect on it

        (1) Three important exceptions to rule that forged endorsements cannot transfer title are imposter rule, fictitious payee rule, and negligence of maker or drawer—these cause maker or drawer to be liable

            (a) **Imposter rule** applies when maker or drawer issues a note or draft to an imposter thinking s/he actually is the real payee—when that imposter forges the real payee's name, this effectively negotiates this note or draft so that a subsequent holder (if not part of scheme) can collect from maker or drawer

                1] Note that this rule normally places loss on person who was in best position to avoid this scheme (i.e., maker or drawer)

                    a] Of course, upon payment, maker or drawer may try to collect from imposter

                        EXAMPLE: J. Loux owes Larsen (whom she has not met) $2,000. Sawyer, claiming to be Larsen, gets Loux to issue him a check for $2,000. Sawyer forges Larsen's endorsement and transfers the check to P. Jenkins. Jenkins can collect from Loux because of the imposter rule exception.

                        EXAMPLE: If in the example above, J. Loux had given the check to the real Larsen and he lost it, the imposter rule would not apply even if someone found the check and forged Larsen's endorsement. No one after the forgery can collect on the check.

                2] This imposter rule exception also applies if an imposter pretends to be **agent** of the named payee

            (b) **Fictitious payee rule** applies when maker, drawer, or his/her agent (employee) issues a note or a check to a fictitious payee—then maker, drawer, or employee forges the endorsement—subsequent parties can enforce the note or check against the maker or drawer

                1] Actually payee may be a real person as long as maker, drawer, or other person supplying name never intended for that payee to ever get payment

                    EXAMPLE: R. Stewart submits a time card for a nonexistent employee and the employer issues the payroll check. Stewart forges the endorsement and transfers it to L. Reed. Reed wins against the employer even though the employer was unaware of the scheme at the time.

            (c) If person's negligence substantially contributes to the forgery that person is prevented from raising the defense of forgery and thus holder wins

                EXAMPLE: D. Wolter has a signature stamp and leaves it lying around. Unauthorized use of the stamp is not a defense against a holder as Wolter's negligence substantially contributed to the forgery. If the forger could be caught, Wolter could sue the forger for losses.

I. Additional Issues

1.   Certain types of draft names come up—although they follow general rules of drafts, definitions are helpful

    a.   Trade acceptance is a draft in which a seller of goods extends credit to buyer by drawing a draft on that buyer directing him/her to pay seller a sum of money on a specified date

      (1) Trade acceptance also requires signature of buyer on face of instrument—called acceptance—buyer is also called acceptor at this point

      (2) Then seller may negotiate trade acceptance at a discount to another party to receive immediate cash

      (3) Seller is normally both drawer and payee of a trade acceptance

  b. Banker's acceptance is a draft in which drawee and drawer are a bank

  c. Sight draft is one payable upon presentment to drawee

  d. Time draft is one payable at a specified date or payable a certain period of time after a specified date

  e. Money order is a draft purchased by one party to pay payee in which the third party is typically post office, a bank, or a company

2. Definitions for certain types of checks are also helpful

  a. Traveler's check is purchased from a bank (or company)—drawer (traveler) must sign twice for purposes of identification (once at the time s/he purchases the check and again at the time s/he uses the check)—drawee is bank or company—payee is one who gets paid

      (1) Technically, drawee must be a bank to be a true "check"—if drawee is not a bank then traveler's check is actually a draft

  b. Cashier's check is a check in which drawer and drawee are the same bank with a separate party being the payee

      (1) This is still considered a "three-party" instrument even though drawer and drawee are same bank

  c. Certified check is a check that payor bank has agreed in advance to pay so that bank becomes primarily liable

  d. Teller's check (bank draft) is draft drawn by one bank on another bank

J. Banks

1. Banks include savings and loan associations, credit unions, and trust companies

2. Relationship between bank and depositor is debtor-creditor

  a. Even though the depositor has funds in the bank, a payee cannot force a drawee to make payment

  b. Only drawer has an action against drawee-bank for wrongfully dishonoring a check—based on contract between customer (drawer) and bank

  c. Bank required to report to IRS any transaction or series of related transactions greater than $10,000

      (1) Ordinary checks are exempted but cash and other types of checks such as cashier's checks come under reporting requirement

  d. Bank must report to IRS suspected crimes involving $1,000 or more in funds

3. Checks

  a. Banks are not obligated to pay on a check presented more than six months after date

      (1) But they may pay in good faith and charge customer's account

  b. Even if check creates an overdraft, a bank may charge customer's account

  c. Bank is liable to drawer for damages caused by wrongful dishonor of a check

      (1) Wrongful dishonor may occur if the bank in error believes funds are insufficient when they are sufficient

  d. Payment of bad checks (e.g., forgery of drawer or altered checks)

      (1) Bank is liable to drawer for payment on bad checks unless drawer's negligence contributed because bank presumed to know signatures of its drawers

      (2) Bank cannot recover from a HDC to whom bank paid on a bad check

(3) If drawer fails to notify bank of forgery or alterations within thirty days of bank statement, the drawer is held liable on subsequent forgeries or alterations done in same way by same person

    (a) In any event, drawer must give notice of forgeries or alterations within one year to keep bank liable or else drawer is liable

        1] This applies to even nonrepeat cases as well as when bank was paying in bad faith

> *EXAMPLE: G. Wilson forges the name of M. Gibson on a check in an artful way. A subsequent HDC cashes this check at the drawee bank. The bank is liable on this check and cannot recover from either the HDC or M. Gibson as long as Gibson notifies the bank of the forgery within one year. The loss falls on the bank based on the idea that the bank should know its drawer's signature.*

    (b) Forgeries of endorsements are treated differently—depositor has three years to notify bank and also bank may charge check back to party that presented check to bank whether or not the party was a HDC

        1] Recall that one cashing check gave warranty that all signatures are genuine

> *EXAMPLE: D issues a check to P. P loses the check which is found by X. X forges the endorsement and transfers it to H. Finally, H cashes the check at the drawee bank. D soon notifies the bank of the forgery. The bank may charge it back to H (whether or not a HDC) but not to D.*

e. Bank is not liable for early payment of postdated check unless drawer notified bank to not pay check until date on check

f. Oral **stop payment order** is good for fourteen days; written stop payment order is good for six months and is renewable

  (1) Stop payment order must be given so as to give bank reasonable opportunity to act on it

  (2) Bank is liable to drawer if it pays after effective stop payment order only when drawer can prove that the bank's failure to obey the order caused drawer's loss. If drawer has no valid defense to justify dishonoring instrument, then bank has no liability for failure to obey stop payment order.

> *EXAMPLE: W. Paisley buys a T.V. set from the Burke Appliance Store and pays for the set with a check. Later in the day Paisley finds a better model for the same price at another store. Paisley telephones his bank and orders the bank to stop payment on the check. If the bank mistakenly pays Paisley's check two days after receiving the stop payment order, the bank will not be liable if Paisley could not rightfully rescind his agreement with the Burke Appliance Store. With these facts, Paisley suffered no damages from the bank's mistake.*

  (3) If drawer stops payment on the check, s/he is still liable to holder of check unless s/he has a valid defense (e.g., if holder qualifies as a holder in due course then drawer must be able to assert a real defense to free him/herself of liability)

g. Bank is entitled to a depositor's endorsement on checks deposited with the bank

  (1) If missing, bank may supply endorsement to negotiate check

h. Banks may choose which checks are charged to account first when several checks received in same day

K. Electronic Fund Transfer Act and Regulation E

1. Applied to consumer electronic fund transfers
2. For lost or stolen debit cards, customer is liable for

  a. Limit of $50 if notifies bank within two days of discovery of loss or theft
  b. Limit of $500 if notifies bank after two days, but before sixty days after unauthorized use appears on customer's bank statement
  c. Limit of $500 does not apply if fails to notify bank before sixty-day period
  d. Note how these rules are very different from those that apply to lost or stolen credit cards

3. Unsolicited debit cards may be sent to consumer only if the debit card is not functional but can be made functional at consumer's actual request

4. Bank is liable for failure to pay electronic fund transfer when customer has sufficient funds in account

L. Fund Transfers under UCC Article 4A

1. Applies to commercial electronic fund transfers only

2. When party gives payment order to bank and that bank or another bank pays too much money or to wrong party, that bank in error is liable for error.

    a. Bank has burden of recovery for wrongfully paid amount

M. Transfer of Negotiable Documents of Title

1. Transfer of documents of title is very similar to transfer of negotiable instruments under commercial paper

2. Types of documents of title

    a. Bill of lading is a document issued by a carrier (a person engaged in the business of transporting or forwarding goods) and given to seller evidencing receipt of the goods for shipment

    b. A warehouse receipt is a document issued by a warehouseman (a person engaged in the business of storing goods for hire) and given to seller evidencing receipt of goods for storage

3. Form

    a. Document of title is negotiable if face of the document contains words of negotiability (order or bearer)

        (1) Document of title containing promise to deliver goods to the order of a named person is an order document

            (a) If person is named on face of document or, if there are endorsements, on back of document and last endorsement is a special endorsement, then document is an order document

                1] Proper negotiation requires delivery of document and endorsement by named individual(s)

        (2) Document of title containing a promise to deliver the goods to bearer is bearer document

            (a) If "bearer" is stated on face of document or, if there are endorsements on back of document and last endorsement is a blank endorsement, it is a bearer document

                1] Proper negotiation merely requires delivery of document

    b. Nonnegotiable (straight) documents of title are assigned, not negotiated

        (1) Assignee will never receive any better rights than assignor had

4. Due negotiation—document of title is "duly negotiated" when negotiated to a holder who takes it in good faith in the ordinary course of business without notice of a defense and pays value

    a. Value does not include payment of a preexisting (antecedent) debt—this is an important difference from value concept required to create a holder in due course for commercial paper

5. Holder by due negotiation acquires rights very similar to those acquired by a holder in due course

    a. These rights include

        (1) Title to document

        (2) Title to goods

        (3) All rights accruing under law of agency or estoppel, including rights to goods delivered after document was issued, and

        (4) The direct obligation of the issuer to hold or deliver the goods according to terms of document

    b. A holder by due negotiation defeats similar defenses to those defeated by a holder in due course for commercial paper (personal but not real defenses)

    c. A document of title procured by a thief upon placing stolen goods in a warehouse confers no rights in the underlying goods.

        (1) This defense is valid against subsequent holder to whom document of title has been duly negotiated

        (2) Therefore, original owner of goods can assert better title to goods than a holder who has received document through due negotiation

6. Rights acquired in absence of due negotiation

    a. Transferee of a document, whether negotiable or nonnegotiable, to whom document has been delivered, but not duly negotiated, acquires title and rights which his/her transferor had or had actual authority to convey

7. Transferor for value warrants that

    a. Document is genuine

    b. S/he has no knowledge of any fact that would impair its validity or worth, and

    c. His/her negotiation or transfer is rightful and fully effective with respect to document of title and goods it represents

MULTIPLE-CHOICE QUESTIONS (1-50)

1. Under the Negotiable Instruments Article of the UCC, an endorsement of an instrument "for deposit only" is an example of what type of endorsement?
   a. Blank.
   b. Qualified.
   c. Restrictive.
   d. Special.

2.

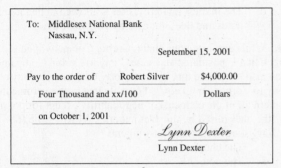

> To: Middlesex National Bank
>   Nassau, N.Y.
>
>   September 15, 2001
>
> Pay to the order of   Robert Silver $4,000.00
>
> Four Thousand and xx/100   Dollars
>
> on October 1, 2001
>
>   *Lynn Dexter*
>   Lynn Dexter

The above instrument is a
   a. Draft.
   b. Postdated check.
   c. Trade acceptance.
   d. Promissory note.

3. Which of the following statements regarding negotiable instruments is **not** correct?
   a. A certificate of deposit is a type of note.
   b. A check is a type of draft.
   c. A promissory note is a type of draft.
   d. A certificate of deposit is issued by a bank.

4. Based on the following instrument:

> May 19, 2001
>
> I promise to pay to the order of A. B. Shark $1,000 (one thousand and one hundred dollars) with interest thereon at the rate of 12% per annum.
>
>   *T. T. Tile*
>   T. T. Tile
>
>   **Guaranty**
>
> I personally guaranty payment by T. T. Tile.
>
>   *N. A. Abner*
>   N. A. Abner

The instrument is a
   a. Promissory demand note.
   b. Sight draft.
   c. Check.
   d. Trade acceptance.

5. Under the Commercial Paper Article of the UCC, which of the following documents would be considered an order to pay?
   I. Draft
   II. Certificate of deposit

   a. I only.
   b. II only.
   c. Both I and II.
   d. Neither I nor II.

6. An instrument that is otherwise negotiable on its face states "Pay to Jenny Larson." Which of the following statements is(are) correct?
   I. It is negotiable if it is a check.
   II. It is negotiable if it is a draft drawn on a corporation.
   III. It is negotiable if it is a promissory note.

   a. I only.
   b. I and II only.
   c. II and III only.
   d. I, II, and III.

7. Under the Commercial Paper Article of the UCC, for a note to be negotiable it must
   a. Be payable to order or to bearer.
   b. Be signed by the payee.
   c. Contain references to all agreements between the parties.
   d. Contain necessary conditions of payment.

8. On February 15, 2001, P.D. Stone obtained the following instrument from Astor Co. for $1,000. Stone was aware that Helco, Inc. disputed liability under the instrument because of an alleged breach by Astor of the referenced computer purchase agreement. On March 1, 2001, Willard Bank obtained the instrument from Stone for $3,900. Willard had no knowledge that Helco disputed liability under the instrument.

> February 12, 2001
>
> Helco, Inc. promises to pay to Astor Co. or bearer the sum of $4,900 (four thousand four hundred and 00/100 dollars) on March 12, 2001 (maker may elect to extend due date to March 31, 2001) with interest thereon at the rate of 12% per annum.
>
>   HELCO, INC.
>
>   By: *A. J. Help*
>
>   A. J. Help, President
>
> Reference: Computer purchase agreement dated
>   February 12, 2001

The reverse side of the instrument is endorsed as follows:

> Pay to the order of Willard Bank, without recourse
>
>   *P.D. Stone*
>   P.D. Stone

The instrument is
   a. Nonnegotiable, because of the reference to the computer purchase agreement.
   b. Nonnegotiable, because the numerical amount differs from the written amount.
   c. Negotiable, even though the maker has the right to extend the time for payment.
   d. Negotiable, when held by Astor, but nonnegotiable when held by Willard Bank.

9. A draft made in the United States calls for payment in Canadian dollars.
   a. The draft is nonnegotiable because it calls for payment in money of another country.
   b. The draft is nonnegotiable because the rate of exchange may fluctuate thus violating the sum certain rule.

c.   The instrument is negotiable if it satisfies all of the other elements of negotiability.

d.   The instrument is negotiable only if it has the exchange rate written on the draft.

10.   An instrument reads as follows:

$10,000	Ludlow, Vermont	February 1, 2001

I promise to pay to the order of Custer Corp. $10,000 within ten days after the sale of my two-carat diamond ring. I pledge the sale proceeds to secure my obligation hereunder.

R. Harris

R. Harris

Which of the following statements correctly describes the above instrument?

a.   The instrument is nonnegotiable because it is **not** payable at a definite time.

b.   The instrument is nonnegotiable because it is secured by the proceeds of the sale of the ring.

c.   The instrument is a negotiable promissory note.

d.   The instrument is a negotiable sight draft payable on demand.

11.   Kline is holding a promissory note in which he is the payer and Breck is the promissor. One of the terms of the note states that payment is subject to the terms of the contract dated March 1 of the current year between Breck and Kline. Does this term destroy negotiability?

a.   No, if the contract is readily available.

b.   No, since the note can be enforced without regard to the mentioned contract.

c.   No, as long as the terms in the mentioned contract are commercially reasonable.

d.   Yes, since this term causes the note to have a conditional promise.

12.   Based on the following instrument:

	May 19, 2001

I promise to pay to the order of A. B. Shark $1,000 (one thousand and one hundred dollars) with interest thereon at the rate of 12% per annum.

T. T. Tile

T. T. Tile

Guaranty

I personally guaranty payment by T. T. Tile.

N. A. Abner

N. A. Abner

The instrument is

a.   Nonnegotiable even though it is payable on demand.

b.   Nonnegotiable because the numeric amount differs from the written amount.

c.   Negotiable even though a payment date is **not** specified.

d.   Negotiable because of Abner's guaranty.

13.   A note has an interest rate that varies based on the stated rate of 2% above the prime rate as determined by XYZ Bank in New York City. Under the Revised Article 3 of the Uniform Commercial Code, which of the following is true?

a.   This interest rate provision destroys negotiability since it does not constitute a sum certain.

b.   This note is not negotiable because the holder has to look outside the instrument to determine what the prime rate is.

c.   The interest rate provision destroys negotiability because the prime rate can vary before the time the note comes due.

d.   The interest rate provision is allowed in negotiable notes and does not destroy negotiability.

14.   While auditing your client, Corbin Company, you see a check that is postdated and states "Pay to Corbin Company." You also see a note that is due in forty days and also says "Pay to Corbin Company." You note that both instruments contain all of the elements of negotiability except for possibly the ones raised by this fact pattern. Which of the following is(are) negotiable instruments?

a.   The check.

b.   The note.

c.   Both the check and the note.

d.   Neither the check nor the note.

15.   Under the Revised Article 3 of the Uniform Code, which of the following is true if the maker of a note provides that payment must come out of a designated fund?

a.   This is allowed even though the maker is not personally obligated to pay.

b.   Since the instrument is not based on the general credit of the maker, the instrument is not negotiable.

c.   The promise to pay is conditional; therefore, the note is not negotiable.

d.   The instrument is not negotiable if the designated fund has insufficient funds.

16.   Wyden holds a check that is written out to him. The check has the amount in words as five hundred dollars. The amount in figures on this check states $200. Which of the following is correct?

a.   The check is cashable for $500.

b.   The check is cashable for $200.

c.   The check is not cashable because the amounts differ.

d.   The check is not cashable because the amounts differ by more than 10%.

17.   Under the Commercial Paper Article of the UCC, which of the following requirements must be met for a transferee of order paper to become a holder?

I. Possession
II. Endorsement of transferor

a.   I only.

b.   II only.

c.   Both I and II.

d.   Neither I nor II.

18.   The following endorsements appear on the back of a negotiable promissory note payable to Lake Corp.

Pay to John Smith only
Frank Parker, President of Lake Corp.

John Smith

Pay to the order of Sharp, Inc. without recourse, but only if Sharp delivers computers purchased by Mary Harris by March 15, 2001.
Mary Harris

Sarah Sharp, President of Sharp, Inc.

Which of the following statements is correct?
   a.   The note became nonnegotiable as a result of Parker's endorsement.
   b.   Harris' endorsement was a conditional promise to pay and caused the note to be nonnegotiable.
   c.   Smith's endorsement effectively prevented further negotiation of the note.
   d.   Harris' signature was **not** required to effectively negotiate the note to Sharp.

19. A note is made payable to the order of Ann Jackson on the front. On the back, Ann Jackson signs it in blank and delivers it to Jerry Lin. Lin puts "Pay to Jerry Lin" above Jackson's endorsement. Which of the following statements is **false** concerning this note?
   a.   After Lin wrote "Pay to Jerry Lin," the note became order paper.
   b.   After Jackson endorsed the note but before Lin wrote on it, the note was bearer paper.
   c.   Lin needs to endorse this note to negotiate it further, even though he personally wrote "Pay to Jerry Lin" on the back.
   d.   The note is not negotiable because Lin wrote "Pay to Jerry Lin" instead of "Pay to the order of Jerry Lin."

20. You are examining some negotiable instruments for a client. Which of the following endorsements can be classified as a special restrictive endorsement?
   a.   Pay to Alex Ericson if he completes the contracted work within ten days, (signed) Stephanie Sene.
   b.   Pay to Alex Ericson without recourse (signed) Stephanie Sene.
   c.   For deposit only, (signed) Stephanie Sene.
   d.   Pay to Alex Ericson, (signed) Stephanie Sene.

21. On February 15, 2001, P.D. Stone obtained the following instrument from Astor Co. for $1,000. Stone was aware that Helco, Inc. disputed liability under the instrument because of an alleged breach by Astor of the referenced computer purchase agreement. On March 1, 2001, Willard Bank obtained the instrument from Stone for $3,900. Willard had no knowledge that Helco disputed liability under the instrument.

February 12, 2001

Helco, Inc. promises to pay to Astor Co. or bearer the sum of $4,900 (four thousand four hundred and 00/100 dollars) on March 12, 2001 (maker may elect to extend due date to March 31, 2001) with interest thereon at the rate of 12% per annum.

HELCO, INC.

By: *A. J. Help*

A. J. Help, President

Reference: Computer purchase agreement dated February 12, 2001

The reverse side of the instrument is endorsed as follows:

Pay to the order of Willard Bank, without recourse

P.D. Stone

P.D. Stone

Which of the following statements is correct?
   a.   Willard Bank **cannot** be a holder in due course because Stone's endorsement was without recourse.
   b.   Willard Bank must endorse the instrument to negotiate it.
   c.   Neither Willard Bank **nor** Stone are holders in due course.
   d.   Stone's endorsement was required for Willard Bank to be a holder in due course.

22. Under the Commercial Paper Article of the UCC, which of the following circumstances would prevent a person from becoming a holder in due course of an instrument?
   a.   The person was notified that payment was refused.
   b.   The person was notified that one of the prior endorsers was discharged.
   c.   The note was collateral for a loan.
   d.   The note was purchased at a discount.

23. One of the requirements needed for a holder of a negotiable instrument to be a holder in due course is the value requirement. Ruper is a holder of a $1,000 check written out to her. Which of the following would not satisfy the value requirement?
   a.   Ruper received the check from a tax client to pay off a four-month-old debt.
   b.   Ruper took the check in exchange for a negotiable note for $1,200 which was due on that day.
   c.   Ruper received the check in exchange for a promise to do certain specified services three months later.
   d.   Ruper received the check for a tax service debt for a close relative.

24. Larson is claiming to be a holder in due course of two instruments. One is a draft that is drawn on Picket Company and says "Pay to Brunt." The other is a check that says "Pay to Brunt." Both are endorsed by Brunt on the back and made payable to Larson. Larson gave value for and acted in good faith concerning both the draft and the check. Larson also claims to be ignorant of any adverse claims on either instrument which are not overdue or have not been dishonored. Which of the following is(are) true?

I. Larson is a holder in due course of the draft.
II. Larson is a holder in due course of the check.

   a.   I only.
   b.   II only.
   c.   Both I and II.
   d.   Neither I nor II.

25. In order to be a holder in due course, the holder, among other requirements, must give value. Which of the following will satisfy this value requirement?

I. An antecedent debt.
II. A promise to perform services at a future date.

   a.   I only.
   b.   II only.

c.   Both I and II.
d.   Neither I nor II.

26. Bond fraudulently induced Teal to make a note payable to Wilk, to whom Bond was indebted. Bond delivered the note to Wilk. Wilk negotiated the instrument to Monk, who purchased it with knowledge of the fraud and after it was overdue. If Wilk qualifies as a holder in due course, which of the following statements is correct?
  a.   Monk has the standing of a holder in due course through Wilk.
  b.   Teal can successfully assert the defense of fraud in the inducement against Monk.
  c.   Monk personally qualifies as a holder in due course.
  d.   Teal can successfully assert the defense of fraud in the inducement against Wilk.

27. To the extent that a holder of a negotiable promissory note is a holder in due course, the holder takes the note free of which of the following defenses?
  a.   Minority of the maker where it is a defense to enforcement of a contract.
  b.   Forgery of the maker's signature.
  c.   Discharge of the maker in bankruptcy.
  d.   Nonperformance of a condition precedent.

28. Under the Commercial Paper Article of the UCC, in a nonconsumer transaction, which of the following are real defenses available against a holder in due course?

	Material alteration	*Discharge of bankruptcy*	*Breach of contract*
a.	No	Yes	Yes
b.	Yes	Yes	No
c.	No	No	Yes
d.	Yes	No	No

29. On February 15, 2001, P.D. Stone obtained the following instrument from Astor Co. for $1,000. Stone was aware that Helco, Inc. disputed liability under the instrument because of an alleged breach by Astor of the referenced computer purchase agreement. On March 1, 2001, Willard Bank obtained the instrument from Stone for $3,900. Willard had no knowledge that Helco disputed liability under the instrument.

February 12, 2001

Helco, Inc. promises to pay to Astor Co. or bearer the sum of $4,900 (four thousand four hundred and 00/100 dollars) on March 12, 2001 (maker may elect to extend due date to March 31, 2001) with interest thereon at the rate of 12% per annum.

HELCO, INC.

By: *A. J. Help*
A. J. Help, President

Reference: Computer purchase agreement dated February 12, 2001

The reverse side of the instrument is endorsed as follows:

Pay to the order of Willard Bank, without recourse

P.D. Stone
P.D. Stone

If Willard Bank demands payment from Helco and Helco refuses to pay the instrument because of Astor's breach of the computer purchase agreement, which of the following statements would be correct?
  a.   Willard Bank is **not** a holder in due course because Stone was **not** a holder in due course.
  b.   Helco will **not** be liable to Willard Bank because of Astor's breach.
  c.   Stone will be the only party liable to Willard Bank because he was aware of the dispute between Helco and Astor.
  d.   Helco will be liable to Willard Bank because Willard Bank is a holder in due course.

30. Northup made out a negotiable promissory note that was payable to the order of Port. This promissory note was meant to purchase some furniture that Port used to own, but he lied to Northup when he claimed he still owned it. Port immediately negotiated the note to Johnson who knew about Port's lie. Johnson negotiated the note to Kenner who was a holder in due course. Kenner then negotiated the note back to Johnson. When Johnson sought to enforce the promissory note against Northup, she refused claiming fraud. Which of the following is correct?
  a.   Johnson, as a holder through a holder in due course, can enforce the promissory note.
  b.   Northup wins because Johnson does not have the rights of a holder in due course.
  c.   Northup wins because she has a real defense on this note.
  d.   Johnson's knowledge of the lie does not affect his rights on this note.

31. Goran wrote out a check to Ruz to pay for a television set he purchased at a flea market from Ruz. When Goran got home, he found out the box did not have the television set but some weights. Goran immediately gave his bank a stop payment order over the phone. He followed this up with a written stop payment order. In the meantime, Ruz negotiated the check to Schmidt who qualified as a holder in due course. Schmidt gave the check as a gift to Buck. When Buck tried to cash the check, the bank and Goran both refused to pay. Which of the following is correct?
  a.   Buck cannot collect on the check from the bank because Goran has a real defense.
  b.   Buck cannot collect on the check from Goran because Goran has a personal defense.
  c.   Buck can require the bank to pay because Buck is a holder through a holder in due course.
  d.   Buck can require Goran to pay on the check even though the check was a gift.

32. Under the Negotiable Instruments Article of the UCC, which of the following parties will be a holder but **not** be entitled to the rights of a holder in due course?
  a.   A party who, knowing of a real defense to payment, received an instrument from a holder in due course.
  b.   A party who found an instrument payable to bearer.
  c.   A party who received, as a gift, an instrument from a holder in due course.
  d.   A party who, in good faith and without notice of any defect, gave value for an instrument.

33. A holder in due course will take free of which of the following defenses?

a. Infancy, to the extent that it is a defense to a simple contract.
b. Discharge of the maker in bankruptcy.
c. A wrongful filling-in of the amount payable that was omitted from the instrument.
d. Duress of a nature that renders the obligation of the party a nullity.

34. Cobb gave Garson a signed check with the amount payable left blank. Garson was to fill in, as the amount, the price of fuel oil Garson was to deliver to Cobb at a later date. Garson estimated the amount at $700, but told Cobb it would be no more than $900. Garson did not deliver the fuel oil, but filled in the amount of $1,000 on the check. Garson then negotiated the check to Josephs in satisfaction of a $500 debt with the $500 balance paid to Garson in cash. Cobb stopped payment and Josephs is seeking to collect $1,000 from Cobb. Cobb's maximum liability to Josephs will be

a. $0
b. $ 500
c. $ 900
d. $1,000

35. A maker of a note will have a real defense against a holder in due course as a result of any of the following conditions **except**

a. Discharge in bankruptcy.
b. Forgery.
c. Fraud in the execution.
d. Lack of consideration.

36. Which of the following parties has(have) primary liability on a negotiable instrument?

I. Drawer of a check.
II. Drawee of a time draft before acceptance.
III. Maker of a promissory note.

a. I and II only.
b. II and III only.
c. I and III only.
d. III only.

37. Which of the following actions does **not** discharge a prior party to a commercial instrument?

a. Good faith payment or satisfaction of the instrument.
b. Cancellation of that prior party's endorsement.
c. The holder's oral renunciation of that prior party's liability.
d. The holder's intentional destruction of the instrument.

38. Under the Negotiable Instruments Article of the UCC, when an instrument is indorsed "Pay to John Doe" and signed "Faye Smith," which of the following statements is(are) correct?

	Payment of the instrument is guaranteed	The instrument can be further negotiated
a.	Yes	Yes
b.	Yes	No
c.	No	Yes
d.	No	No

39.

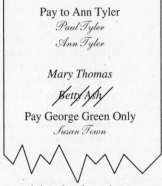

Pay to Ann Tyler
Paul Tyler
Ann Tyler

Mary Thomas
Betty Ash
Pay George Green Only
Susan Town

Susan Town, on receiving the above instrument, struck Betty Ash's endorsement. Under the Commercial Paper Article of the UCC, which of the endorsers of the above instrument will be completely discharged from secondary liability to later endorsers of the instrument?

a. Ann Tyler.
b. Mary Thomas.
c. Betty Ash.
d. Susan Town.

40. A subsequent holder of a negotiable instrument may cause the discharge of a prior holder of the instrument by any of the following actions **except**

a. Unexcused delay in presentment of a time draft.
b. Procuring certification of a check.
c. Giving notice of dishonor the day after dishonor.
d. Material alteration of a note.

41. A check has the following endorsements on the back:

Paul Folk
without recourse

George Hopkins
payment guaranteed

Ann Quarry
collection guaranteed

Rachel Ott

Which of the following conditions occurring subsequent to the endorsements would discharge all of the endorsers?

a. Lack of notice of dishonor.
b. Late presentment.
c. Insolvency of the maker.
d. Certification of the check.

42. Robb, a minor, executed a promissory note payable to bearer and delivered it to Dodsen in payment for a stereo system. Dodsen negotiated the note for value to Mellon by delivery alone and without endorsement. Mellon endorsed the note in blank and negotiated it to Bloom for value. Bloom's demand for payment was refused by Robb because the note was executed when Robb was a minor. Bloom gave prompt notice of Robb's default to Dodsen and Mellon. None of the holders of the note were aware of Robb's minority. Which of the following parties will be liable to Bloom?

	Dodsen	Mellon
a.	Yes	Yes
b.	Yes	No
c.	No	No
d.	No	Yes

43. Vex Corp. executed a negotiable promissory note payable to Tamp, Inc. The note was collateralized by some of Vex's business assets. Tamp negotiated the note to Miller for value. Miller endorsed the note in blank and negotiated it to Bilco for value. Before the note became due, Bilco agreed to release Vex's collateral. Vex refused to pay Bilco when the note became due. Bilco promptly notified Miller and Tamp of Vex's default. Which of the following statements is correct?

    a. Bilco will be unable to collect from Miller because Miller's endorsement was in blank.

    b. Bilco will be able to collect from either Tamp or Miller because Bilco was a holder in due course.

    c. Bilco will be unable to collect from either Tamp or Miller because of Bilco's release of the collateral.

    d. Bilco will be able to collect from Tamp because Tamp was the original payee.

44. Under the Commercial Paper Article of the UCC, which of the following statements best describes the effect of a person endorsing a check "without recourse"?

    a. The person has **no** liability to prior endorsers.

    b. The person makes **no** promise or guarantee of payment on dishonor.

    c. The person gives **no** warranty protection to later transferees.

    d. The person converts the check into order paper.

45. A check is postdated to November 20 even though the check was written out on November 3 of the same year. Which of the following is correct under the Revised Article 3 of the Uniform Commercial Code?

    a. The check is payable on demand on or after November 3 because part of the definition of a check is that it be payable on demand.

    b. The check ceases to be demand paper and is payable on November 20.

    c. The postdating destroys negotiability.

    d. A bank that pays the check is automatically liable for early payment.

46. Stanley purchased a computer from Comp Electronics with a personal check. Later that day, Stanley saw a better deal on the computer so he orally stopped payment on the check with his bank. The bank, however, still paid Comp Electronics when the check was presented three days later. Which of the following is correct?

    a. The bank is liable to Stanley for failure to follow the oral stop payment order.

    b. The bank is not liable to Stanley because the stop payment order was not in writing.

    c. The bank is not liable to Stanley if Comp Electronics qualifies as a holder in due course.

    d. Comp Electronics is liable to Stanley to return the amount of the check.

47. A trade acceptance is an instrument drawn by a

    a. Seller obligating the seller or designee to make payment.

    b. Buyer obligating the buyer or designee to make payment.

    c. Seller ordering the buyer or designee to make payment.

    d. Buyer ordering the seller or designee to make payment.

48. Under the Documents of Title Article of the UCC, which of the following statements is(are) correct regarding a common carrier's duty to deliver goods subject to a negotiable bearer bill of lading?

  I. The carrier may deliver the goods to any party designated by the holder of the bill of lading.

  II. A carrier who, without court order, delivers goods to a party claiming the goods under a missing negotiable bill of lading is liable to any person injured by the misdelivery.

    a. I only.

    b. II only.

    c. Both I and II.

    d. Neither I nor II.

49. Which of the following is **not** a warranty made by the seller of a negotiable warehouse receipt to the purchaser of the document?

    a. The document transfer is fully effective with respect to the goods it represents.

    b. The warehouseman will honor the document.

    c. The seller has **no** knowledge of any facts that would impair the document's validity.

    d. The document is genuine.

50. Under the UCC, a warehouse receipt

    a. Will **not** be negotiable if it contains a contractual limitation on the warehouseman's liability.

    b. May qualify as both a negotiable warehouse receipt and negotiable commercial paper if the instrument is payable either in cash or by the delivery of goods.

    c. May be issued only by a bonded and licensed warehouseman.

    d. Is negotiable if by its terms the goods are to be delivered to bearer or the order of a named person.

OTHER OBJECTIVE QUESTIONS

Problem 1   (15 to 25 minutes)

This question has four separate fact patterns each followed by five legal conclusions relating to the fact pattern preceding those five numbered legal conclusions. Determine whether each conclusion is correct (C) or incorrect(I).

Fact Pattern I: An instrument purports to be a negotiable instrument. It otherwise fulfills all the elements of negotiability and it states "Pay to Rich Crane."

1. It is negotiable if it is a check and Rich Crane has possession of the check.

2. It is negotiable if it is a draft drawn on a corporation.

3. It is negotiable if it is a promissory note due one year later with 5% interest stated on its face.

4. It is negotiable if it is a certificate of deposit.

5. It is negotiable even if it is a cashier's check.

Fact Pattern II: Another instrument fulfills all of the elements of negotiability except possibly one, that is, the instrument does not identify any payee.

6. The instrument is **not** negotiable if it is a draft.

7. The instrument is bearer paper if it is a check.

8. The instrument is negotiable if it is a promissory note.

9. The instrument is bearer paper if it is a promissory note.

10. The instrument is negotiable only if it also states the word "negotiable" on its face.

Fact Pattern III: A promissory note states that the maker promises to pay to the order of ABC Company $10,000 plus interest at 2% above the prime rate of XYZ Bank in New York City one year from the date on the promissory note.

11. The interest rate provision destroys negotiability because the prime rate can fluctuate during the year.

12. The interest rate provision destroys negotiability because one has to look outside the note to see what the prime rate of XYZ Bank is.

13. The maker is obligated to pay only the $10,000 because the amount of interest is not a sum certain.

14. The maker must pay $10,000 plus the judgment rate of interest because the amount of interest cannot be determined without referring to facts outside the instrument.

15. Any holder of this note could not qualify as a holder in due course because of the interest provision.

Fact Pattern IV: An individual fills out his personal check. He postdates the check for ten days later and notes on the face of the check that it is for "Payment for textbooks."

16. The instrument is demand paper because it is a check and is thus payable immediately.

17. The check is not payable before the date on its face.

18. If a bank pays on this check before its stated date, the bank is liable to the drawer.

19. The notation "Payment for textbooks" destroys negotiability because it makes payment conditional.

20. The notation "Payment for textbooks" does **not** destroy negotiability but only if the check was actually used to pay for textbooks.

Problem 2   (10 to 15 minutes)

During an audit of Trent Realty Corp.'s financial statements, Clark, CPA, reviewed the following instruments:

a.
                                        Instrument 1

$300,000	Belle, MD
	September 15, 2000

For value received, ten years after date, I promise to pay to the order of Dart Finance Co. Three Hundred Thousand and 00/100 dollars with interest at 9% per annum compounded annually until fully paid.

This instrument arises out of the sale of land located in MD.

It is further agreed that:

1.   Maker will pay all costs of collection including reasonable attorney fees.
2.   Maker may prepay the amount outstanding on any anniversary date of this instrument.

                                    G. Evans
                        _____
                                    G. Evans

The following transactions relate to Instrument 1.

•   On March 15, 2001, Dart endorsed the instrument in blank and sold it to Morton for $275,000.
•   On July 10, 2001, Evans informed Morton that Dart had fraudulently induced Evans into signing the instrument.
•   On August 15, 2001, Trent, which knew of Evans' claim against Dart, purchased the instrument from Morton for $50,000.

Required:

Items 1 through 5 relate to Instrument 1. For each item, select from List I the correct answer. An answer may be selected once, more than once, or not at all.

                                                              List I

1.   Instrument 1 is a (type of instrument)   A.   Draft
                                                              B.   Promissory Note
2.   Instrument 1 is (negotiability)   C.   Security Agreement
                                                              D.   Holder
3.   Morton is considered a (type of ownership)   E.   Holder in due course
                                                              F.   Holder with rights of a holder in due course under the
4.   Trent is considered a (type of ownership)   shelter provision
                                                              G.   Negotiable
5.   Trent could recover on the instrument from [liable   H.   Nonnegotiable
     party(s)]   I.   Evans, Morton, and Dart
                                                              J.   Morton and Dart
                                                              K.   Only Dart

b.   ***Instrument 2***

Front	*Back*
To: Pure Bank	*M. West*
Upton, VT	
	Pay to C. Larr
April 5, 2001	*T. Keetin*
Pay to the order of M. West $1,500.00	
One Thousand Five Hundred and 00/100 Dollars	*C. Larr*
on May 1, 2001	without recourse
W. Fields	
_____	
W. Fields	

Required:

Items 6 through 13 relate to Instrument 2. For each item, select from List II the correct answer. An answer may be selected once, more than once, or not at all.

6. Instrument 2 is a (type of instrument)

7. Instrument 2 is (negotiability)

8. West's endorsement makes the instrument (type of instrument)

9. Keetin's endorsement makes the instrument (type of instrument)

10. Larr's endorsement makes the instrument (type of instrument)

11. West's endorsement would be considered (type of endorsement)

12. Keetin's endorsement would be considered (type of endorsement)

13. Larr's endorsement would be considered (type of endorsement)

List II

A. Bearer paper
B. Blank
C. Check
D. Draft
E. Negotiable
F. Nonnegotiable
G. Note
H. Order paper
I. Qualified
J. Special

PROBLEMS

Problem 1   (15 to 20 minutes)

Prince, Hall, & Charming, CPAs, has been retained to examine the financial statements of Hex Manufacturing Corporation. Shortly before beginning the examination for the year ended December 31, 2001, Mr. Prince received a telephone call from Hex's president indicating that he thought some type of embezzlement was occurring because the corporation's cash position was significantly lower than in prior years. The president then requested that Prince immediately undertake a special investigation to determine the amount of embezzlement, if any.

After a month of investigation, Prince uncovered an embezzlement scheme involving collusion between the head of payroll and the assistant treasurer. The following is a summary of Prince's findings:

• . The head of payroll supplied the assistant treasurer with punched time cards for fictitious employees. The assistant treasurer prepared invoices, receiving reports, and purchase orders for fictitious suppliers. The assistant treasurer prepared checks for the fictitious employees and suppliers which were signed by the treasurer. Then, either the assistant treasurer or the head of payroll would endorse the checks and deposit them in various banks where they maintained accounts in the names of fictitious payees. All of the checks in question have cleared Omega Bank, the drawee.

• The embezzlement scheme had been operating for ten months and more than $120,000 had been embezzled by the time the scheme was uncovered. The final series of defalcations included checks payable directly to the head of payroll and the assistant treasurer. These checks included skillful forgeries of the treasurer's signature that were almost impossible to detect. This occurred while the treasurer was on vacation. These checks have also cleared Omega Bank, the drawee.

Required:

Answer the following, setting forth reasons for any conclusions stated.

Will Hex or Omega bear the loss with respect to the following categories of checks:

a. Those which were signed by the treasurer but payable to fictitious payees?

b. Those which include the forged signature of the treasurer?

Problem 2   (15 to 20 minutes)

River Oaks is a wholesale distributor of automobile parts. River Oaks received the promissory note shown below from First Auto, Inc., as security for payment of a $4,400 auto parts shipment. When River Oaks accepted the note as collateral for the First Auto obligation, River Oaks was aware that the maker of the note, Hillcraft, Inc., was claiming that the note was unenforceable because Alexco Co. had breached the license agreement under which Hillcraft had given the note. First Auto had acquired the note from Smith in exchange for repairing several cars owned by Smith. At the time First Auto received the note, First Auto was unaware of the dispute between Hillcraft and Alexco. Also, Smith, who paid Alexco $3,500 for the note, was unaware of Hillcraft's allegations that Alexco had breached the license agreement.

```
                PROMISSORY NOTE
                        Date:  1/14/01

    Hillcraft, Inc.            promises to pay to
    Alexco Co. or bearer         the sum of $4,400
    Four Thousand and 00/100      Dollars
on or before      May 15, 2002 (maker may elect
to extend due date by 30 days)        with interest
thereon at the rate of 9 1/2% per annum.


                        Hillcraft, Inc.

                    By  P.J.Hill
                        P.J. Hill, President
Reference:  Alexco Licensing Agreement
```

The reverse side of the note was endorsed as follows:

```
Pay to the order of First Auto without recourse

     E. Smith
     E. Smith
Pay to the order of River Oaks Co.
  First Auto
  By  G. First
  G. First, President
```

First Auto is now insolvent and unable to satisfy its obligation to River Oaks. Therefore, River Oaks has demanded that Hillcraft pay $4,400, but Hillcraft has refused, asserting:

• The note is nonnegotiable because it references the license agreement and is not payable at a definite time or on demand.

• River Oaks is not a holder in due course of the note because it received the note as security for amounts owed by First Auto.

• River Oaks is not a holder in due course because it was aware of the dispute between Hillcraft and Alexco.

• Hillcraft can raise the alleged breach by Alexco as a defense to payment.

• River Oaks has no right to the note because it was not endorsed by Alexco.

• The maximum amount that Hillcraft would owe under the note is $4,000, plus accrued interest.

Required:

State whether each of Hillcraft's assertions are correct and give the reasons for your conclusions.

MULTIPLE-CHOICE ANSWERS

1. c __ __	12. c __ __	22. c __ __	34. d __ __	45. b __ __
2. a __ __	13. d __ __	24. b __ __	35. d __ __	46. c __ __
3. c __ __	14. a __ __	25. a __ __	36. d __ __	47. c __ __
4. a __ __	15. a __ __	26. a __ __	37. c __ __	48. c __ __
5. a __ __	16. a __ __	27. d __ __	38. a __ __	49. b __ __
6. a __ __	17. c __ __	28. b __ __	39. c __ __	50. d __ __
7. a __ __	18. d __ __	29. d __ __	40. c __ __	
8. c __ __	19. d __ __	30. b __ __	41. d __ __	
9. c __ __	20. a __ __	31. d __ __	42. d __ __	
10. a __ __	21. b __ __	32. b __ __	43. c __ __	1st: __/50 = __%
11. d __ __	22. a __ __	33. c __ __	44. b __ __	2nd: __/50 = __%

MULTIPLE-CHOICE ANSWER EXPLANATIONS

B. Types of Commercial Paper

1. **(c)** This is a very common type of restrictive endorsement. Answer (a) is incorrect because a blank endorsement is one that does not specify any endorsee. Answer (b) is incorrect because a qualified endorsement is one in which the endorser disclaims liability to pay the holder or any subsequent endorser for the instrument if it is later dishonored. An example of this is the endorser putting in the words "without recourse" on the back of the instrument. Answer (d) is incorrect because a special endorsement refers to when the endorser indicates a specific person who needs to subsequently endorse it.

2. **(a)** This instrument is a draft because it is a three-party instrument where a drawer (Dexter) orders a drawee (Middlesex National Bank) to pay a fixed amount in money to the payee (Silver). Answer (b) is incorrect because in order for the instrument to qualify as a check, the instrument must be payable on demand. In this situation, the instrument held by Silver is a time draft which specifies the payment date as October 1, 2001. Answer (d) is incorrect because a promissory note is a two-party instrument in which one party promises to pay a fixed amount in money to the payee. Answer (c) is incorrect because a trade acceptance is a special type of draft in which a seller of goods extends credit to the buyer by drawing a draft on that buyer directing the buyer to pay a fixed amount in money to the seller on a specified date. The seller is therefore both the drawer and payee in a trade acceptance.

3. **(c)** Under the Revised Article 3 of the UCC, there are two basic categories of negotiable instruments (i.e., promissory notes and drafts). A certificate of deposit is a promissory note issued by a bank. A check is a draft drawn on a bank and payable on demand unless it is postdated.

4. **(a)** A promissory demand note is a two-party instrument in which the maker (T. T. Tile) promises to pay to the order of the payee (A. B. Shark) and the payment is made upon demand with no time period stated. N. A. Abner made a guaranty but it is still a two-party note. Answers (b), (c), and (d) are all incorrect because sight drafts, checks, and trade acceptances are all three-party instruments requiring a drawee.

5. **(a)** Drafts and checks are three-party instruments in which the drawer orders the drawee to pay the payee. Notes and certificates of deposit are two-party instruments in which the maker promises to pay the payee.

C. Requirements of Negotiability

6. **(a)** All negotiable instruments are required to be payable to order or bearer with the exception of checks. This instrument says "Pay to Jenny Larson"; therefore, it can only be negotiable if it is a check. All of these instruments in the question would be negotiable if they said "Pay to the order of Jenny Larson," including a check.

7. **(a)** One of the elements of negotiability is that the note be payable to order or to bearer. Under the revised UCC, this is true for all negotiable instruments except checks that do not need the words "to the order of" or "bearer." Answer (b) is incorrect because signing by the payee is a method of negotiation but is not a requirement to make the instrument negotiable. Answer (c) is incorrect because such references are not required. Answer (d) is incorrect because the elements of negotiability do not require the stating of any conditions of payment. In fact, such conditions can destroy negotiability.

8. **(c)** This promissory note is negotiable because it meets all of the requirements of negotiability. It is written and signed. It contains an unconditional promise to pay a fixed amount in money. It is payable at a definite time under the UCC even though the maker may extend the due date to March 31, 2001, because this option of the maker to extend the time is limited to a definite date. And finally, the instrument is payable to bearer because it states "Pay to Astor Co. or bearer." Answer (a) is incorrect because the reference to the computer purchase agreement does not condition payment on this agreement, it simply refers to it. Answer (b) is incorrect because when the words and numbers are contradictory, the written words control and thus, the instrument still contains a fixed amount. Answer (d) is incorrect because once an instrument is negotiable and remains unaltered, it is negotiable for all parties.

9. **(c)** The Revised Article 3 of the UCC allows a negotiable instrument to be payable in any medium of exchange of the US or a foreign government. Therefore, answer (a) is incorrect. Answer (b) is incorrect because negotiability is maintained despite the fact that rate of exchange can fluctuate. This is a fact of doing business internationally. Answer (d) is incorrect because the exchange rate can be determined readily.

10. **(a)** This instrument satisfies all of the requirements for negotiability except for the requirement that it be payable on demand or at a definite time. Since it is payable ten days after the sale of the maker's diamond ring, the time of payment is not certain as to the time of occurrence. Answer (b) is incorrect because a negotiable instrument may contain a promise to provide collateral. Answer (c) is incorrect because although it is a two-party note, it is not negotiable because it is not payable at a definite time. Answer (d) is incorrect because it is not negotiable and is not a draft. A draft requires a drawer ordering a drawee to pay the payee.

11. **(d)**   Since this note is subject to the terms of another document, the promise in the note is conditional, causing negotiability to be destroyed. Answer (a) is incorrect because since one must look to a document outside of the note, this destroys negotiability. Answer (b) is incorrect because the note itself makes its promise conditioned on the contract. Thus, the contract cannot be ignored. Answer (c) is incorrect because the contract, which is outside of the note, must be examined. This destroys the note's negotiability.

12. **(c)**   For a note to be negotiable, it must be written and signed by the maker, contain an unconditional promise to pay a fixed amount in money, be payable at a definite time or on demand, and be payable to order or to bearer. This note fulfills all of these requirements. It is therefore negotiable and does not require that the payment date be specified because it is payable on demand. Answer (a) is incorrect because the note fulfills all the requirements of negotiability. Answer (b) is incorrect because in cases of inconsistencies between words and figures, the words control. Answer (d) is incorrect because although the guaranty may make the note more desirable, it was already negotiable.

13. **(d)**   Under the Revised Article 3 of the UCC, interest rates are allowed to be variable or fluctuate. Negotiability is not destroyed. Answer (a) is incorrect because the sum certain rule allows the interest rate to vary based on such things as the prime rate of interest of a given bank. Answer (b) is incorrect because negotiability is not destroyed by needing to resort to information outside of the negotiable instrument. Answer (c) is incorrect because it is allowed for the interest to vary while the negotiable instrument is still outstanding.

14. **(a)**   Under the Revised Article 3 of the UCC, a check may be postdated and need not be payable to order. The words "Pay to Corbin Company" are allowed for checks. However, all negotiable instruments other than checks need to be payable to order or to bearer.

15. **(a)**   Under the Revised Article 3 of the UCC, unlike under earlier versions, payment on a negotiable instrument may be designated to come from a particular source or fund. The maker or drawer does not have to be personally obligated. Therefore, answer (b) is incorrect. Answer (c) is incorrect because this provision is not deemed to make the instrument not negotiable for reason of a conditional promise. Answer (d) is incorrect because lack of payment due to insufficient funds does not destroy negotiability.

D.   Interpretation of Ambiguities in Negotiable Instruments

16. **(a)**   When the amount in words differs from the amount in figures on a negotiable instrument, the words control over the figures. Answer (b) is incorrect because the law has settled this ambiguity in favor of the words on negotiable instruments. Answer (c) is incorrect because the

instrument is still negotiable and can be cashed. Answer (d) is incorrect because there is no such rule involving 10%.

E.   Negotiation

17. **(c)**   Although negotiating bearer paper only requires delivery, negotiating order paper requires both delivery and endorsement by the transferor. Delivery requires that the holder get possession of the instrument.

18. **(d)**   Since John Smith endorsed the instrument in blank (i.e., did not specify any endorsee) it became bearer paper. Since it was bearer paper in Harris's hands, she did not need to endorse it to negotiate it to the next party, Sharp. Answer (a) is incorrect because when Parker endorsed "Pay to John Smith only" he made the instrument require John Smith's signature to negotiate it further. Parker's endorsement will not restrict negotiations beyond John Smith's and it does not destroy negotiability. Answer (b) is incorrect as although conditions on the front generally destroy the negotiability of an instrument, conditions put into an endorsement do not. Answer (c) is incorrect because the wording "Pay to John Smith only" will not restrict further negotiation after John Smith. When John Smith endorsed it in blank, it became bearer paper.

19. **(d)**   The words "Pay to the order of Jerry Lin" are not necessary because the note is already negotiable on its face where it was payable to the order of Ann Jackson. Answer (a) is not chosen because although when Jackson endorsed the note in blank, it became bearer paper, it was converted back to order paper when Lin put "Pay to Jerry Lin" above Jackson's endorsement. Answer (b) should not be chosen because when Jackson endorsed it without specifying any payee, the note became bearer paper. Answer (c) should not be chosen because it became order paper once "Pay to Jerry Lin" was written, whether he personally did it or not.

20. **(a)**   This endorsement is special because it indicates "Pay to Alex Ericson" and it is restrictive because of the phrase "if he completes…." Answer (b) is incorrect because this endorsement is special and qualified. Answer (c) is incorrect because although it is restrictive, it is also a blank endorsement. Answer (d) is incorrect because although it is a special endorsement stating "Pay to Alex Ericson," it is not restrictive.

21. **(b)**   Although the note was originally a bearer instrument, Stone endorsed it with a special endorsement when s/he indicated "Pay to the order of Willard Bank, without recourse" above the endorsement. This means that Willard Bank must endorse the note to negotiate it further. Answer (a) is incorrect because qualified endorsements such as "without recourse" disclaim some liability but do not prevent subsequent parties from becoming a holder in due course. Answer (c) is incorrect because although Stone is not a holder in due course because s/he had notice that the maker disputed liability under the note, Willard Bank is a holder in due course because Willard was unaware that Helco disputed liability on the note. Additionally, Willard meets the other requirements to be a holder in due course, because he was a holder of a negotiable note, gave value ($3,900) for it, took in good faith, and had no notice, not only of the alleged breach by Astor, but of any other relevant problems such as being overdue or having been dishonored.

Answer (d) is incorrect because the note was bearer paper when Stone received it and thus did not require an endorsement.

F. Holder in Due Course

22.   (a)   To be a holder in due course, the holder must, among other things, take without notice that the instrument is overdue, has been dishonored, or that any person has a defense or claim to it. In this case, the person was notified that payment was refused. Answer (b) is incorrect because a prior endorser being discharged does not mean that person necessarily had a defense to the instrument. Answer (c) is incorrect because the use of a note as collateral does not prevent a holder from becoming a holder in due course. Answer (d) is incorrect because reasonable discounts are allowed and do not indicate bad faith or that a person has a defense or claim to the instrument.

23.   (c)   An executory promise does not satisfy the value requirement to be a holder in due course until the promise is actually performed. Answer (a) is incorrect because Ruper received the check to pay off a previous debt owed to her. Taking in satisfaction of a previous debt constitutes value to be a holder in due course. Answer (b) is incorrect because she took the check in exchange for another negotiable instrument. The fact that the check was for less than the face value of the negotiable note does not violate the value requirements. Answer (d) is incorrect because taking the check to pay off an antecedent debt constitutes value whether the debtor was a relative or not.

24.   (b)   In order to be a holder in due course, the individual must be a holder of a negotiable instrument as well as fulfilling the additional requirements referred to in the question. In this case, the draft is not negotiable because it is not payable to order or to bearer. However, the check is negotiable because checks do not have to be payable to order or to bearer to be negotiable.

25.   (a)   Even though an antecedent debt would not be valid for the consideration requirement under contract law, it is valid for the value requirement under negotiable instruments law. A promise to perform services at a future date is an executory promise and is not value until actually performed.

G. Rights of a Holder in Due Course

26.   (a)   Monk is not personally a HDC because although he was a holder of the negotiable note for which he gave value, he did not take in good faith because he had knowledge of the fraud before he purchased the note. Furthermore, he had notice that the note was overdue. Therefore, answer (c) can be ruled out. Answer (a) however, is correct because even though Monk was not a HDC, he obtained the instrument from Wilk who was a HDC. Therefore, Monk qualifies as a holder through a HDC and thus obtains all of the rights of a HDC. Answers (b) and (d) are incorrect because fraud in the inducement is a personal defense. Wilk, as a HDC, and Monk, as a holder through a HDC, both take the note free of personal defenses.

27.   (d)   A holder in due course takes an instrument free of personal defenses but is subject to real defenses. Answer (d) is correct because it involves a breach of contract or nonperformance of a condition precedent which describes a personal defense. Answer (c) is incorrect because bankruptcy is a real defense. Answer (a) is incorrect because when a minor may disaffirm a contract, it is treated as a real defense. Answer (b) is incorrect because a forgery of a maker's or drawer's signature is a real defense.

28.   (b)   Real defenses include bankruptcy and material alterations of the instrument. Material alterations include a change of any monetary amount. They also include changes in the interest rate, if any, on the instrument or changes in the date if the date affects when it is paid or the amount of interest to be paid. Personal defenses include the more typical defenses such as breach of contract, breach of warranty, and fraud in the inducement.

29.   (d)   Helco is claiming breach of contract which is a personal defense. The general rule is that transfer of a negotiable instrument to a holder in due course cuts off all personal defenses against the holder in due course. Since Willard Bank is a holder in due course, Helco is liable to Willard Bank. Answer (a) is incorrect because Willard Bank meets all of the requirements to be a holder in due course. That is, Willard is a holder of a negotiable instrument, gave value, took in good faith, and took without notice of certain problems such as Helco's disputed liability. The fact that Stone was not a holder in due course does not change this. Answer (b) is incorrect because Willard Bank as a holder in due course wins against Helco's claim of Astor's breach. The breach of contract would only constitute a personal defense. Answer (c) is incorrect because Helco is liable to Willard Bank.

30.   (b)   When a negotiable instrument is negotiated from a holder in due course to another holder, this other holder normally obtains the rights of a holder in due course. However, an important exception applies to this case. Since Johnson knew of the lie when he first acquired the note, he was not a HDC and cannot improve his status by reacquiring from a HDC. Answer (a) is incorrect because he did not qualify as a HDC due to his knowledge of the defense. Answer (c) is incorrect because fraud in the inducement is a personal, not real, defense. Answer (d) is incorrect because his knowledge of the lie prevents his becoming a HDC at first and prevents his later becoming a holder through a holder in due course.

31.   (d)   Even though Buck did not personally qualify as a HDC, he was a holder through a holder in due course and can collect from the drawer despite the drawer's personal defense. Answer (a) is incorrect because Goran's defense is a personal defense. Also, the bank is permitted to follow the customer's stop payment order. Answer (b) is incorrect because Buck as a holder through a holder in due course can collect despite the personal defense. Answer (c) is incorrect because the bank is permitted to refuse payment and then Buck collects from the drawer.

32.   (b)   A party who found an instrument payable to bearer is a holder but not a holder through a holder in due course. To be the latter, s/he must obtain a negotiable instrument from a holder in due course. If this had been the case, s/he would have obtained the rights of a holder in due course. However, since s/he found the instrument, it cannot be established that the previous holder was a holder in due course. Answer (a) is incorrect because s/he did receive the instrument from a holder in due course. S/he, therefore, does obtain the rights of a holder in due course even though s/he cannot be a holder in due course him/herself because of having notice of the defense on the instrument. Answer (c) is incorrect because the party received the instrument from a holder in due course and thus becomes a holder through a holder in due course. Answer (d) is incorrect because this party personally qualifies as a holder in due course, thereby obtaining those rights.

33.   (c)   An unauthorized completion of an incomplete instrument is a personal defense, and, as such, will not be valid against a HDC. Infancy (unless the instrument is exchanged for necessaries), bankruptcy of the maker, and extreme duress are all real defenses which are good against a HDC.

34.   (d)   Since Cobb left the amount blank on the signed check and Garson filled it in contrary to Cobb's instructions, this is a case of unauthorized completion which is a personal defense. Garson then negotiated the check to Josephs who is a holder in due course because he gave value for the negotiable instrument and took in good faith without notice of any problems. He gave value for the full $1,000 since cash and taking the check for a previous debt are both value under negotiable instrument law. Therefore, Josephs may collect the full $1,000 and win over the personal defense that Cobb has.

35.   (d)   A maker of a note may use real defenses against a holder in due course but not personal defenses. Lack of consideration is a personal defense. Discharge in bankruptcy, forgery, and fraud in the execution are all real defenses, which create a valid defense against a holder in due course.

H. Liability of Parties

36.   (d)   The maker of a note has primary liability on that note. No one has primary liability on a draft or check unless the drawee accepts it. This is true because although the drawee has been ordered by the drawer to pay, the drawee has not agreed to pay unless it accepts the draft or check.

37.   (c)   When there are multiple endorsers on a negotiable instrument, each is liable to subsequent endorsers or holders. Oral renunciation of a prior party's liability does not discharge that party's liability. Answer (a) is incorrect because once the primary party pays on the instrument, all endorsers are discharged from liability. Answer (b) is incorrect because cancellation of a prior party's endorsement does discharge that party's liability. Answer (d) is incorrect because when a holder intentionally destroys a negotiable instrument, the prior endorsers are discharged.

38.   (a)   When a negotiable instrument is indorsed and a specific person is indicated, the instrument is order paper and can be further negotiated by that person. Note also that payment of the instrument is guaranteed. If the primary party to the negotiable instrument does not pay, the indorser(s) are obligated to pay on the instrument when the holder demands payment or acceptance in a timely manner.

39.   (c)   Striking out the endorsement of a person discharges that person's secondary liability and discharges subsequent endorsers who have already endorsed. This does not, however, discharge any of the prior parties. Therefore,

in this case, Betty Ash is discharged from secondary liability to the later endorsers.

40.   (c)   Various acts or failures of a holder can cause a discharge of prior holders of an instrument. Among these are an unexcused delay in presenting an instrument, cancellation or renunciation of the instrument, fraudulent or material alteration, and certification of a check. Notice of dishonor generally should be given by midnight of the third business day after the dishonor or notice of the dishonor. Banks must give notice by midnight of the next banking day. In either case, answer (c) is correct. Answers (a), (b), and (d) are all incorrect because they are all acts that cause the discharge of prior holders.

41.   (d)   When a holder procures certification of a check, all prior endorsers are discharged. This is true because when a bank certifies a check, it has accepted the check and agreed to honor it as presented. Answers (a) and (b) are incorrect because although lack of notice of dishonor to other endorsers and late presentment of the instrument will normally discharge all endorsers, this is not true if the lack of notice of dishonor or the late presentment is excused. They can be excused in such cases as the delay is beyond the party's control or the presentment is waived. Furthermore in this fact pattern, Hopkins endorsed the check "payment guaranteed" and Quarry endorsed it "collection guaranteed." When words of guaranty are used, presentment or notice of dishonor are not required to hold the users liable. Answer (c) is incorrect because when the maker is insolvent the endorsers will likely be sought after for payment.

42.   (d)   Since Dodsen did not endorse the note, s/he gave transfer warranties and presentment warranties only to the immediate transferee (i.e., Mellon). Mellon gave these warranties to Bloom. Therefore although Mellon will be liable to Bloom, Dodsen will not be.

43.   (c)   Normally, Bilco could seek collection on the defaulted note from the previous endorsers, Tamp and Miller. However, in this case, Bilco agreed to release the collateral underlying this note. Since this materially affects the rights of Tamp and Miller to use this collateral, this act releases them. Answer (a) is incorrect because except for the release of the collateral, Bilco could have collected from his/her immediate transferor even without the endorsement. Answers (b) and (d) are incorrect because the release of the collateral releases Tamp and Miller.

44.   (b)   When a person endorses a negotiable instrument, s/he is normally secondarily liable to later endorsers. This liability means that the endorser can be required to make good on the instrument. If s/he endorses without recourse, the endorser can avoid this liability. Answer (a) is incorrect because the endorser is not liable to prior endorsers anyway whether or not s/he endorses without recourse. Answer (c) is incorrect because the endorser still gives the transferor's warranties with some modification. Answer (d) is incorrect because a check is converted into order paper only if the endorser also specifies a payee.

J. Banks

45.   (b)   Under the Revised Article 3, postdating a check does not destroy negotiability but makes the check properly payable on or after the date written on the check. Although the postdated check is not properly payable before the date on the instrument, if a bank pays it earlier, it is not liable unless the drawer had notified the bank that the check was postdated.

46.   (c)   If the bank fails to follow a stop payment order, it is liable to the customer only if the customer had a valid defense on the check and therefore suffers a loss. Comp Electronics, the payee, can qualify as a HDC and Stanley would have to pay anyway despite the stop payment order. Answer (a) is incorrect because the bank did not cause Stanley a loss. Answer (b) is incorrect because oral stop payment orders are valid for fourteen days. Answer (d) is incorrect because from the facts given, there is no evidence that Comp Electronics breached the contract.

M. Transfer of Negotiable Documents of Title

47.   (c)   A trade acceptance is a special type of draft in which a seller of goods extends credit to the buyer by drawing the draft on the buyer ordering the buyer to make payment to the seller on a specified date.

48.   (c)   A negotiable bearer bill of lading is a document of title that under the UCC allows the bearer the rights to the goods mentioned including the right to designate who will receive delivery of the goods. The carrier is required to deliver the goods to the holder of negotiable bearer bill of lading or to that holder's designee. The carrier is liable for any misdelivery for any damages caused.

49.   (b)   A person who negotiates a negotiable document of title for value extends the following warranties to the immediate purchaser: (1) negotiation by the transferor is rightful and fully effective with respect to the goods it represents, (2) the transferor has no knowledge of any facts that would impair the document's validity or worth, and (3) the document is genuine. However, the transferor of a negotiable warehouse receipt does not necessarily warrant that the warehouseman will honor the document.

50.   (d)   A negotiable warehouse receipt is a document issued as evidence of receipt of goods by a person engaged in the business of storing goods for hire. The warehouse receipt is negotiable if the face of the document contains the words of negotiability (order or bearer). Answer (a) is incorrect because the negotiability of the warehouse receipt is not destroyed by the inclusion of a contractual limitation on the warehouseman's liability. Answer (b) is incorrect because to qualify as commercial paper, the instrument must be payable only in money. If an instrument is payable in money or by the delivery of goods, it is a nonnegotiable instrument. Answer (c) is incorrect because the UCC does not state that only a bonded and licensed warehouseman can issue a warehouse receipt.

OTHER OBJECTIVE ANSWERS AND ANSWER EXPLANATIONS

Problem 1

1.   **(C)**   Even though the instrument states "Pay to Rich Crane," it is negotiable because a check does **not** have to be payable to order or bearer.

2.   **(I)**   A draft to be negotiable must be payable to order or to bearer. "Pay to the order of Rich Crane" would have made it negotiable.

3.   **(I)**   Promissory notes to be negotiable must be payable to order or to bearer.

4.   **(I)**   Certificates of deposit, unlike checks, must be payable to order or to bearer.

5.   **(C)**   A cashier's check is an actual check and thus does **not** have to be payable to order or to bearer.

6.   **(I)**   If an instrument does not name any payee, it is considered to be payable to bearer. Thus, negotiability is not destroyed.

7.   **(C)**   If no payee is named, it is bearer paper.

8.   **(C)**   Since no payee was named, it is bearer paper and thus negotiability is maintained.

9.   **(C)**   Like the cases of drafts, checks, and certificates of deposit, it is bearer paper.

10.   **(I)**   There is no such requirement to state "negotiable" on its face.

11.   **(I)**   The negotiability of an instrument is not destroyed simply because the interest rate used may fluctuate.

12.   **(I)**   Negotiability is not destroyed even if one has to look outside of the document to determine what the actual rate is.

13.   **(I)**   Even though the interest rate may fluctuate, the maker is still obligated to pay the $10,000 plus the interest.

14.   **(I)**   The maker must pay the $10,000 plus the interest described on the promissory note.

15.   **(I)**   Since this note is negotiable despite the possible fluctuation of the interest rate, a holder could qualify to be a holder in due course under those applicable rules.

16.   **(I)**   Normally a check is demand paper. However, when it is postdated, it is not payable until that date.

17.   **(C)**   The postdating overrides the normal characteristic that it is payable on demand.

18.   **(I)**   The bank is not liable unless the drawer has given the bank prior notice of the postdating.

19.   **(I)**   Notations on negotiable instruments that note what it is for do not put conditions on the payment and thus do not destroy negotiability.

20.   **(I)**   These notations can be ignored because they are not conditions of payment.

Problem 2

Part a.

1.   **(B)**   Instrument 1 is a two-party instrument in which Evans promises to pay a fixed amount in money to Dart, therefore it qualifies as a promissory note. A promissory note may be payable on demand or at a specific point in time.

2.   **(G)**   Instrument 1 meets the requirements of negotiability. It is written and signed by the maker. It contains an unconditional promise or order to pay a fixed amount in money, at a definite time or on demand. The document is also payable to order. The fact that it is payable on a certain date subject to acceleration does not destroy its negotiability.

3.   **(E)**   To qualify as a holder in due course, an individual must be a holder of a properly negotiated negotiable instrument, give value for the instrument, and take the instrument in good faith and without notice that it is overdue, has been dishonored, or that any person has a defense or claim to it.

4.   **(F)**   When a negotiable instrument is negotiated from a holder in due course to a second holder, the second holder usually acquires the rights of a holder in due course through the shelter provision. The shelter provision applies to holders who have not previously held the instrument with knowledge of any defenses.

5.   **(I)**   A holder with rights of a holder in due course under the shelter provision obtains all the rights of a holder in due course. A holder in due course takes an instrument free of personal defenses, including fraud in the inducement. Therefore, Evans' claim that Dart had fraudulently induced Evans into signing the instrument would not prevent Trent from recovering from Evans. Trent would also be able to recover from Morton and Dart based on his holder in due course status.

Part b.

6.   **(D)** Instrument 2 is a draft because it is a three-party instrument where a drawer (Fields) orders a drawee (Pure Bank) to pay a fixed amount in money to the payee (West). It is not a check because it is not payable on demand.

7.   **(E)** The draft qualifies as a negotiable instrument as it meets all of the required elements of negotiability. The draft is written and signed by the drawer. It contains an unconditional order to pay a fixed amount in money. It is made payable to order and is payable at a definite time.

8.   **(A)** A blank endorsement which does not specify any endorsee converts order paper to bearer paper.

9.   **(H)** An endorsement which indicates the specific person to whom the endorsee wishes to negotiate the instrument is a special endorsement. The use of a special endorsement converts bearer paper into order paper.

10.   **(A)** Because Larr's endorsement does not specify any endorsee, the endorsement converts the order paper into bearer paper.

11.   **(B)** West's endorsement is a blank endorsement because it does not specify any endorsee.

12.   **(J)** Because Keetin's endorsement indicates a specific person to whom the instrument is being negotiated, the endorsement is a special endorsement.

13.   **(I)** Larr's endorsement is a qualified endorsement because Larr disclaimed liability by signing without recourse.

ANSWER OUTLINE

Problem 1   Fictitious Payee; Drawee Bank's Acceptance
              of Check with Forgery of Drawer's Signature

a.   Checks paid to fictitious payees
       Hex will bear the ultimate loss on these items
           General Rule—forged signatures of drawers and
           forged endorsements are real defenses valid
           against holder in due course
       Exception—fictitious payees rule shifts loss to em-
       ployer-drawer
           Rule states that real defense not created when
           agent or employee of the drawer with name of
           payee intending latter to have no such interest

b.   Checks containing forged signature of treasurer
       Forging of treasurer's signature is an unauthorized
       signature and not valid
       Bank is obligated to know the signatures of its cus-
       tomers and will bear the loss unless:
           Bank proves Hex contributed to forgery
           Bank proves Hex failed to exercise reasonable care
           and promptness in discovering unauthorized sig-
           natures on returned checks

UNOFFICIAL ANSWER

Problem 1   Fictitious Payee; Drawee Bank's Acceptance
              of Check with Forgery of Drawer's Signature

a.   Checks paid to fictitious payees.   Hex will bear the
ultimate loss on these items (the fictitious or nonexistent
"employees" and the fictitious suppliers). As a general rule,
forged signatures of drawers and forged endorsements are
real defenses which are valid even against a holder in due
course. However, when some of these activities are engaged
in by the employees of an employer-drawer of the checks, a
different rule is applied. Essentially, this rule negates these
real defenses in certain cases thereby shifting the loss to the
employer-drawer. The key rule is contained in the Uniform
Commercial Code's Article on Commercial Paper which
deals with "Imposters; Signature of Payee." In essence, this
rule makes the endorsement or signature of the agent or employee of the drawer (Hex) "effective" where the agent has
supplied the drawer the name of the payee intending the
latter to have no such interest.

Insofar as Omega is concerned, it will be treated as if it
had honored valid orders to pay and need not refund to Hex
the amounts it paid. The orders are valid since the forged
endorsements are not treated as unauthorized.

**b.   Checks which contain the forged signature of the
treasurer.**   From the facts it is apparent that the treasurer
had the authority to sign checks and not the assistant treasurer or head of payroll. Thus, the forging of the treasurer's
signature was an "unauthorized signature" under the UCC.

As to these checks, the UCC provides that such signatures are wholly inoperative since the guilty parties had no
authority to sign the treasurer's or any other authorized
party's name as the drawer on behalf of Hex.

As between Hex and Omega, there is an obligation on
the part of the bank to know the signature of its drawer-
depositors. Since Omega has paid the items, it cannot re-
coup the loss from Hex. However, the bank has two possible ways to escape liability to Hex. First, it can resort to the
UCC section which imposes upon a customer to whom items
(checks) are returned, a duty to exercise reasonable care and

promptness in discovering and reporting unauthorized signatures. Another possibility is to establish negligence on the
part of Hex which substantially contributed to the forgeries.
Unless the bank can demonstrate that one of these exceptions applies, it will bear the loss.

ANSWER OUTLINE

Problem 2   Requisites for Negotiability; Transfer and
              Negotiation; Holders and Holders in Due
              Course; Liabilities and Rights

Hillcraft's assertion that the note is nonnegotiable is incorrect
    Reference to license agreement is okay because it does not
    make note subject to it
    Negotiability unaffected by maker's time extensions for a
    definite period of time
Hillcraft's assertion that River Oaks is not a HDC is incorrect
    Under UCC, value given when note is payment/security
    for antecedent debt
Hillcraft's assertion that River Oaks is not a HDC due to the
dispute is correct
    Holder isn't a HDC if takes note with notice of dispute
Hillcraft's assertion that it can raise the breach as a defense
is incorrect
    River Oaks has rights of HDC since took note from HDC
    River Oaks therefore does not take subject to Hillcraft's
    personal defense on note
Hillcraft's assertion that River Oaks has no right to the note
is incorrect
    Payee line on face makes it bearer paper
    Proper negotiation of bearer paper needs no endorsement
Hillcraft's assertion that its maximum liability is $4,000,
plus accrued interest, is correct
    Words take precedence over numbers if in conflict

UNOFFICIAL ANSWER

Problem 2   Requisites for Negotiability; Transfer and
              Negotiation; Holders and Holders in Due
              Course; Liabilities and Rights

Hillcraft's first assertion, that the note is nonnegotiable
because it references the license agreement and is not payable at a definite time or on demand, is incorrect. The note
is negotiable despite the reference to the license agreement
because it does not make the note subject to the terms of the
agreement; rather, the reference is regarded only as a recital
of its existence.

Also, Hillcraft's right to extend the time for payment
does not make the note nonnegotiable because the extension
period is for a definite period of time.

Hillcraft's second assertion, that River Oaks is not a
holder in due course (HDC) because it received the note as
security for an existing debt and, therefore, did not give
value for it, is incorrect. Under the UCC Commercial Paper
Article, a holder does give value for an instrument when it is
taken in payment of, or as security for, an antecedent claim.

Hillcraft's third assertion, that River Oaks is not a HDC
because River Oaks was aware of Alexco's alleged breach
of the license agreement, is correct. If a holder of a note is
aware of a dispute when it acquires the note, that holder
cannot be a HDC because it took with notice.

Hillcraft's fourth assertion, that it can raise the alleged breach by Alexco as a defense to payment of the note, is incorrect. Even though River Oaks is not a HDC under the UCC "shelter provision," it is entitled to the protection of a HDC because it took the instrument from First Auto, which was a HDC. Therefore, River Oaks did not take the note subject to Hillcraft's defense based on the alleged breach by Alexco. Hillcraft's defense is considered a personal defense and can only be used by Hillcraft against Alexco.

Hillcraft's fifth assertion, that River Oaks has no right to the note because it was not endorsed by Alexco, is incorrect. River Oaks acquired rights to the Hillcraft note without Alexco's endorsement because the note was a bearer instrument as a result of it being payable to "Alexco Company or bearer." A bearer instrument can be negotiated by delivery alone.

Hillcraft's final assertion, that the maximum amount Hillcraft would owe under the note is $4,000, plus accrued interest, is correct. If there is a conflict between a number written in numerals and also described by words, the words take precedence. Therefore, Hillcraft's maximum potential principal liability is $4,000 under the note.

SECURED TRANSACTIONS

Overview

The concept of secured transactions is important to modern business. A creditor often requires some security from the debtor beyond a mere promise to pay. In general, the creditor may require the debtor to provide some collateral to secure payment on the debt. If the debt is not paid, the creditor then can resort to the collateral. Under revised Article 9 of the UCC, the collateral is generally personal property or fixtures. You need to understand the concept of attachment as discussed in this module. You also need to understand the important concept of perfection discussed in this module that allows a secured party to obtain greater rights over many third parties. Be sure to understand the three methods by which perfection can be accomplished. The examination also covers rules of priorities when competing interests exist in the same collateral.

A. Scope of Secured Transactions

1. Comes from revised UCC Article 9
2. Applies to transactions in which creditor intends to obtain greater security in debt by taking a security interest in personal property or fixtures (which are used as collateral)

   a. Types of collateral

      (1) Goods—things that are movable at the time security interest attaches

         (a) Consumer goods (bought or used for personal, family, or household use)
         (b) Inventory (goods other than farm products held for sale or lease, or raw materials, work in process or other items consumed by the business)
         (c) Farm products (crops, livestock, and supplies used in farming)
         (d) Equipment (any goods that are not consumer goods, inventory, or farm products)

      (2) Investment property

         (a) Includes securities, securities accounts, commodities, or commodity accounts

      (3) Promissory note

         (a) Drafts, checks, and certificates of deposit are not covered by the revised UCC Article 9

      (4) Chattel paper (writings that evidence both monetary obligation and security interest in specific goods)

         (a) Electronic chattel paper
         (b) Tangible chattel paper

      (5) Documents of title such as bills of lading and warehouse receipts
      (6) Letter-of-credit rights

         (a) Written or electronic

      (7) Intangibles

         (a) Accounts (rights to payment whether or not earned by performance)

      (8) Commercial tort claim

         (a) Excludes personal injury or death tort claims

3. Revised Article 9 of the UCC does **not** apply

   a. If collateral is real property
   b. To assignment of wage claims
   c. To statutory liens

B. Attachment of Security Interests

1. Attachment is a term used to describe the moment when security interest is enforceable against a debtor by the secured party
2. Security interest is said to attach when all of the following occur in any order (these are important)

   a. Secured party gives value (value is any consideration that supports any contract)

      (1) Preexisting claim (although not consideration) is value

      EXAMPLE: D already owes S $5,000 on a previous debt. Subsequently, D signs a security agreement giving S an interest in some furniture owned by D. Value has been given by S based on the previous debt.

EXAMPLE: A bank grants a loan to allow B to purchase a washer and dryer. This extension of credit is a typical type of value.

    b. Debtor has rights in collateral

        (1) Debtor must have rights in collateral

            (a) Ownership interest or

            (b) Some right to possession

            (c) Need not have title

EXAMPLE: M obtains a loan from a bank to purchase a sofa. She signs a security agreement granting the credit union a security interest in any sofa that she will buy with this loan. Attachment cannot occur until she buys a sofa. Note that the other two elements of attachment have occurred.

    c. And either

        (1) Collateral must be in possession of secured party by debtor's agreement (third party may possess if debtor agrees); or

        (2) Secured party must have "control" of collateral if it is investment property, deposit account, electronic chattel paper, or a letter-of-credit right; or

        (3) A record of security agreement must exist

            (a) Record may be in traditional writing or in electronic or other form that is retrievable in perceptible form

            (b) Security agreement must be signed or in case of electronic form, it must be authenticated

                1] Exception to need to sign or authenticate in case of pledge when secured party has possession or control of collateral

C. Perfecting a Security Interest

1. Entails steps **in addition to** attachment (with one exception discussed later) to give secured party priority over many other parties that may claim collateral

    a. Attachment focuses primarily on rights between creditor and debtor

    b. However, perfection focuses on rights between various **other parties** that may claim an interest in same collateral

        (1) Generally, perfecting a security interest gives (constructive) **notice to other parties** that the perfecting party claims an interest (security interest) in certain collateral

        (2) Only an attached security interest can be perfected

2. There are three primary ways that an attached security interest may be perfected—these are important

    a. Most security interests either can or must be perfected by filing financing statement(s) in the appropriate office

    b. Secured party takes possession of collateral, or in certain cases takes control

    c. In a few cases, security interest is perfected automatically upon attachment

3. Depending on the type of collateral there may be only one or several ways to perfect

4. Perfection by filing financing statement(s)

    a. These requirements are streamlined from previous law

        (1) Contents of financing statement

            (a) Debtor's name

            (b) Secured party's name or representative

            (c) Indication of collateral covered

                1] Descriptions such as "all assets" are sufficient

            (d) Signature of debtor is no longer required if debtor approves

            (e) Minor errors in financing statement do not invalidate it if they are not seriously misleading

        (2) Location of filing

            (a) Generally filing is needed only in one office in the jurisdiction

(3) Filings last for five years but can be continued with a continuation statement

(4) Secured party may prefile financing statement if expressly authorized by debtor

5. Perfection by secured party's control of collateral

   a. This is the only way to perfect in cases of certificated securities, money, tangible chattel paper

     EXAMPLE: P wishes to borrow money from a bank using several shares of stock that she owns. In addition to completing the three steps needed for attachment, the bank must possess the shares in order to perfect. Filing is not effective in this case.

     (1) Electronic chattel paper must be perfected by filing or by control but not possession

       (a) Secured party can have control of electronic chattel paper when there is only one authoritative copy

     (2) Nonnegotiable instruments can be perfected either by filing or control

   b. Possession by third parties is effective if all parties know of this

   c. Perfection is accomplished by control rather than actual possession for investment property, deposit accounts, letter-of-credit rights

   d. Secured party must use reasonable care to preserve collateral and may charge reasonable expenses to do so

6. Automatic perfection

   a. Under the following conditions, perfection is accomplished by completing attachment with no further steps

     (1) **Purchase money security interest in consumer goods**

       (a) Purchase money security interest (PMSI) occurs in two important cases

         1] Seller retains security interest in same item sold on credit to secure payment

         2] Another party such as bank provides loan for and retains security interest in same item purchased by debtor

       (b) "In consumer goods" means that goods are bought primarily for personal, family, or household purposes

        EXAMPLE: B buys a refrigerator for his home from Friendly Appliance Dealer on credit. Friendly has B sign a written security agreement. Because all three elements needed for attachment took place, this is automatic perfection. This is true because the refrigerator is a purchase money security interest in consumer goods.

        EXAMPLE: Same as previous example except that Second Intercity Bank provides the loan having B sign a security agreement. This is also a purchase money security interest in consumer goods. Perfection takes place when all three elements of attachment occur.

        EXAMPLE: In the two examples above, if B had purchased the refrigerator for use in a restaurant, the collateral would be equipment. Therefore, automatic perfection would not occur. However, the secured party could file a financing statement to perfect the security interest in both cases.

       (c) Perfection by attachment does not occur for motor vehicles—perfected by a lien on certificate of title filed with state

       (d) Automatic perfection is **not** effective against bona fide purchaser for value who buys goods from consumer for consumer use

         1] **Is effective**, however, if secured party had **filed**

          EXAMPLE: B purchases a washer and dryer from Dear Appliances for use in his home giving Dear a security interest, then sells the washer and dryer to C for a fair price for C's household use. C is unaware of the security interest that Dear has in the washer and dryer. Dear's perfection on attachment is not effective against C.

          EXAMPLE: Same example as above except that Dear had filed a financing statement. Dear wins because filing is effective even against a subsequent bona fide purchaser such as C even if he buys for consumer use.

          *EXAMPLE: In the two examples above, if C had purchased the items from B for other than consumer use, C is **not** free of Dear's security interest. This is so because the rule only applies to bona fide purchasers for consumer use. The extra step of filing would not be needed.*

         2] **Is effective** if subsequent purchaser knows of security interest before buying

> *EXAMPLE: An appliance dealer sells a freezer to Jack for family use. Assume attachment has occurred. Jack then sells it to Cindy who is aware of the security interest that the dealer still has in the freezer. Even if Cindy is buying this for household use, she takes subject to the security interest.*

    (2) Sale of promissory notes

    (3) Assignment of health care insurance to health care provider

    (4) Temporary automatic perfection for twenty days for instruments, certificated securities, negotiable documents, and proceeds of sale of perfected security interest

D. Other Issues under Secured Transactions

1. After-acquired property and future goods may also become part of collateral if agreement so states

   > *EXAMPLE: An agreement states that the collateral consists of all of debtor's furniture now located in his office as well as all office furniture subsequently acquired. The security interest in the new furniture cannot attach until the debtor acquires rights in the other office furniture.*

   a. Typically used for inventory and accounts receivable when debtor also has rights to sell inventory and collect accounts (e.g., a floating lien)

       (1) Sometimes used for equipment

   > *EXAMPLE: A, an automobile dealer, to obtain a loan, grants a bank a security interest covering "all automobiles now possessed and hereafter acquired." As the dealer obtains rights in the new inventory of automobiles, the security interest attaches as to those newly acquired automobiles.*

   b. Certain restrictions exist if debtor buys consumer goods to protect consumer

       (1) An after acquired property clause applying to consumer goods is only effective against the consumer for ten days from date of purchase

2. Although security interests in tort claims now come under revised Article 9, this security interest will not attach to an after-acquired commercial tort claim

3. Computer software embedded in goods is treated as part of those goods and not as software

4. Field warehousing is used to perfect security interest (analogous to possession or control)

   a. Debtor keeps inventory on his/her premises under control of third party such as bonded warehouseman or secured party's employee

   b. Secured party keeps control over inventory such as use of separate room or fenced-off portion with sign showing secured party's control

5. Consignments

   a. Consignment of security interest

       (1) If it is a "true consignment," consignee is simply a sales agent who does not own the goods but sells them for consignor

           (a) "True consignment" exists when

               1] Consignor retains title to goods

               2] Consignee has no obligation to buy goods

               3] Consignor has right to all proceeds (pays consignee commission)

   > *EXAMPLE: Manufacturer (consignor) gives possession of goods to a marketing representative (consignee) to sell those goods on commission.*

           (b) To perfect his/her interest, a consignor must

               1] File a financing statement under secured transactions law and give notice to the consignee's creditors who have perfected security interests in the same type of goods

                   a] Notice must contain description of the goods to be delivered and be given before the consignee receives possession of goods

   > *EXAMPLE: P delivers goods to A on consignment. The consignment is a "true consignment" in that P has title to the goods and pays A a commission for selling the goods. Any goods that are unsold are returned by A to P. A does not pay for any unsold goods. Creditors of A can assert claims against the goods that A possesses unless P has given notice to the creditors. The general way to accomplish this is by filing under the secured transactions law.*

       (2) If it is not a true consignment because it is actually a **sale** from creditor to debtor in which debtor then owns the goods, look for a security agreement

(a) Attachment and perfection occur as in typical secured transaction

E. Priorities

1. If more than one party claims a security interest in same collateral, rules of priority should be examined
2. Although the rules on priorities are complex with many exceptions the following will give the general, important rules to prepare you for the exam
3. General rules of priorities

   a. If both parties have perfected, then first to either file or perfect generally has priority

      (1) This is true even if filing takes place before attachment

      EXAMPLE: K obtains a written security agreement on day one on collateral that D owns and possesses. On day two, K files a financing statement but does not loan the money (value) until day ten. L obtains a written security agreement on the same collateral on day three and gives value on day four and files on day six. K has priority because he filed first even though attachment and perfection did not occur until later (day ten). To test your understanding, note that for L, attachment took place on day four and perfection on day six.

      EXAMPLE: C obtains a security agreement from D on some jewelry that D owns. C loans D $1,000 and takes possession of the jewelry. The day before, D had signed a security agreement granting E a security interest in the same jewelry. E gives D $900 as a loan and files a financing statement one week later on the jewelry. C has priority over E since C perfected before E perfected and filed.

   b. Perfected security interests win over unperfected ones
   c. If neither is perfected, then the first to attach prevails although at least one party will be motivated to perfect
   d. General creditors (unsecured creditors) lose to secured creditors (perfected or unperfected)

4. Other principles on priorities

   a. Buyers in the ordinary course of business take free of any security interest whether perfected or not (be sure to know this one)

      (1) In general, buying in the ordinary course of business means buying from inventory of a person or company that normally deals in those goods
      (2) Buyer has priority even if s/he knows that security agreement exists but buyer must have possession
      (3) Purpose is to allow purchasers to buy from merchants without fear of security agreements between merchants and other parties

      EXAMPLE: S, a dealer in stereos, obtained financing from L by securing the loan with her inventory in stereos. B purchases one of the stereos from that inventory. B takes free of the security interest that L has in the inventory of S whether it is perfected or not.

   b. Distinguish between buyers in the ordinary course of business and the subsequent bona fide purchaser from consumers

      (1) The latter defeats only a purchase money security interest in consumer goods (perfection on attachment) unless filing takes place—applies to sale by consumer to consumer
      (2) The former applies whether buyer is consumer or not but seller is dealer in those goods

      EXAMPLE: See previous example. The result is the same whether or not B was a consumer when he bought in the ordinary course of business from S.

      EXAMPLE: Refer again to the same example using S, L, and B. Now let's add on one more security interest in that B is buying the stereo on credit from S and for his own personal use. Attachment has occurred. There is perfection by attachment because between B and S, it is a purchase money security interest in consumer goods. If B sells the stereo to N, his neighbor, for consumer use, then N takes free of the perfected security interest (unless S had filed or N had notice of the security interest).

   c. In the case of a purchase money security interest, if the secured party files within ten days after the debtor receives the collateral, then this defeats other security interests by use of a ten-day grace period

      (1) Note that this purchase money security interest (PMSI) does not require consumer goods

      EXAMPLE: On August 1, B purchased some equipment from S on credit. All elements of attachment are satisfied on this date. On August 3, B borrows money from a bank using equipment purchased from S as collateral. Attachment is accomplished and a financing statement is correctly filed by the bank on August 3. On August 7, S then files a financing statement. Because of the ten-day grace period, S has priority over the bank.

> EXAMPLE: *Same as above except that S files after the ten-day grace period or not at all. The bank has priority.*

   (2) If inventory, no ten-day grace period is allowed for perfection to have priority

      (a) Party with purchase money security interest must give notice to other secured party

      (b) Party with purchase money security interest must perfect prior to debtor's taking possession

   (3) Knowledge of preexisting security interest has no effect

d. Holder in due course of negotiable instruments wins over perfected or unperfected security interest

e. Security interest, perfected or unperfected, wins over subsequent perfected security interest if latter party **knew** of previous security interest

f. Possessor of negotiable document of title has priority over others

g. Lien creditor (e.g., repairman or contractor)

   (1) Has priority over an unperfected security interest

      (a) Knowledge of security interest is immaterial

   (2) Has priority over a security interest perfected after attachment of the lien unless it is a purchase money security interest perfected within the ten-day grace period

   (3) A security interest perfected before the lien usually has priority

   (4) Lien by statute (not by judgment or court order) has priority over a prior perfected security interest unless state statute expressly provides otherwise

> EXAMPLE: *A person such as a repairman, in the ordinary course of business, furnishes services or materials with respect to goods subject to a security interest. The repairman (artisan lien) has priority.*

h. Trustee in bankruptcy as a lien creditor

   (1) Trustee has the rights of a lien creditor from the date of filing of petition in bankruptcy

      (a) So has priority over a security interest perfected after date of filing petition unless it is a purchase money security interest perfected within the ten-day grace period

   (2) Trustee also takes the position of any existing lien creditor

F. Rights of Parties upon Default

1. If collateral consists of claims (e.g., receivables), the secured party has the right of collection from third parties

   a. Secured party may notify third party to pay secured party directly

   b. Secured party must account for any surplus and debtor is liable for any deficiency

   c. Secured party may deduct his/her reasonable expenses

2. Secured party may retain collateral already in his/her possession or may take possession or control from debtor

   a. May do so him/herself if s/he can without breach of the peace

   b. Otherwise, s/he must use judicial process to foreclose on collateral

   c. Secured party has duty to take reasonable care of collateral in his/her possession

      (1) Expenses to protect collateral are responsibility of debtor

3. If secured party proposes to satisfy obligation by retaining the collateral, s/he must

   a. Send written notice to debtor

   b. Must notify other secured parties (who have sent written notice of their interest), unless consumer goods

   c. Can only retain consumer goods if debtor has paid less than 60% of the purchase price or obligation

      (1) If 60% or more has been paid, secured party must sell collateral within ninety days after taking possession or be liable to the debtor unless debtor waives this right to sale **after** the default

4. Secured party may sell collateral

   a. May be a public or a private sale

   b. Must use commercially reasonable practices—this right cannot be waived by debtor

    c. Must sell within a reasonable time

    d. Must notify debtor of time and place of public sale or time after which private sale will occur unless collateral is perishable, threatens to decline in value, or is type sold on a recognized market

        (1) Must also notify other secured parties (who have sent written notice of their interest) unless collateral consists of consumer goods

    e. Secured party may buy at any public sale and also at a private sale if rights of debtor protected

    f. Subordinate claims are entitled to any surplus

        (1) Debtor is entitled to surplus (if any) after all claims and expenses are paid or is liable for deficiency (if any)

5. Debtor has right to redeem collateral before secured party disposes of it by paying

    a. Entire debt, and

    b. Secured party's reasonable expenses

6. Most remedies can be varied by agreement if reasonable

    a. Provision that secured party must account for any surplus to debtor cannot be varied by agreement

7. Good-faith purchaser (i.e., for value and with no knowledge of defects in sale) of collateral takes free of debtor's rights and any secured interest or lien subordinate to it

    a. Receives debtor's title

    b. If sale was improper, remedy of debtor is money damages against secured party who sold collateral, not against good-faith purchaser

MULTIPLE-CHOICE QUESTIONS (1-30)

1. Under the Revised UCC Secured Transaction Article, when collateral is in a secured party's possession, which of the following conditions must also be satisfied to have attachment?
   a. There must be a written security agreement.
   b. The public must be notified.
   c. The secured party must receive consideration.
   d. The debtor must have rights to the collateral.

2. Under the Revised UCC Secured Transaction Article, which of the following after-acquired property may be attached to a security agreement given to a secured lender?

	Inventory	Equipment
a.	Yes	Yes
b.	Yes	No
c.	No	Yes
d.	No	No

3. Gardner Bank loaned Holland Company $20,000 to purchase some inventory to resell in its store. Gardner had Holland sign a security agreement that listed as collateral all present and future inventory of Holland as well as the proceeds of any sales of the inventory. Later, Boldon Company, who was aware of Gardner's security interest, extended credit to Holland but Holland failed to pay back either Gardner or Boldon. Boldon has sought to defeat the security interest pointing out that Gardner never filled out a financing statement. Which of the following is correct?
   a. Gardner has an enforceable security interest that is valid against Holland and has priority over Boldon's interests.
   b. Gardner does not have an enforceable security interest valid against Holland or against Boldon.
   c. Gardner does have an enforceable security interest valid against Holland but not valid against Boldon.
   d. Gardner does not have an enforceable security interest valid against Holland but does have one valid against Boldon.

4. Article 9 of the UCC which governs security interests has added some items that now are covered by security interests law. Which of the following is true?
   a. Security interests in tort claims already assessed by a court of law are covered.
   b. After-acquired commercial tort claims are covered.
   c. Both a. and b.
   d. Neither a. nor b.

5. Under the Revised Secured Transactions Article of the UCC, which of the following requirements is necessary to have a security interest attach?

	Debtor had rights in the collateral	Proper filing of a security agreement	Value given by the creditor
a.	Yes	Yes	Yes
b.	Yes	Yes	No
c.	Yes	No	Yes
d.	No	Yes	Yes

6. Under the Revised UCC Secured Transaction Article, which of the following events will always prevent a security interest from attaching?
   a. Failure to have a written security agreement.
   b. Failure of the creditor to have possession of the collateral.
   c. Failure of the debtor to have rights in the collateral.
   d. Failure of the creditor to give present consideration for the security interest.

7. Perfection of a security interest permits the secured party to protect its interest by
   a. Avoiding the need to file a financing statement.
   b. Preventing another creditor from obtaining a security interest in the same collateral.
   c. Establishing priority over the claims of most subsequent secured creditors.
   d. Denying the debtor the right to possess the collateral.

8. Under the Revised UCC Secured Transaction Article, what is the effect of perfecting a security interest by filing a financing statement?
   a. The secured party can enforce its security interest against the debtor.
   b. The secured party has permanent priority in the collateral even if the collateral is removed to another state.
   c. The debtor is protected against all other parties who acquire an interest in the collateral after the filing.
   d. The secured party has priority in the collateral over most creditors who acquire a security interest in the same collateral after the filing.

9. A secured creditor wants to file a financing statement to perfect its security interest. Under the Revised UCC Secured Transaction Article, which of the following must be included in the financing statement?
   a. A listing or description of the collateral.
   b. An after-acquired property provision.
   c. The creditor's signature.
   d. The collateral's location.

10. Which of the following transactions would illustrate a secured party perfecting its security interest by taking possession of the collateral?
   a. A bank receiving a mortgage on real property.
   b. A wholesaler borrowing to purchase inventory.
   c. A consumer borrowing to buy a car.
   d. A pawnbroker lending money.

11. Under the Revised UCC Secured Transaction Article, which of the following actions will best perfect a security interest in a negotiable instrument against any other party?
   a. Filing a security agreement.
   b. Taking possession of the instrument.
   c. Perfecting by attachment.
   d. Obtaining a duly executed financing statement.

12. Grey Corp. sells computers to the public. Grey sold and delivered a computer to West on credit. West executed and delivered to Grey a promissory note for the purchase price and a security agreement covering the computer. West purchased the computer for personal use. Grey did not file a financing statement. Is Grey's security interest perfected?
   a. Yes, because Grey retained ownership of the computer.

b. Yes, because it was perfected at the time of attachment.
c. No, because the computer was a consumer good.
d. No, because Grey failed to file a financing statement.

13. In which of the following cases does a seller have automatic perfection of a security interest as soon as attachment takes place?

I. Purchase money security interest in consumer goods.
II. Purchase money security interest in inventory.
III. Purchase money security interest in equipment.

a. I only.
b. I and II only.
c. II and III only.
d. I, II and III.

14. Mars, Inc. manufactures and sells VCRs on credit directly to wholesalers, retailers, and consumers. Mars can perfect its security interest in the VCRs it sells without having to file a financing statement or take possession of the VCRs if the sale is made to

a. Retailers.
b. Wholesalers that sell to distributors for resale.
c. Consumers.
d. Wholesalers that sell to buyers in the ordinary course of business.

15. Under the Revised Secured Transaction Article of the UCC, which of the following purchasers will own consumer goods free of a perfected security interest in the goods?

a. A merchant who purchases the goods for resale.
b. A merchant who purchases the goods for use in its business.
c. A consumer who purchases the goods from a consumer purchaser who gave the security interest.
d. A consumer who purchases the goods in the ordinary course of business.

16. Under the Revised UCC Secured Transaction Article, what is the order of priority for the following security interests in store equipment?

I. Security interest perfected by filing on April 15, 2001.
II. Security interest attached on April 1, 2001.
III. Purchase money security interest attached April 11, 2001 and perfected by filing on April 20, 2001.

a. I, III, II.
b. II, I, III.
c. III, I, II.
d. III, II, I.

17. Noninventory goods were purchased and delivered on June 15, 2001. Several security interests exist in these goods. Which of the following security interests has priority over the others?

a. Security interest in future goods attached June 10, 2001.
b. Security interest attached June 15, 2001.
c. Security interest perfected June 20, 2001.
d. Purchase money security interest perfected June 24, 2001.

18. Under the Revised Secured Transaction Article of the UCC, what would be the order of priority for the following security interests in consumer goods?

I. Financing agreement filed on April 1.
II. Possession of the collateral by a creditor on April 10.
III. Financing agreement perfected on April 15.

a. I, II, III.
b. II, I, III.
c. II, III, I.
d. III, II, I.

19. A party who filed a security interest in inventory on April 1, 2001, would have a superior interest to which of the following parties?

a. A holder of a mechanic's lien whose lien was filed on March 15, 2001.
b. A holder of a purchase money security interest in after-acquired property filed on March 20, 2001.
c. A purchaser in the ordinary course of business who purchased on April 10, 2001.
d. A judgment lien creditor who filed its judgment on April 15, 2001.

20. W & B, a wholesaler, sold on credit some furniture to Broadmore Company, a retailer. W & B perfected its security interest by filing a financing statement. Lean purchased some furniture from Broadmore for his home. He was unaware of W & B's perfected security interest. McCoy purchased some furniture from Broadmore for her home. She was aware that Broadmore's inventory was subject to security interests since Broadmore was having financial problems and had to buy the furniture on credit. Norsome purchased some furniture from Broadmore for use in his business. Broadmore defaults on its loans from W & B, who wants to repossess the furniture purchased and delivered to Lean, McCoy, and Norsome. From which parties can W & B legally repossess the furniture?

a. McCoy.
b. Lean and McCoy.
c. Norsome.
d. None of these parties.

21. Rand purchased a sofa from Abby Department Store for use in her home. Abby had her sign a security agreement for the balance Rand owed. Rand did not pay the balance and sold the sofa to her neighbor, Gram, for use in his home. Gram did not realize that Rand had not paid off the balance. Abby filed a financing statement after Rand defaulted. This filing was also after Gram purchased the sofa from Rand. Which of the following is correct?

a. Abby can repossess the sofa from Gram since it has a written security agreement covering the sofa.
b. Abby can repossess the sofa from Gram since it perfected its security agreement by filing.
c. Abby can repossess the sofa from Gram since it obtained automatic perfection.
d. Abby has no right to repossess the sofa from Gram.

22. Wine purchased a computer using the proceeds of a loan from MJC Finance Company. Wine gave MJC a security interest in the computer. Wine executed a security agreement and financing statement, which was filed by MJC. Wine used the computer to monitor Wine's personal investments. Later, Wine sold the computer to Jacobs, for Jacobs' family use. Jacobs was unaware of MJC's security interest. Wine now is in default under the MJC loan. May MJC repossess the computer from Jacobs?

a. No, because Jacobs was unaware of the MJC security interest.

b. No, because Jacobs intended to use the computer for family or household purposes.

c. Yes, because MJC's security interest was perfected before Jacobs' purchase.

d. Yes, because Jacobs' purchase of the computer made Jacobs personally liable to MJC.

23. Rally Co. has purchased some inventory from Kantar Corporation to sell to customers who will use the inventory primarily for consumer use. Which of the following is **not** correct?

a. If Kantar sells the inventory to Rally on credit and takes out a security interest using the inventory as collateral, this a purchase money security interest.

b. If Kantar sells the inventory to Rally on credit and takes out a security interest using the inventory as collateral, this is a purchase money security interest in consumer goods.

c. If Kantar sells the inventory to Rally but Rally pays for it by getting a loan from a bank who takes out a security interest using the inventory as collateral, this is a purchase money security interest.

d. If a customer purchases some inventory on credit from Rally for home use and signs a written security agreement presented by Rally that lists the inventory as collateral for the credit, this is a purchase money security interest in consumer goods.

24. On June 15, Harper purchased equipment for $100,000 from Imperial Corp. for use in its manufacturing process. Harper paid for the equipment with funds borrowed from Eastern Bank. Harper gave Eastern a security agreement and financing statement covering Harper's existing and after-acquired equipment. On June 21, Harper was petitioned involuntarily into bankruptcy under Chapter 7 of the Federal Bankruptcy Code. A bankruptcy trustee was appointed. On June 23, Eastern filed the financing statement. Which of the parties will have a superior security interest in the equipment?

a. The trustee in bankruptcy, because the filing of the financing statement after the commencement of the bankruptcy case would be deemed a preferential transfer.

b. The trustee in bankruptcy, because the trustee became a lien creditor before Eastern perfected its security interest.

c. Eastern, because it had a perfected purchase money security interest without having to file a financing statement.

d. Eastern, because it perfected its security interest within the permissible time limits.

Items 25 and 26 are based on the following:

Drew bought a computer for personal use from Hale Corp. for $3,000. Drew paid $2,000 in cash and signed a security agreement for the balance. Hale properly filed the security agreement. Drew defaulted in paying the balance of the purchase price. Hale asked Drew to pay the balance. When Drew refused, Hale peacefully repossessed the computer.

25. Under the Revised UCC Secured Transaction Article, which of the following remedies will Hale have?

a. Obtain a deficiency judgment against Drew for the amount owed.

b. Sell the computer and retain any surplus over the amount owed.

c. Retain the computer over Drew's objection.

d. Sell the computer without notifying Drew.

26. Under the Revised UCC Secured Transaction Article, which of the following rights will Drew have?

a. Redeem the computer after Hale sells it.

b. Recover the sale price from Hale after Hale sells the computer.

c. Force Hale to sell the computer.

d. Prevent Hale from selling the computer.

27. Under the Revised UCC Secured Transaction Article, which of the following statements is correct concerning the disposition of collateral by a secured creditor after a debtor's default?

a. A good-faith purchaser for value and without knowledge of any defects in the sale takes free of any subordinate liens or security interests.

b. The debtor may not redeem the collateral after the default.

c. Secured creditors with subordinate claims retain the right to redeem the collateral after the collateral is sold to a third party.

d. The collateral may only be disposed of at a public sale.

28. Bean defaulted on a promissory note payable to Gray Co. The note was secured by a piece of equipment owned by Bean. Gray perfected its security interest on May 29, 2001 Bean had also pledged the same equipment as collateral for another loan from Smith Co. after he had given the security interest to Gray. Smith's security interest was perfected on June 30, 2001. Bean is current in his payments to Smith. Subsequently, Gray took possession of the equipment and sold it at a private sale to Walsh, a good-faith purchaser for value. Walsh will take the equipment

a. Free of Smith's security interest because Bean is current in his payments to Smith.

b. Free of Smith's security interest because Walsh acted in good faith and gave value.

c. Subject to Smith's security interest because the equipment was sold at a private sale.

d. Subject to Smith's security interest because Smith is a purchase money secured creditor.

29. Under the Revised Secured Transactions Article of the UCC, which of the following remedies is available to a secured creditor when a debtor fails to make a payment when due?

	Proceed against the collateral	*Obtain a general judgment against the debtor*
a.	Yes	Yes
b.	Yes	No
c.	No	Yes
d.	No	No

30. In what order are the following obligations paid after a secured creditor rightfully sells the debtor's collateral after repossession?

I. Debt owed to any junior security holder.

II. Secured party's reasonable sale expenses.

III. Debt owed to the secured party.

a. I, II, III.

b. II, I, III.

c. II, III, I.

d. III, II, I.

OTHER OBJECTIVE QUESTIONS

Problem 1   (5 to 10 minutes)

On January 2, 2002, Gray Interiors Corp., a retailer of sofas, contracted with Shore Furniture Co. to purchase 150 sofas for its inventory. The purchase price was $250,000. Gray paid $50,000 cash and gave Shore a note and security agreement for the balance. On March 1, 2002, the sofas were delivered. On March 10, 2002, Shore filed a financing statement.

On February 1, 2002, Gray negotiated a $1,000,000 line of credit with Float Bank, pledged its present and future inventory as security, and gave Float a security agreement. On February 20, 2002, Gray borrowed $100,000 from the line of credit. On March 5, 2002, Float filed a financing statement.

On April 1, 2002, Dove, a consumer purchaser in the ordinary course of business, purchased a sofa from Gray. Dove was aware of both security interests.

Required:

Items 1 through 6 refer to the above fact pattern. For each item, determine whether (A), (B), or (C) is correct.

1. Shore's security interest in the sofas attached on
   A. January 2, 2002.
   B. March 1, 2002.
   C. March 10, 2002.

2. Shore's security interest in the sofas was perfected on
   A. January 2, 2002.
   B. March 1, 2002.
   C. March 10, 2002.

3. Float's security interest in Gray's inventory attached on
   A. February 1, 2002.
   B. March 1, 2002.
   C. March 5, 2002.

4. Float's security interest in Gray's inventory was perfected on
   A. February 1, 2002.
   B. February 20, 2002.
   C. March 5, 2002.

5. A. Shore's security interest has priority because it was a purchase money security interest.
   B. Float's security interest has priority because Float's financing statement was filed before Shore's.
   C. Float's security interest has priority because Float's interest attached before Shore's.

6. A. Dove purchased the sofa subject to Shore's security interest.
   B. Dove purchased the sofa subject to both the Shore and Float security interests.
   C. Dove purchased the sofa free of either the Shore or Float security interests.

PROBLEMS

Problem 1   (15 to 20 minutes)

Dunn & Co., CPAs, is auditing the 2000 financial statements of its client, Safe Finance. While performing the audit, Dunn learned of certain transactions that occurred during 2000 that may have an adverse impact on Safe's financial statements. The following transactions are of most concern to Dunn:

• On May 5, Safe sold certain equipment to Lux, who contemporaneously executed and delivered to Safe a promissory note and security agreement covering the equipment. Lux purchased the equipment for use in its business. On May 8, City Bank loaned Lux $50,000, taking a promissory note and security agreement from Lux that covered all of Lux's existing and after-acquired equipment. On May 11, Lux was involuntarily petitioned into bankruptcy under the liquidation provisions of the Bankruptcy Code and a trustee was appointed. On May 12, City filed a financing statement covering all of Lux's equipment. On May 14, Safe filed a financing statement covering the equipment it had sold to Lux on May 5.

• On July 10, Safe loaned $600,000 to Cam Corp., which used the funds to refinance existing debts. Cam duly executed and delivered to Safe a promissory note and a security agreement covering Cam's existing and after-acquired inventory of machine parts. On July 12, Safe filed a financing statement covering Cam's inventory of machine parts. On July 15, Best Bank loaned Cam $200,000. Contemporaneous with the loan, Cam executed and delivered to Best a promissory note and security agreement covering all of Cam's inventory of machine parts and any after-acquired inventory. Best had already filed a financing statement covering Cam's inventory on June 20, after Best agreed to make the loan to Cam. On July 14, Dix, in good faith, purchased certain machine parts from Cam's inventory and received delivery that same day.

Required:

Define a purchase money security interest. In separate paragraphs, discuss whether Safe has a priority security interest over

• The trustee in Lux's bankruptcy with regard to the equipment sold by Safe on May 5.
• City with regard to the equipment sold by Safe on May 5.
• Best with regard to Cam's existing and after-acquired inventory of machine parts.
• Dix with regard to the machine parts purchased on July 14 by Dix.

Problem 2   (15 to 20 minutes)

On February 20, 2002, Pine, Inc. ordered a specially manufactured computer system consisting of a disk drive and a central processing unit (CPU) from Xeon Corp., a seller of computers and other office equipment. A contract was signed and the total purchase price was paid to Xeon by Pine on the same date. The contract required Pine to pick up the computer system at Xeon's warehouse on March 9, 2002, but was silent as to when risk of loss passed to Pine. The computer system was completed on March 1, 2002, and set aside for Pine's contemplated pickup on March 9, 2002.

On March 3, 2002, the disk drive was stolen from Xeon's warehouse. On March 9, 2002, Pine picked up the CPU. On March 15, 2002, Pine returned the CPU to Xeon for warranty repairs. On March 18, 2002, Xeon mistakenly sold the CPU to Meed, a buyer in the ordinary course of business.

On April 12, 2002, Pine purchased and received delivery of five word processors from Jensen Electronics Corp. for use in its business. The purchase price of the word processors was $15,000. Pine paid $5,000 down and executed an installment purchase note and a security agreement for the balance. The security agreement contained a description of the word processors. Jensen never filed a financing statement. On April 1, 2002, Pine had given its bank a security interest in all of its assets. The bank had immediately perfected its security interest by filing. Pine has defaulted on the installment purchase note.

Required:

Discuss the following assertions, indicating whether such assertions are correct and the reasons therefor.

• As of March 3, 2002, the risk of loss on the disk drive remained with Xeon.
• Meed acquired no rights in the CPU as a result of the March 18, 2002 transaction.
• Jensen's security interest in the word processors never attached and therefore, Jensen's security interest is not enforceable against Pine.
• Jensen has superior security interest to Pine's bank.

MULTIPLE-CHOICE ANSWERS

1. d	8. d	15. d	22. c	29. a
2. a	9. a	16. c	23. b	30. c
3. a	10. d	17. d	24. d	
4. a	11. b	18. a	25. a	
5. c	12. b	19. d	26. c	
6. c	13. a	20. d	27. a	1st: __/30 = __%
7. c	14. c	21. d	28. b	2nd: __/30 = __%

MULTIPLE-CHOICE ANSWER EXPLANATIONS

B.   Attachment of Security Interests

1.   (d)   Under the Revised Article 9 on Secured Transactions, attachment of a security interest takes place when the secured party gives value, the debtor has rights in the collateral, and one of the following three is true:

   a.   The secured party must possess the collateral if the debtor agrees to it

   b.   The secured party must have control of certain types of collateral, or

   c.   The secured party must have a signed security agreement (or an authenticated electronic transmission).

2.   (a)   An after-acquired property clause in a security agreement allows the secured party's interest in such property to attach once the debtor acquires the property, without the need to make a new security agreement. These clauses are typically used for inventory and accounts receivable, and can also be used for equipment.

3.   (a)   The security interest did attach because there was a signed security agreement, Gardner gave value, and Holland had rights in the collateral. Upon attachment, Gardner's security interest is fully enforceable against Holland. Even though Gardner never perfected the security interest, it still has priority over Boldon's interests because Boldon was aware of the security interest.

4.   (a)   Security interests in tort claims are covered under the Revised UCC Secured Transactions Article; this is not true of after-acquired commercial tort claims.

5.   (c)   In order for attachment of a security interest to occur, three elements must take place. First, the secured party must give value, second, the debtor must have rights in the collateral, and third, there must be a security agreement. This security agreement may be oral if the secured party has possession or control of the collateral. Otherwise, it must be in writing and signed by the debtor. An exception to the signature requirement is made if it is an authenticated electronic transmission.

6.   (c)   In order for a security interest to attach, there must be a valid security agreement, the secured party must have given value, and the debtor must have rights in the collateral. If any one of these items is missing, attachment cannot take place. Answer (a) is incorrect because the security interest may be oral if the secured party has possession or control of the collateral. Answer (b) is incorrect because if the security agreement is in writing, the secured party does not need possession of the collateral to achieve attachment. Answer (d) is incorrect because the secured party must give value, not necessarily consideration. A preexisting claim, although not consideration, does count as value.

C.4.   Filing a Financing Statement

7.   (c)   Perfection of a security interest is important in that it establishes for a secured party priority over the claims that may be made by most subsequent secured creditors. Answer (a) is incorrect because there are three methods of obtaining perfection and one of them is filing a financing statement. Answer (b) is incorrect because subsequent creditors may still obtain security interests in the same collateral although they will normally obtain a lower priority. Answer (d) is incorrect because of times the debtor retains possession of the collateral.

8.   (d)   Perfection by filing a financing statement will not defeat all other parties who acquire an interest in the same collateral; rather, perfection by filing gives the secured party most possible rights in the collateral. Note, purchasers from a merchant in the ordinary course of business take the collateral free from any prior perfected security interest. The only time a purchaser would take the collateral subject to a prior perfected security interest would be when the purchaser knew that the merchant was selling the goods in violation of a financing statement. A creditor need not perfect the security interest in order to enforce it against the debtor. The filing of a financing statement does not protect the debtor's rights but rather the creditor's rights.

9.   (a)   Filing a financing statement is one method of perfecting a security interest in personal property. Under the Revised UCC Secured Transaction Article, a financing statement must include the following: the names of the debtor and creditor, and a listing or description of the collateral. An after-acquired property provision, the creditor's signature, and the collateral's location are not required to be included in the financing statement.

C.5.   Perfection by Possession

10.   (d)   One way to perfect a security interest is for the secured party to take possession of the collateral in addition to attaining attachment. A pawnbroker lending money is such a case. There is a security agreement which may be oral since the secured party has possession of the collateral. The secured party gives value by lending the money. The third step in attachment is that the debtor has rights in the collateral such as ownership. Since these steps constitute attachment, perfection is accomplished by the pawnbroker, the secured party, taking possession of the collateral. The secured transactions laws apply to security interests in personal property, not real property. The wholesaler (car buyer), not the secured party, will have possession of the collateral.

11.   (b)   In general, the best way to perfect a security interest in a negotiable instrument is to take possession of the instrument. This is true because negotiable instruments are easily negotiated to other holders who can become holders in due course. Answer (a) is incorrect because a holder can become a holder in due course even if a security agreement is filed. Answer (c) is incorrect because perfecting by attachment requires a purchase money security interest in consumer goods. Answer (d) is incorrect because this cannot even accomplish perfection until it is filed.

C.6. Automatic Perfection

12. (b)   Since West purchased the computer for personal use and the computer itself was the collateral for the security agreement, the fact pattern involves a purchase money security interest in consumer goods. Therefore, once attachment took place, perfection was automatic. Answer (c) is incorrect because since the computer was a consumer good, perfection was automatic upon attachment. Answer (d) is incorrect because filing a financing statement is not required for perfecting a purchase money security interest in consumer goods. Answer (a) is incorrect because retaining or obtaining possession, not ownership, by the secured party is a way to perfect. In any event, Grey Corp. did not retain either ownership or possession since they sold and delivered the computer to West.

13. (a)   Automatic perfection (perfection by attachment) takes place in the case of a purchase money security interest (PMSI) in consumer goods only. Answers (b), (c), and (d) are incorrect because they include PMSI in inventory or equipment which do not qualify for automatic perfection.

14. (c)   Mars holds a purchase money security interest in the goods sold, which allowed the buyers of these goods to secure the credit for their purchase. When a purchase money security interest is in consumer goods, the secured party (Mars) obtains perfection when attachment takes place without the need to file a financing statement or take possession or control of the collateral. Answers (a), (b), and (d) are incorrect because in those cases the goods comprise inventory, not consumer goods.

E. Priorities

15. (d)   Buyers in the ordinary course of business take goods free of any security interest whether perfected or not. The buyer can be, but need not be, a consumer. Answer (a) is incorrect because a merchant who purchases consumer goods for resale may not be buying in the ordinary course of business. Answer (b) is incorrect because the merchant who buys the consumer goods for use in his/her business may not be buying in the ordinary course of business. Answer (c) is incorrect because although a consumer can take goods free of a security interest when buying from another consumer, this requires certain facts along with a purchase money security interest in consumer goods. There are no facts in the question to show this.

16. (c)   In general, a purchase money security interest in noninventory has priority over nonpurchase money security interests if it was perfected within ten days after the debtor received the collateral. Item III, therefore, has the first priority because the purchase money security interest was perfected on April 20, 2001, which was within twenty days of the attachment. Item I has priority over Item II because the security interest in Item I was perfected, while the security interest in Item II was not.

17. (d)   A purchase money security interest in noninventory goods has a special rule. Since it was perfected within twenty days after the debtor got possession of the collateral, it has priority over all of the others. Answers (a) and (b) are incorrect because unperfected security interests have a lower priority than perfected security interests. Answer (c) is incorrect because although this security interest was perfected before the purchase money security interest, the latter has priority if perfected within twenty days of the debtor taking possession of the collateral.

18. (a)   Since security interest I was perfected first when the financing agreement was filed on April 1, it has the first priority. Security interest II was perfected on April 10 when the creditor took possession of the collateral. It has the second priority. Security interest III has the third priority since it was perfected last on April 15.

19. (d)   The party perfected by filing a security interest in inventory on April 1, 2001. S/he would therefore have priority over a judgment lien creditor who filed later on April 15, 2001. Answer (a) is incorrect because the mechanic's lien was filed on March 15 before the perfection of the security interest. Therefore, the mechanic's lien has priority over the perfected security interest. Answer (b) is incorrect because the holder of the purchase money security interest in after-acquired property filed and perfected before April 1. Answer (c) is incorrect because a purchaser in the ordinary course of business is free of other security interests even if they are perfected before s/he purchases the inventory.

20. (d)   Lean, McCoy, and Norsome all purchased the furniture in the ordinary course of business. As such, all three parties take free of the security interest even if it was perfected. This is true whether they purchased the furniture for consumer or business use and whether they knew of the security agreement or not.

21. (d)   Abby had a perfected security agreement because of the purchase money security interest in consumer goods. This, however, is not effective against a good-faith purchaser for value who buys from a consumer for consumer use as in the case of Gram. Perfection by filing is, however, effective in such a case but only if the filing is done before Gram purchases the sofa. Answer (a) is incorrect because the attachment of the written security interest makes it enforceable against Rand, not Gram. Answer (b) is incorrect because the filing of the financing statement took place after Gram bought the sofa. Answer (c) is incorrect because, although Abby did accomplish automatic perfection by way of the PMSI in consumer goods, this type of perfection was not effective against Gram because he was a good-faith purchaser for value who bought it from a consumer (Rand) for consumer use.

22. (c)   MJC obtained a security interest in the computer purchased by Wine and perfected it by filing. Even though when Jacobs later purchased it for consumer use he was unaware of MJC's security interest, MJC still has priority. This is true because the filing is constructive notice to all subsequent parties. MJC has priority and may repossess the computer even if Jacobs was unaware of the filed security interest. The filing gives MJC priority over Jacob despite his intended use for family. Jacobs is not personally liable to MJC because he made no contract and did not agree to take on liability with MJC.

23. **(b)** Because Kantar has a security interest in the inventory it sold and is also using the same inventory as collateral for the credit, this is a purchase money security interest. However, because the items Rally purchased are inventory, not consumer goods, in **Rally's** hands, this is not a PMSI in consumer goods. Answer (a) is not chosen because this does describe a PMSI since Kantar retained a security interest in the same items sold on credit to secure payment. Answer (c) is not chosen because a PMSI includes a third party giving a loan who retains a security interest in the same items purchased by the loan. Answer (d) is not chosen because this is a PMSI in consumer goods since the customer purchased the items for his/her home use.

24. **(d)** When a purchase money security interest uses noninventory as collateral, it has priority over prior competing interests as long as it is perfected within twenty days of the debtor obtaining possession of the collateral. Since the collateral in this fact pattern was equipment, and Eastern filed within twenty days, Eastern has priority over the trustee in bankruptcy. Perfection was not automatic since it was a purchase money security interest in equipment, not in consumer goods. Furthermore, since the secured party did not have possession of the collateral, the way to perfect this security interest is by filing a financing statement.

F. Rights of Parties upon Default

25. **(a)** After Hale repossesses the computer and sells it in a commercially reasonable fashion, Hale may obtain a deficiency judgment for the amount still owed after the proceeds from the sale pay the expenses of repossession and sale and the debt owed to Hale. Any remaining proceeds go to the debtor after repossession and sale expenses and secured parties are paid. For consumer goods, such as the personal computer in this fact pattern, the goods must be sold if the debtor has paid more than 60% of the debt secured by the consumer goods. In this fact pattern, Drew paid two-thirds of the debt. Hale must notify Drew in writing of the impending sale unless Drew had agreed otherwise in writing.

26. **(c)** Since Drew has paid two-thirds of the price, which is over 60% payment on the secured debt for consumer goods, Hale is obligated to sell the computer rather than keep it in satisfaction of the debt. The debtor may redeem before, not after, the sale. Hale may keep the proceeds needed to pay off repossession and sale expenses and the debt owed to Hale. Any excess would go to Drew. Hale has the right to sell the repossessed computer to pay off the secured debt unless Drew properly redeems the interest s/he has in the computer.

27. **(a)** Upon the debtor's default, the secured party may take possession of the collateral and sell it. A good-faith purchaser for value buys the collateral free of any liens or security interests. Answer (b) is incorrect because the debtor has the right to redeem the collateral before the secured party disposes of it. The debtor does this by paying the debt in full as well as the secured party's reasonable expenses. Answer (c) is incorrect as a good-faith purchaser of the collateral takes it free of the debtor's rights and any secured interest or lien subordinate to it. Answer (d) is incorrect because although the collateral may be disposed of by a public sale, it also may be disposed of by a private sale if the sale uses commercially reasonable practices.

28. **(b)** A good-faith purchaser for value at a private sale will take the property free from any security interest or subordinate liens in the property, but remains subject to security interests which are senior to that being discharged at the sale. In this case, Smith perfected his security interest later than Gray and has a subordinate interest in the property. Thus, Walsh takes the equipment free from this subordinate security interest. The fact that Bean is current in his payments to Smith would not affect Smith's interest in the property. As long as Walsh is a good-faith purchaser for value, it doesn't matter if the equipment is sold at a public or private sale. Smith is not a purchase money secured creditor since the proceeds of Smith's loan to Bean were not used to purchase the equipment acting as collateral.

29. **(a)** If the debtor defaults on the debt, the secured party may proceed against the collateral. This extra protection is one of the main reasons for having secured transactions. If the creditor chooses, s/he may obtain a general judgment against the debtor.

30. **(c)** Under the UCC, after a secured creditor rightfully sells the debtor's collateral after repossession, the secured party's reasonable sale expenses are paid first. Next, the debt owed to the secured party is paid. Any junior security holders then get paid to the extent of any money remaining.

OTHER OBJECTIVE ANSWERS AND ANSWER EXPLANATIONS

Problem 1

1.   **(B)** Gray gave Shore a security agreement on January 2. Shore also gave value but Gray did not receive the goods or have rights in them until March 1. Therefore, it was not until March 1 that attachment occurred.

2.   **(C)** Perfection took place on March 10, when Shore filed the financing statement, since attachment had already been accomplished. Note that the filing was needed for perfection since this was not a purchase money security interest in consumer goods but in inventory.

3.   **(A)** Float gave value by giving the $1,000,000 line of credit on February 1. On this same date, Gray gave Float a security agreement. Since Gray had rights in the collateral it already possessed, attachment took place on February 1 for that inventory possessed.

4.   **(C)** Perfection occurred on March 5, when Float filed the financing statement, since attachment had already taken place previously.

5.   **(B)** Generally, when two parties have perfected security interests in the same collateral, the first to either file or perfect has priority. When a purchase money security interest exists in the collateral, however, the general rule may vary, depending on whether the collateral is inventory or noninventory. In this case the collateral is inventory. A purchase money security interest in inventory may obtain priority over previously perfected conflicting security interests if (1) the purchase money security holder perfects his interest in the inventory at the time the debtor receives the inventory, and (2) the purchase money security holder provides written notice of his purchase money security interest and a description of the inventory to all holders of conflicting security interests who have filed financing statements covering the same type of inventory. If the purchase money security holder does not take these steps, the general rule applies. Answer (A) is incorrect because Shore did not take the necessary steps for its purchase money security interest to obtain priority. Answer (B) is correct because the general rule applies, and Float filed first. Answer (C) is incorrect because when both security interests are perfected, priority is not based on the order of attachment.

6.   **(C)** A buyer in the ordinary course of business takes free of any security interests even if perfected and even if the buyer is aware of the security interests. Therefore, answers (A) and (B) are incorrect because Dove purchased the goods in the ordinary course of business.

ANSWER OUTLINE

Problem 1   Purchase Money Security Interest; Priority of Bankruptcy Trustee; Purchase Money Secured Party in Equipment and Buyer in Ordinary Course of Business

Purchase Money Security Interest

Interest in personal property or fixtures

Secures payment or performance

Occurs when either

(1)   Seller retains interest in item sold on credit, or

(2)   Creditor retains interest in item purchased with loaned funds

Priorities

Safe has priority over trustee (i.e., lien creditor from date of filing petition)

   Generally, unperfected security interest is subordinate to person becoming lien creditor before the security interest is perfected

   Safe as a purchase money secured party in equipment has twenty-day grace period for filing

   Safe filed within twenty-day grace period

     Safe has priority over City

     A purchase money security interest in equipment, if perfected no later than the end of the twenty-day grace period, prevails over a conflicting security interest

     Safe filed within ten days of Lux's possession of the equipment

   Best has priority over Safe

     If both conflicting security interests require filing to be perfected, the first party to **file** has priority

       Best filed before Safe

   Dix has priority over Safe

     A buyer in the ordinary course of business takes free of prior perfected security interest

     Dix qualifies as a buyer in the ordinary course of business

UNOFFICIAL ANSWER

Problem 1   Purchase Money Security Interest; Priority of Bankruptcy Trustee; Purchase Money Secured Party in Equipment and Buyer in Ordinary Course of Business

A purchase money security interest is an interest in personal property or fixtures that secures payment or performance of an obligation and that is (1) taken or retained by the seller of the collateral to secure all or part of its price, or (2) taken by a person who by making advances or incurring an obligation gives value to enable the debtor to acquire rights in or the use of collateral if such value is, in fact, so used.

Safe's security interest has priority over the rights of the trustee in bankruptcy. The Revised UCC Article on Secured Transactions states that a lien creditor includes a trustee in bankruptcy from the date of the filing of the petition. Under the general rule, an unperfected security interest is subordinate to the rights of a person who becomes a lien creditor before the security interest is perfected. However, if the secured party files with respect to a purchase money security interest before or within twenty days after the debtor receives possession of the collateral, he takes priority over the rights of a lien creditor that arise between the time the security interest attaches and the time of filing. Under the facts of our case, Safe has a purchase money security interest in the equipment because the security interest was taken by

Safe to secure the price. Therefore, because Safe filed a financing statement on May 14 (within ten days after Lux received possession of the equipment), it has a priority security interest over the trustee in bankruptcy (lien creditor) whose claim arose between the time the security interest attached (May 5) and the time of filing (May 14).

Safe has a priority security interest in the equipment over City. A purchase money security interest in collateral other than inventory has priority over a conflicting security interest in the same collateral if the purchase money security interest is perfected at the time the debtor receives possession of the collateral or within ten days thereafter. Because Safe has a purchase money security interest in the equipment that was perfected by filing a financing statement on May 14 (within ten days after Lux received possession of the equipment on May 5), Safe has a priority security interest over City despite City's perfection of its security interest on May 12.

Best's security interest in the inventory has priority over Safe's security interest. In general, conflicting perfected security interests rank according to priority in time of filing or perfection. Priority dates from the time a filing is first made covering the collateral or the time the security interest is first perfected, whichever is earlier, provided that there is no period thereafter when there is neither a filing nor perfection. In this case, because both Best's and Safe's security interests were perfected by filing, the first to file (Best) will have a priority security interest. The fact that Best filed a financing statement prior to making the loan will not affect Best's priority.

Safe will not have a priority security interest over Dix because Dix is a buyer in the ordinary course of business and will take free of Safe's perfected security interest. Dix is a buyer in the ordinary course of business because Dix acted in good faith when purchasing the machine parts in the regular course of Cam's business. The Revised UCC Article on Secured Transactions states that a buyer in the ordinary course of business takes free of a security interest created by his seller even though the security interest is perfected, and even though the buyer knows of its existence. Therefore, Dix will take the machine parts purchased from Cam's inventory on July 14, free from Safe's security interest, which was perfected on July 12.

ANSWER OUTLINE

Problem 2   Risk of Loss; Rights under Entrusting of Possession of Goods; Attachment of Security Interests; Perfection of Security Interests

Correct, risk of loss remained with Xeon

   When agreement is silent and seller is merchant, risk passes to buyer when buyer receives goods

Incorrect, Meed did acquire rights in CPU

   Entrusting situation: merchant acquires power to transfer ownership and title

     Entruster (Xeon) must be rightful owner

     Merchant must deal in goods of like kind

     Buyer must be in ordinary course of business

Incorrect, Jensen's security interest attached and is enforceable

   Security interest in collateral attaches if

     Secured party has security agreement, signed by debtor containing description of collateral

May be oral if collateral is in secured party's possession
Secured party gave value
Debtor has rights in collateral
Incorrect, Jensen does not have superior interest to bank
Purchase money security interest is not in consumer goods—no automatic perfection
Jensen must file to perfect
Bank has superior interest because it perfected; Jensen did not

UNOFFICIAL ANSWER

Problem 2 Risk of Loss; Rights under Entrusting of Possession of Goods; Attachment of Security Interests; Perfection of Security Interests

The assertion that as of March 3, 2002, the risk of loss on the disk drive remained with Xeon is correct. Under the UCC Sales Article, if the agreement between the parties is otherwise silent, risk of loss passes to the buyer on the buyer's receipt of the goods if the seller is a merchant. Under the facts, Xeon is a merchant because it sells computer systems. Therefore, the risk of loss remained with Xeon because the disk drive was never received by Pine.

The assertion that Meed acquired no rights in the CPU as a result of the March 18, 2002, transaction is incorrect. Under the UCC Sales Article, any entrusting of possession of goods to a merchant who deals in goods of that kind gives the merchant power to transfer all rights of the entruster to the buyer in the ordinary course of business. Entrusting includes any delivery and any acquiescence in retention of possession regardless of any condition expressed between the parties to the delivery or acquiescence, and regardless of whether the possessor's disposition of the goods has been such as to be larcenous under criminal law. For the merchant to acquire the power to transfer ownership and title, the entruster must be the rightful owner. Under the facts of this case, Pine had title at the time the CPU was returned to Xeon for repairs and this constituted an entrusting that gave Xeon the power to transfer all of Pine's rights in the CPU to Meed.

The assertion that Jensen's security interest in the word processors never attached and therefore Jensen's security interest is not enforceable against Pine with respect to the word processors is incorrect. A security interest in collateral will attach if: the collateral is in the possession of the secured party under an agreement, or the debtor has signed a security agreement that contains a description of the collateral; the secured party has given value; and the debtor has rights in the collateral. Based on the facts, Jensen's security interest attached on April 12, 2002, when Jensen sold and Pine received the word processors and Jensen received a security agreement executed by Pine that described the word processors. On attachment, Jensen's security interest became enforceable against Pine.

The assertion that Jensen has a superior security interest to Pine's bank is incorrect. Although Jensen has a purchase money security interest to the extent the security interest is taken by Jensen to secure the purchase price, Jensen's security interest will not be perfected by attachment alone. Jensen must file a financing statement to perfect its security interest because the collateral involved is goods used for business purposes and not consumer goods. Therefore, Jensen has an unperfected security interest in the word processors and the bank obtained a superior security interest by perfecting.

Keep practicing! Wiley's CPA Examination Review Software has over 2,800 questions.

Available at www.wiley.com/cpa

BANKRUPTCY

Overview

The overall objective of bankruptcy law is to allow honest insolvent debtors to surrender most of their assets and obtain release from their debts. A secondary purpose is to give creditors fair opportunity to share in the debtor's limited assets in proportion to their claims.

Bankruptcy is typically tested by either a few multiple-choice questions or an essay question. These questions normally emphasize when involuntary and voluntary proceedings can be conducted, the federal exemp-

tions, the role of the trustee in bankruptcy, preferential transfers, priorities, and conditions under which debts may be discharged in bankruptcy. Although bankruptcy under Chapter 7 is emphasized on the CPA examination, you should also be familiar with the other portions of this module. Recently, for example, Chapter 11 on Business Reorganizations has received some increased treatment.

Various dollar amounts in this module have been increased so the dollar amounts in various textbooks may be too low under current bankruptcy law

A. Alternatives to Bankruptcy Proceedings

1. Creditors may choose to do nothing

   a. Expense of collection may exceed what creditors could recover
   b. Creditors may expect debtor to pull through

2. Creditors may rush to satisfy their claims individually through legal proceedings (i.e., legal judgments, garnishing of wages, etc.)

   a. Bankruptcy proceedings may result anyway, especially if some creditors are dissatisfied

3. Receiverships

   a. This provides for general administration of debtor's assets by a court appointee (a receiver) for benefit of all parties

4. Agreements can be used to avoid bankruptcy such as composition agreements with creditors whereby creditors agree to accept less

   a. Creditors who do not agree may force debtor into bankruptcy

B. Bankruptcy in General

1. Bankruptcy is based mostly on federal law
2. Bankruptcy provides a method of protecting creditors' rights and granting the debtor relief from his/her indebtedness

   a. Debtor is permitted to have a fresh start
   b. Creditors are treated more fairly according to the priorities stated in bankruptcy laws to effect an equitable distribution of debtor's property

C. Chapter 7 Voluntary Bankruptcy Petitions

1. Voluntary bankruptcy petition is a formal request by debtor for an order of relief

   a. Petition is filed with court along with list of debtor's assets and liabilities
   b. Debtor need not be insolvent—merely needs to state that s/he has debts
   c. Debtor is automatically given an order of relief upon filing of petition

      (1) Court may dismiss voluntary petition if petitioning debtor obligations are primarily consumer debts and granting of relief would be substantial abuse of Chapter 7—(debtor may then proceed under Chapter 13)

   d. Petition may be filed by husband and wife jointly

2. Any person, partnership, or corporation may file voluntary bankruptcy petition with some exceptions

   a. Insurance companies, banks, and savings and loans may not

D. Chapter 7 Involuntary Bankruptcy Petitions

1. Involuntary bankruptcy petition may be filed with bankruptcy court by creditors requesting an order for relief

2. Requirements to file petition

    a. If there are fewer than twelve creditors, a single creditor may file the petition as long as his/her claim aggregates $11,625 in excess of any security s/he may hold

        (1) Claims must not be contingent

        (2) If necessary, more than one creditor may join together to have combined debts of more than $11,625 of unsecured claims

        *EXAMPLE: Poor-R-Us Company is not paying its debts as they become due. Its creditors are A (owed $12,000), B (owed $7,000), and C (owed $5,000). A alone may file the involuntary petition to force the company into bankruptcy; however, if A does not wish to do so, neither B nor C **separately** may force the company into bankruptcy because of failure to meet the $11,625 test. B and C may join together to file the petition.*

        EXAMPLE: XYZ Corporation is unable to pay current obligations. XYZ has three creditors: L (owed $12,000 which is secured by personal property), M (owed $24,000 of which one-half is secured), and N (owed $16,000 of which none is secured). L may not file an involuntary bankruptcy petition but can use the personal property to pay off the debt. Either M or N can file the petition.

    b. If there are twelve or more creditors, then at least three must sign the petition and they must have claims that aggregate $11,625 in excess of any security held by them

        (1) Claims must not be contingent

        (2) Claims subject to bona fide dispute are not counted in above $11,625 tests

        EXAMPLE: Poor, Inc. is unable to meet its current obligations as they are becoming due because of severe business difficulties. It owes over $20,000 to a dozen different creditors. One of the unsecured creditors, Green, is owed $12,000. Green may not force Poor, Inc. into Chapter 7 bankruptcy because even though Green is owed more than $11,625, Green must be joined by two other creditors, even if their claims are very small.

        EXAMPLE: Same facts as above except that Poor, Inc. has only eleven creditors. Now Green alone may force Poor, Inc. into bankruptcy under Chapter 7.

    c. Creditors who file petition in bankruptcy may need to post a bond that indemnifies debtor for losses caused by contesting petition to avoid frivolous petitions

        (1) Bankruptcy court may award damages including attorneys' fees to debtor who successfully challenges involuntary bankruptcy petition against creditors filing petition

            (a) If petition was made in bad faith, punitive damages may also be awarded

3. Exempt from involuntary bankruptcy are

    a. Persons (individuals, partnerships, or corporations) owing less than $11,625

    b. Farmers

    c. Charitable organizations

4. When valid petition in bankruptcy is filed, it stops enforcement of most collections of debts and legal proceedings

    EXAMPLE: A judgment lien against property in the bankrupt's estate may not be enforced once the petition in bankruptcy is filed so that an orderly disposition of this debt and others can be accomplished.

    a. Does not stop collection of alimony

5. Bankruptcy not available for deceased person's estate

    a. But once bankruptcy has begun, it is not stopped if bankrupt (debtor) dies

6. An order of relief will be granted if the requirements for filing are met, and

    a. The petition is uncontested; or

    b. The petition is contested; and

        (1) The debtor is generally not paying his/her debts as they become due; or

        (2) During the 120 days preceding the filing of the petition, a custodian was appointed or took possession of substantially all of the property of the debtor

        EXAMPLE: Debtor assigns his property for the benefit of his creditor.

    c. Note that the above rules involve a modified insolvency in the "equity sense" (i.e., debtor not paying debts as they become due). The rest of the Bankruptcy Act uses insolvency in the "bankruptcy sense" (i.e., liabilities exceed fair market value of all nonexempt assets). The use of insolvency in the equity sense for involuntary proceedings is important.

E. Chapter 7 Bankruptcy Proceedings (also called a liquidation or straight bankruptcy)

  1. Take place under federal law

    a. An order of relief is sought
    b. Court appoints interim trustee
    c. Filing petition automatically stays other legal proceedings against debtor's estate until bankruptcy case is over or until court orders otherwise
    d. Debtor may regain property in possession of interim trustee by filing court approved bond

    EXAMPLE: Mortgage foreclosure by savings and loan will be suspended against debtor.

  2. First creditors' meeting

    a. Debtor furnishes a schedule of assets, their locations, and a list of creditors
    b. Claims of debtors are deemed allowed unless objected to, in which case the court will determine their validity

      (1) Claims must be filed within six months of first creditors' meeting
      (2) Contingent and unliquidated claims are estimated
      (3) Any attorneys' fees above those ruled reasonable by court are disallowed when objected to by creditors

    c. Trustee may be elected by creditors in Chapter 7 proceeding

      (1) If no election requested by creditors, interim trustee appointed by court continues in office

  3. Trustee—the representative of the estate

    a. Trustee has right to receive compensation for services rendered based on value of those services (rather than only on size of estate)
    b. Duties—to collect, liquidate, and distribute the estate, keeping accurate records of all transactions
    c. Trustee represents estate of bankrupt (debtor)
    d. Estate of debtor consists of

      (1) Property presently owned by debtor (as of the filing date)
      (2) Property owed to debtor by third parties that can be recovered by trustee
      (3) Income from property owned by estate after petition is filed
      (4) Property received by debtor within 180 days after filing of petition by following methods: inheritance, life insurance, divorce decree, property settlement with spouse, bequest, or devise

        (a) Part of estate of debtor even if debtor has right to receive above within 180 days after the filing of petition

      (5) Leases disguised as secured or unsecured installment sales contracts

        (a) Typically happens when lessee automatically owns "leased" property for no additional consideration or when lessee has option to buy "leased" property for nominal consideration, especially when leased property has a significant market value

          1] However, if agreement is a true lease, it is not part of the lessee's estate

          EXAMPLE: Y has been leasing property to Z under which Z may purchase the property for $10 at the expiration of the lease. It is estimated that the property will be worth $6,000, however, at that time. If Z takes out or is forced into Chapter 7 bankruptcy, this property will be included as part of Z's estate.

          EXAMPLE: Same facts as above except that Y perfects its security interest. Now Y can sell the property to satisfy Y's debt.

      (6) Property acquired by debtor, other than by methods listed above, after filing is considered "new estate" and not subject to creditors' claims in bankruptcy proceeding

4. Exemptions to which debtor is entitled

   a. Keeps any interests in joint tenancy property if those interests are exempt under other nonbankruptcy law, and

   b. Debtor usually has option of choosing either

      (1) **Both** exemptions under state law and federal law other than under federal Bankruptcy Code

         (a) Typical state exemptions (limited in monetary value) include

            1] Small amount of money
            2] Residence
            3] Clothing
            4] Tools of trade
            5] Insurance

         (b) Examples of exemptions under federal nonbankruptcy law

            1] Veteran's benefits
            2] Social security benefits
            3] Unemployment compensation or benefits
            4] Disability benefits
            5] Alimony

      (2) Or, exemptions provided by federal Bankruptcy Code

         (a) Allowable federal exemptions include

            1] $17,425 equity in principal residence and burial plot
            2] $2,775 equity in one motor vehicle
            3] $1,750 in books and tools of one's trade
            4] $450 per item qualifying for personal, family, or home use (has an aggregate ceiling of $9,300)
            5] $1,150 in jewelry
            6] Dividends and life insurance up to $9,300
            7] Social security benefits
            8] Unemployment compensation
            9] Disability, illness, or unemployment benefits
            10] Alimony
            11] Veteran's benefits
            12] Prescribed health aids
            13] Public assistance
            14] Pensions and retirement benefits needed for support and ERISA qualified
            15] Lost earnings payments
            16] Wrongful death payments that bankrupted party depended on
            17] Wages up to maximum of specified formula (75% of person's disposable income or 30 times federal minimum wage
            18] Crime victim's compensation
            19] Interest in any property not to exceed $925 plus $8,725 of any unused portion of the homestead exemption (item [1] above); can be used to protect any type of property including cash
            20] Specified personal injury awards up to $17,425 (not to include pain and suffering or monetary loss)

   c. Above exemptions doubled for married couples

5. Duties of trustee under Chapter 7 bankruptcy (i.e., a liquidation)

   a. In general, to liquidate and sell assets owned to pay creditors based on priorities discussed later and to examine propriety of claims brought by creditors

      (1) Considers how best to sell, use, or lease property of estate to act in best interest of estate

    (2) Acquires all legal assets owed to estate for equitable distribution to creditors

    (3) Trustee makes interim reports and presents final accounting of the administration of the estate to the court

6. Powers of trustee

  a. Trustee may take any legal action necessary to carry out duties

    (1) Trustee may utilize any defense available to the debtor against third parties

    (2) Trustee may continue or cease any legal action started by the debtor for the benefit of the estate

  b. Trustee, with court approval, may employ professionals (e.g., accountants and lawyers) to assist trustee in carrying out duties that require professional expertise

    (1) Employed professional must not hold any interest adverse to that of debtor (i.e., to avoid conflicts of interest)

    (2) Employed professional has right to receive compensation for reasonable value of services performed

      (a) Reasonable fee is based on amount and complexity of services rendered, not on size of estate

    (3) Trustee, with court approval, may act in professional capacity if capable and be compensated separately for professional services rendered

  c. Trustee must within sixty days of the order for relief assume or reject any executory contract, including leases, made by the debtor

    (1) Any not assumed are deemed rejected

    (2) Trustee must perform all obligations on lease of nonresidential property until lease is either assumed or rejected

    (3) Rejection of a contract is a breach of contract and injured party may become an unsecured creditor

    (4) Trustee may assign or retain leases if good for bankrupt's estate and if allowed under lease and state law

    (5) Rejection or assumption of lease is subject to court approval

  d. Trustee may set aside liens (those which arise automatically under law) if lien

    (1) Becomes effective when bankruptcy petition is filed or when debtor becomes insolvent

    (2) Is not enforceable against a bona fide purchaser when the petition is filed

    (3) In the case of a security interest, is not perfected before filing of bankruptcy petition

  e. Trustee **may set aside transfers made within one year prior** to the filing of the bankruptcy petition if

    (1) The transfer was made with intent to hinder, delay, or defraud any creditor. The debtor need not be insolvent at time of transfer.

    (2) Debtor received less than a reasonably equivalent value in exchange for such transfer or obligation and the debtor

      (a) Was insolvent at the time, or became insolvent as a result of the transfer

      (b) If the fact that the transfer was a fraudulent conveyance was the only grounds for avoiding the transfer; once avoided by trustee, transferee that gave value in good faith has a lien on property transferred to the extent of value given

  f. Trustee may also set aside preferential transfers of nonexempt property to a creditor made within the **previous ninety days** while insolvent in the "bankruptcy sense"

    (1) Preferential transfers are those made for **antecedent debts** that enable the creditor to receive more than s/he would have otherwise under a Chapter 7 liquidation proceeding

      (a) Includes a security interest given by debtor to secure antecedent debt

EXAMPLE: Debtor paid off a loan to BB Bank sixty days before Debtor filed a bankruptcy petition. This is a preferential transfer.

EXAMPLE: Debtor gave CC Bank a security interest in some office furniture he owns to secure a previous loan CC Bank had granted him. This is a preferential transfer if Debtor gave the security interest within ninety days of the filing of bankruptcy. The reason for this is that it gives the creditor (bank) greater rights than it had before.

EXAMPLE: Debtor prepaid some installments on an installment loan on equipment.

*EXAMPLE: Debtor made a gift to charity. This is **not** a transfer for an antecedent debt.*

    (2) Preferential transfers **made to insiders** within the **previous twelve months** may be set aside

        (a) Insiders are close blood relatives, officers, directors, controlling stockholders of corporations, or general partners of partnerships

EXAMPLE: S is a secured creditor of XYZ Co. that is in Chapter 7 bankruptcy. S is not an insider.

EXAMPLE: One year ago Herb purchased a car on credit from Ike. Thirty days before filing for bankruptcy, Herb, while insolvent, makes a payment to Ike concerning the auto. This is a preferential transfer. If Ike were Herb's brother, this preference could have been set aside if it had occurred, for example, 120 days before the filing of the petition while Herb was insolvent (insider preference).

    (3) Exceptions to trustee's power to avoid preferential transfers

        (a) A contemporaneous exchange between creditor and debtor whereby debtor receives new value

EXAMPLE: Herb, while insolvent, purchases a car for cash from Ike within ninety days of filing a petition in bankruptcy. The trustee could not avoid this transaction because Herb, the debtor, received present (i.e., contemporaneous) value (the car) for the cash transferred to Ike, the creditor. This is not a voidable preference.

        (b) Transfer made in the ordinary course of business is not a voidable preference, nor is the perfected security interest that arises from it (if filed within forty-five days of creation of that debt)

EXAMPLE: Debtor pays the utility bill for the business.

        (c) A security interest given by debtor to acquire property that is perfected within ten days after such security interest attaches

        (d) A consumer debtor's payment of $600 or less to any creditor

  7. Trustee may be sued or sue on behalf of estate

F. Claims

1. Property rights—where claimant has a property right, property is turned over to claimant, because not considered part of debtor's estate

    a. Reclamation is a claim against specific property by a person claiming it to be his/hers

EXAMPLE: A person rented a truck for a week and in the meantime he becomes bankrupt. The lessor will make a reclamation.

    b. Trust claim is made by beneficiary for trust property when the trustee is bankrupt

EXAMPLE: Trustee maintains a trust account for beneficiary under a trust set up in a will. Trustee becomes bankrupt. The trust account is not part of trustee's estate. The beneficiary may claim the trust account as his property.

    c. Secured claim when creditor has a security interest (e.g., mortgage in property or security interest under UCC)

      (1) As long as trustee does not successfully attack the security—basically, security interest must be without defects to prevail against trustee (i.e., perfected security interests)

      (2) Secured status may be achieved by subrogation (e.g., surety is subrogated to creditor's collateral)

    d. Setoffs are allowed to the extent the bankrupt and creditor have mutual debts whether unsecured or not

2. Filing of claims

    a. All claims must be filed within six months after the first creditors' meeting

3. Proof of claims

    a. Timely claims are deemed allowed unless creditor objects

        (1) Contingent and unliquidated claims may be estimated

    b. Claims below are not allowed if an objection is made

        (1) Unenforceable claims (by law or agreement)

        (2) Unmatured interest as of date of filing bankruptcy petition

        (3) Claims that may be offset

        (4) Property tax claim in excess of the property value

        (5) Insider or attorney claims in excess of reasonable value of services as determined by court

        (6) Alimony, maintenance, and support claims for amounts due after bankruptcy petition is filed (they are not dischargeable)

        (7) Landlord's damages for lease termination in excess of specified amounts

        (8) Damages for termination of an employment contract in excess of one year's wages

        (9) Certain employment tax claims

4. Priority of claims (be sure to know)

    a. Property rights (e.g., secured debts)

        (1) Technically, they are not a part of the priorities because they never become part of the bankrupt estate.

            (a) But security interests perfected before the ninety-day period (one year for insiders) can be thought of as having the highest priority up to the value of the collateral since it can be repossessed

    b. Unsecured claims are paid at each level of priority before any lower level is paid

        (1) If there are insufficient assets to pay any given level then assets are prorated at that level (the next levels get $0)

    c. Levels of priority

        (1) Administration costs

            (a) Includes fees to accountants, attorneys, trustees, and appraisers as well as expenses incurred only in recovering, preserving, selling, or discovering property that should be included in debtor's estate

                EXAMPLE: Bee, Ware, and Watch, a partnership of CPAs, performed professional services for Dee-Funct Company before it was forced into bankruptcy by its creditors. These fees are not put in the first priority but the last because they do not qualify as administration costs.

            (b) Also includes reasonable fees, salary, or wages needed for services such as operating the business after the bankruptcy action begins

        (2) Claims arising in ordinary course of debtor's business after involuntary bankruptcy petition is filed but before order for relief is entered

        (3) Wages of bankrupt's employees ($4,650 maximum each) accrued within ninety days before the petition in bankruptcy was filed (any excess is treated as a general claim)

            (a) This priority does not include officers' salaries

        (4) Contributions to employee benefit plans within the prior 180 days, limited to $4,650 per employee, reduced by amount received as wage preference

        (5) Claims on raising or storage of grain up to $4,650 for each individual

        (6) Consumer deposits for undelivered goods or services limited to $2,100 per individual

        (7) Alimony and child support

        (8) Taxes (federal, state, and local)

        (9) General (unsecured) creditors that filed timely proofs of claims

            (a) Includes amounts owed to secured creditors in excess of amount for which security sells

> *EXAMPLE: X has been forced into Chapter 7 bankruptcy proceedings. X had assets that have been sold for $14,000 cash. Fees to accountants, attorneys, and the trustee total $3,000. Expenses to sell property total $1,000. Wages owed to two employees for the previous month's work are $4,500 and $4,000 respectively. Past taxes amount to $900 and two general creditors have claims amounting to $1,000 and $500 respectively. Under the priorities just given, the $3,000 and the $1,000 are administrative costs and are paid first. The wages owed to the two employees are paid next leaving $1,500. The $900 in taxes is paid next, leaving $600. This must now be paid out proportionately; therefore, the general creditors received $400 and $200 respectively.*

(b) Unsecured claims filed late (unless excused) are paid after timely claims

G. Discharge of a Bankrupt

1. A discharge is the release of a debtor from all his/her debts not paid in bankruptcy except those not dischargeable

    a. Granting an order of relief to an individual is an automatic application for discharge
    b. Corporations and partnerships cannot receive a discharge

2. Debtor must be adjudged an "honest debtor" to be discharged
3. Acts that bar discharge of **all** debts

    a. Improper actions during bankruptcy proceeding

        (1) Making false claims against the estate
        (2) Concealing property
        (3) Transfer of property after filing with intent to defeat the law (i.e., fraudulent transfer)
        (4) Making any false entry in or on any document of account relating to bankrupt's affairs
        (5) These acts are also punishable by fines and imprisonment

    b. Failing to satisfactorily explain any loss of assets
    c. Refusing to obey court orders
    d. Removing or destroying property within twelve months prior to filing of petition with intent to hinder, delay, or defraud any creditor
    e. Destroying, falsifying, concealing, or failing to keep books of account or records unless such act is justified under the circumstances
    f. Being discharged in bankruptcy proceedings within the past six years
    g. "Substantial abuse" of bankruptcy by individual debtor with primarily consumer debts
    h. A preferential transfer does **not** bar discharge (but can be set aside)

H. Debts Not Discharged by Bankruptcy (even though general discharge allowed)

1. Taxes within three years of filing bankruptcy petition
2. Loans for payment of federal taxes
3. Unscheduled debts unless creditor had actual notice of proceedings (i.e., where bankrupt failed to list creditor and debt)

> *EXAMPLE: In a petition in bankruptcy, a mistake was made so that a debt owed to ABC Company was listed as owed to XYZ Company. The debt to ABC is not discharged unless ABC somehow was aware of the mistake.*

4. Alimony, separate maintenance, or child support
5. Liability due to theft or embezzlement
6. Debts arising from debtor's fraud about his/her financial condition or fraud in connection with purchase or sale of securities

> *EXAMPLE: Obtaining credit using false information such as materially fraudulent financial statements that the creditor relied on.*

7. Willful and/or malicious injuries to a person or property of another (intentional torts)

    a. Unintentional torts (i.e., negligence) and breaches of contract are dischargeable

8. Educational loans of a governmental unit or nonprofit institution which became due within prior five years unless liability would impose "undue hardship" on debtor or debtor's dependents
9. Governmental fines or penalties imposed within prior three years
10. Those from a prior bankruptcy proceeding in which the debtor waived discharge or was denied discharge

11. Liability incurred by driving while legally intoxicated
12. To avoid the practice of "loading up on luxury goods" before bankruptcy, there is a presumption of nondischargeability for

    a. Consumer debts to a single debtor of $1,150 or more for luxury goods or services
    b. Certain cash advances based on consumer credit exceeding $1,150

13. Any debt from violation of securities laws

I. Revocation of Discharge

1. Discharge may be revoked if

    a. Bankrupt committed fraud during bankruptcy proceedings unknown to creditors seeking revocation

       EXAMPLE: A bankrupt conceals assets in order to defraud creditors.

       (1) Must be applied for within one year of discharge

    b. Bankrupt acquired rights or title to property of estate and fraudulently failed to report this
    c. Bankrupt refused to obey lawful court order or refused to testify when not in violation of his/her constitutional right against self incrimination

J. Reaffirmation

1. Debtor promises to pay a debt that will be discharged. The Code makes it difficult to reaffirm dischargeable debt.

    a. To be enforceable, reaffirmation of dischargeable debt must satisfy the following conditions:

       (1) Reaffirmation must take place before discharge granted
       (2) Must be approved by bankruptcy court
       (3) Debtor is allowed sixty days to rescind reaffirmation once agreed to

          (a) Debtor must have received appropriate warnings from the court or attorney on effects of reaffirmation, and
          (b) If also involves consumer debt not secured by real property, court must approve new agreement as being in best interests of debtor and not imposing undue hardship on debtor

K. Business Reorganization—Chapter 11

1. Goal is to keep financially troubled firm in business

    a. It is an alternative to liquidation under Chapter 7 (straight bankruptcy)
    b. In general, allows debtor to keep assets of business

2. Can be initiated by debtor (voluntary) or creditors (involuntary)

    a. Available to individuals, partnerships, or corporations including railroads. Other entities ineligible to be debtors under Chapter 7 are ineligible under Chapter 11.
    b. If involuntary, same requirements must be met as needed to initiate a Chapter 7 involuntary proceeding

3. Each class of similar creditors and shareholders creates separate committees to make master reorganization plan

    a. Investigation of debtor's financial affairs is conducted
    b. Committees meet together and negotiate reorganization plan if possible
    c. If debtor's management capable of continuing business, no trustee is appointed
    d. If debtor's management is not considered capable of running business, then trustee is appointed to conduct business
    e. Approval of reorganization plan needs

       (1) Over 1/2 of creditors in each committee owed at least 2/3 of the total debt in that class, and
       (2) Acceptance of stockholders' holding at least 2/3 in amount of the stock

(3) Complete reorganization plan can still be approved by court if court determines plan is fair even if some committees fail to approve it

4. Important provision is court-supervised rehabilitation plan

   a. Allows for continued operation of business unless court orders otherwise
   b. Provides for payment of part or all of debts over extended period

      (1) Payment to creditors comes primarily from future income

   c. Must divide claims into classes of similar claims and treat each class equally
   d. Plan may provide for some creditors to receive stock in place of debt

      (1) Preferred shareholders may be converted to common shareholders
      (2) Common shareholders may forfeit shares of stock
      (3) Typically, claimants receive reduced amounts

5. After court confirms plan and issues final decree

   a. Debtor is discharged from debts that arose before confirmation of plan except those that were agreed to continue or will continue under Bankruptcy Code

      (1) New agreed-upon substituted debts are enforceable

6. Court may convert Chapter 11 reorganization into Chapter 7 straight bankruptcy if fairer
7. SEC has limited power to participate in bankruptcy reorganizations
8. When debtor keeps and operates business, debtor has right to retain employees and professionals it used before reorganization

   EXAMPLE: Debtor, after a Chapter 11 reorganization, wishes to keep its CPA firm. This is permitted.

L. Debts Adjustment Plans—Chapter 13

1. Most individuals are eligible if

   a. Have regular income, and
   b. Owe unsecured debts of less than $290,525, and
   c. Owe secured debts of less than $871,550
   d. Debt ceilings adjusted for inflation every three years

2. Initiated when debtor files voluntary petition in bankruptcy court

   a. Creditors may not file involuntary petition under Chapter 13
   b. Petition normally includes composition or extension plan

      (1) Composition—creditors agree to accept less than full amounts due
      (2) Extension—provides debtor up to three years (five years if court approves) for payments to creditors

   c. Filing of petition stays all collection and straight bankruptcy proceedings against debtor
   d. Debtor has exclusive right to propose plan

      (1) If debtor does not file plan, creditors may force debtor into involuntary proceeding under Chapter 7

   e. Plan will be confirmed or denied by court without approval of unsecured creditors

      (1) However, unsecured creditors must receive as much as they would get under Chapter 7, and

         (a) Either be paid in full, or
         (b) Have all debtor's disposable income committed to plan
         (c) Plan may put claims in different classifications but may not discriminate unfairly against any of designated classes

            1] Each claimant within same classification must receive same treatment

   f. Court must appoint trustee in Chapter 13 cases

    g. Debtor engaged in business may continue to operate that business subject to limitations imposed by court

    h. Completion of plan discharges debtor from debts dischargeable

    i. If composition were involved, then discharge bars another discharge for six years unless debtor paid 70% of debts covered

MULTIPLE-CHOICE QUESTIONS (1-29)

1. Which of the following statements is correct concerning the voluntary filing of a petition in bankruptcy?

a. If the debtor has twelve or more creditors, the unsecured claims must total at least $11,625.

b. The debtor must be insolvent.

c. If the debtor has less than twelve creditors, the unsecured claims must total at least $11,625.

d. The petition may be filed jointly by spouses.

2. A voluntary petition filed under the liquidation provisions of Chapter 7 of the Federal Bankruptcy Code

a. Is **not** available to a corporation unless it has previously filed a petition under the reorganization provisions of Chapter 11 of the Federal Bankruptcy Code.

b. Automatically stays collection actions against the debtor **except** by secured creditors.

c. Will be dismissed unless the debtor has twelve or more unsecured creditors whose claims total at least $11,625.

d. Does **not** require the debtor to show that the debtor's liabilities exceed the fair market value of assets.

3. On February 28, 2002, Master, Inc. had total assets with a fair market value of $1,200,000 and total liabilities of $990,000. On January 15, 2002, Master made a monthly installment note payment to Acme Distributors Corp., a creditor holding a properly perfected security interest in equipment having a fair market value greater than the balance due on the note. On March 15, 2002, Master voluntarily filed a petition in bankruptcy under the liquidation provisions of Chapter 7 of the Federal Bankruptcy Code. One year later, the equipment was sold for less than the balance due on the note to Acme.

If a creditor challenged Master's right to file, the petition would be dismissed

a. If Master had less than twelve creditors at the time of filing.

b. Unless Master can show that a reorganization under Chapter 11 of the Federal Bankruptcy Code would have been unsuccessful.

c. Unless Master can show that it is unable to pay its debts in the ordinary course of business or as they come due.

d. If Master is an insurance company.

4. Which of the following conditions, if any, must a debtor meet to file a voluntary bankruptcy petition under Chapter 7 of the Federal Bankruptcy Code?

	Insolvency	*Three or more creditors*
a.	Yes	Yes
b.	Yes	No
c.	No	Yes
d.	No	No

5. Brenner Corporation is trying to avoid bankruptcy but its four creditors are trying to force Brenner into bankruptcy. The four creditors are owed the following amounts:

Anteed Corporation	-	$5,000 of unsecured debt
Bounty Corporation	-	$4,500 of unsecured debt and $8,500 of secured debt
Courtney Corporation	-	$2,000 of unsecured debt
Dauntless Corporation	-	$1,000 of unsecured debt

Which of the creditors must sign the petition to force Brenner into bankruptcy?

a. Bounty is sufficient.

b. At least Anteed and Bounty are needed.

c. At least Bounty, Courtney, and Dauntless are needed.

d. All of these four creditors are needed.

Items 6 through 10 are based on the following:

Dart Inc., a closely held corporation, was petitioned involuntarily into bankruptcy under the liquidation provisions of Chapter 7 of the Federal Bankruptcy Code. Dart contested the petition.

Dart has not been paying its business debts as they became due, has defaulted on its mortgage loan payments, and owes back taxes to the IRS. The total cash value of Dart's bankruptcy estate after the sale of all assets and payment of administration expenses is $100,000.

Dart has the following creditors:

• Fracon Bank is owed $75,000 principal and accrued interest on a mortgage loan secured by Dart's real property. The property was valued at and sold, in bankruptcy, for $70,000.

• The IRS has a $12,000 recorded judgment for unpaid corporate income tax.

• JOG Office Supplies has an unsecured claim of $3,000 that was timely filed.

• Nanstar Electric Co. has an unsecured claim of $1,200 that was not timely filed.

• Decoy Publications has a claim of $14,000, of which $2,000 is secured by Dart's inventory that was valued and sold, in bankruptcy, for $2,000. The claim was timely filed.

6. Which of the following statements would correctly describe the result of Dart's opposing the petition?

a. Dart will win because the petition should have been filed under Chapter 11.

b. Dart will win because there are **not** more than 12 creditors.

c. Dart will lose because it is **not** paying its debts as they become due.

d. Dart will lose because of its debt to the IRS.

7. Which of the following events will follow the filing of the Chapter 7 involuntary petition?

	A trustee will be appointed	*A stay against creditor collection proceedings will go into effect*
a.	Yes	Yes
b.	Yes	No
c.	No	Yes
d.	No	No

For **items 8 through 10** assume that the bankruptcy estate was distributed.

8. What dollar amount would Nanstar Electric Co. receive?

a. $0

b. $ 800

c. $1,000

d. $1,200

9. What total dollar amount would Fracon Bank receive on its secured and unsecured claims?

a. $70,000

b. $72,000

c. $74,000

d. $75,000

10. What dollar amount would the IRS receive?

a. $0

b. $ 8,000

c. $10,000

d. $12,000

11. Which of the following is **not** allowed as a federal exemption under the Federal Bankruptcy Code?

a.   Some specified amount of equity in one motor vehicle.

b.   Unemployment compensation.

c.   Some specified amount of value in books and tools of one's trade.

d.   All of the above are allowed.

12. Flax, a sole proprietor, has been petitioned involuntarily into bankruptcy under the Federal Bankruptcy Code's liquidation provisions. Simon & Co., CPAs, has been appointed trustee of the bankruptcy estate. If Simon also wishes to act as the tax return preparer for the estate, which of the following statements is correct?

a.   Simon is prohibited from serving as both trustee and preparer under any circumstances because serving in that dual capacity would be a conflict of interest.

b.   Although Simon may serve as both trustee and preparer, it is entitled to receive a fee only for the services rendered as a preparer.

c.   Simon may employ itself to prepare tax returns if authorized by the court and may receive a separate fee for services rendered in each capacity.

d.   Although Simon may serve as both trustee and preparer, its fees for services rendered in each capacity will be determined solely by the size of the estate.

13. Which of the following transfers by a debtor, within 90 days of filing for bankruptcy, could be set aside as a preferential payment?

a.   Making a gift to charity.

b.   Paying a business utility bill.

c.   Borrowing money from a bank secured by giving a mortgage on business property.

d.   Prepaying an installment loan on inventory.

Items 14 and 15 are based on the following:

On August 1, 2002, Hall filed a voluntary petition under Chapter 7 of the Federal Bankruptcy Code. Hall's assets are sufficient to pay general creditors 40% of their claims.

The following transactions occurred before the filing:

• On May 15, 2002, Hall gave a mortgage on Hall's home to National Bank to secure payment of a loan National had given Hall two years earlier. When the loan was made, Hall's twin was a National employee.

• On June 1, 2002, Hall purchased a boat from Olsen for $10,000 cash.

• On July 1, 2002, Hall paid off an outstanding credit card balance of $500. The original debt had been $2,500.

14. The National mortgage was

a.   Preferential, because National would be considered an insider.

b.   Preferential, because the mortgage was given to secure an antecedent debt.

c.   Not preferential, because Hall is presumed insolvent when the mortgage was given.

d.   Not preferential, because the mortgage was a security interest.

15. The payment to Olsen was

a.   Preferential, because the payment was made within ninety days of the filing of the petition.

b.   Preferential, because the payment enabled Olsen to receive more than the other general creditors.

c.   Not preferential, because Hall is presumed insolvent when the payment was made.

d.   Not preferential, because the payment was a contemporaneous exchange for new value.

16. Under the liquidation provisions of Chapter 7 of the Federal Bankruptcy Code, a debtor will be denied a discharge in bankruptcy if the debtor

a.   Fails to list a creditor.

b.   Owes alimony and support payments.

c.   Cannot pay administration expenses.

d.   Refuses to satisfactorily explain a loss of assets.

17. On May 1, 2002, two months after becoming insolvent, Quick Corp., an appliance wholesaler, filed a voluntary petition for bankruptcy under the provisions of Chapter 7 of the Federal Bankruptcy Code. On October 15, 2001, Quick's board of directors had authorized and paid Erly $50,000 to repay Erly's April 1, 2001, loan to the corporation. Erly is a sibling of Quick's president. On March 15, 2002, Quick paid Kray $100,000 for inventory delivered that day.

Which of the following is **not** relevant in determining whether the repayment of Erly's loan is a voidable preferential transfer?

a.   Erly is an insider.

b.   Quick's payment to Erly was made on account of an antecedent debt.

c.   Quick's solvency when the loan was made by Erly.

d.   Quick's payment to Erly was made within one year of the filing of the bankruptcy petition.

18. Brook Corporation has filed for bankruptcy. Of the following debts Brook owes, indicate their priorities from the highest to the lowest.

I.   Federal taxes unpaid for the previous year.

II.   Wages of $3,000 owed to employees.

III.   Balance of $5,000 owed to a creditor that had a security interest. This creditor got paid fully by selling off the collateral except for this $5,000 deficiency.

    a.   I, II, III.

    b.   I, III, II.

    c.   II, I, III.

    d.   III, I, II.

19. Kessler Company has filed a voluntary bankruptcy petition. Kessler's debts include administration costs owed to accountants, attorneys, and appraisers. It also owes federal and state taxes. Kessler still owes various employees for the previous month's wages accrued before the petition was filed. None of these wages are owed to the officers and at most total $4,000 per employee. The company also owes several creditors for claims arising in the ordinary course of business. All of these latter claims arose before Kessler filed the bankruptcy petition. What are the priorities from highest to lowest of these listed debts and claims?

    a.   The claims arising in the ordinary course of business; the administration costs; the employees' wages; the federal and state taxes.

    b.   The administration costs; the employees' wages; the federal and state taxes; the claims arising in the ordinary course of business.

    c.   The federal and state taxes; the administration costs; the claims arising in the ordinary course of business; the employees' wages.

    d.   The claims arising in the ordinary course of business; the federal and state taxes; the administration costs; the employees' wages.

20. Which of the following acts will not bar a general discharge in bankruptcy?

    a.   The debtor tried to hide some property to prevent the estate from getting it.

    b.   The debtor intentionally injured a creditor during an argument about the bankruptcy proceedings.

    c.   The debtor is unwilling to explain satisfactorily why some assets are missing.

    d.   The debtor intentionally destroyed records of his assets.

21. Chapter 7 of the Federal Bankruptcy Code will deny a debtor a discharge when the debtor

    a.   Made a preferential transfer to a creditor.

    b.   Accidentally destroyed information relevant to the bankruptcy proceeding.

    c.   Obtained a Chapter 7 discharge ten years previously.

    d.   Is a corporation or a partnership.

22. Eckson was granted an order for relief after having filed a petition in bankruptcy. Which of the following actions would bar a general discharge in bankruptcy?

  I.   Ten months before the bankruptcy proceedings, Eckson had obtained credit from Cardinal Corporation by using false information on the credit application.

  II. Six months before he filed the petition, Eckson removed a vehicle from his land with the intent to defraud a creditor.

 III. During the bankruptcy proceedings, Eckson made a false entry on some records pertaining to his assets.

    a.   I only.

    b.   I and II only.

    c.   II and III only.

    d.   I, II, and III.

23. Which of the following acts by a debtor could result in a bankruptcy court revoking the debtor's discharge?

  I.   Failure to list one creditor.

  II. Failure to answer correctly material questions on the bankruptcy petition.

    a.   I only.

    b.   II only.

    c.   Both I and II.

    d.   Neither I nor II.

24. Which of the following debts will **not** be discharged by bankruptcy even though a general discharge is allowed?

  I.   Debt owed to a corporation because the debtor was caught embezzling from it.

  II. Money owed to a bank because the debtor was found to have committed fraud about her financial condition to get a loan.

 III. Damages owed to a major customer because the debtor intentionally breached an important contract.

    a.   I only.

    b.   II only.

    c.   I and II only.

    d.   I, II, and III.

25. Which of the following claims will **not** be discharged in bankruptcy?

    a.   A claim that arises from alimony or maintenance.

    b.   A claim that arises out of the debtor's breach of contract.

    c.   A claim brought by a secured creditor that remains unsatisfied after the sale of the collateral.

    d.   A claim brought by a judgment creditor whose judgment resulted from the debtor's negligent operation of a motor vehicle.

26. By signing a reaffirmation agreement on April 15, 2002, a debtor agreed to pay certain debts that would be discharged in bankruptcy. On June 20, 2002, the debtor's attorney filed the reaffirmation agreement and an affidavit with the court indicating that the debtor understood the consequences of the reaffirmation agreement. The debtor obtained a discharge on August 25, 2002. The reaffirmation agreement would be enforceable only if it was

    a.   Made after discharge.

    b.   For debts aggregating less than $5,000.

    c.   Not for a household purpose debt.

    d.   Not rescinded before discharge.

27. Strong Corp. filed a voluntary petition in bankruptcy under the reorganization provisions of Chapter 11 of the Federal Bankruptcy Code. A reorganization plan was filed and agreed to by all necessary parties. The court confirmed the plan and a final decree was entered.

Which of the following statements best describes the effect of the entry of the court's final decree?

    a.   Strong Corp. will be discharged from all its debts and liabilities.

    b.   Strong Corp. will be discharged only from the debts owed creditors who agreed to the reorganization plan.

    c.   Strong Corp. will be discharged from all its debts and liabilities that arose before the date of confirmation of the plan.

    d.   Strong Corp. will be discharged from all its debts and liabilities that arose before the confirmation of the plan, except as otherwise provided in the plan, the order of confirmation, or the Bankruptcy Code.

28. Which of the following statements is correct with respect to the reorganization provisions of Chapter 11 of the Federal Bankruptcy Code?

    a.   A trustee must always be appointed.

    b.   The debtor must be insolvent if the bankruptcy petition was filed voluntarily.

    c.   A reorganization plan may be filed by a creditor anytime after the petition date.

    d.   The commencement of a bankruptcy case may be voluntary or involuntary.

29. Under Chapter 11 of the Federal Bankruptcy Code, which of the following would **not** be eligible for reorganization?

    a.   Retail sole proprietorship.
    b.   Advertising partnership.
    c.   CPA professional corporation.
    d.   Savings and loan corporation.

OTHER OBJECTIVE QUESTIONS

Problem 1   (15 to 25 minutes)

On April 15, 2002, Wren Corp., an appliance wholesaler, was petitioned involuntarily into bankruptcy under the liquidation provisions of Chapter 7 of the Federal Bankruptcy Code.

When the petition was filed, Wren's creditors included:

Secured creditors	*Amount owed*
Fifth Bank—1st mortgage on warehouse owned by Wren	$50,000
Hart Manufacturing Corp.—perfected purchase money security interest in inventory	30,000
TVN Computers, Inc.—perfected security interest in office computers	15,000

Unsecured creditors	*Amount owed*
IRS—1999 federal income taxes	$20,000
Acme Office Cleaners—services for January, February, and March 2002	750
Ted Smith (employee)—February and March 2002 wages	4,850
Joan Sims (employee)—March 2002 commissions	1,500
Power Electric Co.—electricity charges for January, February, and March 2002	600
Soft Office Supplies—supplies purchased in 2001	2,000

The following transactions occurred before the bankruptcy petition was filed:

- On December 31, 2001, Wren paid off a $5,000 loan from Mary Lake, the sister of one of Wren's directors.
- On January 30, 2002, Wren donated $2,000 to Universal Charities.
- On February 1, 2002, Wren gave Young Finance Co. a security agreement covering Wren's office fixtures to secure a loan previously made by Young.
- On March 1, 2002, Wren made the final $1,000 monthly payment to Integral Appliance Corp. on a two-year note.
- On April 1, 2002, Wren purchased from Safety Co., a new burglar alarm system for its factory, for $5,000 cash.

All of Wren's assets were liquidated. The warehouse was sold for $75,000, the computers were sold for $12,000, and the inventory was sold for $25,000. After paying the bankruptcy administration expenses of $8,000, secured creditors, and priority general creditors, there was enough cash to pay each nonpriority general creditor fifty cents on the dollar.

Required:

a.   Items 1 through 5 represent the transactions that occurred before the filing of the bankruptcy petition. For each transaction, determine if the transaction would be set aside as a preferential transfer by the bankruptcy court. Choose (Y) if the transaction would be set aside or (N) if the transaction would **not** be set aside.

1. Payment to Mary Lake

2. Donation to Universal Charities

3. Security agreement to Young Finance Co.

4. Payment to Integral Appliance Corp.

5. Purchase from Safety Co.

b.   Items 6 through 10 represent creditor claims against the bankruptcy estate. Select from List I each creditor's order of payment in relation to the other creditors named in items 6 through 10.

		List I	
6.	Bankruptcy administration expense	A.	First
7.	Acme Office Cleaners	B.	Second
		C.	Third
8.	Fifth Bank	D.	Fourth
9.	IRS	E.	Fifth
10.	Joan Sims		

c.   Items 11 through 15 also represent creditor claims against the bankruptcy estate. For each of the creditors listed in Items 11 through 15, select from List II the amount that creditor will receive.

		List II			
11.	TVN Computers, Inc.	A.	$0	H.	$ 4,850
12.	Hart Manufacturing Corp.	B.	$ 300	I.	$12,000
		C.	$ 600	J.	$13,500
13.	Ted Smith	D.	$ 1,000	K.	$15,000
14.	Power Electric Co.	E.	$ 1,200	L.	$25,000
		F.	$ 4,300	M.	$27,500
15.	Soft Office Supplies	G.	$ 4,750	N.	$30,000

Problem 2   (5 to 10 minutes)

On May 1, 2002, Able Corp. was petitioned involuntarily into bankruptcy under the provisions of Chapter 7 of the Federal Bankruptcy Code.

When the petition was filed, Able had the following unsecured creditors:

Creditor	*Amount owed*
Cole	$12,000
Lake	2,000
Young	1,500
Thorn	1,000

The following transactions occurred before the bankruptcy petition was filed:

- On January 15, 2002, Able paid Vista Bank the $1,000 balance due on an unsecured business loan.
- On February 28, 2002, Able paid $1,000 to Owen, an officer of Able, who had lent Able money.
- On March 1, 2002, Able bought a computer for use in its business from Core Computer Co. for $2,000 cash.

Required:

Items 1 through 3 refer to the bankruptcy filing. For each item, determine whether the statement is True(T) or False (F).

1. Able can file a voluntary petition for bankruptcy if it is solvent.

2. Lake, Young, and Thorn can file a valid involuntary petition.

3. Cole alone can file a valid involuntary petition.

Items 4 through 6 refer to the transactions that occurred before the filing of the involuntary bankruptcy petition. Assuming the bankruptcy petition was validly filed, for each item determine whether the statement is True (T) or False (F).

4. The payment to Vista Bank would be set aside as a preferential transfer.

5. The payment to Owen would be set aside as a preferential transfer.

6. The purchase from Core Computer Co. would be set aside as a preferential transfer.

Problem 3   (5 to 10 minutes)

On June 2, 2002, Rusk Corp. was petitioned involuntarily into bankruptcy. At the time of the filing, Rusk had the following creditors:

- Safe Bank, for the balance due on the secured note and mortgage on Rusk's warehouse.
- Employee salary claims.
- 2000 federal income taxes due.
- Accountant's fees outstanding.
- Utility bills outstanding.

Prior to the bankruptcy filing, but while insolvent, Rusk engaged in the following transactions:

- On February 1, 2002, Rusk repaid all corporate directors' loans made to the corporation.
- On May 1, 2002, Rusk purchased raw materials for use in its manufacturing business and paid cash to the supplier.

Required:

Items 1 through 5 relate to Rusk's creditors and the February 1 and May 1 transactions. For each item, select from List I whether only statement I is correct, whether only statement II is correct, whether both statements I and II are correct, or whether neither statement I nor II is correct.

List I

A. I only.

B. II only.

C. Both I and II.

D. Neither I nor II.

1. I.   Safe Bank's claim will be the first paid of the listed claims because Safe is a secured creditor.
    II.   Safe Bank will receive the entire amount of the balance of the mortgage due as a secured creditor regardless of the amount received from the sale of the warehouse.

2. I.   The employee salary claims will be paid in full after the payment of any secured party.
    II.   The employee salary claims up to $4,650 per claimant will be paid before payment of any general creditors' claims.

3. I.   The claim for 2002 federal income taxes due will be paid as a secured creditor claim.
    II.   The claim for 2002 federal income taxes due will be paid prior to the general creditor claims.

4. I. The February 1 repayments of the directors' loans were preferential transfers even though the payments were made more than ninety days before the filing of the petition.

II. The February 1 repayments of the directors' loans were preferential transfers because the payments were made to insiders.

5. I. The May 1 purchase and payment was **not** a preferential transfer because it was a transaction in the ordinary course of business.

II. The May 1 purchase and payment was a preferential transfer because it occurred within ninety days of the filing of the petition.

PROBLEMS

Problem 1   (15 to 20 minutes)

On February 1, 2002, Drake, a sole proprietor operating a retail clothing store, filed a bankruptcy petition under the liquidation provisions of the Bankruptcy Code. For at least six months prior to the filing of the petition, Drake had been unable to pay current business and personal obligations as they came due. Total liabilities substantially exceeded the total assets. A trustee was appointed who has converted all of Drake's nonexempt property to cash in the amount of $96,000. Drake's bankruptcy petition reflects a total of $310,000 of debts, including the following:

• A judgment against Drake in the amount of $19,500 as a result of an automobile accident caused by Drake's negligence.

• Unpaid federal income taxes in the amount of $4,300 for the year 1996 (Drake filed an accurate tax return for 1996).

• A $3,200 obligation payable on June 1, 2002, described as being owed to Martin Office Equipment, when, in fact, the debt is owed to Bartin Computer Supplies (Bartin has no knowledge of Drake's bankruptcy and the time for filing claims has expired).

• Unpaid child support in the amount of $780 arising from a support order incorporated in Drake's 1994 divorce judgment.

Prior to the filing of the petition, Drake entered into the following transactions:

• January 13, 2002—paid Safe Bank $7,500, the full amount on an unsecured loan given by Safe on November 13, 2001 (Drake had used the loan proceeds to purchase a family automobile).

• October 21, 2001—conveyed to his brother, in repayment of a $2,000 debt, a painting that cost Drake $125 and which had a fair market value of $2,000.

• November 15, 2001—borrowed $23,000 from Home Savings and Loan Association, giving Home a first mortgage on Drake's residence, which has a fair market value of $100,000.

• November 9, 2001—paid $4,300 to Max Clothing Distributors for clothing delivered to Drake sixty days earlier (Drake had for several years purchased inventory from Max and his other suppliers on sixty-day credit terms).

Required:

Answer the following questions, setting forth reasons for any conclusions stated.

a. Will the four debts described above be discharged in Drake's bankruptcy?

b. What factors must the bankruptcy trustee show to set aside a transaction as a preferential transfer?

c. State whether each transaction entered into by Drake is a preferential or nonpreferential transfer.

Problem 2   (15 to 20 minutes)

Techno, Inc. is a computer equipment dealer. On February 3, 2002, Techno was four months behind in its payments to Allied Building Maintenance, Cleen Janitorial Services, Inc., and Jones and Associates, CPAs, all of whom provide monthly services to Techno. In an attempt to settle with these three creditors, Techno offered each of them a reduced lump-sum payment for the past due obligations and full payment for future services. These creditors rejected Techno's offer and on April 9, 2002, Allied, Cleen and Jones filed an involuntary petition in bankruptcy against Techno under the provisions of Chapter 7 of the Federal Bankruptcy Code. At the time of the filing, Techno's liability to the three creditors was $19,100, all of which was unsecured.

Techno, at the time of the filing, had liabilities of $229,000 (owed to twenty-three creditors) and assets with a fair market value of $191,000. During the entire year before the bankruptcy filing, Techno's liabilities exceeded the fair market value of its assets.

Included in Techno's liabilities was an installment loan payable to Dollar Finance Co., properly secured by cash registers and other equipment.

The bankruptcy court approved the involuntary petition.

On April 21, 2002, Dollar filed a motion for relief from automatic stay in bankruptcy court claiming it was entitled to take possession of the cash registers and other equipment securing its loan. Dollar plans to sell these assets immediately and apply the proceeds to the loan balance. The fair market value of the collateral is less than the loan balance and Dollar claims to lack adequate protection. Also, Dollar claims it is entitled to receive a priority distribution, before distribution to unsecured creditors, for the amount Techno owes Dollar less the proceeds from the sale of the collateral.

During the course of the bankruptcy proceeding, the following transactions were disclosed:

• On October 6, 2001, Techno paid its president $9,900 as repayment of an unsecured loan made to the corporation on September 18, 1999.

• On February 19, 2002, Techno paid $1,150 to Alexis Computers, Inc. for eight color computer monitors. These monitors were delivered to Techno on February 9, 2002, and placed in inventory.

• On January 12, 2002, Techno bought a new delivery truck from Maple Motors for $7,900 cash. On the date of the bankruptcy filing, the truck was worth $7,000.

Required:

Answer the following questions and give the reasons for your conclusions.

a. What circumstances had to exist to allow Allied, Cleen, and Jones to file an involuntary bankruptcy petition against Techno?

b.   1. Will Dollar's motion for relief be granted?
    2. Will Dollar's claim for priority be approved by the bankruptcy court?

c. Are the payments to Techno's president, Alexis, and Maple preferential transfers?

1. d __ __	8. a __ __	15. d __ __	21. d __ __	27. d __ __
2. d __ __	9. c __ __	16. d __ __	22. c __ __	28. d __ __
3. d __ __	10. d __ __	17. c __ __	23. b __ __	29. d __ __
4. d __ __	11. d __ __	18. c __ __	24. c __ __	
5. d __ __	12. c __ __	19. b __ __	25. a __ __	
6. c __ __	13. d __ __	20. b __ __	26. d __ __	1st: __/29 = __%
7. a __ __	14. b __ __			2nd: __/29 = __%

MULTIPLE-CHOICE ANSWER EXPLANATIONS

C. Chapter 7 Voluntary Bankruptcy Petitions

1. (d) Voluntary bankruptcy petition is a formal request by the debtor for an order of relief. This voluntary bankruptcy petition may be filed jointly by a husband and a wife. Answer (b) is incorrect because the debtor in a voluntary bankruptcy petition need not be insolvent but needs to state that s/he has debts. Answers (a) and (c) are incorrect because there is no requirement as to the minimum amount of the debtor's liabilities in a voluntary proceeding.

2. (d) Under Chapter 7 of the Federal Bankruptcy Code, a debtor may file a voluntary petition without showing that s/he is insolvent. S/he merely has to state the existence of debts. Therefore, the debtor is not required to show that liabilities exceed the fair market value of assets. Answer (a) is incorrect because a corporation may generally file a voluntary bankruptcy petition and there is not a requirement that it has previously filed under Chapter 11. Answer (b) is incorrect because when the debtor is automatically given an order for relief upon filing the petition, the actions to collect money by creditors are stayed. Secured creditors will resort to the collateral, however. Answer (c) is incorrect because the debtor is voluntarily going into bankruptcy and there is no requirement that twelve or more unsecured creditors be owed at least $11,625. Note that this requirement, as written, does not exist for an involuntary bankruptcy petition either.

3. (d) Most debtors may file a voluntary bankruptcy petition. Among those that may not are insurance companies, banks, and saving and loan associations. Answer (a) is incorrect because the number of creditors is not relevant for a voluntary bankruptcy petition. Answer (b) is incorrect because there is no need to show that a Chapter 11 bankruptcy would have been unsuccessful. Answer (c) is incorrect because the inability of the debtor to pay its debts as they become due is not relevant to a voluntary bankruptcy.

4. (d) A debtor may file a voluntary bankruptcy petition without showing that s/he is insolvent. The debtor may merely state that s/he has debts. There is also no requirement as to the number of creditors needed.

D. Chapter 7 Involuntary Bankruptcy Petitions

5. (d) Since there are fewer than twelve creditors, it is true that only one creditor is needed to file the petition. However, no one creditor is owed at least $11,625 of unsecured debt. Therefore, the claims can be aggregated to total at least $11,625 of unsecured debt. The only way this can be accomplished is by aggregating the claims of all four creditors. Note that Bounty Corporation is not enough because the secured debt is not counted in the total.

6. (c) When the debtor contests the petition s/he can still be forced into bankruptcy if the debtor is generally not paying his/her debts as they become due. Answer (a) is incorrect because the petition may be filed under either Chapter 7 (straight bankruptcy) or Chapter 11 (business reorganization). When the bankruptcy is involuntary, Chapter 7 and Chapter 11 are alternatives and have the same requirements for filing against business debtors. Answer (b) is incorrect because although the rules are different when there are fewer than twelve creditors versus when there are twelve or more creditors, Dart can be forced into bankruptcy when Decoy Publications files the petition because Decoy is owed over $11,625 of unsecured debt. Answer (d) is incorrect because there is no exception for the IRS.

7. (a) Once a valid petition in bankruptcy is filed, this automatically stays other legal proceedings against the debtor's estate. Also, the court appoints an interim trustee.

8. (a) The bankruptcy estate contains $100,000 after the sale of all assets and payment of administration expenses. The secured debt of $70,000 to Fracon Bank and the secured debt of $2,000 to Decoy Publications are satisfied first. (This actually takes place as a higher priority over the administrative expenses.) Therefore, after paying this $72,000 there is $28,000 left. The $12,000 of unpaid income tax has the next highest priority of those listed. This leaves $16,000 for the general creditors who filed on time. There are three of these, that is, Fracon who is owed $5,000 in excess of what the sale of the property brought, JOG who is owed $3,000, and Decoy who is still owed $12,000 in excess of the security interest. These three creditors together are owed $20,000 ($5,000 + $3,000 + $12,000). Since this is more than the $16,000 left, these 3 general creditors' debts are prorated. The last priority of unsecured claimants who filed late get nothing. Therefore, Nanstar Electric gets $0.

9. (c) The bankruptcy estate contains $100,000 after the sale of all assets and payment of administration expenses. The secured debt of $70,000 to Fracon Bank and the secured debt of $2,000 to Decoy Publications are satisfied first. (This actually takes place as a higher priority over the administrative expenses.) Therefore, after paying this $72,000 there is $28,000 left. The $12,000 of unpaid income tax has the next highest priority of those listed. This leaves $16,000 for the general creditors who filed on time. There are three of these, that is, Fracon who is owed $5,000 in excess of what the sale of the property brought, JOG who is owed $3,000, and Decoy who is still owed $12,000 in excess of the security interest. These three creditors together are owed $20,000 ($5,000 + $3,000 + $12,000). Since this is more than the $16,000 left, these three general creditors' debts are prorated. Fracon Bank gets money from both the unsecured and secured claims. From the unsecured claim, Fracon receives a prorated share or

$$\frac{\$5,000}{\$5,000 + \$3,000 + \$12,000} \times \$16,000 = \$4,000$$

Add this prorated share of $4,000 to the $70,000 Fracon received from the sold property to arrive at $74,000.

10. (d) The bankruptcy estate contains $100,000 after the sale of all assets and payment of administration expenses. The secured debt of $70,000 to Fracon Bank and the secured debt of $2,000 to Decoy Publications are satisfied first. (This actually takes place as a higher priority over the administrative expenses.) Therefore, after paying this $72,000 there is $28,000 left. The $12,000 of unpaid income tax has the next highest priority of those listed.

E. Chapter 7 Bankruptcy Proceedings

11. (d) Federal exemptions allowed under the Federal Bankruptcy Code include $2,775 equity in one motor vehicle and $1,750 in books and tools of one's trade. They also include, among others, unemployment compensation.

12. (c) A trustee in bankruptcy has the power to employ court approved professionals, such as accountants and attorneys, to handle estate matters which require professional expertise. These professionals have the right to reimbursement for services rendered. A trustee is not deemed to have the appropriate expertise required to prepare tax returns; thus, a trustee may employ a CPA to perform this function. Simon, as trustee, has the power to employ himself to prepare tax returns if authorized by the court and may receive a separate fee for services rendered. Simon may serve as both trustee and preparer if authorized to do so by the court. Simon has the right to receive fees for services rendered as both a trustee and a preparer. The fee for services rendered in each capacity is determined on the basis of the value of the services rendered, not solely the size of the estate.

E.6.f.(3) Exceptions to Trustee's Power to Avoid Preferential Transfers

13. (d) Preferential transfers are payments made for antecedent debts which enable the creditor to receive more than s/he would under a Chapter 7 liquidation proceeding. A gift is not payment for an antecedent debt. Transfers made in the ordinary course of business are exceptions to the trustee's power to avoid a preferential transfer. A contemporaneous exchange between a creditor and the debtor whereby the debtor receives new value is not a preferential transfer. Prepaying an existing installment loan on inventory is making a payment on an antecedent debt which enables the creditor to receive more than s/he would in a liquidation proceeding.

14. (b) Under Chapter 7 of the Federal Bankruptcy Code, the trustee may set aside preferential transfers made to a creditor within ninety days prior to the filing of the petition for bankruptcy. Preferential transfers are those made for antecedent debts that allow the creditor to receive more than s/he would have under the bankruptcy law. All of these conditions were met for the National mortgage. Answer (a) is incorrect because National would not be considered an insider. Even though Hall's twin was a National employee, he was not an officer, director, or controlling stockholder of National. Furthermore, the preferential transfer was not made to him personally but to National Bank. Answer (c) is incorrect because to set aside a preferential transfer, the debtor must have made the transfer while he was insolvent

in the bankruptcy sense. Therefore, if Hall was presumed insolvent when the mortgage was given, the trustee is able to set aside the preferential transfer. Note that insolvency is irrelevant to whether a transfer is preferential or nonpreferential. Answer (d) is incorrect because when Hall gave National Bank the mortgage to secure payment of the two-year-old loan, this was a preferential transfer because it attempted to give National Bank more priority than it would have had as a general unsecured creditor.

15. (d) An exception to the trustee's powers to avoid preferential transfers is a contemporaneous exchange between the debtor and creditor for new values. When Hall paid the $10,000 cash, he received the boat he had purchased from Olsen. Therefore, this $10,000 payment was a contemporaneous exchange for new value. Answer (a) is incorrect because this fact pattern fits the contemporaneous exchange exception. It does not matter that the exchange occurred within ninety days of the filing. Answer (b) is incorrect because Olsen received the $10,000 cash in exchange for the boat. Olsen therefore has not been put in a better position than other general creditors, as Hall received new value for the cash. Answer (c) is incorrect because the issue of presumption of insolvency is not relevant when determining whether a transfer is preferential or nonpreferential.

16. (d) Improper actions during a bankruptcy that bar a discharge of all of the debts include concealing property and refusing to explain a loss of assets. Answer (a) is incorrect because this action means that this particular creditor's claim will not be discharged but does not bar a general discharge of the other debts. Answer (b) is incorrect because although alimony and support payments are not discharged themselves, their existence does not bar a general discharge. Answer (c) is incorrect because the inability to pay does not bar a general discharge.

17. (c) The trustee in bankruptcy may set aside preferential transfers made within ninety days before the filing of the bankruptcy petition while the debtor is insolvent. The time is extended to the previous twelve months if the preferential transfer was made to an insider. In this question, Quick's solvency when the loan was made by Erly is not relevant because this loan was made thirteen months before the filing of the petition for bankruptcy. Answer (a) is incorrect because since payment to Erly was made more than three months but less than twelve months before the filing, it is important that Erly is an insider. Answer (b) is incorrect because the definition of a preferential transfer incorporates transfers made for an antecedent debt. Answer (d) is incorrect because since Erly is an insider, it is relevant that the payment to Erly was made within one year of the filing of the bankruptcy petition.

F. Claims

18. (c) Of those listed, wages of the bankrupt's employees receive the highest priority for up to $4,650 each. Federal taxes have a low priority but are ahead of general creditors. Any deficiency for secured creditors after the collateral is sold is paid along with the general creditors.

19. (b) The highest priority includes the administration costs. Of those listed, the wages to employees up to $4,650 each accrued within ninety days before the petition was filed have the next priority. Federal and state taxes have the second lowest priority but are next because the claims in the ordinary course of business arose **before** the petition was filed and therefore get the lowest priority as general creditors.

G.   Discharge of a Bankrupt

20.   **(b)**   This is an intentional tort and the liability for these injuries would not be discharged in bankruptcy; however, this does not bar a general discharge of the debts. Answer (a) is incorrect because this is one of the prime acts that the law attempts to prevent. Answer (c) is incorrect because failing to satisfactorily explain a loss of assets can bar a general discharge. Answer (d) is incorrect because this is an act that can bar a general discharge.

21.   **(d)**   Corporations and partnerships cannot receive a discharge under Chapter 7 of the Federal Bankruptcy Code. Answer (a) is incorrect because although preferential transfers can be set aside, this would not prevent the discharge in bankruptcy. Answer (b) is incorrect because the rule is that destroying information relevant to the bankruptcy proceeding can bar a general discharge unless the act was justified under the circumstances. The accidental nature of the act in answer (b) is not a good case to bar the discharge. Answer (c) is incorrect because the rule states that the discharge is not allowed if the debtor has been discharged in bankruptcy within the past six years rather than ten years.

22.   **(c)**   Actions that bar a general discharge in bankruptcy include removing or destroying property within twelve months prior to filing the petition with an intent to hinder, delay, or defraud a creditor. Also included is making a false entry in a document related to the bankrupt's affairs. Obtaining credit by fraud involving the debtor's financial condition causes that debt to be nondischargeable. It, however, does not prevent a general discharge of all debts.

23.   **(b)**   The bankruptcy court can revoke the debtor's discharge if the debtor committed fraud during the bankruptcy proceedings, refused to obey lawful court orders, or failed to answer correctly material questions on the bankruptcy petition. Failure to list a creditor causes that creditor's debt not to be discharged but does not cause a revocation of the discharge.

H.   Debts Not Discharged by Bankruptcy

24.   **(c)**   There is a list of various types of debts that will not be discharged in bankruptcy, even though a general discharge is allowed. Among these are liabilities from theft, embezzlement, and committing fraud about one's financial condition. Note that liabilities from ordinary negligence or from breaches of contract, whether intentional or not, are dischargeable in bankruptcy.

25.   **(a)**   Debts that are not discharged in bankruptcy include alimony, separate maintenance, and child support. A claim from a breach of contract is a typical type of claim discharged. Any amount unsatisfied after sale of the collateral is paid along with the rest of the general creditors if sufficient funds remain after all of the other creditors are paid. These are discharged in bankruptcy. Although intentional torts are not dischargable in bankruptcy, claims based on mere negligence are.

J.   Reaffirmation

26.   **(d)**   To get debtors to reaffirm debts that have been discharged in bankruptcy, creditors must comply with certain procedures. In general, the reaffirmation must take place before the discharge is granted and it must be approved by the bankruptcy court. The debtor is given sixty days to rescind the reaffirmation after s/he agrees to it. Answer (a) is incorrect because it must be agreed to before discharge. Answer (b) is incorrect because there is no such limitation on the dollar amounts. Answer (c) is incorrect because the reaffirmation agreement is valid for almost all debt including household purpose debt.

K.   Business Reorganization—Chapter 11

27.   **(d)**   Under the reorganization provisions of Chapter 11 of the Federal Bankruptcy Code, a court supervised rehabilitation plan is adopted. It typically allows for the continued operation of the business and provides for the payment of all or part of the debts over an extended period of time. The payments to the creditors often come largely from future earnings. Answer (a) is incorrect because the court typically does not discharge the debtor from all of its debts under a Chapter 11 bankruptcy but provides for payments of debts out of future earnings. Answer (b) is incorrect because the plans can apply to any creditors whether they were in the portion that agreed to the plan or not. Answer (c) is incorrect because the debtor under Chapter 11 is often required to pay all or part of the debts out of future earnings.

28.   **(d)**   The Chapter 11 bankruptcy petition may either be filed voluntarily by the debtor or filed by the creditors to force the debtor into bankruptcy. Answer (a) is incorrect because a trustee need not be appointed. Answer (b) is incorrect because the debtor need not be insolvent to file a voluntary bankruptcy petition. Answer (c) is incorrect because only the debtor has the right to file the reorganization plan during the first 120 days the order for relief occurs.

29.   **(d)**   Under Chapter 11 of the Federal Bankruptcy Code, individuals, partnerships, and corporations are eligible for reorganization. Savings and loan companies, banks, and insurance companies are not eligible.

OTHER OBJECTIVE ANSWERS AND ANSWER EXPLANATIONS

Problem 1

Part a.

The trustee in bankruptcy may set aside preferential transfers of nonexempt property made to a creditor within the ninety days prior to the filing of the bankruptcy petition while the debtor was insolvent. Preferential transfers are those made for antecedent debts which enable the creditor to receive more than s/he would otherwise be entitled to under a Chapter 7 liquidation proceeding. Preferential transfers made to insiders within the previous twelve months may also be set aside.

1. **(Y)** This payment may be set aside because Mary Lake is an insider since she is the sister of one of Wren's directors. The preferential transfer to her on December 31, 2001, falls within the twelve months prior to the filing of the bankruptcy petition on April 15, 2002.

2. **(N)** This transaction represents a donation rather than payment on an antecedent debt, therefore it would not be set aside as a preferential transfer.

3. **(Y)** The transaction would be set aside as a preferential transfer. On February 1, 2002, Wren gave Young Finance Co. a security agreement to secure a loan previously made by Young. Preferential transfers include the granting of a security interest by the debtor to secure an antecedent debt.

4. **(N)** Transfers in the ordinary course of business are not voidable preferences.

5. **(N)** In this case, Wren purchased a new burglar alarm system for its factory for $5,000 cash. A contemporaneous exchange between a creditor and debtor whereby the debtor receives new value is not a preferential transfer.

Part b.

6. **(B)** Following satisfaction of the secured debts, bankruptcy administration expenses have the highest priority. Therefore, the administrative expenses will have second priority.

7. **(E)** Acme Office Cleaners is a general creditor and, therefore, receives the lowest priority for services performed before the bankruptcy petition was filed.

8. **(A)** The claim of Fifth Bank will be the first claim satisfied because it had a 1st mortgage on the warehouse owned by Wren. This warehouse was sold for $75,000, which more than satisfies the $50,000 owed to Fifth Bank.

9. **(D)** The IRS has priority for taxes due just before the priority of general creditors, therefore the IRS has fourth priority.

10. **(C)** Joan Sims, the employee, will have third priority because the bankrupt's employees have highest priority for wages and commission accrued within three months before the filing of the bankruptcy petition (up to a maximum of $4,650 each) after the administration costs have been satisfied.

Part c.

The fact pattern states that after paying the secured creditors, the bankruptcy administration expenses, and the priority general creditors, each nonpriority general creditor receives fifty cents on the dollar.

11. **(J)** TVN will receive $13,500. This is true because TVN's collateral sold for $12,000. TVN receives all of this $12,000 as a secured creditor owed $15,000. TVN becomes a general creditor for the remaining debt of $3,000 and receives fifty cents on the dollar for this which amounts to $1,500. TVN, therefore, receives $13,500 in total.

12. **(M)** Hart's collateral was sold for $25,000. The remaining $5,000 of the debt owed to Hart is paid at fifty cents on the dollar which amounts to $2,500. Hart, therefore, receives a total of $27,500.

13. **(G)** Ted Smith receives $4,650 as a priority for wages earned within the previous three months. Any wages in excess of the $4,650 are treated as a general claim; therefore, he receives fifty cents on the dollar for the remaining $200 owed to him for a total of $4,750.

14. **(B)** Power Electric Co., as a general creditor, receives half of the $600 of charges which amounts to $300.

15. **(D)** Soft Office Supplies is a general creditor, and thus, receives fifty cents on the dollar for the $2,000 debt owed for a total of $1,000.

Problem 2

1. **(T)** A debtor need not be insolvent to file a voluntary petition for bankruptcy. S/he merely needs to state that s/he has debts. Thus, Able could file even if solvent.

2. **(F)** In order to file a valid involuntary petition when there are fewer than twelve creditors, a single creditor may file the petition as long as s/he is owed at least $11,625 of unsecured debt. More than one creditor may be used to reach the $11,625 requirement. However, Lake, Young, and Thorn may not file a valid involuntary petition because they are collectively owed only $4,500.

3.   (T) In order to file a valid involuntary petition when there are fewer than twelve creditors, a single creditor can file the petition as long as s/he is owed at least $11,625 of unsecured debt. Cole may file alone as s/he is owed $12,000.

4.   (F) The trustee may set aside preferential transfers of nonexempt property to a creditor made within the previous ninety days while insolvent. The payment made to Vista Bank is not a preferential transfer because it was made more than ninety days before May 1, 2002, the date the involuntary petition was filed.

5.   (T) The trustee may set aside preferential transfers of nonexempt property to a creditor made within the previous ninety days while insolvent. If the creditor was an insider, the time period is extended to within one year prior to the filing of the bankruptcy petition. The payment to Owen is a preferential transfer because Owen, an officer of Able Corp., is an insider, and the payment was made within one year prior to the filing of the petition.

6.   (F) The payment to Core is not a preferential transfer because contemporaneously, Able received new value; that is, the computer. A contemporaneous exchange between creditor and debtor whereby the debtor receives new value is an exception to the trustee's power to set aside as a preferential transfer.

Problem 3

1.   (A) Statement I is correct since secured creditors receive payments before unsecured creditors (up to the value of the collateral) or receive the collateral itself. Statement II is incorrect because a secured creditor gets paid first only up to the value of the security. Any debt above the value of the security is given the lowest priority along with the general creditors.

2.   (B) Statement I is incorrect and statement II is correct because employees have the highest priority after the secured creditor of all the ones listed in the question up to $4,650 per claimant.

3.   (B) Statement I is incorrect because there is no collateral backing the 2002 federal income tax claim. It will thus not be paid as a secured creditor. Statement II is correct because taxes (federal, state, or local) have a higher priority than the general creditors.

4.   (C) Statement I is correct because preferential transfers to insiders may be set aside when made within the previous **twelve** months. Thus, the February 1 repayment of corporate directors' loans are preferential transfers. Statement II is correct because the preferential transfer rule of ninety days is extended to twelve months in the case of insiders.

5.   (A) Both transfers in the ordinary course of business and contemporaneous exchanges between creditors and debtors (whereby the debtors receive new value) are exceptions to the trustee's power to avoid preferential transfers. In this case, Rusk had purchased on May 1 raw materials for use in its manufacturing business and paid cash to the supplier. These facts constitute an exception to the trustee's power to avoid a preferential transfer. Statement II is incorrect because the May 1 purchase and payment constitute an exception to the preferential transfer avoiding powers.

ANSWER OUTLINE

Problem 1   Dischargeability of Debts in Bankruptcy; Preferential Transfer

a.   Judgment against Drake for auto accident is dischargeable
    1996 unpaid federal income taxes are dischargeable
    1996 taxes are not within three years of the filing
    Obligation to Bartin is not dischargeable
        Debt was not included in bankruptcy petition
        Bartin did not know of Drake's bankruptcy before
          time for filing claim expired
    Unpaid child support is not dischargeable

b.   Preferential transfer established if
    Payment made within ninety days prior to filing
    Antecedent debt owed by debtor
    Debtor was insolvent
    Benefited creditor
    Creditor received more than it would in liquidation

c.   Payment to Safe is a preferential transfer
    Transfer to Drake's brother is a preferential transfer
        Brother is an insider
        Payment made within one year of filing
    Mortgage given to Home is not a preferential transfer
        Mortgage was not an antecedent debt
    Payment to Max is not a preferential transfer
        Payment was made in ordinary course of business
          under ordinary terms

UNOFFICIAL ANSWER

Problem 1   Dischargeability of Debts in Bankruptcy; Preferential Transfer

a.   The judgment against Drake arising from this negligence is dischargeable in his bankruptcy.

    The unpaid federal income taxes are also dischargeable because they became due and owing more than three years prior to the filing of the bankruptcy petition.

    The obligation to Bartin will not be discharged because the debt was not included in Drake's bankruptcy petition schedules and the creditor did not have notice or actual knowledge of the bankruptcy in time to file a proof of claim.

    The unpaid child support is not dischargeable in Drake's bankruptcy.

b.   To establish a preferential transfer that can be set aside, the bankruptcy trustee must show

    •   A voluntary or involuntary transfer of nonexempt property to a creditor.
    •   The transfer was made during the ninety days immediately preceding the bankruptcy filing (or within one year in the case of an "insider").
    •   The transfer was on account of an antecedent debt.
    •   The transfer was made while the debtor was insolvent.
    •   The transfer allows the creditor to receive a greater percentage than would otherwise be received in the bankruptcy proceeding.

c.   The payment to Safe will be regarded as a preference and may be set aside by the trustee.

    The transfer by Drake to his brother can be set aside as a preference since his brother would be considered an insider and payment was made within one year of filing.

Giving the mortgage to Home is not a preference because it was not on account of an antecedent debt.

    The payment to Max is not a preference because it was made in the ordinary course of the business of Max and Drake under ordinary business terms.

ANSWER OUTLINE

Problem 2   Requirements for Involuntary Bankruptcy; Claims and Preferences—Secured Creditor; Preferential Transfer

a.   Involuntary bankruptcy petition against debtor having twelve or more creditors:
    May be filed by three or more creditors having unsecured claims of at least $11,625
    Debtor must not be paying undisputed debts as due

b.   1.   Dollar's motion for relief will be granted
        Dollar is entitled to take possession of collateral
          securing its loan
            Secured creditor may take possession of collateral if there is no equity in it
        Dollar may sell collateral and apply proceeds to loan balance
    2.   Bankruptcy court will not approve Dollar's claim for priority
        Dollar is entitled to the value of its collateral
        Dollar is an unsecured creditor for any deficiency

c.   Payment to Techno's president is a preferential transfer
    President is an insider
    Payment on unsecured loan during year preceding bankruptcy filing is preferential
    Payment to Alexis is not a preferential transfer made in the ordinary course of business
    Payment to Maple for truck is not a preferential transfer
    Contemporaneous exchange for new value

UNOFFICIAL ANSWER

Problem 2   Requirements for Involuntary Bankruptcy; Claims and Preferences—Secured Creditor; Preferential Transfer

a.   An involuntary bankruptcy petition may be filed against a debtor having twelve or more creditors by at least three creditors having unsecured claims of at least $11,625, provided the debtor is not paying its undisputed debts as they become due.

b.   1.   Dollar's motion for relief will be granted. Dollar's claim that it is entitled to take possession of the collateral securing its loan is correct. Generally, a secured creditor is allowed to take possession of its collateral if there is no equity in it (that is, the debt balance exceeds the collateral's fair market value). Dollar would then be entitled to sell the collateral and apply the proceeds to the loan balance.

    2.   Dollar's claim that is entitled to a priority distribution to the extent that the proceeds from the sale of its collateral are less than the loan balance will not be approved by the bankruptcy court. Dollar is entitled to the value of its collateral. As to any deficiency, Dollar will be treated as an unsecured creditor.

c.   The payment to Techno's president would be regarded as a preferential transfer. Because the president is an "in-

ANSWER OUTLINE

Problem 1 Minority; Reasonable Covenant not to Compete; Surety's Defenses

Beach's minority defense is invalid
  Misrepresentation of age does not invalidate defense
  However, failure to disaffirm within reasonable time after reaching majority constitutes implied ratification
Beach's assertion that Reid's violation of noncompetition covenant constitutes breach is valid
  Noncompetition clause is reasonable in light of circumstances present
Abel's defense based on Beach's fraud is invalid
  Since Reid knew nothing of Beach's fraud, he has no duty to inform Abel
Abel's defense based on Beach's minority is invalid
  Surety cannot use minority of principal debtor as defense to payment
Abel's defense based on Reid's violation of noncompetition covenant is valid
  Surety may use material breach of underlying contract by creditor as defense to payment
  Reid's violation of noncompetition clause constitutes breach

UNOFFICIAL ANSWER

Problem 1 Minority; Reasonable Covenant not to Compete; Surety's Defenses

Beach's minority at the time the contract with Reid was entered into will not be a valid defense. Despite Beach's misrepresentation of his age, the agreement with Reid was voidable at Beach's option while Beach was a minor. However, Beach's use and operation of the travel agency for at least seven months after reaching majority constituted an implied ratification of the contract. Some states may construe Beach's mere failure to disaffirm the contract within a reasonable time after reaching majority to be a ratification of the contract. Furthermore, a small number of states provide that minority is not a defense where the minor has entered into a business contract.

Beach's assertion that he is not liable due to Reid's violation of the contract clause prohibiting Reid from competing with Beach is correct because violation of the non-

competition covenant is a material breach of the contract. Since the case at issue involves the sale of a business including its goodwill, the legal validity of a clause prohibiting competition by the seller is determined by its reasonableness regarding the time and geographic area covered. Each case must be considered on its own facts, with a determination of what is reasonable under the particular circumstances. It appears that, according to the facts of this case, the prohibition against Reid's operating a competing travel agency within a one-mile radius of Beach's travel agency for two years is reasonable.

Abel's claim that he is not liable to Reid because of Beach's fraud in supplying him with false financial statements is incorrect. Although a creditor has a duty to disclose to the surety all material facts that would increase the surety's risk, the breach of such duty is not a valid defense of the surety if the creditor lacks knowledge of such facts. Therefore, unless Abel can show that Reid knew or had reason to know of the fraud committed by Beach, Abel will not be relieved of his surety undertaking.

Abel's claim that he is not liable to Reid because of Beach's minority is without merit. Beach's minority is a personal defense that in a proper case may be exercised only at Beach's option. Therefore, whether Beach has the power to disaffirm his contract with Reid will have no effect on Abel's surety obligations to Reid.

Abel's assertion that his liability to Reid will be discharged because of Reid's failure to comply with the express promise not to compete with Beach is correct. Unlike the defense of the principal debtor's minority, a material breach of the underlying contract between the principal debtor and creditor may be properly asserted by the surety. The creditor's failure to perform in accordance with the material terms of the underlying contract without justification will discharge the principal debtor's obligation to perform, thereby increasing the risk of the principal debtor's nonperformance. Thus, the surety will also be discharged from liability due to his own increased risk of loss on the surety contract. It seems clear that Reid's opening of a travel agency across the street from Beach's business after only nineteen months constituted a material breach of the sale contract. Therefore, Abel will be discharged from his surety obligation.

AGENCY

Overview

Agency is a relationship in which one party (agent) is authorized to act on behalf of another party (principal). The law of agency is concerned with the rights, duties, and liabilities of the parties in an agency relationship. Important to this relationship is the fact that the agent has a fiduciary duty to act in the best interest of the principal.

A good understanding of this module is important because partnership law is a special application of agency law.

The CPA exam emphasizes the creation and termination of the agency relationship, the undisclosed as well as the disclosed principal relationship, unauthorized acts or torts committed by the agent within the course and scope of the agency relationship and principal's liability for agent's unauthorized contracts.

A. Characteristics

1. Agency is a relationship between two parties, whereby one party (agent) agrees to act on behalf of the other party (principal). A contract is not required but is frequently present.

   a. Agent is subject to control of principal
   b. Agent is a fiduciary and must act for the benefit of principal
   c. Agent can be used for other purposes, but we are primarily concerned with agents that agree to act for the principal in business transactions with third parties
   d. Agent's specific authority is determined by the principal but generally agent has authority to bind the principal contractually with third parties

2. Employee (servant)

   a. Employee is a type of agent in which employee's physical conduct is subject to control by employer (master)

      (1) Employer is a type of principal and may be called such when the agent is an employee
      (2) Employer is generally liable for employee's torts if committed within course and scope of employment relationship

         (a) Known as doctrine of respondeat superior (vicarious liability)

         EXAMPLE: S is an employee of M. One day while delivering inventory for M, she negligently hits a third party with the delivery truck. Although S is liable because she committed the tort, M is also liable.

         (b) Course and scope of employment is defined broadly

            1] Note that this makes employer liable for torts of employee even if employer not actually negligent him/herself

         EXAMPLE: M, the employer, gives S $30 and asks him to go buy donuts for the employees who are working overtime. He takes his own car and injures a third party through his own negligence. The employer is also liable for this tort.

         (c) Employee need not be following instructions of employer (i.e., rule applies even if employee violated employer's instructions in committing tort)

         EXAMPLE: P works for Q delivering widgets. One rule that Q has is that all employees must look behind the truck before backing out after all deliveries. P violated this rule and injured R. Q is still liable even s/he though had taken steps to prevent this type of accident.

         (d) Contributory negligence (i.e., third party's negligence) is generally a defense for both the agent and his/her principal

            1] Some jurisdictions have adopted comparative negligence which means that defendant at fault pays but that amount of damages is determined by comparing each party's negligence

3. Independent contractor distinguished from employee

   a. Not subject to control of employer as to methods of work
   b. Not subject to regular supervision as an employee
   c. Employer controls results only (independent contractor controls the methods)
   d. Generally, employer is not liable for torts committed by independent contractor

      (1) Unless independent contractor is employed to do something inherently dangerous (e.g., blasting)

      (2) Unless employer was negligent in hiring independent contractor

  e. Independent contractor may also be an agent in certain cases

    EXAMPLE: A public accounting firm represents a client in tax court.

4. Examples of agents and agencies

  a. Power of attorney

    (1) Principal, in writing, grants authority to agent

      (a) Only principal need sign

    (2) Agent need not be an attorney but anyone with capacity to be agent

    (3) Power of attorney may grant general authority or restricted authority

  b. Broker—special agent acting for either buyer or seller in business transactions (e.g., real estate broker)

  c. Exclusive—only agent the principal may deal with for a certain purpose during life of the contract (e.g., real estate broker who has sole right to sell property except for personal sale by principal)

  d. Del credere—a sales agent who, prior to the creation and as a condition of the agency, guarantees the accounts of the customers to his/her principal (if the customers fail to pay)

    (1) Guarantee is not within the Statute of Frauds (i.e., it is not required to be in writing)

  e. E-agent is computer program or electronic method to take some action without specific human review

    EXAMPLE: P authorizes an on-line search to find the lowest price of a certain product found through on-line stores.

  f. Relationship resembling agency

    (1) Agency coupled with an interest—agent has an interest in subject matter through a security interest

      (a) For example, mortgagee with right to sell property on default of mortgagor

        1] Agreement stipulating agent is to receive profits or proceeds does not by itself create an agency coupled with an interest

      (b) Principal does not have the power to terminate agency coupled with an interest

      (c) Actually not an agency relationship because one who creates this relationship surrenders power—fact patterns may still use terms of principal and agent

5. Types of principals

  a. Disclosed—when the third party knows agent is acting for a principal and who the principal is

    (1) Principal becomes a party to authorized contracts made by the agent in the principal's name

    (2) Agent is not liable under contract

      EXAMPLE: Signed "Andy Andrews as agent for Pam Paringer."

      EXAMPLE: Signed "Pam Paringer, by Andy Andrews, agent."

      EXAMPLE: Signed "Pam Paringer, by Andy Andrews."

  b. Partially disclosed—when the third party knows or should know the agent is acting for a principal but does not know who the principal is

    (1) Both agent and principal are liable under the contract

      EXAMPLE: Signed, "Andy Andrews, agent."

      (a) Principal is liable for all parts of contract authorized by principal

      (b) Agent is liable for all of contract

      (c) Agent generally has same authority as if principal disclosed

  c. Undisclosed—when the third party has no notice that the agent is acting for a principal

(1) Both agent and principal are liable under authorized contracts if agent so intended to act for principal

EXAMPLE: Signed, "Andy Andrews."

(a) Similar to partially disclosed principal (i.e., principal is liable for parts of contract s/he authorized and agent is liable for all of contract)

(b) Agent generally has same authority as if principal disclosed

6. Types of agents

a. General agent—agent is given broad powers

b. Special agent—authority of agent is limited in some significant way such as authority over one transaction

c. Subagent

(1) Generally, agents have no authority to hire subagents unless principal so authorizes

B. Methods of Creation

1. Appointment

a. Express—by agreement between the principal and agent

(1) Generally the agency contract need not be in writing in situations where the agent enters into agreements which themselves fall under the Statute of Frauds

EXAMPLE: A, in his capacity as agent of P, signs a contract for the sale of goods costing $600. Even though the sales contract must normally be in writing under the UCC version of the Statute of Frauds, the agency agreement between A and P need not be expressed in writing.

(a) But if agency contract cannot be completed within one year, it must be in writing

EXAMPLE: P agrees to pay A as his agent and to keep him as his agent for two years.

(b) In some states, agency contract needs to be written if agent is to buy or sell a specific piece of real estate named in agency contract

b. Implied—based on customs and industry practices as to extent of agent's authority

2. Representation—principal represents to third party that someone is his/her agent

a. Creates apparent (ostensible) authority

b. Does not require reliance by third party

c. Directed toward third party causing third party to believe (as opposed to implied appointment when agent is led to believe)

EXAMPLE: Principal writes to a third party that A is his agent and has authority. Even if A has no actual authority, he is an apparent agent.

3. By estoppel—principal is not allowed to deny agency relationship when s/he causes third party to believe it exists

a. Imposed by law rather than by agreement

b. The third party must rely to his/her detriment on this appearance of agency before the principal is estopped from denying it

EXAMPLE: A, who is not an agent of P, bargained, while in P's presence with X, to buy goods for P. If P remains silent, he will not be able to deny the agency.

4. Necessity—when a situation arises that makes it a matter of public policy to presume an agency relationship (e.g., in an emergency to contract for medical aid)

5. Ratification—approval after the fact of an unauthorized act done by an agent or one not yet an agent

a. By affirming the act or by accepting the benefits of the act

b. Other party to the contract can withdraw before principal ratifies

c. Ratification is effective retroactively back to time of agent's act

d. Undisclosed principal cannot ratify unauthorized acts of agent

e. Requirements to be valid

(1) Act must be one that would have been valid if agent had been authorized (i.e., lawful and dele-gable)

   (a) Torts can be ratified, but not crimes

(2) Principal must have been in existence and competent when the act was done

(3) Principal must be aware of all material facts

(4) Act must be ratified in its entirety (i.e., cannot ratify the beneficial part and refuse the rest)

> EXAMPLE: *Receptionist has no authority to contract for X Company but signs a service contract on behalf of X Company. Officers of X Company make use of service contract. The receptionist's act is ratified.*

C. Authority

1. Actual authority

  a. Express—consists of all authority expressly given by the principal to his/her agent

  b. Implied—authority that can be reasonably implied from express authority and from the conduct of the principal

    (1) Includes authority to do what is customary under the circumstances

> EXAMPLE: *A has been engaged by P to be the general manager of P's retail store. A may buy and sell inventory in the business. She may also hire and fire the business employees. A may not, however, do such things as selling the business itself, selling the fixtures or the building, or advertising for the company to go into a complete new line or service.*

2. Apparent (ostensible) authority—third party(ies) must have reasonable belief based on principal's representations

  a. For example, an agent insofar as third persons are concerned can do what the predecessor did or what agents in similar positions in the general business world are deemed authorized to do for their principals

  b. Secret limitations have no effect on third parties

> EXAMPLE: *Principal makes agent manager of his store but tells him not to purchase goods on his own. Agent has apparent authority to purchase as similar managers would.*

> EXAMPLE: *P authorizes A to go to San Francisco to buy a piece of property to open up an office for P. P tells A to not pay more than $150,000. A makes a contract with T to buy some property for P. A signs the contract as agent for P but agrees to $160,000. T was unaware of the limitation on the purchase price. P is bound to the contract with T for the full $160,000.*

  c. Apparent authority exists only for those who know of principal's representations whether directly or indirectly

  d. Agent has apparent authority after termination of agency until those with whom the agent has dealt are given actual notice; others who know of agency relationship require constructive notice

    (1) Notice may come from any source

3. Estoppel—not true authority, but an equitable doctrine to protect a third party who has detrimentally relied, by estopping the principal from denying the existence of authority

  a. Often indistinguishable from effects of apparent authority or ratification

  b. Only creates rights in the third party(ies)

> EXAMPLE: *A sells P's racehorse to T on P's behalf. P did not give authority, but since the racehorse continues to lose races, P does not object. When the horse begins to win races, P claims A never had authority to sell. If A does not have apparent authority and if P did not technically ratify, P can be estopped from denying the authority on equitable grounds.*

D. Capacity to Be Agent or Principal

1. Principal must be able to give legal consent

  a. Minors (person under age of majority, that is, 18 or 21) can, in most jurisdictions, appoint an agent

    (1) But minor may disaffirm agency

  b. Unincorporated associations are not legal entities and therefore cannot appoint agents

(1) Individual members will be responsible as principals if they appoint an agent

c. If act requires some legal capacity (e.g., legal age to sell land), then principal must meet this requirement or agent cannot legally perform even if s/he has capacity. Capacity cannot be increased by appointment of an agent.

2. An agent must merely have sufficient mental and physical ability to carry out instructions of his/her principal

    a. Can bind principal even if agent is a minor or legally unable to act for self
    b. Corporations, unincorporated associations, and partnerships may act as agents
    c. A mental incompetent or an infant of tender years may not be an agent

E. Obligations and Rights

1. Principal's obligations to agent

    a. Compensate agent as per agreement, or, in the absence of an agreement, pay a reasonable amount for the agent's service
    b. Reimburse agent for reasonable expenses and indemnify agent against loss or liability for duties performed at the principal's direction which are not illegal
    c. Not to interfere with his/her work
    d. Inform agent of risks (e.g., physical harm, pecuniary loss)
    e. May have remedies of discharging agent, restitution, damages, and accounting, or an injunction

2. Agent's obligations to principal

    a. Agent is a fiduciary and must act in the best interest of the principal and with loyalty
    b. Carry out instructions of principal exercising reasonable care and skill
    c. To account to the principal for profits and everything that rightfully belong to the principal and not commingle funds
    d. Duty not to compete or act adversely to principal

       (1) Includes not acting for oneself unless principal knows and agrees

    e. Give any information to principal that s/he would want or need to know
    f. After termination, must cease acting as agent

3. Principal's liability to third parties

    a. Disclosed principal is liable on contracts

       (1) Where agent has actual authority, implied authority, apparent authority, or contract is later ratified
       (2) Also held liable for any representations made by agent with authority to make them
       (3) Principal not liable where third party has any notice that agent is exceeding his actual authority

    b. Undisclosed or partially disclosed principal is liable unless

       (1) Third party holds agent responsible (third party has choice)
       (2) Agent has already fully performed contract
       (3) Undisclosed principal is expressly excluded by contract
       (4) Contract is a negotiable instrument

          (a) Only fully disclosed (in instrument) principal is liable on a negotiable instrument

    c. If a writing is required under Statute of Frauds, principal will only be liable if contract is signed
    d. Principal has his/her own personal defenses (e.g., lack of capacity) and defenses on the contract (e.g., nonperformance by the third party)

       (1) Principal does not have agent's personal defenses (e.g., right of setoff where third party owes agent debt)

    e. Notice to agent is generally considered notice to the principal

4. Agent's liability to third parties

    a. Agent is liable on contract when

        (1) Principal is undisclosed or partially disclosed

            (a) Agent is not relieved from liability until principal performs or third party elects to hold principal liable

        (2) S/he contracts in his/her own name

        (3) S/he guarantees principal's performance and principal fails

        (4) S/he signs a negotiable instrument and does not sign as an agent or does not include the principal's name (undisclosed principal)

        (5) S/he knows principal does not exist or is incompetent

        (6) S/he acts without authority

    b. Agent is not liable when

        (1) Principal is disclosed and agent signs all documents showing s/he is agent

        (2) Principal ratifies unauthorized act

        (3) Third party elects to hold partially disclosed or undisclosed principal liable

    c. Agent has his/her personal defenses (e.g., right of offset if third party owes him/her debt) and defenses on the contract (e.g., nonperformance by the third party)

        (1) Agent does not have principal's personal defenses (e.g., lack of capacity)

    d. Agent is liable if s/he does not deliver property received from third party for principal

    e. Agent is liable for his/her own crimes and torts

5. Third party's liability to principal and agent

    a. Third party has no contractual liability to agent unless

        (1) Agent is a party to the contract (i.e., undisclosed or partially disclosed principal), or

        (2) Agent has an interest in the contract (e.g., agent invests in the contract)

    b. Third party is liable to disclosed, partially disclosed, and undisclosed principals

        (1) Third party has personal defenses against principal (e.g., lack of capacity), and defenses on the contract (e.g., nonperformance by principal)

        (2) Against undisclosed principal, third party also has personal defenses against agent

F. Termination of Principal-Agent Relationship

1. Acts of the parties

    a. By agreement

        (1) Time specified in original agreement (e.g., agency for one year)

        (2) Mutual consent

        (3) Accomplishment of objective (e.g., agency to buy a piece of land)

    b. Principal or agent may terminate agency

        (1) Party that terminates is liable for breach of contract if termination is before specified period of time

            (a) One still has power to terminate relationship even though s/he has no right to terminate (i.e., results in breach of contract)

            EXAMPLE: A and P agree to be agent and principal for six months. P terminates A after two months. P is liable to A for breach of contract for the damages that this wrongful termination causes A. However, P does have the power to remove A's authority to act on behalf of P.

        (2) If either party breaches duties owed, other party may terminate agency without liability

        (3) If no time is specified in agency, then either party may terminate without liability

        (4) Principal does not have power to terminate agency coupled with an interest

    c. Death of either agent or principal

    d. Agency coupled with an interest is irrevocable

       (1) Refers to cases in which agent has actual interest in property involved in this agency

2. Third parties who have dealt with agent or have known of agency must be given notice if agency terminated by acts of the parties

    a. Otherwise, agent still binds principal by apparent authority

    b. Constructive notice (e.g., publishing in a newspaper or a trade journal) is sufficient to third parties who have not previously dealt with agent

      EXAMPLE: P fired A, who had been P's agent for a few years. P published in the newspaper that A was no longer his agent. A subsequently made a contract with X purporting to bind P to the contract. X had never dealt with P and A before but was aware that A had been P's agent. X was not aware that A had been fired because he had not read the notice. X cannot hold P to the contract because of the constructive notice. X does not have to read it for the constructive notice to be valid.

    c. Actual notice (e.g., orally informing or sending a letter, etc.) must be given to third parties who have previously dealt with agent unless third party learns of termination from another source

      EXAMPLE: A, while acting as an agent of P, had previous dealings with T. P fires A but A makes a contract with T purporting to act as P's agent. T can still hold P liable unless he received actual notice of termination.

      EXAMPLE: Same as above except that the principal gave constructive notice. T may hold P liable.

      EXAMPLE: Same as above except that although P only gave constructive notice through a trade journal, T happened to read it. This qualifies as actual notice. Therefore, unlike above, T may not hold P liable.

3. Termination by operation of law

    a. If subject of agreement becomes illegal or impossible

    b. Death, insanity, or court determined incompetence of either party

      (1) Exception is an agency coupled with an interest

        EXAMPLE: If mortgagee has power to sell the property to recover his loan, this authority to sell as mortgagor's agent is not terminated by mortgagor's death.

    c. Bankruptcy of principal terminates the relationship

      (1) Bankruptcy of agent does not affect unless agent's solvency is needed for performance

    d. If terminated by operation of law, no notice need be given

MULTIPLE-CHOICE QUESTIONS (1-25)

1. Noll gives Carr a written power of attorney. Which of the following statements is correct regarding this power of attorney?

    a. It must be signed by both Noll and Carr.

    b. It must be for a definite period of time.

    c. It may continue in existence after Noll's death.

    d. It may limit Carr's authority to specific transactions.

2. A principal and agent relationship requires a

    a. Written agreement.

    b. Power of attorney.

    c. Meeting of the minds and consent to act.

    d. Specified consideration.

3. Lee repairs high-speed looms for Sew Corp., a clothing manufacturer. Which of the following circumstances best indicates that Lee is an employee of Sew and **not** an independent contractor?

    a. Lee's work is not supervised by Sew personnel.

    b. Lee's tools are owned by Lee.

    c. Lee is paid weekly by Sew.

    d. Lee's work requires a high degree of technical skill.

4. Harris, while delivering parts to a customer for his employer, negligently ran into and injured Wolfe. Harris had been asked by his employer to make these deliveries even though Harris was using his personal pickup truck. Neither Harris nor the employer had insurance to cover this injury. Which of the following is correct?

    a. Wolfe can hold Harris liable but not the employer because Harris was driving his own vehicle.

    b. Wolfe can hold the employer liable but not Harris because the employer had asked Harris to make the deliveries.

    c. Wolfe can hold either Harris or the employer or both liable.

    d. Wolfe can hold either Harris or the employer liable but not both.

5. Chiron employed Sherwin as a mechanic. Chiron has various rules that all employed mechanics must follow. One day a customer was injured severely when her car's brakes failed. It was shown that her car's brakes failed because Sherwin did not follow one of the specific rules of Chiron. Which of the following is correct?

    a. Sherwin is liable to the customer but Chiron is not because the accident was caused by Sherwin breaking one of Chiron's specific rules.

    b. The customer should sue Sherwin for fraud, not negligence, because Sherwin broke a rule of the employer.

    c. The customer can hold Chiron liable but not Sherwin, because her contract to get the car repaired was with Chiron.

    d. The customer may choose to recover damages from both Chiron and Sherwin.

6. Pine, an employee of Global Messenger Co., was hired to deliver highly secret corporate documents for Global's clients throughout the world. Unknown to Global, Pine carried a concealed pistol. While Pine was making a delivery, he suspected an attempt was being made to steal the pack-

age, drew his gun and shot Kent, an innocent passerby. Kent will **not** recover damages from Global if

    a. Global discovered that Pine carried a weapon and did nothing about it.

    b. Global instructed its messengers **not** to carry weapons.

    c. Pine was correct and an attempt was being made to steal the package.

    d. Pine's weapon was unlicensed and illegal.

7. When an agent acts for an undisclosed principal, the principal will **not** be liable to third parties if the

    a. Principal ratifies a contract entered into by the agent.

    b. Agent acts within an implied grant of authority.

    c. Agent acts outside the grant of actual authority.

    d. Principal seeks to conceal the agency relationship.

8. Trent was retained, in writing, to act as Post's agent for the sale of Post's memorabilia collection. Which of the following statements is correct?

  I. To be an agent, Trent must be at least twenty-one years of age.

  II. Post would be liable to Trent if the collection was destroyed before Trent found a purchaser.

    a. I only.

    b. II only.

    c. Both I and II.

    d. Neither I nor II.

9. Blue, a used car dealer, appointed Gage as an agent to sell Blue's cars. Gage was authorized by Blue to appoint subagents to assist in the sale of the cars. Vond was appointed as a subagent. To whom does Vond owe a fiduciary duty?

    a. Gage only.

    b. Blue only.

    c. Both Blue and Gage.

    d. Neither Blue nor Gage.

10. Which of the following under agency law is **not** a type of authority that an agent might have?

    a. Actual express.

    b. Actual implied.

    c. Resulting.

    d. Apparent.

11. Which of the following actions requires an agent for a corporation to have a written agency agreement?

    a. Purchasing office supplies for the principal's business.

    b. Purchasing an interest in undeveloped land for the principal.

    c. Hiring an independent general contractor to renovate the principal's office building.

    d. Retaining an attorney to collect a business debt owed the principal.

12. Frost's accountant and business manager has the authority to

    a. Mortgage Frost's business property.

    b. Obtain bank loans for Frost.

    c. Insure Frost's property against fire loss.

    d. Sell Frost's business.

13. Ames, claiming to be an agent of Clar Corporation, makes a contract with Trimon in the name of Clar Corporation. Later, Clar Corporation, for the first time, learns what Ames has done and notifies Trimon of the truth that Ames was not an agent of Clar Corporation. Which of the following statements is incorrect?

   a. Clar Corporation may ratify this contract if it does so with the entire contract.
   b. Trimon may withdraw from the contract before Clar attempts to ratify it.
   c. Clar Corporation may ratify this contract by performing under the contract without stating that it is ratifying.
   d. Trimon may enforce this contract even if Clar Corporation does not wish to be bound.

14. Which of the following generally may ratify a contract that was agreed to by his/her agent without authority from the principal?

	Fully disclosed principal	Partially disclosed principal	Undisclosed principal
a.	Yes	Yes	Yes
b.	Yes	Yes	No
c.	Yes	No	No
d.	No	No	Yes

15. Beele authorized McDonald to be his agent to go to Denver and purchase some real estate that would be suitable to open up a branch office for Beele's business. He tells McDonald not to pay more than $125,000 for the real estate. McDonald contacts York to buy some real estate she owns. York calls Beele and Beele tells York that McDonald is his agent to buy the real estate. Nothing is mentioned about the $125,000 limitation. After negotiations between McDonald and York, McDonald signs a contract purchasing the real estate for $140,000. McDonald signed it indicating on the contract that he was signing as agent for Beele.

Further facts show that the real estate is worth $140,000. Which of the following is correct?

   a. There is a fully enforceable contract between Beele and York for $140,000.
   b. Beele may enforce the contract with York for $125,000.
   c. There is no contract between Beele and York because McDonald did not have authority to purchase the real estate for $140,000.
   d. York may require that Beele pay $140,000 because the real estate was worth $140,000 not $125,000.

16. Young Corp. hired Wilson as a sales representative for six months at a salary of $5,000 per month plus 6% of sales. Which of the following statements is correct?

   a. Young does **not** have the power to dismiss Wilson during the six-month period without cause.
   b. Wilson is obligated to act solely in Young's interest in matters concerning Young's business.
   c. The agreement between Young and Wilson is **not** enforceable unless it is in writing and signed by Wilson.
   d. The agreement between Young and Wilson formed an agency coupled with an interest.

17. Which of the following statement(s) concerning agency law is(are) true?

   I. A contract is needed to have an agency relationship.
   II. The agent owes a fiduciary duty to the principal.
   III. The principal owes a fiduciary duty to the agent.

   a. I and II only.
   b. I and III only.
   c. II only.
   d. I, II, and III.

18. Easy Corp. is a real estate developer and regularly engages real estate brokers to act on its behalf in acquiring parcels of land. The brokers are authorized to enter into such contracts, but are instructed to do so in their own names without disclosing Easy's identity or relationship to the transaction. If a broker enters into a contract with a seller on Easy's behalf,

   a. The broker will have the same actual authority as if Easy's identity has been disclosed.
   b. Easy will be bound by the contract because of the broker's apparent authority.
   c. Easy will **not** be liable for any negligent acts committed by the broker while acting on Easy's behalf.
   d. The broker will **not** be personally bound by the contract because the broker has express authority to act.

19. An agent will usually be liable under a contract made with a third party when the agent is acting on behalf of a(n)

	Disclosed principal	Undisclosed principal
a.	Yes	Yes
b.	Yes	No
c.	No	Yes
d.	No	No

20. When a valid contract is entered into by an agent on the principal's behalf, in a nondisclosed principal situation, which of the following statements concerning the principal's liability is correct?

	The principal may be held liable once disclosed	The principal must ratify the contract to be held liable
a.	Yes	Yes
b.	Yes	No
c.	No	Yes
d.	No	No

21. Which of the following rights will a third party be entitled to after validly contracting with an agent representing an undisclosed principal?

   a. Disclosure of the principal by the agent.
   b. Ratification of the contract by the principal.
   c. Performance of the contract by the agent.
   d. Election to void the contract after disclosure of the principal.

22. Able, as agent for Baker, an undisclosed principal, contracted with Safe to purchase an antique car. In payment, Able issued his personal check to Safe. Able could not cover the check but expected Baker to give him cash to deposit before the check was presented for payment. Baker did not do so and the check was dishonored. Baker's identity became known to Safe. Safe may **not** recover from

   a. Baker individually on the contract.
   b. Able individually on the contract.
   c. Baker individually on the check.
   d. Able individually on the check.

23. Thorp was a purchasing agent for Ogden, a sole proprietor, and had the express authority to place purchase orders with Ogden's suppliers. Thorp placed an order with Datz, Inc. on Ogden's behalf after Ogden was declared incompetent in a judicial proceeding. Thorp was aware of Ogden's incapacity. Which of the following statements is correct concerning Ogden's liability to Datz?

    a. Ogden will be liable because Datz was **not** informed of Ogden's incapacity.

    b. Ogden will be liable because Thorp acted with express authority.

    c. Ogden will **not** be liable because Thorp's agency ended when Ogden was declared incompetent.

    d. Ogden will **not** be liable because Ogden was a nondisclosed principal.

24. Generally, an agency relationship is terminated by operation of law in all of the following situations **except** the

    a. Principal's death.

    b. Principal's incapacity.

    c. Agent's renunciation of the agency.

    d. Agent's failure to acquire a necessary business license.

25. Bolt Corp. dismissed Ace as its general sales agent and notified all of Ace's known customers by letter. Young Corp., a retail outlet located outside of Ace's previously assigned sales territory, had never dealt with Ace. Young knew of Ace as a result of various business contacts. After his dismissal, Ace sold Young goods, to be delivered by Bolt, and received from Young a cash deposit for 20% of the purchase price. It was not unusual for an agent in Ace's previous position to receive cash deposits. In an action by Young against Bolt on the sales contract, Young will

    a. Lose, because Ace lacked any implied authority to make the contract.

    b. Lose, because Ace lacked any express authority to make the contract.

    c. Win, because Bolt's notice was inadequate to terminate Ace's apparent authority.

    d. Win, because a principal is an insurer of an agent's acts.

OTHER OBJECTIVE QUESTIONS

Problem 1   (5 to 10 minutes)

Lace Computer Sales Corp. orally contracted with Banks, an independent consultant, for Banks to work part-time as Lace's agent to perform Lace's customers' service calls. Banks, a computer programmer and software designer, was authorized to customize Lace's software to the customers' needs, on a commission basis, but was specifically told not to sell Lace's computers.

On September 15, Banks made a service call on Clear Co. to repair Clear's computer. Banks had previously called on Clear, customized Lace's software for Clear, and collected cash payments for the work performed. During the call, Banks convinced Clear to buy an upgraded Lace computer for a price much lower than Lace would normally charge. Clear had previously purchased computers from other Lace agents and had made substantial cash down payments to the agents. Clear had no knowledge that the price was lower than normal. Banks received a $1,000 cash down payment and promised to deliver the computer the next week. Banks never turned in the down payment and left town. When Clear called the following week to have the computer delivered, Lace refused to honor Clear's order.

Required:

Items 1 through 5 relate to the relationships between the parties. For each item, select from List I whether only statement I is correct, whether only statement II is correct, whether both statements I and II are correct, or whether neither statement I nor II is correct.

List I
A. I only.
B. II only.
C. Both I and II.
D. Neither I nor II.

1.   I.   Lace's agreement with Banks had to be in writing for it to be a valid agency agreement.
      II.   Lace's agreement with Banks empowered Banks to act as Lace's agent.

2.   I.   Clear was entitled to rely on Banks' implied authority to customize Lace's software.
      II.   Clear was entitled to rely on Banks' express authority when buying the computer.

3.   I.   Lace's agreement with Banks was automatically terminated by Banks' sale of the computer.
      II.   Lace must notify Clear before Banks' apparent authority to bind Lace will cease.

4.   I.   Lace is **not** bound by the agreement made by Banks with Clear.
      II.   Lace may unilaterally amend the agreement made by Banks to prevent a loss on the sale of the computer to Clear.

5.   I.   Lace, as a disclosed principal, is solely contractually liable to Clear.
      II.   Both Lace and Banks are contractually liable to Clear.

PROBLEMS

Problem 1   (7 to 10 minutes)

John Nolan, a partner in Nolan, Stein, & Wolf partnership, transferred his interest in the partnership to Simon and withdrew from the partnership. Although the partnership will continue, Stein and Wolf have refused to admit Simon as a partner.

Subsequently, the partnership appointed Ed Lemon as its agent to market its various product lines. Lemon entered into a two-year written agency contract with the partnership which provided that Lemon would receive a 10% sales commission. The agency contract was signed by Lemon and, on behalf of the partnership, by Stein and Wolf.

After six months, Lemon was terminated without cause. Lemon asserts that

- He is an agent coupled with an interest.
- The agency relationship may not be terminated without cause prior to the expiration of its term.
- He is entitled to damages because of the termination of the agency relationship.

Required:

Answer the following, setting forth reasons for any conclusions stated.

Discuss the merits of Lemon's assertions.

MULTIPLE-CHOICE ANSWERS

1. d __ __	7. c __ __	13. d __ __	19. c __ __	25. c __ __
2. c __ __	8. d __ __	14. b __ __	20. b __ __	
3. c __ __	9. c __ __	15. a __ __	21. c __ __	
4. c __ __	10. c __ __	16. b __ __	22. c __ __	
5. d __ __	11. b __ __	17. c __ __	23. c __ __	1st: __/25 = __%
6. d __ __	12. c __ __	18. a __ __	24. c __ __	2nd: __/25 = __%

MULTIPLE-CHOICE ANSWER EXPLANATIONS

A.   Characteristics

1.   **(d)**   A power of attorney is written authority conferred to an agent. It is conferred in a formal writing. A power of attorney can be general or it can grant the agent only restricted authority. Answer (a) is incorrect because the power of attorney must be signed only by the person granting such authority. Answer (b) is incorrect because the power of attorney does not have to be for a definite, specified time period. Answer (c) is incorrect because the death of the principal constitutes the termination of an agency relationship by operation of law.

2.   **(c)**   The relationship between a principal and agent is based upon the consent of both parties, also involving a meeting of the minds. Answer (d) is incorrect because specified consideration is not needed to create an agency relationship; the relationship between the principal and the agent need not be contractual. Answer (a) is incorrect because although the principal and agent relationship may be written, a written agreement is not required. Answer (b) is incorrect because power of attorney is not needed to create an agency relationship.

3.   **(c)**   An employee is generally subject to control as to the methods used to complete the work. An independent contractor is typically paid for the completion of the project rather than on an hourly, weekly, or monthly basis. Answer (a) is incorrect because supervision by Sew Corp. personnel shows an employment relationship. Answer (b) is incorrect because independent contractors typically provide their own tools. Answer (d) is incorrect because the work of both employees and independent contractors can require a high degree of skill.

A.2.   Employee (Servant)

4.   **(c)**   Since Harris was acting within the scope of his employment when he negligently injured Wolfe, both Harris and his employer are liable. Wolfe can recover from either one or both. Answer (a) is incorrect because both are liable since Harris was acting within the scope of the employment. The ownership of the vehicle does not change this. Answer (b) is incorrect because Harris is liable for his own tort even though the employer can also be held liable. Answer (d) is incorrect because Wolfe may recover the full damages from either or may recover a portion of the damages from both.

5.   **(d)**   Because the repairs Sherwin did were within the scope of the employment, the employer is also liable. This is true even if the employer was diligent in creating excellent rules that were not followed by an employee. Answer (a) is incorrect because the repairs were within the scope of the employment. Answer (b) is incorrect because the customer can sue for negligence and hold both parties liable. Answer (c) is incorrect because the customer may recover from both under tort law.

6.   **(d)**   In general, the employer is not responsible for the crimes of the employee unless the employer aided or permitted the illegal activity, even if the activity was within the scope of the employment. Answer (a) is incorrect because if the employer did nothing to instruct the employee about the use of the weapon, this could help establish negligence on the part of the employer and would not prevent the use of the doctrine of respondeat superior, which makes employers liable for the tortious acts of their employees within the scope of the employment. Answer (b) is incorrect because the employer is liable for torts of the employee committed within the course and scope of the employment even if the employee was violating the employer's instructions. Answer (c) is incorrect because even if the employee's suspicions were correct, the shooting of an innocent passerby should establish at least negligence for which the employer and the employee are liable.

A.5.   Types of Principals

7.   **(c)**   A principal, whether disclosed, partially disclosed, or undisclosed is liable on contracts where the agent has actual or apparent authority, or where the principal ratifies an agent's contract. Actual authority includes express or implied authority projected by the principal to the agent. Apparent authority of an agent is authority perceived by a third party based on the principal's representations. Therefore, apparent authority can exist only where there is a disclosed or a partially disclosed principal. It follows, then, that an undisclosed principal will **not** be liable to third parties if the agent acts outside the grant of **actual** authority.

B.   Methods of Creation

8.   **(d)**   An agent must merely have sufficient mental and physical ability to carry out instructions of his/her principal. An agent can bind the principal even if the agent is a minor. If the memorabilia collection was destroyed before Trent found a purchaser, Post would not be liable to Trent. Upon the loss or destruction of the subject matter on which the agency relationship is based, the agency relationship is terminated.

9.   **(c)**   The fiduciary duty is an important duty owed by agents to their principals. Gage as Blue's agent was authorized by Blue to appoint subagents to assist in the sales transactions. Since Gage did appoint Vond as a subagent, legally Bond is an agent both of Blue and Gage. Therefore, Vond owes a fiduciary duty to both Blue and Gage making (a), (b), and (d) all incorrect.

10.   **(c)**   Resulting authority is not one of the types of authority that an agent might have. Answer (a) is not chosen because actual express authority is a common type of authority and consists of all authority expressly given by the principal to his/her agent. Answer (b) includes the authority that can be reasonably implied from the express authority and the conduct of the principal. Answer (d) is not chosen because even though a party was never authorized by a principal to be an agent, if the principal leads a third party to believe that the party did have authority, this is apparent agency.

11. **(b)** An agency agreement normally does not need to be in writing. Exceptions to this general rule include agency contracts that cannot be completed within one year and agreements whereby the agent is to buy specific real estate for the principal. This question incorporates the latter. Typical agency agreements need not be in writing; these would include purchasing office supplies, retaining an independent contractor to do renovation work, or hiring an attorney to collect a business debt.

12. **(c)** An agent has implied authority to do what is customary for agents of that type to do under the circumstances. It would be customary for one who is a principal's accountant and business manager to have authority to insure the principal's property against fire loss. Answers (a), (b), and (d) are incorrect because they involve authority that is beyond customary, ordinary authority.

B.5. Ratification

13. **(d)** Since Ames had no express, implied, or actual authority, Trimon cannot enforce the contract. Answer (a) is not chosen because ratifications under agency law require that the contract be ratified in its entirety or not at all. Answer (b) is not chosen because until Clar ratifies the contract in its entirety, Trimon may withdraw from the contract since Ames had no authority to make the contract. Answer (c) is not chosen because ratification can be accomplished by actions as well as words.

14. **(b)** When the third party is aware that there is a principal, that principal, fully disclosed or partially disclosed, may generally ratify the contract when he or she is aware of all material facts and if ratification of the entire contract takes place.

C. Authority

15. **(a)** Since Beele authorized McDonald to be his agent, the secret limitation has no effect on York. York may enforce the contract for the full $140,000. Answer (b) is incorrect because Beele authorized McDonald to be his agent. Even though his agent was instructed to pay at most $125,000 in the contract, this was a secret limitation that did not limit York who was unaware of it. Answer (c) is incorrect because McDonald was given authority to purchase real estate on Beele's behalf. The limitation on the dollar amount was not known by York and therefore does not limit her. Answer (d) is incorrect because although York can enforce the contract against Beele, it is because Beele gave authority to McDonald rather than how much the real estate is worth.

E. Obligations and Rights

16. **(b)** As a fiduciary to the principal, an agent must act in the best interest of the principal. Therefore, the agent has an obligation to refrain from competing with or acting adversely to the principal, unless the principal knows and approves of such activity. Answer (c) is incorrect because the Statute of Frauds would not require that the described agency relationship be contained in a signed writing since it

is possible for the contract to be performed within one year. Answer (d) is incorrect because the mere right of the agent to receive a percentage of proceeds is not sufficient to constitute an agency coupled with an interest. In order to have an agency coupled with an interest, the agent must have either a property interest or a security interest in the subject matter of the agency relationship. Answer (a) is incorrect because in all agency relationships, except agencies coupled with an interest, the principal always has the power to dismiss the agent. However, the principal does not necessarily have the right to terminate the relationship. In certain situations the dismissed agent could sue for breach of contract.

17. **(c)** In an agency relationship, the agent owes a fiduciary duty to the principal but the principal does not owe a fiduciary duty to the agent. Also, even though there is often a contract between the principal and agent, this is not a requirement, for example, when the agent consents to act for the principal as a friend.

E.3. Principal's Liability to Third Parties

18. **(a)** When the principal is undisclosed in an agency relationship, the agent generally has the same authority as if the principal were disclosed. The main difference is in the liability of the agent to third parties. Answer (b) is incorrect because the principal is liable on the contract because of the express authority given to the agent to make the contract on behalf of the principal. Apparent authority exists when the principal represents the agent to third parties to be his/her agent. In this case, the principal wished to be undisclosed. Answer (c) is incorrect because principal can be held liable for negligence committed by the agent within the course and scope of the agency. Answer (d) is incorrect because the agent can be held liable on the contract by third parties when the principal is undisclosed.

19. **(c)** An agent is liable to a third party on a contract when the principal is undisclosed or partially disclosed. If the principal is fully disclosed, the agent is not liable.

E.4. Agent's Liability to Third Parties

20. **(b)** When an agent enters into a contract with a third person on behalf of an undisclosed principal, the agent is personally liable, unless the third person discovers the existence and identity of the principal and chooses to hold the principal to the contract instead of the agent. Ratification is the approval after the fact of an unauthorized act done by an agent or of an act done by someone who is not yet an agent. Undisclosed principals cannot ratify unauthorized acts of the agent.

21. **(c)** When a third party contracts with an agent representing an undisclosed principal, the agent is liable for performance of the contract. The third party is not entitled to disclosure of the principal. Answer (b) is incorrect because ratification of a contract by the principal is the approval required after the fact related to an unauthorized act by the agent or one not yet an agent. Answer (d) is incorrect because the third party generally is not allowed the option of voiding the contract after disclosure of the principal.

22. **(c)** One who issues a personal check is liable on it; however, any party or principal who is not disclosed on the check is not liable on the negotiable instrument. Answers (a) and (b) are incorrect because the third party can elect to hold either the agent or the principal liable when the

agent makes a contract for an undisclosed principal. Answer (d) is incorrect because the party who signs a check is
liable on it.

F.   Termination of Principal-Agent Relationship

23.   (c)   The declaration of Ogden's incapacity constitutes the termination of the agency relationship by operation
of law. When an agency relationship is terminated by operation of law, the agent's authority to enter into a binding
agreement on behalf of the principal ceases. There is no
requirement that notice be given to third parties when the
agency relationship is terminated by operation of law. In
this case, Ogden will not be liable to Datz because Thorp
was without authority to enter into the contract. Answer (a)
is incorrect because insanity of the principal terminates the
agency relationship even though the third parties are unaware of the principal's insanity. Answer (b) is incorrect
because Thorp's authority terminated upon the declaration
of Ogden's incapacity. Answer (d) is incorrect because an
undisclosed principal is liable unless the third party holds
the agent responsible, the agent has fully performed the
contract, the undisclosed principal is expressly excluded by
contract or the contract is a negotiable instrument. However, Ogden will not be liable as Thorp was without authority to enter into the agreement.

24.   (c)   An agency relationship is terminated by operation of law if the subject of the agreement becomes illegal or
impossible, the principal or the agent dies or becomes in-
sane, or the principal becomes bankrupt. Answers (a), (b),
and (d) are incorrect because they will cause the termination
of an agency relationship by operation of law. Answer (c),
agent's renunciation of the agency, will not cause the termination of an agency relationship.

25.   (c)   When the agency relationship is terminated by
an act of the principal and/or agent, third parties are entitled
to notice of the termination from the principal. Failure of
the principal to give the required notice gives the agent apparent authority to act on behalf of the principal. Specifically, the principal must give actual notice to all parties who
had prior dealings with the agent or principal. Constructive
or public notice must be given to parties who knew of the
existence of the agency relationship, but did not actually
have business dealings with the agent or principal. Since
Bolt Corp. did not give proper constructive notice to Young
Corp., Ace had apparent authority to bind the principal and,
therefore, Young Corp. will win. Accordingly, answer (a) is
incorrect. Answer (b) is incorrect because although Ace
lacked express authority, apparent authority was present due
to the inadequacy of Bolt's notice. Answer (d) is incorrect
because a principal is not an absolute insurer of his agent's
acts. A principal is liable for his agent's torts only if the
principal expressly authorizes the conduct or the tort is
committed within the scope of the agent's employment.

OTHER OBJECTIVE ANSWERS AND ANSWER EXPLANATIONS

Problem 1

1.   (B) Statement I is incorrect because normally an agency agreement need not be in writing unless the agency contract cannot be completed in one year. Statement II is correct because Lace authorized Banks to be Lace's agent.

2.   (A) Statement I is correct because Banks was given actual, express authority by Lace to perform Lace's customers' service calls and to customize Lace's software to the customer's needs. As an extension to this actual, express authority, Clear can also rely on what is customary and ordinary for such an agent to be able to do under implied authority. Statement II is incorrect because Banks did not have express authority to sell the computer. In fact, Banks was told **not** to sell Lace's computers.

3.   (B) Banks breached his/her fiduciary duty to Lace and breached his/her duty to follow instructions when s/he sold the computer. This, however, does not automatically terminate their agreement. Statement II is correct because Banks had dealt with Clear before as Lace's agent. Therefore, Clear must receive actual notice to terminate the apparent authority.

4.   (D) Statement I is incorrect because Banks had apparent authority to sell the computer even though Banks did not have actual authority to do so. Statement II is incorrect because Lace is bound by the contract with Clear. Any modification of the contract must be made by both parties to the contract, not just one.

5.   (A) Statement I is correct because since Lace was a disclosed principal, only Lace, the principal, is liable under the contract to Clear, the third party. Banks, the agent, is not. For the same reason, statement II is incorrect.

ANSWER OUTLINE

Problem 1   Principal's Power and Right to Terminate
Agency

Lemon's first assertion is incorrect

Agency coupled with an interest requires agent to have an
interest in property which is subject of agency

Lemon's commission agreement does not qualify as an
agency coupled with an interest

Lemon's second assertion is incorrect

Principal has the power to discharge the agent, although
the principal may not have the right to do so

Lemon's third assertion is correct

If principal wrongfully discharges agent, principal is liable for damages under breach of contract

UNOFFICIAL ANSWER

Problem 1   Principal's Power and Right to Terminate
Agency

Lemon's first assertion that he is an agent coupled with
an interest is incorrect. An agency coupled with an interest
in the subject matter arises when the agent has an interest in
the property that is the subject of the agency. The fact that
Lemon entered into a two-year written agency agreement
with the partnership that would pay Lemon a commission
clearly will not establish an interest in the subject matter of
the agency. The mere expectation of profits to be realized or
proceeds to be derived from the sale of the partnership's
products is not sufficient to create an agency coupled with
an interest. As a result, the principal-agency relationship
may be terminated at any time.

Lemon's second assertion that the principal-agency relationship may not be terminated without cause prior to the
expiration of its term is incorrect. Where a principal-agency
relationship is based upon a contract to engage the agent for
a specified period of time, the principal may discharge the
agent despite the fact such discharge is wrongful. Although
the principal does not have the right to discharge the agent,
he does have the power to do so. Thus, Lemon may be discharged without cause.

Lemon's third assertion that he is entitled to damages
because of the termination of the agency relationship is correct. Where a principal wrongfully discharges its agent, the
principal is liable for damages based on breach of contract.
Under the facts, Lemon's discharge by the partnership without cause constitutes a breach of contract for which Lemon
may recover damages.

PARTNERSHIPS AND JOINT VENTURES

Overview

A partnership is an association of two or more persons to carry on a business as co-owners for profit. For most purposes, the partnership is not considered a separate legal entity, but a specialized form of agency. The major areas tested on partnerships are the characteristics of a partnership, comparisons with corporations, the rights and liabilities of the partnership itself, the rights, duties, and liabilities of the partners among themselves and to third parties, the allocation of profits and losses, and the rights of various parties, including creditors, upon dissolution.

The law of joint ventures is similar to that of partnerships with some exceptions. Note that the joint venture is more limited in scope than the partnership form of business. The former is typically organized to carry out one single business undertaking or a series of related undertakings; whereas, the latter is formed to conduct ongoing business.

A. Nature of Partnerships

1. A partnership is an association of two or more persons to carry on a business as co-owners for profit

    a. To carry on a business includes almost every trade, occupation, or profession

        (1) It does not include passive co-ownership of property (e.g., joint tenants of a piece of land)

    b. Co-ownership of the "business" (and not merely of assets used in a business) is an important element in determining whether a partnership exists

        (1) Co-ownership of property (including capital) is one element
        (2) The most important and necessary element of co-ownership (and thereby partnership) is profit sharing

            (a) Need not be equal
            (b) Receipt of a share of profits is prima facie evidence (raises a presumption) of a partnership

                1] Presumption rebutted by establishing that profit sharing was only for payment of debt, interest on loan, services performed, rent, etc.

        (3) Another important element of co-ownership is joint control

            (a) Each partner has an equal right to participate in management. May be contracted away to a managing partner

2. Partnership relationship creates a fiduciary relationship between partners

    a. Fiduciary relationship arises because each partner is an agent for partnership and for each other in partnership business

3. Partnership relationship is based on contract but arrangements may be quite informal

    a. Agreement can be inferred from conduct (e.g., allowing someone to share in management and profits may result in partnership even though actual intent to become partner is missing)

4. In general, partnerships are governed by the Revised Uniform Partnership Act (RUPA) and by agency law

    a. Draws heavily on agency law because each partner is an agent as well as a principal of partnership

        (1) Most rules can be changed in individual cases by agreement between parties affected (e.g., rights and duties between partners)

        EXAMPLE: A, B, and C form a partnership in which all three partners agree that A is liable for all of the product liability cases against the partnership. This agreement is enforceable between A, B, and C but not against other parties that never agreed to this. Therefore, as long as A is solvent, B and C can collect from A even though a third party recovers from all of them on a product liability problem.

5. Generally, any person (entity) who has the capacity to contract may become a partner

    a. Corporations
    b. Minors—but contract of partnership is voidable
    c. Partnerships can become partners

6. Common characteristics of partnerships

    a. Limited duration

    b. Transfer of ownership requires agreement

    c. Under RUPA partnerships are separate entities

        (1) May sue and be sued

        (2) May own property in partnership name

    d. Unlimited liability of partners for partnership debts

    e. Ease of formation, can be very informal

B. Types of Partnerships and Partners

  1. Limited partnership is a special statutory relationship consisting of one or more general partners and one or more limited partners

    a. Limited partners only contribute capital and are usually only liable to that extent (analogous to shareholder)

    b. Limited partners do not take part in management of partnership

  2. General partners are ones who share in management of business and have unlimited liability

C. Formation of Partnership

  1. By agreement, express or implied

    a. Agreement to share profits is prima facie evidence that partnership exists

        (1) Need not agree to share losses because agreement to share profits assumes sharing of losses

        (2) Sharing of gross receipts does not establish partnership

    b. Partnership not implied if profits received for some other purpose such as for payment of debt or wages

  2. Creation of a partnership may be very informal, either oral or written

    a. Written partnership agreement not required unless within Statute of Frauds (e.g., partnership that cannot be completed within one year)

        EXAMPLE: A, B, and C form a partnership that, although they expect it to last for several years, has no specific time period specified. This partnership agreement may be oral.

        EXAMPLE: X, Y, and Z organize XYZ partnership which by agreement will last at least five years. This partnership agreement must be in writing.

        (1) Usually wise to have in writing

    b. Filing not required

  3. Articles of copartnership (partnership agreement)—not legally necessary, but a good idea to have

  4. Fictitious name statutes require partners to register fictitious or assumed names

    a. Failure to comply does not invalidate partnership but may result in fine

    b. The purpose is to allow third parties to know who is in partnership

D. Partner's Rights

  1. Partnership agreement, whether oral or written, would be controlling

    a. Following rules are used unless partnership agreement states otherwise

  2. Partnership interest

    a. Refers to partner's right to share in profits and return of contribution on dissolution

    b. Is considered personal property

        (1) Even if partnership property is real estate

    c. Does not include specific partnership property, merely right to use it for partnership purposes

    d. Freely assignable without other partner's consent

        (1) Assignee is not substituted as a partner without consent of all other partners

        (2) Assignee does **not** receive right to manage partnership, to have an accounting, to inspect books, to possess or own any individual partnership property—merely receives rights in the

assigning partner's share of profits and return of partner's capital contribution (unless partners agree otherwise)

(a) Typically, assignments are made to secure a loan

> EXAMPLE: *C, a CPA, wishes to obtain a large loan. He is a member of a CPA firm and assigns rights in his partnership to the bank to secure the loan.*

(3) Assignor remains liable as a partner
(4) Does not cause dissolution unless assignor also withdraws

3. Partnership property

a. Includes

(1) Property acquired with partnership funds unless different intent is shown
(2) Property not acquired in partnership name is, however, partnership property if

(a) Partner acquires title to it in his/her capacity as a partner, or
(b) Property acquired with partnership funds
(c) Otherwise, property presumed to be owned by individual partners even if used in partnership

b. Not assignable or subject to attachment individually, only by a claim on partnership

(1) All partners can agree and assign property
(2) Any partner can assign or sell if for the apparent purpose of carrying on the business of the partnership in the usual way

c. Upon partner's death, his/her estate is entitled to deceased partner's share of profits and capital, but not to any specific partnership property

(1) Remaining partners have duty to account to the heirs of the deceased for value of interest
(2) Remaining partners own partnership property as tenants in partnership
(3) Heirs not automatically partners

4. Participate in management

a. Right to participate equally in management

(1) Ordinary business decisions by a majority vote
(2) Unanimous consent needed to make fundamental changes

b. Power to act as an agent for partnership in partnership business
c. Also has right to inspect books and have full knowledge of partnership affairs
d. Silent partner is one who does not help manage

(1) Still has personal, unlimited liability

5. Share in profits and losses

a. Profits and losses are shared equally unless agreement specifies otherwise

(1) Even if contributed capital is not equal
(2) For example, agreement may specify one partner to receive greater share of profits for doing more work, etc., while losses still shared equally

b. If partners agree on unequal profit sharing but are silent on loss sharing, losses are shared per the profit-sharing proportions

(1) May choose to share losses in a different proportion from profits

> EXAMPLE: *A, B, and C form a partnership with capital contributions as follows: A, $100,000; B, $20,000; and C, $20,000. Their agreement is silent on how to split profits or losses. Therefore, profits and losses will be split equally.*

> EXAMPLE: *Same as above except that they agree to give A 50% of the profits and B and C each get 25%. Profits as well as losses will be split based on these stated percentages.*

EXAMPLE: Assume that A, B, and C agree to a 50%, 25%, 25% split if there is a profit but to a 20%, 40%, 40% split, respectively, for any annual losses. If there is a $100,000 annual loss, A will suffer $20,000 and B and C each will suffer $40,000 of the loss.

6. Other rights

   a. Indemnification for expenses incurred on behalf of the partnership

   b. General partners may be creditors, secured or unsecured, of the partnership

      (1) May receive interest on loans

      (2) No interest on capital contributions unless in partnership agreement

   c. No right to salary for work performed because this is a duty

      (1) Common for partners to agree to pay salaries, especially if only one or two do most of the work

   d. May obtain formal accounting of partnership affairs

7. Every partner owes a fiduciary duty to every other partner (this is important)

   a. May pursue own self-interest as long as it is not competition and does not interfere with partner's duty to partnership

   b. Any wrongly derived profits must be held by partner for others

   c. Must abide by partnership agreement

   d. Liable to others partners for liability caused by going beyond actual authority

8. Incoming partners new to partnership have same rights as previous partners

   a. Requires consent of all partners to admit new partner

   b. Profit sharing, loss sharing, and capital contributions are by agreement between all partners

E. Relationship to Third Parties

1. Partners are agents of the partnership

   a. Can bind partnership to contracts with third parties

      (1) Even where no actual authority, can bind partnership where there is apparent (ostensible) authority, authority by estoppel, or implied authority

         (a) Apparent (ostensible) or purported partnership created when parties misrepresent to others that they are partners

            1] Similar in concept to apparent (ostensible) agency

            2] Partnership may make public recording of limitation on partner authority or statement of partnership authority to limit possible liability

            3] Individuals called apparent (ostensible) partners and are liable to third parties as if they were actual partners

               a] Usually liable even if allows others to misrepresent him/her as partner

         (b) Partnership by estoppel created when parties misrepresent to others that they are partners and others are hurt as they rely on this

            1] Many courts treat partnership by estoppel and apparent partnership as essentially the same

            2] Not actual partners but liable as if were actual partners

            3] Individuals called partners by estoppel

EXAMPLE: A, B, and C form a partnership to sell widgets. Contrary to the wishes of B and C, A decides to buy in the partnership name some "super-widgets" from T. Even though A did not have actual authority to buy these, T can enforce the contract based on apparent authority. A, of course, breached his fiduciary duty to B and C.

   b. Partners normally have implied authority to buy and sell goods, receive money, and pay debts for partnership

(1) Each partner is agent of partnership to carry out typical business of firm or business of the kind carried on by partnership

(2) Third parties can rely on implied authority even though secret limitations may exist which were unknown to those third parties

EXAMPLE: A and B have a partnership to sell furniture in a retail outlet. A and B agreed that neither would buy more than $10,000 of furniture from suppliers without the consent of the other. A, however, buys $20,000 of furniture from a regular supplier who was unaware of this limitation. When the supplier attempts to deliver, B refuses the furniture. Since A had implied authority, the supplier can enforce the contract for the full $20,000.

c. Partnership is not liable for acts of partners outside of express, implied, or apparent authority

EXAMPLE: A partner of a hardware store attempts to buy some real estate in the name of the partnership. Here apparent authority does not exist.

d. Partnership is liable for partner's torts committed in course and scope of business and for partner's breach of trust (i.e., misapplication of third party's funds)

EXAMPLE: A partner takes a third party's money on behalf of the partnership to invest in government bonds. Instead he uses it himself to build an addition onto his home.

EXAMPLE: A partner, while driving on partnership business, injures a third party. If the partner is negligent, the partnership is also liable.

2. Unanimous consent of partners is needed (so no implied authority for)

a. Admission of a new partner
b. Amending the partnership agreement
c. Assignment of partnership property
d. Making partnership a surety or guarantor
e. Admitting to a claim against partnership in court
f. Submitting partnership claim to arbitrator
g. Any action outside the scope of the partnership business

3. Partner's liability is personal, that is, extends to all his/her personal assets, (not just investment in partnership,) to cover all debts and liabilities of partnership

a. Partners are jointly and severally liable for all debts

(1) RUPA requires creditors to first attempt collection from partnership before partners unless partnership is bankrupt

b. Partners may split losses or liability between themselves according to any proportion agreed upon; however, third parties can still hold each partner personally liable despite agreement

(1) If any partner pays more than his/her agreed share, s/he can get reimbursed from other partners

EXAMPLE: X, Y, and Z as partners agreed to split losses 10%, 20%, and 70% respectively. A third party recovers $100,000 from X only based on a partnership tort. X can get $20,000 from Y and $70,000 from Z so that she ends up paying only her 10%.

EXAMPLE: Same as before except that Y is insolvent. X can recover the proportionate share from Z or $87,500 ($100,000 x 70%/80%).

EXAMPLE: A, B, and C are partners who agree to split losses 10%, 10%, and 80%, respectively. Y sues the partners for a tort based on the partnership business. C takes out bankruptcy. Y can recover from A and B and is not bound by the agreement between A, B, and C.

c. New partners coming into a partnership are liable for existing debts only to the extent of their capital contributions

(1) Unless new partners assume personal liability for old debts

d. Partners withdrawing are liable for existing liabilities
e. Partners withdrawing are liable for subsequent liabilities unless notice of withdrawal or death is given to third parties

(1) Actual notice to creditors who previously dealt with partnership

      (2) Constructive (e.g., published) notice is sufficient for others who merely knew of partnership's existence

    f.   Estates of deceased partners are liable for partners' debts

    g.   Liability of withdrawing partner may be limited by agreement between partners but agreement is not binding on third parties (unless they join in on agreement)

    h.   Partners are not criminally liable unless they personally participate in some way or statute prescribes liability to all members of management (e.g., environment regulation or sale of alcohol to a minor)

F. Termination of a Partnership

  1. Termination happens when

    a.   First, dissolution occurs (i.e., partners stop carrying on business together)

    b.   Second, winding up takes place (i.e., process of settling of partnership affairs)

  2. Dissolution can occur by

    a.   Prior agreement (e.g., partnership agreement)

    b.   Present agreement of partners

    c.   By decree of court in such cases as

        (1) Partner continually or seriously breaches partnership agreement

        (2) Partner guilty of conduct that harms business

    d.   Assignment, selling, or pledging of partnership interest does **not** cause dissolution even if no consent of other partners

    e.   Under RUPA, unlike previous law, partner's withdrawal, death, or bankruptcy does **not** automatically cause dissolution of partnership

        (1) Flows from concept that partnership is actually a legal entity

        (2) Partners that own majority of partnership may choose to continue general partnership within ninety days of partners' withdrawal, death, or bankruptcy

        (3) Any partner has power to dissociate from partnership even if had agreed not to, but is liable for breach of such a contract

  3. Winding up

    a.   Remaining partners may elect to wind up and terminate partnership or not wind up and continue business

  4. Order of distribution upon termination of general partnership

    a.   To creditors including partners as creditors

    b.   Capital contributions and profits or losses are calculated together

        (1) Partners may receive money or even need to pay money at this stage

  5. Partners are personally liable to partnership for any deficits in their capital accounts and to creditors for insufficiency of partnership assets

    a.   Priority between partnership creditors and partner's personal creditors

        (1) Partnership creditors have first priority to partnership assets; any excess goes to personal creditors

        (2) Usually, personal creditors have first priority to personal assets; any excess goes to partnership creditors

  6. Partners can bind other partners and the partnership on contracts until third parties who have known of the partnership are given notice of dissolution

    a.   Actual notice must be given to third parties who have dealt with the partnership prior to dissolution

b. Constructive notice (e.g., notice in newspaper) is adequate for third parties who have only known of the partnership

G. Limited Partnerships

1. Revised Uniform Limited Partnership Act (RULPA) is designed to modernize law because today many limited partnerships are very large with many limited partners.

    a. RULPA has been adopted by majority of states

2. Creation of limited partnership

    a. Unlike general partnership that requires no formal procedures to create it, limited partnership requires compliance with state statute to create it
    b. Must file certificate of limited partnership with Secretary of State

        (1) Includes names of all general partners

            (a) Names of limited partners not required
            (b) Must amend certificate of partnership to show any additions or deletions of general partners

                1] Must also amend if any general partner becomes aware of false information in certificate

    c. Requires at least one general partner who retains unlimited personal liability and at least one limited partner

        (1) Liability of limited partner(s) is limited to amount of capital contributions (with some exceptions below)

    d. Name of limited partner may not be used in name of limited partnership unless name is also name of a general partner.

        (1) If a limited partner **knowingly** allows his/her name to be part of limited partnership name, then is liable to creditors who extend credit to business (unless creditors knew that limited partner was not a general partner)

    e. "Limited partnership" words must be in firm's name
    f. Partnership interests may be purchased with cash, property, services rendered, promissory note
    g. Defective formation of limited partnership causes limited partners to be liable as general partners

        (1) Under RULPA, partner who believes s/he is limited partner may avoid liability of general partner if upon learning of defective formation either

            (a) Withdraws from partnership and renounces all future profits, or
            (b) Files amendment or new certificate that cures defect

        (2) However, limited partner is liable for past transactions before withdrawal or amendment to any third party transacting business while believing partner was general partner

    h. Must maintain continuous office in state
    i. Foreign limited partnership is one doing business in given state but was formed in another state

        (1) Foreign limited partnership must register with Secretary of State before doing business in state

3. Rights of partners in limited partnership

    a. General partners manage partnership
    b. Limited partners invest

        (1) Limited partner who manages partnership substantially like general partner obtains liability like general partner to third parties who believed s/he was general partner
        (2) Limited partner allowed to do following without risking loss of limited protection

            (a) Acting as an agent or employee of limited partnership or a general partner
            (b) Consulting with and advising general partner about business

        (c) Approving or disapproving amendments to limited partnership agreement

        (d) Voting on dissolution or winding up of limited partnership

        (e) Voting on loans of limited partnership

        (f) Voting on change in nature of business

        (g) Voting on removal of a general partner

        (h) Bringing derivative lawsuit on behalf of limited partnership

c. Profit or loss sharing

    (1) Profits or losses are shared as agreed upon in certificate agreement

        (a) Losses and any liability are limited to capital contributions for limited partners

        (b) If no agreement on profit and losses, then shared based on percentages of capital contributions

            1] Note how this differs from a general partnership in which losses and profits are shared equally unless agreed otherwise

d. Admission of new limited partner requires written agreement of all partners unless partnership agreement provides otherwise

    (1) Admission of new general partner requires approval of only general partners

e. Limited partnership interests may be assigned in part or in whole

    (1) If all interest assigned, then ceases to be partner unless otherwise agreed

    (2) Assignee becomes actual limited partner if all other partners consent or if assignor gives assignee that status pursuant to authority (if given in certificate of partnership)

        (a) In such case, former limited partner is generally not released from liability to limited partnership

    (3) Assignment does not cause dissolution of partnership

f. Limited partners have right to inspect partnership books and tax return information

g. Can be a limited and general partner at same time

    (1) Has rights, powers, and liability of a general partner

    (2) Has rights against other partners with respect to contribution as a limited partner and also as a general partner

h. Limited partners may own competing interests

i. Limited partner may be a secured or unsecured creditor of partnership

j. Limited partner may not withdraw capital contribution if it impairs creditors

4. Duties of partners

a. General partners owe fiduciary duties to general and limited partners—limited partners in general do not owe fiduciary duties

5. Dissolution of limited partnership takes place upon following events

a. Completion of time period specified in certificate

b. Upon event specified in partnership agreement

c. Unanimous written consent of all partners

d. Dissolution of court decree when not practical to continue partnership

e. Withdrawal of general partner by retirement, removal, death, bankruptcy

    (1) Unless all partners agree in writing to continue business

    (2) Or unless partnership agreement allows partners to continue business

    (3) Withdrawal of limited partner does not cause dissolution

6. If partnership not continued, winding up takes place with the following distribution of assets of partnership in order of priority

a. To creditors including partners who are creditors

   b. To partners and ex-partners to pay off unpaid distributions
   c. To partners to return capital contributions
   d. To partners for partnership interests in proportions they share in distributions
   e. Note that in these priorities general and limited partners share equally
   f. Also, note that partners can vary their rights by agreement of all parties affected

   7. Upon dissolution, partners that remain typically complete winding-up process

H. Joint Ventures

   1. Definition of joint venture—association of two or more persons (or entities) organized to carry out a single business undertaking (or series of related undertakings) for profit

   a. Generally, corporations may engage in joint ventures

   EXAMPLE: X corporation, O corporation, and N corporation decide to form a joint venture to bring oil from the north to the south of Alaska.

   2. Law of joint ventures is similar to that of partnerships with some exceptions

   a. Each joint venturer is not necessarily an agent of other joint venturers—limited power to bind others
   b. Death of joint venturer does not automatically dissolve joint venture
   c. Joint venture is interpreted as special form of partnership

   (1) Fiduciary duties of partners in partnership law apply
   (2) Each member has right to participate in management
   (3) Liability is unlimited and each joint venturer is personally liable for debts of joint venture

I. Limited Liability Companies (LLC)

   1. Laws for this relatively new form of business have been developing in the majority of states to be fairly uniform

   a. Few states have passed uniform statute in this area governing LLC so this material will cover the laws passed by what is now a majority of states (and therefore testable on CPA exam)

   2. LLC is not considered a corporation but majority of states provide

   a. All owners (often called members) have limited liability and therefore no personal liability

   (1) Compare with limited partnership in which only limited partners can have limited liability

   b. LLC must be formed according to limited liability company statute of the state in which it is formed

   (1) LLC is foreign LLC in other states that it does business, and laws of state where it was formed typically govern LLC in all states

   c. LLC is separate legal entity so can sue or be sued in own name

   (1) Foreign LLC must register with Secretary of State before doing business in state or cannot sue in state courts

   d. Most states require that name of LLC include either phrase of limited liability company or initials LLC to notify outside parties

   (1) Many states allow phrase of limited company or just two initials of LC

   e. To form LLC, members adopt operating agreement

   (1) It is contract that specifies rights and duties of members
   (2) Typically entire operating agreement is required by state law to be in writing

   (a) Some states allow all or part of operating agreement to be oral

   3. Member of LLC has no interest in any specific property in LLC but has interest (personal property interest) in LLC in general

   a. Member has right to distributions according to profit and loss sharing agreed upon in operating agreement

      (1) In absence of agreement, majority of jurisdictions allocate profits and losses in proportion to what contribution members had made

   b. Member has management interest

      (1) Includes rights to manage affairs of firm, vote within firm, and get information about LLC
      (2) Unless agreed otherwise, each member has equal voice in management

   c. Member may assign financial interest in LLC unless operating agreement specifies otherwise

      (1) Assignee does not become member, only receives assignor's share of profits assigned unless other members agree otherwise
      (2) Member's interest not freely transferable

4. Duties in LLC

   a. Members of LLC may designate others to manage LLC, in which case these rules apply

      (1) Managers of LLC have duty of due care and important fiduciary duty (including duty of loyalty)

         (a) When members manage LLC themselves, members instead have these duties

      (2) Whether managers are appointed or not, **all** members and **all** managers, if any, still have limited liability in LLC
      (3) Managers, when appointed, are agents of LLC and members are not agents

         (a) If no managers are appointed then members are actual agents rather than managers

5. Dissolution of LLC

   a. Most state LLC statutes cause LLC to dissolve when

      (1) All members agree in writing to dissolution
      (2) Time period passes or event happens as specified in operating agreement
      (3) Member withdraws, is voted out, dies, goes bankrupt, or becomes incompetent

         (a) Most states allow remainder of members unanimously to continue LLC

      (4) Court order dissolves it

6. Distribution of assets upon dissolution are made in following priorities:

   a. To creditors including managers and members except for their shares in the distribution of profits
   b. To members and past members for unpaid distributions unless agreed otherwise
   c. To members to receive back capital contributions, unless agreed otherwise
   d. To members for their distributions as agreed in operating agreement, or if not agreed upon, in proportion to contributions they had made

J. Limited Liability Partnerships (LLP)

1. Vast majority of states now allow LLP
2. Formation of LLP

   a. Must file with Secretary of State
   b. Majority of states require only majority, not unanimous, approval of partners to become LLP
   c. All states require firm to designate it as LLP either by using phrase of limited liability partnership, phrase of registered limited liability partnership, or initials LLP to notify public
   d. Generally, laws of state in which the LLP is formed govern affairs of the LLP in all other states
   e. The LLP often works well for professionals who want to do business as professionals in a partnership but still pass through tax benefits while limiting personal liability of the partners
   f. Most states allow an easy transition from conventional partnership into limited liability partnership

      (1) Typically, its organizational structure remains same or is very similar

  g. Most common law and statutory law from partnership law applies to LLP

3. Liability provisions of partners in LLP

  a. Under traditional general partnerships and limited partnerships, big disadvantage is that general partners in both firms have unlimited personal liability for partnership obligations

  b. Under LLP, partners avoid some personal liability for mistakes or malpractice of other partners

      (1) Popular for professionals

  c. LLP statutes on limits to liability vary by state, but typically state statutes provide for liability limits of partners in at least some ways, such as "innocent" partners are not liable for errors or negligence of other partners

      (1) Parameters to this limit on liability are still largely unsettled

         (a) To what extent is supervising partner liable for a negligent partner's errors?—Supervising partner typically is held liable

         (b) Some states do not recognize foreign (out of state) LLP

         (c) When more than one partner is liable for negligence, some states allow liability to be proportioned

         (d) Some state statutes limit liability for all debts of LLP

         (e) Other state statutes give protection only for negligent acts in LLP

         (f) Others give protection for partnership torts or contract liability that arise from misconduct of partners or employees

MULTIPLE-CHOICE QUESTIONS (1-29)

1. A general partnership must
   a. Pay federal income tax.
   b. Have two or more partners.
   c. Have written articles of partnership.
   d. Provide for apportionment of liability for partnership debts.

2. Which of the following statements is correct with respect to a limited partnership?
   a. A limited partner may not be an unsecured creditor of the limited partnership.
   b. A general partner may not also be a limited partner at the same time.
   c. A general partner may be a secured creditor of the limited partnership.
   d. A limited partnership can be formed with limited liability for all partners.

3. A partnership agreement must be in writing if
   a. Any partner contributes more than $500 in capital.
   b. The partners reside in different states.
   c. The partnership intends to own real estate.
   d. The partnership's purpose **cannot** be completed within one year of formation.

4. Sydney, Bailey, and Calle form a partnership under the Revised Uniform Partnership Act. During the first year of operation, the partners have fundamental questions regarding the rights and obligations of the partnership as well as the individual partners. Which of the following questions can correctly be answered in the affirmative?
   I. Is the partnership allowed legally to own property in the partnership's name?
   II. Do the partners have joint and several liability for breaches of contract of the partnership?
   III. Do the partners have joint and several liability for tort actions against the partnership?
   a. I only.
   b. I and II only.
   c. II and III only.
   d. I, II, and III.

5. Which of the following is not true of a general partnership?
   a. Ownership by the partners may be unequal.
   b. It is a separate legal entity.
   c. An important characteristic is that the partners share in the profits equally.
   d. Each partner has an equal right to participate in management.

6. The partnership agreement for Owen Associates, a general partnership, provided that profits be paid to the partners in the ratio of their financial contribution to the partnership. Moore contributed $10,000, Noon contributed $30,000, and Kale contributed $50,000. For the year ended December 31, 2001, Owen had losses of $180,000. What amount of the losses should be allocated to Kale?
   a. $ 40,000
   b. $ 60,000
   c. $ 90,000
   d. $100,000

7. Lark, a partner in DSJ, a general partnership, wishes to withdraw from the partnership and sell Lark's interest to Ward. All of the other partners in DSJ have agreed to admit Ward as a partner and to hold Lark harmless for the past, present, and future liabilities of DSJ. As a result of Lark's withdrawal and Ward's admission to the partnership, Ward
   a. Acquired only the right to receive Ward's share of DSJ profits.
   b. Has the right to participate in DSJ's management.
   c. Is personally liable for partnership liabilities arising before and after being admitted as a partner.
   d. Must contribute cash or property to DSJ to be admitted with the same rights as the other partners.

8. Cobb, Inc., a partner in TLC Partnership, assigns its partnership interest to Bean, who is not made a partner. After the assignment, Bean asserts the rights to
   I. Participate in the management of TLC.
   II. Cobb's share of TLC's partnership profits.

Bean is correct as to which of these rights?
   a. I only.
   b. II only.
   c. I and II.
   d. Neither I nor II.

9. The apparent authority of a partner to bind the partnership in dealing with third parties
   a. Will be effectively limited by a formal resolution of the partners of which third parties are aware.
   b. Will be effectively limited by a formal resolution of the partners of which third parties are unaware.
   c. Would permit a partner to submit a claim against the partnership to arbitration.
   d. Must be derived from the express powers and purposes contained in the partnership agreement.

10. In a general partnership, which of the following acts must be approved by all the partners?
   a. Dissolution of the partnership.
   b. Admission of a partner.
   c. Authorization of a partnership capital expenditure.
   d. Conveyance of real property owned by the partnership.

11. Under the Revised Uniform Partnership Act, partners have joint and several liability for
   a. Breaches of contract.
   b. Torts committed by one of the partners within the scope of the partnership.
   c. Both of the above.
   d. None of the above.

12. Which of the following actions require(s) unanimous consent of the partners under partnership law?
   I. Making partnership a surety.
   II. Admission of a new partner.
   a. I only.
   b. II only.
   c. Both I and II.
   d. Neither I nor II.

13. Which of the following statements best describes the effect of the assignment of an interest in a general partnership?
   a. The assignee becomes a partner.

b. The assignee is responsible for a proportionate share of past and future partnership debts.

c. The assignment automatically dissolves the partnership.

d. The assignment transfers the assignor's interest in partnership profits and surplus.

14. Under the Revised Uniform Partnership Act, in which of the following cases will property be deemed to be partnership property?

I. A partner acquires property in the partnership name.

II. A partner acquires title to it in his/her own name using partnership funds.

III. Property owned previously by a partner is used in the partnership business

    a. I only.

    b. I and II only.

    c. II only.

    d. I, II, and III.

15. Wind, who has been a partner in the PLW general partnership for four years, decides to withdraw from the partnership despite a written partnership agreement that states, "no partner may withdraw for a period of five years." Under the Uniform Partnership Act, what is the result of Wind's withdrawal?

    a. Wind's withdrawal causes a dissolution of the partnership by operation of law.

    b. Wind's withdrawal has **no** bearing on the continued operation of the partnership by the remaining partners.

    c. Wind's withdrawal is **not** effective until Wind obtains a court-ordered decree of dissolution.

    d. Wind's withdrawal causes a dissolution of the partnership despite being in violation of the partnership agreement.

16. Dowd, Elgar, Frost, and Grant formed a general partnership. Their written partnership agreement provided that the profits would be divided so that Dowd would receive 40%; Elgar, 30%; Frost, 20%; and Grant, 10%. There was no provision for allocating losses. At the end of its first year, the partnership had losses of $200,000. Before allocating losses, the partners' capital account balances were: Dowd, $120,000; Elgar, $100,000; Frost, $75,000; and Grant, $11,000. Grant refuses to make any further contributions to the partnership. Ignore the effects of federal partnership tax law.

After losses were allocated to the partners' capital accounts and all liabilities were paid, the partnership's sole asset was $106,000 in cash. How much would Elgar receive on dissolution of the partnership?

    a. $37,000

    b. $40,000

    c. $47,500

    d. $50,000

17. Sharif, Hirsch, and Wolff formed a partnership with Sharif and Hirsch as general partners. Wolff was the limited partner. They failed to agree upon a profit-sharing plan but put in capital contributions of $120,000, $140,000, and $150,000, respectively. At the end of the first year how should they divide the profits?

    a. Sharif and Hirsch each receives half and Wolff receives none.

b. Each of the three partners receives one-third.

c. The profits are shared in proportion to their capital contribution.

d. None of the above.

18. Which of the following is(are) true of a limited partnership?

I. Limited partnerships must have at least one general partner.

II. The death of a limited partner terminates the partnership.

    a. I only.

    b. II only.

    c. Neither I nor II.

    d. Both I and II.

19. Alchorn, Black, and Chan formed a limited partnership with Chan becoming the only limited partner. Capital contributions from these partners were $20,000, $40,000, and $50,000, respectively. Chan, however, helped in the management of the partnership and Ham, who had several contracts with the partnership, thought Chan was a general partner. Ham won several breach of contract actions against the partnership and the partnership does not have sufficient funds to pay these claims. What is the potential liability for Alchorn, Black, and Chan?

    a. Unlimited liability for all three partners.

    b. Unlimited liability for Alchorn and Black; $50,000 for Chan.

    c. Up to each partner's capital contribution.

    d. None of the above.

20. To create a limited partnership, a certificate of limited partnership must be filed with the Secretary of State. Which of the following must be included in this certificate under the Revised Uniform Limited Partnership Act?

I. Names of all of the general partners.

II. Names of the majority of the general partners.

III. Names of all of the limited partners.

IV. Names of the majority of the limited partners.

    a. I only.

    b. II only.

    c. I and III only.

    d. I and IV only.

21. Mandy is a limited partner in a limited partnership in which Strasburg and Hua are the general partners. Which of the following may Mandy do without losing limited liability protection?

I. Mandy acts as an agent of the limited partnership.

II. Mandy votes to remove Strasburg as a general partner.

    a. I only.

    b. II only.

    c. Both I and II.

    d. Neither I nor II.

22. Hart and Grant formed Hart Limited Partnership. Hart put in a capital contribution of $20,000 and became a general partner. Grant put in a capital contribution of $10,000 and became a limited partner. During the second year of operation, a third party filed a tort action against the partnership and both partners. What is the potential liability of Hart and Grant respectively?

a. $20,000 and $0.
b. $20,000 and $10,000.
c.   Unlimited liability and $0.
d.   Unlimited liability and $10,000.

23. The admission of a new general partner to a limited partnership requires approval by

I.   A majority of the general partners.
II.   All of the general partners.
III.   A majority of the limited partners.
IV.   All of the limited partners.

   a.   I only.
   b.   II only.
   c.   I and III only.
   d.   II and IV only.

24. The admission of a new limited partner to a limited partnership requires approval by

I.   A majority of the general partners.
II.   All of the general partners.
III.   A majority of the limited partners.
IV.   All of the limited partners.

   a.   I only.
   b.   II only.
   c.   I and III only.
   d.   II and IV only.

25. Which of the following is **not** true of a joint venture?
   a.   Each joint venturer is personally liable for the debts of a joint venture.
   b.   Each joint venturer has the right to participate in the management of the joint venture.
   c.   The joint venturers owe each other fiduciary duties.
   d.   Death of a joint venturer dissolves the joint venture.

26. Which form(s) of a business organization can have characteristics common to both the corporation and the general partnership?

	Limited liability company	Subchapter S corporation
a.	Yes	Yes
b.	Yes	No
c.	No	Yes
d.	No	No

27. Which of the following is **not** characteristic of the typical limited liability company?
   a.   Death of a member (owner) causes it to dissolve unless the remaining members decide to continue the business.
   b.   All members (owners) are allowed by law to participate in the management of the firm.
   c.   The company has, legally, a perpetual existence.
   d.   All members (owners) have limited liability.

28. Which of the following is true of the typical limited liability company?
   a.   It provides for limited liability for some of its members (owners), that is, those identified as limited members (owners).
   b.   The members' (owners') interests are not freely transferable.
   c.   Voting members (owners) but not all members can help choose the managers of the company.
   d.   No formalities are required for its formation.

29. In which of the following respects do general partnerships and limited liability partnerships **differ**?

I.   In the level of liability of the partners for torts they themselves commit.
II.   In the level of liability of the partners for torts committed by other partners in the same firm.
III.   In the amount of liability of the partners for contracts signed by other partners on behalf of the partnership.
IV.   In the amount of liability of the partners for contracts they themselves signed on behalf of the firm.

   a.   I only.
   b.   II only.
   c.   I and IV only.
   d.   II and III only.

OTHER OBJECTIVE QUESTIONS

Problem 1   (5 to 10 minutes)

In 1999, Anchor, Chain, and Hook created ACH Associates, a general partnership. The partners orally agreed that they would work full time for the partnership and would distribute profits based on their capital contributions. Anchor contributed $5,000; Chain $10,000; and Hook $15,000.

For the year ended December 31, 2000, ACH Associates had profits of $60,000 that were distributed to the partners. During 2001, ACH Associates was operating at a loss. In September 2001, the partnership dissolved.

In October 2001, Hook contracted in writing with Ace Automobile Co. to purchase a car for the partnership. Hook had previously purchased cars from Ace Automobile Co. for use by ACH Associates partners. ACH Associates did not honor the contract with Ace Automobile Co. and Ace Automobile Co. sued the partnership and the individual partners.

Required:

Items 1 through 6 refer to the above facts. For each item, determine whether (A) or (B) is correct.

1. A. The ACH Associates oral partnership agreement was valid.
    B. The ACH Associates oral partnership agreement was invalid because the partnership lasted for more than one year.

2. A. Anchor, Chain, and Hook jointly owning and conducting a business for profit establishes a partnership relationship.
    B. Anchor, Chain, and Hook jointly owning income-producing property establishes a partnership relationship.

3. A. Anchor's share of ACH Associates' 2000 profits was $20,000.
    B. Hook's share of ACH Associates' 2000 profits was $30,000.

4. A. Anchor's capital account would be reduced by 1/3 of any 2001 losses.
    B. Hook's capital account would be reduced by 1/2 of any 2001 losses.

5. A. Ace Automobile Co. would lose a suit brought against ACH Associates because Hook, as a general partner, has no authority to bind the partnership.
    B. Ace Automobile Co. would win a suit brought against ACH Associates because Hook's authority continues during dissolution.

6. A. ACH Associates and Hook would be the only parties liable to pay any judgment recovered by Ace Automobile Co.
    B. Anchor, Chain, and Hook would be jointly and severally liable to pay any judgment recovered by Ace Automobile Co.

PROBLEMS

Problem 1   (15 to 20 minutes)

On January 5, Stein, Rey, and Lusk entered into a written general partnership agreement by which they agreed to operate a stock brokerage firm. The agreement stated that the partnership would continue upon the death or withdrawal of a partner. The agreement also provided that no partner could reduce the firm's commission below 2% without the consent of all of the other partners. On March 10, Rey, without the consent of Stein and Lusk, agreed with King Corp. to reduce the commission to 1 1/2% on a large transaction by King. Rey believed this would entice King to become a regular customer of the firm. King was unaware of any of the terms of the partnership agreement.

On May 15, Stein entered into a contract conveying Stein's partnership to Park and withdrew from the partnership. That same day, all of the partners agreed to admit Park as a general partner. Notice of Stein's withdrawal and Park's admission as a partner was properly published in two newspapers. In addition, third parties who had conducted business with the partnership prior to May 15 received written notice of Stein's withdrawal.

Required:

a. In separate paragraphs, discuss whether:

    1. The partnership could recover the 1/2% commission from King.

    2. The partnership could recover the 1/2% commission from Rey.

b. In separate paragraphs, discuss:

    1. Park's liability for partnership obligations arising both before and after being admitted to the partnership.

    2. Stein's liability for partnership obligations arising both before and after withdrawing from the partnership.

Problem 2   (15 to 20 minutes)

Prime Cars Partnership is a general partnership engaged in the business of buying, selling, and servicing used cars. Prime's original partners were Baker and Mathews, who formed the partnership years ago under a written partnership agreement, which provided that

• Profits and losses would be allocated 60% to Baker and 40% to Mathews.

• Baker would be responsible for supervising Prime's salespeople and for purchasing used cars for inventory. Baker could not, without Mathews' consent, enter into a contract to purchase more than $15,000 worth of used cars at any one time.

• Mathews would be responsible for supervising Prime's service department.

On May 1, 2001, Baker entered into a contract on Prime's behalf with Jaco Auto Wholesalers, Inc., to purchase eleven used cars from Jaco for a total purchase price of $40,000. Baker's agreement with Jaco provided that the cars would be delivered to Prime on September 1. Baker did not advise Mathews of the terms and conditions of the contract with Jaco. Baker had regularly done business with Jaco on behalf of Prime in the past, and on several occasions had purchased $12,000 to $15,000 of used cars from Jaco. Jaco was unaware of the limitation on Baker's authority.

Baker also frequently purchased used cars for Prime from Top Auto Auctions, Ltd., a corporation owned by Baker's friend. Whenever Prime purchased cars from Top, Baker would personally receive up to 5% of the total purchase price from Top as an incentive to do more business with Top. Baker did not tell Mathews about these payments.

On August 1, 2001, Baker and Mathews agreed to admit KYA Auto Restorers, Inc. as a partner in Prime to start up and supervise a body shop facility. KYA made a $25,000 capital contribution and Prime's partnership agreement was amended to provide that Prime's profits and losses would be shared equally by the partners.

On September 1, 2001, Mathews learned of the Jaco contract and refused to accept delivery of the cars. Mathews advised Jaco that Baker had entered into the contract without Mathews' consent as required by their agreement. Jaco has demanded a payment of $10,000 from Prime from Jaco's lost profits under the contract.

Mathews has also learned about the incentive payments made to Baker by Top.

Mathews has taken the following positions:

• Prime is not liable to Jaco because Baker entered into the contract without Mathews' consent.

• In any event, Mathews is not liable to Jaco for more than 40% of Jaco's lost profits because of original partnership provisions concerning the sharing of profits and losses.

• Baker is liable to Mathews for any liability incurred by Mathews under the Jaco contract.

• Baker is liable to Prime for accepting the incentive payments from Top.

KYA contends that none of its $25,000 capital contribution should be applied to the Jaco liability and that, in any event, KYA does not have any responsibility for the obligation.

Required:

a. State whether Mathews' positions are correct and give the reasons for your conclusions.

b. State whether KYA's contentions are correct and give the reasons for your conclusions.

Problem 3   (15 to 25 minutes)

Best Aviation Associates is a general partnership engaged in the business of buying, selling and servicing used airplanes. Best's original partners were Martin and Kent. They formed the partnership on January 1, 2000, under an oral partnership agreement which provided that the partners would share profits equally. There was no agreement as to how the partners would share losses. At the time the partnership was formed, Martin contributed $320,000 and Kent contributed $80,000.

On December 1, 2001, Best hired Baker to be a salesperson and to assist in purchasing used aircraft for Best's inventory. On December 15, 2001, Martin instructed Baker to negotiate the purchase of a used airplane from Jackson without disclosing that Baker was acting on Best's behalf. Martin thought that a better price could be negotiated by Baker if Jackson was not aware that the aircraft was being acquired for Best. Baker contracted with Jackson without disclosing that the airplane was being purchased for Best. The agreement provided that Jackson would deliver the airplane to Baker on January 2, 2001, at which time the purchase price was to be paid. On January 2, 2002, Jackson attempted to deliver the used airplane purchased for Best by Baker. Baker, acting on Martin's instructions, refused to accept delivery or pay the purchase price.

On December 20, 2001, Kent assigned Kent's partnership interest in Best to Green. On December 31, 2001, Kent advised Martin of the assignment to Green. On January 11, 2002, Green contacted Martin and demanded to inspect the partnership books and to participate in the management of partnership affairs, including voting on partnership decisions.

On January 13, 2002, it was determined that Best had incurred an operating loss of $160,000 in 2001. Martin demanded that Kent contribute $80,000 to the partnership to account for Kent's share of the loss. Kent refused to contribute.

On January 28, 2002, Laco Supplies, Inc., a creditor of Best, sued Best and Martin for unpaid bills totaling $92,000. Best had not paid the bills because of a cash shortfall caused by the 2001 operating loss.

Jackson has taken the following position:

  • Baker is responsible for any damages incurred by Jackson as a result of Best's refusal to accept delivery or pay the purchase price.

Martin has taken the following positions:

  • Green is not entitled to inspect the partnership books or participate in the management of the partnership.

  • Only the partnership is liable for the amounts owed to Laco, or, in the alternative, Martin's personal liability is limited to 50% of the total of the unpaid bills.

Kent has taken the following positions:

  • Only Martin is liable for the 2001 operating loss because of the assignment to Green of Kent's partnership interest.

  • Any personal liability of the partners for the 2001 operating loss should be allocated between them on the basis of their original capital contributions.

Required:

a. Determine whether Jackson's position is correct and state the reasons for your conclusions.

b. Determine whether Martin's positions are correct and state the reasons for your conclusions.

c. Determine whether Kent's positions are correct and state the reasons for your conclusions.

MULTIPLE-CHOICE ANSWERS

1. b __ __	8. b __ __	15. d __ __	22. d __ __	29. b __ __
2. c __ __	9. a __ __	16. a __ __	23. b __ __	
3. d __ __	10. b __ __	17. c __ __	24. d __ __	
4. d __ __	11. c __ __	18. a __ __	25. d __ __	
5. c __ __	12. c __ __	19. a __ __	26. a __ __	
6. d __ __	13. d __ __	20. a __ __	27. c __ __	1st: __/29 = __%
7. b __ __	14. b __ __	21. c __ __	28. b __ __	2nd: __/29 = __%

MULTIPLE-CHOICE ANSWER EXPLANATIONS

A. Nature of Partnerships

1. **(b)** A general partnership is an association of two or more persons to carry on a business as co-owners for profit. There must be at least two partners involved in order for a partnership to exist. Answer (a) is incorrect because a general partnership is normally not recognized as a taxable entity under federal income tax laws. Answer (c) is incorrect because execution of written articles of partnership is not required to create a general partnership. A partnership agreement may be oral or in writing. Answer (d) is incorrect because a partnership does not have to provide for apportionment of liability for partnership debt. Note that even if the partners agreed to split partnership liability in a specified proportion, third parties can still hold each partner personally liable despite the agreement.

B. Types of Partnerships and Partners

2. **(c)** A general partner has a voice in management and has unlimited personal liability. Anyone, including a secured creditor of the limited partnership, may be a general partner if he/she takes on these responsibilities. Answer (a) is incorrect because an unsecured creditor of the limited partnership may also be a limited partner. A limited partner is defined as having no voice in management and his/her liability is limited to the extent of his/her capital contribution. Answer (b) is incorrect because a general partner may also be a limited partner at the same time. This partner would have the rights, powers, and liability of a general partner, and the rights against other partners with respect to his/her contribution as both a limited and a general partner. Answer (d) is incorrect because every limited partnership must have at least one general partner who will be liable for the partnership obligations.

C. Formation of Partnership

3. **(d)** A partnership agreement may be expressed or implied based upon the activities and conduct of the partners. The expressed agreement may be oral or in writing with, in general, one exception. A partnership agreement that cannot be completed within one year from the date on which it is entered into must be in writing. Answer (b) is incorrect because the partners may reside in different states without having to put the partnership agreement in writing. Answer (a) is incorrect because the $500 amount applies to the sale of goods which must be in writing, not partnerships. Answer (c) is incorrect because the purpose of the partnership is irrelevant. Agreements to buy and sell real estate must be in writing, while an agreement to form a partnership whose principal activity will involve the buying and selling of real estate normally need not be in writing unless the stated duration exceeds one year.

4. **(d)** Under RUPA, the partnership is a legal entity that can own property in its own name. The partners also have joint and several liability for all debts whether they are based in contract or tort.

5. **(c)** The partners may agree to share profits as well as losses unequally. Answer (a) is incorrect because the partners may agree that ownership in the partnership is unequal. Answer (b) is incorrect because under RUPA, the partnership is a separate legal entity. Answer (d) is incorrect because the partners may agree to unequal management rights.

D. Partner's Rights

6. **(d)** Profits and losses in a general partnership are shared equally unless otherwise specified in the partnership agreement. If partners agree on unequal profit sharing but are silent on loss sharing, then losses are shared per the profit sharing proportions. The partnership agreement for Owen Associates provided that profits be paid to the partners in the ratio of their financial contribution to the partnership. The ratios are as follows:

Total contributed $10,000 + 30,000 + 50,000 = $90,000

Moore	$10,000 ÷ 90,000 = 1/9
Noon	$30,000 ÷ 90,000 = 1/3
Kale	$50,000 ÷ 90,000 = 5/9

For the year ended December 31, 2001, Owen had losses of $180,000. Therefore, Kale would be allocated $100,000 of the losses ($180,000 x 5/9).

7. **(b)** An incoming partner has the same rights as all of the existing partners. Thus, an incoming partner has the right to participate in the management of the partnership. Answer (c) is incorrect since a person admitted as a partner into an existing partnership is only liable for existing debts of the partnership to the extent of the incoming partner's capital contribution. Answer (d) is incorrect because a partner need not make a capital contribution to be admitted with the same rights as the other partners.

8. **(b)** A partner is free to assign his interest in any partnership to a third party. However, the assignee does not become a partner by virtue of this assignment, but merely succeeds to the assignor's rights as to profits and return of partner's capital contribution. The assignee does not receive the right to manage, to have an accounting, to inspect the books, or to possess or use any individual partnership property. Since Bean was not made a partner, he is entitled to Cobb's share of TLC's profits, but does not have the right to participate in the management of TLC.

MODULE 14 PARTNERSHIPS AND JOINT VENTURES

E.   Relationship to Third Parties

9.   (a)   A partner's apparent authority is derived from the reasonable perceptions of third parties due to the manifestations or representations of the partnership concerning the authority each partner possesses to bind the partnership. However, if third parties are aware of a formal resolution which limits the partner's actual authority to bind the partnership, then that partner's apparent authority will also be limited. Answer (b) is incorrect because if third parties are unaware of such a resolution which limits the partner's actual authority, then the partner retains apparent authority to bind the partnership. Answer (c) is incorrect because third parties should be aware that in order for a partner to submit a claim against the partnership to arbitration, unanimous consent of the partners is needed. Therefore, a partner has no apparent authority to take such an action. Answer (d) is incorrect because as stated above, the apparent authority of a partner to bind the partnership is not derived from the express powers and purposes contained in the partnership agreement.

10.   (b)   In a general partnership, unanimous consent is required of all of the partners to admit a new partner. Answer (a) is incorrect because any one partner can cause a dissolution by actions such as withdrawing. Answer (c) is incorrect because each partner is an agent of the general partnership and thus may purchase items for the business of the firm. Answer (d) is incorrect; an individual partner may sell real property on behalf of the partnership because s/he is an agent of the partnership.

11.   (c)   Under the Revised Uniform Partnership Act, partners have joint and several liability for not only torts but also breaches of contract. This is a change from previous law.

12.   (c)   Although individual partners normally have implied authority to buy and sell goods for the partnership, they do not have implied authority to do such things as making the partnership a surety or admitting a new partner. These require the consent of all partners.

13.   (d)   A partner's interest in a partnership is freely assignable without the other partners' consent. A partner's interest refers to the partners' right to share in profits and return of contribution. Answer (a) is incorrect because the assignee does not become a partner without the consent of all the other partners. Answer (b) is incorrect because the assignor remains liable as a partner. The assignee has only received the partner's right to share in profits and capital return. Answer (c) is incorrect because assignment of a partner's interest does not cause dissolution unless the assignor also withdraws.

F.   Termination of a Partnership

14.   (b)   Under RUPA, partnership property not only includes property purchased in the partnership name but also includes property purchased by a partner, who is an agent of the partnership, with partnership funds. Note that a partner may use property in the partnership business without it becoming partnership property.

15.   (d)   Even if a partner has agreed not to withdraw before a certain period of time, s/he has the power to do so anyway. That partner's withdrawal is a break of contract and causes a dissolution of the partnership. Answer (a) is incorrect because this dissolution is caused by an act of a partner rather than by operation of law. Answer (b) is incorrect because Wind's withdrawal does have an effect on the remaining partners because they must decide on what new terms they will operate or else wind up and terminate the partnership. Answer (c) is incorrect because the dissolution is effective once Wind does withdraw from the partnership. A court decree is not necessary.

16.   (a)   The best approach to answer this question is to make a chart as follows:

	Dowd 40%	Elgar 30%	Frost 20%	Grant 10%
Capital Balance	$120,000	$100,000	$75,000	$11,000
Allocation of Loss $200,000	(80,000)	(60,000)	(40,000)	(20,000)
Remaining balance	40,000	40,000	35,000	(9,000)
Distribution of deficit of insolvent Partner:				9,000
40/90 x 9,000	(4,000)			
30/90 x 9,000		(3,000)		
20/90 x 9,000			(2,000)	
Balance	36,000	37,000	33,000	0
Cash distribution $106,000	(36,000)	(37,000)	(33,000)	0
	0	0	0	0

A capital deficit may be corrected by the partner investing more cash or assets to eliminate the deficit or by distributing the deficit to the other partners in their resulting profit and loss sharing ratio. The latter was done in this case, as the facts in the question indicated that Grant refuses to make any further contributions to the partnership. The remaining cash is then used to pay the three partners' capital balances.

G.   Limited Partnerships

17.   (c)   Under the Revised Uniform Limited Partnership Act, when the partners do not agree how to split profits, the split is made in proportion to their capital contributions. Note that this is different for general partners under the Revised Uniform Partnership Act.

18.   (a)   Limited partnerships must have at least one general partner who has the unlimited personal liability of the firm. Unlike a general partner, the death of a limited partner does not cause a dissolution or termination of a partner.

19.   (a)   Since Chan acted like a general partner and Ham thought he was a general partner, Chan has the liability of a general partner to Ham. Answers (b), (c), and (d) are incorrect because Ham believed Chan was a general partner based on Chan's actions. Therefore, Chan had the liability of a general partner, that is, unlimited liability.

20.   (a)   Under the Revised Uniform Limited Partnership Act, none of the names of the limited partners need to be listed in the certificate of limited partnership that is filed with the Secretary of State. However, all of the general partners must be listed.

21.   (c)   A limited partner is allowed, without losing the protection of limited liability, to act as an agent of the limited partnership. The limited partner may also vote on the removal of a general partner.

22.   (d)   If the liability is more than the partnership can pay, each partner loses its capital contribution and then the general partner has personal, unlimited liability for the debt.

23.   (b)   The admission of a new general partner to a limited partnership under the Revised Uniform Limited Partnership Act requires the approval of all the general partners. Approval of the limited partners is not needed.

24.   (d)   Unlike the admission of a new general partner, the admission of a new limited partner requires the written approval of not only all of the general partners but also all of the limited partners.

H.   Joint Ventures

25.   (d)   The law of joint ventures is similar to the law of partnerships with some exceptions. One of these exceptions is that the death of a joint venturer does not automatically dissolve the joint venture. Answers (a), (b), and (c) are all incorrect because these are all examples in which joint venture law and partnership law are similar, involving liability, right to participate in management, and fiduciary duties.

I.   Limited Liability Companies (LLC)

26.   (a)   A limited liability company provides for limited liability of its members, similar to the limited liability of the shareholders of a corporation. However, it typically has a limited duration of existence, similar to that of a partnership in which the death or withdrawal of a member or partner causes the business to dissolve unless the remaining members or partners choose to continue the business. The limited liability company can also be taxed similar to a partnership if formed to do so. The subchapter S corporation has the limited liability of the corporation but is taxed similar to a partnership.

27.   (c)   Limited liability companies typically have a limited life. Provisions often provide that they exist for thirty years at most and dissolve if a member dies. Therefore (a) is an incorrect response. Answer (b) is also not chosen because members (owners) are permitted to participate in the management of the LLC or can choose the management. Answer (d) is an incorrect response because one of the main benefits of an LLC is the limited liability of its members (owners).

28.   (b)   In the typical limited liability company (LLC), unlike the common corporation, the interests of the members are not freely transferable. The other members have to agree to admit new members. Answer (a) is incorrect because it provides for limited liability of all of its members. Answer (c) is incorrect because all members have a voice in the management of the LLC. Answer (d) is incorrect because a limited liability company must be formed pursuant to the filing requirements of the relevant state statute.

J.   Limited Liability Partnerships (LLP)

29.   (b)   In a limited liability partnership (LLP), where permitted by state statute, the basic difference between it and a general partnership is limited liability in some cases. In the LLP, partners have limited liability for the torts of the other partners. This is not true of a general partnership. Answer (a) is wrong because both in the LLP and the general partnership, the partners have unlimited liability for their own torts. Answers (c) and (d) are wrong because any contracts signed on behalf of the firm make all of the partners jointly liable in both the LLP and the general partnership.

OTHER OBJECTIVE ANSWERS AND ANSWER EXPLANATIONS

Problem 1

1.   **(A)** The creation of a partnership usually may be either oral or written. A written partnership agreement is not required unless it falls within the Statute of Frauds (e.g., the partnership cannot be completed within one year).

2.   **(A)** A partnership is an association of two or more persons to carry on a business as co-owners for profit. Co-ownership of property is one element of a partnership; however the most important and necessary element of a partnership is profit sharing. Another important element of co-ownership is joint control.

3.   **(B)** Partnership profits and losses are shared equally unless the partnership agreement specifies otherwise. The agreement for ACH Associates specified that the partners would distribute profits based on their capital contributions. As such, Anchor's share of ACH Associates' 2000 profits would be

$$\frac{\$5,000}{15,000 + 10,000 + 5,000} \times \$60,000 = \$10,000$$

Hook's share of ACH Associates' 2000 profits would be

$$\frac{\$15,000}{15,000 + 10,000 + 5,000} \times \$60,000 = \$30,000$$

4.   **(B)** Since the partners agreed on profit sharing in the creation of the partnership, but were silent on loss sharing, losses are shared on the same basis as profits. Therefore, Anchor's capital account would be reduced by

$$\frac{\$5,000}{15,000 + 10,000 + 5,000} = 16.6\% \text{ or } 1/6 \text{ of the 2001 losses}$$

Hook's capital account would be reduced by

$$\frac{\$15,000}{15,000 + 10,000 + 5,000} = .5 \text{ or } 1/2 \text{ of the 2001 losses}$$

5.   **(B)** During dissolution, partners can bind other partners and the partnership on contracts until third parties who have known of the partnership are given notice of dissolution. Actual notice must be given to third parties who have dealt with the partnership prior to the dissolution. Constructive notice is adequate for third parties who have only known of the partnership.

6.   **(B)** Under the Revised Uniform Partnership Act, the partners are jointly and severally liable for all debts of the partnership. Creditors are required to first attempt collection from the partnership unless it is bankrupt. Once ACH Associates has paid off what it can, the partners are jointly and severally liable.

ANSWER OUTLINE

Problem 1   Partner as Agent of Partnership; Apparent
Authority; Partner's Obligations under
Partnership Agreement; Liability of Newly
Admitted Partner; Liability of Withdrawing
Partner

The partnership cannot recover 1/2% commission from King
   Rey had apparent authority to reduce commission to
   1 1/2%
   It is reasonable for King to believe that Rey had authority
   to perform transaction
   King lacked knowledge of the partnership restriction limiting Rey's authority to bind partnership
Partnership can recover 1/2% commission from Rey
   Rey violated his duty to act in accordance with partnership agreement
Park is only liable for existing debts of partnership to extent
   of capital contributed
   Park is personally liable for partnership obligations arising
   after being admitted to partnership
Stein is personally liable for partnership obligations arising
   prior to withdrawing from partnership, unless Stein obtains
   a release from existing creditors
   Stein has no liability for partnership obligations arising
   after actual and constructive notice of withdrawing is
   properly given

UNOFFICIAL ANSWER

Problem 1   Partner as Agent of Partnership; Apparent
Authority; Partner's Obligations under
Partnership Agreement; Liability of Newly
Admitted Partner; Liability of Withdrawing
Partner

a.   1.   The partnership cannot recover the 1/2% commission from King because Rey had the apparent authority to
reduce the commission to 1 1/2%. The Uniform Partnership
Act states that every partner is an agent of the partnership
for the purpose of its business, and the act of every partner
for apparently carrying on in the usual way the business of
the partnership, binds the partnership, unless the partner so
acting has, in fact, no authority to act for the partnership in
the particular matter, and the person with whom the partner
is dealing has knowledge of the fact that the partner has no
such authority. In determining whether Rey had the apparent authority to bind the partnership, one must examine the
circumstances and conduct of the parties and whether King
reasonably believed such authority to exist. Because brokerage commissions are generally not uniform, it would be
reasonable for King to believe that Rey had the authority to
perform the transaction at 1 1/2% commission. Furthermore, King lacked knowledge of the restriction in the partnership agreement that prohibited Rey from reducing a
commission below 2% without the other partners' consent.
Therefore, King will not be liable for the 1/2% commission.

2.   The partnership can recover the 1/2% commission
from Rey because Rey violated the partnership agreement by
reducing the commission to 1 1/2% without the partners'
consent. Rey owes a duty to act in accordance with the
partnership agreement.

b.   1.   Under the Revised Uniform Partnership Act, a
person admitted as a partner into an existing partnership is
liable for all the obligations of the partnership arising before
being admitted as though that person had been a partner

when such obligations were incurred, except that this liability may be satisfied only out of partnership property. Thus,
Park will not be personally liable for the partnership obligations arising prior to being admitted as a partner but would
be liable based upon the extent of partnership interests held.
Park will be personally liable for partnership obligations
arising after being admitted to the partnership.

2.   Stein will continue to be personally liable for partnership obligations arising prior to withdrawing from the
partnership, unless Stein obtains a release from the existing
creditors. Stein will have no liability for partnership obligations arising after actual and constructive notice of withdrawing was properly given. However, Stein may be personally liable for partnership obligations arising after withdrawing but prior to notice being given. Actual notice of
Stein's withdrawal was given by written notification to partnership creditors that had conducted business with the partnership prior to May 15. Constructive notice of Stein's
withdrawal was given by proper publication in two newspapers to those third parties who had not dealt with the partnership, but may have known of its existence.

ANSWER OUTLINE

Problem 2   Liability and Authority of Partners; Allocation
of Profits and Losses

a.   Mathews' assertion that Prime is not liable to Jaco is
   incorrect
   Baker was an agent of Prime with apparent authority
   because
      General nature of Prime's business
      Baker previously dealt with Jaco for Prime
   Jaco not bound by limit because had no knowledge
   Mathews' assertion that his maximum liability to Jaco
   is 40% of lost profits is incorrect
      Partner is personally liable for partnership's debts
      Jaco not bound by Prime's profit/loss sharing agree-
      ments because did not agree to them
   Mathews' assertion that Baker is liable to him is correct
      Partner is liable to other partners for partnership con-
      tracts outside actual authority
      Baker liable to Mathews for breaking $15,000 limit
   Mathews' assertion that Baker is liable to Prime for accepting payments is correct
      Fiduciary duty owed to partnership and partners
      Partners can't take benefits of partnership business
      without partnership's consent
         Partner liable to other partners

b.   KYA's contentions are incorrect
   New partner is liable for preadmission debts up to
   capital contribution and interest in partnership
   KYA's liability is $25,000 and interests

UNOFFICIAL ANSWER

Problem 2   Liability and Authority of Partners; Allocation of Profits and Losses

a.   1.   Mathews' first position is incorrect. A partner is considered an agent of the partnership in carrying out its usual business. In this case, Baker lacked actual authority to bind Prime to the Jaco contract; however, Baker did have, from Jaco's perspective, apparent authority to do so because of the general character of Prime's business and, more important, because Baker had previously purchased cars from Jaco on Prime's behalf. Jaco was not bound by the limitation on Baker's authority unless Jaco was aware of it.

2.   Mathews' second position is also incorrect. As a general rule, a partner is liable for the debts of the partnership, and a third party is not bound by the profit and loss sharing agreements between partners because the third party is not a party to the partnership agreement. Therefore, Jaco can look to Prime's assets and Mathews' personal assets to satisfy the obligation.

3.   Mathews' third position is correct. A partner is liable to other partners for any liability associated with contracts entered into ostensibly on behalf of the partnership but outside the partner's actual authority. In this case, because Baker violated the agreement with Mathews concerning the $15,000 limitation on used car purchases, Baker will be liable to Mathews for any liability that Mathews may have to Jaco.

4.   Mathews' fourth position is also correct. A partner owes a fiduciary duty (that is, a duty of loyalty) to the partnership and every other partner. A partner may not benefit directly or indirectly at the expense of the partnership. A partner must account to the partnership for any benefits derived from the partnership's business without the consent or knowledge of the other partners. In this case, Baker was not entitled to accept and retain the incentive payments made by Top. Doing so violated Baker's fiduciary duty to Prime and Mathews. Baker must account to Prime for all the incentive payments received.

b.   KYA's contention that its $25,000 capital contribution cannot be used to satisfy Prime's obligation to Jaco is incorrect. A new partner is liable for partnership liabilities that arose prior to new partners' admission, but the liability is limited to the partner's capital contribution and interest in partnership property. Therefore, KYA's liability is limited to its capital contribution and its interest as a partner in Prime's assets.

ANSWER OUTLINE

Problem 3   Liabilities and Authority of Partners; Assignees, and Agents Acting for Undisclosed Principles

Jackson's position that Baker is responsible for Jackson's damages is correct

  Baker is personally liable for any contracts entered into as agent acting on behalf of undisclosed principal (Dodd)

Martin's first position that Green is not entitled to inspect the partnership books or participate in partnership management is correct

  An assignee of partnership interest is entitled to receive assignor's share of profits only, not to inspect partnership records or participate in partnership management

Martin's second position that only partnership is liable for unpaid bills, or that Martin's personal liability for unpaid bills is limited, is incorrect

  Although partnership is primarily liable for unpaid bills, Martin and Kent, as Best's partners, are personally liable for unpaid debt

  Laco can seek full recovery against Martin or Kent

Kent's first position that only Martin is liable for 2001 operating loss is incorrect

  Partner's assignment of partnership interest does not terminate that partner's liability for partnership's losses and debts

Kent's second position that 2001 operating loss should be allocated based on original capital contributions is incorrect

  Martin and Kent had not agreed on method for allocating losses

  2001 loss will be allocated in same way that profits were to be allocated (equally)

UNOFFICIAL ANSWER

Problem 3   Liabilities and Authority of Partners; Assignees, and Agents Acting for Undisclosed Principles

a.   Jackson is correct. Baker, as an agent acting on behalf of an undisclosed principal (Best), is personally liable for any contracts entered into in that capacity.

b.   Martin's first position that Green is not entitled to inspect the partnership books or participate in partnership management is correct. Green, as an assignee of Kent's partnership interest, is entitled to receive Kent's share of partnership profits only. Green is not entitled, as an assignee of Kent's partnership interest, to inspect the partnership records or to participate in the management of the partnership.

  Martin's second position that only the partnership is responsible for the debt owed Laco is incorrect. Although the partnership is primarily liable for the unpaid bills, both Martin and Kent, as Best's partners, are personally liable for the unpaid amount of the debt. Laco will be entitled to seek recovery against Martin or Kent for the full amount owed.

c.   Kent's first position that only Martin is liable for the 1998 operating loss because of the assignment of Kent's partnership interest to Green is incorrect. A partner's assignment of a partnership interest does not terminate that partner's liability for the partnership's losses and debts.

  Kent's second position that any personal liability of the partners for the 2001 operating loss should be allocated on the basis of their original capital contributions is incorrect. The 2001 loss will be allocated in the same way that profits were to be allocated between the parties, that is, equally, because Martin and Kent had not agreed on the method for allocating losses between themselves.

CORPORATIONS

Overview

A corporation is an artificial person that is created by or under law and which operates under a common name through its elected management. It is a legal entity, separate and distinct from its shareholders. The corporation has the authority vested in it by statute and its corporate charter. The candidate should understand the characteristics and advantages of the corporate form over other forms of business organization.

Basic to preparation for questions on corporation law is an understanding of the following: the liabilities of a promoter who organizes a new corporation; the liability of shareholders; the liability of the corporation with respect to the preincorporation contracts made by the promoter; the fiduciary relationship of the promoter to the stockholders and to the corporation; the various circumstances under which a stockholder may be liable for the debts of the corporation; the rights of shareholders particularly concerning payment of dividends; the rights and duties of officers, directors, and other agents or employees of the corporation to the corporation, to stockholders, and to third persons; subscriptions; and the procedures necessary to merge, consolidate, or otherwise change the corporate structure.

A. Characteristics and Advantages of Corporate Form

1. Limited liability

   a. Generally a shareholder in a corporation risks only his/her investment

2. Transferability of interest

   a. Shares in corporations are represented by stocks and can be freely bought, sold, or assigned unless shareholders have agreed to restrictions

3. Continuous life

   a. Unlike a partnership, a corporation is not terminated by death of a shareholder, or his/her incapacity

      (1) Regarded as perpetual, and continues to exist until dissolved, merged, or otherwise terminated

4. Separate entity

   a. A corporation is a legal entity in itself and is treated separately from its stockholders

      (1) Can take, hold, and convey property
      (2) Can contract in own name with shareholders or third parties
      (3) Can sue and be sued

5. Financing

   a. Often easier to raise large amounts of capital than in other business organizations by issuance of stock or other securities (e.g., bonds)
   b. More flexible because can issue different classes of stock and/or bonds to suit its needs and market demands

6. Corporate management

   a. Persons who manage corporations are not necessarily shareholders
   b. Management of a corporation is usually vested in board of directors elected by shareholders

7. Note that unincorporated association is similar to partnership so that managing members have unlimited personal liability and no ownership shares need be distributed

B. Disadvantages of Form

1. Taxation (can be an advantage depending on circumstances)

   a. Tax burdens may be heavier than on individuals operating sole proprietorship because of federal "double taxation"

      (1) Corporate taxation
      (2) Distributed earnings taxed to shareholders
      (3) Subchapter S status can alleviate

         (a) Subchapter S corporation (also called S corporation) is treated as corporation for liability purposes but is treated almost like partnership for tax purposes

  (4) Various tax breaks may partially or completely avoid double taxation

2. Costs of incorporating, because must meet formal creation requirements
3. Formal operating requirements must be met

C. Types of Corporations

1. Domestic corporation is one that operates and does business within the state in which it was incorporated

2. Foreign corporation is one doing business in any state except one in which it was incorporated

  a. Foreign corporations, if "doing business" in a given state, are not exempt from many requirements and details that domestic corporations must meet

    (1) Corporation is doing business in that state if transactions are continuous rather than isolated transactions

  b. Foreign corporations file documentation similar to that for incorporation
  c. If foreign corporation does not qualify to do business in a state

    (1) May be denied access to courts to sue
    (2) Is liable to the state for any fees, taxes, interest, and penalties as if it had qualified to do business

3. Professional corporations are ones under state laws that allow professionals to incorporate (e.g., doctors, accountants, attorneys)

  a. Typically, shares may be owned only by licensed professionals
  b. Retain personal liability for their professional acts
  c. Obtain other corporation benefits (e.g., limited liability for corporate debts, some tax benefits)

4. Closely held corporation (also called close corporation or closed corporation) is one whose stock is owned by a limited number of persons usually with restrictions on the transfer of stock to keep it out of the hands of outsiders

5. **De facto** corporation has been formed in fact but has not been formed properly under the law

  a. Usually defective because of some small error

    (1) There must have been a good-faith attempt to form
    (2) There must have been at least an attempt to substantially comply with the incorporation statute

    EXAMPLE: An organization filed all the necessary papers but did not pay the filing fee.

  b. It is necessary that there has been exercise of corporate power by this group

   *EXAMPLE: The organization in the example above is completely idle, holds no organizational meeting, and transacts no business in the corporate name. It is not even a **de facto** corporation.*

  c. Shareholders in a **de facto** corporation still have limited liability to third parties

    (1) If **de facto** incorporation is not achieved, the stockholders are treated as partners for purposes of liability

  d. A **de facto** corporation may only be challenged by the state directly (quo warranto proceeding) and may not be challenged by third parties
  e. Under Model Business Corporation Act essentially same end is achieved by providing that

    (1) Once state issues certificate of incorporation, this is conclusive evidence that all conditions have been met to be a corporation

      (a) However, state may revoke or cancel certificate of incorporation or dissolve corporation

6. **De jure** corporation has been formed correctly in compliance with the incorporation statute
7. Corporation by estoppel is a term used to prevent injustice when an organization has not qualified as either a **de jure** or a **de facto** corporation but has held itself out as one or has been recognized as being a corporation

EXAMPLE: Purchaser who makes a promissory note payable to a "corporation" cannot refuse to pay on the grounds that the "corporation" does not exist even though it was actually a partnership.

EXAMPLE: "Corporation" owes a debt to a supplier. The "corporation" cannot avoid the obligation by claiming that it is not a valid corporation.

D. Formation of Corporation

1. Promoters are persons who form corporations and arrange capitalization to begin corporations

   a. Promoter handles issuing of the prospectus, promoting stock subscriptions, and drawing up charter
   b. Promoter has a fiduciary relationship with corporation, and is not permitted to act against interests of corporation

      (1) Does not prevent personal profit if fully disclosed

   c. Promoter is not an agent of the corporation, because the corporation is still not in existence

      (1) Any agreements (preincorporation contracts) made by promoter are not binding on the future corporation until adopted after corporation comes into existence

         (a) Normally promoter is personally liable on contract. Adoption by corporation does not relieve promoter; novation is required to relieve promoter

            1] Promoter has liability even if promoter's name does not appear on contract
            2] However, promoter is not liable if third party clearly states that s/he would look only to corporation for performance

         (b) The corporation may adopt the promoter's actions formally or by actions

            EXAMPLE: Promoter, P, makes a contract for a corporation that is to be formed, called C. After C is formed, it begins performance of the contract made by P. C is now liable on the contract.

            EXAMPLE: Same as above except that C formally adopts the preincorporation agreement and states so in the corporate minutes. C is liable on this contract even before the corporation begins performance of the contract.

         (c) Corporation is not liable to promoter for his/her services unless adopted by corporation

2. Formed only under state incorporation statutes ("Creature of statute")
3. Incorporation

   a. Articles of Incorporation (charter) are filed with the state and contain

      (1) Proposed name of corporation
      (2) Purpose of corporation
      (3) Powers of corporation
      (4) Name of registered agent of corporation
      (5) Name of incorporators

         (a) Incorporators may be promoters

      (6) Number of authorized shares of stock, types of stock, and whether stock has par value, stated value, or neither

   b. First shareholders' meeting

      (1) Stock certificates issued to shareholders
      (2) Resignation of temporary directors and election of new

   c. At same meeting or subsequent meeting, directors

      (1) Elect officers
      (2) Adopt or reject preincorporation contracts
      (3) Begin business of corporation
      (4) Adopt initial bylaws

4. Articles of Incorporation may be subsequently amended

   a. Approval of any adversely affected shareholders of amendment needed

(1) Often majority vote or sometimes two-thirds vote required

    (a) Dissenting minority shareholders may assert right of appraisal and therefore receive fair value for shares

        1] Fair value is value just before vote

E. Corporate Financial Structure

1. Definitions

  a. Uncertificated securities—securities not represented by written documents

  b. Authorized stock—amount permitted to be issued in Articles of Incorporation (e.g., amount and types)

  c. Issued stock—authorized and delivered to shareholders

  d. Unissued stock—authorized but not yet issued

  e. Outstanding stock—issued and not repurchased by the corporation (i.e., it is still owned by shareholders)

  f. Treasury stock—issued but not outstanding (i.e., corporation repurchased it)

    (1) Are not votable and do not receive dividends

    (2) Corporation does not recognize gain or loss on transactions with its own stock

    (3) Must be purchased out of unreserved or unrestricted earned surplus as defined below and as permitted by state law

        (a) If Articles of Incorporation so permit or if majority of voting shareholders permit, unrestricted capital surplus (see below) may also be used

    (4) May be distributed as part of stock dividend

    (5) May be resold without regard to par value

    (6) Can be resold without regard to preemptive rights

    (7) No purchase of treasury stock may be made if it renders corporation insolvent

  g. Canceled stock—stock purchased or received by corporation that is canceled

    (1) No longer issued or outstanding

    (2) Makes room for more stock to be issued

  h. Par-value stock

    (1) Par value is amount set in Articles of Incorporation

    (2) Stock should be issued for this amount or more

    (3) May subsequently be traded for any amount

    (4) Creditors may hold purchaser liable if stock originally purchased at below par

        (a) Contingently liable for difference between amount paid and par value

        (b) Subsequent purchaser also liable unless purchased in good faith without notice that sale was below par

  i. No-par stock—stock issued without a set par value

    (1) May have a stated value

  j. Stated capital (legal capital)—number of shares issued times par value (or stated value)

    (1) If no par or stated value, then includes total consideration received by corporation

        (a) Under limited circumstances, portion may be allocated by board of directors to capital surplus as permitted by law

    (2) Dividends normally may not be declared or paid out of it

    (3) Following also increase stated capital by number of shares increased times par value (or stated value)

        (a) Exercise of stock option

        (b) Small common stock dividend

(4) Following do not change stated capital

    (a) Acquisition or reissuance of treasury stock under cost method
    (b) Stock splits

        1] Increase number of shares issued and decrease par or stated value (e.g., 2-for-1 stock split doubles the number of shares issued and cuts in half the par or stated value)
        2] Do not distribute assets or capital

    (c) Payment of organization costs

k. Earned surplus (retained earnings)—cumulative amount of income (net of dividends) retained by the corporation during its existence or since a deficit was properly eliminated

    (1) Note that under modern terminology, this is correctly referred to as retained earnings as indicated above; since laws written using old terms, CPA candidates should be familiar with old as well as new terms as learned in accounting

l. Net assets—excess of total assets over total debts
m. Surplus—excess of net assets over stated capital
n. Capital surplus—entire surplus of corporation less earned surplus

    (1) Note that paid-in capital is considered capital surplus

o. Contributed capital—total consideration received by corporation upon issuance of stock

2. Classes of stock

a. Common stock usually gives each shareholder one vote per share and is entitled to dividends if declared by the directors

    (1) Has no priority over other stock for dividends
    (2) Shareholders entitled to share in final distribution of assets
    (3) Votes may be apportioned to shares in other ways (e.g., one vote per ten shares)
    (4) Corporation may issue more than one class of common stock with varying terms (e.g., class may have no voting rights or different par value, etc.)

b. Preferred stock is given preferred status as to liquidations and dividends, but dividends are still discretionary

    (1) Usually nonvoting stock
    (2) Dividend rate is generally a fixed rate
    (3) Cumulative preferred means that if a periodic dividend is not paid at the scheduled time, it accumulates and must be satisfied before common stock may receive a dividend

        (a) These arrearages are not liabilities of corporation until declared by board of directors

            1] Disclosed in footnotes to financial statements

        (b) Noncumulative preferred means that if the dividend is passed, it will never be paid
        (c) Held to be implicitly cumulative unless different intent shown

    (4) Participating preferred stock participates further in corporate earnings remaining after a fixed amount is paid to preferred shares

        (a) Participation with common shares is generally on a fixed percentage basis

c. Callable (or redeemable) stock may be redeemed at a fixed price by the corporation

    (1) Call price is fixed in Articles of Incorporation or may be subject to agreement among shareholders themselves

d. Convertible preferred gives shareholder option to convert preferred stock to common stock at a fixed exchange rate

3. Marketing of stock

a. Stock subscriptions are contracts to purchase a given number of shares in an existing corporation or one to be organized

   (1) Subscription to stock is a written offer to buy and is not binding until accepted by the corporation

   (2) Under the Model Business Corporation Act, stock subscriptions are irrevocable for six months

   (3) Once accepted, the subscriber becomes liable

       (a) For the purchase, and

       (b) As a corporate shareholder

   (4) An agreement to subscribe in the future is not a subscription

b. Watered stock

   (1) Stock is said to be watered when the cash or property exchanged is less than par value or stated value

   (2) Stock must be issued for consideration equal to or greater than the par or stated value under most state laws

       (a) No-par stock may be issued for consideration that the directors determine to be reasonable

   (3) Creditors of the corporation may recover from the stockholders the amount of water in their shares; that is, the amount the stockholders would have paid to the corporation had they paid the full amount required (i.e., par value less amount paid)

       (a) If the corporation becomes insolvent

       (b) Subsequent purchaser of watered stock is not liable unless s/he had knowledge thereof

c. Valid consideration or value for shares

   (1) Consists of cash, property, services performed

       (a) Directors have duty to set value on property received

           1] Directors' value set is conclusive unless fraud shown

   (2) Executory promises are **not** sufficient, for example,

       (a) Promise to perform services cannot be counted

       (b) Promise to pay is not sufficient

       (c) Promissory note (whether negotiable or not) likewise is not sufficient

4. Bonds

  a. Evidence of debt of corporation

    (1) Owner of a bond is not an owner of corporation but a creditor

F. Powers of Corporation

1. Corporations generally have following powers

  a. To acquire their own shares (treasury stock) or retire their own shares

    (1) Typically limited to amount of surplus

  b. To make charitable contributions

  c. To guarantee obligations of others only if in reasonable furtherance of corporation's business

  d. Loans to directors require shareholder approval

  e. Loans to employees (even employees who are also directors) do not need shareholder approval and are appropriate if they benefit corporation

  f. Generally, a corporation may also be a partner of a partnership

G. Liabilities of Corporations

1. Crimes

a. Corporations are liable for crimes they are capable of committing
b. Punishment generally consists of fines or forfeiture, although directors have been faced with prison sentences for crimes of the corporation

2. Contracts

   a. Rules under agency law apply in corporate dealings

3. Torts

   a. Corporations are liable for the damages resulting from torts committed by their officers, directors, agents, or employees within the course and scope of their corporate duties

      EXAMPLE: Fraudulent deceit against a customer.

      EXAMPLE: Employee assaults a complaining customer.

   b. Defense that the tort occurred in connection with **ultra vires** acts is not valid

4. **Ultra vires** acts

   a. Illegal and **ultra vires** acts are not the same

      (1) Illegal acts are acts in violation of statute or public policy

         EXAMPLE: False advertising.

      (2) Whereas **ultra vires** acts are merely beyond the scope of the corporate powers (i.e., a legal act may be **ultra vires**)

         EXAMPLE: Although legal to become a surety, the Articles of Incorporation may not allow it.

   b. The state and stockholders have right to object to **ultra vires** acts
   c. **Ultra vires** contract will be upheld to the extent of performance by both sides

      (1) Directors or officers may be sued by shareholders on behalf of the corporation or by the corporation itself if there are damages to the corporation

H. Directors and Officers of Corporations

1. Directors are elected by shareholders
2. Directors' duties and powers

   a. A director as an individual has no power to bind the corporation—must act as a board member at a duly constituted meeting of the board

      (1) Majority vote of those present is needed for most business decisions if quorum is present
      (2) Action may be taken by board with no meeting

         (a) Unless prohibited by Articles of Incorporation or by corporate bylaws, and
         (b) There must be unanimous written consent by board members for action to be taken

   b. Powers and duties in general

      (1) Declaration of dividends
      (2) Selection of officers
      (3) Must comply with Articles of Incorporation—they do not amend these—these are amended by voting of shareholders
      (4) Typically delegate some authority (e.g., day to day or routine matters to officers and agents)
      (5) Directors are not entitled to compensation unless so provided in articles, bylaws, or by a resolution of the board passed before the services are rendered

         (a) May be reimbursed for expenses incurred on behalf of corporation

3. Director's liability

   a. General rule is that directors must exercise ordinary care and due diligence in performing the duties entrusted to them by virtue of their positions as directors

    (1) Directors are liable for own torts committed even if acting for corporation

        (a) Corporation is **also** liable if committed within the scope of corporate duties

    (2) Business judgment rule—as long as director is acting in good faith s/he will not be liable for errors of judgment unless s/he is negligent

    (3) Directors are chargeable with knowledge of the affairs of the corporation

        (a) If director does not prevent (intentionally or negligently) wrongs of other directors, may be held liable

        (b) Normally may rely on reports of accountants, officers, etc. if reasonable judgment used

    (4) If corporation does not actually exist (not even a de facto corporation) then director as well as others in business have personal liability

  b. Directors liable for negligence if their action was the cause of the corporation's loss

    (1) Corporation may indemnify directors (also officers, employees, agents) against suits based on their duties for the corporation if acted in good faith and in best interests of corporation

        (a) Also applies to criminal actions if s/he reasonably believed that actions were lawful

    (2) Corporation may purchase liability insurance for officers and directors

        (a) Corporation pays premiums
        (b) Policies usually cover litigation costs as well as judgment or settlement costs

  c. Directors owe a fiduciary duty to the corporation

    (1) Owe fiduciary duties of loyalty and due care to the corporation
    (2) Conflicts of interest

        (a) Transactions of a corporation with director(s) or other corporation in which director(s) has interest are valid as long as at least one of the following can be established

          1] Conflict of interest is disclosed or known to board and majority of disinterested members approve of transaction
          2] Conflict of interest is disclosed or known to shareholders and those entitled to vote approve it by a majority
          3] Transaction is fair and reasonable to corporation

          EXAMPLE: A plot of land already owned by a director is sold at the fair market value to the corporation. This contract is valid even without approval if the land is needed by the corporation.

  d. Directors are personally liable for **ultra vires** acts of the corporation unless they specifically dissented on the record

    EXAMPLE: Loans made to stockholders by a corporation.

  e. Directors are personally liable to corporation for approving and paying dividends that impair corporation's solvency

    (1) Directors who act in good faith may use defense of business judgment rule

4. Officers

  a. Typically operate day-to-day business

    (1) Delegated from directors

  b. An officer of the corporation is an agent and can bind corporation by his/her individual acts if within the scope of his/her authority

    (1) Corporation is not bound by acts of an agent beyond the scope of authority
    (2) President usually has authority for transactions that are part of usual and regular course of business

        (a) No authority for extraordinary transactions

        (3) Acts of officers may be ratified by board

  c. Officers and directors may be the same persons

  d. Officers are selected by the directors for a fixed term under the bylaws

        (1) If a term is not definite, it is governed by the directors

  e. Officers have a fiduciary duty to corporation

  f. Courts are recognizing a fiduciary duty owed by majority shareholders to minority shareholders when the majority shareholders have de facto control over the corporation

5. Officers, like directors, are liable for own torts, even if committed while acting for corporation

  a. Corporation is also liable if officer was acting within the scope of his/her authority

I. Stockholder's Rights

1. Right to transfer stock by endorsement and delivery or by separate assignment

  a. Stock certificates are negotiable instruments

  b. Limitations on transfer may be imposed, but they must be reasonable

        (1) UCC requires that any restrictions must be plainly printed on the certificate to be effective against third party

        (2) These limitations are most often imposed in closely held corporations

> EXAMPLE: *Existing shareholders of the corporation may have first option to buy.*

2. Stockholder has no right to manage corporation unless s/he is also officer or director

  a. Retains limited liability unlike limited partner who participates in management

3. Right to vote for election of directors, decision to dissolve the corporation, and any other fundamental corporate changes

  a. Governed by the charter and class of stock owned

  b. Stockholders may have agreements that are enforceable which provide that they will vote a certain way on issues or vote for specified people for the board of directors

  c. Cumulative voting may be required (i.e., a person gets as many votes as s/he has shares times the number of directors being elected)

> EXAMPLE: *100 shares x 5 directors is 500 votes.*

        (1) Gives minority shareholders an opportunity to get some representation by voting all shares for one or two directors

  d. Can vote by proxy—an assignment of voting rights

  e. Directors have the power to amend or repeal the bylaws unless reserved to the shareholders by the Articles of Incorporation

  f. Amendment of the Articles of Incorporation and approval of fundamental corporate changes such as a merger, consolidation, or sale of all assets generally require majority approval by shareholders

4. Right to dividends

  a. Shareholder generally has no right to dividends unless they are declared by the board of directors

        (1) Power to declare is discretionary based on the board's assessment of business needs

        (2) When there is a surplus together with available cash, the shareholders may be able to compel declaration of dividends if board's refusal to declare a dividend is in bad faith or its refusal is unreasonable, but this is difficult to establish

  b. Dividends become a liability of corporation only when declared

        (1) True for all types of stock such as common stock or even cumulative preferred stock

> EXAMPLE: *Knave Corporation declares dividends of $10,000 to the 10,000 $1 cumulative preferred stockholders (there is no average on these shares) and $20,000 to the 500 common stockholders. The following year is so bad*

that Knave Corporation is liquidated. Furthermore, no dividends are declared and general creditors are owed more than the corporation has. None of the shareholders get any dividends in this following year.

    c. Cash dividends may be paid out of unrestricted and unreserved earned surplus (retained earnings) unless corporation already is or will be insolvent because of dividend

        (1) Some states have other regulations, sometimes allowing reductions in other accounts, too

        (2) Under Model Business Corporation Act, dividends are prohibited that cause total liabilities to exceed total assets after effect of the distribution is considered

5. Right of stockholders to inspect books and records exists

    a. These books and records include minute books, stock certificate books, stock ledgers, general account books

    b. Demand must be made in good faith and for a proper purpose

        (1) May get list of shareholders to help wage a proxy fight to attempt to control corporation

        (2) May not get list of shareholders or customers to use for business mailing list

6. Preemptive right

    a. This is the right to subscribe to new issues of stock (at FMV) so that a stockholder's ownership will not be diluted without the opportunity to maintain it

EXAMPLE: A corporation has one class of common stock. Stockholder A owns 15%. A new issue of the same class of stock is to be made. Stockholder A has the right to buy 15% of it.

    b. Usually only applies to common stock, not preferred

    c. Not for treasury stock

    d. There is no preemptive right to purchase stock unless Articles of Incorporation so provide

7. Stockholder's right to sue

    a. Stockholder can sue in his/her own behalf where his/her interests have been directly injured, for example

        (1) Denial of right to inspect records

        (2) Denial of preemptive right if provided for

    b. Stockholders can sue on behalf of the corporation (i.e., a derivative suit)

        (1) In cases where a duty to the corporation is violated and corporation does not enforce, for example

            (a) Director violates his/her fiduciary duty to corporation

            (b) Illegal declaration of dividends (e.g., rendering corporation insolvent)

            (c) Fraud by officer on corporation

        (2) Unless demand would be futile, must first demand that directors sue in name of corporation and then may proceed if they refuse

            (a) Suit may be barred if directors make good faith business judgment that the suit is not in corporation's best interests

        (3) Damages go to corporation

8. Right to a pro rata share of distribution of assets on dissolution after creditors have been paid

J. Stockholder's Liability

1. Generally stockholder's liability is limited to his/her price paid for stock

2. May be liable to creditors for

    a. Original issue stock sold at below par value

        (1) Contingently liable for the difference between par value and original issuance price

    b. Unpaid balance on no-par stock

    c. Dividends paid which impair capital if the corporation is insolvent

3. Piercing the corporate veil—courts disregard corporate entity and hold stockholders personally liable

    a. Rarely happens but may occur if

        (1) Corporation used to perpetrate fraud (e.g., forming an under-capitalized corporation)
        (2) Owners/officers do not treat corporation as separate entity
        (3) Shareholders commingle assets, bank accounts, financial records with those of corporation
        (4) Corporate formalities not adhered to

4. Majority shareholders owe fiduciary duty to minority shareholders and to corporation

K. Substantial Change in Corporate Structure

1. Merger

    a. Union of two corporations where one is absorbed by other

        (1) Surviving corporation issues its own shares (common and/or preferred) to shareholders of original corporations

2. Consolidation

    a. Joining of two (or more) corporations into a single new corporation
    b. All assets and liabilities are acquired by the new company
    c. New corporation is liable for debts of old corporations

3. Requirements to accomplish a merger or consolidation

    a. Boards of both corporations must prepare and submit plan to shareholders of both corporations
    b. Approval of board of directors of both companies
    c. Shareholders of both corporations must be given copy or summary of merger plan
    d. Majority vote of shareholders of each corporation
    e. Surviving corporation gets all assets and liabilities of merging corporations
    f. Dissatisfied shareholders of subsidiary may dissent and assert appraisal rights, thereby receiving the FMV of their stock

L. Dissolution

1. Dissolution is the termination of corporation's status as a legal entity

    a. Liquidation is the winding up of affairs and distribution of assets
    b. Dissolution does not finally occur until liquidation is complete

2. May be done by voluntary dissolution or involuntary dissolution by state for cause

    a. Voluntary dissolution occurs when board of directors passes resolution to dissolve

        (1) Resolution must be ratified by majority of stockholders entitled to vote

3. Shareholder may petition for judicial dissolution if directors or shareholders are deadlocked

MULTIPLE-CHOICE QUESTIONS (1-36)

1. Which of the following statements best describes an advantage of the corporate form of doing business?
   a. Day-to-day management is strictly the responsibility of the directors.
   b. Ownership is contractually restricted and is **not** transferable.
   c. The operation of the business may continue indefinitely.
   d. The business is free from state regulation.

2. Which of the following is not considered to be an advantage of the corporate form of doing business over the partnership form?
   a. A potential perpetual and continuous life.
   b. The interests in the corporation are typically easily transferable.
   c. The managers in the corporation and shareholders have limited liability.
   d. Persons who manage corporation are not necessarily shareholders.

3. Bond Company is incorporated in Florida but not in Georgia. Bond has branch offices in both states. Which of the following is correct?

   I. Bond is a domestic corporation in Georgia.
   II. Bond is a domestic corporation in Florida.
   III. Bond needs to incorporate also in Georgia.

   a. I and II only.
   b. II only.
   c. II and III only.
   d. I, II, and III.

4. Colby formed a professional corporation along with two other attorneys. They took out loans in the name of the corporation. During the first year, Colby failed to file some papers on time for a client causing the client to lose a very good case. For which does Colby have the corporate protection of limited liability?

   I. The negligence for failure to file the papers on time.
   II. The corporate loans.

   a. I only.
   b. II only.
   c. Both I and II.
   d. Neither I nor II.

5. Which of the following statements is correct with respect to the differences and similarities between a corporation and a limited partnership?
   a. Stockholders may be entitled to vote on corporate matters but limited partners are prohibited from voting on any partnership matters.
   b. Stock of a corporation may be subject to the registration requirements of the federal securities laws but limited partnership interests are automatically exempt from those requirements.
   c. Directors owe fiduciary duties to the corporation and limited partners owe such duties to the partnership.
   d. A corporation and a limited partnership may be created only under a state statute and each must file a copy of its organizational document with the proper governmental body.

6. Under the Revised Model Business Corporation Act, which of the following must be contained in a corporation's articles of incorporation?
   a. Quorum voting requirements.
   b. Names of stockholders.
   c. Provisions for issuance of par and nonpar shares.
   d. The number of shares the corporation is authorized to issue.

7. Which of the following facts is(are) generally included in a corporation's articles of incorporation?

	Name of registered agent	*Number of authorized shares*
a.	Yes	Yes
b.	Yes	No
c.	No	Yes
d.	No	No

8. Absent a specific provision in its Articles of Incorporation, a corporation's board of directors has the power to do all of the following, **except**
   a. Repeal the bylaws.
   b. Declare dividends.
   c. Fix compensation of directors.
   d. Amend the Articles of Incorporation.

9. Which of the following statements is correct concerning the similarities between a limited partnership and a corporation?
   a. Each is created under a statute and must file a copy of its certificate with the proper state authorities.
   b. All corporate stockholders and all partners in a limited partnership have limited liability.
   c. Both are recognized for federal income tax purposes as taxable entities.
   d. Both are allowed statutorily to have perpetual existence.

10. Johns owns 400 shares of Abco Corp. cumulative preferred stock. In the absence of any specific contrary provisions in Abco's Articles of Incorporation, which of the following statements is correct?
   a. Johns is entitled to convert the 400 shares of preferred stock to a like number of shares of common stock.
   b. If Abco declares a cash dividend on its preferred stock, Johns becomes an unsecured creditor of Abco.
   c. If Abco declares a dividend on its common stock, Johns will be entitled to participate with the common stock shareholders in any dividend distribution made after preferred dividends are paid.
   d. Johns will be entitled to vote if dividend payments are in arrears.

11. Gallagher Corporation issued 100,000 shares of $40 par value stock for $50 per share to various investors. Subsequently, Gallagher purchased back 10,000 of those shares for $30 per share and held them as treasury stock. When the price of the stock recovered somewhat, Gallagher sold this treasury stock to Thomas for $35 per share. Which of the following statements is correct?

   I. Gallagher's purchase of the stock at below par value is illegal.
   II. Gallagher's purchase of the stock at below par value is void as an ultra vires act.

III. Gallagher's resale of the treasury stock at below par value is valid.

    a.   I only.
    b.   II only.
    c.   III only.
    d.   I and II only.

12. An owner of common stock will **not** have any liability beyond actual investment if the owner

    a.   Paid less than par value for stock purchased in connection with an original issue of shares.
    b.   Agreed to perform future services for the corporation in exchange for original issue par value shares.
    c.   Purchased treasury shares for less than par value.
    d.   Failed to pay the full amount owed on a subscription contract for no-par shares.

13. Which of the following securities are corporate debt securities?

	Convertible bonds	Debenture bonds	Warrants
a.	Yes	Yes	Yes
b.	Yes	No	Yes
c.	Yes	Yes	No
d.	No	Yes	Yes

14. Which of the following rights is a holder of a public corporation's cumulative preferred stock always entitled to?

    a.   Conversion of the preferred stock into common stock.
    b.   Voting rights.
    c.   Dividend carryovers from years in which dividends were **not** paid, to future years.
    d.   Guaranteed dividends.

15. All of the following distributions to stockholders are considered asset or capital distributions, **except**

    a.   Liquidating dividends.
    b.   Stock splits.
    c.   Property distributions.
    d.   Cash dividends.

16. Which of the following is(are) valid consideration for the purchase of stock of a corporation?

  I. Real estate.
  II. A written promise to pay money.

    a.   I only.
    b.   II only.
    c.   Both I and II.
    d.   Neither I nor II.

17. Brawn subscribed to 1,000 shares of $1 par value stock of Caldo Corporation at the agreed amount of $20 per share. She paid $5,000 on April 1 and then paid $9,000 on August 1. Caldo Corporation filed for bankruptcy on December 1 and the creditors of the corporation sought to hold Brawn liable under her subscription agreement. Which of the following is true?

    a.   Brawn has no liability to the creditors because subscription contract was with the corporation, not the creditors.
    b.   Brawn has no liability to the creditors because she has paid more than $1,000 to the corporation which is the par value of the 1,000 shares.
    c.   Brawn is liable for $6,000 to the creditors for the amount unpaid on the subscription price.

    d.   Brawn is liable for $6,000 to the creditors based on the doctrine of ultra vires.

18. Corporations generally have which of the following powers without shareholder approval?

  I. Power to acquire their own shares.
  II. Power to make charitable contributions.
  III. Power to make loans to directors.

    a.   I only.
    b.   I and II only.
    c.   II and III only.
    d.   I, II, and III.

19. Murphy is an employee of Landtry Corporation. Which of the following acts would make the corporation liable for Murphy's actions?

  I. Murphy deceived a customer to convince him to purchase one of Landtry's products.
  II. Murphy hit a customer with his fist breaking his jaw. The management had warned Murphy that he and not the corporation would be responsible for any aggression against customers.

    a.   I only.
    b.   II only.
    c.   Both I and II.
    d.   Neither I nor II.

20. Norwood was a promoter of Parker Corporation. On March 15, Norwood purchased some real estate from Burrows in Parker's name and signed the contract "Norwood, as agent of Parker Corporation." Parker Corporation, however, did not legally come into existence until June 10. Norwood never informed Burrows on or before March 15 that Parker Corporation was not yet formed. After the corporation was formed, the board of directors refused to adopt the preincorporation contract made by Norwood concerning the real estate deal with Burrows. Burrows sued Parker, Norwood, and the board of directors. Which of the following is correct?

    a.   None of these parties can be held liable.
    b.   Norwood only is liable.
    c.   Norwood and Parker are liable but not the board of directors.
    d.   Norwood, Parker, and the board of directors are all liable.

21. Under the Revised Model Business Corporation Act, which of the following statements is correct regarding corporate officers of a public corporation?

    a.   An officer may **not** simultaneously serve as a director.
    b.   A corporation may be authorized to indemnify its officers for liability incurred in a suit by stockholders.
    c.   Stockholders always have the right to elect a corporation's officers.
    d.   An officer of a corporation is required to own at least one share of the corporation's stock.

22. The officers of West Corporation wish to buy some used equipment for West Corporation. The used equipment is actually owned by Parks, a director of West Corporation. For this transaction to **not** be a conflict of interest for Parks, which of the following is(are) required to be true?

I. Parks sells the used equipment to West Corporation in a contract that is fair and reasonable to the corporation.

II. Parks' ownership of the used equipment is disclosed to the shareholders of West who approve it by majority vote.

III. Parks' ownership of the used equipment is disclosed to the board of directors, who approve it by a majority vote of the disinterested directors.

    a. Any one of I, II, or III.
    b. I and II are both required.
    c. I and III are both required.
    d. All three of I, II, and III are required.

23. The following are two statements concerning a fiduciary duty in a corporation.

I. Officers and directors of a corporation owe a fiduciary duty to that corporation.

II. Majority shareholders of a corporation can owe a fiduciary duty to the minority shareholders.

Which of the statements is(are) correct?
    a. I only.
    b. II only.
    c. Both I and II.
    d. Neither I nor II.

24. Hogan is a director of a large corporation. Hogan owns a piece of land that the corporation wishes to purchase and Hogan desires to sell this land at the fair market price. If he sells the land to the corporation, has he breached any fiduciary duty?
    a. No, a director does not owe a fiduciary duty to his corporation.
    b. No, since Hogan is selling the land to his corporation in a fair and reasonable contract.
    c. Yes, unless he discloses his conflict of interest to the shareholders who must then approve the sale of by a simple majority.
    d. Yes, unless he discloses his conflict of interest to the shareholders who must then approve the sale by a two-thirds vote.

25. Acorn Corp. wants to acquire the entire business of Trend Corp. Which of the following methods of business combination will best satisfy Acorn's objectives without requiring the approval of the shareholders of either corporation?
    a. A merger of Trend into Acorn, whereby Trend shareholders receive cash or Acorn shares.
    b. A sale of all the assets of Trend, outside the regular course of business, to Acorn for cash.
    c. An acquisition of all the shares of Trend through a compulsory share exchange for Acorn shares.
    d. A cash tender offer, whereby Acorn acquires at least 90% of Trend's shares, followed by a short-form merger of Trend into Acorn.

26. Price owns 2,000 shares of Universal Corp.'s $10 cumulative preferred stock. During its first year of operations, cash dividends of $5 per share were declared on the preferred stock but were never paid. In the second year, dividends on the preferred stock were neither declared nor paid. If Universal is dissolved, which of the following statements is correct?

    a. Universal will be liable to Price as an unsecured creditor for $10,000.
    b. Universal will be liable to Price as a secured creditor for $20,000.
    c. Price will have priority over the claims of Universal's bond owners.
    d. Price will have priority over the claims of Universal's unsecured judgment creditors.

27. Under the Revised Model Business Corporation Act, when a corporation's bylaws grant stockholders preemptive rights, which of the following rights is(are) included in that grant?

	The right to purchase a proportionate share of a newly issued stock	*The right to a proportionate share of corporate assets remaining on corporate dissolution*
a.	Yes	Yes
b.	Yes	No
c.	No	Yes
d.	No	No

28. Under the Revised Model Business Corporation Act, which of the following actions by a corporation would entitle a stockholder to dissent from the action and obtain payment of the fair value of his/her shares?

I. An amendment to the articles of incorporation that materially and adversely affects rights in respect of a dissenter's shares because it alters or abolishes a preferential right of the shares.

II. Consummation of a plan of share exchange to which the corporation is a party as the corporation whose shares will be acquired, if the stockholder is entitled to vote on the plan.

    a. I only.
    b. II only.
    c. Both I and II.
    d. Neither I nor II.

29. To which of the following rights is a stockholder of a public corporation entitled?
    a. The right to have annual dividends declared and paid.
    b. The right to vote for the election of officers.
    c. The right to a reasonable inspection of corporate records.
    d. The right to have the corporation issue a new class of stock.

30. The limited liability of a stockholder in a closely held corporation may be challenged successfully if the stockholder
    a. Undercapitalized the corporation when it was formed.
    b. Formed the corporation solely to have limited personal liability.
    c. Sold property to the corporation.
    d. Was a corporate officer, director, or employee.

31. The corporate veil is most likely to be pierced and the shareholders held personally liable if
    a. The corporation has elected S corporation status under the Internal Revenue Code.
    b. The shareholders have commingled their personal funds with those of the corporation.

    c.   An ultra vires act has been committed.

    d.   A partnership incorporates its business solely to limit the liability of its partners.

32. A parent corporation owned more than 90% of each class of the outstanding stock issued by a subsidiary corporation and decided to merge that subsidiary into itself. Under the Revised Model Business Corporation Act, which of the following actions must be taken?

    a.   The subsidiary corporation's board of directors must pass a merger resolution.

    b.   The subsidiary corporation's dissenting stockholders must be given an appraisal remedy.

    c.   The parent corporation's stockholders must approve the merger.

    d.   The parent corporation's dissenting stockholders must be given an appraisal remedy.

33. Under the Revised Model Business Corporation Act, a merger of two public corporations usually requires all of the following **except**

    a.   A formal plan of merger.

    b.   An affirmative vote by the holders of a majority of each corporation's voting shares.

    c.   Receipt of voting stock by all stockholders of the original corporations.

    d.   Approval by the board of directors of each corporation.

34. Which of the following statements is a general requirement for the merger of two corporations?

    a.   The merger plan must be approved unanimously by the stockholders of both corporations.

    b.   The merger plan must be approved unanimously by the boards of both corporations.

    c.   The absorbed corporation must amend its articles of incorporation.

    d.   The stockholders of both corporations must be given due notice of a special meeting, including a copy or summary of the merger plan.

35. Which of the following must take place for a corporation to be voluntarily dissolved?

    a.   Passage by the board of directors of a resolution to dissolve.

    b.   Approval by the officers of a resolution to dissolve.

    c.   Amendment of the certificate of incorporation.

    d.   Unanimous vote of the stockholders.

36. A corporate stockholder is entitled to which of the following rights?

    a.   Elect officers.

    b.   Receive annual dividends.

    c.   Approve dissolution.

    d.   Prevent corporate borrowing.

OTHER OBJECTIVE QUESTIONS

Problem 1   (15 to 20 minutes)

Frost, Glen, and Bradley own 50%, 40%, and 10%, respectively, of the authorized and issued voting common stock of Xeon Corp. They had a written stockholders' agreement that provided they would vote for each other as directors of the corporation.

At the initial stockholders' meeting, Frost, Glen, Bradley, and three others were elected to a six-person board of directors. The board elected Frost as president of the corporation, Glen as secretary, and Bradley as vice president. Frost and Glen were given two-year contracts with annual salaries of $50,000. Bradley was given a two-year contract for $10,000 per year.

At the end of its first year of operation, Xeon was in financial difficulty. Bradley disagreed with the way Frost and Glen were running the business.

At the annual stockholders' meeting, a new board of directors was elected. Bradley was excluded because Frost and Glen did not vote for Bradley. Without cause, the new board fired Bradley as vice president even though twelve months remained on Bradley's contract.

Despite the corporation's financial difficulties, the new board, relying on the assurances of Frost and Glen and based on fraudulent documentation provided by Frost and Glen, declared and paid a $200,000 dividend. Payment of the dividend caused the corporation to become insolvent.

- Bradley sued Frost and Glen to compel them to follow the written stockholders' agreement and reelect Bradley to the board.
- Bradley sued the corporation to be reinstated as an officer of the corporation, and for breach of employment contract.
- Bradley sued each member of the board for declaring and paying an unlawful dividend, and demanded its repayment to the corporation.

Required:

Determine whether each of the following legal conclusions is correct or incorrect.

1. Bradley will win in the suit against Frost and Glen for failing to vote Bradley to the board of directors.

2. It is against public policy for stockholders to agree among themselves to vote for each other for the board of directors.

3. The agreement in which Frost, Glen, and Bradley agreed to vote for each other as directors of the corporation is not an enforceable contract because it lacks consideration.

4. The corporation has a right to discharge Bradley as vice president because it had a new board of directors that is not bound by previous contracts.

5. Frost and Glen are not bound to vote for Bradley because Bradley disagreed with the way they were running the business.

6. The corporation is legally bound to complete the two-year contract it had with Bradley, and thus must rehire him.

7. Bradley can sue the corporation for monetary damages because the new board dismissed Bradley.

8. The new board members are required to be shareholders of Xeon Corp. in order to serve on the board.

9. Bradley must sell his/her common stock because s/he is no longer on the board of directors.

10. Bradley will win the suit against each of the members of the board of directors for declaring and paying the dividend.

11. Bradley will win the suit against Frost and Glen to have them held personally responsible for the declaration and payment of the dividends.

12. Assuming that Bradley wins against the board of directors for the payment of the dividends, the remedy is that Bradley gets 10% of the amount of the dividends as damages.

13. Assuming that Bradley wins in the lawsuit against the directors for the dividends, the remedy is that the board members must pay the corporation for the dividends.

14. The directors are personally liable for decisions the board makes that cause the corporation to lose money.

15. The directors owe a fiduciary duty to the corporation.

Problem 2   (5 to 10 minutes)

In 1997, Amber Corp., a closely held corporation, was formed by Adams, Frank, and Berg as incorporators and stockholders. Adams, Frank, and Berg executed a written voting agreement which provided that they would vote for each other as directors and officers. In 2001, stock in the corporation was offered to the public. This resulted in an additional 300 stockholders. After the offering, Adams holds 25%, Frank holds 15%, and Berg holds 15% of all issued and outstanding stock. Adams, Frank, and Berg have been directors and officers of the corporation since the corporation was formed. Regular meetings of the board of directors and annual stockholders meetings have been held.

Required:

Items 1 through 6 refer to the formation of Amber Corp. and the rights and duties of its stockholders, directors, and officers. For each item, determine whether (A), (B), or (C) is correct.

1. A.   Amber Corp. must be formed under a state's general corporation statute.
    B.   Amber Corp.'s Articles of Incorporation must include the names of all stockholders.
    C.   Amber Corp. must include its corporate bylaws in the incorporation documents filed with the state.

2. Amber Corp.'s initial bylaws ordinarily would be adopted by its
    A.   Stockholders.
    B.   Officers.
    C.   Directors.

3. Amber Corp.'s directors are elected by its
    A.   Officers.
    B.   Outgoing directors.
    C.   Stockholders.

4. Amber Corp.'s officers ordinarily would be elected by its
    A.   Stockholders.
    B.   Directors.
    C.   Outgoing officers.

5. Amber Corp.'s day-to-day business ordinarily would be operated by its
    A.   Directors.
    B.   Stockholders.
    C.   Officers.

6. A.   Adams, Frank, and Berg must be elected as directors because they own 55% of the issued and outstanding stock.
    B.   Adams, Frank, and Berg must always be elected as officers because they own 55% of the issued and outstanding stock.
    C.   Adams, Frank, and Berg must always vote for each other as directors because they have a voting agreement.

PROBLEMS

Problem 1   (15 to 20 minutes)

Walsh is evaluating two different investment opportunities. One requires an investment of $100,000 to become a limited partner in a limited partnership that owns a shopping center. The other requires an investment of $100,000 to purchase 3% of the voting common stock of a corporation engaged in manufacturing. Walsh is uncertain about the advantages and disadvantages of being a limited partner versus being a shareholder. The issues of most concern to Walsh are

• The right to transfer a limited partnership interest versus shares of stock.

• The liability as a limited partner versus that of a shareholder for debts incurred by a limited partnership or a corporation.

• The right of a limited partner versus that of a shareholder to participate in daily management.

• The right of a limited partner to receive partnership profits versus the right of a shareholder to receive dividends from a corporation.

Required:

Briefly identify and discuss the basic differences and similarities in the formation of a limited partnership and a corporation. Discuss in separate paragraphs the issues raised by Walsh. (Ignore tax and securities laws.)

Problem 2   (15 to 20 minutes)

Mace, Inc. wishes to acquire Creme Corp., a highly profitable company with substantial retained earnings. Creme is incorporated in a state that recognizes the concepts of stated capital (legal capital) and capital surplus.

In conjunction with the proposed acquisition, Mace engaged Gold & Co., CPAs, to audit Creme's financial statements. Gold began analyzing Creme's stated capital account and was provided the following data:

• Creme was initially capitalized in 1995 by issuing 40,000 shares of common stock, 50¢ par value, at $15 per share. The total number of authorized shares was fixed at 100,000 shares.

• Costs to organize Creme were $15,000.

• During 1997, Creme's board of directors declared and distributed a 5% common stock dividend. The fair market value of the stock at that time was $20 per share.

• On June 1, 1998, the president of Creme exercised a stock option to purchase 1,000 shares of common stock at $21 per share when the market price was $25 per share.

• During 1999, Creme's board of directors declared and distributed a 2-for-1 stock split on its common stock when the market price was $28 per share.

• During 2000, Creme acquired as treasury stock 5,000 shares of its common stock at a market price of $30 per share. Creme uses the cost method of accounting and reporting for treasury stock.

• During 2001, Creme reissued 3,000 shares of the treasury stock at the market price of $32 per share.

Required:

Answer the following, setting forth reasons for any conclusions stated.

a. Discuss what effect each of the transactions described above would have on stated capital (legal capital), indicating the dollar amount of change.

b. Discuss the requirements necessary to properly declare and pay cash dividends.

Problem 3   (15 to 25 minutes)

Edwards, a director and a 10% stockholder in National Corp., is dissatisfied with the way National's officers, particularly Olsen, the president, have been operating the corporation. Edwards has made many suggestions that have been rejected by the board of directors, and has made several unsuccessful attempts to have Olsen removed as president.

National and Grand Corp. had been negotiating a merger that Edwards has adamantly opposed. Edwards has blamed Olsen for initiating the negotiation and has urged the board to fire Olsen. National's board refused to fire Olsen. In an attempt to defeat the merger, Edwards approached Jenkins, the president of Queen Corp., and contracted for Queen to purchase several of National's assets. Jenkins knew Edwards was a National director, but had never done business with National. When National learned of the contract, it notified Queen that the contract was invalid.

Edwards filed an objection to the merger before the stockholders' meeting called to consider the merger proposal was held. At the meeting, Edwards voted against the merger proposal.

Despite Edward's efforts, the merger was approved by both corporations. Edwards then orally demanded that National purchase Edwards' stock, citing the dissenters rights provision of the corporation's by-laws, which reflects the Model Business Corporation Act.

National's board has claimed National does not have to purchase Edward's stock.

As a result of the above

• Edwards initiated a minority stockholder's action to have Olsen removed as president and to force National to purchase Edwards' stock.

• Queen sued National to enforce the contract and/or collect damages.

• Queen sued Edwards to collect damages.

Required:

Answer the following questions and give the reasons for your answers.

a. Will Edwards be successful in a lawsuit to have Olsen removed as president?

b. Will Edwards be successful in a lawsuit to have National purchase the stock?

c. 1. Will Queen be successful in a lawsuit against National?

2. Will Queen be successful in a lawsuit against Edwards?

MULTIPLE-CHOICE ANSWERS

1. c	_ _	9. a	_ _	17. c	_ _	25. d	_ _	33. c	_ _
2. c	_ _	10. b	_ _	18. b	_ _	26. a	_ _	34. d	_ _
3. b	_ _	11. c	_ _	19. c	_ _	27. b	_ _	35. a	_ _
4. b	_ _	12. c	_ _	20. b	_ _	28. c	_ _	36. c	_ _
5. d	_ _	13. c	_ _	21. b	_ _	29. c	_ _		
6. d	_ _	14. c	_ _	22. a	_ _	30. a	_ _		
7. a	_ _	15. b	_ _	23. c	_ _	31. b	_ _	1st: __/36 = __%
8. d	_ _	16. a	_ _	24. b	_ _	32. b	_ _	2nd: __/36 = __%

MULTIPLE-CHOICE ANSWER EXPLANATIONS

A. Characteristics and Advantages of Corporate Form

1. **(c)** One advantage of the corporate form of business is that it has a continuous life and is not terminated by the death of a shareholder or manager. Answer (a) is incorrect because although the power to manage the corporation is vested in the board of directors, they usually delegate the day-to-day management responsibilities to various managers. Answer (b) is incorrect because in most corporations, ownership is not contractually restricted. In fact, free transferability of the shares of stock is a major advantage of the corporate form of business. Answer (d) is incorrect because corporations are not free from state regulation.

2. **(c)** A major advantage is that shareholders have limited liability, that is, typically limited to what they paid for the stock. However, managers do not have limited liability for their actions as managers. If a manager is also a shareholder, that person has limited liability for the ownership in the stock but can still be sued for misdeeds as a manager. Answers (a), (b), and (d) are all considered to be advantages of a corporation. Note that since a person can manage a corporation without necessarily being an owner, this can encourage professional managers to get involved.

C. Types of Corporations

3. **(b)** Bond is a domestic corporation in Florida since it incorporated there. It is a foreign corporation in Georgia since it did not incorporate there. Bond does not need to incorporate in Georgia but must qualify to do business there because it has branch offices in Georgia. This qualifying normally entails filing required documents with the state.

4. **(b)** In a professional corporation, the professional has most of the benefits of a corporation such as limited liability for corporate debts. However, the professional has personal liability for professional acts. Colby cannot avoid liability for the damage caused the client due to negligence in a professional act.

D. Formation of Corporation

5. **(d)** Corporations and limited partnerships may only be created pursuant to state statutes. Normally, both the Articles of Incorporation and a Certificate of Limited Partnership must be filed with the Secretary of State. Answer (c) is incorrect since limited partners do not owe fiduciary duties to the partnership. Answer (a) is incorrect since limited partners have the right to vote on partnership matters such as the dissolution or winding up of the partnership, loans of the partnership, a change in the nature of the business of a partnership, and the removal of a general partner without jeopardizing their limited partner status. Answer (b)

is incorrect since sale of limited partnership interests is not automatically exempted from the general securities laws' registration requirements.

6. **(d)** Under the Revised Model Business Corporation Act, a corporation's articles of incorporation generally must include the name of the corporation, the purpose of the corporation, the powers of the corporation, the name of the incorporators, the name of the registered agent of the corporation and the number of shares of stock the corporation is authorized to issue.

7. **(a)** The articles of incorporation are filed with the state and contain the names of the corporation, registered agent, and incorporators. This document also contains the purpose and powers of the corporation as well as a description of the types of stock and number of authorized shares.

8. **(d)** Normally, the board of directors of a corporation has the power to adopt, amend, and repeal the bylaws. It also has the power to declare dividends and fix the compensation of the directors. However, it does not have the power to amend the Articles of Incorporation.

9. **(a)** Corporations and limited partnerships may only be created pursuant to state statutes. Normally, both the Articles of Incorporation and a Certificate of Limited Partnership must be filed with the Secretary of State. Answer (b) is incorrect because a limited partnership requires at least one general partner who retains unlimited personal liability. Answer (c) is incorrect because a limited partnership is treated the same as a general partnership for tax purposes in that it is not recognized as a separate taxable entity. Answer (d) is incorrect because a limited partnership is not statutorily allowed perpetual existence.

E. Corporate Financial Structure

10. **(b)** The Articles of Incorporation must include, among other things, the amount of capital stock authorized and the types of stock to be issued. Specific provisions applicable to stock must also be stated. Examples of stock provisions which must be authorized by the Articles of Incorporation include number of authorized shares, whether the stock is to be par value or no-par value, and classes of stock, including voting rights and dividend provisions. Preferred stock is given preferred status as to liquidations and dividends. This is part of the definition of preferred stock and need not be specifically included in the Articles of Incorporation in order to be enforceable. Therefore, Johns becomes an unsecured creditor upon Abco's declaration of preferred stock dividend. In order for Johns to be entitled to convert his/her preferred shares to common shares, to participate with common shareholders in any dividend distribution made after preferred dividends are paid, or to be entitled to vote if dividend payments are in arrears, it must be stated in the Articles of Incorporation.

11.   (c)   Gallagher originally sold the stock at above par value. It may buy back and resell the shares without regard to par value.

12.   (c)   A corporation may resell treasury shares without regard to par value. Therefore, an owner of common stock who purchased treasury shares for less than par value will not have any liability beyond actual investment. Answer (a) is incorrect because an owner of common stock who paid less than par value for stock purchased in connection with an original issue of shares is contingently liable in many states to creditors for the difference between the amount paid and par value. Answer (b) is incorrect because a promise to perform future services in exchange for original issue par value shares is an executory promise which is not considered valid consideration for shares. An owner of common stock who agreed to perform future services for the corporation in exchange for original issue par value shares is liable to creditors for the difference between any valid consideration (i.e., cash, property, or services performed) given and par value. Answer (d) is incorrect because once the corporation accepts an offer to buy stock subscriptions, the subscriber becomes liable for the purchase. Therefore, an owner of common stock who failed to pay the full amount owed on a subscription contract for no-par shares is liable for the difference between any amounts already paid and the full amount owed according to the contract.

13.   (c)   Corporate debt securities include the following: (1) registered bonds, (2) bearer bonds, (3) debenture bonds, (4) mortgage bonds, (5) redeemable bonds, and (6) convertible bonds. A warrant is not a corporate debt security, but rather is written evidence of a stock option which grants its owner the option to purchase a specified amount of shares of stock at a stated price within a specified period of time.

14.   (c)   Preferred shares of stock are shares that have a contractual preference over other classes of stock as to liquidations and dividends. If a preferred stock is cumulative, the shareholder would be entitled to dividend carryovers from years in which dividends were not paid, to future years and would receive all dividends in arrears before any dividend is paid to owners of common stock. Answers (a) and (b) are incorrect because in order for a shareholder to be entitled to convert preferred stock into common stock or to have voting rights, it must be stated in the articles of incorporation. These are not rights that a holder of preferred stock would always be entitled to. Answer (d) is incorrect because although a preferred stockholder has preference over other classes of stock as to declared dividends, the board of director's power to declare dividends is discretionary and thus dividends are not guaranteed.

15.   (b)   A stock split increases the number of shares outstanding and proportionately decreases the par value per share. However, the total outstanding par value does not change and therefore no charge is made to retained earnings or capital. Liquidating dividends represent a return of the stockholders' capital and are considered a capital distribution. Both cash and property distributions are considered asset distributions. Property distributions are recorded at the fair market value of the asset at the date of transfer.

E.3.   Marketing of Stock

16.   (a)   Cash, property, and services performed are valid consideration for the purchase of corporate stock. Executory promises, however, are not.

17.   (c)   Since Brawn had a contract to purchase 1,000 shares at $20 per share, this is binding. Therefore, the creditors can recover in bankruptcy the remainder of the price not paid. Answer (a) is incorrect because the creditors have the right to see that the bankruptcy estate includes this amount owed the corporation. Answer (b) is incorrect because the contract required that the full $20,000 be paid, not just the par value. Answer (d) is incorrect because ultra vires acts are acts that are beyond the scope of the powers of the corporation. These do not apply to this fact pattern.

F.   Powers of Corporation

18.   (b)   Corporations generally have the power to acquire or retire their own shares without shareholder approval. They can also make charitable contributions without such approval. Loans to directors require shareholder approval.

G.   Liabilities of Corporation

19.   (c)   A business is liable for the torts of its employees committed within the course and scope of employment. This is true even if management has warned the employee that he and not the corporation will be liable. The injured third party can hold both the employee and the corporation liable in either case.

H.   Directors and Officers of Corporations

20.   (b)   Since the corporation never adopted the contract by words or actions, it is not liable. The board of directors is not personally liable either because they never agreed to the contract. However, Norwood is personally liable on the contract because he signed the contract and agency law will not protect him. This is true because he was not an agent, even though he claimed to be, because there was no principal to authorize him when the contract was made on March 15.

21.   (b)   Under the Revised Model Business Corporation Act, a corporation is authorized to indemnify its officers for expenses, attorney fees, judgments, fines and amounts paid in settlement incurred in a suit by stockholders when the liability is a result of the officer's good faith, nonnegligent actions on behalf of the best interest of the corporation. Answer (a) is incorrect because a corporate officer may also serve as a director. Answer (c) is incorrect because officers are appointed by the directors of a corporation who are in turn elected by the shareholders. Answer (d) is incorrect because there is no requirement that an officer must own any shares of the corporation's stock.

22.   (a)   The transaction the director wishes to have with the corporation is not a conflict of interest if any one of the following is true. (1) The transaction is fair and reasonable for the corporation. (2) The shareholders are given the relevant facts and they approve it by a majority vote. (3) The board of directors are given the relevant facts and they approve it by a majority vote of the disinterested members of the board of directors.

23. **(c)**   Officers and directors are in important positions in a corporation. As such, they owe a fiduciary duty to the corporation to act in the best interests of the corporation. Courts have also recognized that because majority shareholders can exercise a lot of power in a corporation from their stockholdings and voting rights, they owe a fiduciary duty to the minority shareholders when these majority shareholders have de facto control over the corporation by virtue of their concentrated ownership.

24. **(b)**   A contract between a director and his/her corporation is valid if it is reasonable to the corporation. Hogan has not breached his fiduciary duty with the corporation since he is selling the land at fair market value. Answer (a) is incorrect because a director does owe a fiduciary duty to his/her corporation to act in its best interests. Answers (c) and (d) are incorrect because since the transaction is fair and reasonable to the corporation, the shareholders need not approve it.

I. Stockholder's Rights

25. **(d)**   When Acorn pays cash and buys 90% or more of Trend's shares, it has control of the Trend stock. It can then accomplish a short-form merger of Trend Corp. into Acorn Corp. Answer (a) is incorrect because this can require the approval of Acorn shareholders. Answer (b) is incorrect because this is not a regular sale of Trend's assets and will require shareholder approval. Answer (c) is incorrect because the entire compulsory exchange for Acorn shares to accomplish the acquisition does require shareholder approval.

26. **(a)**   Upon declaration, a cash dividend on preferred stock becomes a legal debt of the corporation, and the preferred shareholders become unsecured creditors of the corporation. However, any dividends not paid in any year concerning cumulative preferred stock are not a liability of the corporation until they are declared. Therefore, Universal will be liable to Price as an unsecured creditor for $10,000, which is the amount of the declared dividends. Answers (c) and (d) are incorrect because Price has become a general unsecured creditor for the declared dividends and will have the same priority as the debenture (unsecured) bond owners and the unsecured judgment creditors. Answer (b) is incorrect because the undeclared dividends did not become a legal liability to Universal.

27. **(b)**   The preemptive right gives the shareholder the right to purchase newly issued stock so as to keep the same overall percentage of ownership of the corporation. The way this is done is by allowing him/her to purchase a proportionate share. Otherwise, his/her ownership of the overall corporation may become diluted.

28. **(c)**   When the rights of individual shareholders may be adversely affected, the shareholder is given the right to dissent and receive payment of the fair value of his/her shares. This is true even if the dissenting shareholder has voting rights when s/he is being outvoted. In I., the shareholder has this right because his/her preference rights are being abolished. In II., the dissenting shareholder has this right because his/her shares being acquired by another corporation may affect the value and rights of the shares of stock.

29. **(c)**   Shareholders have the right to inspect the corporate records if done in good faith for a proper purpose. Answer (a) is incorrect because shareholders do not have a right to dividends. It is the decision of the board of directors whether or not to declare dividends. Answer (b) is incorrect because although at least one class of stock must have voting rights to elect the **board of directors**, the **officers** may be selected by the board of directors. Answer (d) is incorrect because the shareholders cannot force an issuance of a new class of stock.

J. Stockholder's Liability

30. **(a)**   Normally, the liability of shareholders of corporations is limited to their capital contribution. However, the court will "pierce the corporate veil" and hold the shareholders personally liable for the debts of the corporation if the corporate entity is being used to defraud people or to achieve other injustices. Thus, if the shareholders establish a corporation, knowing that it would have less capital than required for it to pay its debts, then the court will "pierce the corporate veil" and hold the shareholders personally liable. Answer (c) is incorrect because a shareholder may sell property to the corporation without becoming personally liable for the debts of the corporation. Answer (d) is incorrect because shareholders may also be corporate officers, directors or employees without jeopardizing their limited liability status. Answer (b) is incorrect because the formation of a corporation solely to limit personal liability is a valid purpose so long as it is done without intent to defraud.

31. **(b)**   The court will disregard the corporate entity and hold the shareholders individually liable when the corporate form is used to perpetrate a fraud or is found to be merely an agent or instrument of its owners. An example of when the corporate veil is likely to be pierced is if the corporation and its shareholders commingle assets and financial records. In such a situation, the shareholders lose their limited liability and will be held personally liable for the corporation's legal obligations. Answer (a) is incorrect because the election of S corporation status is allowable under the law and is not, in itself, grounds for piercing the corporate veil. Answer (d) is incorrect because the desire of shareholders to limit their personal liability is a valid reason to form a corporation. Limited personal liability is one advantage of the corporate entity. Answer (c) is incorrect since the court will hold personally liable only those corporate officers responsible for the commission of an **ultra vires** act. The court will not pierce the corporate veil and hold the shareholders personally liable for such an act.

K. Substantial Change in Corporate Structure

32. **(b)**   Under the Revised Model Business Corporation Act, a corporation that owns at least 90% of the outstanding shares of each class of stock of the subsidiary may merge the subsidiary into itself without approval by the shareholders of the parent or subsidiary. The approval of the shareholders or the subsidiary's board of directors is unnecessary since the parent owns 90% of the subsidiary. This ownership assures that the plan of the merger would be approved. The only requirement is a merger resolution by the board of directors of the parent corporation. Furthermore, the dissenting shareholders of the subsidiary must be given an appraisal remedy, that is the right to obtain payment from the parent for their shares. The shareholders of the parent do not have this appraisal remedy because the merger has not materially changed their rights.

33.   (c)   In order for a merger of two public corporations to be accomplished, it is required that a formal plan of merger be prepared and that the merger plan be approved by a majority of the board of directors and stockholders of both corporations.

34.   (d)   As one of the steps leading up to a merger of two corporations, the stockholders need to be given notice of the merger plan. This is true of the stockholders of both corporations, so a special meeting is called inviting both sets of stockholders. Answers (a) and (b) are incorrect because unanimous approval is not needed by either the stockholders or the boards of either corporation. Answer (c) is incorrect because the absorbed corporation will no longer exist after the merger plan is accomplished.

L. Dissolution

35.   (a)   A corporation voluntarily dissolves when its board of directors passes a resolution to dissolve and liquidate. Answer (d) is incorrect because this resolution must be ratified by a majority of stockholders who are entitled to vote. Following ratification, the corporation must file a certificate of dissolution with the proper state authority, cease business, wind up its affairs, and publish notice of its dissolution. Answers (b) and (c) are incorrect because they are not requirements of a voluntary dissolution.

36.   (c)   Shareholders have the right to vote on the dissolution of the corporation. Stockholders also have the right to elect the directors of the corporation, who in turn elect the officers. Answer (b) is incorrect as shareholders do not have the right to receive dividends unless they are declared by the board of directors. Answer (d) is incorrect as shareholders are not necessarily involved in the management of the corporation and cannot prevent corporate borrowing.

OTHER OBJECTIVE ANSWERS AND ANSWER EXPLANATIONS

Problem 1

1.   **(C)** Stockholders may agree among themselves on how they will vote for the board of directors. This agreement is a contract that is enforceable under the law.

2.   **(I)** Stockholders are allowed to make agreements on how they will vote.

3.   **(I)** The contract is supported by consideration in that each has agreed to vote for the others.

4.   **(I)** When the original board of directors elected Bradley to be vice president, it gave him/her a two-year contract. The board was acting as an agent and thus bound the corporation as the principal to the contract for the two-year term. The principal remains liable on the contract even if the agent is later changed.

5.   **(I)** Bradley has not breached his/her contract even though s/he disagreed with the way Frost and Glen were running the business. In absence of a breach, Frost and Glen are still obligated under the contract.

6.   **(I)** Bradley can sue for monetary damages but cannot require the corporation to rehire him/her.

7.   **(C)** Since there was still time left on the two-year contract for $10,000 per year, the appropriate remedy is to compensate Bradley for the damages after s/he was fired.

8.   **(I)** One of the important elements of a corporation is that the management and ownership can be separate.

9.   **(I)** One can be a shareholder without being on the board. Bradley never agreed to give up his/her shares.

10.   **(I)** In general, directors are personally liable to the corporation for approving and paying dividends that impair the corporation's solvency. However, the directors other than Frost and Glen relied upon the information given by Frost and Glen. Although Frost and Glen are personally liable, the others are not under the business judgment rule.

11.   **(C)** Frost and Glen are personally liable for the dividend payments that impaired the corporation's solvency. Unlike the other directors, Frost and Glen gave the assurances and the fraudulent documentation.

12.   **(I)** Directors who approve such dividends are generally personally liable to the corporation, not the shareholders.

13.   **(C)** The payment goes to the corporation.

14.   **(I)** This statement is not always true because as long as the director is acting in good faith, s/he is not liable for errors of judgment in the absence of negligence. This is known as the business judgment rule.

15.   **(C)** The directors owe a fiduciary duty to the corporation which includes loyalty and due care.

Problem 2

1.   **(A)** A corporation must be formed under state incorporation statutes. The articles of incorporation are filed with the state and contain the proposed name of the corporation, the purpose of the corporation, the powers of the corporation, the name of the registered agent of the corporation, the name of the incorporators, and the number of authorized shares of stock, types of stock, and whether the stock has a par value, stated value, or neither.

2.   **(C)** Since the bylaws are necessary to the organization of the corporation, the adoption of the bylaws is one of the first items of business performed by the board of directors promptly after incorporation.

3.   **(C)** The shareholders of a corporation elect the board of directors to manage the business of the corporation. The board of directors then appoints officers to run the day-to-day operations.

4.   **(B)** The board of directors appoints officers.

5.   **(C)** The officers run the day-to-day operations of the corporation.

6.   **(C)** In most jurisdictions, shareholders may enter into a written agreement to vote in a specified manner for the election or removal of directors or for any matter subject to shareholder approval. These voting agreements are not limited to a time frame. Since Adams, Frank, and Berg entered into a written voting agreement, they must always vote for each other as directors. However, all three will not necessarily be elected as directors or officers because by use of cumulative voting, the minority shareholders may be able to vote in one of their candidates.

ANSWER OUTLINE

Problem 1 Comparisons of Limited Partnership with Corporation; Formation; Transfer of Interests; Liability; Participation in Management; Share of Profits

Formation

Limited Partnership

- Two or more persons
- Governed by state limited partnership statute
- One or more general partners required
- File certificate of limited partnership with the state

Corporation

- May only be formed under state incorporation statute
- Must file Articles of Incorporation with the state
- One or more incorporators must sign Articles of Incorporation

Liability

Limited Partner liable to extent of capital contribution unless participates in daily management

Shareholder generally liable to extent of capital contribution

Rights

Transfer

- Limited Partnership interest assignable unless otherwise agreed
- Shares of stock freely transferable unless otherwise agreed

Management Participation

- Limited Partner cannot participate without losing limited liability status
- Shareholders may not participate unless they are an officer or director
- Shareholders owning voting stock may vote for board of directors

Profits

- Limited Partner entitled to share of profits based on the partnership agreement
- Shareholders generally not entitled to dividends until declared by the board of directors

UNOFFICIAL ANSWER

Problem 1 Comparisons of Limited Partnership with Corporation; Formation; Transfer of Interests; Liability; Participation in Management; Share of Profits

A limited partnership is formed by two or more persons under a state's limited partnership statute, having as members one or more general partners and one or more limited partners. Two or more persons desiring to form a limited partnership must execute a certificate of limited partnership that must be filed in the office of the secretary of state, or other appropriate state or local office. A corporation may be formed only under a state incorporation statute that requires that one or more incorporators sign Articles of Incorporation which must be filed with the secretary of state.

Unless otherwise provided in the partnership agreement, or other agreements among the partners, a limited partnership interest is assignable in whole or in part. Similarly, in the absence of a restriction in the corporation's organizational documents or other agreements among the shareholders, shares of stock are freely transferable.

A limited partner's liability for partnership debts is generally limited to the partner's investment (capital contribution) in the partnership if the interest is fully paid and nonassessable and the partner does not participate in the daily management of the business. Likewise, a shareholder's liability for a corporation's debts is generally limited to the shareholder's investment (capital contribution) in the corporation.

A limited partner cannot participate in the daily operations of the partnership's business without losing limited liability. A shareholder who is not also an officer or a director cannot participate in the daily operations of the corporation's business. However, a shareholder owning voting stock has the right to vote for a board of directors, which will manage the business affairs of the corporation. The board of directors elects officers to run the daily operations of the corporation.

A limited partner is entitled to receive a share of the partnership's profits in the manner provided in the partnership agreement. On the other hand, whether a shareholder receives dividends is generally within the discretion of the board of directors.

ANSWER OUTLINE

Problem 2 Stated Capital; Treasury Stock; Cash Dividends

a. Stated capital is the number of shares issued, valued at par value

Organization costs do not affect stated capital

Stock dividend would increase stated capital by the number of shares issued, valued at par value

Stock option would increase stated capital by the number of shares issued, valued at par value

Stock split does not affect stated capital

 Instead the par value of the stock is decreased and the number of shares is increased

The acquisition of treasury stock under cost method has no effect on stated capital

The reissuance of treasury stock has no effect on stated capital

b. Cash dividends may be declared and paid if the corporation is solvent and payment of dividends would **not** cause insolvency. Some states permit payment of dividends only out of retained earnings.

UNOFFICIAL ANSWER

Problem 2 Stated Capital; Treasury Stock; Cash Dividends

a. The initial capitalization of Creme in 1995 would result in $20,000 being allocated to stated capital. Stated capital includes the par value of all shares of the corporation having a par value that have been issued. Therefore, the $20,000 is calculated as follows: 40,000 shares issued x 50¢ par value = $20,000.

The $15,000 of expenses incurred in organizing Creme would not affect stated capital. The Model Business Corporation Act permits payment of organization expenses out of the consideration received by it in payment for its shares if the payment does not render such shares assessable or unpaid. Thus, stated capital remains at $20,000.

The 5% stock dividend would increase stated capital by $1,000 calculated as follows: 40,000 shares x 5% stock dividend = 2,000 shares x 50¢ par value = $1,000. The market price of the shares would have no effect on stated capital. Thus, stated capital is $21,000.

The exercise of the stock option by Creme's president would increase stated capital by $500 calculated as follows: 1,000 shares x 50¢ par value = $500. Neither the price paid by Creme's president nor the market price of the shares on the date the option was exercised would affect stated capital. Thus, stated capital is $21,500.

The 2-for-1 stock split would not affect stated capital. Instead the par value of 50¢ per share would be reduced to 25¢ per share and the 43,000 shares of stock issued would be increased to 86,000 shares. Thus, stated capital remains at $21,500.

The acquisition of 5,000 shares as treasury stock at $30 per share by Creme would have no effect on stated capital under the cost method. Thus, stated capital remains at $21,500.

The reissuance of the 3,000 shares of treasury stock at $32 per share would also have no effect on stated capital under the cost method. Thus, stated capital remains at $21,500.

b.   Cash dividends may be declared and paid if the corporation is solvent and payment of the dividends would not render the corporation insolvent. Furthermore, each state imposes additional restrictions on what funds are legally available to pay dividends. One of the more restrictive tests adopted by many states permits the payment of dividends only out of unrestricted and unreserved earned surplus (retained earnings). The Model Business Corporation Act prohibits dividend distributions if, after giving effect to the distribution, the corporation's total assets would be less than its total liabilities.

ANSWER OUTLINE

Problem 3   Power of Individual Stockholders; Purchase of Stock under a Merger; Authority of a Director

a.   Edwards will not win the suit to remove Olsen
   Only Board of Directors have right to hire/fire officers
   Stockholders do not vote on hiring/firing of officers
   Influence only by voting for directors

b.   Edwards will lose suit to have National purchase stock
   Stockholder has right to request the corporation repurchase his/her stock if dissent from a merger if:
   1. File objection to merger prior to stockholders meeting at which the merger proposed
   2. Vote against the merger proposal
   3. Demand in writing that corporation repurchase stock
   Edwards will lose because no written demand submitted

c.   1.   Queen will lose suit against National to enforce contract
         Edwards had no authority to contractually bind
            Director does not have authority to bind corporation contractually unless expressly granted

            No express authority bestowed
2.   Queen will win against Edwards
      Edwards granted no authority to act for National
      Edwards personally liable for damages

UNOFFICIAL ANSWER

Problem 3   Power of Individual Stockholder; Purchase of Stock under a Merger; Authority of a Director

a.   Edwards will not win the suit to have Olsen removed as president. The right to hire and fire officers is held by the board of directors. Individual stockholders, regardless of the size of their holding, have no vote in the selection of officers. Individual stockholders may exert influence in this area by voting for directors at the annual stockholders' meeting.

b.   Edwards will lose the suit to have National purchase the stock. A stockholder who dissents from a merger may require the corporation to purchase his or her shares if the statutory requirements are met and would be entitled to the fair value of the stock (appraisal remedy). To compel the purchase, Edwards would have had to file an objection to the merger before the stockholders meeting at which the merger proposal was considered, vote against the merger proposal, and make a written demand that the corporation purchase the stock at an appraised price. Edwards will lose because the first two requirements were met but Edwards failed to make a written demand that the corporation purchase the stock.

c.   1.   Queen will lose its suit against National to enforce the contract, even though Edwards was a National director. Jenkins may have assumed that Edwards was acting as National's agent, but Edwards had no authority to contract with Queen. A director has a fiduciary duty to the stockholders of a corporation but, unless expressly authorized by the board of directors or the officers of the corporation, has no authority to contract on behalf of the corporation. There is no implied agency authority merely by being a director.

2.   Queen will win its suit against Edwards because Edwards had no authority to act for National. Edwards will be personally liable for Queen's damages.

FEDERAL SECURITIES ACTS

Overview

The bulk of the material tested on the exam from this area comes from the Securities Act of 1933, as amended, and the Securities Exchange Act of 1934, as amended. Topics included under the scope of the 1933 Act are registration requirements, exempt securities, and exempt transactions. The purposes of the 1933 Act are to provide investors with full and fair disclosure of a security offering and to prevent fraud. The basic prohibition of the 1933 Act is that no sale of a security shall occur in interstate commerce without registration and without furnishing a prospectus to prospective purchasers unless the security or the transaction is exempt from registration.

The purpose of the 1934 Act is the establishment of the Securities Exchange Commission to assure fairness in the trading of securities subsequent to their original issuance. The basic scope of the 1934 Act is to require periodic reports of financial and other information concerning registered securities, and to prohibit manipulative and deceptive devices in both the sale and purchase of securities.

The exam often includes an essay question on the Federal Securities Acts; however, this is sometimes combined with accountant's liability or is included within a question concerning corporate or limited partnership law.

A. Securities Act of 1933 (Generally applies to initial issuances [primary offerings] of securities)

1. Purposes of the Act are to provide potential investors with full and fair disclosure of all material information relating to issuance of securities (such that a prudent decision to invest or refrain from investing can be made) and to prevent fraud or misrepresentation

   a. Accomplished by

      (1) Requiring a registration statement to be filed with Securities Exchange Commission (SEC) before either a public sale or an offer to sell securities in interstate commerce

         (a) This is the fundamental thrust of the 1933 Act
         (b) SEC is a government agency comprised of commissioners and its staff that was created to administer and enforce the Federal Securities Laws. The Commission interprets the acts, conducts investigations, adjudicates violations, and performs a rule-making function to implement the acts.

            1] Can subpoena witnesses
            2] Can obtain injunction preventing sale of securities
            3] Cannot assess monetary penalties without court proceedings
            4] Cannot prosecute criminal acts

      (2) Requiring prospectuses to be provided to investors with, or before, the sale or delivery of the securities to provide public with information given to SEC in registration statement
      (3) Providing civil and criminal liabilities for failure to comply with these requirements and for misrepresentation or fraud in the sale of securities even if not required to be registered

   b. SEC does not evaluate the merits or value of securities

      (1) SEC can only compel full and fair disclosure
      (2) In theory, public can evaluate merit of security when provided with full and fair disclosure
      (3) SEC's function is not to detect fraud or to stop offerings where fraud or unethical conduct is suspected

   c. The major items you need to know are

      (1) That a registration statement and prospectus are usually required
      (2) Which transactions are exempt from registration
      (3) Which securities are exempt from registration
      (4) What the liability is for false or misleading registration statements

2. Definitions

   a. Security—any note, stock, bond certificate of interest, debenture, investment contract, etc., or any interest or instrument commonly known as a security

      (1) General idea is that investor intends to make a profit on the investment through the efforts of others rather than through his/her own efforts

EXAMPLE: W is a general partner of WDC partnership in Washington, D.C. Usually, W's interest would not be considered a security because a general partner's interest typically involves participation in the business rather than mere investment.

(a) Includes limited partnership interests

(b) Includes rights and warrants to subscribe for the above

(c) Includes treasury stock

(d) Investment contract is a security when money is invested in a common enterprise with profits to be derived from the effort of others

EXAMPLE: Blue Corporation in Florida owns several acres of orange trees. Blue is planning on selling a large portion of the land with the orange trees to several individuals in various states on a row-by-row basis. Each purchaser gets a deed and is required to purchase a management contract whereby Blue Corporation maintains all the land and oranges and then remits the net profits to the various purchasers. Even though it may appear that each individual purchased separately the land with the oranges and a management contract, the law looks at the "big picture" here. Since in reality the individuals are investing their money, and the profits are derived from the efforts of others, the law treats the above fact pattern as involving securities. Therefore, the Securities Acts apply.

b. Person—individual, corporation, partnership, unincorporated association, business trust, government

c. Controlling person—has power, direct/indirect, to influence the management and/or policies of an issuer, whether by stock ownership, contract, position, or otherwise

EXAMPLE: A 51% stockholder is a controlling person by virtue of a majority ownership.

EXAMPLE: A director of a corporation also owns 10% of that same corporation. By virtue of the stock ownership and position on the board of directors, he has a strong voice in the management of the corporation. Therefore, he is a controlling person.

d. Insiders—(applies to the Securities Exchange Act of 1934) include officers, directors, and owners of more than 10% of any class of issuer's equity securities

(1) Note that debentures not included because not equity securities

(2) For purposes of this law to avoid a "loophole," insiders include "beneficial owners" of more than 10% of the equity stock of issuer

(a) To determine amount of "beneficial ownership," add to the individual's equity ownership, equity stock owned by

1] Owner's spouse

2] Owner's minor children

3] Owner's relative in same house

4] Owner's equity stock held in trust in which owner is beneficiary

EXAMPLE: X owns 6% of the common stock of ABC Company in Philadelphia. Her spouse owns 3% of ABC Company's common stock. Stock was also placed in the name of their two minor children, each owning 1% of ABC Company's common stock. X has beneficial ownership of 11% of the equity securities of ABC Company so she is an insider for the 1934 Act. Note that her husband also qualifies as an insider.

EXAMPLE: Use the same facts as in the previous example except that all four individuals owned debentures of ABC Company. Since these are not equity securities, none qualifies as an insider.

EXAMPLE: L is an officer who owns 4% of the common stock of XYZ Company in Washington, DC. Since L is an officer, s/he is an insider even though the ownership level is below 10%.

e. Underwriter—any person who has purchased from issuer with a view to the public distribution of any security or participates in such undertaking

(1) Includes any person who offers or sells for issuer in connection with the distribution of any security

(2) Does not include person who sells or distributes on commission for underwriter (i.e., dealers)

f. Sales of securities are covered by these laws

(1) Issuance of securities as part of business reorganization (e.g., merger or consolidation) constitutes a sale and must be registered with SEC unless the issue otherwise qualifies as an exemption from the registration requirements of 1933 Act

(2) Issuance of stock warrants is considered a sale so that requirements of 1933 Act must be met

       (3) Employee stock purchase plan is a sale and therefore must comply with the provisions of the 1933 Act

          (a) Company must also supply a prospectus to each employee to whom stock is offered

       (4) Stock dividends or splits are not sales

   g. Registration statement—the statement required to be filed with SEC before initial sale of securities in interstate commerce

       (1) Includes financial statements and all other relevant information about the registrant's property, business, directors, principal officers, together with prospectus

       (2) Also, includes any amendment, report, or document filed as part of the statement or incorporated therein by reference

       (3) It is against law to sell, offer to sell, or offer to purchase securities before filing registration statement

       (4) Registration statement and prospectus become public upon filing

          (a) Effective date of registration statement is 20th day after filing

          (b) Against law to sell securities until effective date but issuer may **offer** securities upon filing registration statement.

          (c) Such offers may be made

             1] Orally

             2] By tombstone ads that identify security, its price, and who will take orders

             3] By a "red-herring prospectus"

                a] Legend in red ink (thus, red-herring) is printed on this preliminary prospectus indicating that the prospectus is "preliminary" and that a registration statement has been filed but has not become effective.

   h. Prospectus—any notice, circular, advertisement, letter, or communication offering any security for sale (or merger)

       (1) May be a written, radio, or television communication

          (a) SEC adopted new "plain English" rule for important sections of companies' prospectuses, including risk factor sections

       (2) After the effective date of registration statement, communication (written or oral) will not be considered a prospectus if

          (a) Prior to or at same time, a written prospectus was also sent, or

          (b) If it only states from whom written prospectus is available, identifies security, states price, and who will execute orders for it (i.e., tombstone ad)

3. Registration requirements

   a. Registration is required under the Act if

       (1) The securities are to be offered, sold, or delivered in interstate commerce or through the mail

          (a) Interstate commerce means trade, commerce, transportation, or communication (e.g., telephone call) among more than one state or territory of US

             1] Interpreted very broadly to include trade, commerce, etc. that is within one state but affects interstate commerce

              EXAMPLE: A corporation issues securities to individuals living only in Philadelphia. It is further shown that this issuance affects trade in Delaware. Interstate commerce is affected because although Philadelphia is of course in one state, the effects on at least one other state allow the Federal Securities Acts to take effect under our Constitution. Therefore, registration of these securities is required under the Federal Law unless exemptions are found as discussed later.

       (2) Unless it is an exempted security or exempted transaction as discussed later

   b. Issuer has primary duty of registration

(1) Any person who sells unregistered securities that should have been registered may be liable to a purchaser (unless transaction or security is exempt)

(2) Liability cannot be disclaimed in writing or orally by issuer

c. Information required, in general, in registration statements

(1) Financial statements audited by independent CPA

(2) Names of issuer, directors, officers, general partners, underwriters, large stockholders, counsel, etc.

(3) Risks associated with the securities

(4) Description of property, business, and capitalization of issuer

(5) Information about management of issuer

(6) Description of security to be sold and use to be made by issuer of proceeds

d. Prospectus is also filed as part of registration statement

(1) Generally must contain same information as registration statement, but it may be condensed or summarized

e. Registration statement and prospectus are examined by SEC

(1) Amendments are almost always required by SEC

(2) SEC may issue stop-order suspending effectiveness of registration if statement appears incomplete or misleading

(3) Otherwise registration becomes effective on 20th day after filing (or on 20th day after filing amendment)

(a) Twenty-day period is called the waiting period

(4) It is unlawful for company to sell the securities prior to approval (effective registration date)

(a) However, preliminary prospectuses are permitted once registration statement is filed

f. Applies to both corporate and noncorporate issuers

g. Registration covers a single distribution, so second distribution must also be registered

h. Shelf registration is exception to requirement that each new distribution of nonexempt securities requires a new filing

(1) Allows certain qualified issuers to register securities once and then offer and sell them on a delayed or continuous basis "off the shelf"

(2) Advantage is that issuer can respond better to changing market conditions affecting stock

i. Different registration forms are available

(1) Form S-1

(a) This is basic long-form registration statement

(2) Forms S-2 and S-3

(a) These forms adopted by SEC to ease much of burden of disclosures required under federal securities regulation

(b) Require less detailed disclosures than Form S-1

(c) Integrate information required under 1933 and 1934 Acts

1] Firms already on file with SEC under 1934 Act may incorporate much information by reference to avoid additional disclosure

(3) Forms SB-1 and SB-2

(a) These forms permitted for small businesses under Regulation S-B

1] Reduce amount of financial and nonfinancial information required when registering under 1933 Act and when reporting quarterly information under 1934 Act

2] Small business issuer is generally one that has revenues less than $25 million

4. Exempt securities (need not be registered but still subject to antifraud provisions under the Act)

a. Commercial paper (e.g., note, draft, check, etc.) with a maturity of nine months or less

   (1) Must be for commercial purpose and not investment

   > *EXAMPLE: OK Corporation in Washington, DC wishes to finance a short-term need for more cash for current operations. OK will do this by issuing some short-term notes which all have a maturity of nine months or less. These are exempt from the registration requirements.*

b. Intrastate issues—securities offered and sold only within one state

   (1) Issuer must be resident of state and doing 80% of business in the state and must use at least 80% of sale proceeds in connection with business operations in the state
   (2) All offerees and purchasers must be residents of state
   (3) For nine months after last sale by issuer, resales can only be made to residents of state
   (4) All of particular issue must qualify under this rule or this exemption cannot be used for any sale of the issue

   > *EXAMPLE: A regional corporation in need of additional capital makes an offer to the residents of the state in which it is incorporated to purchase a new issue of its stock. The offer expressly restricts sales to only residents of the state and all purchasers are residents of the state.*

c. Small issues (Regulation A)—issuances up to $5,000,000 by issuer in twelve-month period may be exempt if

   (1) There is a notice filed with SEC
   (2) An offering circular (containing financial information about the corporation and descriptive information about offered securities) must be provided to offeree. Financial statements in offering circular need not be audited.
   (3) Note that an offering circular (statement) is required under Regulation A instead of the more costly and time-consuming prospectus
   (4) Nonissuers can sell up to $1,500,000 in twelve-month period

d. Securities of governments, banks, quasi governmental authorities (e.g., local hospital authorities), savings and loan associations, farmers, co-ops, and common carriers regulated by ICC

   (1) Public utilities are not exempt

e. Security exchanged by issuer exclusively with its existing shareholders so long as

   (1) No commission is paid
   (2) Both sets of securities must have been issued by the same person

   > *EXAMPLE: A stock split is an exempt transaction under the 1933 Act and thus, the securities need not be registered at time of split.*

f. Securities of nonprofit religious, educational, or charitable organizations
g. Certificates issued by receiver or trustee in bankruptcy
h. Insurance and annuity contracts

5. Exempt transactions or offerings (still subject, however, to antifraud provisions of the Act; may also be subject to reporting requirements of the 1934 Act)

   a. Sale or offer to sell by any person **other than** an issuer, underwriter, or dealer

      (1) Generally covers sales by individual investors on their own account
      (2) May be transaction by broker on customer's order

         (a) Does not include solicitation of these orders

      (3) Exemption does not apply to sales by controlling persons because considered an underwriter or issuer

   b. **Regulation D** establishes three important exemptions in Rules 504, 505, and 506 under the 1933 Act

      (1) Rule 504 exempts an issuance of securities up to $1,000,000 sold in twelve-month period to any number of investors (this is also known as seed capital exemption)

         (a) General offering and solicitations are permitted under Rule 504

(b) Issuer need not restrict purchasers' right to resell securities
(c) No specific disclosure is required
(d) Must send notice of offering to SEC within fifteen days of first sale of securities

(2) Rule 505 exempts issuance of up to $5,000,000 in twelve-month period

    (a) No general offering or solicitation is permitted within twelve-month period
    (b) Permits sales to thirty-five unaccredited (nonaccredited term sometimes used) investors and to unlimited number of accredited investors within twelve months

        1] Accredited investors are, for example, banks, savings and loan associations, credit unions, insurance companies, broker dealers, certain trusts, partnerships and corporations, also natural persons having joint or individual net worth exceeding $1,000,000 or having joint or individual net income of $200,000 for two most recent years
        2] SEC must be notified within fifteen days of first sale

    (c) The issuer must restrict the purchasers' right to resell the securities; in general must be held for two years or else exemption is lost
    (d) These securities typically state that they have not been registered and that they have resale restrictions
    (e) Unlike under Rule 504, if nonaccredited investor purchases these securities, audited balance sheet must be supplied (i.e., disclosure is required) as well as other financial statements or information, if readily available

        1] If purchased only by accredited investors, no disclosure required

(3) Rule 506 allows private placement of unlimited amount of securities

    (a) In general, same rules apply here as outlined under Rule 505
    (b) However, an additional requirement is that the unaccredited investors (up to thirty-five) must be sophisticated investors (individuals with knowledge and experience in financial matters) or be represented by individual with such knowledge and experience

    EXAMPLE: A growing corporation is in need of additional capital and decides to make a new issuance of its stock. The stock is only offered to ten of the president's friends who regularly make financial investments of this sort. They are interested in purchasing the stock for an investment and each of them is provided with the type of information that is regularly included in a registration statement.

(4) Disclosures for offerings under $2,000,000 have been simplified to be similar to disclosures under Regulation A
(5) A controlling person who sells restricted securities may be held to be an underwriter (and thus subject to the registration provisions) unless requirements of Rule 144 are met when controlling person is selling through a broker

    (a) If the following are met, the security can be sold without registration

        1] Broker performs no services beyond those of typical broker who executes orders and receives customary fee
        2] Ownership (including beneficial ownership) for at least two years
        3] Only limited amounts of stock may be sold—based on a specified formula
        4] Public must have available adequate disclosure of issuer corporation
        5] Notice of sale must be filed with SEC

c. Postregistration transactions by dealer (i.e., dealer is not required to deliver prospectus)

(1) If transaction is made at least forty days after first date security was offered to public, or
(2) After ninety days if it is issuer's first public issue
(3) Does not apply to sales of securities that are leftover part of an allotment from the public issue

6. Antifraud provisions

a. Apply even if securities are exempt or the transactions are exempt as long as interstate commerce is used (use of mail or telephone qualifies) to sell or offer to sell securities
b. Included are schemes to defraud purchaser or making sale by use of untrue statement of material fact or by omission of material fact

(1) Proof of negligence is sometimes sufficient rather than proof of scienter

(2) Protects purchaser, not seller

7. Civil liability (i.e., private actions brought by purchasers of securities)

   a. Purchaser may recover if can establish that

      (1) Was a purchase of a security issued under a registration statement containing a misleading statement or omission of a material fact, and

        (a) May also recover if issuer or any person sold unregistered securities for which there is no exemption

      (2) Suffered economic loss

      (3) Privity of contract is **not** necessary

        EXAMPLE: *Third parties who have never dealt with issuer but bought securities from another party have a right to recover when the above is established despite lack of privity.*

      (4) Need **not** prove that defendant intended to deceive

      (5) Purchaser need **not** rely on registration statement to recover

   b. Purchaser of securities may recover from

      (1) The issuer

      (2) Any directors, partners, or underwriters of issuer

      (3) Anyone who signed registration statement

      (4) Experts of authorized statements (e.g., attorneys, accountants, engineers, appraisers)

   c. Burden of proof is shifted to defendant in most cases; however, except for the issuer, defendant may use "due diligence" defense

      (1) Due diligence defense can be used successfully by defendant by proving that

        (a) As an expert, s/he had reasonable grounds after reasonable investigation to believe that his/her own statements were true and/or did not contain any omissions of material facts by the time the registration statement became effective

          EXAMPLE: *Whitewood, a CPA, performs a reasonable audit and discovers no irregularities.*

        (b) S/he relied on an expert for the part of the registration statement in question and did believe (and had reasonable grounds for such belief) that there were no misstatements or material omissions of fact

          EXAMPLE: *Greenwood, a CPA, relies on an attorney's work as a foundation for his own work on contingent liabilities.*

        (c) S/he did reasonably believe that after a reasonable investigation, statements not in the province of an expert were true or that material omissions did not exist

          EXAMPLE: *Lucky, an underwriter, made a reasonable investigation on the registration statement and did reasonably believe no impropriety existed even though misstatements and omissions of material facts existed. Note that the issuer is liable even if s/he exercised the same care and held the same reasonable belief because the issuer is liable without fault and cannot use the due diligence defense.*

   d. Seller of security is liable to purchaser

      (1) If interstate commerce or mail is used, and

      (2) If registration is not in effect and should be, or

      (3) If registration statement contains misstatements or omissions of material facts

      (4) For amount paid plus interest less any income received by purchaser

      (5) Even if seller no longer owns any of the securities

      (6) Buyer may ask for rescission instead of damages

   e. Statute of limitations is

      (1) Two years after discovery is made or after discovery should have reasonably been made of fraud

      (2) In any event no longer than five years after offering of securities

8. Criminal liability

    a. If person intentionally (willfully) makes an untrue statement or intentionally omits a material fact, or willfully violates SEC Act or regulation

        (1) Reckless disregard of the truth may also qualify
        (2) Tampering with documents to be used in official proceedings do qualify

    b. If person uses interstate commerce or mail to fraudulently sell any security
    c. Person is subject to fine or imprisonment up to twenty years or both

        (1) Injunctions are also available

    d. Criminal liability available even if securities are exempt or transactions are exempt

        (1) For example, criminal sanctions available if fraudulent means used to sell securities even though exemption available

9. Increased protection for whistleblowers of public companies

B. Securities Exchange Act of 1934 (Generally applies to subsequent trading of securities—must comply separately with 1933 Act if applicable, that is, initial issuances rather than subsequent trading)

1. Purposes of the Act

    a. To federally regulate securities exchanges and securities traded thereon
    b. To require periodic disclosure by issuers of equity securities
    c. To require adequate information be provided in various transactions
    d. To prevent unfair use of information by insiders
    e. To prevent fraud and deceptive practices

2. Following securities must be registered with SEC

    a. Over-the-counter and other equity securities traded in interstate commerce where corporation has assets of more than $10 million and 500 or more shareholders

        (1) Equity securities—stock, rights to subscribe to, or securities convertible into stock (not ordinary bonds)

    b. Securities that are traded on any national securities exchange must be registered

        (1) Securities exempted under 1933 Act may still be regulated under 1934 Act

    c. Securities offered by issuer who was required to register under 1933 Act

3. Required disclosures in registration include

    a. Names of officers and directors
    b. Nature of business
    c. Financial structure of firm
    d. Any bonus and profit-sharing provisions

4. Sanctions available to SEC under the 1934 Act

    a. Revocation or suspension of registration
    b. Denial of registration
    c. Permanent or temporary suspension of trading of securities (injunction)
    d. May order accounting and disgorgement of gains made illegally
    e. May sanction individuals violating foreign laws
    f. May require large traders to identify selves

5. Exempt securities

    a. Obligations of US government, guaranteed by, or in which US government has interest
    b. Obligations of state or political subdivision, or guaranteed thereby
    c. Securities of federally chartered bank or savings and loan institution
    d. Securities of common carrier regulated by ICC
    e. Industrial development bonds

6. Issuers of securities registered under the 1934 Act must file the following reports with SEC

   a. Annual reports (Form 10-K) must be certified by independent public accountant

   b. Quarterly reports (Form 10-Q) must be filed for each of first three fiscal quarters of each fiscal year of issuer

      (1) Not required to be certified by CPA

   c. Monthly reports (Form 8-K) when material events occur such as change in corporate control, significant change or revaluation of assets, or change in amount of issued securities

      (1) Filed within fifteen days after material event occurs

   d. Similar reports must be given to shareholders

      (1) However, annual report need not be given if issuer had to disclose under 1934 Act only because it made a registered offering under 1933 Act

7. Whether registered under 1934 Act or not, securities registered during previous year under 1933 Act must have periodic reports filed with SEC by issuers

8. Proxy solicitations

   a. Proxy—grant of authority by shareholder to someone else to vote his/her shares at meeting

   b. Proxy solicitation provisions apply to solicitation (by any means of interstate commerce or the mails) of holders of securities required to be registered under the 1934 Act—must be reported to SEC

   c. Proxy statement must be sent with proxy solicitation

      (1) Must contain disclosure of all material facts concerning matters to be voted upon

         (a) Either misstatements or omissions of material facts are violations of proxy rules

         (b) Material means that it would likely affect vote of average shareholder on proposed action

      (2) Purpose is for fairness in corporate action and election of directors

   d. Requirements of proxy itself

      (1) Shall indicate on whose behalf solicitation is made

      (2) Identify clearly and impartially each matter to be acted on

   e. Some of inclusions in proxy material

      (1) Proposals by shareholders that are a proper subject for shareholders to vote on

      (2) Financial statements for last two years, certified by independent accountant, if

         (a) Solicitation is on behalf of management, and

         (b) It is for annual meeting at which directors are to be elected

   f. Any person who owns at least 5% or has held stock for six months or more has right of access to lists of shareholders for lawful purpose

   g. The proxy statement, proxy itself, and any other soliciting material must be filed with SEC

   h. Brokers are required to forward proxies for customers' shares held by broker

   i. Incumbent management is required to mail proxy materials of insurgents to shareholders if requested and expenses are paid by the insurgents

   j. Remedies for violation of proxy solicitation rules

      (1) Civil action by aggrieved shareholder for damages caused by material misinformation or omissions of material facts

      (2) Or injunctions possible

      (3) Or court may set aside vote taken and require a new proxy solicitation with full and fair disclosure

9. Tender offers

   a. Tender offer is invitation by buyer (bidder) to shareholders of targeted company to tender shares they own for sale for price specified over a period of time

   b. Reporting and disclosure requirements apply to tender offers to provide shareholders full disclosure by both the bidder and targeted company

10. Short-swing profits

   a. Corporation is entitled to recover profits from any insider who sells stock of company within six months of its purchase

   b. Profits that can be recovered are calculated by matching highest sale price with lowest purchase price found within six months

   c. Losses cannot be used to offset these profits

11. Antifraud provisions—very broad scope

   a. Unlawful to manipulate process and create appearance of active trading (not good-faith transactions by brokers)

   b. Unlawful to use any manipulative or deceptive devices in purchase or sale of securities

     (1) Applies to all securities, whether registered or not (as long as either mail, interstate commerce, or a national stock exchange is used)—this is important

     (2) Includes any act, practice, or scheme which is deceptive or manipulative (against SEC rules and/or regulations)—most importantly, it is unlawful to make any false statement of a material fact or any omission of a material fact that is necessary to make statement(s) not misleading (in connection with purchase or sale of security, whether registered or not)

       (a) This is Rule 10b-5 promulgated by the SEC under Section 10(b) of the Act

         1] There are no exemptions under Rule 10b-5

     (3) Plaintiff must prove

       (a) Defendant made material false statement or omission of material fact in connection with purchase or sale of securities

         1] The basic test of materiality is whether a reasonable person would attach importance to the fact in determining his/her choice of action in the transaction

            EXAMPLE: A broker offers to sell a stock and omits to tell the purchaser that the corporation is about to make an unfavorable merger.

       (b) Defendant acted with scienter which is either

         1] Knowledge of falsity, or

         2] Reckless disregard for the truth

         3] Note that negligence is not sufficient

         4] Note that with antifraud provisions under the **1933** Act scienter need not necessarily be proven

       (c) Defendant must have relied upon false statements or omissions

       (d) Defendant who suffers damages may

         1] Sue for monetary damages, or

         2] Rescind transaction

     (4) Applies to brokers who intend to never deliver securities or who intend to misappropriate proceeds of sales

       (a) SEC by US Supreme Court ruling has power to sue brokers for fraud

     (5) Applies to any seller, buyer, or person who lends his/her name to statements used in the buying and selling of securities. Cross reference this to the 1933 Act that only applies to sellers or offerors of securities

     (6) Applies to insider who buys or sells on inside information until it is disseminated to public

     (7) Even if exempt from registration under 1934 Act, still subject to antifraud provisions

     (8) SEC urges affirmative disclosure of material information affecting issuer and securities

       (a) No statutory duty to do so

      (b) Must forego trading if one has such knowledge until public has information

          1] Includes insiders and anyone with knowledge (e.g., accountant, attorney, engineer)

          2] May not tip information to others, nor may tipees trade the securities

12. Civil liability

    a. Any person who intentionally (willfully) manipulates a security may be liable to the buyer or seller of that security if the buyer or seller is damaged

      (1) Note that both buyers and sellers may recover under the 1934 Act

    b. Any person who makes a misleading (or of course false) statement about any material fact in any application, report, or document is liable to an injured purchaser or seller if s/he

      (1) Relied on the statement, and

      (2) Did not know it was false or misleading

      (3) Privity of contract is not necessary

      (4) However, the party sued can avoid liability if s/he can prove s/he

          (a) Acted in good faith, and

          (b) Had no knowledge that the statement(s) was (were) materially misleading or false

13. Criminal liability

    a. Available for intentional violation of the Act, regulations, or rules

    b. Also available for intentional false or misleading statements on material facts in applications, reports, or documents under the Act

14. Reporting requirements of insiders under 1934 Act

    a. Must file statement with SEC

      (1) Discloses amount of equity securities

      (2) Time of statement disclosure

          (a) When securities registered, or

          (b) When registration statement becomes effective, or

          (c) Within ten days of person attaining insider status

      (3) Insider must report any changes in ownership within ten days

15. Foreign Corrupt Practices Act

    a. Unlawful for any domestic company or its officers or employees or agents to offer or give to foreign officials or to political party or political officials something of value to influence decisions

      (1) Excluded are routine governmental actions that do not involve official's discretion such as processing applications or permits

      (2) Amendment includes attempt by supplier to obtain any improper advantage is unlawful

    b. Requires companies having registered securities to maintain system of internal control and to maintain accurate accounting and to protect integrity of independent audits

    c. Actions of foreign citizens or organizations committed within US also covered

16. Regulation Fair Disclosure (Reg FD) from SEC requires corporation to disseminate its data equally among investors and analysts to help avoid conflicts of interest by analysts

    a. If one mistakenly gives out inside information s/he must disclose it publicly as soon as is practicable and always within 24 hours or less

    b. It now applies also to giving nonpublic information to shareholders who are likely to trade based upon it

C. Sarbanes-Oxley Act of 2002

1. New federal law that contains many reforms that affect both this Module and Module 17

    a. Act also directs SEC to conduct several studies and to promulgate regulations for corporations, accounting profession, other professions, directors, officers that are expected to affect issues for CPA exam

       (1) New laws and new regulations are expected from this for at least the next three to five years—new information will be available when it is relevant for your preparation for CPA exam

2. Act covers all public companies
3. Section 906 certification provision of Act requires that each periodic report that contains financial reports of the issuer must be accompanied with written statement of CEO or CFO that certifies that reports comply fully with relevant securities laws and also fairly present the financial condition of company in all material aspects

    a. Any officer who makes certification while knowing it does not comply with SEC requirements can be fined up to $1,000,000 or imprisoned for up to ten years, or both

       (1) Officers can be fined for up to $5,000,000 or imprisoned for up to twenty years, or both, for willful violation of this certification requirement

4. Section 302 certification makes officers responsible for maintaining effective internal controls and requires signing officers to disclose all significant internal control deficiencies to issuer's auditors and audit committee

    a. Also, requires that they report any fraud (whether material or not) involving management or employees with role in internal controls

5. Act amends Securities Exchange Act of 1934 to make it illegal for issuer to give various types of personal loans to or for any executive officer or director
6. When issuer is required to disclose an accounting restatement under securities laws and when misconduct was present, CEO and CFO must reimburse issuer for any bonus received generally for previous twelve months as well as profits from sale of issuer's securities during previous twelve-month period
7. The following provisions take effect 180 days after July 30, 2002, which is the date of the Act

    a. Attorneys required to report to chief legal counsel or CEO such things as material violations of securities laws or breach of fiduciary duties

       (1) Attorneys must report this to audit committee (or another committee) of board of directors if counsel or CEO does not take action

    b. Companies must disclose material off-balance-sheet liabilities and transactions
    c. Pro forma information disclosed to public in financial reports, press releases, etc., must not contain any untrue statement of a material fact or omit any material fact

       (1) Pro forma information must also be reconciled with financial statements prepared in accordance with GAAP

D. Internet Securities Offering (ISO) (Direct Public Offerings [DPO])

1. ISO used primarily by small businesses to accumulate capital
2. SEC created electronic database of corporate information

    a. Allows access to much data formerly available only to big institutions

       (1) Thus tends to level playing field between small investors and large investors
       (2) Also, tends to level playing field between small and large businesses

    b. Allows electronic filing
    c. Companies may market securities faster and more cheaply by circumventing paperwork of investment bankers
    d. These securities are typically riskier because often avoid screening processes of various professionals

3. In general, securities laws and regulations apply to ISO
4. Prospectuses may be placed on-line

5. Secondary market for securities may also be accomplished on websites

E. Electronic Signatures and Electronic Records

1. Federal law specifies that no agreement, record, or signature required by federal securities laws or state laws can be denied legal effect because it is electronic record or contains electronic signature

   a. Also applies to electronic signatures between investment advisors, brokers, dealers, and customers
   b. SEC may specify manner of file retention but may not discriminate against any specific technology in effort to promote advances in technology

F. State "Blue-Sky" Laws

1. These are state statutes regulating the issuance and sale of securities

   a. They contain antifraud and registration provisions

2. Must be complied with **in addition** to federal laws
3. Exemptions from federal laws are not exemptions from state laws

MULTIPLE-CHOICE QUESTIONS (1-42)

1. A preliminary prospectus, permitted under SEC Regulations, is known as the
  a. Unaudited prospectus.
  b. Qualified prospectus.
  c. "Blue-sky" prospectus.
  d. "Red-herring" prospectus.

2. Under the Securities Exchange Act of 1934, which of the following types of instruments is excluded from the definition of "securities"?
  a. Investment contracts.
  b. Convertible debentures.
  c. Nonconvertible debentures.
  d. Certificates of deposit.

3. A tombstone advertisement
  a. May be substituted for the prospectus under certain circumstances.
  b. May contain an offer to sell securities.
  c. Notifies prospective investors that a previously-offered security has been withdrawn from the market and is therefore effectively "dead."
  d. Makes known the availability of a prospectus.

4. Under the Securities Act of 1933, which of the following statements most accurately reflects how securities registration affects an investor?
  a. The investor is provided with information on the stockholders of the offering corporation.
  b. The investor is provided with information on the principal purposes for which the offering's proceeds will be used.
  c. The investor is guaranteed by the SEC that the facts contained in the registration statement are accurate.
  d. The investor is assured by the SEC against loss resulting from purchasing the security.

5. Which of the following statements concerning the prospectus required by the Securities Act of 1933 is correct?
  a. The prospectus is a part of the registration statement.
  b. The prospectus should enable the SEC to pass on the merits of the securities.
  c. The prospectus must be filed after an offer to sell.
  d. The prospectus is prohibited from being distributed to the public until the SEC approves the accuracy of the facts embodied therein.

Items 6 and 7 are based on the following facts:

Sandy Corporation is considering the following issuances:

  I. Notes with maturities of three months to be used for commercial purposes and having a total aggregate value of $500,000.
  II. Notes with maturities of two years to be used for investment purposes and having a total aggregate value of $300,000.
  III. Notes with maturities of two years to be used for commercial purposes and having a total aggregate value of $200,000.

6. Which of the above notes is(are) exempt securities and need not be registered under the Securities Act of 1933?

  a. I only.
  b. II only.
  c. I and III only.
  d. I, II, and III.

7. Which of the above notes is(are) subject to the antifraud provisions of the Securities Act of 1933?
  a. I only.
  b. II only.
  c. I and III only.
  d. I, II, and III.

8. Which of the following is **not** a security under the definition for the Securities Act of 1933?
  a. Any note.
  b. Bond certificate of interest.
  c. Debenture.
  d. All of the above are securities under the Act.

9. Which of the following requirements must be met by an issuer of securities who wants to make an offering by using shelf registration?

	Original registration statement must be kept updated	*The offer must be a first-time issuer of securities*
a.	Yes	Yes
b.	Yes	No
c.	No	Yes
d.	No	No

10. Which of the following securities would be regulated by the provisions of the Securities Act of 1933?
  a. Securities issued by not-for-profit, charitable organizations.
  b. Securities guaranteed by domestic governmental organizations.
  c. Securities issued by savings and loan associations.
  d. Securities issued by insurance companies.

11. Which of the following securities is exempt from registration under the Securities Act of 1933?
  a. Shares of nonvoting common stock, provided their par value is less than $1.00.
  b. A class of stock given in exchange for another class by the issuer to its existing stockholders without the issuer paying a commission.
  c. Limited partnership interests sold for the purpose of acquiring funds to invest in bonds issued by the United States.
  d. Corporate debentures that were previously subject to an effective registration statement, provided they are convertible into shares of common stock.

12. Universal Corp. intends to sell its common stock to the public in an interstate offering that will be registered under the Securities Act of 1933. Under the Act,
  a. Universal can make offers to sell its stock before filing a registration statement, provided that it does **not** actually issue stock certificates until after the registration is effective.
  b. Universal's registration statement becomes effective at the time it is filed, assuming the SEC does **not** object within twenty days thereafter.
  c. A prospectus must be delivered to each purchaser of Universal's common stock unless the purchaser qualifies as an accredited investor.

d. Universal's filing of a registration statement with the SEC does **not** automatically result in compliance with the "blue-sky" laws of the states in which the offering will be made.

13. If securities are exempt from the registration provisions of the Securities Act of 1933, any fraud committed in the course of selling such securities can be challenged by

	SEC	Person defrauded
a.	Yes	Yes
b.	Yes	No
c.	No	Yes
d.	No	No

14. Issuers of securities are normally required under the Securities Act of 1933 to file a registration statement with the Securities Exchange Commission before these securities are either offered or sold to the general public. Which of the following is a reason why the SEC adopted the registration statement forms called Form S-2 and Form S-3?
a. To require more extensive reporting.
b. To be filed along with Form S-1.
c. To reduce the burden that issuers have under the securities laws.
d. To reduce the burden of disclosure that issuers have for intrastate issues of securities.

15. Regulation D provides for important exemptions to registration of securities under the Securities Act of 1933. Which of the following would be exempt?

I. Issuance of $500,000 of securities sold in a twelve-month period to forty investors.
II. Issuance of $2,000,000 of securities sold in a twelve-month period to ten investors. The issuer restricts the right of the purchasers to resell for two years.

a. I only.
b. II only.
c. Both I and II.
d. Neither I nor II.

16. Pix Corp. is making a $6,000,000 stock offering. Pix wants the offering exempt from registration under the Securities Act of 1933. Which of the following provisions of the Act would Pix have to comply with for the offering to be exempt?
a. Regulation A.
b. Regulation D, Rule 504.
c. Regulation D, Rule 505.
d. Regulation D, Rule 506.

17. Eldridge Corporation is seeking to offer $7,000,000 of securities under Regulation D of the Securities Act of 1933. Which of the following is(are) true if Eldridge wants an exemption from registration under the Securities Act of 1933?

I. Eldridge must comply with Rule 506 of Regulation D.
II. These securities could be debentures.
III. These securities could be investment contracts.

a. I only.
b. I and II only.
c. II and III only.
d. I, II, and III.

18. An offering made under the provisions of Regulation A of the Securities Act of 1933 requires that the issuer
a. File an offering circular with the SEC.
b. Sell only to accredited investors.
c. Provide investors with the prior four years' audited financial statements.
d. Provide investors with a proxy registration statement.

19. Which of the following facts will result in an offering of securities being exempt from registration under the Securities Act of 1933?
a. The securities are nonvoting preferred stock.
b. The issuing corporation was closely held prior to the offering.
c. The sale or offer to sell the securities is made by a person other than an issuer, underwriter, or dealer.
d. The securities are AAA-rated debentures that are collateralized by first mortgages on property that has a market value of 200% of the offering price.

20. Regulation D of the Securities Act of 1933
a. Restricts the number of purchasers of an offering to thirty-five.
b. Permits an exempt offering to be sold to both accredited and nonaccredited investors.
c. Is limited to offers and sales of common stock that do not exceed $1.5 million.
d. Is exclusively available to small business corporations as defined by Regulation D.

21. Frey, Inc. intends to make a $2,000,000 common stock offering under Rule 505 of Regulation D of the Securities Act of 1933. Frey
a. May sell the stock to an unlimited number of investors.
b. May make the offering through a general advertising.
c. Must notify the SEC within fifteen days after the first sale of the offering.
d. Must provide all investors with a prospectus.

22. Under Regulation D of the Securities Act of 1933, which of the following conditions apply to private placement offerings? The securities
a. Cannot be sold for longer than a six-month period.
b. Cannot be the subject of an immediate unregistered reoffering to the public.
c. Must be sold to accredited institutional investors.
d. Must be sold to fewer than twenty nonaccredited investors.

23. Which of the following statements concerning an initial intrastate securities offering made by an issuer residing in and doing business in that state is correct?
a. The offering would be exempt from the registration requirements of the Securities Act of 1933.
b. The offering would be subject to the registration requirements of the Securities Exchange Act of 1934.
c. The offering would be regulated by the SEC.
d. The shares of the offering could **not** be resold to investors outside the state for at least one year.

24. Pix Corp. is making a $6,000,000 stock offering. Pix wants the offering exempt from registration under the

Securities Act of 1933. Which of the following requirements would Pix have to comply with when selling the securities?

    a.   No more than thirty-five investors.
    b.   No more than thirty-five nonaccredited investors.
    c.   Accredited investors only.
    d.   Nonaccredited investors only.

25. Which of the following transactions will be exempt from the full registration requirements of the Securities Act of 1933?

    a.   All intrastate offerings.
    b.   All offerings made under Regulation A.
    c.   Any resale of a security purchased under a Regulation D offering.
    d.   Any stockbroker transaction.

26. Under Rule 504 of Regulation D of the Securities Act of 1933, which of the following is(are) required?

  I. No general offering or solicitation is permitted.
  II. The issuer must restrict the purchasers' right to resell the securities.

    a.   I only.
    b.   II only.
    c.   Both I and II.
    d.   Neither I nor II.

27. Dean, Inc., a publicly traded corporation, paid a $10,000 bribe to a local zoning official. The bribe was recorded in Dean's financial statements as a consulting fee. Dean's unaudited financial statements were submitted to the SEC as part of a quarterly filing. Which of the following federal statutes did Dean violate?

    a.   Federal Trade Commission Act.
    b.   Securities Act of 1933.
    c.   Securities Exchange Act of 1934.
    d.   North American Free Trade Act.

28. The Securities Exchange Commission promulgated Rule 10b-5 under Section 10(b) of the Securities Exchange Act of 1934. Which of the following is(are) purpose(s) of the Act?

	To rate securities so investors can choose more wisely	To encourage disclosure of information relevant to investors	To deter fraud involving securities
a.	No	No	Yes
b.	No	Yes	Yes
c.	Yes	Yes	Yes
d.	Yes	Yes	No

29. Integral Corp. has assets in excess of $4 million, has 350 stockholders, and has issued common and preferred stock. Integral is subject to the reporting provisions of the Securities Exchange Act of 1934. For its 2001 fiscal year, Integral filed the following with the SEC: quarterly reports, an annual report, and a periodic report listing newly appointed officers of the corporation. Integral did not notify the SEC of stockholder "short swing" profits; did not report that a competitor made a tender offer to Integral's stockholders; and did not report changes in the price of its stock as sold on the New York Stock Exchange. Under SEC reporting requirements, which of the following was Integral required to do?

    a.   Report the tender offer to the SEC.
    b.   Notify the SEC of stockholder "short swing" profits.

    c.   File the periodic report listing newly appointed officers.
    d.   Report the changes in the market price of its stock.

30. Which of the following factors, by itself, requires a corporation to comply with the reporting requirements of the Securities Exchange Act of 1934?

    a.   Six hundred employees.
    b.   Shares listed on a national securities exchange.
    c.   Total assets of $2 million.
    d.   Four hundred holders of equity securities.

31. The registration provisions of the Securities Exchange Act of 1934 require disclosure of all of the following information **except** the

    a.   Names of owners of at least 5% of any class of nonexempt equity security.
    b.   Bonus and profit-sharing arrangements.
    c.   Financial structure and nature of the business.
    d.   Names of officers and directors.

32. Under the Securities Act of 1933, which of the following statements is correct concerning a public issuer of securities who has made a registered offering?

    a.   The issuer is required to distribute an annual report to its stockholders.
    b.   The issuer is subject to the proxy rules of the SEC.
    c.   The issuer must file an annual report (Form 10-K) with the SEC.
    d.   The issuer is **not** required to file a quarterly report (Form 10-Q) with the SEC, unless a material event occurs.

33. Which of the following persons is **not** an insider of a corporation subject to the Securities Exchange Act of 1934 registration and reporting requirements?

    a.   An attorney for the corporation.
    b.   An owner of 5% of the corporation's outstanding debentures.
    c.   A member of the board of directors.
    d.   A stockholder who owns 10% of the outstanding common stock.

34. The Securities Exchange Commission promulgated Rule 10b-5 from power it was given the Securities Exchange Act of 1934. Under this rule, it is unlawful for any person to use a scheme to defraud another in connection with the

	Purchase of any security	Sale of any security
a.	Yes	Yes
b.	Yes	No
c.	No	Yes
d.	No	No

35. The antifraud provisions of Rule 10b-5 of the Securities Exchange Act of 1934

    a.   Apply only if the securities involved were registered under either the Securities Act of 1933 or the Securities Exchange Act of 1934.
    b.   Require that the plaintiff show negligence on the part of the defendant in misstating facts.
    c.   Require that the wrongful act must be accomplished through the mail, any other use of interstate commerce, or through a national securities exchange.
    d.   Apply only if the defendant acted with intent to defraud.

Items 36 through 38 are based on the following:

Link Corp. is subject to the reporting provisions of the Securities Exchange Act of 1934.

36. Which of the following situations would require Link to be subject to the reporting provisions of the 1934 Act?

	Shares listed on a national securities exchange	More than one class of stock
a.	Yes	Yes
b.	Yes	No
c.	No	Yes
d.	No	No

37. Which of the following documents must Link file with the SEC?

	Quarterly reports (Form 10-Q)	Proxy Statements
a.	Yes	Yes
b.	Yes	No
c.	No	Yes
d.	No	No

38. Which of the following reports must also be submitted to the SEC?

	Report by any party making a tender offer to purchase Link's stock	Report of proxy solicitations by Link stockholders
a.	Yes	Yes
b.	Yes	No
c.	No	Yes
d.	No	No

39. Which of the following events must be reported to the SEC under the reporting provisions of the Securities Exchange Act of 1934?

	Tender offers	Insider trading	Soliciting proxies
a.	Yes	Yes	Yes
b.	Yes	Yes	No
c.	Yes	No	Yes
d.	No	Yes	Yes

40. Adler, Inc. is a reporting company under the Securities Exchange Act of 1934. The only security it has issued is voting common stock. Which of the following statements is correct?

    a. Because Adler is a reporting company, it is **not** required to file a registration statement under the Securities Act of 1933 for any future offerings of its common stock.

    b. Adler need **not** file its proxy statements with the SEC because it has only one class of stock outstanding.

    c. Any person who owns more than 10% of Adler's common stock must file a report with the SEC.

    d. It is unnecessary for the required annual report (Form 10-K) to include audited financial statements.

41. Which of the following is correct concerning annual reports (Form 10-K) and quarterly reports (Form 10-Q)?

    a. Both Form 10-K and Form 10-Q must be certified by independent public accountants and both must be filed with the SEC.

    b. Both Form 10-K and Form 10-Q must be certified by independent public accountants but neither need be filed with the SEC.

    c. Although both Form 10-K and Form 10-Q must be filed with the SEC, only Form 10-K need be certified by independent public accountants.

    d. Form 10-K must be certified by independent public accountants and must also be filed with the SEC; however, Form 10-Q need not be certified by independent public accountants nor filed with the SEC.

42. Burk Corporation has issued securities that must be registered with the Securities Exchange Commission under the Securities Exchange Act of 1934. A material event took place a week ago, that is, there was a change in the control of Burk Corporation. Which of the following statements is correct?

    a. Because of this material event, Burk Corporation is required to file with the SEC, Forms 10-K and 10-Q.

    b. Because of this material event, Burk Corporation is required to file Form 8-K.

    c. Burk Corporation need not file any forms with the SEC concerning this material event if the relevant facts are fully disclosed in the audited financial statements.

    d. Burk Corporation need not file any form concerning the material event if Burk Corporation has an exemption under Rules 504, 505, or 506 of Regulation D.

OTHER OBJECTIVE QUESTIONS

Problem 1   (15 to 25 minutes)

This question is based on the following information.

Butler Manufacturing Corp. planned to raise capital for a plant expansion by borrowing from banks and making several stock offerings. Butler engaged Weaver, CPA, to audit its December 31, 2001 financial statements. Butler told Weaver that the financial statements would be given to certain named banks and included in the prospectuses for the stock offerings.

In performing the audit, Weaver did not confirm accounts receivable and, as a result, failed to discover a material overstatement of accounts receivable. Also, Weaver was aware of a pending class action product liability lawsuit that was not disclosed in Butler's financial statements. Despite being advised by Butler's legal counsel that Butler's potential liability under the lawsuit would result in material losses, Weaver issued an unqualified opinion on Butler's financial statements.

In May 2002, Union Bank, one of the named banks, relied on the financial statements and Weaver's opinion in giving Butler a $500,000 loan.

Butler raised an additional $16,450,000 through the following stock offerings, which were sold completely:

•   June 2002—Butler made a $450,000 unregistered offering of Class B nonvoting common stock under Rule 504 of Regulation D of the Securities Act of 1933. This offering was sold over one year to thirty nonaccredited investors and twenty accredited investors by general solicitation. The SEC was notified eight days after the first sale of this offering.

•   September 2002—Butler made a $10,000,000 unregistered offering of Class A voting common stock under Rule 506 of Regulation D of the Securities Act of 1933. This offering was sold over one year to 200 accredited investors and thirty nonaccredited investors through a private placement. The SEC was notified fourteen days after the first sale of this offering.

•   November 2002—Butler made a $6,000,000 unregistered offering of preferred stock under Rule 505 of Regulation D of the Securities Act of 1933. This offering was sold during a one-year period to forty nonaccredited investors by private placement. The SEC was notified eighteen days after the first sale of this offering.

Shortly after obtaining the Union loan, Butler began experiencing financial problems but was able to stay in business because of the money raised by the offerings. Butler was found liable in the product liability suit. This resulted in a judgment Butler could not pay. Butler also defaulted on the Union loan and was involuntarily petitioned into bankruptcy. This caused Union to sustain a loss and Butler's stockholders to lose their investments. As a result

- The SEC claimed that all three of Butler's offerings were made improperly and were not exempt from registration.
- Union sued Weaver for

  - Negligence
  - Common Law Fraud

- The stockholders who purchased Butler's stock through the offerings sued Weaver, alleging fraud under Section 10(b) and Rule 10b-5 of the Securities Exchange Act of 1934.

These transactions took place in a jurisdiction providing for accountant's liability for negligence to known and intended users of financial statements.

Required:

    a.   **Items 1 through 5** are questions related to the June 2002 offering made under Rule 504 of Regulation D of the Securities Act of 1933. For each item, indicate your answer by choosing either yes (Y) or no (N).

  1.   Did the offering comply with the dollar limitation of Rule 504?
  2.   Did the offering comply with the method of sale restrictions?
  3.   Was the offering sold during the applicable time limit?
  4.   Was the SEC notified timely of the first sale of the securities?
  5.   Was the SEC correct in claiming that this offering was not exempt from registration?

    b.   **Items 6 through 10** are questions related to the September 2002 offering made under Rule 506 of Regulation D of the Securities Act of 1933. For each item, indicate your answer by choosing either yes (Y) or no (N).

  6.   Did the offering comply with the dollar limitation of Rule 506?
  7.   Did the offering comply with the method of sale restrictions?
  8.   Was the offering sold to the correct number of investors?
  9.   Was the SEC notified timely of the first sale of the securities?
10.   Was the SEC correct in claiming that this offering was not exempt from registration?

    c.   **Items 11 through 15** are questions related to the November 2001 offering made under Rule 505 of Regulation D of the Securities Act of 1933. For each item, indicate your answer by choosing either yes (Y) or no (N).

11.   Did the offering comply with the dollar limitation of Rule 505?
12.   Was the offering sold during the applicable time limit?
13.   Was the offering sold to the correct number of investors?
14.   Was the SEC notified timely of the first sale of the securities?
15.   Was the SEC correct in claiming that this offering was not exempt from registration?

Problem 2   (5 to 10 minutes)

Coffee Corp., a publicly held corporation, wants to make an $8,000,000 exempt offering of its shares as a private placement offering under Regulation D, Rule 506, of the Securities Act of 1933. Coffee has more than 500 shareholders and assets in excess of $1 billion, and has its shares listed on a national securities exchange.

Required:

Items 1 through 5 relate to the application of the provisions of the Securities Act of 1933 and the Securities Exchange Act of 1934 to Coffee Corp. and the offering. For each item, select from List II whether only statement I is correct, whether only statement II is correct, whether both statements I and II are correct, or whether neither statement I nor II is correct.

> *List II*
> A. I only.
> B. II only.
> C. Both I and II.
> D. Neither I nor II.

1. I. Coffee Corp. may make the Regulation D, Rule 506, exempt offering.
   II. Coffee Corp., because it is required to report under the Securities Exchange Act of 1934, may **not** make an exempt offering.

2. I. Shares sold under a Regulation D, Rule 506, exempt offering may only be purchased by accredited investors.
   II. Shares sold under a Regulation D, Rule 506, exempt offering may be purchased by any number of investors provided there are **no** more than thirty-five nonaccredited investors.

3. I. An exempt offering under Regulation D, Rule 506, must **not** be for more than $10,000,000.
   II. An exempt offering under Regulation D, Rule 506, has **no** dollar limit.

4. I. Regulation D, Rule 506, requires that all investors in the exempt offering be notified that for nine months after the last sale **no** resale may be made to a nonresident.
   II. Regulation D, Rule 506, requires that the issuer exercise reasonable care to assure that purchasers of the exempt offering are buying for investment and are **not** underwriters.

5. I. The SEC must be notified by Coffee Corp. within five days of the first sale of the exempt offering securities.
   II. Coffee Corp. must include an SEC notification of the first sale of the exempt offering securities in Coffee's next filed Quarterly Report (Form 10-Q).

PROBLEMS

Problem 1   (15 to 20 minutes)

Various Enterprises Corporation is a medium sized conglomerate listed on the American Stock Exchange. It is constantly in the process of acquiring smaller corporations and is invariably in need of additional money. Among its diversified holdings is a citrus grove which it purchased eight years ago as an investment. The grove's current fair market value is in excess of $2 million. Various also owns 800,000 shares of Resistance Corporation which it acquired in the open market over a period of years. These shares represent a 17% minority interest in Resistance and are worth approximately $2 1/2 million. Various does its short-term financing with a consortium of banking institutions. Several of these loans are maturing; in addition to renewing these loans, it wishes to increase its short-term debt from $3 to $4 million.

In light of the above, Various is considering resorting to one or all of the following alternatives in order to raise additional working capital.

• An offering of 500 citrus grove units at $5,000 per unit. Each unit would give the purchaser a 0.2% ownership interest in the citrus grove development. Various would furnish management and operation services for a fee under a management contract and net proceeds would be paid to the unit purchasers. The offering would be confined almost exclusively to the state in which the groves are located or in the adjacent state in which Various is incorporated.

• An increase in the short-term borrowing by $1 million from the banking institution which currently provides short-term funds. The existing debt would be consolidated, extended, and increased to $4 million and would mature over a nine-month period. This would be evidenced by a short-term note.

• Sale of the 17% minority interest in Resistance Corporation in the open market through its brokers over a period of time and in such a way as to minimize decreasing the value of the stock. The stock is to be sold in an orderly manner in the ordinary course of the broker's business.

Required:

Answer the following, setting forth reasons for any conclusions stated.

In separate paragraphs discuss the impact of the registration requirements of the Securities Act of 1933 on each of the above proposed alternatives.

Problem 2   (15 to 25 minutes)

Perry, a staff accountant with Orlean Associates, CPAs, reviewed the following transactions engaged in by Orlean's two clients: World Corp. and Unity Corp.

WORLD CORP.

During 2001, World Corp. made a $4,000,000 offering of its stock. The offering was sold to fifty nonaccredited investors and 150 accredited investors. There was a general advertising of the offering. All purchasers were provided with material information concerning World Corp. The offering was completely sold by the end of 2001. The SEC was notified thirty days after the first sale of the offering.

World did not register the offering and contends that the offering and any subsequent resale of the securities are completely exempt from registration under Regulation D, Rule 505, of the Securities Act of 1933.

UNITY CORP.

Unity Corp. has 750 equity stockholders and assets in excess of $100,000,000. Unity's stock is traded on a national stock exchange. Unity contends that it is not a covered corporation and is not required to comply with the reporting provisions of the Securities Exchange Act of 1934.

Required:

a. **1.** State whether World is correct in its contention that the offering is exempt from registration under Regulation D, Rule 505, of the Securities Act of 1933. Give the reason(s) for your conclusion.

2. State whether World is correct in its contention that on subsequent resale the securities are completely exempt from registration. Give the reason(s) for your conclusion.

b. **1.** State whether Unity is correct in its contention that it is not a covered corporation and is not required to comply with the reporting requirements of the Securities Exchange Act of 1934 and give the reason(s) for your conclusion.

2. Identify and describe two principal reports a covered corporation must file with the SEC.

MULTIPLE-CHOICE ANSWERS

1. d __ __	10. d __ __	19. c __ __	28. b __ __	37. a __ __
2. d __ __	11. b __ __	20. b __ __	29. c __ __	38. a __ __
3. d __ __	12. d __ __	21. c __ __	30. b __ __	39. a __ __
4. b __ __	13. a __ __	22. b __ __	31. a __ __	40. c __ __
5. a __ __	14. c __ __	23. a __ __	32. c __ __	41. c __ __
6. a __ __	15. c __ __	24. b __ __	33. b __ __	42. b __ __
7. d __ __	16. d __ __	25. b __ __	34. a __ __	
8. d __ __	17. d __ __	26. d __ __	35. c __ __	1st: __/42 = __%
9. b __ __	18. a __ __	27. c __ __	36. b __ __	2nd: __/42 = __%

MULTIPLE-CHOICE ANSWER EXPLANATIONS

A. Securities Act of 1933

1. **(d)** A preliminary prospectus is usually called a "red-herring" prospectus. The preliminary prospectus indicates that a registration statement has been filed but has not become effective.

2. **(d)** Securities include debentures, stocks, bonds, some notes, and investment contracts. The main idea is that the investor intends to make a profit on the investment through the efforts of others. A certificate of deposit is a type of commercial paper, not a security.

3. **(d)** A tombstone advertisement is allowed to inform potential investors that a prospectus for the given company is available. It is not an offer to sell or the solicitation of an offer to buy the securities. Answer (a) is incorrect because the tombstone ad informs potential purchasers of the prospectus and cannot be used as a substitute for the prospectus. Answer (b) is incorrect because it informs of the availability of the prospectus and cannot be construed as an offer to sell securities. Answer (c) is incorrect because the tombstone ad notifies potential purchasers of the prospectus. It does not notify that the securities have been withdrawn from the market.

4. **(b)** The registration of securities under the Securities Act of 1933 has as its purpose to provide potential investors with full and fair disclosure of all material information relating to the issuance of securities, including such information as the principal purposes for which the offering's proceeds will be used. Answer (a) is incorrect because information on the stockholders of the offering corporation is not required to be reported. Answer (c) is incorrect because the SEC does not guarantee the accuracy of the registration statements. Answer (d) is incorrect because although the SEC does seek to compel full and fair disclosure, it does not evaluate the securities on merit or value, or give any assurances against loss.

5. **(a)** If no exemption is applicable under the Securities Act of 1933, public offerings must be registered with the SEC accompanied by a prospectus. Answer (b) is incorrect because the SEC does not pass on nor rate the securities. Answer (c) is incorrect because the prospectus is given to prospective purchasers of the securities. Answer (d) is incorrect because the SEC does not pass on the merits or accuracy of the prospectus.

6. **(a)** Notes are exempt securities under the Securities Act of 1933 if they have a maturity of nine months or less and if they are also used for commercial purposes rather than investments. The actual dollar amounts in the question are not a factor. The notes described in II are not exempt for two reasons; they have a maturity of two years and are used for investment purposes. The notes in III are not exempt because the maturity is two years even though they are for commercial purposes.

7. **(d)** Whether the securities are exempt from registration or not, they are still subject to the antifraud provisions of the Securities Act of 1933.

8. **(d)** The definition of a security is very broad under the Securities Act of 1933. The basic idea is that the investor intends to make a profit through the efforts of others rather than through his/her own efforts. Notes, bond certificates of interest, and debentures are all considered securities.

9. **(b)** If an issuer of securities wants to make an offering by using shelf registration, the actual issuance takes place over potentially a long period of time. Therefore, s/he must keep the original registration statement updated. There is no requirement that the offeror must be a first-time issuer of securities.

10. **(d)** Under the 1933 Act, certain securities are exempt. Although insurance and annuity contracts are exempt, securities issued by the insurance companies are not. Answer (a) is incorrect because securities of nonprofit organizations are exempt. Answer (b) is incorrect because securities issued by or guaranteed by domestic government organizations are exempt. Answer (c) is incorrect because securities issued by savings and loan associations are exempt.

11. **(b)** Securities exchanged for other securities by the issuer exclusively with its existing shareholders are exempt from registration under the 1933 Act as long as no commission is paid and both sets of securities are issued by the same issuer. Answer (a) is incorrect because nonvoting common stock is not exempted under the Act. The amount of the par value is irrelevant. Answer (c) is incorrect because although the securities of governments are themselves exempt, the limited partnership interests are not. Answer (d) is incorrect because no such exemption is allowed.

12. **(d)** Even though the issuer may comply with the Federal Securities Act of 1933, it must also comply with any applicable state "blue-sky" laws that regulate the securities at the state level. Answer (a) is incorrect because it is unlawful for the company to offer or sell the securities prior to the effective registration date. Answer (b) is incorrect because registration becomes effective on the twentieth day after filing unless the SEC issues a stop order. Answer (c) is incorrect because a prospectus is any notice, circular, advertisement, letter, or communication offering the security for sale. No general offering or solicitation is allowed under Rules 505 or 506 of Regulation D whether the purchaser is accredited or not.

13. (a) Even if the securities are exempt under the Securities Act of 1933, they are still subject to the antifraud provisions. Both the person defrauded and the SEC can challenge the fraud committed in the course of selling the securities.

14. (c) The SEC adopted the Forms S-2 and S-3 to decrease the work that issuers have in preparing registration statements by permitting them to give less detailed disclosure under certain conditions than Form S-1 which is the basic long form. Answer (a) is incorrect because these forms decrease, not increase, reporting required. Answer (b) is incorrect because when permitted, these forms are used instead of Form S-1 which is the standard long-form registration statement. Answer (d) is incorrect because the purpose of the forms was not directed at intrastate issues.

A.5.   Exempt Transactions or Offerings

15. (c) The issuance described in I is exempt because Rule 504 exempts an issuance of securities up to $1,000,000 sold in a twelve-month period to any number of investors. The issuer is not required to restrict the purchasers' resale. The issuance described in II is also exempt because Rule 505 exempts an issuance up to $5,000,000 sold in a twelve-month period. It permits sales to thirty-five unaccredited investors and to any number of accredited investors. Since there were only ten investors, this is met. The issuer also restricted the purchasers' right to resell for two years as required.

16. (d) Under Regulation D, Rule 504 exempts an issuance of securities up to $1,000,000 sold in a twelve-month period. Rule 505 exempts an issuance of up to $5,000,000 in a twelve-month period. So Rule 506 has to be resorted to for amounts over $5,000,000. Regulation A can be used only for issuances up to $1,500,000.

17. (d) When more than $5,000,000 in securities are being offered, an exemption from the registration requirements of the Securities Act of 1933 is available under Rule 506 of Regulation D. Securities under the Act include debentures and investment contracts.

18. (a) Under Regulation A of the 1933 Act, the issuer must file an offering circular with the SEC. Answer (b) is incorrect because the rules involving sales to unaccredited and accredited investors are in Regulation D, not Regulation A. Answer (c) is incorrect because although financial information about the corporation must be provided to offerees, the financial statements in the offering circular need not be audited. Answer (d) is incorrect because the issuer is not required to provide investors with a proxy registration statement under Regulation A.

19. (c) Sales or offers to sell by any person **other than** an issuer, underwriter, or dealer are exempt under the 1933 Act. Answer (a) is incorrect because the Act covers all types of securities including preferred stock. Answer (b) is incorrect because closely held corporations are not automatically exempt. Answer (d) is incorrect because debentures, as debt

securities, are covered under the Act even if they are highly rated or backed by collateral.

20. (b) Regulation D of the Securities Act of 1933 establishes three important exemptions in Rules 504, 505, and 506. Although Rules 505 and 506 have some restrictions on sales to nonaccredited investors, all three rules under Regulation D allow sales to both nonaccredited and accredited investors with varying restrictions. Answer (a) is incorrect because although Rules 505 and 506 allow sales to up to thirty-five nonaccredited investors, all three rules allow sales to an unlimited number of accredited investors. Answer (c) is incorrect because Rule 506 has no dollar limitation. Rule 505 has a $5,000,000 limitation in a twelve-month period and Rule 504 has a $1,000,000 limitation in a twelve-month period. Answer (d) is incorrect because Regulation D is not restricted to only small corporations.

21. (c) Under Rule 505 of Regulation D, the issuer must notify the SEC of the offering within fifteen days after the first sale of the securities. Answer (a) is incorrect because under Rule 505, the issuer may sell to an unlimited number of **accredited** investors and to thirty-five unaccredited investors. Answer (b) is incorrect because no general offering or solicitation is permitted. Answer (d) is incorrect because the accredited investors need not receive any formal information. The unaccredited investors, however, must receive a formal registration statement that gives a description of the offering.

22. (b) The private placement exemption permits sales of an unlimited number of securities for any dollar amount when sold to accredited investors. This exemption also allows sales to up to thirty-five nonaccredited investors if they are also sophisticated investors under the Act. Resales of these securities are restricted for two years after the date that the issuer sells the last of the securities. Answer (a) is incorrect because there is no such restriction of sale. Answer (c) is incorrect because sales may be made to an unlimited number of accredited investors and up to thirty-five nonaccredited investors. Answer (d) is incorrect because sales can be made to up to thirty-five nonaccredited investors.

23. (a) When the issuer is a resident of that state, doing 80% of its business in that state, and only sells or offers the securities to residents of the same state, the offering qualifies for an exemption under the 1933 Act as an intrastate issue. Answer (b) is incorrect as the offering also qualifies for an exemption under the 1934 Act. Therefore, as the offering is exempted from both the 1933 and 1934 Acts, it would not be regulated by the SEC. Answer (d) is incorrect because resales can only be made to residents of that state nine months after the issuer's last sale.

24. (b) Rule 506 permits sales to thirty-five unaccredited investors and to an unlimited number of accredited investors. The unaccredited investors must also be sophisticated investors (i.e., individuals with knowledge and experience in financial matters).

25. (b) Under Regulation A, an offering statement is required instead of the more costly disclosure requirements of full registration under the Securities Act of 1933. Answer (a) is incorrect because not all intrastate offerings are exempt. They must meet specified requirements to be exempt. Answer (c) is incorrect because many securities sold under Regulation D cannot be resold for two years. Answer (d) is incorrect because there is no such exemption for stockbroker transactions.

26. **(d)** Under Rule 504 of Regulation D, general offerings and solicitations are permitted. Also, the issuer need not restrict the purchasers' right to resell. Note that both I and II are requirements of Rules 505 and 506 of Regulation D.

B. Securities Exchange Act of 1934

27. **(c)** Under the Securities Exchange Act of 1934, issuers of securities registered under this Act must file quarterly reports (Form 10-Q) for the first three quarters of each fiscal year. The financial data in these may be unaudited; however, material misinformation is a violation of the 1934 Act. Answer (a) is incorrect—the Federal Trade Commission Act does not apply to this action. Answer (b) is incorrect because the Securities Act of 1933 applies to the initial issuance of securities and not to the secondary market of publicly traded securities. Answer (d) is incorrect because NAFTA is an agreement designed to promote free trade between the US, Mexico, and Canada.

28. **(b)** Purposes of Section 10(b) of the Securities Exchange Act of 1934 include deterring fraud in the securities industry and encouraging disclosure of relevant information so investors can make better decisions. The SEC does not rate the securities.

29. **(c)** Under the Securities Exchange Act of 1934, issuers of securities registered under this Act must file annual and quarterly reports with the SEC. The company must also file current reports covering certain material events such as a change in the amount of issued securities, a change in corporate control, or a change in newly appointed officers. Answer (a) is incorrect because a competitor's making a tender offer need not be reported to the SEC. Answer (b) is incorrect because Integral Corp. need not notify the SEC of stockholder "short swing profits." Answer (d) is incorrect because the company need not report information on the market price of its stock to the SEC. This market price information is already public information because the stock is traded on the New York Stock Exchange.

30. **(b)** Securities must be registered with the SEC if they are traded on any national securities exchange. Securities must also be registered if they are traded in interstate commerce where the corporation has more than $10 million in assets **and** 500 or more shareholders.

31. **(a)** The Securities Exchange Act of 1934 has registration provisions that require specified disclosures including bonus and profit-sharing arrangements, the financial structure and nature of this business, and names of officers and directors.

32. **(c)** Under the Federal Securities Act of 1933, which incorporates the filing requirements of the Federal Securities Exchange Act of 1934, the issuer must file with the SEC an annual report on Form 10-K. Answer (a) is incorrect because the issuer must file the annual report with the SEC but is not required to distribute it to its stockholders. Answer (b) is incorrect because the solicitation of proxies triggers certain proxy solicitation rules. Answer (d) is incorrect because it is the current report on Form 8-K that is filed

when material events occur. The Form 10-Q is filed each of the first three quarters of each year and is known as the quarterly report.

33. **(b)** Under the 1934 Act, insiders include officers and directors of the corporation as well as owners of 10% or more of the stock of the corporation. Accountants, attorneys, and consultants can also be insiders subject to further regulation under the 1934 Act. Creditors, that is, owners of debentures are not considered to be insiders.

34. **(a)** Under Rule 10b-5, it is unlawful to use schemes to defraud in connection with the purchase **or** sale of any security. Note that this rule was made from powers given the SEC under the Securities Exchange Act of 1934, which applies to purchases in addition to sales of securities.

35. **(c)** For the Securities Exchange Act of 1934 to apply, including the antifraud provisions of Rule 10b-5, there must be shown a federal constitutional basis such as use of the mail, interstate commerce, or a national securities exchange. Answer (a) is incorrect because the antifraud provisions apply whether or not the securities had to be registered under either the 1933 Act or the 1934 Act. Answer (b) is incorrect because under Rule 10b-5, the plaintiff must prove more than negligence (i.e., either knowledge of falsity or reckless disregard for the truth in misstating facts). Answer (d) is incorrect because the plaintiff could recover if the defendant acted with reckless disregard for the truth.

36. **(b)** If the shares are listed on a national securities exchange, they are subject to the reporting provisions of the 1934 Act. There is no provision concerning a corporation owning more than one class of stock that by itself requires that it be subject to the reporting provisions of the 1934 Act.

37. **(a)** Under the 1934 Act, Link must file with the SEC annual reports (Form 10-K), quarterly reports (form 10-Q), current reports (Form 8-K) of certain material events, and proxy statements when proxy solicitations exist.

38. **(a)** When there is a proxy solicitation, Link must make a report of this to the SEC. Also, reports of tender offers to purchase securities need to be submitted to the SEC.

39. **(a)** A tender offer is a request to the shareholders of a given company to tender their shares for a stated price. If the tender offer was unsolicited, the corporation must report this to the SEC under the reporting provisions of the Securities Exchange Act of 1934. Also, trading by insiders such as officers, directors, or shareholders owning at least 10% of the stock of a corporation registered with the SEC must also be reported to the SEC under the 1934 Act. Likewise, solicitation of proxies must be reported to the SEC.

40. **(c)** Under the Securities Exchange Act of 1934 which applies if interstate commerce or the mail is used, any purchaser of more than 5% of a class of equity securities must file a report with the SEC. Answer (d) is incorrect because the required annual report (Form 10-K) must be certified by independent public accountants. Answer (a) is incorrect because each company must also comply with the filing requirements under the Securities Act of 1933. Answer (b) is incorrect because there is no exemption from filing proxy statements simply because the company has only one class of stock.

41. **(c)** Forms 10-K (annual reports) and 10-Q (quarterly reports) must be filed with the SEC. Forms 10-K containing financial statements must be certified by independent public accountants. However, this is not true of Forms 10-Q which cover the first three fiscal quarters of each fiscal year of the issuer.

42. **(b)** When certain material events take place, such as a change in corporate control, the corporation covered under the 1934 Act must file Form 8-K, a current report, with the SEC within fifteen days after the material event occurs. Answer (a) is incorrect because Burk Corporation must file Forms 10-K, annual reports, and Forms 10-Q, quarterly reports, whether or not a material event has taken place. Answer (c) is incorrect because there is no such exception provided. Answer (d) is incorrect because Rules 504, 505, and 506 under Regulation D apply to the initial issuance of securities under the Securities Act of 1933 and do not relieve Burk Corporation from the filing requirements with the SEC under the 1934 Act.

OTHER OBJECTIVE ANSWERS AND ANSWER EXPLANATIONS

Problem 1

1. **(Y)** Rule 504 exempts an issuance of securities up to $1,000,000 sold in a twelve-month period to any number of investors. Butler made the offering for $450,000.

2. **(Y)** This offering involved a general solicitation which is now allowed under Rule 504.

3. **(Y)** This offering was sold over the applicable twelve-month period in Rule 504.

4. **(Y)** The SEC was sent notice of this offering eight days after the first sale. Under Rule 504, the SEC must be notified within fifteen days of the first sale of the securities.

5. **(N)** Even though this stock was sold by general solicitation, this is allowed under Rule 504.

6. **(Y)** Rule 506 allows private placement of an unlimited dollar amount of securities.

7. **(Y)** These securities were sold through private placement which is appropriate under Rule 506.

8. **(Y)** Rule 506 allows sales to up to thirty-five nonaccredited investors who are sophisticated investors with knowledge and experience in financial matters. It allows sales to an unlimited number of accredited investors.

9. **(Y)** The SEC was notified fourteen days after the first sale of the offering which is within the fifteen-day rule.

10. **(N)** Since this offering met the requirements discussed in 6. through 9. above, the SEC was incorrect.

11. **(N)** Rule 505 exempts an issuance of securities up to $5,000,000. Butler made a $6,000,000 unregistered offering of preferred stock.

12. **(Y)** The offering was sold during the applicable twelve-month period.

13. **(N)** Rule 505 permits sales to thirty-five nonaccredited investors. Butler went over this limit by selling to forty nonaccredited investors.

14. **(N)** The SEC was notified eighteen days after the first sale of this offering which is over the fifteen-day requirement.

15. **(Y)** This offering was not exempt from registration because it went over the $5,000,000 limit and the stock was sold to more than thirty-five nonaccredited investors.

Problem 2

1. **(A)** Statement I is correct because under Regulation D, Rule 506, the corporation may make a private placement of an unlimited amount of securities if it meets certain requirements. Statement II is incorrect. Coffee Corp. may still make an exempt offering under the Securities Act of 1933 even if it will be subject to the requirements of the Securities Exchange Act of 1934.

2. **(B)** Statement I is incorrect because up to thirty-five non-accredited investors may purchase shares under Regulation D, Rule 506, if they are sophisticated investors. Statement II is correct because Rule 506 does allow sales to up to thirty-five nonaccredited investors **assuming they are also** sophisticated investors, that is, individuals with knowledge and experience in financial matters, or individuals represented by people with such knowledge and experience.

3. **(B)** Statement I is incorrect and Statement II is correct for the same reason. Regulation D, Rule 506, has no dollar limit on the placement of securities as long as other requirements are met.

4. **(B)** Statement I is incorrect because Regulation D has no requirements putting restrictions on resales to nonresidents. Statement II is correct because Regulation D requires that the issuer take reasonable steps to see that purchasers of the exempt offering are not underwriters and are buying for investment.

5. **(D)** Statement I is incorrect. Under Regulation D, the SEC must be notified within fifteen days of the first sale of the securities. Statement II is incorrect because the Quarterly Reports do not require SEC notification of the first sale of exempt securities.

ANSWER OUTLINE

Problem 1   Registration Requirements under 1933 Act

Since sale of interest in citrus groves meets definition of
   security, must comply with registration requirement of
   1933 Act
    Unless one of the three exemptions are present
      Small offering exemption
      Intrastate offering exemption
      Private offering exemption
    None met; therefore, Various must comply
Short-term note qualifies as exempt security under 1933 Act
    Since it is commercial paper with maturity of nine months
     or less
      And proceeds to be used for current operations
   Also qualifies as exempt transaction as private offering
Issue is whether Various is a controlling person of Resis-
   tance Corporation
    If not controlling person, sale of these shares exempted
     from registration requirements
      Under casual sales exemption
    If controlling person, Various must meet registration re-
     quirements of 1933 Act
      Unless sale of shares meets requirements of Rule 144

UNOFFICIAL ANSWER

Problem 1   Registration Requirements under 1933 Act

    The sale of the ownership interests in the citrus groves
qualifies as a security under the 1933 Act. A security is the
sale of any interest in a scheme where a person invests
money in a common enterprise and is led to expect profits
solely from the endeavors of others. The purchasers of the
citrus grove units would be expecting profits from the operation and management of these units by Various. Consequently, unless an exemption can be found under the 1933
Act, Various must file a registration statement with the SEC,
and such statement must be approved before the issuance of
these interests. The only possible exemptions would be an
intrastate offering, a small offering and a private offering.
The sale of citrus grove interests would not constitute an
intrastate offering because interests are offered to persons
residing in more than one state. This offering would not
qualify as a small offering in that the aggregate value would
exceed $1,500,000. Also, it does not appear that it is a pri-
vate offering, since the offering is not limited to a small
number of sophisticated investors.

    The issuance of a short-term note by Various would not
require the filing of a registration statement with the SEC.
Commercial paper having a maturity date not exceeding nine
months is exempt from the registration requirements of the
1933 Act. This is only true if the proceeds gained from the
issuance of this paper have been or are to be used for current
operations. However, if the proceeds are to be used for
long-term capital investments, this exemption would not
apply. Since the problem states the instrument would be
used to finance current operations, it appears that the note
would qualify as an exemption to the 1933 Securities Act
requirement for filing. It appears that the requirements for a
private placement would be met in this situation. The offering is limited to one sophisticated investor, since institutional investors such as banks and insurance companies are
considered to be sophisticated in nature.

    Concerning Various' sale of the Resistance shares, the
important fact is to determine whether Various qualifies as a

controlling person of Resistance Corporation. If Various
does not qualify as a controlling person, the sale of these
shares would be exempted from the registration requirements of the 1933 Act under the casual sales exemption.
The casual sales exemption states that a transaction by any
person other than an issuer, underwriter, or dealer is exempt
from registration. A controlling person in a corporation has
been construed to mean anyone with direct or indirect power
to determine the policies of the business. Obviously, ownership of a majority share of existing stock in a company
would constitute control. However, in past court decisions,
as little as 10% ownership of outstanding shares has been
determined to constitute control when combined with such
other factors as being a member of the board of directors; an
officer of the corporation; or the fact that the remaining
shares are distributed over a large number of shareholders.
Thus, the fact that Various only owns 17% would not keep it
from being a controlling person. If held to be a controlling
person, Various' sale of shares would not fall within the
casual sales exemption of the 1933 Act. Since this exemption is not met, Various would have to file a registration
statement when selling these shares even though the sale is
accomplished through a broker. However, the SEC does
permit controlling persons to sell limited quantities of their
securities without registration of their security if their sale
complies with requirements of Rule 144. Rule 144 requires:
adequate information concerning the company be publicly
available; sale of no more than 1% of all outstanding shares
of that class during any three month period; that all sales
take place in broker's transactions, with the broker receiving
only the ordinary brokerage commission and the broker not
engaging in any solicitations of offers to buy from prospective purchasers. Thus, even if Various was considered to be
a controlling person, upon compliance with the above requirements, Various would still be able to sell a limited
number of its shares without registration.

ANSWER OUTLINE

Problem 2   Exemptions from Registration under Regula-
            tion D of the Securities Act of 1933; Re-
            porting Requirements of the Securities Ex-
            change Act of 1934

a. **1.**   World's first contention is incorrect because it
        violated the following rules under Rule 505:

        • Sales are limited to thirty-five nonaccredited
          investors
        • A general advertising is not permitted
        • The SEC must be notified within fifteen days
          of first sale

    2.   World's second contention is incorrect because se-
        curities originally sold under Regulation D are re-
        stricted securities
       They must be registered prior to resale unless an-
       other exemption applies

b. **1.**   Unity's contention is incorrect for either of two
        reasons:

        • Unity has 500 or more stockholders and assets
          in excess of $10,000,000
        • Unity's securities are traded on a national se-
          curity exchange

2. Covered corporations must file following with SEC:

- Quarterly Reports (10-Qs)
- Annual Reports (10-Ks)
- Current Reports (8-Ks)

These reports should present a complete, current picture of business operations and matters affecting the value of securities

UNOFFICIAL ANSWER

Problem 2   Exemptions from Registration under Regulation D of the Securities Act of 1933; Reporting Requirements of the Securities Exchange Act of 1934

a.   1.   World is incorrect in its first contention that the offering is exempt from registration under Regulation D, Rule 505, of the Securities Act of 1933. World did not comply with the requirements of Rule 505 for the following reasons: the offering was sold to more than thirty-five nonaccredited investors; there was a general advertising of the offering; and the SEC was notified more than fifteen days after the first sale of the offering.

2.   World is also incorrect in its second contention that the resale of the securities would be completely exempt from registration if the offering were exempt. Securities originally purchased under a Regulation D limited offering exemption are restricted securities. They must be registered prior to resale unless sold subject to another exemption.

b.   1.   Unity is incorrect in its contention that it is not required to comply with the reporting requirements of the Securities Exchange Act of 1934. Unity must comply because it has more than 500 stockholders and total assets in excess of $10,000,000. Alternately, Unity must comply because its shares are traded on a national securities exchange.

2.   A covered corporation must file the following reports with the SEC: Quarterly Reports (10-Qs); Annual Reports (10-Ks); and Current Reports (8-Ks). These reports are intended to provide a complete, current statement of all business operations and matters affecting the value of the corporation's securities.

Keep practicing! Wiley's CPA Examination Review Software has over 2,800 questions.

Available at www.wiley.com/cpa

PROFESSIONAL RESPONSIBILITIES

Overview

The Code of Professional Conduct consists of two sections

(1) Principles—which provide the framework
(2) Rules—which govern the performance of professional services

The first part of this module contains many rules and interpretations. These are covered over many pages in part A. of this module. Because this entire area is detailed and has typically been tested with just a few multiple-choice questions, less priority and weight should be given to this area in your study. The remainder of this module, however, should be studied well.

Accountants' legal liability is often tested on the CPA exam by use of essay questions that require the candidate to apply the legal principles contained in this module to hypothetical fact patterns. Multiple-choice questions are also used which require application as well as knowledge of this material.

Accountants' civil liability arises primarily from contract law, the law of negligence, fraud, the Securities Act of 1933, and the Securities Exchange Act of 1934. The first three are common law and largely judge-made law, whereas the latter two are federal statutory law.

The agreement between an accountant and his/her client is generally set out in a carefully drafted engagement letter. Additionally, the accountant has a duty to conduct his/her work with the same reasonable care as an average accountant. This duty defines the standard used in a negligence case. It is important to understand

1. When an accountant can be liable to his/her client.
2. When an accountant can be liable to third parties.
3. That an accountant is liable to the client and to all third parties that relied on the financial statements when the accountant committed fraud, constructive fraud, or was grossly negligent; furthermore in these cases, the accountant can be assessed punitive damages.
4. The extent of liability under the Securities Act of 1933 and the Securities Exchange Act of 1934 as well as how they differ from each other and from common law.

The CPA examination also tests the dual nature of the ownership of the accountant's working papers. Although the accountant owns the working papers and retains them as evidence of his/her work, confidentiality must be maintained. Therefore, the CPA cannot allow this information to reach another without the client's consent. In general, privileged communications between a CPA and the client are not sanctioned under federal statutory law or common law, but the privilege is in existence in states that have passed statutes granting such a right.

A. Code of Conduct and Other Responsibilities

1. Code of Professional Conduct

    a. The Code is applicable to all AICPA members, not merely those in public practice
    b. Compliance with the Code depends primarily on members' understanding and voluntary actions, and only secondarily on

        (1) Reinforcement by peers,
        (2) Public opinion, and
        (3) Disciplinary proceedings.

            (a) Possible disciplinary proceedings include from joint trial board panel **admonishment, suspension** (for up to two years), or **expulsion** from AICPA, or acquittal

    c. The Code provides **minimum** levels of acceptable conduct relating to all services performed by CPAs, unless wording of a standard specifically excludes some members

        (1) For example, some standards do not apply to CPAs not in public practice

    d. Overall structure of the Code goes from very generally worded standards to more specific and operational rules

        (1) Interpretations and rulings remaining from the prior Code are even more specific

    e. The Principles section consists of six Articles

        I.   Responsibilities
        II. The Public Interest
        III. Integrity
        IV. Objectivity and Independence
        V.   Due Care
        VI. Scope and Nature of Services

2.   Code of Professional Conduct—Principles

   a.   Outline of six Articles in Section 1 of the Code

   Article I—Responsibilities. In carrying out their responsibilities as professionals, members should exercise sensitive professional and moral judgments in all their activities.

   Article II—The Public Interest. Members should accept the obligation to act in a way that will serve the public interest, honor the public trust, and demonstrate commitment to professionalism.

   (1) A distinguishing mark of a professional is acceptance of responsibility to public.

   (a) The accounting profession's public consists of clients, credit grantors, governments, employers, investors, business and financial community, and others.

   (b) In resolving conflicting pressures among groups an accountant should consider the public interest (the collective well-being of the community).

   Article III—Integrity. To maintain and broaden public confidence, members should perform all professional responsibilities with the highest sense of integrity.

   (1) Integrity can accommodate the inadvertent error and honest difference of opinion, but it cannot accommodate deceit or subordination of principle.

   (2) Integrity

   (a) Is measured in terms of what is right and just

   (b) Requires a member to observe **principles of objectivity, independence, and due care**

   Article IV—Objectivity and Independence. A member should maintain objectivity and be free of conflicts of interest in discharging professional responsibilities. A member in public practice should be independent in fact and appearance when providing auditing and other attestation services.

   (1) Overall

   (a) Objectivity a state of mind

   1] Objectivity imposes obligation to be impartial, intellectually honest, and free of conflicts of interest.

   2] Independence precludes relationships that may appear to impair objectivity in rendering attestation services.

   (b) Regardless of the service performed, members should protect integrity of their work, maintain objectivity, and avoid any subordination of their judgment.

   (2) Members in public practice require maintenance of objectivity and independence (includes avoiding conflict of interest).

   (a) Attest services—require independence in fact and in appearance

   (3) Members **not in public practice**

   (a) Are unable to maintain appearance of independence, but must maintain objectivity

   (b) When employed by others to prepare financial statements, or to perform auditing, tax, or consulting services, must remain objective and candid in dealings with members in public practice

   Article V—Due Care. A member should observe the profession's technical and ethical standards, strive continually to improve competence and the quality of services, and discharge professional responsibility to the best of the member's ability.

   (1) Competence is derived from both education and experience.

   (2) Each member is responsible for assessing his or her own competence and for evaluating whether education, experience, and judgment are adequate for the responsibility taken.

Article VI—Scope and Nature of Services. A member in public practice should observe the Principles of the Code of Professional Conduct in determining the scope and nature of services to be provided.

(1) Members should

    (a) Have in place appropriate internal quality control procedures for services rendered

    (b) Determine whether scope and nature of other services provided to an audit client would create a conflict of interest in performance of audit

    (c) Assess whether activities are consistent with role as professionals

3. Code of Professional Conduct—Rules, Interpretations, and Rulings

    a. Combined outline of Section 2 of the code (rules) integrated with interpretation and rulings

Rule 101 Independence. A member in public practice shall be independent in the performance of professional services as required by standards promulgated by designated bodies.

Interpretation 101-1. Independence is impaired if

(1) During the period of the professional engagement a covered member

    (a) Had or was committed to acquire any direct or material indirect financial interest in the client.

    (b) Was a trustee of any trust or executor or administrator of any estate if such trust or estate had or was committed to acquire any direct or material indirect financial interest in the client.

    (c) Had a joint closely held investment that was material to the covered member.

    (d) Except as specifically permitted in interpretation 101-5, had any loan to or from the client, any officer or director of the client, or any individual owning 10% or more of the client's outstanding equity securities or other ownership interests.

(2) During the period of the professional engagement, a partner or professional employee of the firm, his or her immediate family, or any group of such persons acting together owned more than 5% of a client's outstanding equity securities or other ownership interests.

(3) During the period covered by the financial statements or during the period of the professional engagement, a partner or professional employee of the firm was simultaneously associated with the client as a

    (a) Director, officer, or employee, or in any capacity equivalent to that of a member of management;

    (b) Promoter, underwriter, or voting trustee; or

    (c) Trustee for any pension or profit-sharing trust of the client.

Application of the Independence Rules to a Covered Member's Immediate Family

(1) Except as stated in the following paragraph, a covered member's immediate family is subject to Rule 101 [ET Section 101.01], and its interpretations and rulings.

(2) The exceptions are that independence would not be considered to be impaired solely as a result of the following:

    (a) An individual in a covered member's immediate family was employed by the client in a position other than a key position.

    (b) In connection with his or her employment, an individual in the immediate family of one of the following covered members participated in a retirement, savings, compensation, or similar plan that is sponsored by a client or that invests in a client (provided such plan is normally offered to all employees in similar positions):

        1] A partner or manager who provides ten or more hours of nonattest services to the client; or

        2] Any partner in the office in which the lead attest engagement partner primarily practices in connection with the attest engagement.

(3) For purposes of determining materiality under Rule 101 [ET Section 101.01], the financial interests of the covered member and his or her immediate family should be aggregated.

Application of the Independence Rules to Close Relatives

(1) Independence would be considered to be impaired if

    (a) An individual participating on the attest engagement team has a close relative who had

        1] A key position with the client; or
        2] A financial interest in the client that

            a] Was material to the close relative and of which the individual has knowledge; or
            b] Enabled the close relative to exercise significant influence over the client.

    (b) An individual in a position to influence the attest engagement or any partner in the office in which the lead attest engagement partner primarily practices in connection with the attest engagement has a close relative who had

        1] A key position with the client; or
        2] A financial interest in the client that

            a] Was material to the close relative and of which the individual has knowledge; and
            b] Enabled the close relative to exercise significant influence over the client.

Important Definitions

(1) **Covered member.** A covered member is

    (a) An individual on the attest engagement team;
    (b) An individual in a position to influence the attest engagement;
    (c) A partner or manager who provides nonattest services to the attest client beginning once he or she provides ten hours of nonattest services to the client within any fiscal year and ending on the later of the date

        (1) The firm signs the report on the financial statements for the fiscal year during which those services were provided; or
        (2) He or she no longer expects to provide ten or more hours of nonattest services to the attest client on a recurring basis;

    (d) A partner in the office in which the lead attest engagement partner primarily practices in connection with the attest engagement;
    (e) The firm, including the firm's employee benefit plans; or
    (f) An entity whose operating, financial, or accounting policies can be controlled (as defined by generally accepted accounting principles [GAAP] for consolidation purposes) by any of the individuals or entities described in (a) through (e) or by two or more such individuals or entities if they act together.

(2) **Individual in a position to influence the attest engagement.** An individual in a position to influence the attest engagement is one who

    (a) Evaluates the performance or recommends the compensation of the attest engagement partner;
    (b) Directly supervises or manages the attest engagement partner, including all successively senior levels above that individual through the firm's chief executive;
    (c) Consults with the attest engagement team regarding technical or industry-related issues specific to the attest engagement; or
    (d) Participates in or oversees, at all successively senior levels, quality control activities, including internal monitoring, with respect to the specific attest engagement.

(3) **Period of the professional engagement.** The period of the professional engagement begins when a member either signs an initial engagement letter or other agreement to perform attest services or begins to perform an attest engagement for a client, whichever is earlier. The period lasts for the entire duration of the professional relationship (which could cover many pe-

riods) and ends with the formal or informal notification, either by the member or the client, of the termination of the professional relationship or by the issuance of a report, whichever is later. Accordingly, the period does not end with the issuance of a report and recommence with the beginning of the following year's attest engagement.

(4) **Key position.** A key position is a position in which an individual

   (a) Has primary responsibility for significant accounting functions that support material components of the financial statements;
   (b) Has primary responsibility for the preparation of the financial statements; or
   (c) Has the ability to exercise influence over the contents of the financial statements, including when the individual is a member of the board of directors or similar governing body, chief executive officer, president, chief financial officer, chief operating officer, general counsel, chief accounting officer, controller, director of internal audit, director of financial reporting, treasurer, or any equivalent position.

(5) **Close relative.** A close relative is a parent, sibling, or nondependent child.
(6) **Immediate family.** Immediate family is a spouse, spousal equivalent, or dependent (whether or not related).

Interpretation 101-2. A former partner (shareholder, or equivalent) is not considered a member of the firm and does not affect firm independence when the former partner

(1) Has retirement benefits **fixed** as to amount and dates, although benefits may be adjusted for inflation
(2) Does not participate in firm business after a reasonable transition
(3) Does not **appear** to participate in the firm's business

   (a) For example, the former partner's name should not be associated with the CPA firm in an office building directory, or in membership lists of business, professional, or civic organizations
   (b) Simply providing an office to the former partner (including secretarial and telephone services) is acceptable

Interpretation 101-3. When a CPA performs nonattest services for an attest client it **may or may not** impair independence.

(1) Must meet following requirements to retain appearance that CPA is not employee of client

   (a) Evaluate the effect of nonattest services on independence
   (b) Must not perform management functions or make management decisions
   (c) Responsibility for decisions must remain with client's board of directors and management
   (d) Establish understanding with client regarding the services, preferable in an engagement letter
   (e) Make sure that client understands its responsibility to

      1] Designate a management-level individual(s) to oversee services
      2] Evaluate the adequacy of the services and findings
      3] Make management decisions, including accepting responsibility for the results
      4] Establish and maintain internal controls

(2) The Sarbanes-Oxley Act of 2002 places traditional restrictions on nonattest services for audits of public companies (see Section F.)

Interpretation 101-4. CPA who is a director of a nonprofit organization where board is large and representative of community leadership is **not** lacking independence if

(1) Position purely honorary
(2) Position identified as honorary on external materials
(3) CPA participation restricted to use of name
(4) CPA does not vote or participate in management affairs

Interpretation 101-5. Loans from financial institution clients and related terminology.

(1) Independence is not impaired by certain "grandfathered" and other loans from financial institution clients

    (a) Grandfathered loans that are permitted (home mortgages, other secured loans, loans immaterial to CPA) that were obtained

        1] Prior to January 1, 1992, under standards then in effect

        2] From a financial institution for which independence was not required, and the financial institution subsequently became an attest client

        3] Obtained from a financial institution for which independence was not required, and the loan was sold to an attest client **or**

        4] Obtained by a CPA prior to becoming a member of CPA firm of which the financial institution is an attest client

    NOTE: All of the above must be kept current and not renegotiated after the above dates. Also, the collateral on other secured loans must equal or exceed the remaining loan balance.

    (b) Other permitted loans from a financial institution attest client

        1] Automobile loans and leases collateralized by automobile

        2] Loans of surrender value under an insurance policy

        3] Borrowings fully collateralized by cash deposits at same financial institution (e.g., "passbook loans")

        4] Credit cards and cash advances on checking accounts of $5,000 or less

(2) Terminology

    (a) Loan—Financial transactions that generally provide for repayment terms and a rate of interest

    (b) Financial institution—An entity that makes loans to the general public as part of its normal business operations

    (c) Normal lending procedures, terms, and requirements—Comparable to those received by other borrowers during period, when considering

        1] Amount of loan and collateral

        2] Repayment terms

        3] Interest rate, including "points"

        4] Closing costs

        5] General availability of such loans to public

Interpretation 101-6. Effect of threatened litigation

(1) Client-CPA actual or threatened litigation

    (a) Commenced by present management alleging audit deficiencies, impairs

    (b) Commenced by auditor against present management for fraud, deceit impairs

    (c) Expressed intention by present management alleging deficiencies in audit work impairs if auditor believes **strong possibility** of claim

    (d) Immaterial not related to audit **usually** does **not** impair (i.e., billing disputes)

(2) Litigation by client security holders or other third parties generally does not impair unless material client-CPA cross-claims develop.

(3) If independence is impaired, CPA should disassociate and/or disclaim an opinion for lack of independence.

Interpretation 101-7. (Deleted)

Interpretation 101-8. A CPA's financial interests in nonclients may impair independence when those nonclients have financial interests in the CPA's clients.

Interpretation 101-9. (Deleted)

Interpretation 101-10. Describes members' duties for independence when auditing entities included in governmental financial statements

(1) Generally, auditor of a material fund type, fund account group, or component unit of entity that should be disclosed in notes of general-purpose financial statements, but is not auditing primary government, should be independent with respect to those financial statements and primary government

(2) Also should be independent if, although funds and accounts are separately immaterial, they are material in the aggregate

Interpretation 101-11. Modified application of Rule 101 for certain engagements to issue restricted-use reports under the Statements on Standards for Attestation Engagements

(1) Rule 101: Independence and its interpretations and rulings apply to all attest engagements. However, for purposes of performing engagements to issue reports under the Statements on Standards for Attestation Engagements (SSAE) that are restricted to identified parties, only the following covered members, and their immediate families, are required to be independent with respect to the responsible party[1] in accordance with Rule 101:

   (a) Individuals participating on the attest engagement team;

   (b) Individuals who directly supervise or manage the attest engagement partner; and

   (c) Individuals who consult with the attest engagement team regarding technical or industry-related issues specific to the attest engagement.

(2) In addition, independence would be considered to be impaired if the firm had a financial relationship covered by interpretation 101-1.A with the responsible party that was material to the firm.

(3) In cases where the firm provides non-attest services to the responsible party that are proscribed under interpretation 101-3 and that do not directly relate to the subject matter of the attest engagement, independence would not be considered to be impaired.

(4) In circumstances where the individual or entity that engages the firm is not the responsible party or associated with the responsible party, individuals on the attest engagement team need not be independent of the individual or entity, but should consider their responsibilities under interpretation 102-2 with regard to any relationships that may exist with the individual or entity that engages them to perform these services.

(5) This interpretation does not apply to an engagement performed under the Statement on Auditing Standards or Statement on Standards for Accounting and Review Services, or to an examination or review engagement performed under the Statements on Standards for Attestation Engagements.

Interpretation 101-12. Independence is impaired if during professional engagement or while expressing an opinion, member's firm had any material cooperative arrangement with client.

(1) Cooperative arrangement exists when member's firm and client participate jointly in business activity such as

   (a) Joint ventures to develop or market a product or service

   (b) Arrangements to provide services or products to a third party

   (c) Arrangements to combine services or products of the member's firm with those of client to market them with references to both parties

   (d) Arrangements under which member firm or client act as distributor of other's products or services

(2) Joint participation with client is not a cooperative arrangement and is thus allowed if all of the following three conditions are present.

   (a) Participation of the firm and client are governed by separate agreements

   (b) Neither firm nor client assumes any responsibility for the other

   (c) Neither party is an agent of the other

---

[1] *As defined in the SSAE.*

Interpretation 101-13.

(1) Member may be asked by client to perform extended audit services (i.e., member may assist client in internal audit activities or member may extend audit services beyond what GAAS requires). Member performing extended audit services does not impair independence if member does not act or appear to act as a manager or employee of client.

(2) Example that would impair independence includes performing ongoing monitoring or control activities (i.e., reviewing loan originations for client). Another example that would impair independence is if member determines which internal control recommendations should be used by client.

Rule 102 Integrity and Objectivity. In performance of **any** professional service, a member shall (a) maintain objectivity and integrity, (b) avoid conflicts of interest, and (c) not knowingly misrepresent facts or subordinate judgment.

(1) In tax matters, resolving doubt in favor of client does not, by itself, impair integrity or objectivity.

Interpretation 102-1. Knowingly making or permitting false and misleading entries in an entity's financial statements or records is a violation.

Interpretation 102-2. A conflict of interest may occur if a member performing a professional service has a **significant relationship** with another person, entity, product, or service that **could be viewed** as impairing the member's objectivity.

(1) If the member believes that the professional service can be performed with objectivity, and if the relationship is disclosed to and consent is obtained from the client, employer, or other appropriate parties, the rule does not prohibit performance of the professional service.

(2) Nothing in this interpretation overrides Rule 101 (on independence), its interpretations, and rulings.

Interpretation 102-3. When a member deals with his/her employer's external accountant, the member must be candid and not knowingly misrepresent facts or knowingly fail to disclose material facts.

Interpretation 102-4. If a member and his/her supervisor have a disagreement concerning the preparation of financial statements or the recording of transactions, the member should

(1) Allow the supervisor's position if that position is an acceptable alternative with authoritative support and/or does not result in a material misstatement.

(2) Report the problem to higher levels in firm if supervisor's position could cause material misstatements in records.

(3) Consider quitting firm if after reporting the problem to upper management, action is not taken. Consider reporting this to regulatory authorities and external accountant.

Interpretation 102-5. Those involved in educational services such as teaching full- or part-time at a university, teaching professional education courses, or engaged in research and scholarship are subject to Rule 102.

Interpretation 102-6. Sometimes members are asked by clients to act as advocates in support of clients' position on tax services, consulting services, accounting issues, or financial reporting issues. Member is still subject to Rule 102. Member is also still subject to Rules 201, 202, and 203. Member is also subject to Rule 101 for professional services requiring independence.

*NOTE: While CPA candidates should read the rulings to better understand the ethics rules and interpretations, it is **not** necessary to memorize them; consider them to be illustrations. Gaps in sequence are due to deleted sections.*

Rule 101, 102 Ethics Rulings

Independence and Integrity Ethics Rulings

1. If a member accepts more than a token gift from a client, independence may be impaired.

2. A member may join a trade association which is a client, without impairing independence, but may not serve in a capacity of management.

3. If a member is cosigner of a client's checks, independence is impaired.

4. Independence is impaired if a member prepares a client's payroll and conditions of Interpretation 101-3 are not met.

7. Independence is impaired if a member supervises client office personnel on a monthly basis.

8. Extensive accounting and consulting services, including interpretation of statements, forecasts, etc., do not impair independence.

9. Independence is impaired if the member cosigns checks or purchase orders or exercises general supervision over budgetary controls.

10. The independence of an elected legislator (a CPA) in a local government is impaired with respect to that governmental unit.

11. Mere designation as executor or trustee, without actual services in either capacity, does not impair independence, but actual service does.

12. If a member is a trustee of a foundation, independence is impaired.

14. Independence of a member serving as director or officer of a local United Way or similar organization is not impaired with respect to a charity receiving funds from that organization unless the organization exercises managerial control over that charity.

16. Independence is impaired if a member serves on the board of a nonprofit social club if the board has ultimate responsibility for the affairs of the club.

17. The acquisition of equity or debt securities as a condition for membership in a country club does not normally impair independence; serving on the club's governing board or taking part in its management does impair independence.

19. Independence is impaired if a member serves on a committee administering a client's deferred compensation program.

20. Membership on governmental advisory committees does not impair independence with respect to that governmental unit.

21. A member serving as director of an enterprise would not be independent with respect to the enterprise's profit sharing and retirement trust.

29. A member's independence is impaired when owning bonds in a municipal authority.

31. A member's ownership of an apartment in a co-op apartment building would impair the member's and the firm's independence.

33. A member impairs independence upon joining a client's employee benefit plan.

35. A member's ownership of shares in a mutual investment fund which owns stock in the CPA's clients normally would not impair independence.

36. A member who is a member of an investment club, holding stock in a client, lacks independence.

38. A member serving with a client bank in a cofiduciary capacity, with respect to a trust, does not impair independence with respect to the bank or trust department (if the estate's or trust's assets were not material).

39. A member who acts as a transfer agent and/or registrar is not independent with respect to the company.

41. Independence is not impaired when a member's retirement plan is invested and managed by an insurance company in a separate account, not a part of the general assets of the insurance company.

48. A university faculty member cannot be independent to a student senate fund because the student senate is a part of the university which is the member's employer.

51. A member who provides legal services to a client is not independent with respect to the client.

52. Independence is impaired when prior year fees for professional services, whether billed or unbilled, remain unpaid for more than one year prior to the date of the report.

54. A member's independence is not impaired by performing appraisal, valuation, or actuarial services for a client, if all significant judgments are determined or approved by the client and if the client is able to provide an informed judgment on the results of the services.

55. A member's independence is not impaired if the member is involved in hiring and instructing new personnel during a systems implementation. The client must make all significant management decisions and the member must restrict supervisory activities to initial instruction and training.

56. Independence is impaired by recruiting and hiring a controller and/or cost accountant for a client company. The member may, however, recommend position descriptions and candidate specifications as well as initially screen and recommend qualified candidates.

58. Independence is impaired when a member owns a building and leases space to a client.

60. If a member audits an employee benefit plan, independence is impaired with respect to employer if a partner or professional employee of the firm had significant influence over such employer, was in a key position with the employer, or was associated with the employer as a promoter, underwriter, or voting trustee.

61. Participation by a member's spouse in an employee stock ownership plan of a client does not impair independence until a right of possession of the stock exists.

64. Independence with respect to a fund-raising foundation is impaired if a member serves on the board of directors of the entity for whose benefit the foundation exists (unless position is purely honorary).

65. Member who is **not** in public practice may use CPA designation in connection with financial statements and correspondence of member's employer. May also use CPA designation on business cards if along with employment title. Member may **not** imply independence from employer. Member cannot state that transmittal is in conformity with GAAP.

66. Independence is impaired by a member's retirement or savings plan which includes a direct or material indirect financial interest in an attest client.

67. If a client financial institution merely services a member's loan, independence is not impaired.

68. A member may not hold a direct financial interest in an attestation client, even when held in a blind trust.
69. A member with a material limited partnership interest is not independent of other limited partnerships that have the same general partner.
70. Maintaining state or federally insured deposits (e.g., checking accounts, savings accounts, certificates of deposit) in a financial institution does not impair independence; uninsured deposits do not impair independence if the uninsured amounts are immaterial.
71. CPA Firm A is not independent of an entity audited by Firm B. CPA Firm B may only use Firm A personnel in a manner similar to internal auditors without impairing Firm B's independence.
72. A member (and the member's firm) are not independent if the member serves on the advisory board of a client unless the advisory board (1) is truly advisory, (2) has no authority to make or appear to make management decisions, and (3) membership is distinct with minimal, if any, common membership with management and the board of directors.
73. The "period of the professional engagement" during which independence is required starts when services requiring independence begin, and ends when there is notification of termination of the professional relationship.
74. A member must be independent to issue an audit opinion or a review report, but need not be independent to issue a compilation report (such lack of independence is disclosed).
75. Membership in a credit union does not impair audit independence if (1) the member qualifies as a credit union member on grounds other than by providing professional services, (2) the member does not exert significant influence over the credit union, (3) the member's loans (if any) from credit union are normal (see Interpretation 101-1), and (4) the conditions of ruling 70 have been met.
77. When a member is offered (or seeks) employment with a client, that member should remove himself/herself from the engagement until the employment offer is rejected or employment is no longer being considered; when a member becomes aware that an individual participated on the engagement in those circumstances, that member should consider the need to reperform work or other appropriate procedures.
79. A member's independence is impaired if s/he is a general partner in a partnership that invests in a client of the member's firm; if s/he is a limited partner, independence is impaired if the partnership invests in a material portion of the client.
81. A member's investment in a limited partnership impairs independence with respect to the limited partnership; when the investment is material, independence is impaired with respect to both the general partner of the limited partnership and any subsidiaries of the limited partnership.
82. When a member is the campaign treasurer for a mayoral candidate, independence is impaired with respect to the candidate's campaign organization, but independence is not impaired with respect to the candidate's political party or the municipality.
85. A member may serve as a bank director, but this is generally not desirable when s/he has clients that are bank customers; performing both services is allowed, however, if the relationship is disclosed and acceptable to all appropriate parties. Revealing confidential client information without client permission is a violation of the Code, even when the failure to disclose such information may breach the member's fiduciary responsibility as a director.
86. A partially secured, "grandfathered loan" will not impair independence if the portion of the loan that exceeds the value of the collateral is not material to the member's net worth.
87. The date a loan commitment was made may be used as the date of a transaction for purposes of determining whether a loan qualifies as "grandfathered."
88. A loan from a financial institution to a limited partnership in which CPAs have a combined interest exceeding 50% of the total limited partnership interest impairs independence unless the loan qualifies as "grandfathered."
89. A member's independence with respect to a financial institution is impaired if that member is a general partner in a partnership financed by the financial institution unless the loan qualifies as "grandfathered."
90. If a member has outstanding credit card loans to a financial institution of over $5,000, independence will not be impaired if that member reduces the outstanding balance to $5,000 or less on a current basis.
91. Independence is not impaired when a member has an "operating lease" from a client made under normal terms; independence is impaired by a "capital lease" from a client unless the "loan" related to the lease qualifies as "grandfathered."
92. A material joint investment in a vacation home with an officer, director, or principal stockholder of an attest client will impair independence.
93. When a member serves as a director or officer for the United Way or a similar organization and that organization provides funds to local charities that are the member's clients, a conflict of interest will not be considered to exist if the relationship is disclosed and consent is obtained from the appropriate parties.
94. Independence is not impaired if client in the engagement letter agrees to release, indemnify, defend, and hold harmless the member from any liability and costs from misrepresentations of management.
95. An agreement by the member and a client to use alternative dispute resolution techniques in lieu of litigation before a dispute arises does not impair independence.
96. A commencement of an alternative dispute resolution does not impair independence unless the member's and client's positions are materially adverse so that the proceedings are similar to litigation, such as binding arbitration.

97. If a member performs internal audit procedures for client, independence is impaired if the member performs a management function such as helping in client's approval of loans. Testing system of internal control does not impair independence.

98. A loan from a nonclient who is a subsidiary of a client does impair independence. Loan from a nonclient parent does not impair independence with respect to a client subsidiary if the subsidiary is not material to the parent.

99. If a member is asked by a company to provide personal financial planning or tax services for its executives and the member may give the executives recommendations adverse to the company, before accepting and while doing this work, the member should consider Rule 102 on Integrity and Objectivity and Rule 301 on Confidential Client Information. The member can perform the work if s/he believes it can be done with objectivity.

100. A member who was independent when his/her report was issued, may resign the report or consent to its use at a later date when his/her independence is impaired, if no postaudit work is performed while impaired.

101. Member serving as expert witness does not serve as advocate but as one having specialized knowledge, training, and experience—should arrive at position objectively.

102. If a member indemnifies client for damages, losses or costs arising from lawsuits, claims, or settlements relating directly or indirectly to clients acts, this impairs independence.

Rule 201 General Standards. Member must comply with the following standards for all professional engagements:

(1) Only undertake professional services that one can reasonably expect to complete with professional competence
(2) Exercise due professional care

    (a) Member may need to consult with experts to exercise due care

(3) Adequately plan and supervise engagements
(4) Obtain sufficient relevant data to afford a reasonable basis for conclusions and recommendations

Interpretation 201-1. Competence to complete an engagement includes

(1) Technical qualifications of CPA and staff
(2) Ability to supervise and evaluate work
(3) Knowledge of technical subject matter
(4) Capability to exercise judgment in its application
(5) Ability to research subject matter and consult with others

Interpretations 201-2, 3, 4. (Deleted)

Rule 202 Compliance with Standards. A member who performs auditing, review, compilation, consulting services, tax or other services shall comply with standards promulgated by bodies designated by Council.

NOTE: The designated bodies are

(1) Financial Accounting Standards Board
(2) Governmental Accounting Standards Board
(3) AICPA designated bodies

    (a) Accounting and Review Services Committee
    (b) Auditing Standards Board
    (c) Management Advisory Services Executive Committee

Rule 203 Accounting Principles. Member cannot provide positive or negative assurance that financial statements are in conformity with GAAP if statements contain departures from GAAP having a material effect on statements taken as a whole except when unusual circumstances would make financial statements following GAAP misleading.

(1) When unusual circumstances require a departure from GAAP, CPA must disclose in report the departure, its effects (if practicable), and reasons why compliance would result in a misleading statement.

Interpretation 203-1. CPAs are to allow departure from SFAS only when results of SFAS will be misleading.

(1) Requires use of professional judgment
(2) Examples of possible circumstances justifying departure are

    (a) New legislation
    (b) New form of business transaction

Interpretation 203-2. FASB Interpretations are covered by Rule 203

(1) Also unsuperseded ARB and APB

Interpretation 203-3. (Deleted)

Interpretation 203-4. Rule 203 also applies to communications such as reports to regulatory authorities, creditors, and auditors.

Rule 201, 202, 203 Ethics Rulings

7. A CPA who is in partnership with non-CPAs may sign the report with the firm name, his own name, and indicate "certified public accountant."
8. A member selecting subcontractors for consulting services engagements is obligated to select subcontractors on the basis of professional qualifications, technical skills, etc.
9. A member should be in a position to supervise and evaluate work of a specialist in his employ.
10. If a member prepares financial statements as a stockholder, partner, director, or employee of an entity, any transmittal should indicate the member's relationship and should not imply independence. If transmittal indicates financial statements are in accordance with GAAP, Rule 203 must be met. If financial statements are on member's letterhead, member should disclose lack of independence.
11. Rule 203 applies to members performing litigation support services.

Rule 301 Confidential Client Information. Member in public practice shall not disclose confidential client information without client consent except for

(1) Compliance with Rule 202 and 203 obligations
(2) Compliance with enforceable subpoena or summons
(3) AICPA review of professional practice
(4) Initiating complaint or responding to inquiry made by a recognized investigative or disciplinary body

Interpretation 301-1. (Deleted)

Interpretation 301-2. (Deleted)

Interpretation 301-3. A member who is considering selling his/her practice, or merging with another CPA, may allow that CPA to review confidential client information without the specific consent of the client.

(1) The member should take appropriate precautions (e.g., obtain a written confidentiality agreement) so that the prospective purchaser does not disclose such information.

*NOTE: This exception only relates to a review in conjunction with a purchase or merger. It **does not** apply to the review of working papers **after** a CPA has purchased another's practice. AU 315, discussed in detail later in this module, requires that the successor who wishes to review predecessor auditor working papers should request the client to authorize the predecessor to make such working papers available.*

Rule 302 Contingent Fees.

(1) A member in public practice shall not

    (a) Perform for a contingent fee any professional services when the member or member's firm also performs any of the following services for that client

        1] Audits or reviews of financial statements
        2] Compilations when the member is independent and expects that a third party may use the financial statements
        3] Examinations of prospective financial information

    (b) Prepare an original or amended tax return or claims for a tax refund for a contingent fee for any client

(2) Solely for purposes of this rule, (a) fees fixed by courts or other public authorities, or (b) in tax matters, fees determined based on the results of a judicial proceeding or findings of governmental agency, are not regarded as contingent and are therefore permitted

Interpretation 302-1. Examples related to contingent fees

(1) A contingent fee **would be permitted** in various circumstances in which the amounts due are not clear; examples are

   (a) Representing a client in an examination by a revenue agent
   (b) Filing amended tax returns based on a tax issue that is the subject of a test case **involving a different taxpayer**

(2) A contingent fee **would not be permitted** for preparing an amended tax return for a client claiming a refund that is clearly due to the client because of an inadvertent omission

Rule 301, 302 Ethics Rulings

1. A member may utilize outside computer services to process tax returns as long as there is no release of confidential information.
2. With client permission, a member may provide P&L percentages to a trade association.
3. A CPA withdrawing from a tax engagement due to irregularities on the client's return should urge successor CPA to have client grant permission to reveal reasons for withdrawal.
5. A member may use a records retention agency to store client records as long as confidentiality is maintained.
6. A member may be engaged by a municipality to verify taxpayer's books and records for the purpose of assessing property tax. The member must maintain confidentiality.
7. Members may reveal the names of clients without client consent unless such disclosure releases confidential information.
14. A member has a responsibility to honor confidential relationships with nonclients. Accordingly, members may have to withdraw from consulting services engagements where the client will not permit the member to make recommendations without disclosing confidential information about other clients or nonclients.

15. If the member has conducted a similar consulting services study with a negative outcome, the member should advise potential clients of the previous problems providing that earlier confidential relationships are not disclosed. If the earlier confidential relationship may be disclosed (through client knowledge of other clients), the member should seek approval from the first client.
16. In divorce proceedings a member who has prepared joint tax returns for the couple should consider both individuals to be clients for purposes of requests for confidential information relating to prior tax returns. Under such circumstances the CPA should consider reviewing the legal implications of disclosure with an attorney.
17. A contingent fee or a commission is considered to be "received" when the performance of the related services is complete and the fee or commission is determined.
18. Identical to Ruling 85 under Rule 101.
19. A member's spouse may provide services to a member's attest client for a contingent fee and may refer products or services for a commission.
20. When a member learns of a potential claim against him/her, the member may release confidential client information to member's liability carrier used solely to defend against claim.
21. Identical to Ruling 99 under Rule 102.

Rule 501 Acts Discreditable. A member shall not commit an act discreditable to the profession.

Interpretation 501-1. Retention of client records after client has demanded them is discreditable.

(1) A CPA may keep analyses and schedules prepared by the client for the CPA and need not make them available to the client.
(2) A CPA may keep workpapers with information not reflected in the client's books (adjusting, closing, consolidating entries, etc.) until payment of fees due is received.

Interpretation 501-2. Discrimination on basis of race, color, religion, sex, age, or national origin is discreditable.

Interpretation 501-3. In audits of governmental grants, units, or other recipients of governmental monies, failure to follow appropriate governmental standards, procedures, etc. is discreditable.

Interpretation 501-4. Negligently making (or permitting or directing another to make) false or misleading journal entries is discreditable.

Interpretation 501-5. When a governmental body, commission, or other regulatory agency has requirements beyond those required by GAAS, members are required to follow them.

(1) Failure to follow these requirements is considered an act discreditable to the profession, unless the member discloses in the report that such requirements were not followed and the reasons therefor.

Interpretation 501-6. Member who solicits or discloses May 1996 or later Uniform CPA Examination question(s) and/or answer(s) without AICPA written authorization has committed an act discreditable to profession in violation of Rule 501.

Rule 502 *Advertising and Other Forms of Solicitation.* In public practice, shall not seek to obtain clients by false, misleading, deceptive advertising or other forms of solicitation.

Interpretation 502-1. (Deleted)

Interpretation 502-2. Advertising that is false, misleading or deceptive is prohibited, including advertising that

(1) Creates false or unjustified expectations
(2) Implies ability to influence a court, tribunal, regulatory agency or similar body or official
(3) Contains unrealistic estimates of future fees
(4) Would lead a reasonable person to misunderstand or be deceived

Interpretations 502-3, 4. (Deleted)

Interpretation 502-5. CPA may render services to clients of third parties as long as all promotion efforts are within Code.

Rule 503 *Commissions and Referral Fees.*

(1) A member in public practice may not accept a commission for recommending a product or service to a client when the member or member's firm also performs any of the following services for that client

    (a) Audits or reviews of financial statements
    (b) Compilations when the member is independent and expects that a third party may use the financial statements
    (c) Examinations of prospective financial information

(2) A member who receives a commission [not prohibited in (1) above] shall disclose that fact to the client
(3) A member who accepts a referral fee for recommending or referring any service of a CPA to any person or entity, or who pays a referral fee to obtain a client, must disclose such acceptance or payment to the client

Rule 504. (Deleted)

Rule 505 *Form of Practice and Name.* Member may practice public accounting in form of proprietorship, partnership, professional corporation, etc. and may not practice under a misleading name.

(1) May include past partners.
(2) An individual may practice in name of a former partnership for up to two years (applies when all other partners have died or withdrawn).
(3) A firm name may include a fictitious name or indicate specialization if name is not misleading.
(4) Firm may not designate itself as member of AICPA unless all partners or shareholders are members.
(5) Appendix B to Code of Professional Conduct allows non-CPA ownership of CPA firms under certain conditions.

(a) 66 2/3% (super majority) of ownership (both voting rights and financial interest) must belong to CPAs. Non-CPA owners must be involved in own principal occupation, not practice accounting, and not hold selves out as CPAs.

(b) CPAs must have ultimate responsibility in firm, not non-CPAs.

(c) Non-CPA owners must abide by AICPA Code of Professional Conduct, CPE requirements and hold a baccalaureate degree.

(d) Non-CPAs not eligible to be members of AICPA.

Interpretation 505-1. For a CPA in public practice, the allowable interest in an organization providing accounting services depends upon state law regarding practice in the corporate form.

(1) If the corporate form is permitted, the CPA may have an unlimited investment in any accounting organization.

(2) If the corporate form is not permitted, the member's relationship to the corporation must be solely as an investor, and the investment cannot allow the member significant influence over the corporation.

Interpretation 505-2. Applicability of rules to members who operate a separate business that provides accounting services.

(1) A member in public practice who participates in the operation of a separate business that performs accounting, tax, etc. services must observe all of the Rules of Conduct.

(2) A member not otherwise in the practice of public accounting must observe the Rules of Conduct if the member holds out as a CPA and performs for a client any professional services included in public accounting.

Rule 501, 502, 503, 505 Ethics Rulings and Other Responsibilities Ethics Rulings

Due to rescinding the advertising and solicitation prohibition, the majority of the ethics rulings have been suspended.

2. A member may permit a bank to collect notes issued by a client in payment of fees.

3. A CPA employed by a firm with non-CPA practitioners must comply with the rules of conduct. If a partner of such a firm is a CPA, the CPA is responsible for all persons associated with the firm to comply with the rules of conduct.

33. A member who is a course instructor has the responsibility to determine that the advertising materials promoting the course are within the bounds of Rule 502.

38. A member who is controller of a bank may place his CPA title on bank stationery and in paid advertisements listing the officers and directors of the bank.

78. CPAs who are also attorneys may so indicate on their letterhead.

82. A member may write a financial management newsletter (being advertised for sale) with his name featured prominently.

108. Members interviewed by the press should observe the Code of Professional Conduct and not provide the press with any information for publication that the member could not publish himself.

117. A member may be a director of a consumer credit company if he is not the auditor.

134. Members who share offices, employees, etc., may not indicate a partnership exists unless a partnership agreement **is** in effect.

135. CPA firms that are members of an association cannot use letterhead that indicates a partnership rather than an association.

136. Where a firm consisting of a CPA and a non-CPA is dissolved, and an audit is continued to be serviced by both, the audit opinion should be signed by both individuals, such that a partnership is not indicated.

137. The designation "nonproprietary partner" should not be used to describe personnel as it may be misleading.

138. A member may be a partner of a firm of public accountants when all other personnel are not certified, and at the same time practice separately as a CPA.

139. A member in practice with a non-CPA would have to conform to the Code of Conduct, and would not be permitted to represent itself as a partnership of CPAs.

140. A partnership practicing under the name of the managing partner who is seeking election to high office may continue to use the managing partner's name plus "and Company" if the managing partner is elected and withdraws from the partnership.

141. A CPA in partnership with a non-CPA is ethically responsible for all acts of the partnership and those of the non-CPA partner.

144. A CPA firm may use an established firm name in a different state even though there is a difference in the roster of partners.

145. Newly merged CPA firms may practice under a title that includes the name of a previously retired partner from one of the firms.

146. CPA firms may not designate themselves as Members of the American Institute of Certified Public Accountants unless all their partners or shareholders are members of the AICPA.

158. If a member who is in the practice of public accounting also participates in the operation of a separate business that provides data processing services to public, the member must comply with all rules of conduct in connection with this business.

176. A CPA firm's name, logo, etc., may be imprinted on newsletters and similar publications if the CPA has a reasonable basis to conclude that the information is not fake, misleading, or deceptive.

177. Performing centralized billing services for a doctor is a public accounting service and must be conducted in accordance with the Code.

179. CPA firms which are members of an association (for purposes of joint advertising, training, etc.) should practice in their own names, although they may indicate membership in the association.

182. A member need only return records originally provided to the member by the client for a terminated engagement (in this case preparation of a tax return).

183. A CPA firm may designate itself "Accredited Personal Financial Specialists" on its letterhead and in marketing materials if all partners or shareholders of the firm currently have the AICPA-awarded designation.

184. Identical to Ruling 18 under Rule 302.

185. A member may purchase a product from a supplier and resell it to a client at a profit without disclosing the profit to the client.

186. A member may contract for support services from a computer-hardware maintenance servicer and bill them to a client at a profit without disclosing the profit to the client.

187. Identical to Ruling 19 under Rule 302.

188. When a member refers products to clients through distributors and agents, the member may not perform for those clients the services described in Rule 503 [part (1) of the outline of Rule 503].

189. When individuals associated with a client entity have an internal dispute, and have separately asked a member for client records, the member need only supply them once, and to the individual who previously has been designated or held out as the client's representative.

4. Responsibilities in Consulting Services

    a. In January of 1991 a new series of pronouncements on consulting services, *Statements on Standards for Consulting Services* (SSCS), became effective. This series of pronouncements replaces the three *Statements on Standards for Management Advisory Services*. These standards apply to CPAs in public practice who provide consulting services.

    b. Outline of SSCS 1 Definitions and Standards

        (1) Comparison of consulting and attest services

            (a) **Attest services**—Practitioner expresses a conclusion about the reliability of a written assertion that is the responsibility of another party (the asserter)

            (b) **Consulting services**—Practitioner develops the findings, conclusions and recommendations presented, generally only for the use and benefit of the client; the nature of the work is determined solely by agreement between the practitioner and the client

            (c) Performance of consulting services **for an attest client** requires that the practitioner maintain independence and does not in and of itself impair independence

            NOTE: While one must remain objective in performing consulting services, independence is not required unless the practitioner also performs attest (e.g., audit) services for that client.

        (2) Definitions

            (a) **Consulting services practitioner**—A CPA holding out as a CPA (i.e., a CPA in public practice) while engaged in the performance of a consulting service for a client

            (b) **Consulting process**—Analytical approach and process applied in a consulting service

               1] This definition **excludes** services subject to other AICPA technical standards on auditing (SAS), other attest services (SSAE), compilations and reviews (SSARS), most tax engagements, and recommendations made during one of these engagements as a direct result of having performed these excluded services

            (c) **Consulting services**—Professional services that employ the practitioner's technical skills, education, observations, experiences, and knowledge of the consulting process

        (3) Types of consulting services

            (a) **Consultations**—Provide counsel in a short time frame, based mostly, if not entirely, on existing personal knowledge about the client

           1]   Examples: reviewing and commenting on a client business plan, suggesting software for further client investigation

     (b) **Advisory services**—Develop findings, conclusions and recommendations for client consideration and decision making

           1]   Examples: Operational review and improvement study, analysis of accounting system, strategic planning assistance, information system advice

     (c) **Implementation services**—Place an action plan into effect

           1]   Examples: Installing and supporting computer system, executing steps to improve productivity, assisting with mergers

     (d) **Transaction services**—Provide services related to a specific client transaction, generally with a third party

           1]   Examples: Insolvency services, valuation services, information related to financing, analysis of a possible merger or acquisition, litigation services

     (e) **Staff and other support services**—Provide appropriate staff and possibly other support to perform tasks specified by client

           1]   Examples: Data processing facilities management, computer programming, bankruptcy trusteeship, controllership activities

     (f) **Product services**—Provide client with a product and associated support services

           1]   Examples: Sale, delivery, installation, and implementation of training programs, computer software, and systems development

   (4) Standards for Consulting Services

     (a) General Standards of Rule 201 of Code of Professional Conduct

           1]   Professional competence
           2]   Due professional care
           3]   Planning and supervision
           4]   Sufficient relevant data

     (b) Additional standards established for this area (under Rule 202 of Code of Professional Conduct)

           1]   Client interest—Must serve client interest while maintaining **integrity** and **objectivity**
           2]   Understanding with client—Establish either in **writing or orally**
           3]   Communication with client—Inform client of any conflicts of interest, significant reservations about engagement, significant engagement findings

     (c) Professional judgment must be used in applying SSCS

           1]   Example: Practitioner not required to decline or withdraw from a consulting engagement when there are mutually agreed upon limitations with respect to gathering relevant data

   5. Responsibilities in Personal Financial Planning

     a. Definition, scope and standards of personal financial planning

       (1) Personal financial planning engagements are only those that involve developing strategies and making recommendations to assist a client in defining and achieving personal financial goals
       (2) Personal financial planning engagements involve all of following

         (a) Defining engagement objectives
         (b) Planning specific procedures appropriate to engagement
         (c) Developing basis for recommendations
         (d) Communicating recommendations to client

(e) Identifying tasks for taking action on planning decisions

(3) Other engagements may also include

(a) Assisting client to take action on planning decisions
(b) Monitoring client's progress in achieving goals
(c) Updating recommendations and helping client revise planning decisions

(4) Personal financial planning does not include services that are limited to, for example

(a) Compiling personal financial statements
(b) Projecting future taxes
(c) Tax compliance, including, but not limited to, preparation of tax returns
(d) Tax advice or consultations

(5) CPA should act in conformity with AICPA Code of Professional Conduct

(a) Rule 102, Integrity and Objectivity

1] A member shall maintain objectivity and integrity, be free of conflicts of interest, and not knowingly misrepresent facts or subordinate his/her judgment to others

(b) Rule 201

1] A member shall undertake only those professional services that member can reasonably expect to be completed with professional competence, shall exercise due professional care in the performance of professional services, shall adequately plan and supervise performance of professional services, and shall obtain sufficient relevant data to afford a reasonable basis for conclusions or recommendations

(c) Rule 301, Confidential Client Information

1] Member in public practice shall not disclose any confidential client information without specific consent of client

(d) Rule 302, Contingent Fees

1] Rules must be followed

(6) When a personal financial planning engagement includes providing assistance in preparation of personal financial statements or financial projections, the CPA should consider applicable provisions of AICPA pronouncements, including

(a) Statements on Standards for Accounting and Review Services
(b) Statement on Standards for Attestation Engagements Financial Forecasts and Projections
(c) Audit and Accounting Guide for Prospective Financial Information
(d) Personal Financial Statements Guide

(7) The CPA should document his/her understanding of scope and nature of services to be provided

(a) Consider engagement letter

(8) Personal financial planning engagement should be adequately planned
(9) Engagement's objectives form basis for planning engagement

(a) Procedures should reflect materiality and cost-benefit considerations

(10) Relevant information includes understanding of client's goals, financial position, and available resources for achieving goals

(a) External factors (such as inflation, taxes, and investment markets) and nonfinancial factors (such as client attitudes, risk tolerance, spending habits, and investment preferences) are also relevant information
(b) Relevant information also includes reasonable estimates furnished by client's advisors, or developed by CPA

        (11) Recommendations should ordinarily be in writing and include summary of client's goals and significant assumptions and description of any limitations on work performed

        (12) Unless otherwise agreed, CPA is not responsible for additional services, for example,

           (a) Assisting client to take action on planning decisions

           (b) Monitoring progress in achieving goals

           (c) Updating recommendations and revising planning decisions

    b. Working with other advisers

        (1) If CPA does not provide a service needed to complete an engagement, s/he should restrict scope of engagement and recommend that client engage another adviser

        (2) If client declines to engage another adviser, CPA and client may still agree to proceed with engagement

    c. Implementation engagement functions and responsibilities

        (1) Implementation engagements involve assisting client to take action on planning decisions developed during personal financial planning engagement

        (2) Implementation includes activities such as selecting investment advisers, restructuring debt, creating estate documents, establishing cash reserves, preparing budgets, and selecting and acquiring specific investments and insurance products

        (3) When undertaking implementation engagement, CPA should apply existing professional standards and published guidance

6. Responsibilities in Business and Industry

    a. Internal auditing

        (1) Internal auditors are employed by company to perform audits on that company

           (a) Do financial, operational, and compliance audits

           (b) In financial auditing, evaluate effectiveness of internal control procedures

              1] Used to comply with, among other items, Foreign Corrupt Practices Act that requires companies to have effective internal control

        (2) Internal auditors do not need CPA license but instead may get Certified Internal Auditor (CIA) designation

           (a) Rely on Institute of Internal Auditors for professional guidance rather than AICPA

           (b) Guidelines for internal audits not as well developed as those for external audits

           (c) Some firms have CPA firm perform internal audit functions

              1] This outsourcing to CPAs is controversial

              2] AICPA considers it "extended audit services"

                  a] Acceptable for CPAs if management understands it has ultimate responsibility for internal control

        (3) Standards for Professional Practice of Internal Auditing issued by Institute of Internal Auditing

           (a) Divided into five general sections

              1] Independence—Independent in sense that organization puts no restrictions on auditor's judgment

                  a] Independence defined differently than AICPA; must be independent of **activities** they audit since they are employees of organization they are auditing

                  b] Reporting is often directly to audit committee or board of directors

              2] Professional proficiency

              3] Scope of work

a] Not only accounting and financial controls but also internal control procedures and operational auditing

b] Evaluate compliance with company policies and goals

4] Performance of audit work

a] Requires effective planning and communication of audit results

5] Management of internal auditing department

a] Coordinate with external audit

b] Work of internal auditor supplements but does not substitute for work of outside auditors in financial statement audit

c] External auditors do not control internal auditors but often review work to avoid needless duplication

(4) Internal auditors responsible to management—external auditors responsible to users of financial statements

(a) Audit methods are similar

(b) Decisions about materiality or risk often different because internal auditors responsible to management

(c) Permitted for external auditors to use internal auditors to assist audit

1] May reduce audit fee

b. Operational auditing—looking at improving efficiency and performance in firm or government

(1) There are no generally accepted standards

(2) Reporting is to management

(3) Often about nonfinancial areas (i.e., personnel)

(4) Can be performed by internal, external, or government auditors

c. Compliance auditing—determination on how organization has complied with requirement of specified laws or regulations

(1) CPAs often hired to apply procedures to attest to management's assertion that company is complying with specified regulations—if so, CPA can issue unqualified opinion on compliance

7. Responsibilities in Governmental Auditing

a. Include audits of government organizations as well as those made by government audit agencies such as the GAO (Government Accounting Office)

(1) Audits may be accomplished by government auditors at local, state, or federal level or by CPA firms

b. Auditors must comply with all relevant AICPA and government auditing standards

(1) Must comply with government auditing standards (GAS) established by GAO

(a) These are published in "Yellow Book" and are known as "Yellow Book standards"—auditing standards in Yellow Book usually same as AICPA's GAAS with important exceptions

1] Threshold for materiality often lower because of sensitivity of government activities

2] Makes compliance auditing requirement for laws and regulations

3] Working papers standards are more detailed

(b) Government auditing standards include requirements for continuing education and training for governmental auditing

1] For auditors involved in government audits, twenty-four of eighty hours every two years for CPE must relate to governmental auditing

              (c) GAS pronouncements require reporting on compliance with laws and regulations as well as internal control

              (d) GAS pronouncements also cover financial statement audits

                  1] Whether financial statements are presented fairly in accordance with GAAP

                  2] Whether internal control procedures are in place

              (e) GAS pronouncements also cover performance audits of governmental entities

                  1] Economy and efficiency audits, including looking into whether entity has complied with laws and regulations on its economy and efficiency

                  2] Includes program audits to see if entity has complied with laws and regulations governing program

        (2) Must also comply with generally accepted auditing standards

              (a) These include all relevant AICPA generally accepted auditing standards

              (b) Members of AICPA violate AICPA Code of Professional Conduct if fail to follow GAS

    c. Single Audit Act established use of single organization-wide government audits to reduce duplication

        (1) State and local governments as well as other entities often get funding from several federal government sources—in past, this would require several audits to see that regulations for each source are complied with

        (2) State and local governments receiving $300,000 or more in federal funds in a fiscal year are now audited under the Single Audit Act and OMB Circular A-133 (*Audits of States, Local Governments, and Nonprofit Organizations*)

        (3) If they receive $300,000 or more in a year, they have the option of being audited under the Single Audit Act or under other federal requirements on each individual program

        (4) Single Audit Act mandates two additional reports

              (a) Report on compliance with laws and regulations

              (b) Report on entity's internal control

        (5) Single Audit Act also requires that auditors report on several other areas

              (a) Schedule of federal financial assistance

              (b) Compliance with requirements having material effect on federal financial assistance programs

                  1] Auditors required to report on whether organization has met requirements of laws and regulations that may materially affect each major program

                      a] Program is a major program if its expenditures meet threshold in relation to total expenditures of whole organization on all federal programs

                      b] For example—If organization's total expenditures are less than or equal to $100 million for year, a major program is one that expends $300,000 or 3% of the total expenditures of the organization, whichever is larger

                          i] For organizations over $100 million, rule to determine if it is major program is based on sliding scale in Single Audit Act

              (c) Internal control procedures

              (d) Compliance with general requirements of federal assistance programs that Congress mandates (many of these are for other than financial goals)

                  1] Examples include requirements involving drug-free workplace, prohibitions against civil rights violations, prohibitions against use of federal funds for partisan political purposes

8. Disciplinary Systems of the Profession and State Regulatory Bodies

    a. Joint trial board panel may discipline CPAs—possible results include

    (1) Acquittal

    (2) Admonishment

    (3) Suspension for up to two years

    (4) Expulsion from AICPA

        (a) May still practice public accounting using valid license issued by state

            1] Violation of state code, however, can result in revocation of CPA certificate and loss of ability to practice public accounting

        (b) Any member who departs from rulings or interpretations has burden justifying it in any disciplinary proceedings

        (c) **Automatic expulsion** from AICPA takes place when

            1] Member's CPA certificate is revoked by state board of accountancy or by some other authorized body

            2] Member convicted of felony

            3] Member files or helps to prepare fraudulent tax return for client or self

            4] Member intentionally fails to file tax return that was required

        (d) Professional Ethics Division may investigate ethics violations and may sanction those that are less serious using less severe remedies

        (e) In addition, court decisions have consistently held that even if an individual is not a member of AICPA, that individual is still expected to follow profession's Code of Professional Conduct

        (f) The individual state CPA board and societies monitor ethical matters

            1] Typically ethics complaints can be referred to state societies as well as to AICPA

            2] State boards license CPAs and can revoke or suspend licenses

  b. Securities Exchange Commission actions against accountant

    (1) After a hearing, SEC can revoke or suspend accountant from practicing before SEC if accountant willfully violated federal securities laws or regulations, or has acted unethically or unprofessionally

    (2) SEC can revoke or suspend accountant upon conviction of felony or misdemeanor in which moral turpitude was involved

    (3) SEC can prohibit accountant or accounting firm from doing work for SEC clients

    (4) SEC can penalize accountants with civil fines and mandates to pay profits gained from violations of securities laws and regulations

  c. Joint Ethics Enforcement Program

    (1) Most state societies have agreements with AICPA to allow referrals of ethics complaints to each other

B. Accountant's Legal Liabilities

1. Common Law Liability to Clients

  a. Liability to clients for breach of contract

    (1) Occurs if accountant fails to perform substantially as agreed under contract

        (a) Duties under contract may be

            1] Implied—accountant owes duty in contract to perform in nonnegligent manner

            2] Express—accountant owes duty to perform under terms of the contract

                a] This duty can extend liability beyond that which is standard under a normal audit

                b] Typically, terms are expressed in engagement letter that should specify clearly and in writing the following:

                    i] Type and scope of engagement to avoid misunderstandings between CPA and client ii] Procedures and tests to be used

        iii] That engagement will not necessarily uncover fraud, mistakes, defalcations, or illegal actions unless CPA agrees to greater responsibility

        iv] Engagement letter should be signed by at least client (accountant will typically sign also) but oral contract for audit still enforceable without engagement letter

(b) Accountant (CPA) is said to be in privity of contract with client when contract exists between them

    1] Reverse also true (i.e., client is in privity of contract with CPA)

(c) Accountant is not an insurer of financial statements and thus does not guarantee against losses from fraud

    1] "Normal" audit is not intended to uncover fraud, shortages, or defalcations, in general but is meant to provide audit evidence needed to express opinion on fairness of financial statements

(d) Accountant is not normally liable for failure to detect fraud, etc. **unless**

    1] "Normal" audit or review would have detected it, or

    2] Accountant by agreement has undertaken greater responsibility such as defalcation audit, or

    3] Wording of audit report indicates greater responsibility

    EXAMPLE: A CPA has been hired by a client to perform an audit. A standard engagement letter is used. During the course of the audit, the CPA fails to uncover a clever embezzlement scheme by one of the client's employees. The CPA is not liable for the losses unless a typical, reasonable audit should have resulted in discovery of the scheme.

(e) In an audit or review of financial statements, accountant is under duty to investigate when s/he discovers or becomes aware of suspicious items

    1] Investigation should extend beyond management's explanations

(2) Client should not interfere or prevent accountant from performing

    EXAMPLE: A CPA firm issues its opinion a few days late because of its client's failure to supply needed information. The CPA firm is entitled to the full fee agreed upon under the contract (engagement).

(3) When breach of contract occurs

(a) Accountant is not entitled to compensation if breach is major

    EXAMPLE: M failed to complete the audit by the agreed date. If time is of the essence so that the client receives no benefit from the audit, M is not entitled to compensation.

(b) Accountant is entitled to compensation if there are only minor errors but client may deduct from fees paid any damages caused by breach

(c) Client may recover any damages caused by breach even if accountant is not entitled to fee

(d) In general, punitive damages are not awarded for breach of contract

b. Liability to clients based on negligence

(1) Elements needed to prove negligence against accountant

(a) Accountant had duty to perform with same degree of skill and judgment possessed by average accountant

    1] This is the standard used in cases involving ordinary negligence (or simply called negligence)

        a] Different phrases are used for this standard, that is,

            i] Duty to exercise due care

            ii] Duty of skill of average, reasonable accountant (or CPA) iii] Duty to act as average (or reasonable) accountant (or CPA) would under similar circumstances

iv] Duty of judgment of ordinary, prudent accountant (or CPA)

2] Standard for accountants is guided by

a] State and federal statutes

b] Court decisions

c] Contract with client

d] GAAS and GAAP (persuasive but not conclusive)

i] Failure to follow GAAS virtually establishes lack of due care but reverse not true (i.e., following GAAS does not automatically preclude negligence but is strong evidence for presence of due care)

e] Customs of the profession (persuasive but not conclusive)

EXAMPLE: W, a CPA, issued an unqualified opinion on the financial statements of X Company. Included in the assets was inventory stated at cost when the market was materially below cost. This violation of GAAP can be used to establish that W was negligent. Also, the client can sue under contract law because W has an implied duty in the contract to not be negligent.

EXAMPLE: A CPA, while performing the annual audit, detects material errors in the previously issued audit report. The CPA has a duty to correct these material errors.

EXAMPLE: A CPA failing to warn a client of known internal weakness is falling below this standard.

(b) Accountant breached duty owed of average reasonable accountant

(c) Damage or loss results

1] Limited to actual losses that use of reasonable care would have avoided

2] Punitive damages not normally allowed for ordinary negligence

3] Contributory negligence may be a complete defense by CPA in many states if client's own negligence substantially contributed to accountant's failure to perform audit adequately

(d) Causal relationship must exist between fault of accountant and damages of plaintiff

1] Also, cause should be proximate (i.e., foreseeable)

EXAMPLE: A CPA negligently fails to discover during an audit that several expensive watches are missing from the client's inventory. Subsequently, an employee is caught stealing some watches. He confesses to stealing several before the audit and more after the audit when he found out he did not get caught. Only 5 of the watches can be recovered from the employee, who is unable to pay for those stolen. The CPA may be liable for those losses sustained after the audit if discovery could have prevented them. However, the CPA normally would not be liable for the watches taken before the audit when the loss is not the proximate result of the negligent audit. But if there were watches that could have been recovered at time of audit but can't be now, the CPA could be liable for those watches even though they were taken before audit.

c. Accountant's liability is not based solely on honest errors of judgment; liability requires at least negligence under common law

d. Liability to client for fraud, gross negligence, or constructive fraud

(1) Common law fraud of accountant is established by following elements:

(a) Misrepresentation of material fact or accountant's expert opinion

(b) Scienter, shown by either

1] Intent to mislead with accountant's knowledge of falsity, or

2] Reckless disregard of the truth

(c) Reasonable or justifiable reliance by injured party

(d) Actual damages

(2) Called constructive fraud or gross negligence if when proving above four elements, reckless disregard of the truth is established instead of knowledge of falsity

EXAMPLE: During the course of an audit, a CPA fails to verify the existence of the company's investments which amount to a substantial portion of the assets. Many of these, it is subsequently found, were nonexistent. Even in the absence of intent to defraud, the CPA is liable for constructive fraud based on reckless disregard of the truth.

EXAMPLE: Care and Less Co., CPAs, uncover suspicious items during the course of their audit of Blue Co. Because their audit steps did not require the additional steps needed to check into these suspicious items, the CPAs failed to uncover material errors. Even if a typical audit would not have required these additional audit steps, the CPAs are liable for the damages that result because they have a duty to look into such circumstances when they come to their attention.

    (3) Contributory negligence of client is not a defense available for accountant in cases of fraud, constructive fraud, or gross negligence

    (4) Privity of contract is not required for plaintiff to prove fraud, constructive fraud, or gross negligence

    (5) Punitive damages may be added to actual damages for fraud, constructive fraud, or gross negligence

2. Common Law Liability to Third Parties (Nonclients)

  a. Client is in privity of contract with accountant based on contractual relationship

    (1) In typical accountant-client relationship, there usually is no privity of contract between the accountant and third parties

    (2) Traditionally, accountants could use defense of no privity against suing third parties in contract and negligence cases

      (a) Ultramares decision is leading case in which accountants held liable only to parties for whose primary benefit financial statements are intended

        1] This generally means only client or third-party beneficiaries since these were in privity of contract with accountant

        2] However, anyone (including third parties) who can prove fraud or constructive fraud may recover

      (b) This is a significant **minority** rule today

  b. More recently, many courts have expanded liability to some third parties. The following distinctions should be understood:

    (1) Foreseen party—third party who accountant knew would rely on financial statements, or member of limited class that accountant knew would rely on financial statements, for specified transaction

      (a) **Majority rule** is that accountant is liable to foreseen third parties for negligence

        1] Rationale for not allowing liability to more third parties is that accountants should not be exposed to liability in indeterminate amount to indeterminate class

EXAMPLE: A CPA agrees to perform an audit for ABC Client knowing that the financial statements will be used to obtain a loan from XYZ Bank. Relying on the financial statements, XYZ Bank loans ABC $100,000. ABC goes bankrupt. If XYZ can establish that the financial statements were not fairly stated, thus causing the bank to give the loan, and if negligence can be established, most courts will allow XYZ Bank to recover from the CPA.

EXAMPLE: Facts are the same as in the example above except that XYZ Bank was not specified. Since the CPA knew that some bank would rely on these financial statements, the actual bank is a foreseen party since it is a member of a limited class and most courts will allow for liability.

      (b) Accountant liable for fraud, constructive fraud, or gross negligence to all parties whether foreseen or not

    (2) Distinguish foreseen party and foreseeable party

      (a) Foreseeable party—any party that accountant could reasonably foresee would receive financial statements and use them

        1] **Majority rule** is that accountant **not** liable to mere foreseeable parties for negligence

EXAMPLE: A CPA is informed that financial statements after being audited will be used to obtain a loan from a bank. The audited financial statements are also shown to trade creditors and potential investors. The bank is a foreseen third party but these other third parties are not actually foreseen parties and generally cannot recover from the CPA for ordinary negligence. They may qualify as foreseeable third parties since creditors or investors are the types of parties whom an accountant should reasonably foresee as users of the audited financial statements.

3. Statutory Liability to Third Parties—Securities Act of 1933

   a. General information on the Securities Act of 1933

     (1) Covers regulation of sales of securities registered under 1933 Act

       (a) Requires registration of initial issuances of securities with SEC

       (b) Makes it unlawful for registration statement to contain untrue **material** fact or to omit **material** fact

         1] Material fact—one about which average prudent investor should be informed

         2] Most potential accountant liability occurs because registration statement (and prospectus) includes audited financial statements

         3] Accountant's legal liability arises for untrue material fact or omission of material fact in registration statement (or prospectus)

         4] 1933 Act does not include periodic reports to SEC or annual reports to stockholders (these are in the 1934 Act below)

   b. Parties that may sue

     (1) Any purchaser of registered securities

       (a) Plaintiff need not be initial purchaser of security

       (b) Purchaser generally must prove that specific security was offered for sale through registration statement

         1] Exchange and issuance of stock based on a merger counts as a sale

     (2) Third parties can sue without having privity of contract with accountant under Federal Securities Acts

   c. Liability under Section 11 of the 1933 Act

     (1) This imposes liability on auditors (and other experts) for misstatements or omissions of material fact in certified financial statements or other information provided in registration statements

     (2) Proof requirements

       (a) Plaintiff (purchaser) must prove damages were incurred

       (b) Plaintiff must prove there was material misstatement or omission in financial statements included in registration statement

       (c) If these two are proven, it is sufficient to win against the CPA and shifts burden of proof to accountant who may escape liability by proving one of the following defenses

         1] "Due diligence," that is, after reasonable investigation, accountant had reasonable grounds to believe that statements were true while there was no material misstatement

NOTE: Although the basis of liability is not negligence, an accountant who was at least negligent will probably not be able to establish "due diligence."

         2] Plaintiff knew financial statements were incorrect when investment was made

         3] Lack of causation—loss was due to factors other than the misstatement or omission

         4] Following generally accepted auditing standards is generally valid as a defense for CPA

       (d) Plaintiff **need not** prove reliance on financial statements unless security was purchased at least twelve months after effective date of registration statement

       (e) Plaintiff **need not** prove negligence or fraud

d. Damages

(1) Difference between amount paid and market value at time of suit
(2) If sold, difference between amount paid and sale price
(3) Damages cannot exceed price at which security was offered to public
(4) Plaintiff cannot recover decrease in value after suit is brought

(a) Accountant is given benefit of any increase in market value during suit

e. Statute of limitations

(1) Action must be brought against accountant within one year from discovery (or when discovery should have been made) of false statement or omission
(2) Or if earlier, action must be brought within three years after security offered to public

f. This liability can come from negligence in reviewing events subsequent to date of certified balance sheet

(1) This is referred to as S-1 review when made for registration statement under securities regulations

EXAMPLE: An accountant performed an audit and later performed an S-1 review to review events subsequent to the balance sheet date. The accountant did not detect certain material events during this S-1 review even though there was sufficient evidence to make the accountant suspicious. Further investigation was required to avoid liability.

NOTE: This example was based on the case of Escott v. BarChris Construction Corporation.

4. Statutory Liability to Third Parties—Securities Exchange Act of 1934

a. General information on Securities Exchange Act of 1934

(1) Regulates securities sold on national stock exchanges

(a) Includes securities traded over-the-counter and other equity securities where the corporation has more than $10 million in total assets and the security is held by 500 or more persons at the end of a fiscal year

(2) Requires each company to furnish to SEC an annual report (Form 10-K)

(a) Includes financial statements (not necessarily the same as an annual report to shareholders) attested to by an accountant
(b) Accountant civil liability comes from two sections—10 and 18

1] Section 10 (including Rule 10b-5)—makes it unlawful to

a] Employ any device, scheme, or artifice to defraud
b] Make untrue statement of material fact or omit material fact
c] Engage in act, practice, or course of business to commit fraud or deceit in connection with purchase or sale of security

2] Section 18—makes it unlawful to make false or misleading statement with respect to a material statement unless done in "good faith"

b. Parties who may sue

(1) Purchasers **and** sellers of registered securities

(a) Note that under the 1933 Act, only purchasers may sue
(b) Exchanges and issuances of stock based on merger included in 1934 Act

c. Proof requirements—Section 10, in general including Rule 10b-5

(1) Plaintiff (purchaser or seller) must prove damages resulted in connection with purchase or sale of security in interstate commerce
(2) Plaintiff must prove there was a material misstatement or omission in information released by firm

        (a) Information may, for example, be in form of audited financial statements in report to stockholders or in Form 10-K

    (3) Plaintiff must prove justifiable reliance on financial information

    (4) Plaintiff must prove existence of **scienter** (the intent to deceive, manipulate, or defraud)

        (a) Includes reckless disregard of truth or knowledge of falsity

        (b) Negligence alone will not subject accountant to liability under this section but lack of good faith will

    (5) Note that these proof requirements differ in very significant ways from proof requirements under the 1933 Act

    (6) Plaintiff cannot recover if s/he is reckless or fraudulent

  d. Proof requirements—Section 18

    (1) Plaintiff (purchaser or seller) must prove

        (a) S/he incurred damages

        (b) There was a material misstatement or omission on report (usually Form 10-K) filed with SEC

        (c) S/he read and relied on defective report

    (2) Then burden of proof is shifted to accountant who may escape liability by proving s/he acted in "good faith"

        (a) Although basis of liability here is not negligence, an accountant who has been grossly negligent typically will not be able to establish "good faith"

        (b) An accountant who has been only negligent will probably be able to establish "good faith"

  e. Damages

    (1) Generally, difference between amount paid and market value at time of suit

    (2) If sold, difference between amount paid and sale price

5. Summary of auditors' defenses under Securities Act of 1933 and Securities Exchange Act of 1934*

• **Defenses** available to auditors:	*1934 Act*	*1933 Act*
1. Audit was performed with **due care**	Yes	Yes
2. Misstatement was immaterial	Yes	Yes
3. Plaintiff had prior knowledge of misstatement	Yes	Yes
4. Plaintiff did not rely on information	Yes	No
5. Misstatement was not cause of loss	Yes	Yes

  • Due diligence is a defense for the 1933 Act **only** (Do not use for 1934)

* Prepared by Debra R. Hopkins, Northern Illinois University

C. Legal Considerations Affecting the Accountant's Responsibility

1. Accountant's working papers

  a. Consist of notes, computations, etc. that accountant accumulates when doing professional work for client

  b. Owned by accountant unless there is agreement to the contrary

  c. Ownership is essentially custodial in nature (to serve dual purpose)

    (1) To preserve confidentiality

        (a) Absent client consent, cannot allow transmission of information in working papers to another

            1] However, accountant must produce, upon being given an enforceable subpoena, workpapers requested by court of law or government agency

                a] Subpoenas should be limited in scope and specific in purpose b] Accountant may challenge a subpoena as being too broad and unreasonably burdensome

       (2) Retention by accountant as evidence of nature and extent of work performed for legal or other reasons

2. Privileged communications between accountant and client

    a. Do not exist at common law so must be created by statute

       (1) Only a few states have privileged communications
       (2) Federal law does not recognize privileged communications
       (3) If accountant acting as agent for (hired by) one who has privileged communication such as an attorney, then accountant's communications are privileged

    b. To be considered privileged, accountant-client communication must

       (1) Be located in a jurisdiction where recognized
       (2) Have been intended to be confidential at time of communication
       (3) Not be waived by client

    c. If considered privileged, valid grounds exist for accountant to refuse to testify in court concerning these matters

       (1) This privilege is, in general, for benefit of client
       (2) Can be waived by client
       (3) If part of privileged communication is allowed, all of privilege is lost

    d. Code of Professional Conduct prohibits disclosure of confidential client data unless

       (1) Client consents

          (a) Note that if client is a partnership, each partner is actually a client and therefore each must give consent

       (2) To comply with GAAS and GAAP
       (3) To comply with enforceable subpoena (e.g., courts where privilege not recognized)
       (4) Quality review under AICPA authorization
       (5) Responding to AICPA or state trial board

    e. US Supreme Court has held that tax accrual files are not protected by accountant-client privilege

3. Illegal acts by clients

    a. Situations in which there may be a duty to notify parties outside the client

       (1) Form 8-K disclosures (change of auditors)
       (2) Disclosure to successor auditor (AU315)
       (3) Disclosure in response to subpoena
       (4) Disclosure to funding agency for entities receiving governmental financial assistance

4. CPA certificates are issued under state (not federal) jurisdiction
5. Acts of employees

    a. Accountant is liable for acts of employees in the course of employment

    EXAMPLE: XYZ, a partnership of CPAs, hires Y to help perform an audit. Y is negligent in the audit, causing the client damage. The partners cannot escape liability by showing they did not perform the negligent act.

    b. Insurance typically used to cover such losses

6. Duty to perform audit is not delegable because it is contract for personal services
7. Generally, basis of relationship of accountant to his/her client is that of independent contractor
8. Insurance

    a. Accountants' malpractice insurance covers their negligence
    b. Fidelity bond protects client from accountant's fraud

    c. Client's insurance company is subrogated to client's rights (i.e., has same rights of recovery of loss against accountant that client had)

9. Reliance by auditor on other auditor's work

    a. Principal auditor still liable for all work unless audit report clearly indicates divided responsibility

    b. Cannot rely on unaudited data; must disclaim or qualify opinion

10. Subsequent events and subsequent discovery

    a. Generally not liable on audit report for effect of events subsequent to last day of fieldwork

       (1) Unless report is dated as of the subsequent event
       (2) Liability extends to effective date of registration for reports filed with SEC

    b. Liable if subsequently discovered facts that existed at report date indicate statements were misleading **unless**

       (1) Immediate investigation is conducted, and
       (2) Prompt revision of statements is possible, or
       (3) SEC and persons known to be relying on statements are notified by client or CPA

    c. Accountant liable if s/he makes assurances that there are no material changes after fieldwork or report date when in fact there are material changes

       (1) Therefore accountant should perform sufficient audit procedures before giving this assurance

11. Liability from preparation of unaudited financial statements

    a. Financial statements are unaudited if

       (1) No auditing procedures have been applied
       (2) Insufficient audit procedures have been applied to express an opinion

    b. Failure to mark each page, "unaudited"
    c. Failure to issue a disclaimer of opinion
    d. Failure to inform client of any discovery of something amiss

       (1) For example, circumstances indicating presence of fraud

D. Criminal Liability

1. Sources of liability

    a. Securities Act of 1933 and Securities Exchange Act of 1934

       (1) Can be found guilty for **willful** illegal conduct

           (a) Misleading omission of material facts
           (b) Putting false information in registration statement

       (2) Subject to fine of up to $10,000 and/or up to five years prison
       (3) Examples of possible criminal actions

           (a) CPA aids management in a fraudulent scheme
           (b) CPA covers up prior year financial statement misstatements

    b. Criminal violations of Internal Revenue Code

       (1) For willfully preparing false return (perjury)
       (2) For willfully assisting others to evade taxes (tax evasion)

    c. Criminal liability under RICO (Racketeer Influenced and Corrupt Organizations)

       (1) Covers individuals affiliated with businesses or associations involved in a pattern of racketeering

           (a) Racketeering includes organized crime but also includes fraud under the federal securities laws as well as mail fraud

        1] Accountants subject to criminal penalty through affiliation with accounting firm or business involved in racketeering

      (b) Pattern of racketeering means at least two illegal acts of racketeering in previous ten years

  (2) RICO has also been expanded to allow civil suit by private parties

      (a) Treble damages allowed (to encourage private enforcement)
      (b) Has been held to apply against accountants even without a criminal indictment or conviction

E. Responsibilities of Auditors under Private Securities Litigation Reform Act

1. Auditors who audit financial statements under Federal Securities Exchange Act of 1934 are required to establish procedures to

  a. Detect material illegal acts
  b. Identify material related-party transactions, and
  c. Evaluate ability of firm to continue as going concern

2. If auditor detects possible illegal activity, must inform audit committee or board of directors

  a. If senior management or board fails to take remedial action and if illegal activities are material so that departure from standard audit report or auditor resignation is indicated, auditor shall report this to board of directors

    (1) Board has one day to notify SEC of this report

      (a) If not done, auditor must furnish SEC with copy of auditor's report to board and/or resign from audit

3. Civil liability may be imposed by SEC for auditor's failures under Act

  a. Auditors are protected from private civil suits for these reports to SEC under this Act

4. Amends Federal Securities Act of 1933 and Federal Securities Exchange Act of 1934

  a. Law passed to reduce lawsuits against accounting firms and issuers of securities

    (1) SEC's enforcement of securities laws not affected by act because law governs private litigation

5. Creates "safe harbor" from legal liability for preparation of forward-looking statements

  a. Including projections of income, revenues, EPS, and company plans for products and services
  b. To fall within safe harbor, written or oral forward-looking statement should include cautions and identify assumptions and conditions that may cause projections to vary
  c. Purpose is to encourage company to give investors more meaningful information without fear of lawsuits

6. Discourages class action lawsuits for frivolous purposes

  a. Accomplished by

    (1) Providing for stringent pleading requirements for many private actions under Securities Exchange Act of 1934
    (2) Awards costs and attorneys' fees against parties failing to fulfill these pleading requirements

7. Changes rules on joint and several liability, so that liability of defendants is generally proportionate to their degree of fault

  a. This relieves accountants (and others) from being "deep pockets" except up to their proportional fault
  b. Exception—joint and several liability is imposed if defendant **knowingly** caused harm

EXAMPLE: Plaintiffs suffered $2 million in damages from securities fraud of a company. The auditors of the company are found to be 15% at fault. If the auditors did not act knowingly, they can be held liable for the 15% or $300,000. If they acted knowingly, they can be held liable for up to the full $2 million based on joint and several liability.

    c.   Accountants liable for the proportionate share of damages they actually (and unknowingly) caused plus an additional 50% where principal defendant is insolvent

F. New Responsibilities and Provisions under Sarbanes-Oxley Act

  1. This act is predicted to generate not only provisions summarized here but also new laws and regulations for at least next three to five years—new information for this Module and Module 16 will be available when it is relevant for your preparation for CPA exam

  2. New federal crime involving willful nonretention of audit and review workpapers

    a.   Retention required for five years (in some cases seven years)
    b.   Provides for fines or imprisonment up to ten years or both
    c.   Applies to accountant who audits issuer of securities
    d.   Act requires SEC to issue new rules and then periodically update its rules on details of retaining workpapers and other relevant records connected with audits or reviews

  3. SEC authorized to discipline professionals practicing before SEC

    a.   SEC may censure, temporarily bar or permanently bar him/her for

      (1) Lack of qualifications needed
      (2) Improper professional conduct
      (3) Willful violation of helping another violate securities laws or regulations

  4. Creates new Public Company Accounting Oversight Board

    a.   Violation of rules of this Board treated as violation of Securities Exchange Act of 1934 with its penalties
    b.   Two members must be or have been CPAs

      (1) Three members cannot be or cannot have been CPAs

    c.   Board regulates firms that audit SEC registrants, not accounting firms of private companies
    d.   Main functions of Board are to

      (1) Register and conduct inspections of public accounting firms

        (a) This replaces peer reviews

      (2) Set standards on auditing, quality control, independence, or preparation of audit reports

        (a) May adopt standards of existing professional groups or new groups
        (b) Accounting firm must have second partner review and approve each audit report
        (c) Accounting firm must report on examination of internal control structure along with description of material weaknesses

      (3) Enforce compliance with professional standards, securities laws relating to accountants and audits
      (4) Perform investigations and disciplinary proceedings on registered public accounting firms

  5. Act lists several specific service categories that issuer's public accounting firm cannot legally do, even if approved by audit committee, such as

    a.   Bookkeeping or other services relating to financial statements or accounting records
    b.   Financial information systems design and/or implementation
    c.   Appraisal services
    d.   Internal audit outsourcing services
    e.   Management functions
    f.   Note that Act does **not** restrict auditor from performing these services to nonaudit clients or to private companies
    g.   Act intended to restrict specified categories performed for public audit clients
    h.   Act permits auditor as a registered public accounting firm to perform nonaudit services not specifically prohibited (e.g., tax services) when approved by issuer's audit committee

  6. Act does not now require that accounting firms be rotated

      a.   But does require that both audit partner having primary responsibility for the audit and audit partner who reviews audit can do the audit services for that issuer for only five consecutive years

7. Act requires increased disclosure of off-balance-sheet transactions
8. Act mandates that pro forma financial disclosures be reconciled with figures done under GAAP
9. Act creates new federal laws against destruction or tampering with audit workpapers or documents that are to be used in official proceedings
10. Act increases protection of whistleblowers

MULTIPLE-CHOICE QUESTIONS (1-67)

1. Which of the following best describes what is meant by the term generally accepted auditing standards?
   a. Rules acknowledged by the accounting profession because of their universal application.
   b. Pronouncements issued by the Auditing Standards Board.
   c. Measures of the quality of the auditor's performance.
   d. Procedures to be used to gather evidence to support financial statements.

2. For which of the following can a member of the AICPA receive an automatic expulsion from the AICPA?

   I. Member is convicted of a felony.
   II. Member files his own fraudulent tax return.
   III. Member files fraudulent tax return for a client knowing that it is fraudulent.

   a. I only.
   b. I and II only.
   c. I and III only.
   d. I, II, and III.

3. According to the standards of the profession, which of the following circumstances will prevent a CPA performing audit engagements from being independent?
   a. Obtaining a collateralized automobile loan from a financial institution client.
   b. Litigation with a client relating to billing for consulting services for which the amount is immaterial.
   c. Employment of the CPA's spouse as a client's director of internal audit.
   d. Acting as an honorary trustee for a not-for-profit organization client.

4. The profession's ethical standards most likely would be considered to have been violated when a CPA represents that specific consulting services will be performed for a stated fee and it is apparent at the time of the representation that the
   a. Actual fee would be substantially higher.
   b. Actual fee would be substantially lower than the fees charged by other CPAs for comparable services.
   c. CPA would **not** be independent.
   d. Fee was a competitive bid.

5. According to the ethical standards of the profession, which of the following acts is generally prohibited?
   a. Issuing a modified report explaining a failure to follow a governmental regulatory agency's standards when conducting an attest service for a client.
   b. Revealing confidential client information during a quality review of a professional practice by a team from the state CPA society.
   c. Accepting a contingent fee for representing a client in an examination of the client's federal tax return by an IRS agent.
   d. Retaining client records after an engagement is terminated prior to completion and the client has demanded their return.

6. According to the profession's ethical standards, which of the following events may justify a departure from a Statement of Financial Accounting Standards?

	New legislation	*Evolution of a new form of business transaction*
a.	No	Yes
b.	Yes	No
c.	Yes	Yes
d.	No	No

7. May a CPA hire for the CPA's public accounting firm a non-CPA systems analyst who specializes in developing computer systems?
   a. Yes, provided the CPA is qualified to perform each of the specialist's tasks.
   b. Yes, provided the CPA is able to supervise the specialist and evaluate the specialist's end product.
   c. No, because non-CPA professionals are **not** permitted to be associated with CPA firms in public practice.
   d. No, because developing computer systems is **not** recognized as a service performed by public accountants.

8. Stephanie Seals is a CPA who is working as a controller for Brentwood Corporation. She is not in public practice. Which statement is true?
   a. She may use the CPA designation on her business cards if she also puts her employment title on them.
   b. She may use the CPA designation on her business cards as long as she does not mention Brentwood Corporation or her title as controller.
   c. She may use the CPA designation on company transmittals but not on her business cards.
   d. She may not use the CPA designation because she is not in public practice.

9. According to the standards of the profession, which of the following activities would most likely **not** impair a CPA's independence?
   a. Providing advisory services for a client.
   b. Contracting with a client to supervise the client's office personnel.
   c. Signing a client's checks in emergency situations.
   d. Accepting a luxurious gift from a client.

10. Which of the following reports may be issued only by an accountant who is independent of a client?
   a. Standard report on an examination of a financial forecast.
   b. Report on consulting services.
   c. Compilation report on historical financial statements.
   d. Compilation report on a financial projection.

11. According to the standards of the profession, which of the following activities may be required in exercising due care?

	Consulting with experts	*Obtaining specialty accreditation*
a.	Yes	Yes
b.	Yes	No
c.	No	Yes
d.	No	No

12. Larry Sampson is a CPA and is serving as an expert witness in a trial concerning a corporation's financial statements. Which of the following is(are) true?

  I. Sampson's status as an expert witness is based upon his specialized knowledge, experience, and training.

  II. Sampson is required by AICPA ruling to present his position objectively.

  III. Sampson may regard himself as acting as an advocate.

    a. I only.
    b. I and II only.
    c. I and III only.
    d. III only.

13. According to the ethical standards of the profession, which of the following acts is generally prohibited?
    a. Purchasing a product from a third party and reselling it to a client.
    b. Writing a financial management newsletter promoted and sold by a publishing company.
    c. Accepting a commission for recommending a product to an audit client.
    d. Accepting engagements obtained through the efforts of third parties.

14. To exercise due professional care an auditor should
    a. Critically review the judgment exercised by those assisting in the audit.
    b. Examine all available corroborating evidence supporting managements assertions.
    c. Design the audit to detect all instances of illegal acts.
    d. Attain the proper balance of professional experience and formal education.

15. Kar, CPA, is a staff auditor participating in the audit engagement of Fort, Inc. Which of the following circumstances impairs Kar's independence?
    a. During the period of the professional engagement, Fort gives Kar tickets to a football game worth $75.
    b. Kar owns stock in a corporation that Fort's 401(k) plan also invests in.
    c. Kar's friend, an employee of another local accounting firm, prepares Fort's tax returns.
    d. Kar's sibling is director of internal audit at Fort.

16. On June 1, 2000, a CPA obtained a $100,000 personal loan from a financial institution client for whom the CPA provided compilation services. The loan was fully secured and considered material to the CPA's net worth. The CPA paid the loan in full on December 31, 2001. On April 3, 2001, the client asked the CPA to audit the client's financial statements for the year ended December 31, 2001. Is the CPA considered independent with respect to the audit of the client's December 31, 2001 financial statements?
    a. Yes, because the loan was fully secured.
    b. Yes, because the CPA was **not** required to be independent at the time the loan was granted.
    c. No, because the CPA had a loan with the client during the period of a professional engagement.
    d. No, because the CPA had a loan with the client during the period covered by the financial statements.

17. Which of the following statements is(are) correct regarding a CPA employee of a CPA firm taking copies of information contained in client files when the CPA leaves the firm?

  I. A CPA leaving a firm may take copies of information contained in client files to assist another firm in serving that client.

  II. A CPA leaving a firm may take copies of information contained in client files as a method of gaining technical expertise.

    a. I only.
    b. II only.
    c. Both I and II.
    d. Neither I nor II.

18. Which of the following statements is correct regarding an accountant's working papers?
    a. The accountant owns the working papers and generally may disclose them as the accountant sees fit.
    b. The client owns the working papers but the accountant has custody of them until the accountant's bill is paid in full.
    c. The accountant owns the working papers but generally may **not** disclose them without the client's consent or a court order.
    d. The client owns the working papers but, in the absence of the accountant's consent, may **not** disclose them without a court order.

19. According to the profession's standards, which of the following would be considered consulting services?

	Advisory services	Implementation services	Product services
a.	Yes	Yes	Yes
b.	Yes	Yes	No
c.	Yes	No	Yes
d.	No	Yes	Yes

20. According to the standards of the profession, which of the following events would require a CPA performing a consulting services engagement for a nonaudit client to withdraw from the engagement?

  I. The CPA has a conflict of interest that is disclosed to the client and the client consents to the CPA continuing the engagement.

  II. The CPA fails to obtain a written understanding from the client concerning the scope of the engagement.

    a. I only.
    b. II only.
    c. Both I and II.
    d. Neither I nor II.

21. Which of the following services may a CPA perform in carrying out a consulting service for a client?

  I. Analysis of the client's accounting system.

  II. Review of the client's prepared business plan.

  III. Preparation of information for obtaining financing.

    a. I and II only.
    b. I and III only.
    c. II and III only.
    d. I, II, and III.

22. Under the Statements on Standards for Consulting Services, which of the following statements best reflects a CPA's responsibility when undertaking a consulting services engagement? The CPA must
    a. Not seek to modify any agreement made with the client.
    b. Not perform any attest services for the client.
    c. Inform the client of significant reservations concerning the benefits of the engagement.
    d. Obtain a written understanding with the client concerning the time for completion of the engagement.

23. Which of the following services is a CPA generally required to perform when conducting a personal financial planning engagement?
    a. Assisting the client to identify tasks that are essential in order to act on planning decisions.
    b. Assisting the client to take action on planning decisions.
    c. Monitoring progress in achieving goals.
    d. Updating recommendations and revising planning decisions.

24. Which of the following is correct concerning internal auditing?
    a. The internal auditor often coordinates his/her work with that of the company's external auditors.
    b. The internal auditor must maintain independence in the sense of doing the audit completely independently from the external auditors.
    c. The internal auditor has no responsibility to maintain independence.
    d. The work of the internal auditors, if they are CPAs, substitutes for the work of external auditors.

25. Which of the following is(are) true concerning independent auditors involved in governmental accounting?
  I. They must meet requirements for continuing education that include some governmental auditing.
  II. Members of the AICPA violate the AICPA Code of Professional Conduct if they fail to follow generally accepted government auditing standards.
    a. I only.
    b. II only.
    c. Both I and II.
    d. Neither I nor II.

26. Which of the following is correct regarding the Single Audit Act?
  I. The Act mandates that local and state governments receiving $300,000 or more in federal funds in a fiscal year are to be audited under this Act.
  II. The purpose of this Act is to reduce duplication in organization-wide governmental audits.
  III. For government entities covered under this Act, only one audit every five years is required.
    a. I only.
    b. II only.
    c. I and II only.
    d. II and III only.

27. Cable Corp. orally engaged Drake & Co., CPAs, to audit its financial statements. Cable's management informed Drake that it suspected the accounts receivable were materially overstated. Though the financial statements Drake audited included a materially overstated accounts receivable balance, Drake issued an unqualified opinion. Cable used the financial statements to obtain a loan to expand its operations. Cable defaulted on the loan and incurred a substantial loss.

If Cable sues Drake for negligence in failing to discover the overstatement, Drake's best defense would be that Drake did **not**
    a. Have privity of contract with Cable.
    b. Sign an engagement letter.
    c. Perform the audit recklessly or with an intent to deceive.
    d. Violate generally accepted auditing standards in performing the audit.

28. Which of the following statements best describes whether a CPA has met the required standard of care in conducting an audit of a client's financial statements?
    a. The client's expectations with regard to the accuracy of audited financial statements.
    b. The accuracy of the financial statements and whether the statements conform to generally accepted accounting principles.
    c. Whether the CPA conducted the audit with the same skill and care expected of an ordinarily prudent CPA under the circumstances.
    d. Whether the audit was conducted to investigate and discover all acts of fraud.

29. Ford & Co., CPAs, issued an unqualified opinion on Owens Corp.'s financial statements. Relying on these financial statements, Century Bank lent Owens $750,000. Ford was unaware that Century would receive a copy of the financial statements or that Owens would use them to obtain a loan. Owens defaulted on the loan.

To succeed in a common law fraud action against Ford, Century must prove, in addition to other elements, that Century was
    a. Free from contributory negligence.
    b. In privity of contract with Ford.
    c. Justified in relying on the financial statements.
    d. In privity of contract with Owens.

30. When performing an audit, a CPA
    a. Must exercise the level of care, skill, and judgment expected of a reasonably prudent CPA under the circumstances.
    b. Must strictly adhere to generally accepted accounting principles.
    c. Is strictly liable for failing to discover client fraud.
    d. Is **not** liable unless the CPA commits gross negligence or intentionally disregards generally accepted auditing standards.

31. When performing an audit, a CPA will most likely be considered negligent when the CPA fails to
    a. Detect all of a client's fraudulent activities.
    b. Include a negligence disclaimer in the client engagement letter.
    c. Warn a client of known internal control weaknesses.
    d. Warn a client's customers of embezzlement by the client's employees.

32. A CPA's duty of due care to a client most likely will be breached when a CPA
    a.   Gives a client an oral instead of written report.
    b.   Gives a client incorrect advice based on an honest error of judgment.
    c.   Fails to give tax advice that saves the client money.
    d.   Fails to follow generally accepted auditing standards.

33. Which of the following elements, if present, would support a finding of constructive fraud on the part of a CPA?
    a.   Gross negligence in applying generally accepted auditing standards.
    b.   Ordinary negligence in applying generally accepted accounting principles.
    c.   Identified third-party users.
    d.   Scienter.

34. If a CPA recklessly departs from the standards of due care when conducting an audit, the CPA will be liable to third parties who are unknown to the CPA based on
    a.   Negligence.
    b.   Gross negligence.
    c.   Strict liability.
    d.   Criminal deceit.

35. In a common law action against an accountant, lack of privity is a viable defense if the plaintiff
    a.   Is the client's creditor who sues the accountant for negligence.
    b.   Can prove the presence of gross negligence that amounts to a reckless disregard for the truth.
    c.   Is the accountant's client.
    d.   Bases the action upon fraud.

36. A CPA audited the financial statements of Shelly Company. The CPA was negligent in the audit. Sanco, a supplier of Shelly, is upset because Sanco had extended Shelly a high credit limit based on the financial statements which were incorrect. Which of the following statements is the most correct?
    a.   In most states, both Shelly and Sanco can recover from the CPA for damages due to the negligence.
    b.   States that use the Ultramares decision will allow both Shelly and Sanco to recover.
    c.   In most states, Sanco cannot recover as a mere foreseeable third party.
    d.   Generally, Sanco can recover but Shelly cannot.

37. Under the Ultramares rule, to which of the following parties will an accountant be liable for negligence?

	Parties in privity	Foreseen parties
a.	Yes	Yes
b.	Yes	No
c.	No	Yes
d.	No	No

Items 38 and 39 are based on the following:

While conducting an audit, Larson Associates, CPAs, failed to detect material misstatements included in its client's financial statements. Larson's unqualified opinion was included with the financial statements in a registration statement and prospectus for a public offering of securities made by the client. Larson knew that its opinion and the financial statements would be used for this purpose.

38. In a suit by a purchaser against Larson for common law negligence, Larson's best defense would be that the
    a.   Audit was conducted in accordance with generally accepted auditing standards.
    b.   Client was aware of the misstatements.
    c.   Purchaser was **not** in privity of contract with Larson.
    d.   Identity of the purchaser was **not** known to Larson at the time of the audit.

39. In a suit by a purchaser against Larson for common law fraud, Larson's best defense would be that
    a.   Larson did **not** have actual or constructive knowledge of the misstatements.
    b.   Larson's client knew or should have known of the misstatements.
    c.   Larson did **not** have actual knowledge that the purchaser was an intended beneficiary of the audit.
    d.   Larson was **not** in privity of contract with its client.

40. Quincy bought Teal Corp. common stock in an offering registered under the Securities Act of 1933. Worth & Co., CPAs, gave an unqualified opinion on Teal's financial statements that were included in the registration statement filed with the SEC. Quincy sued Worth under the provisions of the 1933 Act that deal with omission of facts required to be in the registration statement. Quincy must prove that
    a.   There was fraudulent activity by Worth.
    b.   There was a material misstatement in the financial statements.
    c.   Quincy relied on Worth's opinion.
    d.   Quincy was in privity with Worth.

41. Beckler & Associates, CPAs, audited and gave an unqualified opinion on the financial statements of Queen Co. The financial statements contained misstatements that resulted in a material overstatement of Queen's net worth. Queen provided the audited financial statements to Mac Bank in connection with a loan made by Mac to Queen. Beckler knew that the financial statements would be provided to Mac. Queen defaulted on the loan. Mac sued Beckler to recover for its losses associated with Queen's default. Which of the following must Mac prove in order to recover?

   I.   Beckler was negligent in conducting the audit.
  II.   Mac relied on the financial statements.

    a.   I only.
    b.   II only.
    c.   Both I and II.
    d.   Neither I nor II.

Items 42 and 43 are based on the following:

Dart Corp. engaged Jay Associates, CPAs, to assist in a public stock offering. Jay audited Dart's financial statements and gave an unqualified opinion, despite knowing that the financial statements contained misstatements. Jay's opinion was included in Dart's registration statement. Larson purchased shares in the offering and suffered a loss when the stock declined in value after the misstatements became known.

42. In a suit against Jay and Dart under the Section 11 liability provisions of the Securities Act of 1933, Larson must prove that

a. Jay knew of the misstatements.
b. Jay was negligent.
c. The misstatements contained in Dart's financial statements were material.
d. The unqualified opinion contained in the registration statement was relied on by Larson.

43. If Larson succeeds in the Section 11 suit against Dart, Larson would be entitled to
a. Damages of three times the original public offering price.
b. Rescind the transaction.
c. Monetary damages only.
d. Damages, but only if the shares were resold before the suit was started.

Items 44 and 45 are based on the following:

Under the liability provisions of Section 11 of the Securities Act of 1933, a CPA may be liable to any purchaser of a security for certifying materially misstated financial statements that are included in the security's registration statement.

44. Under Section 11, a CPA usually will **not** be liable to the purchaser
a. If the purchaser is contributorily negligent.
b. If the CPA can prove due diligence.
c. Unless the purchaser can prove privity with the CPA.
d. Unless the purchaser can prove scienter on the part of the CPA.

45. Under Section 11, which of the following must be proven by a purchaser of the security?

	Reliance on the financial statements	Fraud by the CPA
a.	Yes	Yes
b.	Yes	No
c.	No	Yes
d.	No	No

46. Ocean and Associates, CPAs, audited the financial statements of Drain Corporation. As a result of Ocean's negligence in conducting the audit, the financial statements included material misstatements. Ocean was unaware of this fact. The financial statements and Ocean's unqualified opinion were included in a registration statement and prospectus for an original public offering of stock by Drain. Sharp purchased shares in the offering. Sharp received a copy of the prospectus prior to the purchase but did not read it. The shares declined in value as a result of the misstatements in Drain's financial statements becoming known. Under which of the following Acts is Sharp most likely to prevail in a lawsuit against Ocean?

	Securities Exchange Act of 1934, Section 10(b), Rule 10b-5	Securities Act of 1933, Section 11
a.	Yes	Yes
b.	Yes	No
c.	No	Yes
d.	No	No

47. Danvy, a CPA, performed an audit for Lank Corporation. Danvy also performed an S-1 review to review events subsequent to the balance sheet date. If Danvy fails to further investigate suspicious facts, under which of these can he be found negligent?
a. The audit but not the review.
b. The review but not the audit.
c. Neither the audit nor the review.
d. Both the audit and the review.

48. Dart Corp. engaged Jay Associates, CPAs, to assist in a public stock offering. Jay audited Dart's financial statements and gave an unqualified opinion, despite knowing that the financial statements contained misstatements. Jay's opinion was included in Dart's registration statement. Larson purchased shares in the offering and suffered a loss when the stock declined in value after the misstatements became known.

In a suit against Jay under the antifraud provisions of Section 10(b) and Rule 10b-5 of the Securities Exchange Act of 1934, Larson must prove all of the following **except**
a. Larson was an intended user of the false registration statement.
b. Larson relied on the false registration statement.
c. The transaction involved some form of interstate commerce.
d. Jay acted with intentional disregard of the truth.

49. Under the antifraud provisions of Section 10(b) of the Securities Exchange Act of 1934, a CPA may be liable if the CPA acted
a. Negligently.
b. With independence.
c. Without due diligence.
d. Without good faith.

50. Under Section 11 of the Securities Act of 1933, which of the following standards may a CPA use as a defense?

	Generally accepted accounting principles	Generally accepted fraud detection standards
a.	Yes	Yes
b.	Yes	No
c.	No	Yes
d.	No	No

51. Dart Corp. engaged Jay Associates, CPAs, to assist in a public stock offering. Jay audited Dart's financial statements and gave an unqualified opinion, despite knowing that the financial statements contained misstatements. Jay's opinion was included in Dart's registration statement. Larson purchased shares in the offering and suffered a loss when the stock declined in value after the misstatements became known.

If Larson succeeds in the Section 10(b) and Rule 10b-5 suit, Larson would be entitled to
a. Only recover the original public offering price.
b. Only rescind the transaction.
c. The amount of any loss caused by the fraud.
d. Punitive damages.

52. Which of the following statements is correct with respect to ownership, possession, or access to a CPA firm's audit working papers?
a. Working papers may **never** be obtained by third parties unless the client consents.
b. Working papers are **not** transferable to a purchaser of a CPA practice unless the client consents.

    c.   Working papers are subject to the privileged communication rule which, in most jurisdictions, prevents any third-party access to the working papers.

    d.   Working papers are the client's exclusive property.

53. Which of the following statements is correct regarding a CPA's working papers? The working papers must be

    a.   Transferred to another accountant purchasing the CPA's practice even if the client hasn't given permission.

    b.   Transferred permanently to the client if demanded.

    c.   Turned over to any government agency that requests them.

    d.   Turned over pursuant to a valid federal court subpoena.

54. To which of the following parties may a CPA partnership provide its working papers, without being lawfully subpoenaed or without the client's consent?

    a.   The IRS.

    b.   The FASB.

    c.   Any surviving partner(s) on the death of a partner.

    d.   A CPA before purchasing a partnership interest in the firm.

55. To which of the following parties may a CPA partnership orvide its working papers without either the client's consent or a lawful subpoena?

	The IRS	The FASB
a.	Yes	Yes
b.	Yes	No
c.	No	Yes
d.	No	No

56. A CPA is permitted to disclose confidential client information without the consent of the client to

  I.   Another CPA who has purchased the CPA's tax practice.

  II.   Another CPA firm if the information concerns suspected tax return irregularities.

 III.   A state CPA society voluntary quality control review board.

    a.   I and III only.

    b.   II and III only.

    c.   II only.

    d.   III only.

57. Thorp, CPA, was engaged to audit Ivor Co.'s financial statements. During the audit, Thorp discovered that Ivor's inventory contained stolen goods. Ivor was indicted and Thorp was subpoenaed to testify at the criminal trial. Ivor claimed accountant-client privilege to prevent Thorp from testifying. Which of the following statements is correct regarding Ivor's claim?

    a.   Ivor can claim an accountant-client privilege only in states that have enacted a statute creating such a privilege.

    b.   Ivor can claim an accountant-client privilege only in federal courts.

    c.   The accountant-client privilege can be claimed only in civil suits.

    d.   The accountant-client privilege can be claimed only to limit testimony to audit subject matter.

58. A violation of the profession's ethical standards most likely would have occurred when a CPA

    a.   Issued an unqualified opinion on the 2002 financial statements when fees for the 2001 audit were unpaid.

    b.   Recommended a controller's position description with candidate specifications to an audit client.

    c.   Purchased a CPA firm's practice of monthly write-ups for a percentage of fees to be received over a three-year period.

    d.   Made arrangements with a financial institution to collect notes issued by a client in payment of fees due for the current year's audit.

59. Which of the following statements concerning an accountant's disclosure of confidential client data is generally correct?

    a.   Disclosure may be made to any state agency without subpoena.

    b.   Disclosure may be made to any party on consent of the client.

    c.   Disclosure may be made to comply with an IRS audit request.

    d.   Disclosure may be made to comply with generally accepted accounting principles.

60. McGee is auditing Nevus Corporation and detects probable criminal activity by one of the employees. McGee believes this will have a material impact on the financial statements. The financial statements of Nevus Corporation are under the Securities Exchange Act of 1934. Which of the following is correct?

    a.   McGee should report this to the Securities Exchange Commission.

    b.   McGee should report this to the Justice Department.

    c.   McGee should report this to Nevus Corporation's audit committee or board of directors.

    d.   McGee will discharge his duty by requiring that a note of this be included in the financial statements.

61. Which of the following is an auditor not required to establish procedures for under the Private Securities Litigation Reform Act?

    a.   To develop a comprehensive internal control system.

    b.   To evaluate the ability of the firm to continue as a going concern.

    c.   To detect material illegal acts.

    d.   To identify material related-party transactions.

62. Which of the following is an auditor required to do under the Private Securities Litigation Reform Act concerning audits under the Federal Securities Exchange Act of 1934?

  I.   Establish procedures to detect material illegal acts of the client being audited.

  II.   Evaluate the ability of the firm being audited to continue as a going concern.

    a.   Neither I nor II.

    b.   I only.

    c.   II only.

    d.   Both I and II.

63. Lin, CPA, is auditing the financial statements of Exchange Corporation under the Federal Securities Exchange Act of 1934. He detects what he believes are probable material illegal acts. What is his duty under the Private Securities Litigation Reform Act?

    a. He must inform the principal shareholders within ten days.

    b. He must inform the audit committee or the board of directors.

    c. He need not inform anyone, beyond requiring that the financial statements are presented fairly.

    d. He should not inform anyone since he owes a duty of confidentiality to the client.

64. The Private Securities Litigation Reform Act

    a. Applies only to securities not purchased from a stock exchange.

    b. Does not apply to common stock of a publicly held corporation.

    c. Amends the Federal Securities Act of 1933 and the Federal Securities Exchange Act of 1934.

    d. Does not apply to preferred stock of a publicly held corporation.

65. Bran, CPA, audited Frank Corporation. The shareholders sued both Frank and Bran for securities fraud under the Federal Securities Exchange Act of 1934. The court determined that there was securities fraud and that Frank was 80% at fault and Bran was 20% at fault due to her negligence in the audit. Both Frank and Bran are solvent and the damages were determined to be $1 million. What is the maximum liability of Bran?

    a. $0

    b. $ 200,000

    c. $ 500,000

    d. $1,000,000

66. Which of the following nonattest services are auditors allowed to perform for a public company?

    a. Bookkeeping services.

    b. Appraisal services.

    c. Tax services.

    d. Internal audit services.

67. Which of the following Boards has the responsibility to regulate CPA firms that audit public companies?

    a. Auditing Standards Board.

    b. Public Oversight Board.

    c. Public Company Accounting Oversight Board.

    d. Accounting Standards Board.

OTHER OBJECTIVE QUESTIONS

Problem 1   (15 to 20 minutes)

Sleek Corp. is a public corporation whose stock is traded on a national securities exchange. Sleek hired Garson Associates, CPAs, to audit Sleek's financial statements. Sleek needed the audit to obtain bank loans and to make a public stock offering so that Sleek could undertake a business expansion program.

Before the engagement, Fred Hedge, Sleek's president, told Garson's managing partner that the audited financial statements would be submitted to Sleek's banks to obtain the necessary loans.

During the course of the audit, Garson's managing partner found that Hedge and other Sleek officers had embezzled substantial amounts of money from the corporation. These embezzlements threatened Sleek's financial stability. When these findings were brought to Hedge's attention, Hedge promised that the money would be repaid and begged that the audit not disclose the embezzlements.

Hedge also told Garson's managing partner that several friends and relatives of Sleek's officers had been advised about the projected business expansion and proposed stock offering, and had purchased significant amounts of Sleek's stock based on this information.

Garson submitted an unqualified opinion on Sleek's financial statements, which did not include adjustments for or disclosures about the embezzlements and insider stock transactions. The financial statements and audit report were submitted to Sleek's regular banks including Knox Bank. Knox, relying on the financial statements and Garson's report, gave Sleek a $2,000,000 loan.

Sleek's audited financial statements were also incorporated in a registration statement prepared under the provisions of the Securities Act of 1933. The registration statement was filed with the SEC in conjunction with Sleek's public offering of 100,000 shares of its common stock at $100 per share.

An SEC investigation of Sleek disclosed the embezzlements and the insider trading. Trading in Sleek's stock was suspended and Sleek defaulted on the Knox loan.

As a result, the following legal actions were taken:

- Knox sued Garson.
- The general public purchasers of Sleek's stock offerings sued Garson.

Required:

Determine whether each legal conclusion below is correct (C) or incorrect(I).

1. Knox cannot recover from Garson for fraud because fraud requires a misrepresentation of a material fact. Garson had issued an unqualified opinion on the financial reports and the opinion does not constitute a material fact.

2. Garson is not liable to Knox for fraud because the scienter requirement was not met.

3. Garson is not liable to Knox for fraud because Hedge promised to repay the money.

4. Garson is not liable to Knox for fraud because Knox was not an actual named party in the audit contract.

5. Garson is not liable to Knox for fraud because of Hedge's contributory negligence or fraud.

6. Assume that Garson did not learn of the embezzlements and that an average accountant would not have caught the embezzlement. Under these facts, Garson is liable to Sleek Corp.

7. Assume that Garson did not learn of the embezzlements because Garson's employees failed to perform part of the audit. Garson is liable to Sleek Corp. under these facts.

8. Assume the same facts as in **7**. Garson is liable to Knox bank.

9. Under the original fact pattern, Garson is liable to the general public purchasers of Sleek's stock offering.

10. Garson can successfully defend against liability under the Securities Act of 1933 by using the due diligence defense.

11. The general public purchasers of the Sleek's stock offering can recover from Garson under the antifraud provisions of Rule 10b-5 of the Securities Exchange Act of 1934 under the original fact pattern.

12. Garson may be held criminally liable based on the original fact pattern.

13. Assuming that Garson was only negligent with no knowledge of the embezzlements or insider trading, Garson can still be successfully sued under Rule 10b-5.

14. Under Rule 10b-5, Garson has the burden of proof to establish lack of liability.

Problem 2   (5 to 10 minutes)

Under Section 11 of the Securities Act of 1933 and Section 10(b), Rule 10b-5, of the Securities Exchange Act of 1934, a CPA may be sued by a purchaser of registered securities.

Required:

Items 1 through 6 relate to what a plaintiff who purchased securities must prove in a civil liability suit against a CPA. For each item determine whether the statement must be proven under Section 11 of the Securities Act of 1933, under Section 10(b), Rule 10b-5, of the Securities Exchange Act of 1934, both Acts, or neither Act.

	Only Section 11	*Only Section 10(b)*	*Both*	*Neither*
	(A)	(B)	(C)	(D)

The plaintiff security purchaser must allege or prove:

1. Material misstatements were included in a filed document.

2. A monetary loss occurred.

3. Lack of due diligence by the CPA.

4. Privity with the CPA.

5. Reliance on the document.

6. The CPA had scienter.

Problem 3   (5 to 10 minutes)

Required:

Determine for each of the following numbered situations whether or not the auditor (a covered member of the firm) is considered to be independent. If the auditor's independence would **not** be impaired select (N). If the auditor's independence would be impaired select (Y).

1. The auditor is a cosigner of a client's checks.

2. The auditor is a member of a country club which is a client.

3. The auditor owns a large block of stock in a client but has placed it in a blind trust.

4. The auditor placed her checking account in a bank which is her client. The account is fully insured by a federal agency.

5. The client has not paid the auditor for services for the past two years.

6. The auditor is leasing part of his building to a client.

7. The auditor joins, as an ordinary member, a trade association which is also a client.

8. The auditor has an immaterial, indirect financial interest in the client.

PROBLEMS

Problem 1   (15 to 20 minutes)

Dill Corp. was one of three major suppliers who sold raw materials to Fogg & Co. on credit. Dill became concerned over Fogg's ability to pay its debts. Payments had been consistently late and some checks had been returned, marked "insufficient funds." In addition, there were rumors concerning Fogg's solvency. Dill decided it would make no further sales to Fogg on credit unless it received a copy of Fogg's current, audited financial statements. It also required Fogg to assign its accounts receivable to Dill to provide security for the sales to Fogg on credit.

Clark & Wall, CPAs, was engaged by Fogg to perform an examination of Fogg's financial statements upon which they subsequently issued an unqualified opinion. Several months later, Fogg defaulted on its obligations to Dill. At this point Dill was owed $240,000 by Fogg. Subsequently, Dill discovered that only $60,000 of the accounts receivable that Fogg had assigned to Dill as collateral was collectible.

Dill has commenced a lawsuit against Clark & Wall. The complaint alleges that Dill has incurred a $180,000 loss as a result of negligent or fraudulent misrepresentations contained in the audited financial statements of Fogg. Specifically, it alleges negligence, gross negligence, and actual and/or constructive fraud on the part of Clark & Wall in the conduct of the audit and the issuance of an unqualified opinion.

State law applicable to this action follows the majority rule with respect to the accountant's liability to third parties for negligence. In addition, there is no applicable state statute which creates an accountant-client privilege. Dill demanded to be provided a copy of the Fogg workpapers from Clark & Wall who refused to comply with the request claiming that they are privileged documents. Clark & Wall has asserted that the entire action should be dismissed because Dill has no standing to sue the firm because of the absence of any contractual relationship with it (i.e., a lack of privity).

Required:

Answer the following, setting forth reasons for any conclusions stated.

a. Will Clark & Wall be able to avoid production of the Fogg workpapers based upon the assertion that they represent privileged communications?

b. What elements must be established by Dill to show negligence on the part of Clark & Wall?

c. What is the significance of compliance with GAAS in determining whether the audit was performed negligently?

d. What elements must be established by Dill to show actual or constructive fraud on the part of Clark & Wall?

Problem 2   (15 to 20 minutes)

Birk Corp. is interested in acquiring Apple & Co. Birk engaged Kaye & Co., CPAs, to audit the 2001 financial statements of Apple. Both Birk and Apple are engaged in the business of providing management consulting services. While reviewing certain contracts entered into by Apple, Kaye became concerned with the proper reporting of the following matters:

•   On December 5, 2001, Apple entered into an oral agreement with Cream Inc., to perform certain management advisory services for Cream for a fee of $150,000 per month. The services were to have commenced on February 15, 2002, and to have ended on December 20, 2002. Apple reported all of the revenues related to the contract on its 2001 financial statements. This constituted 30% of Apple's income for 2001.

•   On February 8, 2001, Apple purchased the assets of Nestar & Co., a small management consulting firm. Apple and Nestar entered into a written agreement with regard to the transaction that required Apple to pay Nestar $80,000 a year for five years. The agreement required Nestar to transfer all of its assets and goodwill to Apple. Further, the agreement required Nestar not to compete with Apple or Apple's successors for a period of three years within the city where the majority of Nestar's clients were located. Nestar's office was also located in this city. Other Nestar clients were located throughout the state.

On February 1, 2002, Birk acquired all of Apple's outstanding stock. Birk's decision was based on the unqualified opinion issued by Kaye on Apple's 2001 financial statements. Within ten days after the merger, Cream decided not to honor the agreement with Apple and gave notice that it had selected another management consulting firm. This caused the market value of the Apple stock acquired by Birk to decrease drastically.

On May 2, 2001, Birk learned that Nestar opened a management consulting firm three blocks from where Nestar's office had been located on February 8, 2001.

Based on the foregoing, Birk has commenced an action against Kaye alleging negligence in performing the audit of Apple's financial statements.

Required:

Answer the following, setting forth reasons for any conclusions stated.

a. Discuss whether the December 5, 2001 agreement between Cream and Apple is enforceable.

b. Discuss whether the agreement of Nestar not to compete with Apple is enforceable against Nestar.

c. Discuss whether Birk will prevail in its action against Kaye & Co., CPAs.

Problem 3 (15 to 20 minutes)

In order to expand its operations, Dark Corp. raised $4 million by making a private interstate offering of $2 million in common stock and negotiating a $2 million loan from Safe Bank. The common stock was properly offered pursuant to Rule 505 of Regulation D.

In connection with this financing, Dark engaged Crea & Co., CPAs, to audit Dark's financial statements. Crea knew that the sole purpose for the audit was so that Dark would have audited financial statements to provide to Safe and the purchasers of the common stock. Although Crea conducted the audit in conformity with its audit program, Crea failed to detect material acts of embezzlement committed by Dark's president. Crea did not detect the embezzlement because of its inadvertent failure to exercise due care in designing its audit program for this engagement.

After completing the audit, Crea rendered an unqualified opinion on Dark's financial statements. The financial statements were relied upon by the purchasers of the common stock in deciding to purchase the shares. In addition, Safe approved the loan to Dark based on the audited financial statements.

Within sixty days after the sale of the common stock and the making of the loan by Safe, Dark was involuntarily petitioned into bankruptcy. Because of the president's embezzlement, Dark became insolvent and defaulted on its loan to Safe. Its common stock became virtually worthless. Actions have been commenced against Crea by:

- The purchasers of the common stock who have asserted that Crea is liable for damages under Section 10(b) and Rule 10b-5 of the Securities Exchange Act of 1934.
- Safe, based upon Crea's negligence.

Required:

In separate paragraphs, discuss the merits of the actions commenced against Crea, indicating the likely outcomes and the reasons therefor.

Problem 4 (15 to 20 minutes)

Wolf Corp. is an audit client of Dunbar Associates, CPAs. Wolf is a reporting company under the provisions of the Securities Exchange Act of 1934. In 2001, Wolf's audit committee engaged Dunbar to perform litigation support services. The services were completed in January 2001, and Dunbar billed Wolf in February 2001.

In February 2002, Dunbar began its annual audit of Wolf's financial statements. During the course of the audit, Dunbar discovered that Wolf's officers had committed management fraud. The officers' fraud resulted in material misstatements in the financial statements that were to be submitted to the SEC with Wolf's annual report (Form 10-K). In March 2002, Dunbar issued an auditor's report containing an unqualified opinion on the financial statements. As of that date, Wolf had not paid Dunbar's outstanding February 2001 bill.

Required:

a. State whether Dunbar committed any violations of the standards of the profession in the areas of independence and due care. Explain your conclusions and indicate what, if any, additional actions Dunbar should have taken.

b. State whether Dunbar committed any violations of the Securities Exchange Act of 1934 and the Private Securities Litigation Reform Act of 1995. Explain your conclusions.

MULTIPLE-CHOICE ANSWERS

1. c __ __	15. d __ __	29. c __ __	43. c __ __	57. a __ __
2. d __ __	16. b __ __	30. a __ __	44. b __ __	58. a __ __
3. c __ __	17. d __ __	31. c __ __	45. d __ __	59. b __ __
4. a __ __	18. c __ __	32. d __ __	46. c __ __	60. c __ __
5. d __ __	19. a __ __	33. a __ __	47. d __ __	61. a __ __
6. c __ __	20. d __ __	34. b __ __	48. a __ __	62. d __ __
7. b __ __	21. d __ __	35. a __ __	49. d __ __	63. b __ __
8. a __ __	22. c __ __	36. c __ __	50. b __ __	64. c __ __
9. a __ __	23. a __ __	37. b __ __	51. c __ __	65. b __ __
10. a __ __	24. a __ __	38. a __ __	52. b __ __	66. c __ __
11. b __ __	25. c __ __	39. a __ __	53. b __ __	67. c __ __
12. b __ __	26. c __ __	40. b __ __	54. c __ __	
13. c __ __	27. d __ __	41. c __ __	55. d __ __	1st: __/67 = __%
14. a __ __	28. c __ __	42. c __ __	56. d __ __	2nd: __/67 = __%

MULTIPLE-CHOICE ANSWER EXPLANATIONS

A.2. Code of Professional Conduct—Principles

1.   (c)   The requirement is to identify the statement that best describes the meaning of generally accepted auditing standards. Answer (c) is correct because generally accepted auditing standards deal with measures of the quality of the performance of audit procedures (AU 150). Answer (d) is incorrect because procedures relate to acts to be performed, not directly to the standards. Answer (b) is incorrect because generally accepted auditing standards have been issued by predecessor groups, as well as by the Auditing Standards Board. Answer (a) is incorrect because there may or may not be **universal** compliance with the standards.

2.   (d)   All of these can result in the automatic expulsion of the member from the AICPA. Answer (a) is incorrect because although the conviction of a felony can result in automatic expulsion, likewise can the other two. Answers (b) and (c) are incorrect because all three can result in automatic expulsion from the AICPA.

A.3. Code of Professional Conduct—Rules, Interpretations, and Rulings

3.   (c)   According to the Code of Professional Conduct, Rule 101 regarding independence, a spouse may be employed by a client if s/he does not exert significant influence over the contents of the client's financial statements. This is a key position as defined by the Interpretation of Rule 101.

4.   (a)   According to Rule 102 of the Code of Professional Conduct, in performing any professional service, a member shall maintain objectivity and integrity, avoid conflicts of interest, and not knowingly misrepresent facts. Answer (a) is correct as this would be knowingly misrepresenting the facts. Answers (b) and (d) are incorrect as these are not intentional misstatements. Answer (c) is incorrect because while one must remain objective while performing consulting services, independence is not required unless the CPA also performs attest services for that client.

5.   (d)   The requirement is to determine which act is generally prohibited. Answer (d) is correct because "If an engagement is terminated prior to completion, the member is required to return only client records" (ET 501). Answer (a) is incorrect because issuing a modified report explaining a failure to follow a governmental regulatory agency's standards when conducting an attest service is not prohibited.

Answer (c) is incorrect because accepting a contingent fee is allowable when representing a client in an examination by a revenue agent of the client's federal or state income tax return (ET 302). Answer (b) is incorrect because revealing confidential client information during a quality review of a professional practice by a team from the state CPA society is not prohibited (ET 301).

6.   (c)   According to Rule 203 of the Code of Professional Conduct, CPAs are allowed to depart from a Statement of Financial Accounting Standards only when results of the Statement of Financial Accounting Standards would be misleading. Examples of possible circumstances justifying departure are new legislation and a new form of business transaction.

7.   (b)   The requirement is to determine whether a CPA may hire a non-CPA systems analyst and, if so, under what conditions. Answer (b) is correct because ET 291 allows such a situation when the CPA is qualified to supervise and evaluate the work of the specialist. Answer (a) is incorrect because the CPA need not be qualified to perform the specialist's tasks. Answer (c) is incorrect because non-CPA professionals are permitted to be associated with CPA firms in public practice. Answer (d) is incorrect because nonprofessionals may be hired, and because developing computer systems is recognized as a service performed by public accountants.

8.   (a)   She may use the CPA designation on her business cards when she does not imply independence but shows her title and her employer. Therefore, answer (b) is incorrect. Answer (c) is incorrect because she may use the CPA designation on her business cards or company transmittals if she does not imply independence. Answer (d) is incorrect because under the above situations, she can use the CPA designation.

9.   (a)   The requirement is to determine the activity that would most likely **not** impair a CPA's independence. Accounting and consulting services do not normally impair independence because the member's role is advisory in nature (ET 191). Answers (b) and (c) are incorrect because management functions are being performed (ET 191). Answer (d) is incorrect because accepting a luxurious gift impairs a CPA's independence (ET 191).

10. (a)   The requirement is to identify the type of report that may be issued only by an independent accountant. Answer (a) is correct because AT 101 requires an accountant be independent for all attestation engagements. An attestation engagement is one in which the accountant expresses a conclusion about the reliability of assertions which are the responsibility of another party. A standard report on an examination of a financial forecast requires the auditor to express an opinion, which requires an accountant to be independent. Answer (b) is incorrect because CS 100 indicates that consulting services are fundamentally different from the attestation function, and therefore do not require independence of the accountant. Answers (c) and (d) are incorrect because AR 100 indicates that an accountant who is not independent is not precluded from issuing a report on a compilation of financial statements.

11. (b)   Per ET 56, due care requires a member to discharge professional responsibilities with competence and diligence. Competence represents the attainment and maintenance of a level of understanding and knowledge that enables a member to render services with facility and acumen. It also establishes the limitations of a member's capabilities by dictating that consultation or referral may be required when a professional engagement exceeds the personal competence of a member or a member's firm. Accordingly, answer (b) is correct as it may be required to consult with experts in exercising due care. Due care does not require obtaining specialty accreditation.

12. (b)   Under ruling 101 under Rule of Conduct 102, when a CPA is acting as an expert witness, s/he should **not** act as an advocate but should give his/her position based on objectivity. The expert witness does this based on specialized knowledge, training, and experience.

13. (c)   The requirement is to determine which act is generally prohibited. Answer (c) is correct because "a member in public practice shall not for a commission recommend or refer to a client any product or service, or for a commission recommend or refer any product or service to be supplied by a client, or receive a commission when the member or the member's firm perform for that client: (1) an audit of a financial statement; or (2) a compilation of a financial statement when the member expects that a third party will use the financial statement and the member's compilation report does not disclose a lack of independence; or (3) an examination of prospective financial information." Answer (a) is incorrect because a member may purchase a product and resell it to a client. Any profit on sale would not constitute a commission (ET 591).

14. (a)   The principle of due care requires the member to observe the profession's technical and ethical standards, strive continually to improve competence and the quality of services, and discharge responsibility to the best of the member's ability. Answer (b) is incorrect as the auditor is not required to examine **all** corroborating evidence supporting management's assertions, but rather to examine evidence on a scope basis based on his/her consideration of materiality and level of risk assessed. Answer (c) is incorrect as the auditor should be aware of the possibility of illegal acts, but an audit provides no assurance that all or any illegal acts will be detected. Answer (d) is not the best answer because competence is derived from both education and experience. The principle of due care requires the member to strive to

improve competence, however, attaining the proper balance of professional experience and formal education is not a criterion for exercising due care.

15. (d)   The fact that a close relative of Kar works for Fort impairs Kar's independence. Answer (a) is incorrect because the gift is of a token amount which does not impair Kar's independence. Answer (b) is incorrect because a joint financial investment must be material to impair independence, and this would generally not occur with respect to a retirement plan. Answer (c) is incorrect because preparation of the client's tax return is not a service that impairs independence.

16. (b)   Independence is not required for the performance of a compilation engagement. Answer (a) is incorrect because if the CPA is required to be independent, a mortgage loan would not be permitted even if it was fully secured. Answer (c) is incorrect because the CPA was not required to be independent of the client. Answer (d) is incorrect because the CPA was not required to be independent of the client.

17. (d)   Both of the statements are incorrect; either would violate Rule 301 on confidential client information. Answer (a) is incorrect because statement I also is incorrect. Answer (b) is incorrect because statement II also is incorrect. Answer (c) is incorrect because statements I and II are both incorrect.

18. (c)   Information in the CPA's working papers is confidential and may not be disclosed except with the client's consent or by court order. Answer (a) is incorrect because disclosure of the information would generally violate Rule 301 on confidential client information. Answers (b) and (d) are incorrect because the CPA owns the working papers.

A.4. Responsibilities in Consulting Services

19. (a)   Types of consulting services include consultations, advisory services, implementation services, transaction services, staff and other support services, and product services.

20. (d)   According to the Statements on Standards for Consulting Services, independence is not required for performance of consulting services unless the CPA also performs attest services for that client. However, the CPA must remain objective in performing the consulting services. Furthermore, the understanding with the client for performing the services can be established either in writing or orally.

21. (d)   CS 100 indicates that the nature and scope of consulting services is determined solely by the practitioner and the client, typically in which the practitioner develops findings, conclusions, and recommendations for the client. All three services listed would fall under the definition of consulting services.

22. (c)   The AICPA Statement on Standards for Consulting Services, Section 100, describes general standards for all consulting services, in addition to those established under the AICPA Code of Professional Conduct. Section 100 addresses the areas of client interest, understanding with the client, and communication with the client. Specifically, this section states that the accountant should inform the client of significant reservations concerning the scope or benefits of the engagement.

23. (a) Personal financial planning engagements are only those that involve developing strategies and making recommendations to assist a client in defining and achieving personal financial goals. Personal financial engagements involve all of the following:

1. Defining engagement objectives
2. Planning specific procedures appropriate to engagement
3. Developing basis for recommendations
4. Communicating recommendations to client
5. Identifying tasks for taking action on planning decisions.

Other engagements may also include, but generally are not **required** to perform, the following:

1. Assisting client to take action on planning decisions
2. Monitoring client's progress in achieving goals
3. Updating recommendations and helping client revise planning decisions.

A.6. Responsibilities in Business and Industry

24. (a) Internal auditors are employees of the organization they are auditing. The external auditors are allowed to use work performed by internal auditors to aid them in the audit. They still must perform an independent audit but can coordinate their work to avoid duplication of effort. Answer (b) is incorrect because independence for internal auditors means that they must be independent of the activities they audit within the firm. Answer (c) is incorrect because although internal auditors do not need to meet the same standards of independence as external auditors, they do need to be independent of the activities they are auditing. Answer (d) is incorrect because their work may supplement but not substitute for the work of the external auditors.

A.7. Responsibilities in Governmental Auditing

25. (c) Independent auditors who are involved in governmental auditing must complete continuing education requirements that include continuing education and training for governmental auditing. It is specified that all members of the AICPA involved in government audits must follow generally accepted government auditing standards or be in violation of the AICPA Code of Professional Conduct.

26. (c) The Single Audit Act was passed by Congress to reduce duplications of many governmental audits that were overlapping because entities often receive federal funds from multiple sources. This act applies to local governments or state governments that in a fiscal year receive $300,000 or more of federal funds. There is no specification that allows a governmental audit only once every five years.

B.1. Common Law Liability to Clients

27. (d) A CPA is not automatically liable for failure to discover a materially overstated account. The CPA can be liable if the failure to discover was due to the CPA's own negligence. Although performing an audit in accordance with GAAS does not guarantee that there is no negligence, it is normally a good defense against negligence. Answer (a) is incorrect because there was privity of contract with Cable. There was an oral agreement constituting a contractual rela-

tionship, therefore this would not be a good defense. Answer (b) is incorrect because an oral contract for an audit is still enforceable without a signed engagement letter. Answer (c) is incorrect because a CPA does not have to perform an audit recklessly or with an intent to deceive to be liable for negligence. Negligence simply means that a CPA failed to exercise due care owed of the average reasonable accountant in performing an audit.

28. (c) In order to meet the required standard of due care in conducting an audit of a client's financial statements, a CPA has the duty to perform with the same degree of skill and judgment expected of an ordinarily prudent CPA under the circumstances. Answer (a) is incorrect because the client's expectations do not guide the standard of due care. Rather, the standard of due care is guided by state and federal statute, court decisions, the contract with the client, GAAS and GAAP, and customs of the profession. Answer (b) is incorrect because it is generally the client's responsibility to prepare its financial statements in accordance with generally accepted accounting principles. Answer (d) is incorrect because a CPA is not normally liable for failure to detect fraud or irregularities unless (1) a "normal" audit would have detected it, (2) the accountant by agreement has undertaken greater responsibility, or (3) the wording of the audit report indicates greater responsibility.

29. (c) The following elements are needed to establish fraud against an accountant: (1) misrepresentation of the accountant's expert opinion, (2) scienter shown by either the accountant's knowledge of falsity or reckless disregard of the truth, (3) reasonable reliance by injured party, and (4) actual damages. Answer (a) is incorrect because contributory negligence of a third party is not a defense available for the accountant in cases of fraud. Answers (b) and (d) are incorrect because privity of contract is not a requirement for an accountant to be held liable for fraud.

30. (a) In the performance of an audit, a CPA has the duty to exercise the level of care, skill, and judgment expected of a reasonably prudent CPA under the circumstances. Answer (b) is incorrect because a CPA performing an audit must adhere to generally accepted **auditing** standards. It is the client's responsibility to prepare its financial statements in accordance with generally accepted accounting principles. Answer (c) is incorrect because an accountant is not liable for failure to detect fraud unless (1) a "normal" audit would have detected it, (2) the accountant by agreement has undertaken greater responsibility such as a defalcation audit, or (3) the wording of the audit report indicates greater responsibility for detecting fraud. Answer (d) is incorrect because a CPA **can** be liable for negligence, which is simply a failure to exercise due care in performing an audit. The CPA does not have to be grossly negligent or intentionally disregard generally accepted auditing standards to be held liable for negligence.

31. (c) A CPA will be liable for negligence when s/he fails to exercise due care. The standard for due care is guided by state and federal statutes, court decisions, contracts with clients, conformity with GAAS and GAAP, and the customs of the profession. Per the AICPA Professional Standards, AU 325, requires that if the auditor becomes aware of weaknesses in the design or operation of the internal control structure, these weaknesses, termed reportable conditions, be communicated to the audit committee of the client. Answer (a) is incorrect because a CPA is not normally liable for failure to detect fraud. Answer (b) is incorrect because including a negligence disclaimer in an engagement letter has no bearing on whether the CPA is negligent. Answer (d) is incorrect because generally a CPA is not required to inform a client's customers of embezzlements although knowledge of the embezzlements may adversely affect the CPA's audit opinion.

32. **(d)** A CPA's duty of due care is guided by the following standards: (1) state and federal statutes, (2) court decisions, (3) contract with the client, (4) GAAS and GAAP, and (5) customs of the profession. Therefore, failure to follow GAAS constitutes a breach of a CPA's duty of due care. Answer (a) is incorrect because issuance of an oral rather than written report does not necessarily constitute a failure to exercise due care. Answers (b) and (c) are incorrect because the standard of due care requires the CPA to exercise the skill and judgment of an ordinary, prudent accountant. An honest error of judgment or failure to provide money saving tax advice would not breach the duty of due care if the CPA acted in a reasonable manner.

33. **(a)** A CPA's liability for constructive fraud is established by the following elements: (1) misrepresentation of a material fact, (2) reckless disregard for the truth, (3) reasonable reliance by the injured party, and (4) actual damages. Gross negligence constitutes a reckless disregard for the truth. Answer (b) is incorrect because ordinary negligence is not sufficient to support a finding of constructive fraud. Answer (c) is incorrect because the liability for constructive fraud does not depend upon the identification of third-party users. Answer (d) is incorrect because the presence of the intent to deceive is needed to satisfy the scienter requirement for fraud. However, even in the absence of the intent to deceive, the CPA can be liable for constructive fraud based on reckless disregard of the truth.

B.2. Common Law Liability to Third Parties (Nonclients)

34. **(b)** A foreseeable third party is someone not identified to the CPA, but who may be expected to receive the accountant's audit report and rely upon it. Even though this party is unknown to the CPA, the CPA is liable for gross negligence or fraud.

35. **(a)** Lack of privity can be a viable defense against third parties in a common law case of negligence or breach of contract. A client's creditor is not in privity of contract with the accountant. Answers (b) and (d) are incorrect because plaintiffs who are suing for fraud, constructive fraud, or gross negligence, which involves a reckless disregard for the truth, need not show privity of contract. Answer (c) is incorrect because the accountant's client is in privity of contract with the accountant due to their contractual agreement.

36. **(c)** Since Sanco was a foreseeable third party instead of an actually foreseen third party by the CPA, Sanco in most states cannot recover. Answer (a) is incorrect because most states do not extend liability to mere foreseeable third parties for simple negligence. Answer (b) is incorrect because the Ultramares decision limited liability to parties in privity of contract with the CPA. Answer (d) is incorrect because the client can recover for damages caused to it when negligence is established.

37. **(b)** Under the Ultramares rule, the accountant is held liable only to parties whose primary benefit the financial statements are intended. This generally means only the client or third-party beneficiaries who are in privity of contract with the accountant. Many courts have more recently departed from the Ultramares decision to allow foreseen third parties to recover from the accountant. However, those courts that adhere to the Ultramares rule do not expand liability to foreseen parties.

38. **(a)** In order to establish common law liability against an accountant based upon negligence, it must be proven that (1) the accountant had the duty to exercise due care, (2) the accountant breached the duty of due care, (3) damage or loss resulted, and (4) a causal relationship exists between the fault of the accountant and the resulting damages. The accountant may escape liability if due care can be established. The standard for due care is guided by state and federal statute, court decisions, contract with client, GAAS and GAAP, and customs of the profession. Although following GAAS does not automatically preclude negligence, it is strong evidence for the presence of due care. Answer (b) is incorrect because although the client may be aware of the misstatement, the auditor has the responsibility to detect the material misstatement if it is such that an average, reasonable accountant should have detected it. Answer (c) is incorrect because the client and Larson intended for the opinion and the financial statements to be used by purchasers. Therefore, a purchaser is considered a third-party beneficiary and is in privity of contract. Answer (d) is incorrect because the accountant need not know the specific identity of a third-party beneficiary to be held liable for negligence.

39. **(a)** To establish a CPA's liability for common law fraud, the following elements must be present: (1) misrepresentation of a material fact or the accountant's expert opinion, (2) scienter, shown by either an intent to mislead or reckless disregard for the truth, (3) reasonable or justifiable reliance by injured party, and (4) actual damages resulted. If Larson did not have actual or constructive knowledge of the misstatements, the scienter element would not be present and thus Larson would not be liable. Answers (b) and (d) are incorrect because neither contributory negligence of the client nor lack of privity of contract are defenses available to the accountant in cases of fraud. Answer (c) is incorrect because an accountant is generally liable to all parties defrauded. Therefore, the accountant need not have actual knowledge that the purchaser was an intended beneficiary.

B.3. Statutory Liability to Third Parties—Securities Act of 1933

40. **(b)** The Securities Act of 1933 requires that a plaintiff need only prove that damages were incurred and that there was a material misstatement or omission in order to establish a prima facie case against a CPA. The Act does not require that the plaintiff prove that s/he relied on the financial information or that there was negligence or fraud present. The Securities Act of 1933 eliminates the necessity for privity of contract.

41. **(c)** Mac is a third party that the accountant knew would rely on the financial statements. Queen's financial statements contained material misstatements. Mac can recover by showing that the accountant was negligent in the audit. Mac also needs to establish that it did rely on the financial statements in order to recover from the accountant for the losses on Queen.

42. **(c)** Under the Securities Act of 1933, a CPA is liable to any third-party purchaser of registered securities for losses resulting from misstatements in the financial statements included in the registration statement. The plaintiff (purchaser) must establish that damages were incurred, and that the misstatements were material misstatements of facts. Answer (a) is incorrect because under the 1933 Act it is not necessary for the purchaser of securities to prove "scienter," or knowledge of material misstatement, on the part of the CPA. Answers (b) and (d) are incorrect because under the 1933 Act, the plaintiff need not prove negligence on the part of the CPA or that there was reliance by the plaintiff on the financial statements included in the registration statement.

43. **(c)** In a Section 11 suit under the 1933 Act, the plaintiff may recover damages equal to the difference between the amount paid and the market value of the stock at the time of the suit. If the stock has been sold, then the damages are the difference between the amount paid and the sale price. Answer (a) is incorrect because damages of triple the original price are not provided for under this act. Answer (b) is incorrect because recission is not a remedy under this act. Answer (d) is incorrect because if the shares have not been sold before the suit, then the court uses the difference between the amount paid and the market value at the time of the suit.

44. **(b)** Under Section 11 of the 1933 Act, if the plaintiff proves damages and the existence of a material misstatement or omission in the financial statements included in the registration statement, these are sufficient to win against the CPA unless the CPA can prove one of the applicable defenses. Due diligence is one of the defenses. Answer (a) is incorrect because contributory negligence is not a defense under Section 11. Answer (c) is incorrect because the purchaser need not prove privity with the CPA. Answer (d) is not correct because the purchaser needs to prove the above two elements but not scienter.

45. **(d)** To impose liability under Section 11 of the Securities Act of 1933 for a misleading registration statement, the plaintiff must prove the following: (1) damages were incurred, and (2) a material misstatement or omission was present in financial statements included in the registration statement. The plaintiff generally is not required to prove the defendant's intent to deceive nor must the plaintiff prove reliance on the registration statement.

46. **(c)** The proof requirements necessary to establish an accountant's liability under the Securities Act of 1933, Section 11 are as follows: (1) the plaintiff must prove damages were incurred, and (2) the plaintiff must prove there was a material misstatement or omission in financial statements included in the registration statement. To establish an accountant's liability under the Securities Exchange Act of 1934, Section 10(b), Rule 10b-5, the following elements must be proven: (1) damages resulted to the plaintiff in connection with the purchase or sale of a security in interstate commerce, (2) a material misstatement or omission existed in information released by the firm, (3) the plaintiff justifiably relied on the financial information, and (4) the

existence of scienter. Because Sharp can prove that damages were incurred and that the statements contained material misstatements, Sharp is likely to prevail in a lawsuit under the Securities Act of 1933, Section 11. However, Sharp would be unable to prove justifiable reliance on the misstated information or the existence of scienter; thus, recovery under the Securities Exchange Act of 1934, Section 10(b), Rule 10b-5, is unlikely.

47. **(d)** If an accountant is negligent, s/he may have liability not only for a negligently performed audit but also for a negligently performed review when there were facts that should require the accountant to investigate further because of their suspicious nature. This is true even though a review is not a full audit.

B.4. Statutory Liability to Third Parties—Securities Exchange Act of 1934

48. **(a)** In order to establish a case under the antifraud provisions of Section 10(b) and Rule 10b-5 of the 1934 Act, the plaintiff has to prove that the defendant either had knowledge of the falsity in the registration statement or acted with reckless disregard for the truth. In addition, the plaintiff must show that the transaction involved interstate commerce so that there is a constitutional basis for using this federal law. S/he also must prove justifiable reliance. The plaintiff need not prove that s/he was an intended user of the false registration statement.

49. **(d)** Under Rule 10b-5 of Section 10(b) of the Securities Exchange Act of 1934, a CPA may be liable if s/he makes a false statement of a material fact or an omission of a material fact in connection with the purchase or sale of a security. Scienter is required which is shown by either knowledge of falsity or reckless disregard for the truth. Of the four answers given, lack of good faith best describes this scienter requirement. Answer (a) is incorrect because negligence is not enough under this rule. Answer (b) is incorrect because independence is not the issue under scienter. Answer (c) is incorrect because although due diligence can be a defense under Section 11 of the Securities Act of 1933, it is not the standard used under Section 10(b) of the Securities Exchange Act of 1934.

50. **(b)** Under Section 11 of the Securities Act of 1933, the CPA may be liable for material misstatements or omissions in certified financial statements. The CPA may escape liability by showing due diligence. This can often be proven by the CPA showing that s/he followed Generally Accepted Accounting Principles. There are not generally accepted fraud detection standards that the CPA can use as a defense.

51. **(c)** In a civil suit under Section 10(b) and Rule 10b-5, the damages are generally the difference between the amount paid and the market value at the time of suit, or the difference between the amount paid and the sales price if sold. Answer (a) is incorrect because recovery of the full original public offering price is not used as the damages. Answer (b) is incorrect because the above described monetary damages are used. Answer (d) is incorrect because punitive damages are not given under this rule.

C.1. Accountant's Working Papers

52. **(b)** In general, the accountant's workpapers are owned by the accountant. However, the CPA's ownership of the working papers is custodial in nature and the CPA is required to preserve confidentiality of the client's affairs. Normally, the CPA firm cannot allow transmission of information included in the working papers to third parties without the client's consent. This prevents a CPA firm from transferring workpapers to a purchaser of a CPA practice unless the client consents. Answer (c) is incorrect because the privileged communication rule does not exist at common law and has only been enacted by a few states. Additionally, the privileged communications rule only applies to communications which were intended to be privileged at the time of communication. Answer (a) is incorrect because working papers may be obtained by third parties without the client's consent when they appear to be relevant to issues raised in litigation (through a subpoena).

53. (d) The working papers are owned by the CPA, but the CPA must preserve confidentiality. They cannot be transmitted to another party unless the client consents or unless the CPA is required to under a valid court or governmental agency subpoena. Answers (a) and (c) are incorrect because these do not preserve the confidentiality. Answer (b) is incorrect because the CPA retains the working papers as evidence of the work done.

54. (c) Any of the partners of a CPA partnership can have access to the partnership's working papers. Third parties outside the firm need to have the client's consent or a legal subpoena.

C.2. Privileged Communications between Accountant and Client

55. (d) To preserve confidentiality, a CPA (including a CPA partnership) may not allow transmission of information in the working papers to other parties. Exceptions are consent of the client or the production of an enforceable subpoena. There are no exceptions for the IRS or the FASB, thus making answers (a), (b), and (c) incorrect.

56. (d) In a jurisdiction having an accountant-client privilege statute, the CPA generally may not turn over workpapers without the client's permission. It is allowable to do so, however, for use in a quality review under AICPA authorization or to be given to the state CPA society quality control panel. Answers (a), (b), and (c) are incorrect because the client would have to give permission for the CPA to turn over the confidential workpapers to the purchaser of the CPA practice, as well as to another CPA firm in regard to suspected tax return irregularities.

57. (a) Privileged communications between the accountant and client are recognized only in a few states. Therefore, if a state statute has been enacted creating such a privilege, Ivor will be able to prevent Thorp from testifying. Answer (b) is incorrect because federal law does not recognize accountant-client privileged communication. Answer (d) is incorrect because Ivor will not be able to prevent Thorp from testifying about the nature of the work performed in the audit unless a privileged communication statute has been enacted in that state. Answer (c) is incorrect because privileged communication does not exist at common law but must be created by state statute. Criminal law is based on common law and varies by state. However, as a general rule, in states that recognize accountant-client privilege, it can be claimed in both civil and criminal suits.

58. (a) The requirement is to identify the situation in which it is most likely that a violation of the profession's ethical standards would have occurred. Answer (a) is correct because independence is impaired if fees remain unpaid for professional services of the preceding year when the report on the client's current year is issued. Accordingly, no report should have been issued on the 2002 financial statements when fees for the 2001 audit were unpaid. Answer (b) is incorrect because CPAs may recommend a position description (ET 191) without violating the profession's ethical standards. Answer (c) is incorrect because a practice may be purchased for a percentage of fees to be received. Answer (d) is incorrect because the Code of Professional Conduct does not prohibit arrangements with financial institutions to collect notes issued by a client in payment of professional fees.

59. (b) A CPA must not disclose confidential information of a client unless the client gives consent to disclose it to that third party. Answer (a) is incorrect because state agencies need a subpoena before the CPA must comply. Answer (c) is incorrect because the IRS does not have the right to force a CPA to turn over confidential information of a client without either the client's consent or an enforceable subpoena. Answer (d) is incorrect because although the CPA can use the client information to defend a lawsuit, the CPA is not normally requested to disclose confidential information to comply with Generally Accepted Accounting Principles.

E. Responsibilities of Auditors under Private Securities Litigation Reform Act

60. (c) Under the Private Securities Litigation Reform Act, the auditor should inform first the audit committee or the board of directors. Answer (a) is incorrect because the Securities Litigation Reform Act does not require that the SEC be informed unless after the audit committee or board of directors is informed, no remedial action is taken. Answer (b) is incorrect because the Justice Department need not be informed of this under the Private Securities Litigation Reform Act. Answer (d) is incorrect because inclusion of the problem in a note of the financial statements is not enough; the audit committee or the board of directors should be informed.

61. (a) The Private Securities Litigation Reform Act requires that auditors of firms covered under the Securities Exchange Act of 1934 establish procedures to do the items in (b), (c), and (d). Developing a comprehensive internal control system is not specifically mentioned, although part of this would be helpful in accomplishing the three stated items.

62. (d) Under the Private Securities Litigation Reform Act, an auditor who audits financial statements under the Federal Securities Exchange Act of 1934 is required to establish procedures to (1) detect illegal acts, (2) identify material related-party transactions, and (3) evaluate the ability of the firm to continue as a going concern.

63. (b) Under the Private Securities Litigation Reform Act, he is required to report this to the audit committee of the firm or the board of directors. Answer (a) is incorrect because he need not report this to the shareholders but to the audit committee or the board of directors. Answers (c) and (d) are incorrect because he is required under the Reform Act to inform the audit committee or the board of directors.

64.   (c)   The Private Securities Litigation Reform Act amends both the 1933 and 1934 Acts. Answer (a) is incorrect because it applies to the 1933 and 1934 Acts which apply to stocks sold on a stock exchange. Answers (b) and (d) are incorrect because this Reform Act applies to securities covered under the 1933 and 1934 Acts which may include both common and preferred stock of a publicly held corporation.

65.   (b)   Bran is liable under the Private Securities Litigation Reform Act for her proportionate fault of the liability since she acted unknowingly. Answer (a) is incorrect because Bran was determined to be 20% at fault. Answers (c) and (d) are incorrect because the Reform Act changes the joint and several liability for unknowing conduct and substitutes proportionate liability.

66.   (c)   The Sarbanes-Oxley Act of 2002 established a number of nonattest services that may not be performed by the auditor for a public company. Tax services may be performed but must be approved by the company's audit committee.

67.   (c)   The Sarbanes-Oxley Act established the Public Accounting Oversight Board to regulate CPA firms that audit public companies.

OTHER OBJECTIVE ANSWERS AND ANSWER EXPLANATIONS

Problem 1

1. **(I)** Although a portion of the requirements of fraud do entail a misrepresentation of a material fact, an expert's opinion can be used instead of a fact.

2. **(I)** Garson was aware of the embezzlements and insider stock transactions. This knowledge constitutes scienter.

3. **(I)** Garson submitted an unqualified opinion on Sleek's financial statements. These did not include any adjustments or disclosures about the embezzlements or insider stock transactions. The financial statements were still incorrect when the unqualified opinion was given.

4. **(I)** Any person who can prove s/he was defrauded can recover based on fraud. S/he need not be a party to the contract or a third party beneficiary.

5. **(I)** Since Knox can prove fraud against Garson, Knox can recover from Garson even though another party may be negligent or fraudulent.

6. **(I)** Fraud cannot be established here. Furthermore, negligence cannot be proven because the average, reasonable accountant standard has not been breached in this fact pattern.

7. **(C)** Since employees of Garson failed to perform part of the audit causing loss to the client, the employees are liable for negligence. The employer, Garson, is also liable to the client for the negligence committed within the scope of the employment.

8. **(C)** Garson is not only liable to the client for the negligence but is also liable to foreseen, known third parties. Before the engagement, Garson's managing partner was told that the audited financial statements would be submitted to the client's banks to obtain loans.

9. **(C)** Section 11 of the Securities Act of 1933 provides that anyone, such as an accountant, who contributes to or allows in a registration statement material misrepresentations or omissions is liable to purchasers who sustain losses.

10. **(I)** Garson knew that the registration statements contained material misrepresentations of facts.

11. **(C)** Under Rule 10b-5, the purchasers can win against Garson by proving that there were material misstatements and omissions concerning the embezzlements and insider trading. The purchasers can also prove justifiable reliance and scienter.

12. **(C)** Garson can be held criminally liable for willful illegal conduct such as including the false information without adjusting for or disclosing the embezzlements.

13. **(I)** Negligence alone will not subject the accountant to liability under Rule 10b-5.

14. **(I)** The burden of proof is on the plaintiff under Rule 10b-5.

Problem 2

1. **(C)** Section 11 of the Securities Act of 1933 imposes liability on auditors for misstatements or omissions of a material fact in certified financial statements or other information provided in registration statements. Similarly, under Section 10(b), Rule 10b-5 of the Securities Exchange Act of 1934, the plaintiff must prove there was a material misstatement or omission in information released by the firm such as audited financial statements. Actually, if the examiners wish to emphasize the phrase "filed document" in the question, then the answer would be (A). Under Section 10(b), the material misstatement may occur in information released by the firm rather than filed. Since the requirements state "...**must** allege or prove," technically the answer would be (D), since the plaintiff could allege or prove **omission** of material facts instead of material **misstatements** stated in the question. Therefore, this question depends upon how technical one decides to get on these points.

2. **(C)** Under both Section 11 of the 1933 Act and Section 10(b) of the 1934 Act, the plaintiff must allege or prove that s/he incurred monetary damages.

3. **(D)** Under Section 11 of the 1933 Act, the burden of proof is shifted to the defendant, accountant. The accountant may then defend him or herself by establishing due diligence. The plaintiff does not have to show lack of due diligence by the CPA. Under Section 10(b), the plaintiff must prove scienter.

4. **(D)** The plaintiff does not have to prove that s/he was in privity with the CPA under either section.

5. **(B)** Under Section 10(b), the plaintiff must prove justifiable reliance on the financial information. This is not true under Section 11 in which the plaintiff need prove only the items in item **1.** and item **2.** discussed above.

6. **(B)** The plaintiff does have to prove that the CPA had scienter under Section 10(b) of the 1934 Act. Scienter is not needed under the 1933 Act, however.

Problem 3

1. **(Y)** Since the auditor is a cosigner on a client's check, the auditor could become liable if the client defaults. This relationship impairs the auditor's independence.

2. **(N)** Independence is not impaired because membership in the country club is essentially a social matter.

3. **(Y)** An auditor may not hold a direct financial interest in a client. Putting it in a blind trust does not solve the impairment of independence.

4. **(N)** If the auditor places his/her account in a client bank, this does not impair independence if the accounts are state or federally insured. If the accounts are not insured, independence is not impaired if the amounts are immaterial.

5. **(Y)** The auditor's independence is impaired when prior years' fees for professional services remain unpaid for more than one year.

6. **(Y)** The auditor's independence is impaired when s/he leases space out of a building s/he owns to a client.

7. **(N)** When the auditor does not serve in management, s/he may join a trade association who is a client.

8. **(N)** Independence is impaired for direct financial interests and material, indirect financial interests but not for immaterial, indirect financial interests.

ANSWER OUTLINE

Problem 1   Accountant-Client Privilege; CPA's Negligence; CPA's Fraud

a.   No accountant-client privilege recognized at common law and no applicable state statute
Right to assert privilege rests with client not accountant

b.   Elements necessary to establish CPA's negligence
   • Legal duty to protect plaintiff from unreasonable risk
   • Failure of CPA to perform with due care or competence
   • Failure to exercise due care caused plaintiff's loss
   • Actual damage resulted from failure to exercise due care
   • Plaintiff was within a known and intended class of third-party beneficiaries

c.   Significance of compliance with GAAS
   • Primary standard against which CPA's conduct tested
   • Considered "the custom of the industry"
   • Failure to meet GAAS will result in finding of CPA's negligence
   • Meeting GAAS not conclusive evidence of CPA's not being negligent

d.   Elements necessary to establish CPA's actual or constructive fraud
   • False representation of fact by CPA
   • Actual fraud requires knowledge by CPA that statement was false (scienter). Constructive fraud inferred from gross negligence or reckless disregard for truth
   • Intention to have plaintiff rely on false statement
   • Reasonable reliance on false statement
   • Damage results from reliance

UNOFFICIAL ANSWER

Problem 1   Accountant-Client Privilege; CPA's Negligence; CPA's Fraud

a.   No. Since there is no accountant-client privilege recognized at common law and there is no applicable state statute which creates an accountant-client privilege, Clark & Wall will be required to produce its workpapers. Furthermore, the right to assert the accountant-client privilege generally rests with the client and not with the accountant.

b.   The elements necessary to establish a cause of action for negligence against Clark & Wall are

   • A legal duty to protect the plaintiff (Dill) from unreasonable risk.
   • A failure by the defendant (Clark & Wall) to perform or report on an engagement with the due care or competence expected of members of its profession.
   • A causal relationship (i.e., that the failure to exercise due care resulted in the plaintiff's loss).
   • Actual damage or loss resulting from the failure to exercise due care.

In addition to the foregoing, Dill must be able to establish that it is within a known and intended class of third-party beneficiaries in order to recover damages from Clark & Wall for negligence. This is necessary because Clark & Wall has asserted that it is not in privity of contract with Dill.

c.   The primary standards against which the accountant's conduct will be tested are GAAS. Such standards are generally known as "the custom of the industry." Failure by Clark & Wall to meet the standards of the profession will undoubtedly result in a finding of negligence. However, meeting the standard of the profession will not be conclusive evidence that Clark & Wall was not negligent, although it is of significant evidentiary value.

d.   The requirements to establish actual or constructive fraud on the part of Clark & Wall are

1.   A false representation of fact by the defendant (Clark & Wall).
2.   For actual fraud, knowledge by the defendant (Clark & Wall) that the statement is false (scienter) or that the statement is made without belief that it is truthful. Constructive fraud may be inferred from gross negligence or a reckless disregard for the truth.
3.   An intention to have the plaintiff (Dill) rely upon the false statement.
4.   "Justifiable" reliance upon the false statement.
5.   Damage resulting from said reliance.

ANSWER OUTLINE

Problem 2   Statute of Frauds; Restraint of Trade; Accountant's Liability for Negligence

The agreement between Cream and Apple is unenforceable
   Statute of Frauds requires an agreement that cannot possibly be performed within one year of its **creation** to be in writing
The agreement between Apple and Nestar is likely to be enforceable
   An agreement not to compete will be enforceable if it protects legitimate property interests and is reasonable with respect to both time and geographic area
   The agreement protects goodwill which a buyer of a business has a right to protect
Birk will prevail against Kaye
   Kaye was required to perform the audit with due care
   Kaye was negligent in issuing an unqualified opinion on financial statements that contained material misstatements

UNOFFICIAL ANSWER

Problem 2   Statute of Frauds; Restraint of Trade; Accountant's Liability for Negligence

a.   The December 5 oral agreement between Cream and Apple is unenforceable because the agreement failed to comply with the requirements of the Statute of Frauds. A contract that cannot possibly be performed within one year from the making of the contract falls within the provisions of the Statute of Frauds. As the facts clearly indicate, the December 5 oral agreement could not possibly be performed within one year of the making of the agreement (December 5, 2001) since the agreement required Apple to continue to perform until December 20, 2002. Therefore, the oral agreement is unenforceable.

b.   The agreement between Nestar and Apple restricting Nestar from competing with Apple for three years within the city where Nestar's office and the majority of Nestar's clients were located is likely to be enforceable. An agreement not to compete will be enforceable if there has been a sale of a business including goodwill and the purpose of the restraint is to protect a property interest of the purchaser; the restraint is reasonable as to the geographic area covered; and the restraint is reasonable as to the time period. Under the facts of this case, the agreement not to compete is likely to be enforceable. The transaction involves the sale of Nestar's management consulting business and goodwill. The purpose of the restraint is to protect the goodwill. The three-year time period is reasonable. The limitation on the geographic area covered by the restraint to only the city where Nestar's office and the majority of Nestar's clients are located appears to be reasonable.

c.   Birk will prevail in its action against Kaye based on negligence. Kaye owed a duty to Birk to conduct the audit with due care. Kaye failed to conduct the audit with due care by issuing an unqualified opinion on Apples' 2001 financial statements when, in fact, Apple had made a material error by reporting all of the revenues related to the unenforceable December 5 agreement on its 2001 financial statements. Kaye's issuance of an unqualified opinion despite the material error caused Birk to suffer damages as evidenced by the drastic decrease in the market value of Apple stock.

ANSWER OUTLINE

Problem 3   Antifraud Provisions under Rule 10b-5 of the 1934 Act; Liability to Third Parties Based on Negligence

Crea will not be liable to purchasers of the common stock
  Regulation D exempts offering from registration requirements but antifraud provisions of federal securities acts continue to apply
  Under Section 10(b) and Rule 10b-5 of 1934 Act the purchaser must show

1. Material misrepresentation or omission
2. Scienter (intentional or willful conduct)
3. Reliance on wrongful conduct
4. Causal connection between purchaser's loss and wrongful conduct

Crea is not liable due to lack of scienter
Crea is probably liable to Safe Bank based on negligence
A CPA is generally liable for ordinary negligence to third parties if audit report is for the identified third party's primary benefit
In order to establish Crea's negligence, Safe must show

1. Crea had legal duty to protect Safe from unreasonable risk
2. Crea failed to exercise due care
3. There was a causal relationship between Safe's loss and Crea's failure to exercise due care
4. Actual damage or loss resulting from Crea's failure to exercise due care

---

Problem 3   Antifraud Provisions under Rule 10b-5 of the 1934 Act; Liability to Third Parties Based on Negligence

Crea will not be liable to the purchasers of the common stock. Although an offering of securities made pursuant to Regulation D is exempt from the registration requirements of the Securities Act of 1933, the antifraud provisions of the federal securities acts continue to apply. In order to establish a cause of action under Section 10(b) and Rule 10b-5 of the Securities Exchange Act of 1934, the purchasers generally must show that: Crea made a material misrepresentation or omission in connection with the purchase or sale of a security; Crea acted with some element of scienter (intentional or willful conduct); Crea's wrongful conduct was material; the purchasers relied on Crea's wrongful conduct; and, that there was a sufficient causal connection between the purchasers' loss and Crea's wrongful conduct.

Under the facts of this case, Crea's inadvertent failure to exercise due care, which resulted in Crea's not detecting the president's embezzlement, will not be sufficient to satisfy the scienter element because such conduct amounts merely to negligence. Therefore, Crea will not be liable for damages under Section 10(b) and Rule 10b-5 of the Securities Exchange Act of 1934.

Crea is likely to be held liable to Safe Bank based on Crea's negligence despite the fact that Safe is not in privity of contract with Crea. In general, a CPA will not be liable for negligence to creditors if its auditor's report was primarily for the benefit of the client, for use in the development of the client's business, and only incidentally or collaterally for the use of those to whom the client might show the financial statements. However, a CPA is generally liable for ordinary negligence to third parties if the audit report is for the identified third party's primary benefit.

In order to establish Crea's negligence, Safe must show that: Crea had a legal duty to protect Safe from unreasonable risk; Crea failed to perform the audit with the due care or competence expected of members of its professions; there was a causal relationship between Safe's loss and Crea's failure to exercise due care; actual damage or loss resulting from Crea's failure to exercise due care. On the facts of this case, Crea will be liable based on negligence since the audited financial statement reports were for the primary benefit of Safe, an identified third party, and Crea failed to exercise due care in detecting the president's embezzlement, which resulted in Safe's loss (i.e., Dark's default in repaying the loan to Safe).

ANSWER OUTLINE

Problem 4   Standards of Profession and Rule 10b-5

a.   Did not violate standards of profession in area of independence by accepting litigation support services engagement
  CPA may perform such services at same time of audit
    Dunbar did violate standard of independence when issued report for client with overdue bill
  Did violate standard of due care in two ways
    Knowingly and intentionally gave unqualified opinion on materially misstated financial statements

Dunbar on discovering fraud by Wolf's officers
should have reported it to Wolf's audit committee
and insisted financial statements be revised

b. Dunbar probably violated Rule 10b-5
Dunbar contributed to filing with SEC of Form 10-K
containing misstatements of material facts
Dunbar probably violated antifraud provisions of 1934
Act and Private Securities Litigation Reform Act
Fraud based on scienter
Dunbar knowingly and intentionally issued un-
qualified opinion after discovered management
fraud
Dunbar probably violated other provisions of Private
Securities Litigation Reform Act
Failed to withdraw from engagement and notify SEC
of material illegal acts of Wolf's officers

UNOFFICIAL ANSWER

Problem 4   Standards of Profession and Rule 10b-5

a.   Dunbar did not violate the standards of the profession in
the area of independence by accepting the litigation support
services engagement. A CPA may perform litigation support services for an attest client at the same time the CPA
performs an audit. However, when Dunbar did not receive
payment of the bill for the litigation support services within
one year and prior to issuing an audit report, Dunbar's independence was impaired. Dunbar should not have issued the
report.

Dunbar violated the standards of the profession in the
area of due care in two ways. First, Dunbar did this by
knowingly and intentionally giving an unqualified opinion
on the materially misstated financial statements.

Second, Dunbar also violated due care by failing to
comply with the standards of the profession regarding the

discovery of management fraud. Under the standards of the
profession, Dunbar, on discovering the fraud committed by
Wolf's officers, should have reported it directly to Wolf's
audit committee. Dunbar should have insisted that the financial statements be revised.

If the client did not revise the financial statements,
Dunbar should have either issued a nonstandard report or
withdrawn from the engagement. Dunbar should then have
reported its action (in either case) to the client's board of
directors. If the client did not advise the SEC of Dunbar's
findings and did not properly notify Dunbar that the SEC
had been advised, Dunbar should have notified the SEC. By
failing to take these steps, Dunbar violated due care.

b.   Dunbar will likely be found to have violated the antifraud provisions of Section 10(b) and Rule 10b-5 of the Securities Exchange Act of 1934. Specifically, Dunbar contributed to the filing with the SEC of written materials
(Form 10-K) containing misstatements of material facts.

Dunbar will also likely be found to have violated the
antifraud provision of both the 1934 Act and the provisions
of the Private Securities Litigation Reform Act of 1995.
Specifically, Dunbar will be found to have committed fraud
because scienter can be established. Dunbar knowingly and
intentionally issued an unqualified opinion after discovering
management fraud that caused material misstatements in the
financial statements.

Dunbar will also likely be found to have violated the
provisions of the Private Securities Litigation Reform Act of
1995. Specifically, Dunbar failed to withdraw from the engagement and notify the SEC of the material illegal acts
committed by Wolf's officers.

Keep practicing! Wiley's CPA Examination Review Software has over 2,800 questions.

Available at www.wiley.com/cpa

REGULATION OF EMPLOYMENT AND ENVIRONMENT

Overview

Issues on this topic are based on the Workers' Compensation Laws and Federal Social Security Rules including the Federal Insurance Contributions Act (FICA) and the Federal Unemployment Tax Act (FUTA). These laws supplement the law of agency. In this area, emphasis is placed on the impact that state and federal laws have on the regulation of employment.

To adequately understand these materials, you should emphasize the theory and purpose underlying the Workers' Compensation Laws. You should also focus on the effect that these laws have on employers and employees. Notice the changes these laws have made on common law.

Upon looking at the Federal Social Security Laws, emphasize the coverage and benefits of the respective programs.

Also, emphasize the various discrimination and environmental laws.

A. Federal Social Security Act

1. Main purpose of Act is as name implies (i.e., attainment of the social security of people in our society)

   a. Basic programs include

      (1) Old age insurance
      (2) Survivor's and disability insurance
      (3) Hospital insurance (Medicare)
      (4) Unemployment insurance

   b. Sources of financing for these programs

      (1) Old-age, survivor's, disability, and hospital insurance programs are financed out of taxes paid by employers, employees, and self-employed under provisions of Federal Insurance Contributions Act and Self-Employment Contributions Act
      (2) Unemployment insurance programs are financed out of taxes paid by employers under the Federal Unemployment Tax Act and various state unemployment insurance laws

2. Federal Insurance Contributions Act (FICA)

   a. Imposes social security tax on employees, self-employed, and employers
   b. Social security tax applies to compensation received that is considered to be wages
   c. In general, tax rates are same for both employer and employee

      (1) Rates changed from time to time

   d. Taxes are paid only up to base amount that is also changed frequently

      (1) If employee pays FICA tax on more than base amount, s/he has right to refund for excess

         (a) May happen when employee works for two or more employers

            1] These two or more employers do not get refunds

   e. FICA is also used to fund Medicare

      (1) Base rate on this Medicare portion has been set at a higher amount

   f. It is employer's duty to withhold employee's share of FICA from employee's wages and remit both employee's amount and employer's equal share to government

      (1) Employer subject to fines for failure to make timely FICA deposits

         (a) Also, employer subject to fine for failure to supply taxpayer identification number

      (2) Employer is required to match FICA contributions of employees on dollar-for-dollar basis

      (3) If employer neglects to withhold, employer may be liable for both employee's and employer's share of taxes (i.e., to pay double tax)

         (a) Once employer pays, s/he has right to collect employee's share from employee
         (b) Employer may voluntarily pay not only its share but also employee's share

1] Employee's share is deductible by employer as additional compensation and is taxable to the employee as compensation

(4) Employer is required to furnish employee with written statement of wages paid and FICA contributions withheld during calendar year

g. Taxes paid by employer are deducted on tax return of employer

(1) But employee may not deduct taxes paid on his/her tax return

h. Neither pension plans nor any other programs may be substituted for FICA coverage

(1) Individuals receiving payments from private pension plans may also receive social security payments

3. Self-Employment Contributions Act

a. Self-employed persons are required to report their own taxable earnings and pay required social security tax
b. Self-employment income is net earnings from self-employment
c. Tax rates paid on self-employment income up to base amount

(1) Since self-employed does not have employer to match the rate, tax rate is that of employer and employee combined
(2) Base amount and tax rate are subject to amendment
(3) Base rate is reduced by any wages earned during year because wages are subject to FICA
(4) Self-employed can deduct half of FICA tax paid on his/her income tax form

4. Unemployment Insurance (Federal Unemployment Tax Act—FUTA)

a. Tax is used to provide unemployment compensation benefits to workers who lose jobs and cannot find replacement work
b. Federal unemployment tax must be paid by employer if employer employs one or more persons covered by act

(1) Deductible as business expense on employer's federal income tax return
(2) Not deductible by employee because not paid by employee

c. Employer must also pay a state unemployment tax

(1) An employer is entitled to credit against his/her federal unemployment tax for state unemployment taxes paid
(2) State unemployment tax may be raised or lowered according to number of claims against employer
(3) If employer pays a low state unemployment tax because of good employment record, then employer is entitled to additional credit against federal unemployment tax

5. Coverage under Social Security Act is mandatory for qualifying employees

a. Person may not elect to avoid coverage
b. Part-time and full-time employees are covered
c. Compensation received must be "wages"

6. Definitions

a. Wages—all compensation for employment

(1) Include

(a) Money wages
(b) Contingent fees
(c) Compensation in general even though not in cash
(d) Base pay of those in the service
(e) Bonuses and commissions
(f) Most tips

(g) Vacation and dismissal allowances

   (2) Exclude

      (a) Wages greater than base amount
      (b) Reimbursed travel expenses
      (c) Employee medical and hospital expenses paid by employer
      (d) Employee insurance premiums paid by employer
      (e) Payment to employee retirement plan by employer

b. Employee—person whose performance is subject to physical control by employer not only as to results but also as to methods of accomplishing those results

   (1) Partners, self-employed persons, directors of corporations, and independent contractors are not covered by unemployment compensation provisions since they are not "employees"

      (a) Are covered as self-employed persons for old-age, survivor's, and disability insurance program purposes

   (2) Independent contractor distinguished from an employee

      (a) Independent contractor not subject to control of employer or regular supervision as employee
      (b) That is, employer seeks results only and contractor controls method

        EXAMPLE: A builder of homes has only to produce the results.

   (3) Officers and directors of corporations are "employees" if they perform services and receive remuneration for these services from corporation

c. Employment—all service performed by employee for person employing him/her

   (1) Must be continuing or recurring work
   (2) Services from following are exempt from coverage

      (a) Student nurses
      (b) Certain public employees
      (c) Nonresident aliens

   (3) Services covered if performed by employee for employer without regard to residence or citizenship

      (a) Unless employer not connected with US

   (4) Domestic workers, agricultural workers, government employees, and casual workers are governed by special rules

d. Self-employment—carrying on trade or business either as individual or in partnership

   (1) Wages greater than base amount are excluded
   (2) Can be both employed (in one job) and self-employed (another business), but must meet requirements of trade or business (i.e., not a hobby, occasional investment, etc.)

e. Employer

   (1) For Federal Unemployment Tax Act (FUTA) need only employ one person or more for some portion of a day for twenty weeks, or pays $1,500 or more in wages in any calendar quarter
   (2) In general, may be individual, corporation, partnership, trust, or other entity

7. Old-age, survivor's, and disability insurance benefits

a. Availability of benefits depends upon attainment by individual of "insured status"

   (1) Certain lengths of working time are required to obtain insured status

b. An individual who is "fully insured" is eligible for following benefits

   (1) Survivor benefits for widow or widower and dependents

       (2) Benefits for disabled worker and his/her dependents

       (3) Old-age retirement benefits payable to retired worker and dependents

          (a) Reduced benefits for retirement at age sixty-two

       (4) Lump-sum death benefits

  c. Individual who is "currently insured" is eligible for following benefits

       (1) Limited survivor benefits

          (a) In general, limited to dependent minors or those caring for dependent minors

       (2) Benefits for disabled worker and his/her dependents

       (3) Lump-sum death benefits

       (4) Survivors or dependents need not have paid in program to receive benefits

       (5) Divorced spouses may receive benefits

  d. Amount of benefits defined by statute which changes from time to time and depends upon

       (1) Average monthly earnings, and

       (2) Relationship of beneficiary to retired, deceased, or disabled worker

          (a) For example, husband, wife, child, grandchild—may be entitled to different benefits

       (3) Benefits increased based on cost of living

       (4) Benefits increased for delayed retirement

8. Reduction of social security benefits

  a. Early retirement results in reduced benefits

       (1) Retirement age is increasing in steps

  b. Returning to work after retirement can affect social security benefits

       (1) Income from private pension plans, savings, investments, or insurance does not affect benefits because not earned income

       (2) Income from limited partnership is considered investment income rather than self-employment income

9. Unemployment benefits

  a. Eligibility for and amount of unemployment benefits governed by state laws

  b. Does not include self-employed

  c. Generally available only to persons unemployed through no fault of their own; however, not available to seasonal workers if paid on yearly basis (e.g., professional sports player in off-season)

  d. One must have worked for specified period of time and/or earned specified amount of wages

B. Workers' Compensation Act

1. Workers' compensation is a form of strict liability whereby employer is liable to employee for injuries or diseases sustained by employee which arise out of and in course of employment

  a. Employee is worker subject to control and supervision of employer

  b. Distinguish independent contractor

       (1) Details of work not supervised

       (2) Final result can of course be monitored (based on contract law)

2. Purpose

  a. To give employees and their dependents benefits for job-related injuries or diseases with little difficulty

       (1) Previously, employee had to sue employer for negligence to receive any benefits in form of damages

       (2) Employee usually cannot waive his/her right to benefits

   b. Cost is passed on as an expense of production
   c. **No fault need be shown**; payment is automatic upon satisfaction of requirements

       (1) Removes employer's common law defenses of

            (a) Assumption of risk
            (b) Negligence of a fellow employee—employer formerly could avoid liability by proving it
                 was another employee's fault
            (c) Contributory negligence—injured employee was also negligent

3. Regulated by states

    a. Except that federal government employees are covered by federal statute
    b. Each state has its own statute

4. Generally, there are two types of statutes

    a. Elective statutes

        (1) If employer rejects, s/he loses the three common law defenses against employee's common
             law suit for damages so most accept

    b. Compulsory statutes

        (1) Require that all employers within coverage of statute provide benefits
        (2) Majority of states have compulsory coverage

5. Insurance used to provide benefits

    a. In lieu of insurance policy, employer may assume liability for workers' compensation claims but
        must show proof of financial responsibility to carry own risk

6. Legislative scope

    a. Workers' compensation coverage extends to all employees who are injured on the job or in the
        course of the employment (i.e., while acting in furtherance of employer's business purpose)
    b. Coverage also extends to occupational diseases and preexisting diseases that are aggravated by
        employment
    c. Coverage does not extend to employee while traveling to or from work
    d. Out-of-state work may be covered if it meets above mentioned criteria
    e. All states have workers' compensation law; most employees covered
    f. Must be employee; coverage does not extend to independent contractors
    g. Public employees are often covered

7. Legal action for damages

    a. Employers covered by workers' compensation insurance are generally exempt from lawsuits by
        employees

        (1) If employee does not receive benefits covered under workers' compensation, s/he may sue in-
             surance company that agreed to cover workers

    b. Benefits under workers' compensation laws received by employee are in lieu of action for dam-
        ages against employer and such a suit is barred

        (1) Employer assumes liability in exchange for employee giving up his/her common law rights to
             sue employer for damages caused by the job (e.g., suit based on negligence)
        (2) When employee is covered by workers' compensation law, his/her sole remedy against em-
             ployer is that which is provided for under appropriate workers' compensation act
        (3) However, if employer **intentionally** injures employee, employee may proceed against em-
             ployer based on intentional tort in addition to recovering under workers' compensation bene-
             fits

    c. Employee is entitled to workers' compensation benefits **without regard to fault**

        (1) Negligence or even gross negligence of injured employee is not a bar to recovery

       (2) Employee's negligence plays no role in determination of amount of benefits awarded

       (3) Failure of employee to follow employer's rules is not a bar to recovery

       (4) However, injuries caused by intentional self-infliction, or intoxication of employee, can bar recovery

    d. When employer fails to provide workers' compensation insurance or when employer's coverage is inadequate, injured employee may sue in common law for damages, and employer cannot resort to usual common law defenses

       (1) When employer uninsured, many states have a fund to pay employee for job-related injuries

          (a) State then proceeds against uninsured company

          (b) Penalties imposed

8. Actions against third parties

    a. Employee's acceptance of workers' compensation benefits does not bar suit against third party whose negligence or unreasonably dangerous product caused injury

       (1) If employee sues and recovers from third party, employer (or its insurance carrier) is entitled to compensation for workers' compensation benefits paid to employee

          (a) Any recovery in excess of workers' compensation benefits received belongs to injured employee

          (b) To the extent that recovery duplicates benefits already obtained from employer (or carrier), that employer (or carrier) is entitled to reimbursement from employee

EXAMPLE: Kraig, an employee of Badger Corporation, was injured in an auto accident while on the job. The accident was due to the negligence of Todd. Kraig can recover under workers' compensation and also fully recover from Todd in a civil court case. However, Kraig must reimburse the workers' compensation carrier to the extent the recovery from Todd duplicates benefits already obtained under workers' compensation laws.

    b. If employee accepts workers' compensation benefits, employer (or its insurance carrier) is subrogated to rights of employee against third party who caused injury

       (1) Therefore, if employee elects not to sue third party, employer (or its insurance carrier) obtains employee's right of action against third person

9. Claims

    a. Employees are required to file claim forms on timely basis

       (1) In some states, failure to file claim on time may bar employee's recovery

10. Benefits

    a. Medical

       (1) Provides for medical care to injured or diseased employee

    b. Disability

       (1) This is partial wage continuation plan

    c. Death

       (1) Various plans and schedules provide payments to widow(er) and minor children

    d. Special provisions

       (1) Normally, statutes call for specific scheduled payments for loss of limb or eye

       (2) Also, if employee's injury is of a nature that prevents his/her returning to his/her occupation, plan may pay cost of retraining

    e. Normally not subject to waiver by employee

C. Torts of Employee

1. Employer is generally liable to third parties for torts of employee if committed within the course and scope of his/her employment

    a. Note that third party may hold both liable up to full damages

D. Employee Safety

1. Occupational Safety and Health Act (OSHA)

    a. OSHA applies to almost all employers except federal government, state governments, and certain industries subject to other safety regulations
    b. Purpose of OSHA is to promote safety standards and job safety
    c. Occupational Safety and Health Administration (OSHA) administers this law

        (1) OSHA develops and enforces standards in work place on health and safety
        (2) OSHA investigates complaints and makes inspections of workplace

            (a) Employers can require OSHA to get search warrant for inspection

                1] Search warrant issued based on probable cause

                    a] High employee complaint rate can form probable cause

        (3) Employers required to keep records of job-related injuries and report serious accidents to OSHA
        (4) Employers required to comply with regulations set by OSHA
        (5) Employers are prohibited from discriminating against or discharging employees for exercising his/her rights under OSHA
        (6) OSHA may assess civil penalties for violations
        (7) Employers may be criminally liable if willful violation results in death of employee

            (a) Possible fine, imprisonment, or both

E. Employment Discrimination

1. Title VII of the Civil Rights Act of 1964 forbids discrimination in employment on the basis of race, color, religion, sex, or national origin

    a. Applies to employers and labor unions having fifteen or more employees whose business affects interstate commerce

        (1) By amendment, applies to federal, state, and local government employees

    b. Job discrimination applies to discrimination in hiring, promotion, transfers, firing, compensation, etc.
    c. Enforced by Equal Employment Opportunity Commission (EEOC) which is a federal government administrative agency, or by lawsuits of private individuals
    d. Not necessarily illegal to treat employees differently, but

        (1) Illegal discrimination occurs when employee treated differently than person of other race, color, religion, sex, or national origin
        (2) Illegal discrimination may occur when employer adopts rules that adversely affect a member of a protected class

        EXAMPLE: *Rules requiring certain standards on weight, height, or strength*

        (3) Illegal discrimination may be proven statistically to show pattern of discrimination
        (4) Defendant may have defenses to Title VII violations

            (a) Bona fide occupational qualification
            (b) Bona fide seniority or merit system
            (c) Professionally developed ability test
            (d) National security reasons

2. Age Discrimination in Employment Act

    a. Generally applies to individuals at least forty years old

        (1) Remedies for violations of Act

            (a) Monetary damages including back pay
            (b) Reinstatement
            (c) Promotion

    b. Applies to most businesses employing at least twenty people
    c. Generally prohibits mandatory retirement under age seventy

3. Vocational Rehabilitation Act of 1973 applies to employers with federal contracts over $2,500

    a. Employers required to take affirmative action to employ and advance qualified handicapped individuals

4. Americans with Disabilities Act (ADA)

    a. Applies to employers with at least fifteen employees
    b. Forbids companies and most other entities from discriminating against qualified persons with a disability in various employment decisions including hiring, firing, promotion, and pay

        (1) Qualified individual with disability means person who can perform essential functions of job either with or without reasonable accommodation

            (a) Reasonable accommodation may include acquiring new equipment, modifying facilities, restructuring jobs, modifying work schedules, etc. unless employer can show undue hardship based on significant expense or hardship

    c. ADA protects disabled persons from discrimination and guarantees them equal access to, among others,

        (1) Public services including public transportation and public accommodations
        (2) Public services operated by private entities

    d. Enforcement may be by attorney general or by private legal action

5. Pregnancy Discrimination Act

    a. Employers prohibited from discriminating against employees becoming pregnant or giving birth

        (1) Unmarried and married woman are covered
        (2) Employers' health and disability insurance must cover pregnancy the same as any other medical condition

6. Vietnam Era Veterans Readjustment Assistance Act

    a. Employers with federal contracts of $10,000 or more must take affirmative action in hiring and promoting qualified veterans of the Vietnam war or qualified disabled veterans

7. Discrimination based on religion

    a. Employer must accommodate employee's religious practices, beliefs, and observances unless it is an undue hardship on employer's business

8. Equal Pay Act

    a. Requires equal pay for equal work for both sexes
    b. Differences in pay may be based on merit, quality of work, or seniority
    c. Enforced by Equal Employment Opportunity Commission (EEOC)

9. Affirmative Action

    a. Policies that

        (1) Encourage employers to correct present conditions or practices that cause discrimination, or

(2) Provide for affirmative steps to increase in work forces the hiring of minorities and females

10. Family and Medical Leave Act

a. Covers employees employed for at least twelve months for at least 1250 hours by employers having at least fifty employees

b. Employees have right to up to twelve workweeks of leave during a twelve-month period for any of following reasons

(1) Employee's own serious health problem
(2) To care for serious health problem of parent, spouse, or child
(3) Birth and care of baby
(4) Child placed with employee for adoption or foster care

c. Leave of twelve weeks may be done intermittently for cases of serious health problems of employee or his/her covered relatives
d. Typically, leave is without pay
e. When employee returns, s/he must get back same or equivalent position
f. Returning employee cannot lose benefits due to leave
g. Employers who deny these rights to employee are civilly liable for damages

11. Health Insurance Portability and Accountability Act

a. Restricts using exclusions for preexisting conditions in employer sponsored group health insurance policies

12. Whistleblower Protection Act

a. Federal law that protects federal employees from retaliation by employers for blowing the whistle on employers
b. Majority of states also have laws that protect whistleblowers from employers' retaliation

F. Federal Fair Labor Standards Act

1. Applies to all businesses that affect interstate commerce
2. All covered employees must be paid at least "the minimum wage"

a. Computer professionals have a much higher minimum wage
b. Employees younger than twenty may be hired for a somewhat lower "opportunity wage" for ninety calendar days

3. Workers who work more than forty hours per week must be paid time and a half

a. Regulates number of hours in standard work week

4. Some employees are not covered under some or all of the minimum wage and time-and-a-half provisions

a. For example, professionals, executives, outside salespersons

5. Some employees must get at least minimum wage but are not covered by the overtime rules

a. For example, taxi drivers, railroad employees

6. Employees may be paid based on various time bases such as hourly, weekly, monthly, etc.
7. Enforced by Department of Labor and may include fines and/or prison

G. National Labor Relations Act (Wagner Act)

1. Provides that employees have right to join, assist, or form labor organizations
2. Employers are required to bargain with union about work-related issues such as firing practices, working hours, retirement rules, safety conditions, and pay, including sick pay and vacation pay

H. Taft-Hartley Act

1. Prohibits certain unfair labor practices of unions such as secondary boycotts and featherbedding (requirements to pay employees for work not actually performed)

2. Provides for cooling-off period, in some cases, before a strike can take place

I. Landrum-Griffin Act

1. Requires extensive financial reporting involving unions
2. Provides for civil and criminal action against misdeeds of union officers
3. Provides for bill of rights for union members in conducting meetings and elections

J. Federal Consolidated Budget Reconciliation Act (COBRA)

1. Provides that when employee quits, s/he may keep same group health insurance coverage for eighteen months for that former employee and spouse

    a. Former employee pays for it

K. Pensions

1. Employee Retirement Income Security Act (ERISA)

    a. Does not require employer to set up pension plan
    b. If employer does set up plan, it must meet certain standards

        (1) Generally, employee contributions to pension plan vest immediately
        (2) In general, employee's rights to employer's contributions to pension plan vest from five to seven years after beginning employment based on formulas in law
        (3) Standards on investment of funds are set up to avoid mismanagement
        (4) Employers cannot delay employee's participation in pension plan
        (5) Covered plans must give annual reports to employees in plan

2. In noncontributory pension plan, employee does not pay but employer pays for all
3. Maximum punishments for violations of Act by individuals increased to imprisonment of ten years and fine of $100,000—by entities, maximum fine is increased to $500,000

L. Worker Adjustment and Retraining Notification Act

1. Provides that employers before they close a plant or have mass layoffs must give sixty days notice to employees as well as to state and local officials
2. Act allows shorter notice period in case of emergencies or failing companies

M. Federal Employee Polygraph Protection Act

1. Private employers may not require employees or prospective employees to take lie detector test or make adverse employment decisions based on such tests or refusals to take them

    a. Government employers exempted
    b. Private employer may use lie detector tests as part of investigation of economic loss when employer has reason to suspect individual

        (1) Employee cannot be disciplined based solely on test
        (2) Employer is limited in topics of questions that violate privacy especially in topics not directly related to investigation of economic loss

N. Environmental Regulation

1. Under common law

    a. Parties may be liable under doctrine of nuisance

        (1) Based on party using property in manner that unreasonably interferes with another's right to use and enjoy property
        (2) Typically, monetary damages is remedy rather than injunction
        (3) Often, plaintiffs need to show their injury is distinct from harm of public in general

    b. Businesses may be liable for negligence

        (1) Plaintiff shows that his/her harm was caused by business polluter who failed to use reasonable care to prevent foreseeable harm

   c. Businesses may be liable under strict liability if involved in ultrahazardous activities

      EXAMPLE: B is in the business of transporting radioactive materials. Strict liability may be used which makes B liable for all damages it causes without the need to prove negligence.

2. Under federal statutory laws

   a. Environmental Protection Agency (EPA)

     (1) Administrative agency set up to ensure compliance with environmental protection laws

     (2) EPA may enforce federal environmental laws by use of administrative orders and/or civil penalties

       (a) May also refer criminal or civil actions to Department of Justice

     (3) EPA also adopts regulations and conducts research on environment and effects of pollution

     (4) Most environmental statutes provide for criminal liability

       (a) Generally, corporate officers must be "blameworthy," based on ability to prevent or correct, to be criminally liable

     (5) EPA generally uses civil suits more than criminal prosecutions because civil suits require preponderance of evidence to win but criminal convictions require proof beyond a reasonable doubt

     (6) Private citizens may also sue violators or may sue EPA to enforce compliance with laws

     (7) States may also sue violators

   b. National Environmental Policy Act

     (1) Requires all federal agencies consider environmental factors in all major decisions

       (a) Requires preparation of environmental impact statement (EIS) when federal action or proposed laws significantly affect environment

         1] Shows expected impact on environment

         2] Describes adverse consequences of action that are unavoidable

         3] Must examine alternatives to achieve goals

         4] For EIS, environment means more than natural environment—can include aesthetic, cultural, and national heritage interests, etc.

       (b) If agency finds no EIS is warranted, it must prepare and make available to public document called "Finding of No Significant Impact" with reasons for no action needed

   c. Clean Air Act

     (1) Provides that EPA set air quality standards for mobile sources, such as autos, and stationary sources, such as factories

     (2) Regulates various toxic pollutants, including those that affect acid rain and ozone layer

     (3) Act allows private citizens to sue violators of Act

       (a) Those winning successful citizens' lawsuits can get attorneys' fees and court costs

     (4) Encourages and requires use of alternative fuels to help meet pollution goals

     (5) Federal government may force recall of automobiles violating emission regulations

     (6) EPA can assess stated civil penalties

       (a) When company finds it cost effective to violate Clean Air Act, EPA may wage penalty equal to benefit company received by not complying

       (b) Criminal fines and imprisonment for knowing violations

     (7) Amendments to Clean Air Act allow companies to trade some rights to pollute

   d. Clean Water Act

     (1) EPA sets standards to reduce, eliminate, or prevent pollution of rivers, seas, ponds, wetlands, streams, etc.

(a) For example, controls dredging or filling of rivers and wetlands

(2) Owners of point sources such as floating vessels, pipes, ditches, and animal feeding operations must obtain permits which control water pollution

(a) Nonpoint sources such as farms, forest lands, and mining are exempt

(3) Broad in scope—includes regulation of discharge of heated water (e.g., by nuclear power plant or electric utilities)

(4) Provides for fines and prison for neglect or knowing violations or endangerment (i.e., knowingly putting person in imminent danger of death or serious bodily harm)

e. Safe Drinking Water Act

(1) Regulates safety of water supplied to homes by public water systems
(2) Prohibits discharge of waste into wells for drinking water

f. Oil Pollution Act

(1) Requires establishment of oil pollution cleanup contingency plans by tanker owners and operators to handle worst case spills under adverse weather conditions
(2) Requires that new tankers have double hulls
(3) Requires phase-in of double hulls on existing oil tankers and barges

g. Noise Control Act

(1) Regulates noise pollution and encourages research on its effects
(2) EPA establishes noise standards for products sold in US
(3) Violations may result in fines, imprisonment, or injunctions

h. Resource Conservation and Recovery Act

(1) Creates permit system to regulate businesses that store, use, or transport hazardous waste
(2) Requires companies to keep strict records of hazardous waste from "cradle to grave" transport
(3) Producers required to label and package correctly hazardous materials that are to be transported
(4) Fines and prison for violators

(a) Can be doubled for certain violations

(5) Also, household waste regulated

i. Toxic Substances Control Act

(1) Mandates testing and regulation of chemicals that pose unreasonable risk to health or environment

(a) Requires testing before marketing allowed

(2) Requires special labeling of toxic substances

j. Federal Insecticide, Fungicide, and Rodenticide Act

(1) Provides that pesticides and herbicides must be registered with EPA before sale
(2) EPA can

(a) Deny registration
(b) Certify them for general or restricted use
(c) Suspend registration if emergency or imminent danger

(3) Limits set for amount of pesticide residue permitted on crops for human or animal consumption
(4) Act has labeling requirements
(5) Violators subject to fine and imprisonment
(6) Private party may petition EPA to suspend or cancel registration

k. Federal Environmental Pesticide Control Act

   (1) All who distribute pesticides must register them with EPA
   (2) EPA uses cost-benefit analysis to decide to register pesticides rather than deciding if they will pose health hazard

l. Comprehensive Environmental, Compensation, and Liability Act (CERCLA)

   (1) Often known as the Superfund legislation
   (2) Levies taxes on manufacturers of certain dangerous chemicals
   (3) Identifies hazardous waste sites needed to be cleaned up
   (4) Regulates generation and transportation of hazardous substances

      (a) Does not regulate petroleum or natural gas

   (5) Government can impose broad liability for cleanup costs and environmental damages

      (a) Parties have **joint and several liability** and include

         1] **Current owners and operators** of site
         2] **Past owners and operators** of site
         3] Persons who **transported** waste to site
         4] Persons who arranged to have waste transported

      (b) With limited exceptions, the standard is based on **strict liability** for all cleanup costs
      (c) One who is responsible for portion of waste can be liable for all cleanup costs
      (d) Liability is retroactive under this statute
      (e) Only three narrow defenses are allowed under this statute: acts of God, war, or unrelated third parties
      (f) CERCLA does **not** make polluters liable to private parties; they generally use private suits under common law

m. Emergency Planning, and Community Right-to-Know Act

   (1) Companies having specified amounts of extremely hazardous substances must notify state and local agencies and also must issue annual reports of releases of specified toxic chemicals that result from operations

      (a) This information is available to public

n. International protection of ozone layer

   (1) Many countries, including US, have agreed to reduce or eliminate certain chemicals believed to harm ozone layer

o. Nuclear Waste Policy Act

   (1) Creates national plan to dispose of highly radioactive nuclear waste
   (2) State may regulate emissions of radioactive particles under Clean Air Act

p. Marine Protection, Research, and Sanctuaries Act

   (1) Regulates dumping into oceans
   (2) Establishing marine sanctuaries

q. Endangered Species Act

   (1) Enforced by both EPA and Department of Commerce
   (2) Protects both endangered as well as threatened species

r. Pollution Prevention Act

   (1) Provides incentives to industry to prevent some pollution from initially being formed

s. SEC requires that companies report in financial statements their environmental liabilities

3. Environmental Compliance Audits

    a. These are systematic, objective reviews designed to evaluate compliance with federal and state regulations and laws on environment

       (1) Some states have environmental audit privilege laws

    b. Purposes of audit

       (1) To discover violations or questionable practices to allow company to avoid litigation
       (2) Voluntary discovery to avoid criminal sanctions
       (3) To meet disclosure requirements under securities laws

O. Telephone Consumer Protection Act

1. Restricts use of prerecorded messages
2. Act requires that in order to use prerecorded messages, a live person must introduce prerecorded message and receive from telephoned person permission to play that message

    a. Act exempts calls by nonprofit organizations, calls made for emergencies, and call to businesses
    b. Act does not cover personal phone calls

MULTIPLE-CHOICE QUESTIONS (1-44)

1. Taxes payable under the Federal Unemployment Tax Act (FUTA) are
   a. Calculated as a fixed percentage of all compensation paid to an employee.
   b. Deductible by the employer as a business expense for federal income tax purposes.
   c. Payable by employers for all employees.
   d. Withheld from the wages of all covered employees.

2. An unemployed CPA generally would receive unemployment compensation benefits if the CPA
   a. Was fired as a result of the employer's business reversals.
   b. Refused to accept a job as an accountant while receiving extended benefits.
   c. Was fired for embezzling from a client.
   d. Left work voluntarily without good cause.

3. After serving as an active director of Lee Corp. for twenty years, Ryan was appointed an honorary director with the obligation to attend directors' meetings with no voting power. In 2001, Ryan received an honorary director's fee of $5,000. This fee is
   a. Reportable by Lee as employee compensation subject to social security tax.
   b. Reportable by Ryan as self-employment income subject to social security self-employment tax.
   c. Taxable as "other income" by Ryan, **not** subject to any social security tax.
   d. Considered to be a gift **not** subject to social security self-employment or income tax.

4. Syl Corp. does **not** withhold FICA taxes from its employees' compensation. Syl voluntarily pays the entire FICA tax for its share and the amounts that it could have withheld from the employees. The employees' share of FICA taxes paid by Syl to the IRS is
   a. Deductible by Syl as additional compensation that is includible in the employees' taxable income.
   b. Not deductible by Syl because it does **not** meet the deductibility requirement as an ordinary and necessary business expense.
   c. A nontaxable gift to each employee, provided that the amount is less than $1,000 annually to each employee.
   d. Subject to prescribed penalties imposed on Syl for its failure to withhold required payroll taxes.

5. Social security benefits may include all of the following **except**
   a. Payments to divorced spouses.
   b. Payments to disabled children.
   c. Medicare payments.
   d. Medicaid payments.

6. Which of the following forms of income, if in excess of the annual exempt amount, will cause a reduction in a retired person's social security benefits?
   a. Annual proceeds from an annuity.
   b. Director's fees.
   c. Pension payments.
   d. Closely held corporation stock dividends.

7. Which of the following payments are deducted from an employee's salary?

	Unemployment compensation insurance	Worker's compensation insurance
a.	Yes	Yes
b.	Yes	No
c.	No	Yes
d.	No	No

8. Which of the following types of income is subject to taxation under the provisions of the Federal Insurance Contributions Act (FICA)?
   a. Interest earned on municipal bonds.
   b. Capital gains of $3,000.
   c. Car received as a productivity award.
   d. Dividends of $2,500.

9. Under the Federal Insurance Contributions Act (FICA), which of the following acts will cause an employer to be liable for penalties?

	Failure to supply taxpayer identification numbers	Failure to make timely FICA deposits
a.	Yes	Yes
b.	Yes	No
c.	No	Yes
d.	No	No

10. Which of the following parties generally is ineligible to collect workers' compensation benefits?
   a. Minors.
   b. Truck drivers.
   c. Union employees.
   d. Temporary office workers.

11. Kroll, an employee of Acorn, Inc., was injured in the course of employment while operating a forklift manufactured and sold to Acorn by Trell Corp. The forklift was defectively designed by Trell. Under the state's mandatory workers' compensation statute, Kroll will be successful in

	Obtaining workers' compensation benefits	A negligence action against Acorn
a.	Yes	Yes
b.	Yes	No
c.	No	Yes
d.	No	No

12. Which of the following provisions is basic to all workers' compensation systems?
   a. The injured employee must prove the employer's negligence.
   b. The employer may invoke the traditional defense of contributory negligence.
   c. The employer's liability may be ameliorated by a coemployee's negligence under the fellow-servant rule.
   d. The injured employee is allowed to recover on strict liability theory.

13. Workers' Compensation Acts require an employer to
   a. Provide coverage for all eligible employees.
   b. Withhold employee contributions from the wages of eligible employees.
   c. Pay an employee the difference between disability payments and full salary.
   d. Contribute to a federal insurance fund.

14. Generally, which of the following statements concerning workers' compensation laws is correct?
   a. The amount of damages recoverable is based on comparative negligence.
   b. Employers are strictly liable without regard to whether or **not** they are at fault.
   c. Workers' compensation benefits are **not** available if the employee is negligent.
   d. Workers' compensation awards are payable for life.

15. Workers' compensation laws provide for all of the following benefits **except**
   a. Burial expenses.
   b. Full pay during disability.
   c. The cost of prosthetic devices.
   d. Monthly payments to surviving dependent children.

16. Which of the following claims is(are) generally covered under workers' compensation statutes?

	Occupational disease	Employment aggravated preexisting disease
a.	Yes	Yes
b.	Yes	No
c.	No	Yes
d.	No	No

17. Under which of the following conditions is an on-site inspection of a workplace by an investigator from the Occupational Safety and Health Administration (OSHA) permissible?
   a. Only if OSHA obtains a search warrant after showing probable cause.
   b. Only if the inspection is conducted after working hours.
   c. At the request of employees.
   d. After OSHA provides the employer with at least twenty-four hours notice of the prospective inspection.

18. Which of the following Acts prohibit(s) an employer from discriminating among employees based on sex?

	Equal Pay Act	Title VII of the Civil Rights Act
a.	Yes	Yes
b.	Yes	No
c.	No	Yes
d.	No	No

19. Under the Age Discrimination in Employment Act, which of the following remedies is(are) available to a covered employee?

	Early Retirement	Back pay
a.	Yes	Yes
b.	Yes	No
c.	No	Yes
d.	No	No

20. Which of the following company policies would violate the Age Discrimination in Employment Act?
   a. The company will not hire any accountant below twenty-five years of age.
   b. The office staff must retire at age sixty-five or younger.

   c. Both of the above.
   d. None of the above.

21. Under the provisions of the Americans With Disabilities Act of 1990, in which of the following areas is a disabled person protected from discrimination?

	Public transportation	Privately operated public accommodations
a.	Yes	Yes
b.	Yes	No
c.	No	Yes
d.	No	No

22. Under the Americans with Disabilities Act, which is(are) true?
  I. The Act requires that companies with at least ten employees set up a specified plan to hire people with disabilities.
 II. The Act requires companies to make reasonable accommodations for disabled persons unless this results in undue hardship on the operations of the company.

   a. I only.
   b. II only.
   c. Both I and II.
   d. Neither I nor II.

23. The Americans With Disabilities Act has as a purpose to give remedies for discrimination to individuals with disabilities. Which of the following is(are) true of this Act?
   I. It protects most individuals with disabilities working for companies but only if the companies do not need to incur any expenses to modify the work environment to accommodate the disability.
  II. It may require a company to modify work schedules to accommodate persons with disabilities.
 III. It may require a company to purchase equipment at company expense to accommodate persons with disabilities.

   a. I only.
   b. I and II only.
   c. II and III only.
   d. III only.

24. Which of the following is **not** true under the Family and Medical Leave Act?
   a. An employee has a right to take a leave from work for the birth and care of her child for one month at half of her regular pay.
   b. An employee has a right to take a leave from work for twelve workweeks to care for his/her seriously ill parent.
   c. An employee, upon returning under the provisions of the Act, must get back the same or equivalent position in the company.
   d. This Act does not cover all employees.

25. The Family Medical Leave Act provides for
   I. Unpaid leave for the employee to care for a newborn baby.
  II. Unpaid leave for the employee to care for the serious health problem of his or her parent.
 III. Paid leave for the employee to care for a serious health problem of his or her spouse.

a. I only.
b. II only.
c. I and II but not III.
d. III but not I or II.

26. Under the Fair Labor Standards Act, which of the following pay bases may be used to pay covered, nonexempt employees who earn, on average, the minimum hourly wage?

	Hourly	Weekly	Monthly
a.	Yes	Yes	Yes
b.	Yes	Yes	No
c.	Yes	No	Yes
d.	No	Yes	Yes

27. Under the Fair Labor Standards Act, if a covered, non-exempt employee works consecutive weeks of forty-five, forty-two, thirty-eight, and thirty-three hours, how many hours of overtime must be paid to the employee?
a. 0
b. 7
c. 18
d. 20

28. Which of the following employee benefits is(are) exempt from the provisions of the National Labor Relations Act?

	Sick pay	Vacation pay
a.	Yes	Yes
b.	Yes	No
c.	No	Yes
d.	No	No

29. Under the Federal Consolidated Budget Reconciliation Act of 1985 (COBRA), when an employee voluntarily resigns from a job, the former employee's group health insurance coverage that was in effect during the period of employment with the company
a. Automatically ceases for the former employee and spouse, if the resignation occurred before normal retirement age.
b. Automatically ceases for the former employee's spouse, but continues for the former employee for an eighteen-month period at the former employer's expense.
c. May be retained by the former employee at the former employee's expense for at least eighteen months after leaving the company, but must be terminated for the former employee's spouse.
d. May be retained for the former employee and spouse at the former employee's expense for at least eighteen months after leaving the company.

30. Under the Employee Retirement Income Security Act of 1974 (ERISA), which of the following areas of private employer pension plans is(are) regulated?

	Employee vesting	Plan funding
a.	Yes	Yes
b.	Yes	No
c.	No	Yes
d.	No	No

31. Under the provisions of the Employee Retirement Income Security Act of 1974 (ERISA), which of the following statements is correct?

a. Employees are entitled to have an employer established pension plan.
b. Employers are prevented from unduly delaying an employee's participation in a pension plan.
c. Employers are prevented from managing retirement plans.
d. Employees are entitled to make investment decisions.

32. Under the Comprehensive Environmental Response, Compensation, and Liability Act (CERCLA), commonly known as Superfund, which of the following parties would be liable to the Environmental Protection Agency (EPA) for the expense of cleaning up a hazardous waste disposal site?

I. The current owner or operator of the site.
II. The person who transported the wastes to the site.
III. The person who owned or operated the site at the time of the disposal.

a. I and II.
b. I and III.
c. II and III.
d. I, II, and III.

33. Which of the following activities is(are) regulated under the Federal Water Pollution Control Act (Clean Water Act)?

	Discharge of heated water by nuclear power plants	Dredging of wetlands
a.	Yes	Yes
b.	Yes	No
c.	No	Yes
d.	No	No

34. Environmental Compliance Audits are used for which of the following purpose(s)?

I. To voluntarily discover violations to avoid criminal sanctions.
II. To discover violations to avoid civil litigation.
III. To meet disclosure requirements to the SEC under the securities laws.

a. I only.
b. I and II only.
c. II only.
d. I, II and III.

35. Which of the following is(are) true under the Federal Insecticide, Fungicide, and Rodenticide Act?

I. Herbicides and pesticides must be certified and can be used only for applications that are approved.
II. Herbicides and pesticides must be registered under the Act before companies can sell them.
III. Pesticides, when used on food crops, can only be used in quantities that are limited under the Act.

a. I only.
b. I and II only.
c. II and III only.
d. I, II, and III.

36. Under the Comprehensive Environmental Response, Compensation and Liability Act as amended by the Superfund Amendments, which of the following is(are) true?

I. The present owner of land can be held liable for cleanup of hazardous chemicals placed on the land by a previous owner.

II. An employee of a company that had control over the disposal of hazardous substances on the company's land can be held personally liable for cleanup costs.

   a.   I only.
   b.   II only.
   c.   Both I and II.
   d.   Neither I nor II.

37. The National Environmental Policy Act was passed to enhance and preserve the environment. Which of the following is **not** true?
   a.   The Act applies to all federal agencies.
   b.   The Act requires that an environmental impact statement be provided if any proposed federal legislation may significantly affect the environment.
   c.   Enforcement of the Act is primarily accomplished by litigation of persons who decide to challenge federal government decisions.
   d.   The Act provides generous tax breaks to those companies that help accomplish national environmental policy.

38. Under the federal statutes governing water pollution, which of the following areas is(are) regulated?

	Dredging of coastal or freshwater wetlands	*Drinking water standards*
a.	Yes	Yes
b.	Yes	No
c.	No	Yes
d.	No	No

39. The Clean Air Act provides for the enforcement of standards for

I. The emissions of radioactive particles from private nuclear power plants.

II. The emissions of pollution from privately owned automobiles.

III. The emissions of air pollution from factories.

   a.   I and II only.
   b.   I and III only.
   c.   II and III only.
   d.   I, II and III.

40. Under the Clean Air Act, which of the following statements is(are) correct regarding actions that may be taken against parties who violate emission standards?

I. The federal government may require an automobile manufacturer to recall vehicles that violate emission standards.

II. A citizens' group may sue to force a coal burning power plant to comply with emission standards.

   a.   I only.
   b.   II only.
   c.   Both I and II.
   d.   Neither I nor II.

41. The Environmental Protection Agency is an administrative agency in the federal government that aids in the protection of the environment. Which of the following is **not** a purpose or function of this agency?
   a.   It adopts regulations to protect the quality of water.
   b.   It aids private citizens to make cases for private civil litigation.
   c.   It may refer criminal matters to the Department of Justice.
   d.   It may refer civil cases to the Department of Justice.

42. Whenever a federal agency recommends actions or legislation that may affect the environment, the agency must prepare an environmental impact statement. Which of the following is **not** required in the environmental impact statement?
   a.   A description of the source of funds to accomplish the action without harming the environment.
   b.   An examination of alternate methods of achieving the goals of the proposed actions or legislation.
   c.   A description in detail of the proposed actions or legislation on the environment.
   d.   A description of any unavoidable adverse consequences.

43. Which of the following is(are) possible when a company violates the Clean Air Act?

I. The company can be assessed a criminal fine.

II. Officers of the company can be imprisoned.

III. The Environmental Protection Agency may assess a civil penalty equal to the savings of costs by the company for noncompliance.

   a.   I only.
   b.   I or II only.
   c.   III only.
   d.   I, II or III.

44. Green, a former owner of Circle Plant, caused hazardous waste pollution at the Circle Plant site two years ago. Sason purchased the plant and caused more hazardous waste pollution. It can be shown that 20% of the problem was caused by Green and that 80% of the problem was caused by Sason. Sason went bankrupt recently. The government wishes to clean up the site and hold Green liable. Which of the following is true?
   a.   The most Green can be held liable for is 20%.
   b.   Green is not liable for any of the cleanup costs since the site was sold.
   c.   Green is not liable for any of the cleanup costs because Green was responsible for less than half of the problem.
   d.   Green can be held liable for all the cleanup costs even if Sason has some funds.

OTHER OBJECTIVE QUESTIONS

Problem 1   (10 to 15 minutes)

Required:

For each of the numbered items, indicate: (**A**) this item is considered to be wages under the Social Security Act, or (**B**) this item is **not** considered to be wages under the Social Security Act.

1.   Wages, paid in money, to a construction worker.

2.   Reimbursed normal travel expenses of a salesperson.

3.   Compensation not paid in cash.

4.   Commissions of a salesperson.

5.   Bonuses paid to employees.

6.   Employee insurance premiums paid by the employer.

7.   Wages paid to a secretary who is working part time.

8.   Vacation allowance pay given to employees who are working full time.

9.   Wages paid to a full-time secretary who wishes to elect not to be covered under the Social Security Act.

10.   Tips of a waitress.

PROBLEM

Problem 1 (15 to 20 minutes)

Maple owns 75% of the common stock of Salam Exterminating, Inc. Maple is not an officer or employee of the corporation, and does not serve on its board of directors. Salam is in the business of providing exterminating services to residential and commercial customers.

Dodd performed exterminating services on behalf of Salam. Dodd suffered permanent injuries as a result of inhaling one of the chemicals used by Salam. This occurred after Dodd sprayed the chemical in a restaurant that Salam regularly services. Dodd was under the supervision of one of Salam's district managers and was trained by Salam to perform exterminating services following certain procedures, which he did. Later that day several patrons who ate at the restaurant also suffered permanent injuries as a result of inhaling the chemical. The chemical was manufactured by Ace Chemical Corp. and sold and delivered to Salam in a closed container. It was not altered by Salam. It has now been determined that the chemical was defectively manufactured and the injuries suffered by Dodd and the restaurant patrons were a direct result of the defect.

Salam has complied with an applicable compulsory workers' compensation statute by obtaining an insurance policy from Spear Insurance Co.

As a result of the foregoing, the following actions have been commenced:

- Dodd sued Spear to recover workers' compensation benefits.
- Dodd sued Salam based on negligence in training him.
- Dodd sued Ace based on strict liability in tort.
- The restaurant patrons sued Maple claiming negligence in not preventing Salam from using the chemical purchased from Ace.

Required:

Discuss the merits of the actions commenced by Dodd and the restaurant patrons, indicating the likely outcomes and your reasons therefor.

1. b _ _	11. b _ _	21. a _ _	31. b _ _	41. b _ _
2. a _ _	12. d _ _	22. b _ _	32. d _ _	42. a _ _
3. b _ _	13. a _ _	23. c _ _	33. a _ _	43. d _ _
4. a _ _	14. b _ _	24. a _ _	34. d _ _	44. d _ _
5. d _ _	15. b _ _	25. c _ _	35. d _ _	
6. b _ _	16. a _ _	26. a _ _	36. c _ _	
7. d _ _	17. c _ _	27. b _ _	37. d _ _	
8. c _ _	18. a _ _	28. d _ _	38. a _ _	
9. a _ _	19. c _ _	29. d _ _	39. d _ _	1st: __/44 = __%
10. d _ _	20. b _ _	30. a _ _	40. c _ _	2nd: __/44 = __%

MULTIPLE-CHOICE ANSWER EXPLANATIONS

A. Federal Social Security Act

1.   (b)   Taxes payable under the Federal Unemployment Tax Act (FUTA) are used to provide unemployment compensation benefits to workers who lose jobs and cannot find replacement work. These taxes paid are deductible by the employer as a business expense for federal income tax purposes. Therefore, answer (b) is correct. Answer (c) is incorrect because only those employers who paid wages of $1,500 or more during any calendar quarter or who employed at least one employee for at least one day a week for twenty weeks must pay FUTA taxes. Answer (d) is incorrect because it is the employer, not the employee, who pays the taxes. Answer (a) is incorrect because the taxes payable under the FUTA are calculated as a fixed percentage of only the first $6,000 of wages of each employee.

2.   (a)   Unemployment compensation is intended for workers who lose jobs through no fault of their own and cannot find replacement work. Answer (a) is correct because a CPA fired as a result of the employer's business reversals is entitled to receive unemployment compensation. Answer (b) is incorrect because an accountant who refuses to accept replacement work offered him/her would not receive unemployment compensation. Answers (c) and (d) are incorrect because unemployment compensation is not intended for an employee whose actions led to his/her loss of a job.

3.   (b)   Directors' fees are generally treated as self-employment income and thus are subject to social security self-employment tax.

4.   (a)   Answer (a) is best since the nondeduction of the FICA tax **and** the payment of it by the employer effectively raises the income of the employee. Answer (d) is not correct because although the employer is required to withhold tax on wages and is liable for payment of such tax whether or not it is collected, the employer's liability can be relieved after showing the employee's related income tax liability has been paid. Therefore, since the employer has paid the taxes, the employer is not subject to penalty. Answer (c) is not correct since no mention is made of a gift. Answer (b) is not correct since no reference is made to wages not being an ordinary and necessary business expense.

5.   (d)   Social security benefits may include payments to spouses, including divorced spouses in some cases, and to children. It may also include medicare payments but not medicaid payments.

6.   (b)   **Earned** income in excess of the annual limitation will cause a reduction in a retired person's social security benefits. Answer (b) is therefore correct, since "director's fees" are considered earned income. Answers (a), (c), and (d) are incorrect because proceeds from an annuity, pension payments, and stock dividends are not considered earned income.

7.   (d)   Unemployment insurance tax must be paid by the employer if the employer employs one or more persons covered by the act. Payments for unemployment insurance are not deducted from employees' salaries. Workers' compensation is a form of strict liability whereby the employer is liable to the employee for injuries or diseases sustained by the employee which arise out of and in the course of employment. The insurance is paid by the employer and the cost is passed on as an expense of doing business. Thus, worker's compensation insurance also is not paid by the employee.

8.   (c)   Social security tax applies to wages, defined as all compensation for employment. Employment compensation does not have to be in the form of cash to be included in wages taxed under the Federal Insurance Contributions Act (FICA). Therefore, a car received as a productivity award is considered employment compensation subject to the social security tax and answers (a), (b), and (d) are incorrect, because these are not wages.

9.   (a)   Both a failure to supply taxpayer identification numbers and a failure to make timely FICA deposits would be violations of the Act. As all employees are required to participate in Social Security, their identification numbers must be supplied in order to track employment and cumulative FICA tax paid to the government. The Act also explicitly states that an employer's failure to collect and deposit taxes in a timely manner subjects him/her to penalties and interest.

B. Workers' Compensation Act

10.   (d)   Workers' compensation benefits arise out of a type of strict liability whereby employers are liable for injuries or diseases sustained by employees which arise from the scope of the employment. Temporary office workers are usually either independent contractors or are employees of a separate employment agency. Answer (a) is incorrect because the employment laws are especially meant to protect minors. Answer (b) is incorrect because truck drivers are not exempted. Answer (c) is incorrect because union affiliation does not create an exemption.

11. **(b)** Under workers' compensation laws, any employee injured during the course of employment is entitled to workers' compensation benefits regardless of fault, as long as the injury is not self-inflicted, and not the result of a fight or intoxication. However, acceptance of benefits under workers' compensation laws precludes an employee from suing the employer for damages in a civil court.

12. **(d)** Workers' compensation is a form of strict liability in which an employer is liable to employees for injuries or diseases sustained in the course of employment, without regard to fault. Answer (a) is incorrect because the injured employee is not required to establish employer negligence to recover a workers' compensation action. Answer (b) is incorrect because contributory negligence of the employee is not a valid defense in workers' compensation cases. The workers' compensation act removes the employer's common law defense of negligence of a fellow employee, therefore answer (c) is incorrect.

13. **(a)** Workers' Compensation Acts require an employer to provide coverage for all eligible employees. Furthermore, the employer is required to cover the cost of injuries to employees, and no amount is deducted from the employees' wages. Therefore, answer (b) is incorrect. Answer (c) is incorrect because under workers' compensation, the disability benefit payments are usually a percentage of weekly earnings. The employer does not have to make up the difference between the benefit payments and the employee's salary. Answer (d) is incorrect because a business covered under workers' compensation laws may be self-insured but it must show proof of financial responsibility to carry this risk.

14. **(b)** Most workers' compensation laws provide that the employer is strictly liable to an employee without regard to negligence of the employer or employee. Therefore, answers (a) and (c) are incorrect. Answer (d) is incorrect because worker's compensation awards may or may not be payable for life.

15. **(b)** The following are some examples of workers' compensation benefits: burial expenses, the cost of prosthetic devices, monthly payments to surviving dependent children, and **partial** wage continuation during disability.

16. **(a)** Both occupational disease and employment aggravated preexisting disease are covered by the statutes in that all consequences of an injury on the job, regardless of whether such injury was actually caused by an accident, are deemed to be "accidental" injuries resulting from employment. If any conditions in the workplace could have possibly contributed to or aggravated consequences, the doctrine of strict employer liability applies.

D. Employee Safety

17. **(c)** OSHA investigates complaints and makes inspections of the workplace. Employers can require that OSHA obtain a search warrant in most cases to conduct the search. Probable cause is needed to obtain a search warrant and complaints by employees can provide the needed probable cause. Answer (a) is incorrect because the employer can allow the search or give permission, in which cases, search warrants are not needed. Answer (b) is incorrect because inspections can be made during working hours. In fact, this may be the only or most effective time to conduct

the inspection. Answer (d) is incorrect because there is no requirement that OSHA give the employers advance notice of the inspections. Such a requirement would make many inspections less effective.

E. Employment Discrimination

18. **(a)** Under the Equal Pay Act, employers cannot pay some employees less money than that paid to employees of the opposite sex when equal work is performed. Under Title VII of the Civil Rights Act, employers cannot discriminate against a prospective employee on the basis of race, color, national origin, religion, or sex.

19. **(c)** The Age Discrimination in Employment Act does not specifically use the term "back pay" but the Act provides equitable relief as deemed appropriate and otherwise authorizes back pay. The Act does provide for employment reinstatement or promotion, but does not provide for early retirement.

20. **(b)** The Age Discrimination in Employment Act generally prohibits mandatory retirement under age seventy. Answers (a) and (c) are incorrect because the Act generally applies to individuals over forty years old. Answer (d) is incorrect because forced retirement under the age of seventy is generally prohibited under the Act.

21. **(a)** The Americans With Disabilities Act of 1990 prohibits all businesses with fifteen employees or more from considering a person's handicap when making a hiring decision. Also, the act requires businesses to make special accommodations available to handicapped employees and customers, unless the cost is too burdensome. Therefore, answer (a) is correct as the act covers both public transportation and privately operated public accommodations.

22. **(b)** The Americans with Disabilities Act provides the disabled with better access to employment, public accommodations, and transportation. The Act requires companies to make reasonable accommodations for the disabled unless this would cause undue hardship for the business. The Act does not require companies to set up a hiring plan.

23. **(c)** The Americans With Disabilities Act requires most companies and entities to not discriminate against qualified individuals with disabilities who can perform the essential functions of the job either with or without reasonable accommodation, unless the company can show undue hardship. Reasonable accommodation may include purchasing new equipment, modifying facilities, or modifying work schedules.

E.10. Family and Medical Leave Act

24. **(a)** A covered employee has the right to a leave from work for specified reasons for twelve workweeks in a twelve-month period but typically receives leave without pay. Answer (b) is incorrect because it mentions one of the specified reasons allowed for a leave. Answer (c) is incorrect because an important right under the Act is to get back the same or similar position upon returning. Answer (d) is an incorrect response because not all employees are covered. To be covered employees must have worked for twelve months, for at least 1,250 hours in those twelve months, and be one of at least fifty employees.

25.   (c)   The Act provides for up to twelve workweeks of unpaid leave for the employee to care for serious health problems of his or her parent, spouse, or child. It also provides the same right to care for his or her newborn baby. Note that (d) is incorrect because it provides for paid leave to care for his or her spouse who is seriously ill.

F. Federal Fair Labor Standards Act

26.   (a)   The Fair Labor Standards Act allows employees to be paid on a piecework basis or salary. Workers must receive at least the equivalent of the minimum hourly rate, but the basis on which the workers are paid can be hourly, weekly, or monthly.

27.   (b)   The Fair Labor Standards Act requires overtime pay to be paid when hours worked in any given week exceed forty hours. Therefore, the additional five hours and two hours worked in the first two weeks constitute overtime.

G. National Labor Relations Act (Wagner Act)

28.   (d)   Among other fringe benefits, sick pay and vacation pay are subjects for collective bargaining. Therefore, sick pay and vacation pay are not exempt from the provisions of the National Labor Relations Act.

J. Federal Consolidated Budget Reconciliation Act

29.   (d)   Under the Federal Consolidated Budget Reconciliation Act of 1985 (COBRA), a former employee may retain group health coverage under the employer for him/herself and his/her spouse at the former employee's expense for at least eighteen months after leaving the company. Answer (a) is incorrect because the former employee and spouse may retain the coverage for at least eighteen months. Answers (b) and (c) are incorrect because not only the former employee but also the spouse may retain the coverage for eighteen months at the former employee's expense.

K. Pensions

30.   (a)   If a pension plan is established, employee contributions to the pension plan vest immediately. In addition, standards on investment of funds are set up to avoid mismanagement.

31.   (b)   The Employee Retirement Income Security Act of 1974 (ERISA) does not require an employer to establish a pension plan. Therefore, answer (a) is incorrect. If the employer does set up a plan, it must meet certain standards. These standards prevent employers from unduly delaying an employee's participation in a pension plan. Therefore, answer (b) is correct. Standards are also set up for the investment of funds to avoid mismanagement. However, employers are able to manage the retirement plans. Therefore, answer (c) is incorrect. Answer (d) is incorrect because ERISA provisions do not require that the employees make the investment decisions. This is a function of the particular company's plan.

N. Environmental Regulation

32.   (d)   CERCLA imposes environmental liability on a broad group of potentially responsible parties. The courts have included the following classes: (1) current owners and operators, (2) owners and operators at the time of waste disposal, (3) generators of hazardous waste, (4) transporters of hazardous waste, and (5) lenders who finance borrowers' hazardous waste sites.

33.   (a)   The Clean Water Act regulates the dredging or filling of wetlands. Without a permit, these are generally prohibited. The discharging of heated water by nuclear power plants is also regulated.

34.   (d)   All of the purposes listed are reasons to have an Environmental Compliance Audit. Since the environmental laws and regulations can be complex and may result in both criminal violations and civil liability, both statements I and II are correct. Statement III is also correct because problems with the environmental laws can be significant under the federal securities laws.

35.   (d)   The Federal Insecticide, Fungicide, and Rodenticide Act does have all three of the provisions. Herbicides and pesticides are required to be registered before they can be sold. Furthermore, they need to be used only for the purposes certified. Also, when used on food crops, the amount that can be used is limited.

36.   (c)   The provisions of the Comprehensive Environmental Response, Compensation, and Liability Act (CERCLA) as amended is very broad in scope. If the EPA cleans up the hazardous chemicals, it can recover the costs from any responsible party including present owners of the facility and any person who arranged for the disposal of the hazardous substance.

37.   (d)   The National Environmental Policy Act is centered around requiring the federal government and its agencies to consider the effects of its actions on the environment. It does not provide tax breaks to companies to accomplish environmental goals. Answer (a) is not chosen because it correctly states that the Act applies to all federal agencies. Answer (b) is not chosen because it is also correct. The Act does require an environmental impact statement if the environment may be significantly hurt. Answer (c) is not chosen because private litigation is the main way this Act is enforced.

38.   (a)   The Clean Water Act regulates the dredging of both coastal and freshwater wetlands. The Safe Drinking Water act regulates the safety of water supplied by public water systems to homes.

39.   (d)   The Clean Air Act regulates emissions into the air from automobiles, factories, and nuclear power plants. Note that emissions from the nuclear power plant are handled by the Clean Air Act rather than the Nuclear Waste Policy Act. The latter creates a national plan to dispose of highly radioactive nuclear waste.

40.   (c)   The Clean Air Act sets air quality standards for mobile sources such as autos, and for stationary sources such as power plants. The federal government has ways to encourage and require compliance, such as requiring manufacturers to recall vehicles that violate emission standards. The Act also allows private citizens to sue violators to enforce compliance.

41.   (b)   The Environmental Protection Agency (EPA) is an administrative agency designed to aid the federal government in national environmental policy. When citizens have private lawsuits about the environment, they would typically seek remedies by resorting to common law or statutory remedies. The Environmental Protection Agency was not set up to help in this manner. This agency does, however, adopt regulations on the environment. Therefore answer (a) is not chosen. Answers (c) and (d) are not chosen because the EPA does refer both criminal and civil cases over to the Department of Justice.

42. **(a)**   The environmental impact statement is not designed to show the cost or source of the funds for the actions or legislation being proposed. Answers (b), (c), and (d) are all not chosen because these are all required as part of the environmental impact statement.

43. **(d)**   The Clean Air Act provides for both criminal and civil penalties against violators. For criminal violations, both fines and prison are possible. Civil penalties can also be assessed by the EPA including an amount equal to any benefits in costs for not complying.

44. **(d)**   Green as a part owner is one of the parties that has joint and several liability for the cleanup costs. Even though Sason also has joint and several liability, Green can be held liable for any portion or all of the cleanup costs without regard to percent of responsibility. Answer (a) is incorrect because Green, having joint and several liability, can be held liable for all of the cleanup costs. Answer (b) is incorrect because past as well as present owners have potential liability. Answer (c) is incorrect because there is no such defense as having less than half of the responsibility.

OTHER OBJECTIVE ANSWERS AND ANSWER EXPLANATIONS

Problem 1

1.   (**A**) Under the Social Security Act, money wages are considered wages.

2.   (**B**) Reimbursed travel expenses are generally excluded from wages.

3.   (**A**) Compensation whether in cash or not is generally considered to be wages.

4.   (**A**) Commissions are a method of compensation.

5.   (**A**) Bonuses are a method of compensation.

6.   (**B**) Insurance premiums paid by employers for employees generally are excluded from wages.

7.   (**A**) Part-time employees are covered under this law.

8.   (**A**) Vacation allowance pay is another form of compensation.

9.   (**A**) Qualifying employees may not elect to avoid the Social Security Act.

10.   (**A**) Tips are another form of wages.

ANSWER OUTLINE

Problem 1   Workers' Compensation; Definition of Employee; Strict Liability; Limited Liability of Shareholders

Dodd is entitled to workers' compensation from Spear
  Dodd is considered an employee because Salam had control over details of Dodd's work and Dodd was subject to Salam's supervision
Dodd will be unsuccessful in his negligence suit
  An employee who receives workers' compensation benefits cannot successfully maintain an action for negligence against his employer seeking additional compensation
Dodd will be successful in his action against Ace based on strict liability in tort
  Elements needed to prove strict tort liability are

  1. Product was unreasonably dangerous when it left the seller's hands
  2. Defect caused the injury
  3. Seller normally sells the product
  4. Product was not substantially changed before reaching the buyer

Maple is not liable to restaurant patrons based on negligence
  Shareholders of corporation are insulated from personal liability for negligence of corporation or corporation's employees

UNOFFICIAL ANSWER

Problem 1   Workers' Compensation; Definition of Employee; Strict Liability; Limited Liability of Shareholders

Dodd is entitled to recover workers' compensation benefits from Spear because Dodd was an employee of Salam, the injury was accidental, and the injury occurred out of and in the course of his employment with Salam. Based on the facts of this case, Dodd would be considered an employee and not an independent contractor because Salam had control over the details of Dodd's work by training Dodd to perform the services in a specified manner and Dodd was subject to Salam's supervision.

Dodd will be unsuccessful in his action against Salam based on negligence in training him because Dodd is an employee of Salam and Salam has complied with the applicable compulsory workers' compensation statute by obtaining workers' compensation insurance. Under workers' compensation, an employee who receives workers' compensation benefits cannot successfully maintain an action for negligence against his employer seeking additional compensation. Therefore, whether Salam was negligent in training Dodd is irrelevant.

Dodd's action against Ace based on strict liability in tort will be successful. Generally, in order to establish a cause of action based on strict liability in tort, it must be shown that: the product was in defective condition when it left the possession or control of the seller; the product was unreasonably dangerous to the consumer or user; the cause of the consumer's or user's injury was the defect; the seller engaged in the business of selling such a product; the product was one which the seller expected to, and did reach the consumer or user without substantial changes in the condition in which it was sold. Under the facts of this case, Ace will be liable based on strict liability in tort because all of the elements necessary to state such a cause of action have been met. The fact that Dodd is entitled to workers' compensation benefits does not preclude Dodd from recovering based on strict liability in tort from a third party (Ace).

Maple will not be liable to the restaurant patrons based on negligence, because shareholders of a corporation are insulated from personal liability for the negligence of the corporation or the corporation's employees. This rule would apply even though Maple owned a controlling interest in the common stock of Salam. Therefore, whether Salam or Dodd was negligent is irrelevant.

Keep practicing! Wiley's CPA Examination Review Software has over 2,800 questions.

Available at www.wiley.com/cpa

PROPERTY

Overview

Property entails items capable of being owned (i.e., the rights related to the ownership of things that society will recognize and enforce). Property is classified as real or personal, and as tangible or intangible. Protection of property and settlement of disputes concerning property is a major function of the legal system.

The candidate should be able to distinguish between personal and real property and between tenancies in common, joint tenancies, and tenancies by the entirety. The candidate also should understand that an instrument given primarily as security for real property is a mortgage and be able to distinguish between the legal results arising from "assumption" of a mortgage and taking "subject to" a mortgage. Other questions concerning mortgages require basic knowledge of the concepts of novation, suretyship, subrogation, redemption, and purchase money mortgages.

Questions on deeds may distinguish between the legal implication of warranty deeds, quitclaim deeds, and special warranty deeds. Both mortgages and deeds should be publicly recorded, and the questions may require the candidate to identify a priority and explain constructive notice. The most important topics under lessor-lessee law are the Statute of Frauds, the effect of a sale of leased property, assignment, and subleasing.

A. Distinctions between Real and Personal Property

1. Real property (realty)—includes land and things attached to land in a relatively permanent manner

   EXAMPLE: A building is erected on a parcel of land. Both the land and the building are real property.

   a. Crops harvested are not real property because they are separate from land
   b. Growing crops are generally part of land and therefore realty

      (1) Growing crops can be sold separately from land in which case they are considered personal property

         (a) True whether buyer or seller will sever growing crops from land

2. Personal property (personalty)—property not classified as real property or a fixture

   a. May be either

      (1) Tangible—subject to physical possession

         EXAMPLE: Automobiles and books are tangible personal property.

      (2) Intangible—not subject to physical possession but subject to legal ownership

         EXAMPLE: Contractual rights to receive payment for automobiles sold are intangible personal property.

3. Fixture—item that was originally personal property but which is affixed to real property in relatively permanent fashion such that it is considered to be part of real property

   a. Several factors are applied in determining whether personal property that has been attached to real property is a fixture

      (1) Affixer's objective intent as to whether property is to be regarded as personalty or realty
      (2) Method and permanence of physical attachment to real property

         (a) If item cannot be removed without material injury to real property, it is generally held that item has become part of realty (i.e., a fixture)

      (3) Adaptability of use of personal property for purpose for which real property is used

         (a) If personal property is necessary or beneficial to use of real property, more likely that item is fixture
         (b) But if use or purpose of item is unusual for type of realty involved, it normally would be personal property

   b. Trade fixture is a fixture installed by tenant in connection with business on leased premises

      EXAMPLE: A tenant who is leasing premises for use as grocery store installs refrigeration unit on property. Refrigeration unit is integral to conducting of business for which tenant occupies premises and therefore qualifies as trade fixture.

      (1) Trade fixtures remain personal property, giving tenant right to remove these items upon expiration of lease

(a) If item is so affixed to real property that removing it would cause substantial damage, then it is considered part of realty

B. Personal Property Can Be Acquired By

1. Gift—a present, voluntary transfer of property without consideration

   a. Necessary elements

      (1) Donative intent by donor
      (2) Delivery
      (3) Acceptance by donee (usually presumed)

   b. Promise to make a gift is unenforceable because it is not a contract due to lack of consideration given by donee
   c. Inter vivos gift is made while donor is living and is irrevocable once completed
   d. Gift causa mortis is a conditional gift in contemplation of death and is automatically revoked if the donor does not die of impending illness or crisis causing gift

2. Will or intestate succession

   a. Property passes under terms of will that is valid at death
   b. If deceased has no valid will (i.e., dies intestate) then property passes under laws of state

3. Finding personal property

   a. Mislaid property

      (1) Happens when owner **voluntarily** puts the property somewhere but forgets to take it
      (2) Finder does **not** obtain title to mislaid property

         (a) Owner of premises becomes caretaker in case true owner of mislaid property comes back

   b. Lost property

      (1) Happens when owner **involuntarily** leaves property somewhere
      (2) Finder has title to lost property which is valid against all parties except the true owner

      EXAMPLE: A loses his watch. B finds it but C attempts to take it from B even though both know it is not C's watch. B has the right to keep it from C.

   c. Abandoned property

      (1) Generally, finder has title valid against all parties including owner that abandoned property

C. Bailments

1. Bailment exists when owner of personal property gives possession without giving title to another (bailee)—bailee has duty to either return personal property to bailor or to dispose of it as directed by owner
2. Requirements for creation

   a. Delivery of personal property to bailee
   b. Possession by bailee
   c. Bailee has duty to return property or dispose of property as directed by owner

3. Types of bailments

   a. For benefit of bailor (i.e., bailee takes care of bailor's property)
   b. For mutual benefit (i.e., bailee takes care of bailor's property for a fee)
   c. For benefit of bailee (i.e., bailor gratuitously allows bailee use of his/her property)

4. Bailee's duty of care

   a. Older view depended on the type of bailment (i.e., slight care if for benefit of bailor, ordinary care if for mutual benefit, extreme care if for benefit of bailee)
   b. Now general rule is bailee must take reasonable care in light of the facts and circumstances

      (1) Type of bailment is part of facts and is used to determine what is reasonable care

        (a) Bailee is absolutely liable for delivery to improper person

          1] But a receipt or ticket that is for identification of bailor entitles bailee to deliver bailed goods to holder of ticket without liability

  c. Bailee has absolute liability for unauthorized use of property
  d. Bailee usually cannot limit liability with exculpatory clauses

> *EXAMPLE: A coat check ticket often limits liability on its back side. If the ticket is to be just a means of identification, then the bailee's liability is not limited. If the bailor is aware of the liability limitations statement, liability may be limited if reasonable.*

5. Bailee has duty to use property as directed to fulfill purpose of bailment only

  a. Liable to bailor for misuse
  b. In cases of theft, destruction of property, or failing to return property, this constitutes tort of conversion
  c. Bailee may normally limit liability for his/her negligence but not for intentional conduct

6. Bailee is not an agent of bailor, so bailor is not responsible for bailee's actions
7. Bailments normally terminated by

  a. Fulfillment of purpose of bailment
  b. Agreement to terminate by both bailor and bailee
  c. Bailee using property inappropriately

8. Common carriers are licensed to provide transportation for public

  a. Liability is based on strict liability, so common carriers are liable for damage to goods being transported even if loss caused by third parties or by accidents

    (1) Exceptions—common carrier not liable for

      (a) Acts of shipper, such as improperly packing goods to be shipped
      (b) Acts of God, such as earthquakes
      (c) Acts of public enemies
      (d) Loss because of inherent nature of goods

    (2) Common carriers allowed to limit liability to dollar amount specified in contract

D. Intellectual Property and Computer Technology Rights

1. Two general but competing goals

  a. Incentives to create products and services

    (1) By granting property rights so creators have incentive to create and market

  b. Provide public access to intellectual property and computer ideas and uses

    (1) By limiting intellectual and computer technology rights so that public has access to this

2. Copyright law

  a. Protects original works (e.g., literary, musical, or artistic works)

    (1) Expressions of ideas are generally copyrightable—ideas may not by themselves be copyrighted
    (2) Amendments to Copyright Act protect computer programs

  b. Copyrights created after January 1, 1978, are valid for life of author plus seventy years

    (1) For corporations, valid for ninety-five years

  c. Registration of copyright not required because copyright begins when author puts expression in tangible form

(1) Registration, however, gives copyright owner, in case of infringement, rights to statutory damages and attorneys' fees

d. Works published after March 1, 1989, no longer need copyright notice on them
e. Fair use doctrine allows use for limited purposes without violating copyright

(1) Examples include portions for comment, news reporting, research, or teaching

EXAMPLE: Professor hands out a copy of a copyrighted work to each member of the class.

f. Consumer Software Copyright Act amends copyright law to include computer programs as creative works protected by federal copyright law

(1) Covers not only portions of computer program readable by humans but also binary language portions normally read by computer
(2) Covers general items in program such as its basic structure and organizations

g. Remedies include stated statutory damages or actual damages including profits attributed to infringement of copyright—injunctions also allowed

(1) Higher damages can be statutorily assessed for willful infringement

h. Criminal penalties of fines and imprisonment are allowed for willful infringement
i. No Electronic Theft Act (NET Act)

(1) Act criminalizes copyright infringement over Internet whether or not for financial gain where retail value of copyrighted works exceeds $1,000

3. Patent Law

a. Covers machines, processes, art, methods, composition of matter, new and useful improvements including genetically engineered plants or animals
b. Mere ideas are not covered

(1) But practical applications may be

c. Invention must be novel, useful, and not obvious
d. Patents administered by US Patent and Trademark Office

(1) Inventor may not obtain patent if invention was on sale or in public use in US at least one year before attempt to obtain patent

e. Generally, patents are valid for twenty years from when patent application was filed

(1) By treaties, patents generally receive international protection for twenty years
(2) Design patents are valid for fourteen years from date of issuance of patent

f. Owner of patent must mark it using word patent to give notice to others
g. US gives patent protection to first inventor to invent

(1) Most countries give protection to the first to file the patent

h. Earlier views of computer software often categorized it as based on ideas and thus not patentable—more recent authority and court decisions protect software and Internet business methods as patentable

EXAMPLE: Pratt Company patented a computer program that used mathematical formulas to constantly improve a curing process for synthetic rubber upon receiving feedback in the process. This computer program was patentable because Pratt did not attempt to patent the mathematical formula to exclude others from using the formula but patented the process.

EXAMPLE: River.com Inc. receives a patent for the company storing customers' shipping (and billing information) with a one-click ordering system to reduce customers' need to reenter data on future orders.

EXAMPLE: Dual Softie, Inc. receives a patent that allows purchasers of automobiles over Internet to select options wished on the auto.

EXAMPLE: Silvernet, Inc. patents a system that pays individuals who respond to on-line surveys.

i. Even when patent issued by US Patent Trade Office (PTO), PTO may reexamine and reject patent

        (1) Patent may be overturned or narrowed in case brought to court

        (2) Unlike earlier, computer-related patents focus now on whether they are novel and nonobvious rather than on whether they can be patented at all

   j. Remedies include injunctions, damages including lost profits traceable to infringement, or assessment of reasonable royalties

        (1) If infringement is willful, inventor may be awarded treble damages and require infringer to also pay attorney's fees

   k. US Supreme Court recently affirmed important part of patent law providing that one cannot escape liability for patent infringement by making only insubstantial changes to a patent and attempting to claim it to be a new patent

   l. Paris convention—allows patent protection in many foreign countries

        (1) Most comprehensive agreement between nations involving intellectual property

        (2) Signed by nearly all industrialized countries and by many developing countries

        (3) Generally, allows a one-year grace period for inventors to file in other countries once inventor files for patent protection in first country

 4. Trade Secrets Law

   a. No federal protection available under registration

   b. Alternative to protection by copyright or patent

   c. Protects formulas, patterns, devices or compilations of information that give business an advantage over competitors

        (1) Must be secret that others have difficulty in acquiring except by improper means

        (2) Owner must take reasonable steps to guard trade secret

        (3) Can cover computer hardware and software

   d. Remedies for violations include breach of contract, breach of fiduciary duties, wrongful appropriation of trade secret, injunction, theft, espionage

        (1) Civil law as well as criminal law may be used

   e. Trade secret protection by law may be lost if

        (1) Owner of trade secret fails to take steps to keep it secret, or

        (2) Other person independently discovers what was subject of trade secret

   f. Methods to help protect trade secret include

        (1) Licensing of software

           (a) Prohibit copying except for backup copies

        (2) Provide in license that it is terminated for any breach of confidentiality

        (3) Sell software in object code instead of source code

        (4) Have employees and buyers sign confidentiality agreements

 5. Semiconductor Chip Protection Act

   a. Amends copyright laws

   b. Prohibits taking apart chips to copy them

        (1) Allows such act if used to create new chip rather than copy

        (2) Not prohibiting copying if design embodies the unoriginal or commonplace

   c. Protection is for ten years from time of registration or first commercial application, whichever is first

   d. Civil sanctions only—no criminal sanctions

 6. Federal Counterfeit Access Device and Computer Fraud and Abuse Act has criminalized many intentional, unauthorized uses of computer to

   a. Obtain classified information to hurt US

b.   Collect credit or financial information protected by privacy laws

> *EXAMPLE: Obtaining credit card limits and credit card numbers by accessing credit card accounts.*

c.   Modify material financial data in computers
d.   Destroy or alter computer data to hurt rightful users

> *EXAMPLE: A person intentionally transfers a computer virus to a company computer.*

7.   Trademarks under Lanham Act

a.   Purposes

(1) To provide identification symbol for company's product
(2) To guarantee consistent quality of all goods from same source
(3) Advertising

b.   Protection for trademark for distinctive graphics, words, shapes, packaging, or sounds

> *EXAMPLE: Coca-Cola has a trademark for its distinctive bottle.*

c.   Marks normally need to be distinctive to be protected

(1) Secondary meaning of things not inherently distinctive can develop to make them protectable

> *EXAMPLE: Microsoft registered "Windows" as a trademark when "Windows" acquired its secondary meaning.*
>
> *EXAMPLE: Windows store cannot be used as a trademark because it sells windows to put on homes and is thus generic rather than distinctive.*

d.   Generic words like software cannot be protected

(1) Many words that were once trademarks have become generic so are no longer protectable

> *EXAMPLE: Escalator was originally a brand name but is no longer protectable due to its generic use. Other examples are Yo-Yo and Dry Ice.*
>
> *EXAMPLE: Xerox takes out advertisements explaining that Xerox is not a verb, but instead say "copy" the document. Xerox is trying to protect its trademark by trying not to let the name grow into common usage.*

e.   Trademark rights in US are obtained initially by its use in commerce

(1) For distinctive marks, generally first seller to use trademark owns it
(2) Company can register trademark

(a) Although this is not required, provides constructive notice to others of claim of trademark

(3) On-line company may register domain name as trademark with US Patent and Trademark Office

(a) Various companies may use same trademark for different types of goods or services but only one company may register the domain name

> *EXAMPLE: Both Star Fences Inc. and Star Insurance Company wish to use Star.com. Only one may do so.*

f.   Loss of trademark rights

(1) Actual abandonment when not used in ordinary course of business

(a) Presumption of abandonment if not used for three years unless owner can prove intent to use trademark

(2) Constructive abandonment—Company allows trademark to lose its distinctiveness by frequent and common usage

g.   Trademark infringement

(1) Can infringe on trademark whether registered or not
(2) Proof of infringement

(a) Establish trademark is valid—federally registered mark is prima facie valid
(b) Priority of usage

       (c) Violation against trademark if similarities will likely cause confusion in minds of prospective or actual purchasers

  h. Remedies for infringement

    (1) Injunction against use
    (2) Lost profits caused by confusion
    (3) Attorneys' fees in some situations

8. Other symbols under Lanham Act

  a. Certification mark

    (1) Used to certify characteristics such as origin by geographical location, origin by organization, mode of manufacture.

      EXAMPLE: Product XYZ receives the Good Housekeeping Seal of Approval.

  b. Collective mark

    (1) Used to identify that product or service is provided by certain collective group, union, or fraternal society.

      EXAMPLE: Product ABC indicates that it was manufactured by a unionized company.

  c. Service mark

    (1) Used to identify that services come from certain company or person

      EXAMPLE: All of the shops of a group of shops called The Green Roof Plaza have similar style of roofs painted in the same shade of green.

  d. Similar to trademarks, these additional three types of trade symbols need to be distinctive and not deceptive so that prospective customers do not confuse these products or services with others

    (1) Registration is not required but advisable because it provides federal protection for ten years

      (a) Renewable for as many additional ten-year periods as desired

9. Invasion of Privacy—Increased computer use puts on more pressure

  a. Computer Matching and Privacy Act

    (1) Regulates computer systems used to determine eligibility for various government programs such as student financial aid

  b. Right to Financial Privacy Act

    (1) Restricts government access to financial institution records without customer approval

  c. Family Educational Rights and Privacy Act

    (1) Grants adult students and parents of minors access and right to correct records at institutions of higher learning

10. Anticybersquatting Consumer Reform Act

  a. Federal law passed by Congress that amends Landham Act protecting trademarks
  b. Illegal to register or use domain name if

    (1) Domain name is identical or similar enough to confuse others with bad intent to profit from trademark

      (a) Bad faith includes using domain name to sell products or services
      (b) Also can include intent to harm goodwill of trademark

  c. Act applies to all domain names even those registered before Act
  d. Plaintiff may elect to sue either for actual damages (including profits) or statutory damages of $1,000 to $100,000

11. Digital Millennium Copyright Act

    a. Federal law based on treaties with other countries to minimize pirating and distribution of copyrighted works

    b. Provides civil and criminal penalties against those that circumvent antipiracy protections or manufacture or sell such equipment to allow circumvention

    c. Act contains exceptions for "fair use" for educational and other noncommercial uses

    d. Internet Service Provider (ISP) is generally not liable for customers' copyright infringement unless ISP became aware of infringement and failed to correct problem

12. Uniform Computer Information Transactions Act (UCITA) requires that the following be in writing

    a. Contracts for licensing of information rights for over $5,000

    b. Contracts for licensing of information services that cannot be performed within one year

13. On-line dispute resolution is becoming increasingly used to resolve disputes

    a. Advantages include low cost, fast communication, and often no need to bring in third parties

    b. Disadvantage includes hard to enforce settlement because no court or sheriff involved

E. Interests in Real Property

1. Present interests

    a. Fee simple absolute

        (1) Highest estate in law (has the most ownership rights)

        (2) May be transferred inter vivos (while living), by intestate succession (without will), or by will (testate at death)

        (3) May be subject to mortgages, state laws, etc.

            EXAMPLE: Most private residences are fee simple absolute estates although they are commonly subject to mortgage.

    b. Fee simple defeasible

        (1) Fee simple determinable—upon the happening of the stated event the estate automatically reverts to the grantor

            EXAMPLE: Conveyance to the holder of an interest was, "to A as long as A uses it for church purposes." The interest will revert back to the grantor or his heirs if the property is not used for church purposes.

        (2) Fee simple subject to condition subsequent—upon the happening of the stated event the grantor must take affirmative action to divest the grantee of the estate

            EXAMPLE: Conveyance to the holder of the interest was "to A, but if liquor is ever served on the premises, the grantor has right to enter the premises." The grantor has power of termination so as to repossess the premises.

    c. Life interest—an interest whose duration is usually measured by the life of the holder but may be measured by lives of others

        EXAMPLE: Conveyance of land, "to A so long as she shall live."

        (1) Upon termination (death), property reverts to grantor or grantor's heirs, or to a named remainderman

        (2) Usual life interest can be transferred by deed only (i.e., not by a will because it ends on death)

        (3) Holder of a life interest (life tenant) is entitled to ordinary use and profits of land but may not commit waste (injure interests of remainderman)

            (a) Must maintain property (in reasonable state of repair)

            (b) May not misuse property

    d. Leaseholds—see Lessor-Lessee at end of Property Module

2. Future interest (holder of this interest has right to or possibility of possession in the future)

    a. Reversion—future interest reverts back to transferor (or his/her heirs) at end of transferee's estate

        (1) Usually kept when conveying a life interest or an interest for a definite period of time

EXAMPLE: X conveys, "to Y for life" or "to Y for ten years." X has a reversion.

b. Remainder—future interest is in a third party at the end of transferee's estate

EXAMPLE: X conveys, "to Y for life, remainder to Z and her heirs."

3. Concurrent interest—two or more persons (cotenants) have undivided interests and concurrent possessory rights in real or personal property—each has a nonexclusive right to possess whole property

a. Tenancy in common

(1) A concurrent interest with no right of survivorship (interest passes to heirs, donee, or purchaser)

EXAMPLE: A and B each own 1/2 of Greenacre as tenants in common. If B dies, then A still owns 1/2 and B's heirs own the other half.

(2) Unless stated otherwise, multiple grantees are presumed to be tenants in common
(3) Tenant in common may convey individual interest in the whole but cannot convey a specific portion of property

(a) Unless there is a judicial partition to split up ownership

1] Creditors may sue to compel a partition to satisfy individual's debts

b. Joint tenancy

(1) A concurrent interest with all rights of ownership going to the surviving joint tenants (i.e., have rights of survivorship)

(a) To create a joint tenancy, all of following unities are required: time, title, interest, and possession
(b) Cannot be transferred by will because upon death, other cotenants own it
(c) Corporation may not be joint tenant

EXAMPLE: A and B each own 1/2 of Redacre as joint tenants. If B dies, A owns all of Redacre because of her right of survivorship. B's heirs do not receive any interest.

(2) If rights in property conveyed without consent of others, new owner becomes a tenant in common rather than joint tenant; remaining cotenants are still joint tenants

EXAMPLE: A, B, and C are joint tenants of Greenacre. A sells his interest to D without the consent of B and C. D is a tenant in common with a one-third interest in the whole. B and C are still joint tenants (with the right of survivorship) each having a one-third undivided interest.

c. Tenancy by the entirety

(1) Joint interest held by husband and wife
(2) It is presumed when both spouses' names appear on title document
(3) To transfer, both must convey
(4) Each spouse has a right of survivorship
(5) Divorce creates a tenancy in common

4. Nonpossessory interests in land

a. Easement is right to enter another's land and use it in limited way

EXAMPLE: A is granted an easement to drive over a certain segment of B's land.

(1) Methods of creation

(a) Express grant in deed
(b) Express reservation in deed

EXAMPLE: S sells B some land whereby in the deed S reserves an easement to walk across the land.

(c) By necessity

EXAMPLE: A owns a piece of land that blocks B's access to any public road. B has the right to use A's land for access to the public road.

b.   Profit is right to enter another's land and remove items such as trees, grass, or gravel

(1) Profits may be created by grant or by reservation

F.   Contracts for Sale of Land

1.   Generally precede transfers of land. Often includes escrows.

EXAMPLE: An earnest money agreement. The purchaser puts the money down to show his seriousness while he investigates the title and arranges for a mortgage.

a.   Generally, agreement must

(1) Be in writing and signed by party to be bound

(a) To satisfy Statute of Frauds under contract law

(2) Identify land and parties
(3) Identify purpose
(4) Contain terms or promises
(5) Contain purchase price

b.   Assignable unless prohibited in contract

2.   If not expressed, there is an implied promise that seller will provide a marketable title (implied warranty of marketability)

a.   A marketable title is one reasonably free from doubt. Does not contain such defects as breaks in chain of title, outstanding liens, or defective instruments in past (chain of title).

(1) Zoning restrictions do not make a title unmarketable

b.   Agreement may provide for marketable or "insurable" title

(1) Insurable title is one that a title insurance company will insure against defects, liens, and invalidity

c.   If title is not marketable, purchaser may

(1) Rescind and recover any down payment
(2) Sue for damages
(3) Sue for specific performance with a reduction in price

3.   Risk of loss before deed is conveyed (e.g., if house burns who bears the burden?)

a.   General rule is purchaser bears the risk of loss, subject to terms of the contract
b.   Courts may look to who has the most ownership rights and benefits (normally buyer)
c.   Either party can insure against risk of loss

G. Types of Deeds

1.   Warranty deeds contain the following covenants (unconditional promises) by grantor

a.   Grantor has title and right to convey it
b.   Free from encumbrances except as disclosed in the deed

EXAMPLE: O conveys by warranty deed Blackacre to P. There is a mortgage still unpaid on Blackacre. Unless O discloses this mortgage to P, O has violated the covenant that the deed be free from encumbrances.

c.   Quiet enjoyment—neither grantor nor third party with rightful claim will disturb grantee's possession

2.   Bargain and sale deed (grant deeds)

a.   Generally, only covenants that grantor has done nothing to impair title (e.g., s/he has not created any encumbrances)
b.   Does not warrant against prior (before grantor's ownership) impairments

3.   Quitclaim deed conveys only whatever interest in land the grantor has. No warranty of title is made by grantor.

    a.   It is insurable, recordable, and mortgagable as with any other deed

H. Executing a Deed

1.   Deed must have description of the real estate

    a.   Purchase price not necessary in deed

2.   There must be delivery for deed to be effective; there must be an intent on part of grantor to pass title (convey) to grantee

    a.   Possession of the deed by grantee raises a presumption (rebuttable) of delivery

    b.   A recorded deed raises a presumption (rebuttable) of delivery

    c.   A deed given to a third party to give to grantee upon performance of a condition is a delivery in escrow

        (1) Escrow agent—intermediary between the two parties who holds deed until grantee pays, then gives deed to grantee and money to grantor

    d.   Destruction of deed does not destroy title

I. Recording a Deed

1.   Gives constructive notice to the world of grantee's ownership (this is important)

    a.   Protects grantee (new owner) against subsequent purchasers

       EXAMPLE: X sells land to Y. Y records his deed. Later X sells land to Z. Z loses against Y because Y recorded the deed giving constructive notice of the prior sale.

        (1) However, deed is valid between immediate parties without recording

    b.   Most recording statutes provide that subsequent purchaser (bona fide) who takes without notice of the first sale has priority

        (1) Under a notice-type statute, a subsequent bona fide (good-faith) purchaser, whether s/he records or not, wins over previous purchaser who did not record before that subsequent purchase

           EXAMPLE: A sells the same piece of property in a state having a notice-type statute to B and C in that order. B did not record the purchase. C is unaware of the sale to B and is thus a bona fide purchaser. C defeats B. Note that C should record the purchase or run the risk of another bona fide purchaser (i.e., D defeating C's claim).

        (2) Under a race-notice type (notice-race) statute, the subsequent bona fide purchaser wins over a previous purchaser only if s/he also records first (i.e., a "race" to file first)

           EXAMPLE: X sells some property to Y and then to Z, a good-faith purchaser. After the sale to Z, Y records the purchase and then Z records the purchase. Although Y wins in a state having a race-notice statute, Z wins in a state having a notice-type statute.

           EXAMPLE: Same as above except that Z does not record, both results above are not affected.

        (3) Under a race statute, the first to record deed wins

    c.   Notice refers to actual knowledge of prior sale or constructive knowledge (i.e., one is deemed to be aware of what is filed in records)

    d.   To be a purchaser, one must give value that does not include antecedent debts

J. Title Insurance

1.   Generally used to insure that title is good and to cover the warranties by seller

    a.   Not required if contract does not require it

2.   Without title insurance, purchaser's only recourse is against grantor and s/he may not be able to satisfy the damages

    a.   Standard insurance policies generally insure against all defects of record and defects grantee may be aware of, but not defects disclosed by survey and physical inspection of premises

    b.   Title insurance company is liable for any damages or expenses if there is a title defect or encumbrance that is insured against

(1) Certain defects are not insured by the title policy

(a) These exceptions must be shown on face of policy

c. Title insurance does not pass to subsequent purchasers

K. Adverse Possession

1. Possessor of land who was not owner may acquire title if s/he holds it for the statutory period

a. The statutory period is the running of the statute of limitations. Varies by state from five to twenty years.
b. The statute begins to run upon the taking of possession
c. True owner must commence legal action before statute runs or adverse possessor obtains title
d. Successive possessors may tack (cumulate required time together)

(1) Each possessor must transfer to the other. One cannot abandon or statute begins over again for the next possessor.

e. True owner of a future interest (e.g., a remainder, is not affected by adverse possession)

EXAMPLE: X dies and leaves his property to A for life, remainder to B. A pays little attention to the property and a third party acquires it by adverse possession. When A dies, B is entitled to the property regardless of the adverse possession but the statute starts running against B.

2. Necessary elements

a. Open and notorious possession

(1) Means type of possession that would give reasonable notice to owner

b. Hostile possession

(1) Must indicate intentions of ownership

(a) Does not occur when possession started permissively or as cotenants
(b) Not satisfied if possessor acknowledges other's ownership

(2) Color of title satisfies this requirement. When possession is taken under good-faith belief in a defective instrument or deed purporting to convey the land.

c. Actual possession

(1) Possession of land consistent with its normal use (e.g., farm land is being farmed)

d. Continuous possession

(1) Need not be constant, but possession as normally used

e. Exclusive possession

(1) Possession to exclusion of all others

L. Easement by Prescription

1. Person obtains right to use another's land (i.e., easement) in way similar to adverse possession
2. Same elements are used as for adverse possession except for exclusive possession—state laws require several years to obtain this

EXAMPLE: X cuts across Y's land for several years in such a way that s/he meets all of the same requirements as those needed for adverse possession except for exclusive possession. X obtains an easement to use the path even if Y later tries to stop X.

M. Mortgages

1. Lien on real property to secure payment of loan

a. Mortgage is an interest in real property and thus must satisfy Statute of Frauds

(1) Must be in writing and signed by party to be charged

(a) Party to be charged in this case is mortgagor (i.e., party taking out mortgage)

      (2) Must include description of property and debt to be incurred

    b. Debt is usually evidenced by a promissory note which is incorporated into mortgage
    c. Mortgage must be delivered to mortgagee (i.e., lender)
    d. Mortgage may be given to secure future advances
    e. Purchase-money mortgage is created when seller takes a mortgage from buyer at time of sale

      (1) Or lender furnishes money with which property is purchased

2. Mortgage may be recorded and receives the same benefits as recording a deed or recording an assignment of contract

    a. Gives constructive notice of the mortgage

      (1) But mortgage **is effective** between mortgagor and mortgagee and third parties, who have actual notice, even without recording

    b. Protects mortgagee against subsequent mortgagees, purchasers, or other takers
    c. Recording statutes for mortgages are like those used for recording deeds

      (1) Under a notice-type statute, a subsequent good-faith mortgagee has priority over previous mortgagee who did not file

        (a) This is true whether subsequent mortgagee files or not; but of course if s/he does not file, a subsequent good-faith mortgagee will have priority.

          EXAMPLE: Banks A, B, and C, in that order, grant a mortgage to a property owner. None of these record the mortgage and none knows of the others. Between A and B, B has priority. However, C has priority over B.

          EXAMPLE: Same facts as before, however, B does record before C grants the mortgage. B has priority over A again. B also has priority over C because now C has constructive notice of B and thus has lower priority.

        (b) Notice is either actual notice or constructive notice based on recording

      (2) Under a race-notice type (notice-race) statute, the subsequent good-faith mortgagee wins over a previous mortgagee only if s/he also records first
      (3) Under a race statute, the first mortgagee to record mortgage wins
      (4) First mortgage to have priority is satisfied in full (upon default) before next mortgage to have priority is satisfied

        (a) Second mortgagee can require first mortgagee to resort to other property for payment if first mortgagee has other property available as security

3. When mortgaged property is sold the buyer may

    a. Assume the mortgage

      (1) If "assumed," the buyer becomes personally liable (mortgage holder is third-party beneficiary)
      (2) Seller remains liable (unless released by mortgagee by a novation)

        (a) Mortgagee may hold either seller or buyer liable on mortgage

      (3) Normally the mortgagee's consent is needed due to "due on sale clauses"

        (a) Terms of mortgage may permit acceleration of principal or renegotiation of interest rate upon transfer of the property

    b. Take subject to the mortgage

      (1) If buyer takes "subject to" then buyer accepts **no** liability for mortgage and seller is still primarily liable
      (2) Mortgagee may still foreclose on the property even in the hands of buyer

        (a) Buyer may pay mortgage if s/he chooses to avoid foreclosure

      (3) Mortgagee's consent to allow buyer to take subject to the mortgage is not needed unless stipulated in mortgage

    c. Novation—occurs when purchaser assumes mortgage and mortgagee (lender) releases in writing the seller from the mortgage

EXAMPLE: O has mortgaged Redacre. He sells Redacre to T. T agrees to assume mortgage and mortgagee bank agrees in writing to substitute T as the only liable party in place of O. Because of this novation, O is no longer liable on the mortgage.

4. Rights of parties

    a. Mortgagor (owner, debtor) retains possession and right to use land

        (1) May transfer land encumbered by mortgage

    b. Mortgagee (creditor) has a lien on the land

        (1) Even if mortgagor transfers land, it is still subject to the mortgage if it has been properly recorded

    c. Mortgagee has right to assign mortgage to third party without mortgagors' consent

    d. Upon mortgagor's default, mortgagee may assign mortgage to third parties or mortgagee may foreclose on the land

        (1) Foreclosure requires judicial action that directs foreclosure sale

            (a) Court will refuse to confirm sale if price is so low as to raise a presumption of unfairness

            (b) However, court will not refuse to confirm sale merely because higher price might have been received at a later time

        (2) Mortgagor usually can save real estate (redeem the property) by use of equity of redemption

            (a) Pays interest, debt, and expenses

            (b) Exists until foreclosure sale

            (c) Cannot be curtailed by prior agreement

        (3) After foreclosure sale debtor has right of redemption if state law grants statutory right of redemption

            (a) Affords mortgagor one last chance to redeem property

            (b) Pays off loan within statutory period

        (4) If mortgagee forecloses and sells property and mortgagor does not use equity of redemption or right of redemption

            (a) Mortgagee must return any excess proceeds from sale to mortgagor

                1] Equity above balance due does not give right to mortgagor to retain possession of property

            (b) If proceeds from sale are insufficient to pay note, mortgagor is still indebted to the mortgagee for deficiency

                1] Grantee of the mortgagor who **assumed** mortgage would also be liable for deficiency, but one who took **subject to** the mortgage would not be personally liable

5. Mortgage lenders are regulated by Real Estate Settlement Procedures Act (RESPA)

    a. Provides home buyers with extensive information about settlement process and helps protect them from high settlement fees

6. Deed of trust—also a nonpossessory lien on real property to secure a debt

    a. Like a mortgage, debtor retains possession of land and creditor has a lien on it

    b. Legal title is given to a trustee to hold

        (1) Upon default, trustee may sell the land for the benefit of creditor

7. Sale on contract

    a. Unlike a mortgage or a deed of trust, the seller retains title to property

    b. Purchaser takes possession and makes payments on the contract

    c. Purchaser gets title when debt fully paid

8. When mortgaged property is sold or destroyed, the proceeds from sale or insurance go to mortgagee with highest priority until it is completely paid, then the proceeds, if any, go to any mortgagees or other interest holders, with the next highest priority, etc.

N. Lessor-Lessee

1. A lease is a contract and a conveyance

   a. Contract is the primary source of rights and duties
   b. Contract must contain essential terms including description of leased premises
   c. May be oral if less than one year

2. Types of leaseholds

   a. Periodic tenancy

      (1) Lease is for a fixed time such as a month or year but it continues from period to period until proper notice of termination
      (2) Notice of termination normally must be given in the same amount of time as rent or tenancy period (i.e., if tenancy is from month to month then the landlord or tenant usually must give at least one month's notice)

   b. Tenancy for a term (also called tenancy for years)

      (1) Lease is for a fixed amount of time (e.g., lease of two years or six months)
      (2) Ends automatically at date of termination

   c. Tenancy at sufferance

      (1) Created when tenant remains in property after lease expires
      (2) Landlord has option of treating tenant as trespasser and ejecting him/her or treating him/her as tenant and collecting rent

   d. Tenancy at will

      (1) Property is leased for indefinite period of time
      (2) Either party may terminate lease at will

3. Lessor covenants (promises) and tenant's rights

   a. Generally, lessor's covenants are independent of lessee's rights; therefore, lessor's breach does not give lessee right to breach
   b. Right to possession—lessor makes premises available to lessee

      (1) Residential lease for real estate entitles tenant to exclusive possession of property during period of lease unless otherwise agreed in lease

   c. Quiet enjoyment—neither lessor nor a third party with a valid claim will evict lessee unless tenant has breached lease contract
   d. Fitness for use—premises are fit for human occupation (i.e., warranty of habitability)
   e. In general, if premises are destroyed through no fault of either party, then contract is terminated

   EXAMPLE: Landlord's building is destroyed by a sudden flood. Tenant cannot hold landlord liable for loss of use of building.

   f. Lessee may assign or sublease unless prohibited or restricted in lease

      (1) Assignment is transfer by lessee of his/her entire interest reserving no rights

         (a) Assignee is in privity of contract with lessor and lessor may proceed against him/her for rent and breaches under lease agreement
         (b) Assignor (lessee) is still liable to lessor unless there is a novation or release
         (c) Lease may have clause that requires consent of lessor for subleases

            1] In which case, consent to each individual sublease is required
            2] Lack of consent makes sublease voidable

         (d) Clause prohibiting sublease does not prohibit assignment

    (2) A sublease is the transfer by lessee of less than his/her entire interest (e.g., for three months during summer, then lessee returns to it in the fall)

         (a) Lessee (sublessor) is still liable on lease

         (b) Lessor has no privity with sublessee and can take no action against him/her for rent, but certain restrictions of original lease run with the land and are enforceable against sublessee

         (c) Sublessee can assume obligations in sublease and be liable to pay landlord

         (d) Clause prohibiting assignment does not prohibit sublease

  g. Subject to lease terms, trade fixtures attached by lessee may be removed if can be removed without substantial damage to premises

  h. Tenant can use premises for any legal purpose unless lease restricts

4. Lessee's duties and lessor's rights

  a. Rent—due at end of term or period of tenancy unless otherwise agreed in lease

    (1) No right to withhold rent even if lessor is in breach (unless so provided by lease or by statute)

    (2) Nonpayment gives lessor right to sue for it or to bring an eviction suit or both

  b. Lessee has obligation to make ordinary repairs. Lease or statute may make lessor liable.

    (1) Structural repairs are lessor's duty

  c. If tenant wrongfully retains possession after termination, lessor may

    (1) Evict lessee, or

    (2) Treat as holdover tenant and charge with fair rental value, or

    (3) Tenancy becomes one of period-to-period, and lessee is liable for rent the same as in expired lease

5. Termination

  a. Expiration of lease

  b. Proper notice in a tenancy from period-to-period

  c. Surrender by lessee and acceptance by lessor

  d. Death of lessee terminates lease except for a lease for a period of years

    (1) Death of lessor generally does not terminate lease

  e. Eviction

    (1) Actual eviction—ousting directly

    (2) Constructive eviction—allowing conditions which make property unusable if lessor is liable for condition of premises

  f. Transfer of property does not affect tenancy

    (1) New owner cannot rightfully terminate lease unless old owner could have (e.g., breach by tenant)

        (a) However, if tenant purchases property then lease terminates

MULTIPLE-CHOICE QUESTIONS (1-42)

1. Which of the following items is tangible personal property?
- a. Share of stock.
- b. Trademark.
- c. Promissory note.
- d. Oil painting.

2. What is an example of property that can be considered either personal property or real property?
- a. Air rights.
- b. Mineral rights.
- c. Harvested crops.
- d. Growing crops.

3. Which of the following factors help determine whether an item of personal property is a fixture?

I. Degree of the item's attachment to the property.
II. Intent of the person who had the item installed.

- a. I only.
- b. II only.
- c. Both I and II.
- d. Neither I nor II.

4. Getty owned some personal property which was later found by Morris. Both Getty and Morris are claiming title to this personal property. In which of the following cases will Getty win over Morris?

I. Getty had mislaid the property and had forgotten to take it with him.
II. Getty had lost the property out of his van while driving down a road.
III. Getty had abandoned the property but later changed his mind after Morris found it.

- a. I only.
- b. II only.
- c. I and II only.
- d. I, II, and III.

5. Rand discarded an old rocking chair. Stone found the rocking chair and, realizing that it was valuable, took it home. Later, Rand learned that Stone had the rocking chair and wanted it back. Rand subsequently put a provision in his will that his married daughter Walters will get the rocking chair. Who has the actual title to the rocking chair?

	Stone has title	Rand, while living, has title	Walters obtains title upon Rand's death
a.	No	Yes	Yes
b.	No	Yes	No
c.	Yes	Yes	Yes
d.	Yes	No	No

6. Which of the following standards of liability best characterizes the obligation of a common carrier in a bailment relationship?
- a. Reasonable care.
- b. Gross negligence.
- c. Shared liability.
- d. Strict liability.

7. Multicomp Company wishes to protect software it has developed. It is concerned about others copying this software and taking away some of its profits. Which of the following is true concerning the current state of the law?
- a. Computer software is generally copyrightable.

- b. To receive protection, the software must have a conspicuous copyright notice.
- c. Software in human readable source code is copyrightable but in machine language object code is not.
- d. Software can be copyrighted for a period not to exceed twenty years.

8. Which of the following is **not** correct concerning computer software purchased by Gultch Company from Softtouch Company? Softtouch originally created this software.
- a. Gultch can make backup copies in case of machine failure.
- b. Softtouch can typically copyright its software for at least seventy-five years.
- c. If the software consists of compiled computer databases it cannot be copyrighted.
- d. Computer programs are generally copyrightable.

9. Professor Bell runs off fifteen copies to distribute to his accounting class using his computer from a database in some software he had purchased for his personal research. The creator of this software is claiming a copyright. Which of the following is correct?
- a. This is an infringement of a copyright since he bought the software for personal use.
- b. This is not an infringement of a copyright since databases cannot be copyrighted.
- c. This is not an infringement of a copyright because the copies were made using a computer.
- d. This is not an infringement of a copyright because of the fair use doctrine.

10. Intellectual property rights included in software may be protected under which of the following?
- a. Patent law.
- b. Copyright law.
- c. Both of the above.
- d. None of the above.

11. Which of the following statements is **not** true of the law of trademarks in the United States?
- a. Trademark law may protect distinctive shapes as well as distinctive packaging.
- b. Trademark protection can be lost if the trademark becomes so popular that its use becomes commonplace.
- c. Trademarks to receive protection need not be registered.
- d. Trademarks are valid for twenty years after their formation.

12. Diane Trucco recently wrote a novel which is an excellent work of art. She wishes to copyright and publish this novel. Which of the following is correct?
- a. Her copyright is valid for her life plus seventy years.
- b. She must register her copyright to receive protection under the law.
- c. She is required to put on a copyright notice to obtain a copyright.
- d. All of the above are correct.

13. Long, Fall, and Pear own a building as joint tenants with the right of survivorship. Long gave Long's interest in the building to Green by executing and delivering a deed to Green. Neither Fall nor Pear consented to this transfer. Fall and Pear subsequently died. After their deaths, Green's interest in the building would consist of

    a.   A 1/3 interest as a joint tenant.
    b.   A 1/3 interest as a tenant in common.
    c.   No interest because Fall and Pear did **not** consent to the transfer.
    d.   Total ownership due to the deaths of Fall and Pear.

14. What interest in real property generally gives the holder of that interest the right to sell the property?

    a.   Easement.
    b.   Leasehold.
    c.   License.
    d.   Fee simple.

15. Which of the following unities (elements) are required to establish a joint tenancy?

	Time	Title	Interest	Possession
a.	Yes	Yes	Yes	Yes
b.	Yes	Yes	No	No
c.	No	No	Yes	Yes
d.	Yes	No	Yes	No

16. Which of the following is not an interest that a person can have in real property?

    a.   Fee simple absolute.
    b.   Tenancy by default.
    c.   Life interest.
    d.   Remainder.

17. On July 1, 2001, Quick, Onyx, and Nash were deeded a piece of land as tenants in common. The deed provided that Quick owned 1/2 the property and Onyx and Nash owned 1/4 each. If Nash dies, the property will be owned as follows:

    a.   Quick 1/2, Onyx 1/2.
    b.   Quick 5/8, Onyx 3/8.
    c.   Quick 1/3, Onyx 1/3, Nash's heirs 1/3.
    d.   Quick 1/2, Onyx 1/4, Nash's heirs 1/4.

18. Brett conveys his real property by deed to his sister, Jan, for life with the remainder to go to his friend, Randy, for his life. Brett is still living. Randy died first and Jan died second. Who has title to this real property?

    a.   Brett.
    b.   Brett's heirs.
    c.   Jan's heirs.
    d.   Randy's heirs.

19. Court, Fell, and Miles own a parcel of land as joint tenants with right of survivorship. Court's interest was sold to Plank. As a result of the sale from Court to Plank

    a.   Fell, Miles, and Plank each own one-third of the land as joint tenants.
    b.   Fell and Miles each own one-third of the land as tenants in common.
    c.   Plank owns one third of the land as a tenant in common.
    d.   Plank owns one-third of the land as a joint tenant.

20. The following contains three fact patterns involving land. In which of the following is an easement involved?

   I.   O sells land to B in which O retains in the deed the right to use a roadway on B's newly purchased property.
  II.   O sells land to B in which O in the deed has the right to cut and keep ten specified trees on the land sold.

  III. O sells land to B. O continues that year to use a roadway on B's newly purchased property when B is not looking.

    a.   I only.
    b.   I and II only.
    c.   II and III only.
    d.   I, II, and III.

21. A method of transferring ownership of real property that most likely would be considered an arm's-length transaction is transfer by

    a.   Inheritance.
    b.   Eminent domain.
    c.   Adverse possession.
    d.   Sale.

22. Which of the following elements must be contained in a valid deed?

	Purchase price	Description of the land
a.	Yes	Yes
b.	Yes	No
c.	No	Yes
d.	No	No

23. Which of the following warranties is(are) contained in a general warranty deed?

   I.   The grantor has the right to convey the property.
  II.   The grantee will **not** be disturbed in possession of the property by the grantor or some third party's lawful claim of ownership.

    a.   I only.
    b.   II only.
    c.   Both I and II.
    d.   Neither I nor II.

24. For a deed to be effective between the purchaser and seller of real estate, one of the conditions is that the deed must

    a.   Contain the signatures of the seller and purchaser.
    b.   Contain the actual sales price.
    c.   Be delivered by the seller with an intent to transfer title.
    d.   Be recorded within the permissible statutory time limits.

Items 25 and 26 are based on the following:

On February 1, Frost bought a building from Elgin, Inc. for $250,000. To complete the purchase, Frost borrowed $200,000 from Independent Bank and gave Independent a mortgage for that amount; gave Elgin a second mortgage for $25,000; and paid $25,000 in cash. Independent recorded its mortgage on February 2 and Elgin recorded its mortgage on March 12.

The following transactions also took place:

• On March 1, Frost gave Scott a $20,000 mortgage on the building to secure a personal loan Scott had previously made to Frost.

• On March 10, Scott recorded this mortgage.

• On March 15, Scott learned about both prior mortgages.

• On June 1, Frost stopped making payments on all the mortgages.

• On August 1, the mortgages were foreclosed. Frost, on that date, owed Independent, $195,000; Elgin, $24,000; and Scott, $19,000.

A judicial sale of the building resulted in proceeds of $220,000 after expenses were deducted. The above transactions took place in a notice-race jurisdiction.

25. What amount of the proceeds will Scott receive?
- a. $0
- b. $ 1,000
- c. $12,500
- d. $19,000

26. Why would Scott receive this amount?
- a. Scott knew of the Elgin mortgage.
- b. Scott's mortgage was recorded before Elgin's and before Scott knew of Elgin's mortgage.
- c. Elgin's mortgage was first in time.
- d. After Independent is fully paid, Elgin and Scott share the remaining proceeds equally.

27. A purchaser who obtains real estate title insurance will
- a. Have coverage for the title exceptions listed in the policy.
- b. Be insured against all defects of record other than those excepted in the policy.
- c. Have coverage for title defects that result from events that happen after the effective date of the policy.
- d. Be entitled to transfer the policy to subsequent owners.

28. Which of the following is a defect in marketable title to real property?
- a. Recorded zoning restrictions.
- b. Recorded easements referred to in the contract of sale.
- c. Unrecorded lawsuit for negligence against the seller.
- d. Unrecorded easement.

29. Which of the following is not a necessary element for an individual to obtain title of a piece of real estate by adverse possession?
- a. Continuous possession.
- b. Possession that is to the exclusion of others.
- c. Possession permitted by the actual owner.
- d. Open and notorious possession.

30. Rake, twenty-five years ago, put a fence around a piece of land. At the time, Rake knew that fence not only surrounded his land but also a sizable piece of Howe's land. Every summer Rake planted a garden on this land surrounded by the fence. Howe recently sold all of his land to Cross. Cross has found out about the fence line and has asked Rake to either move the fence or pay Cross for the land in question. What is the result?
- a. Rake does not have to move the fence but must pay Cross for the land in question.
- b. Rake does not have to move the fence but must pay Howe for the land in question.
- c. Rake must move the fence.
- d. Rake must neither move the fence nor pay either party for the land in question.

31. Generally, which of the following federal acts regulate mortgage lenders?

	Real Estate Settlement Procedures Act (RESPA)	Federal Trade Commission Act
a.	Yes	Yes
b.	Yes	No
c.	No	Yes
d.	No	No

32. Gilmore borrowed $60,000 from Dix Bank. The loan was used to remodel a building owned by Gilmore as investment property and was secured by a second mortgage that Dix did not record. FCA Loan Company has a recorded first mortgage on the building. If Gilmore defaults on both mortgages, Dix
- a. Will **not** be entitled to any mortgage foreclosure sale proceeds, even if such proceeds are in excess of the amount owed to FCA.
- b. Will be unable to successfully claim any security interest in the building.
- c. Will be entitled to share in any foreclosure sale proceeds pro rata with FCA.
- d. Will be able to successfully claim a security interest that is subordinate to FCA's security interest.

33. Wilk bought an apartment building from Dix Corp. There was a mortgage on the building securing Dix's promissory note to Xeon Finance Co. Wilk took title subject to Xeon's mortgage. Wilk did not make the payments on the note due Xeon and the building was sold at a foreclosure sale. If the proceeds of the foreclosure sale are less than the balance due on the note, which of the following statements is correct regarding the deficiency?
- a. Xeon must attempt to collect the deficiency from Wilk before suing Dix.
- b. Dix will **not** be liable for any of the deficiency because Wilk assumed the note and mortgage.
- c. Xeon may collect the deficiency from either Dix or Wilk.
- d. Dix alone would be liable for the entire deficiency.

34. On April 6, Ford purchased a warehouse from Atwood for $150,000. Atwood had executed two mortgages on the property: a purchase money mortgage given to Lang on March 2, which was not recorded; and a mortgage given to Young on March 9, which was recorded the same day. Ford was unaware of the mortgage to Lang. Under the circumstances
- a. Ford will take title to the warehouse subject only to Lang's mortgage.
- b. Ford will take title to the warehouse free of Lang's mortgage.
- c. Lang's mortgage is superior to Young's mortgage because Lang's mortgage is a purchase money mortgage.
- d. Lang's mortgage is superior to Young's mortgage because Lang's mortgage was given first in time.

35. Which of the following conditions must be met to have an enforceable mortgage?
- a. An accurate description of the property must be included in the mortgage.
- b. A negotiable promissory note must accompany the mortgage.
- c. Present consideration must be given in exchange for the mortgage.
- d. The amount of the debt and the interest rate must be stated in the mortgage.

36. On February 1, Frost bought a building from Elgin, Inc. for $250,000. To complete the purchase, Frost borrowed $200,000 from Independent Bank and gave Independent a mortgage for that amount; gave Elgin a second mortgage for $25,000; and paid $25,000 in cash. Independent recorded its mortgage on February 2 and Elgin recorded its mortgage on March 12.

The following transactions also took place:

• On March 1, Frost gave Scott a $20,000 mortgage on the building to secure a personal loan Scott had previously made to Frost.

• On March 10, Scott recorded this mortgage.

• On March 15, Scott learned about both prior mortgages.

• On June 1, Frost stopped making payments on all the mortgages.

• On August 1, the mortgages were foreclosed. Frost, on that date, owed Independent, $195,000; Elgin, $24,000; and Scott, $19,000.

A judicial sale of the building resulted in proceeds of $220,000 after expenses were deducted. The above transactions took place in a notice-race jurisdiction.

Frost may redeem the property before the judicial sale only if

  a.   There is a statutory right of redemption.

  b.   It is probable that the sale price will result in a deficiency.

  c.   All mortgages are paid in full.

  d.   All mortgagees are paid a penalty fee.

37. A mortgagor's right of redemption will be terminated by a judicial foreclosure sale unless

  a.   The proceeds from the sale are not sufficient to fully satisfy the mortgage debt.

  b.   The mortgage instrument does not provide for a default sale.

  c.   The mortgagee purchases the property for market value.

  d.   The jurisdiction has enacted a statutory right of redemption.

38. Rich purchased property from Sklar for $200,000. Rich obtained a $150,000 loan from Marsh Bank to finance the purchase, executing a promissory note and a mortgage. By recording the mortgage, Marsh protects its

  a.   Rights against Rich under the promissory note.

  b.   Rights against the claims of subsequent bona fide purchasers for value.

  c.   Priority against a previously filed real estate tax lien on the property.

  d.   Priority against all parties having earlier claims to the property.

39. Which of the following provisions must be included to have an enforceable written residential lease?

	A description of the leased premises	*A due date for the payment of rent*
a.	Yes	Yes
b.	Yes	No
c.	No	Yes
d.	No	No

40. Which of the following rights is(are) generally given to a lessee of residual property?

I. A covenant of quiet enjoyment.

II. An implied warranty of habitability.

  a.   I only.

  b.   II only.

  c.   Both I and II.

  d.   Neither I nor II.

41. Which of the following methods of obtaining personal property will give the recipient ownership of the property?

	Lease	*Finding abandoned property*
a.	Yes	Yes
b.	Yes	No
c.	No	Yes
d.	No	No

42. Which of the following forms of tenancy will be created if a tenant stays in possession of the leased premises without the landlord's consent, after the tenant's one-year written lease expires?

  a.   Tenancy at will.

  b.   Tenancy for years.

  c.   Tenancy from period to period.

  d.   Tenancy at sufferance.

OTHER OBJECTIVE QUESTIONS

Problem 1   (15 to 20 minutes)

On June 10, 1998, Bond sold real property to Edwards for $100,000. Edwards assumed the $80,000 recorded mortgage Bond had previously given to Fair Bank and gave a $20,000 purchase money mortgage to Heath Finance. Heath did not record this mortgage. On December 15, 1999, Edwards sold the property to Ivor for $115,000. Ivor bought the property subject to the Fair mortgage but did not know about the Heath mortgage. Ivor borrowed $50,000 from Knox Bank and gave Knox a mortgage on the property. Knox knew of the unrecorded Heath mortgage when its mortgage was recorded. Ivor, Edwards, and Bond defaulted on the mortgages. Fair, Heath, and Knox foreclosed and the property was sold at a judicial foreclosure sale for $60,000. At the time of the sale, the outstanding balance of principal and accrued interest on the Fair mortgage was $75,000. The Heath mortgage balance was $18,000 and the Knox mortgage was $47,500.

Fair, Heath, and Knox all claim that their mortgages have priority and should be satisfied first from the sale proceeds. Bond, Edwards, and Ivor all claim that they are not liable for any deficiency resulting from the sale.

The above transactions took place in a jurisdiction that has a notice-race recording statute and allows foreclosure deficiency judgments.

Required:

a.   Items 1 through 3. For each mortgage, select from List A the priority of that mortgage. A priority should be selected only once.

List A

1. Knox Bank.   A. First Priority.
                             B. Second Priority.
2. Heath Finance.   C. Third Priority.

3. Fair Bank.

b.   Items 4 through 6. For each mortgage, select from List B the reason for its priority. A reason may be selected once, more than once, or not at all.

List B

4. Knox Bank.   A. An unrecorded mortgage has priority over any subse-
                           quently recorded mortgage.
5. Heath Finance.   B. A recorded mortgage has priority over any unrecorded
                           mortgage.
6. Fair Bank.   C. The first recorded mortgage has priority over all subse-
                           quent mortgages.
                       D. An unrecorded mortgage has priority over a subsequently
                           recorded mortgage if the subsequent mortgagee knew of
                           the unrecorded mortgage.
                       E. A purchase money mortgage has priority over a previ-
                           ously recorded mortgage.

c.   Items 7 through 9. For each mortgage, select from List C the amount of the sale proceeds that each mortgagee would be entitled to receive. An amount may be selected once, more than once, or not at all.

List C

7. Knox Bank.   A. $0
                       B. $12,500
8. Heath Finance.   C. $18,000
                       D. $20,000
9. Fair Bank.   E. $42,000
                       F. $47,500
                       G. $60,000

d.   Items 10 through 12. Determine whether each party would be liable to pay a mortgage foreclosure deficiency judgment on the Fair Bank mortgage. If the party would be held liable, select from List D the reason for that party's liability. A reason may be selected once, more than once, or not at all.

List D

10. Edwards.   A. Original mortgagor.
                       B. Assumed the mortgage.
11. Bond.   C. Took subject to the mortgage.
                       D. Not liable.
12. Ivor.

e.   For **items 13 through 15**, determine whether each party would be liable to pay a mortgage foreclosure deficiency judgment on the Heath Finance mortgage. If the party would be held liable, select from List E the reason for that party's liability. A reason may be selected once, more than once, or not at all.

<table>
<tr><td></td><td><u>List E</u></td></tr>
<tr><td>**13.** Edwards.</td><td>A.   Original mortgagor.</td></tr>
<tr><td></td><td>B.   Assumed the mortgage.</td></tr>
<tr><td>**14.** Bond.</td><td>C.   Took subject to the mortgage.</td></tr>
<tr><td>**15.** Ivor.</td><td>D.   Not liable.</td></tr>
</table>

f.   For **items 16 through 18**, determine whether each party would be liable to pay a mortgage foreclosure deficiency judgment on the Knox Bank mortgage. If the party would be held liable, select from List F the reason for that party's liability. A reason may be selected once, more than once, or not at all.

<table>
<tr><td></td><td><u>List F</u></td></tr>
<tr><td>**16.** Edwards.</td><td>A.   Original mortgagor.</td></tr>
<tr><td></td><td>B.   Assumed the mortgage.</td></tr>
<tr><td>**17.** Bond.</td><td>C.   Took subject to the mortgage.</td></tr>
<tr><td>**18.** Ivor.</td><td>D.   Not liable.</td></tr>
</table>

Problem 2

This question, which deals primarily with property, appears in Module 20 because it includes three items dealing with insurance.

PROBLEM

Problem 1   (15 to 20 minutes)

On March 2, 2001, Ash, Bale, and Rangel purchased an office building from Park Corp. as joint tenants with right of survivorship. There was an outstanding note and mortgage on the building, which they assumed. The note and mortgage named Park as the mortgagor (borrower) and Vista Bank as the mortgagee (lender). Vista has consented to the assumption.

Wein, Inc., a tenant in the office building, had entered into a ten-year lease dated May 8, 1998. The lease was silent regarding Wein's right to sublet. The lease provided for Wein to take occupancy on June 1, 1998, and that the monthly rent would be $5,000 for the entire ten-year term. On March 10, 2002, Wein informed Ash, Bale, and Rangel that it had agreed to sublet its office to Nord Corp. On March 17, 2002, Ash, Bale, and Rangel notified Wein of their refusal to consent to the sublet. The following assertions have been made:

• The sublet from Wein to Nord is void because Ash, Bale, and Rangel did not consent.
• If the sublet is not void, Ash, Bale, and Rangel have the right to hold either Wein or Nord liable for payment of the rent.

On April 4, 2002, Ash transferred his interest in the building to his spouse.

Required:

Answer the following, setting forth reasons for any conclusions stated.

a.   For this item only, assume that Ash, Bale, and Rangel default on the mortgage note, that Vista forecloses, and a deficiency results. Discuss the personal liability of Ash, Bale, and Rangel to Vista and the personal liability of Park to Vista.

b.   Discuss the assertions as to the sublet, indicating whether such assertions are correct and the reasons therefor.

c.   For this item only, assume that Ash and Rangel died on April 20, 2002. Discuss the ownership interest(s) in the office building as of April 5, 2002, and April 21, 2002.

MULTIPLE-CHOICE ANSWERS

1. d __ __	10. c __ __	19. c __ __	28. d __ __	37. d __ __
2. d __ __	11. d __ __	20. a __ __	29. c __ __	38. b __ __
3. c __ __	12. a __ __	21. d __ __	30. d __ __	39. b __ __
4. c __ __	13. b __ __	22. c __ __	31. b __ __	40. c __ __
5. d __ __	14. d __ __	23. c __ __	32. d __ __	41. c __ __
6. d __ __	15. a __ __	24. c __ __	33. d __ __	42. d __ __
7. a __ __	16. b __ __	25. d __ __	34. b __ __	
8. c __ __	17. d __ __	26. b __ __	35. a __ __	1st: __/42 = __%
9. d __ __	18. a __ __	27. b __ __	36. c __ __	2nd: __/42 = __%

MULTIPLE-CHOICE ANSWER EXPLANATIONS

A. Distinctions between Real and Personal Property

1. **(d)** Real property is land and objects attached to land in a relatively permanent manner; personal property is property not classified as real. Tangible property is subject to physical possession; intangible property cannot be physically possessed, but can be legally owned. Ownership of intangible property is often represented by a piece of paper, but the property itself is intangible. A share of stock is part ownership of a company; a trademark is ownership of the use of a particular mark, design, word, or picture, and a promissory note is ownership of the right to receive payment of a debt at a future date. These are all usually represented by a piece of paper, but are intangible. An oil painting is personal property subject to physical possession.

2. **(d)** Growing crops generally are part of the land and therefore considered real property. However, the crops can be sold separately from the land, in which case they are considered personal property under the UCC, whether the buyer or the seller will sever the growing crops later from the land. Answer (a) is incorrect because air rights are not discussed in the UCC as one of those that can be either. Answer (b) is incorrect because mineral rights are associated with land or realty. Answer (c) is incorrect because unlike growing crops that may be realty until sold in a contract, harvested crops are personal property separate from the realty.

B. Personal Property

3. **(c)** The factors used to determine whether an item of personal property is considered a fixture are (1) the affixer's intent, (2) the method and permanence of attachment, and (3) whether the personal property is customarily necessary to use the real property.

4. **(c)** When the owner mislays personal property and forgets to take it with him or her, the finder does not obtain title but the owner of the premise acts as caretaker in case the true owner comes back. In the case of lost property (involuntarily left), the finder obtains title; however, the true owner, Getty, wins over this title. In the case of abandoned property, the finder gets valid title that is even valid against Getty.

5. **(d)** When property is discarded with no intention of keeping ownership over it, it is considered abandoned property. In such cases, the one who finds and keeps the abandoned property becomes the owner with title that is good against all other parties, even the owner who abandoned it. Note that Walters cannot obtain title from Rand because Rand no longer owns the rocking chair.

C. Bailments

6. **(d)** The general rule for a bailee is to exercise reasonable care in light of the particular facts and circumstances. However, a common carrier holds itself out as a public delivery service, and is held to a very high standard for property placed in its care. Therefore, answer (d) is correct.

D. Intellectual Property and Computer Technology Rights

7. **(a)** Computer software is covered under the general copyright laws and is therefore usually copyrightable as an expression of ideas. Answer (b) is incorrect because copyrights in general do not need a copyright notice for works published after March 1, 1989. Answer (c) is incorrect because a recent court ruled that programs in both source codes, which are human readable, and in machine readable object code can be copyrighted. Answer (d) is incorrect because copyrights taken out by corporations or businesses are valid for 100 years from creation of the copyrighted item or seventy-five years from its publication, whichever is shorter.

8. **(c)** Computer databases are generally copyrightable as compilations. Answer (a) is not chosen because copies for archival purposes are allowed. Answer (b) is not chosen because in the case of corporations or businesses, the copyright is valid for the shorter of 100 years after the creation of the work or seventy-five years from its date of publication. Answer (d) is not chosen because computer programs are now generally recognized as copyrightable.

9. **(d)** Under the fair use doctrine, copyrighted items can be used for teaching, including distributing multiple copies for class use. Answer (a) is incorrect because although he originally purchased this software for personal use, he may still use it for his class, in which case, the fair use doctrine applies. Answer (b) is incorrect because databases can be copyrighted as derivative works. Answer (c) is incorrect because the use of the computer is not the issue but the fair use doctrine is.

10. **(c)** Both patent and copyright law are used under modern law to protect computer technology rights. Answer (a) is incorrect because copyright law now also protects software. Answer (b) is incorrect because modern law also protects software as patentable. Answer (d) is incorrect because modern law generally protects intellectual property rights in software under both patent law and copyright law.

11. (d) Trademarks are valid indefinitely until they are actually abandoned or the company allows the trademark to lose its distinctiveness. Answer (a) is not chosen because trademarks can protect many distinctive things such as shapes, packaging, or graphic designs. Answer (b) is not chosen because a company must take steps to keep the trademark distinctive or it can lose it through others' common usage. For example, elevator was once a trademark which has since been lost. Answer (c) is not chosen because although a company may register a trademark to better protect its legal rights, it may still receive protection without registering it by proving the facts.

12. (a) Since January 1, 1978, this is the life of a copyright. Answer (b) is incorrect because the copyright is valid when the author puts the work of art in tangible form. Answer (c) is incorrect because works published after March 1, 1989 no longer require a copyright notice placed on them. Answer (d) is incorrect because under current copyright law, (b) and (c) are no longer required.

E. Interests in Real Property

13. (b) In a joint tenancy, each joint tenant has an equal and undivided interest in the property. Each joint tenant can transfer his/her interest in the property without the prior consent of the other joint tenants. When this occurs, the conveyance destroys the joint tenancy and creates a tenancy in common between the remaining joint tenants and the third party. When Long gave his/her interest in the building to Green, Green became a tenant in common with a 1/3 interest in the property. Therefore, answer (a) is incorrect. Answer (d) is incorrect because Green would have total interest in the building after the deaths of Fall and Pear only if Green had been a joint tenant rather than a tenant in common. Answer (c) is incorrect because a joint tenant may convey rights in property without the consent of other joint tenants.

14. (d) A fee simple is generally the most comprehensive interest that a person may have in property under the law of the United States. It allows the owner to sell it or to pass it on to heirs. Answer (a) is incorrect because an easement is not ownership of the land but the right to use it in a way such as using a roadway along with the owner. Answer (b) is incorrect because a leasehold gives the lessee the right to possess the premises under the lease but not the ownership of the premises. Answer (c) is incorrect because a license is permission given by the owner to use or occupy the real estate but not to own it.

15. (a) In a joint tenancy, each joint tenant has an equal and undivided interest in the property. Joint tenancy ownership consists of the unities of time, title, interest, and possession and carries with it the right of survivorship. Thus, all the elements listed in the question are required to establish a joint tenancy and answers (b), (c), and (d) are incorrect.

16. (b) A tenancy by default is not one of the recognized interests in real estate. Answer (a) is incorrect because a fee simple absolute is the highest estate recognized in American law. Answer (c) is incorrect because a life interest is an interest measured by the life of the holder or some other person. Answer (d) is incorrect because a remainder is the future interest that a third party acquires after the interest of a transferee terminates.

17. (d) In a tenancy in common, each tenant essentially owns an undivided fractional share of the property. Each tenant has the right to convey his/her interest in the property and if one of the tenants dies, that tenant's interest passes to his/her heirs. Therefore, if Nash dies, Nash's interest would pass to Nash's heirs and the ownership of the property would be as follows: Quick 1/2, Onyx 1/4, and Nash's heirs 1/4.

18. (a) Jan had title to the property when Brett granted it to her for her life. Randy never got title to it because he died before Jan's life estate terminated. When Jan died, her life estate terminated and the property reverted back to Brett, who was still living. Answer (b) is incorrect because Brett was still living. Answers (c) and (d) are incorrect because Jan and Randy had been granted life estates which automatically terminate upon their deaths.

19. (c) When rights in property held in joint tenancy are conveyed without the consent of the other joint tenants, the new owner becomes a tenant in common rather than a joint tenant. The remaining cotenants are still joint tenants. Thus, after the sale of land from Court to Plank without the consent of the others, Plank owns one third of the land as a tenant in common. Both Fell and Miles will continue to each own one third of the land as joint tenants.

20. (a) Fact pattern I involves an easement in which O reserves the right to use B's land in the deed to B. O does not any longer own the roadway but retains the right to use it. Fact pattern II is a profit rather than an easement in which O has the right to enter B's land to cut and keep the ten trees. Fact pattern III is not an easement because O has not retained nor has s/he been given the right to use the roadway. Note that this is not an easement by prescription in that the use is not open and notorious nor has it occurred for several years.

G. Types of Deeds

21. (d) An arm's-length transaction is a negotiation between unrelated parties acting in his/her interest. A way to test an arm's-length transaction is to consider what a disinterested third party would pay for the property. Answer (d) is correct because a sale involves the transfer of property for consideration in which a third party would generally negotiate and act in his/her interest. Answer (a) is incorrect because the property passes to a party as the decedent directs, subject to certain state limitations. Answer (b) is incorrect because eminent domain is the power of the government to take, with just compensation, private property for public use. Answer (c) is incorrect because adverse possession allows a person to gain title to real property if the person has continuously and openly occupied the land of another for a statutory period of time.

22. (c) In order for a deed to be valid, a description of the land must be included. The purchase price of the land need not be present to form a valid deed.

23. (c) A general warranty deed warrants that (1) the seller has title and the power to convey the property described in the deed, (2) the property is free from any encumbrances, except as disclosed in the deed, and (3) the grantee (purchaser) will not be disturbed in his/her possession of the property by the grantor (seller) or some third party's lawful claim of ownership. Thus, a general warranty deed would contain both of the warranties listed and answers (a), (b), and (d) are incorrect.

I.   Recording a Deed

24.   (c)   In order for a deed to be effective between the purchaser and seller of real estate, the deed must be delivered by the seller with an intent to transfer title. Even though a deed may be executed it does not become effective until delivery is made with the proper intent. Answer (d) is incorrect because a deed need not be recorded in order for it to be valid between the seller and purchaser. Recordation of a deed is important because it gives constructive notice to all third parties of the grantee's ownership; however, it does not affect the resolution of any disputes between the grantor and the grantee. Answer (a) is incorrect since a deed need be signed by only the seller in order for it to be effective; it does not have to be signed by the purchaser. Answer (b) is incorrect since the form of a deed is very different from a contract for the sale of real property. There is no requirement that the deed must contain the actual sales price.

25.   (d)   Under a notice-race statute, if a mortgagee fails to record its mortgage, a subsequent mortgagee who records will have a superior security interest if s/he did not have notice of the prior mortgage. In this situation, Independent Bank was the first to record its mortgage and would receive the $195,000 owed it. Scott would then receive $19,000 because Scott recorded his/her mortgage before Elgin. Since Scott did not have knowledge of Elgin's mortgage until after Scott had recorded his/her mortgage, Scott would have priority over Elgin.

26.   (b)   Under a notice-race statute, a subsequent mortgagee (lender) who loans money without notice of a previous mortgage and records the mortgage first has priority over that previous mortgage. Thus, since Scott recorded his/her mortgage before Elgin and without knowledge of Elgin's mortgage, Scott would have priority in a notice-race jurisdiction. Answer (a) is incorrect because Scott did not know of Elgin's mortgage at the time Scott recorded his/her mortgage. Although Scott later learned about both prior mortgages, this would not affect Scott's priority over Elgin's mortgage. Answer (c) is incorrect because Elgin's mortgage would have priority only if it had been recorded before Scott's. Answer (d) is incorrect because Scott's mortgage had priority over Elgin's. Therefore, Scott would be entitled to receive the full $19,000 before Elgin received any of the proceeds from the judicial sale.

J.   Title Insurance

27.   (b)   Title insurance insures against all defects of record and defects the grantee may be aware of. Any exceptions not insured by the title policy must be shown on the face of the policy. Answer (a) is incorrect because title exceptions are not insured by the title policy. Answer (c) is incorrect because title insurance covers only defects of record. Answer (d) is incorrect because title insurance does not pass to subsequent purchasers.

28.   (d)   Marketable title means that the title to real property is free from encumbrances, such as mortgages, easements, and liens and defects in the chain of title. However, there is an exception. Most courts hold that the seller's obligation to convey marketable title does not require the seller to convey the title free from recorded zoning restrictions, visible public rights-of-way or recorded easements. An unrecorded easement, however, would be a defect in marketable title. Therefore, answer (d) is correct. An unrecorded lawsuit for negligence against the seller would not cause a defect in marketable title.

K.   Adverse Possession

29.   (c)   One of the elements to obtain title to property by adverse possession is that the possession be hostile to the ownership interests of the actual owner. This does not occur when possession is permitted by the actual owner. All of the others are necessary elements to obtain ownership by adverse possession.

30.   (d)   Rake has fulfilled the elements necessary to gain title to this land in question by adverse possession. These are: (1) open and notorious possession, (2) hostile possession shown by the fence, (3) actual possession, (4) continuous possession, and (5) exclusive possession for twenty-five years. Note that it is considered continuous possession even though the gardening is only during the summer, because the fence is constantly there. Answers (a), (b), and (c) are incorrect because since Rake obtained title to the land in question, he does not have to move the fence or pay for the land.

M.   Mortgages

31.   (b)   Congress enacted the Real Estate Settlement Procedures Act (RESPA) in 1974 to provide home buyers with more extensive information about the settlement process and to protect them from unnecessarily high settlement fees. The act applies to all federally related mortgage loans, and nearly all first mortgage loans. Therefore, the general purpose of this act is to regulate mortgage lenders.

The purpose of the Federal Trade Commission Act is to prevent unfair methods of competition and unfair or deceptive practices in commerce. It is a general consumer protection act, and regulates compliance with antitrust laws. Although it may apply to mortgage lenders, its general purpose is not to regulate mortgage lenders.

32.   (d)   Dix's second mortgage on Gilmore's property will allow Dix to claim a security interest subordinate to FCA's first mortgage security interest. Dix's failure to record the second mortgage will not affect their right to successfully enforce the mortgage against Gilmore. Therefore, answer (b) is incorrect. Answer (a) is incorrect because Dix would be entitled to receive mortgage foreclosure sale proceeds if such proceeds were in excess of the amount owed to FCA. Answer (c) is incorrect because FCA's first mortgage must be fully satisfied before any payments can be made to Dix.

33.   (d)   If a buyer takes a mortgage "subject to," then the buyer accepts no liability for the mortgage and the seller is still primarily liable. The mortgagor does not have to attempt to collect from the buyer first; he can go directly against the seller. Therefore, answer (d) is correct, and answers (a) and (c) are incorrect. Answer (b) is incorrect because Wilk did not **assume** the mortgage but bought the building **subject to** the mortgage.

34.   (b)   A purchaser of real estate takes title subject to any mortgage he was aware of or any mortgage that was recorded before the purchase. Ford, therefore, takes title to the warehouse subject to Young's mortgage, but free of

Lang's mortgage. Therefore, answer (b) is correct and answer (a) is incorrect. Answer (c) is incorrect because there is no such provision. Answer (d) is incorrect because the recording statutes change the first in time concept to encourage the recording of mortgages.

35. **(a)** To have an enforceable mortgage it must be in writing and must include a description of the property and debt to be incurred. Therefore, answer (a) is correct. Answer (b) is incorrect, because although debt is usually evidenced by a promissory note, this is not required to be. Answer (c) is incorrect because the promise to pay is adequate consideration. Answer (d) is incorrect because the amount of the debt and the interest rate are not required to be stated in the mortgage.

36. **(c)** A mortgagor has the right to redeem the mortgaged property after default and before a judicial sale by payment of all principal and interest due on the mortgage note. Thus, Frost may redeem the property only if all mortgages are paid in full prior to the judicial sale. Answer (a) is incorrect because the right of redemption is a right that occurs **after** the judicial sale. Most states allow a mortgagor a period of time, usually one year after the foreclosure sale, to reinstate the debt and mortgage by paying to the purchaser at the judicial sale the amount of the purchase price plus the statutory interest rate. Answer (b) is incorrect because Frost may redeem the property prior to the judicial sale by paying all mortgages in full without regard to the probable sale price of the property. Answer (d) is incorrect because Frost would not have to pay penalty fees to the mortgagees.

37. **(d)** After foreclosure of the mortgage, the mortgagor may redeem the property by payment of all principal and interest due on the mortgage note. However, the right of redemption will terminate at the time of the judicial foreclosure sale unless the jurisdiction has enacted a statutory right of redemption. Answers (a), (b), and (c) are incorrect because they do not affect when the mortgagor's right of redemption terminates.

38. **(b)** Recording a mortgage protects the mortgagee against **subsequent** mortgagees, purchasers, or other takers. Therefore, answers (a), (c), and (d) are incorrect because those answers involve parties with existing claims on the property.

N. Lessor-Lessee

39. **(b)** A residential lease agreement must contain the following essential elements: the parties involved, lease payment amount, lease term, and a description of the leased property. The omission of any of these terms will cause the agreement to fail for indefiniteness. The other terms of payment due date, liability insurance requirements, and responsibility for repairs are optional, but not required. They will not cause the contract to fail for indefiniteness.

40. **(c)** The lessee of residential property, although not the owner, generally has the right to possession of the property and the right to quiet enjoyment of the property. The right to quiet enjoyment means that neither the lessor nor a third party with a valid claim will evict the lessee unless the lessee has breached the lease contract. The lessee also has the implied warranty of habitability which means that s/he has the right to inhabit premises that are fit for human occupation.

41. **(c)** A lease is not a sale and does not involve a transfer of title. A lessee may have possession and control of the property but will not have ownership. When property is abandoned, the owner relinquishes possession and title of the property. Subsequent parties who acquire abandoned property with the intent to own it acquire title.

42. **(d)** A tenancy at sufferance is created when a tenant stays in possession of the leased property after the expiration of the lease without the landlord's consent. A tenant at sufferance is a trespasser and the landlord may evict the tenant by instituting legal proceedings. Answer (a) is incorrect because a tenancy at will is an agreement that is not for a fixed period but is terminable at the will of the landlord or tenant. In this situation, the tenant does not have the consent of the landlord to stay in possession of the property and a tenancy at will is not created. Answer (b) is incorrect because a tenancy for years is a tenancy that has a fixed beginning and end at the time of creation of the tenancy. Answer (c) is incorrect because a tenancy from period to period would only be created if the landlord allowed the tenant to remain in possession of the property.

OTHER OBJECTIVE ANSWERS AND ANSWER EXPLANATIONS

Problem 1

Part a.

1. (C) **2.** (B) **3.** (A) Under a notice-race recording statute, a subsequent mortgagee (lender) who loans money without notice of the previous mortgagee and records the mortgage first has priority over that previous mortgagee. Once a mortgagee records, this gives constructive notice to any subsequent parties who then cannot obtain priority over the one who recorded. In this fact pattern, Fair Bank was the first mortgagee. Since Fair Bank also recorded this mortgage first, Fair Bank has the first priority over the subsequent mortgagees. Therefore, the answer to number 3 is (A). Of the two remaining mortgagees, Heath Finance was next in time but did not record the mortgage. Knox Bank was third in time and did record. However, Knox is unable to gain priority over Heath because Knox, when it recorded, knew of the Heath mortgage. Therefore, Knox does not meet all of the rules necessary to have priority over Heath. Thus Heath has the second priority after Fair Bank and Knox has the third priority. Therefore, the answer to number 2 is (B) and number 1 is (C).

Part b.

4. (D) **5.** (D) **6.** (C) This part covers the reason for the priority that applies to each of the mortgagees. Reason (A) states that "an unrecorded mortgage has priority over any subsequently recorded mortgage." This is incorrect for all mortgagees and goes against the policy behind the recording statutes to encourage recording to warn subsequent parties of the previous mortgages. Reason (B) is not a correct statement. It states that "A recorded mortgage has priority over any unrecorded mortgage." In this fact pattern, Knox recorded but Heath did not; however, Knox still has a lower priority because Knox knew of the Heath mortgage when its mortgage was recorded. Reason (C) is the correct answer for Fair Bank. It states that "The first recorded mortgage has priority over all subsequent mortgages." This is true because once Fair Bank recorded, subsequent mortgagees had constructive notice of the Fair Bank mortgage and thus could not obtain priority. The correct answer to number 6 is therefore (C). Reason (D) states that "An unrecorded mortgage has priority over a subsequently recorded mortgage if the subsequent mortgagee knew of the unrecorded mortgage." In this fact pattern, the Heath mortgage was the unrecorded mortgage that still had a higher priority than the recorded Knox mortgage because Knox Bank knew of the Heath mortgage when its mortgage was recorded. Thus Knox never fulfilled the rule which would allow it as the subsequent mortgagee, to gain a higher priority. Therefore, reason (D) is the correct answer for both Knox Bank, number four, and Heath Finance, number 5, because the same rule determines the relative priority of these two parties. Note that reason (E) is not a correct statement for any of the mortgagees because there is no rule that gives purchase money mortgages priority over previously recorded mortgages.

Part c.

7. (A) **8.** (A) **9.** (G) Since Fair Bank has the highest priority, its mortgage will be satisfied first. Since the outstanding balance of the Fair Bank mortgage was greater than the $60,000 received at the judicial foreclosure, Fair Bank receives all of the $60,000 and Knox Bank and Heath Finance each receive nothing.

Part d.

10. (B) **11.** (A) **12.** (D) When a foreclosure sale does not provide enough money to pay off the mortgages, the mortgagee, in states that allow foreclosure deficiency judgments, will attempt to collect any deficiency from the parties involved. In this fact pattern, Bond is liable because s/he was the original mortgagor on the property and as such agreed to pay the mortgage. Thus, (A) is the correct answer for number 11. When Edwards later bought the property from Bond, s/he assumed the Fair Bank mortgage. Edwards, thus, became personally liable on the mortgage even though the seller, Bond, also remained liable. Therefore, (B) is the correct answer for number 10. When Ivor subsequently purchased the property from Edwards, Ivor purchased the property subject to the Fair Bank mortgage. In so doing, s/he did not accept any liability on the mortgage. Note that although reason (C) states "Took subject to the mortgage," the correct answer for number 12 is (D) "Not liable." This is true because the directions to part d. indicate that reasons (A), (B), or (C) are to be chosen as reasons **for liability** and (D) is to be chosen if the party is **not** liable.

Part e.

13. (A) **14.** (D) **15.** (D) When Edwards purchased the property, s/he gave a mortgage to Heath Finance. Therefore, (A) is the correct answer for number thirteen because as the original mortgagor on the Heath mortgage, s/he agreed to be liable on it. Bond is not liable on the Heath mortgage because s/he having owned the property earlier, never agreed to be liable on this mortgage. Therefore, the correct answer to number 14 is (D). Ivor is not liable on the Heath mortgage because s/he never had actual notice or constructive notice of the unrecorded mortgage, and never agreed to be liable on it. Therefore, the correct answer to number 15 is (D).

Part f.

16. (D) **17.** (D) **18.** (A) Since Ivor borrowed from Knox Bank and gave Knox a mortgage on the property, Ivor is liable as the original mortgagor, making (A) the correct reason for number 18. Both Edwards and Bond owned the property prior to the Knox mortgage and never agreed to be liable on it. Therefore, the correct answer to numbers 16 and 17 is (D).

ANSWER OUTLINE

Problem 1   Liability on Assumption of Mortgage; Subletting; Property Interests; Rights of Joint Tenants and Tenants in Common

a.   Ash, Bale, and Rangel are personally liable to Vista
    They assumed the mortgage
    Park is also personally liable to Vista
        Assumption by third party does not relieve Park

b.   Assertion that the sublet is void is false
        A tenant may sublet unless stated otherwise in the lease
    Assertion that Wein or Nord is liable for rent is false
        Sublessee (Nord) is only liable to tenant (Wein)
            Tenant (Wein) is solely liable to landlord (Ash, Bale, and Rangel)

c.   Ash's spouse becomes 1/3 tenant in common on April 4
        Transfer of joint tenant's interest without consent of other joint tenants precludes transferee from becoming a joint tenant
        Rangel's death transfers his 1/3 interest to Bale through right of survivorship
            Bale has 2/3 interest and is now tenant in common since he was the only joint tenant remaining
            Ash's spouse remains 1/3 tenant in common

UNOFFICIAL ANSWER

Problem 1   Liability on Assumption of Mortgage; Subletting; Property Interests; Rights of Joint Tenants and Tenants in Common

a.   Ash, Bale, and Rangel will be personally liable to Vista for the deficiency resulting from the foreclosure sale because they became the principal debtors when they assumed the mortgage. Park will remain liable for the deficiency. Although Vista consented to the assumption of the mortgage by Ash, Bale, and Rangel, such assumption does not relieve Park from its obligation to Vista unless Park obtains a release from Vista or there is a novation.

b.   The assertion that the sublet from Wein to Nord is void because Ash, Bale, and Rangel must consent to the sublet is incorrect. Unless the lease provides otherwise, a tenant may sublet the premises without the landlord's consent. Since the lease was silent regarding Wein's right to sublet, Wein may sublet to Nord without the consent of Ash, Bale, and Rangel.

    The assertion that if the sublet was not void Ash, Bale, and Rangel have the right to hold either Wein or Nord liable for payment of rent is incorrect. In a sublease, the sublessee/subtenant (Nord) has no obligation to pay rent to the landlord (Ash, Bale, and Rangel).

    The subtenant (Nord) is liable to the tenant (Wein), but the tenant (Wein) remains solely liable to the landlord (Ash, Bale, and Rangel) for the rent stipulated in the lease.

c.   Ash's inter vivos transfer of his 1/3 interest in the office building to his spouse on April 4, resulted in his spouse obtaining a 1/3 interest in the office building as a tenant in common. Ash's wife did not become a joint tenant with Bale and Rangel because the transfer of a joint tenant's interest to an outside party destroys the joint tenancy nature of the particular interest transferred. Bale and Rangel will remain as joint tenants with each other.

    As of April 21, the office building was owned by Ash's spouse who had a 1/3 interest as tenant in common and Bale who had a 2/3 interest as tenant in common.

    Ash's death on April 20, will have no effect on the ownership of the office building because Ash had already transferred all of his interest to his wife on April 4.

    Rangel's death on April 20, resulted in his interest being acquired by Bale because of the right of survivorship feature in a joint tenancy. Because there are no surviving joint tenants, Bale will become a tenant in common who owns 2/3 of the office building. Ash's spouse will not acquire any additional interest due to Rangel's death because she was a tenant in common with Rangel.

Keep practicing! Wiley's CPA Examination Review Software has over 2,800 questions.

Available at www.wiley.com/cpa

INSURANCE

Overview

Insurance is a contract whereby the insurer (insurance company) indemnifies the insured (policyholder) against loss on designated property due to specified risks such as fire, storm, etc. The obligation of the insured under the insurance contract is the payment of the stipulated premium. Before an insured can recover under a property insurance policy, the policyholder must have an insurable interest in the property at the time it was damaged or destroyed. Basically, insurance is limited to providing protection against the risk of loss arising from a happening of events caused by the negligence of insured and negligence and intentional acts of third parties. Insurance does not protect against loss due to intentional acts of insured. Insurance contracts like others, require agreement, consideration, capacity, and legality.

Primary emphasis on the exam is placed upon knowledge of fire and casualty insurance. The exam has emphasized insurable interest, coinsurance and pro rata clauses, risks protected against, subrogation, and assignment of insurance contracts.

A. General Considerations

1. Insurance is the distribution of the cost of risk over a large number of individuals subject to the same risk, in order to reimburse the few who actually suffer from the risk
2. Insurance is designed to protect against large unexpected losses, not small everyday losses
3. Intentional acts of insured usually are not insurable (e.g., fire by arson, liability for assault and battery)

   a. Negligence or carelessness is insurable and is generally not a defense of the insurer
   b. Negligence of an insured's employees is also covered

4. Self-insurance is the periodic setting aside of money into a fund to provide for losses

   a. Not true insurance, because it is not a distribution of risk; it is preparation to meet possible losses

B. Insurance Contract

1. Similar to a common law contract. Must contain all essential elements (i.e., agreement, legality, capacity, and consideration)
2. Generally a unilateral contract where the insured prepays the premiums and the insurer promises to indemnify insured against loss
3. Insurance is generally binding at time of unconditional acceptance of the application and communication of this to insured

   a. The application is the offer, and issuance of the policy is acceptance
   b. A company agent (as opposed to an independent agent) usually has power to issue a temporarily binding slip that obligates the insurer during interim before issuance of policy
   c. Physical delivery of written policy is not necessary
   d. Insurer may require conditions to be met before policy becomes effective (e.g., pay a premium)

      (1) A general agent may accept a policy for insured

4. Policy may be voidable at option of insurer if there is

   a. Concealment—the insured failed to inform insurer at time of application of a fact material to insurer's risk

      EXAMPLE: An applicant for auto insurance is unable to drive and does not so inform the insurer.

      (1) Any matter specifically asked by insurer is by law material, and failure to disclose or a misleading answer is concealment
      (2) Need not disclose facts learned after making the contract

   b. Material misrepresentation by insured (e.g., nonexistent subject matter)

      (1) Representation acceptable if substantially true (e.g., value of subject matter does not have to be exact)

   c. Breach of warranty incorporated in the policy

      EXAMPLE: An applicant for fire insurance warrants that a night watchman will be on duty at night at all times to check for fire. If he is not and a loss occurs, this may release the insurer.

5. Statute of Frauds does not require insurance contract to be in writing because it may fall within the one-year rule (but usually is required by state statutes)

6.   Insurable interest

   a.   There must be a relationship between the insured and the insured event so that if the event occurs insured will suffer substantial loss

   b.   In property, there must be both a legal interest and a possibility of pecuniary loss

      (1)   Legal interest may be ownership or a security interest (e.g., general creditors do not have an insurable interest but judgment lien creditors and mortgagees do)

         EXAMPLE: G takes out a fire insurance policy on a building owned by A. G did this because he frequently does some business with A. Although A generally pays his bills as they are due, A owes G $20,000. G, as a general creditor only, has no insurable interest in A's building.

      (2)   Insurable interest need not be present at inception of the policy so long as it is present at time of the loss

      (3)   One can insure only to extent one has an insurable interest (e.g., mortgagee can insure only amount still due)

      (4)   Contract to purchase or possession of property can give an insurable interest

      (5)   Goods identified with contract create insurable interest

   c.   For life insurance, one has an insurable interest in one's own life and the lives of close family relatives or individuals whose death could result in pecuniary loss

      (1)   Company or person has insurable interest in key personnel or key employees

      (2)   For life insurance, insurable interest need be present at inception of policy but not at time of death

         EXAMPLE: Same as example above except that G takes out a life insurance policy on A's life. G does not have an insurable interest.

         EXAMPLE: M and N are partners in a firm in which the skills of both M and N are important. M and N take out life insurance policies on each other. There are valid insurable interests for these policies.

         EXAMPLE: Same as previous example except that M and N terminate their partnership. They do not, however, terminate the life insurance policies on each other's lives. Upon M's death, N can collect on the life insurance policy.

C. Subrogation

1.   This is the right of insurer to step into the shoes of insured as to any cause of action relating to a third party whose conduct caused the loss

   EXAMPLE: While driving his car, X is hit by Y. If X's insurance company pays X, the insurance company is subrogated to X's claim against Y.

   a.   Applies to accident, automobile collision, and fire policies

2.   A general release of a third party, who caused the loss, by insured will release insurer from his/her obligation

   EXAMPLE: While driving his car, X is hit by Y. Y talks X into signing a statement that X releases Y from all liability. X will not be able to recover on his insurance. X's insurance company is released when Y is released.

   a.   Because insurer's right of subrogation has been cut off

   b.   A partial release will release insurer to that extent

D. Liability Insurance

1.   Insurer agrees to protect insured against liability for accidental damage to persons or property

   a.   Usually includes duty to defend in a lawsuit brought by third parties

   b.   Intentional wrongs not covered (e.g., fraud)

   c.   Insurer has no rights against insured for causing the loss because this is what the insurance is to protect against

2.   Malpractice—a form of personal liability

   a.   Used by accountants, doctors, lawyers

   b.   Protects against liability for harm caused by errors or negligence in work

   c.   Does not protect against intentional wrongs (e.g., fraud)

E. Fire Insurance

1. Generally covers direct fire damage and also damage as a result of fire such as smoke, water, or chemicals
2. Blanket policy applies to a class of property that may be changing (inventory) rather than a specific piece of property (specific policy)
3. Valued policy predetermines value of property that becomes the face value of the policy
4. Recovery limited to face value of policy
5. Unvalued (open) policy determines value of property at time of loss which is amount insured collects—maximum amount usually set
6. **Coinsurance clause**

    a. The insured agrees to maintain insurance equal to a specified percentage of the value of his/her property. Then when a loss occurs, insurer only pays a proportionate share if insured has not carried the specified percentage.

    b. Formula

$$\text{Total recovery} = \text{Actual loss x } \frac{\text{Amount of insurance}}{\text{Coinsurance \% x FMV of property at time of loss}}$$

    EXAMPLE: Insured owns a building valued at $100,000. He obtains two insurance policies for $20,000 each and they both contain 80% coinsurance clauses. There is a fire and his loss is $40,000. He will only collect $20,000 ($10,000 each) on his insurance, calculated as follows:

$$\$40,000 \text{ x } \frac{\$20,000 + \$20,000}{80\% \text{ of } \$100,000}$$

    c. This formula is used even though the insured does not maintain insurance equal to specified coverage; in such cases, this formula provides a lower recovery than actual losses

        (1) Therefore, this encourages insured to insure property for amount up to fair market value multiplied by the specified coinsurance percentage

    d. Does not apply when insured property is totally destroyed

    EXAMPLE: On October 10, Harry's warehouse was totally destroyed by fire. At the time of the fire, the warehouse had a value of $500,000 and was insured against fire for $300,000. The policy contained an 80% coinsurance clause. Harry will recover $300,000, the face value of the policy, because total destruction occurred and the coinsurance clause would not apply. If the warehouse had been only partially destroyed, with damages amounting to $300,000, Harry would only recover $225,000 (based on the formula above), because the coinsurance clause would apply.

7. Pro rata clause

    a. Someone who is insured with multiple policies can only collect, from each insurer, the proportionate amount of the loss

        (1) Proportion is the amount insured by each insurer to total amount of insurance

        EXAMPLE: Insured incurs a loss due to fire on property and is entitled to a $10,000 recovery. The property is covered by two insurance policies, one for $8,000 from Company A and one for $12,000 from Company B. Consequently, total insurance coverage on the property was $20,000. Company A will be liable for 40% ($8,000/$20,000) of fire loss, that is, $4,000 (40% x $10,000). Company B will be liable for 60% ($12,000/$20,000) of fire loss, that is, $6,000 (60% x $10,000).

8. Proof of loss

    a. Insured must give insurer a statement of amount of loss, cause of loss, etc., within a specified time

        (1) Failure to comply will excuse insurer's liability unless performance is made impracticable (e.g., death of insured)

9. Mortgagor and mortgagee have insurable interests, and mortgagees usually require insurance for their protection
10. Fire policies are usually not assignable because risk may have changed

    a. Even if property is sold, there can be no assignment of insurance without insurer's consent
    b. A claim against an insurer may be assigned (e.g., house burns and insurance company has not yet paid)

MULTIPLE-CHOICE QUESTIONS (1-8)

1. Which of the following statements correctly describes the requirement of insurable interest relating to property insurance? An insurable interest

    a.   Must exist when any loss occurs.

    b.   Must exist when the policy is issued and when any loss occurs.

    c.   Is created only when the property is owned in fee simple.

    d.   Is created only when the property is owned by an individual.

2. In which of the following cases would Brown not have an insurable interest?

    a.   Brown is a general creditor of Winfield Corporation which is having financial problems.

    b.   Brown is a mortgagee on some real property purchased by Wilson.

    c.   Brown, as an owner of Winfield Company, wishes to insure the life of an officer critical to Winfield.

    d.   Brown wishes to take out a life insurance policy on his partner of a partnership in which both Brown and his partner have important skills for that partnership.

3. Which of the following parties has an insurable interest?

  I. A corporate retailer in its inventory.

  II. A partner in the partnership property.

    a.   I only.

    b.   II only.

    c.   Both I and II.

    d.   Neither I nor II.

4. Massaro is hit by Lux in a two-car accident that is later determined to be completely Lux's fault. Massaro's auto insurance policy paid her for the complete damages to her car and her person. Can Massaro's insurance company collect the amount it paid from another party?

    a.   No, because Massaro's insurance company had been paid for the risk it took.

    b.   Yes, it can recover from Lux or Lux's insurance company based on the right of subrogation.

    c.   Yes, it can recover from Lux's insurance company, if insured, based on the right of contribution.

    d.   Yes, it can recover from Lux or Lux's insurance company, if insured, based on the right of contribution.

5. On February 1, Papco Corp. entered into a contract to purchase an office building from Merit Company for $500,000 with closing scheduled for March 20. On February 2, Papco obtained a $400,000 standard fire insurance policy from Abex Insurance Company. On March 15, the office building sustained a $90,000 fire loss. On March 15, which of the following is correct?

  I. Papco has an insurable interest in the building.

  II. Merit has an insurable interest in the building.

    a.   I only.

    b.   II only.

    c.   Both I and II.

    d.   Neither I nor II.

6. Clark Corp. owns a warehouse purchased for $150,000 in 1995. The current market value is $200,000. Clark has the warehouse insured for fire loss with Fair Insurance Corp. and Zone Insurance Co. Fair's policy is for $150,000 and Zone's policy is for $75,000. Both policies contain the standard 80% coinsurance clause. If a fire totally destroyed the warehouse, what total dollar amount would Clark receive from Fair and Zone?

    a. $225,000

    b. $200,000

    c. $160,000

    d. $150,000

Items 7 and 8 are based on the following:

In 1997, Pod bought a building for $220,000. At that time, Pod purchased a $150,000 fire insurance policy with Owners Insurance Co. and a $50,000 fire insurance policy with Group Insurance Corp. Each policy contained a standard 80% coinsurance clause. In 2001, when the building had a fair market value of $250,000, it was damaged in a fire.

7. How much would Pod recover from Owners if the fire caused $180,000 in damage?

    a. $ 90,000

    b. $120,000

    c. $135,000

    d. $150,000

8. How much would Pod recover from Owners and Group if the fire totally destroyed the building?

    a. $160,000

    b. $200,000

    c. $220,000

    d. $250,000

OTHER OBJECTIVE QUESTIONS

Problem 1 (15 to 25 minutes)

On June 1, 1999, Anderson bought a one-family house from Beach for $240,000. At the time of the purchase, the house had a market value of $200,000 and the land was valued at $40,000. Anderson assumed the recorded $150,000 mortgage Beach owed Long Bank, gave a $70,000 mortgage to Rogers Loan Co., and paid $20,000 cash. Rogers did not record its mortgage. Rogers did not know about the Long mortgage.

Beach gave Anderson a quitclaim deed that failed to mention a recorded easement on the property held by Dalton, the owner of the adjacent piece of property. Anderson purchased a title insurance policy from Edge Title Insurance Co. Edge's policy neither disclosed nor excepted Dalton's easement.

On August 1, 2001, Anderson borrowed $30,000 from Forrest Finance to have a swimming pool dug. Anderson gave Forrest a $30,000 mortgage on the property. Forrest, knowing about the Long mortgage but not the Rogers mortgage, recorded its mortgage on August 10, 2001. After the digging began, Dalton sued to stop the work claiming violation of the easement. The court decided in Dalton's favor.

At the time of the purchase, Anderson had taken out two fire insurance policies; a $120,000 face value policy with Harvest Fire Insurance Co., and a $60,000 face value policy with Grant Fire Insurance Corp. Both policies contained a standard 80% coinsurance clause.

On December 1, 2001, a fire caused $180,000 damage to the house. At that time, the house had a market value of $250,000. Harvest and Grant refused to honor the policies, claiming that the house was underinsured.

Anderson made no mortgage payments after the fire and on June 1, 2002, after the house had been rebuilt, the mortgages were foreclosed. The balances due for principal and accrued interest were as follows: Long, $140,000; Rogers, $65,000; and Forrest, $28,000. At a foreclosure sale, the house and land were sold. After payment of all expenses, $200,000 of the proceeds remained for distribution. As a result of the above events, the following actions took place:

- Anderson sued Harvest and Grant for the face values of the fire insurance policies.
- Anderson sued Beach for failing to mention Dalton's easement in the quitclaim deed.
- Anderson sued Edge for failing to disclose Dalton's easement.
- Long, Rogers, and Forrest all demanded full payment of their mortgages from the proceeds of the foreclosure sale.

The preceding took place in a notice-race jurisdiction.

Required:

a. Items 1 through 3 relate to Anderson's suit against Harvest and Grant. For each item, select from List I the dollar amount Anderson will receive.

	List I
A.	$0
B.	$ 20,000
C.	$ 48,000
D.	$ 54,000
E.	$ 60,000
F.	$ 80,000
G.	$ 96,000
H.	$108,000
I.	$120,000
J.	$144,000
K.	$162,000
L.	$180,000

1. What will be the dollar amount of Anderson's total fire insurance recovery?

2. What dollar amount will be payable by Harvest?

3. What dollar amount will be payable by Grant?

b. Items 4 through 6 relate to Anderson's suit against Beach. For each item, determine whether that statement is true (T) or false (F).

4. Anderson will win the suit against Beach.

5. A quitclaim deed conveys only the grantor's interest in the property.

6. A warranty deed protects the purchaser against any adverse title claim against the property.

c. Items 7 through 9 relate to Anderson's suit against Edge. For each item, determine whether that statement is true (T) or false (F).

7. Anderson will win the suit against Edge.

8. Edge's policy should insure against all title defects of record.

9. Edge's failure to disclose Dalton's easement voids Anderson's contract with Beach.

d. Items 10 through 12 relate to the demands Long, Rogers, and Forrest have made to have their mortgages satisfied out of the foreclosure proceeds. For each item, select from List II the dollar amount to be paid.

			List II
10.	What dollar amount of the foreclosure proceeds will Long receive?	A.	$0
11.	What dollar amount of the foreclosure proceeds will Rogers receive?	B.	$ 28,000
		C.	$ 32,000
12.	What dollar amount of the foreclosure proceeds will Forrest receive?	D.	$ 65,000
		E.	$107,000
		F.	$135,000
		G.	$140,000

Problem 2   (5 to 10 minutes)

Items 1 through 6 are based on the following:

On January 12, 2001, Frank, Inc. contracted in writing to purchase a factory building from Henderson for $250,000 cash. Closing took place on March 15, 2001. Henderson had purchased the building in 1997 for $225,000 and had, at that time, taken out a $180,000 fire insurance policy with Summit Insurance Co.

On January 15, 2001, Frank took out a $140,000 fire insurance policy with Unity Insurance Co. and a $70,000 fire insurance policy with Imperial Insurance, Inc.

On March 16, 2001, a fire caused $150,000 damage to the building. At that time the building had a market value of $250,000. All fire insurance policies contain a standard 80% coinsurance clause. The insurance carriers have refused any payment to Frank or Henderson alleging lack of insurable interest and insufficient coverage. Frank and Henderson have sued to collect on the policies.

Required:

Items 1 through 6 relate to the suits by Frank and Henderson. For each item, determine whether the statement is true (T) or false (F).

1. Frank had an insurable interest at the time the Unity and Imperial policies were taken out.

2. Henderson had an insurable interest at the time of the fire.

3. Assuming Frank had an insurable interest, Frank's coverage would be insufficient under the Unity and Imperial coinsurance clauses.

4. Assuming Henderson had an insurable interest, Henderson's coverage would be insufficient under the Summit coinsurance clause.

5. Assuming only Frank had an insurable interest, Frank will recover $100,000 from Unity and $50,000 from Imperial.

6. Assuming only Henderson had an insurable interest, Henderson will recover $135,000 from Summit.

PROBLEM

Problem 1   (15 to 20 minutes)

On February 1, 1999, Tower and Perry, as tenants in common, purchased a two-unit apartment building for $250,000. They made a down payment of $100,000, and gave a $100,000 first mortgage to Midway Bank and a $50,000 second mortgage to New Bank.

New was aware of Midway's mortgage but, as a result of a clerical error, Midway did not record its mortgage until after New's mortgage was recorded.

At the time of purchase a $200,000 fire insurance policy was issued by Acme Insurance Co. to Tower and Perry. The policy contained an 80% coinsurance clause and a standard mortgagee provision.

Tower and Perry rented an apartment to Young under a month-to-month oral lease. They rented the other apartment to Zimmer under a three-year written lease.

On December 8, 2000, Perry died leaving a will naming the Dodd Foundation as the sole beneficiary of Perry's estate. The estate was distributed on January 15, 2001. That same date, the ownership of the fire insurance policy was assigned to Tower and Dodd with Acme's consent. On January 21, 2001, a fire caused $180,000 in structural damage to the building. At that time, its market value was $300,000 and the Midway mortgage balance was $80,000 including accrued interest. The New mortgage balance was $40,000 including accrued interest.

The fire made Young's apartment uninhabitable and caused extensive damage to the kitchen, bathrooms, and one bedroom of Zimmer's apartment. On February 1, 2001, Young and Zimmer moved out. The resulting loss of income caused a default on both mortgages.

On April 1, 2001, Acme refused to pay the fire loss claiming that the required insurable interest did not exist at the time of the loss and that the amount of the insurance was insufficient to provide full coverage for the loss. Tower and Dodd are involved in a lawsuit contesting the ownership of the building and the claims they have both made for any fire insurance proceeds.

On June 1, 2001, Midway and New foreclosed their mortgages and are also claiming any fire insurance proceeds that may be paid by Acme.

On July 1, 2001, Tower sued Zimmer for breach of the lease and is seeking to collect the balance of the lease term rent.

The above events took place in a notice-race statute jurisdiction.

Required:

Answer the following questions and give the reasons for your conclusions.

a. Who had title to the building on January 21, 2001?

b. Did Tower and/or Dodd have an insurable interest in the building when the fire occurred? If so, when would such an interest have arisen?

c. Does Acme have to pay under the terms of the fire insurance policy? If so, how much?

d. Assuming the fire insurance proceeds will be paid, what would be the order of payment to the various parties and in what amounts?

e. Would Tower succeed in the suit against Zimmer?

MULTIPLE-CHOICE ANSWERS

| 1. a __ __ | 3. c __ __ | 5. c __ __ | 7. c __ __ | 1st: __/8 = __% |
| 2. a __ __ | 4. b __ __ | 6. b __ __ | 8. b __ __ | 2nd: __/8 = __% |

MULTIPLE-CHOICE ANSWER EXPLANATIONS

B.6. Insurable Interest

1. **(a)** In the case of property insurance, the insurable interest must exist when the loss occurs. It need not exist when the policy is issued. Therefore, answer (b) is incorrect. Answers (c) and (d) are incorrect because there are no such requirements that the property be owned in fee simple or by individuals.

2. **(a)** To have an insurable interest in property, there must be both a legal interest and a possibility of pecuniary loss. Although a legal interest may involve ownership or a security interest, general creditors do not have the requisite interest to have an insurable interest. Answer (b) is incorrect because a mortgagee has an insurable interest for the mortgage balance still owed. Answer (c) is incorrect because Brown has an insurable interest in key company personnel whose death could result in pecuniary loss for Brown. Answer (d) is incorrect because Brown has an insurable interest in his partner whose death could cause him great monetary loss.

3. **(c)** An insurable interest in property exists if the insured has both a legal interest in the property and the possibility of incurring a pecuniary loss. The legal interest may be ownership or a security interest. A corporate retailer has an ownership interest in its inventory, and the possibility of incurring a monetary loss. A partner also has an ownership interest in partnership property, with the possibility of incurring a monetary loss.

C. Subrogation

4. **(b)** Once the insurance company pays its insured, Massaro, it steps into Massaro's shoes and obtains the same rights against third parties that Massaro had. Since Lux was at fault in this accident, the insurance company has rights against Lux as well as any insurance company that has insured Lux. Answer (a) is incorrect because the insurance company can nevertheless recover from third parties based on the right of subrogation. Answer (c) is incorrect because the insurance company has the right to collect from Lux as well as an insurer. Answer (d) is incorrect because the relevant concept is the right of subrogation, not contribution.

E. Fire Insurance

5. **(c)** An important element of a property insurance contract is the existence of an insurable interest. The insurable interest requirement is met when an entity has both a legal interest in the property and a possibility of monetary loss if the property is damaged. Since Merit still owns the office building at the time of the fire, they fulfill both these requirements. Papco also has an insurable interest which began on February 1 when they entered into the contract to purchase the building. Papco's legal interest results from their contract to purchase the building. Papco's monetary interest results from their potential loss of future use of the building. Thus, in this situation, both Papco and Merit have an insurable interest.

E.6. Coinsurance Clause

6. **(b)** Although Clark has insurance coverage exceeding the fair value of the warehouse, he may only recover the actual amount of his loss. The coinsurance clause does not apply when the insured property is totally destroyed. Fair Insurance will pay 150/225 of the $200,000 loss, or $133,333, while Zone Insurance will pay 75/225 of the $200,000 loss, or $66,667. Thus, Clark will receive a total of $200,000 from Fair and Zone.

7. **(c)** The recoverable loss is calculated using the coinsurance formula.

$$\text{Actual Loss} \times \frac{\text{Amount of insurance}}{\text{Coinsurance \% } \times \text{ FMV of property at time of loss}}$$

The amount recoverable from Owners is calculated as follows:

$$\$180,000 \times \frac{\$150,000}{80\% \times \$250,000} = \$135,000$$

8. **(b)** When property is covered by a coinsurance clause, the insured party agrees to maintain insurance equal to a given percentage of the value of the property, usually 80%. If the percentage of coverage is less than the specified percentage and partial destruction of the property occurs, then the insured will be liable for a portion of the loss. However, a coinsurance clause applies only when there has been partial destruction of property. If the insured property is totally destroyed, the coinsurance clause does not apply and the insured party will recover the face value of the insurance policy. Thus, Pod will recover $150,000 from Owners Insurance Co. and $50,000 from Group Insurance Co. for a total of $200,000.

OTHER OBJECTIVE ANSWERS AND ANSWER EXPLANATIONS

Problem 1

Part a.

1.   **(K)** In order to calculate the dollar amount of Anderson's total fire insurance recovery, use the coinsurance clause formula, adding together the amount of insurance for both Harvest and Grant, as follows:

$$\text{Recovery} = \text{Actual loss} \times \frac{\text{Amount of insurance}}{\text{Coinsurance \% x FMV of property at time of loss}}$$

$$\text{Recovery} = \$180,000 \times \frac{\$120,000 + \$60,000}{80\% \times \$250,000}$$

$$\text{Recovery} = \$162,000$$

2.   **(H)** In order to calculate the dollar amount that will be payable to Harvest only, use the coinsurance clause formula.

$$\text{Recovery} = \$180,000 \times \frac{\$120,000}{80\% \times \$250,000}$$

$$\text{Recovery} = \$108,000$$

3.   **(D)** In order to calculate the dollar amount payable to Grant only, use the same coinsurance clause formula.

$$\$180,000 \times \frac{\$60,000}{80\% \times \$250,000} = \$54,000$$

Part b.

4.   **(F)** Since Beach had given Anderson a quitclaim deed, Anderson loses in the suit against Beach for failing to mention Dalton's easement in the quitclaim deed.

5.   **(T)** Unlike a warranty deed, a quitclaim deed conveys only whatever interest in land the grantor has. No warranty concerning title or easements is given.

6.   **(T)** A warranty deed contains covenants that generally protect the grantee against any adverse title claim against the property.

Part c.

7.   **(T)** This statement is true because Edge failed to mention a recorded easement on the property. Note that when Edge failed to disclose the recorded easement, this allows Anderson to recover from Edge but does not void the contract between Anderson and the seller of the property.

8.   **(T)** Standard title insurance policies generally insure against all title defects of record. This would be true of the title insurance policy that Anderson purchased from Edge.

9.   **(F)** Since Edge failed to disclose the recorded easement, this allows Anderson to recover from Edge. However, it does not void the contract between Anderson and Beach.

Part d.

10.   **(G)** Under a notice-race statute, the subsequent good faith mortgagee wins over a previous mortgagee only if s/he also records first. In this fact pattern, Long has the first priority because its mortgage was recorded before mortgages were given to Forrest or Rogers. Since $200,000 remained to be distributed, Long gets all of its $140,000.

11.   **(C)** Forrest has the second priority because although its mortgage was granted after Rogers, Rogers did not record its mortgage and Forrest was unaware of it when its mortgage was given. Therefore, Rogers has the third priority. After Long received his $140,000, there is $60,000 left. Forrest has second priority and will receive his full $28,000. Since there is not enough left to pay Rodgers the full $65,000, Rogers only gets the balance remaining of $32,000.

12.   **(B)** Forrest has the second priority because although its mortgage was granted after Rogers, Rogers did not record its mortgage and Forrest was unaware of it when its mortgage was given. Therefore, Rogers has the third priority. After Long received his $140,000, there is $60,000 left. Forrest has second priority and will receive his full $28,000.

Problem 2

1.   **(T)** In property, there must be both a legal interest and a possibility of pecuniary loss. This insurable interest need not be present at the inception of the policy so long as it is present at the time of loss. A contract to purchase or the possession of property can give an insurable interest. Frank had an insurable interest at the time the Unity and Imperial policies were taken out as Frank contracted to purchase the property prior to taking out the insurance policies.

2.   **(F)** A contract to purchase or possession of the property can give an insurable interest. The closing of the sale of the property to Frank took place on March 15, 2001. At this point Henderson no longer had an insurable interest as he no longer had possession nor had he contracted to repurchase the property. Therefore, when the fire occurred on March 16, 2001, Henderson did not have an insurable interest.

3.   **(F)** The recoverable loss is calculated using the coinsurance formula.

$$\text{Actual loss} \text{ x } \frac{\text{Amount of insurance}}{\text{Coinsurance \% x FMV of property at time of loss}}$$

The amount recoverable from Unity is calculated as follows:

$$\$150,000 \text{ x } \frac{\$140,000}{80\% \times \$250,000} = \$105,000$$

The amount recoverable from Imperial is calculated as follows:

$$\$150,000 \text{ x } \frac{\$70,000}{80\% \times \$250,000} = \$52,500$$

The total amount recoverable from the combined insurance policies is therefore sufficient to cover the loss.

4.   **(T)** The recoverable loss is calculated using the coinsurance formula.

$$\text{Actual loss} \text{ x } \frac{\text{Amount of insurance}}{\text{Coinsurance \% x FMV of property at time of loss}}$$

The amount recoverable from Summit is calculated as follows:

$$\$150,000 \text{ x } \frac{\$180,000}{80\% \times \$250,000} = \$135,000$$

Thus, Henderson's coverage would be insufficient.

5.   **(T)** The recoverable loss is calculated using the coinsurance formula.

$$\text{Actual loss} \text{ x } \frac{\text{Amount of insurance}}{\text{Coinsurance \% x FMV of property at time of loss}}$$

The amount recoverable from Unity is calculated as follows:

$$\$150,000 \text{ x } \frac{\$140,000}{80\% \times \$250,000} = \$105,000$$

The amount recoverable from Imperial is calculated as follows:

$$\$150,000 \text{ x } \frac{\$70,000}{80\% \times \$250,000} = \$52,500$$

Combined insurance policies are sufficient but only $150,000 can be recovered. Therefore, Frank can only recover proportionately from Unity and Imperial as follows:

$$\text{Unity —} \quad \frac{140,000}{140,000 + 70,000} = 67\%$$

$$\text{Imperial —} \quad \frac{70,000}{140,000 + 70,000} = 33\%$$

Therefore, Frank will receive $100,000 (67% x $150,000 loss) from Unity and $50,000 (33% x $150,000 loss) from Imperial.

6.   **(T)** The recoverable loss is calculated using the coinsurance formula.

$$\text{Actual loss} \text{ x } \frac{\text{Amount of insurance}}{\text{Coinsurance \% x FMV of property at time of loss}}$$

The amount recoverable from Summit is calculated as follows:

$$\$150,000 \text{ x } \frac{\$180,000}{80\% \times \$250,000} = \$135,000$$

ANSWER OUTLINE

Problem 1   Title of Real Estate; Insurable Interest; Recording of Mortgage; Coinsurance Clause

a. Tower and Perry owned property as tenants in common
    Either party may dispose of property by sale or on death
    On 1/21/01, Tower and Dodd are tenants in common, each owning one-half interest

b. Both Tower and Dodd have insurable interest
    Tower's insurable interest arose when property purchased
    Dodd's insurable interest arose when Dodd inherited Perry's interest in house

c. Acme must honor insurance policy and pay part of loss
    Amount of payment is determined by coinsurance formula

$$\frac{\text{Amount of coverage}}{\text{FMV} \times \text{Coinsurance \%}} \quad \times \quad \text{Amount of loss}$$

    Amount of recovery is

$$\frac{\$200,000}{\$300,000 \times .8} \quad \times \quad \$180,000 \ = \ \$150,000$$

d. In a race-notice statute jurisdiction, New's knowledge of Midway's first mortgage gives Midway priority over New
    Proceeds distributed as follows
       $80,000 to Midway because Midway is contingent beneficiary in policy
       $40,000 to New but not paid until Midway is paid in full
       $30,000 divided equally between Tower and Dodd as tenants in common

e. Tower would not be able to collect rent from Zimmer
    Extensive damage to apartment
    Implied warranty of habitability breached by landlord
    Constructive eviction because premises no longer useful for intended purpose
    Constructive eviction releases both landlord and tenant from obligations under lease

UNOFFICIAL ANSWER

Problem 1   Title of Real Estate; Insurable Interest; Recording of Mortgage; Coinsurance Clause

a. Tower and Perry owned the property as tenants in common. This form of ownership allows either party to dispose of his or her undivided interest by sale or on death. Any person purchasing or inheriting Perry's interest would become a tenant in common with Tower. Thus, on January 21, 2001, Tower and Dodd are tenants in common, each owning a one-half undivided interest in the house.

b. Both Tower and Dodd have an insurable interest in the house. Tower's interest arose when the property was purchased, continued when the insurance policy was purchased, and still existed at the time of the fire loss.
    Dodd's interest arose when Dodd inherited Perry's interest in the house. Acme's consent to the assignment of the policy to Tower and Dodd entitles Dodd to a share of the proceeds of the policy.

c. Acme would have to honor the insurance contract and pay part of the loss. Despite Tower and Perry not maintaining insurance coverage of 80% of the property's market value, the coinsurance clause allows for a percentage of recovery. The formula is as follows:

$$\frac{\text{Amount of coverage}}{\text{Actual market value} \times \text{Coinsurance \%}} \quad \times \quad \text{Amount of loss}$$

This would allow a recovery as follows:

$$\frac{\$200,000}{\$300,000 \times .8} \quad \times \quad \$180,000 \ = \ \$150,000$$

d. The conflict between Midway and New would be resolved in favor of Midway. In a notice-race statute jurisdiction, New's knowledge of Midway's first mortgage would give Midway priority despite New's earlier filing. The insurance proceeds would be distributed as follows:

• $80,000 to Midway representing the balance due on the mortgage including accrued interest. This is due because Midway as a mortgagee is included as a contingent beneficiary in the policy.

• $40,000 to New for the same reasons as above but not paid unless and until Midway is fully paid.

• $30,000 to be divided equally between Tower and Dodd as tenants in common.

e. Tower would not be able to collect rent from Zimmer for the balance of the term of the lease because Zimmer moved as a result of the extensive fire damage to the apartment. The implied warranty of habitability would be considered breached by the landlord and a constructive eviction of Zimmer would be deemed to have taken place because the premises could no longer be used for their intended purpose. Constructive eviction releases both the landlord and the tenant from their obligations under the lease.

TRUSTS AND ESTATES

Overview

This topic includes the administration of a decedent's estate and the administration of a trust.

An estate is the legal entity that comes into existence on a person's death for the purpose of succeeding to the property of the decedent, to establish liability for payment of debts of the decedent, and to distribute any remaining property. The estate is administered in accordance with the decedent's will or the intestate statutes. An executor or administrator is approved by the court and empowered to act for the estate and carry out its responsibilities. An executor or administrator may engage the necessary legal, accounting, and other services. Adequate records must be kept to show proper disposition of the assets of the estate. At the conclusion of an estate, an accounting is generally rendered and the judicial settlement is secured in probate court, thereby closing the estate.

A trust arises where one person holds legal title to certain property for the use and benefit of another. In other words, in a trust, the legal and equitable title are split so that one called a trustee holds legal title for the benefit of another person, called a beneficiary. A trust is administered by a trustee who must perform the duties imposed by law and by the trust instrument and is personally liable if s/he does not follow these requirements.

One of the most frequently tested topics in estates and trusts is allocation of trust principal and income. Candidates should be thoroughly familiar with this distinction (e.g., between cash dividends and stock dividends). Also tested are the rights of beneficiaries to a trust with particular emphasis on the distinction between the rights of income beneficiary and the residual beneficiary, the duties of an administrator or executor of an estate as well as the duties of a trustee. You should also understand for the CPA exam how and when a trust is created and terminated.

A. Estates

1. The execution and validity of a will is generally the province of lawyers. However, some general information regarding wills which pertains to administration of estates is useful to aid you in background knowledge for tested topics.

    a. Emphasis on CPA exam is now on administration of estates and trusts
    b. Preparation of tax returns and schedules used to render an accounting are frequently done by CPA firms

2. General information and definitions

    a. Will takes effect upon death—may be changed or revoked until death
    b. Estate—legal entity holding title to person's property after his/her death
    c. Testate—a person is said to die testate if there is a valid will in existence
    d. Intestate—a person is said to die intestate if there is no will or if will is held invalid

       (1) Estate will pass by intestate succession (i.e., state statute prescribes rules of distribution of an estate)
       (2) Any assets not disposed of by will are distributed by intestate succession laws

    e. Probate—process of proving validity and authenticity of a will by demonstrating that an instrument purporting to be last will and testament of person was duly executed in accordance with legal requirements

3. Validity of will

    a. Testator/testatrix must be competent when s/he executes (makes) will

       (1) Must be of legal age (normally eighteen) at time of execution of will
       (2) Must have mental capacity to make will

          (a) Ability to understand nature and extent of property s/he owns and nature of will

    b. Must be executed in compliance with formal requirements of state statute

       (1) Signature of testator/testatrix required
       (2) Signed by individuals who witnessed testator/testatrix signing will

          (a) Except where handwritten wills allowed

B. Administration of Estates

1. Purpose of administration

    a. To carry out decedent's wishes as expressed in will
    b. To discover, collect, and conserve assets of decedent
    c. To protect creditors by paying from assets all claims and taxes against estate

    d.   To identify beneficiaries and to properly distribute assets of estate according to testator's intentions or law of intestate succession

2. One who is authorized by probate court to administer the estate of decedent is called a personal representative

    a.   Executor/executrix—personal representative named in will by testator to carry out provisions of will and empowered by probate court to act for estate

        (1) Probate court will follow testator's wishes and appoint the person named in will to be the executor, unless person named is disqualified, unavailable, or unwilling to serve

        (2) Person named as executor

            (a) Can decline to serve

            (b) Can be beneficiary of will

    b.   Administrator—person appointed by court to administer estate when decedent dies intestate or if executor named in will cannot or will not serve

    c.   Unless personal representative accepts appointment to serve gratuitously, s/he is entitled to reasonable compensation for services rendered

    d.   Personal representative is required to file with the court an inventory of estate's assets for appraisal

        (1) Taxes also assessed

3. Probate of will is prerequisite to administration of estate

    a.   Will becomes effective upon probate but relates back to time of decedent's death

4. Creditors are given notice and must file their claims within statutory time period

5. Administrator or executor/executrix is fiduciary and must act as such by acting in the best interests, and by carrying out wishes of testator/testatrix or statutory scheme

    a.   Responsible for collecting all debts, paying all expenses, and generally carrying out distribution to those entitled

    b.   Personally liable if s/he fails to execute his/her duties

        (1) Reasonable person standard used

    c.   Must not commingle estate with his/her own property

    d.   Must keep an accounting of all assets and their disposition

        (1) The final accounting rendered should include

            (a) An inventory of all assets of estate

            (b) A statement of all debts of estate

            (c) A statement of disposition of all assets and income from estate

            (d) A statement of expenses, costs, and commissions of administration

        (2) Preparation of tax returns and financial schedules used to render an accounting in estate administration are often done by CPA firms

6. Distribution of estate

    a.   By terms of will

        (1) Surviving spouse, under the concept of statutory share, has right to denounce the provision made in will for him/her and elect instead a stated share (normally 1/3) of decedent's estate

            (a) Protects surviving spouse from being disinherited by will

    b.   By intestate succession when there is no will or if will does not provide for entire estate

        (1) Laws vary from state to state

        (2) Intestate succession applies to real property as well as to personal property

    c.   Property held in joint tenancy passes to surviving joint tenants and, therefore, does not pass through a will or intestate succession

        (1) Property owned as tenants in common does pass through a will or through intestate succession

      d. Abatement—process of determining distribution of estate when it is insufficient to satisfy all debts and gifts

         (1) Debts and administration expenses are paid first, taking from (in order)

            (a) Intestate property (property not provided for in will)
            (b) Residue
            (c) General devises or legacies
            (d) Specific devises or legacies

         (2) Abatement attempts to fulfill wishes of testator to best extent by protecting those bequests most important to testator, such as specific bequests

      e. Dividing an estate per capita among heirs means that heirs with the same degree of relationship to the deceased receive an equal share

      f. Per stirpes means that each person takes his/her deceased parent's share

      EXAMPLE: Grandfather has two children who predeceased him. In his will, the grandfather left property to his grandchildren providing for a per capita distribution. He has two grandchildren from his first child and one grandchild from his second child. Each grandchild would share equally and receive a 1/3 share.

      EXAMPLE: Same as above except that the grandfather provided for a per stirpes distribution. The first two grandchildren each receive a 1/4 share since they divide their parent's share. The third grandchild gets a 1/2 share since he receives the share of his parent.

  7. Postmortem passing of property by means other than wills

      a. Joint tenancy—concurrent ownership of same piece of property with right of survivorship

         (1) Right of survivorship means that other joint tenant(s) get property upon death of one joint tenant

            (a) Heirs do not share in property by will or by intestate succession
            (b) No estate administration involved

            EXAMPLE: M, N, and O own a piece of property as joint tenants. If O dies, then M and N become the two joint tenants even if O tried to pass this interest in a will.

      b. Tenancy in common—concurrent ownership with no right of survivorship

         (1) This interest passes to heirs in a will, or if no will exists, by intestate succession

      c. Life insurance—by selection of beneficiaries who directly receive insurance proceeds by contract, not by will

      d. Employee benefits and pensions

         (1) Provisions for direct death benefits without estate administration

C. Trusts

  1. Definition—a trust is fiduciary relationship wherein trustee holds legal title to property for benefit of beneficiaries

      a. Legal and equitable (beneficial) title are separated

         (1) Trustee holds legal title
         (2) Beneficiaries hold equitable title

      b. Trustor or settlor is the person who creates the trust

         (1) Settlor can reserve right to revoke trust; otherwise, trust is irrevocable

      c. Trustee manages trust property and distributes income to beneficiary(ies) if so provided in trust agreement

      EXAMPLE: S desires to transfer Blackacre to her son, B, who is a minor, but does not want B to control legal title until he is older and capable of managing the property. Therefore, S creates a trust by transferring title of Blackacre to a trustee, J, who will hold and manage the property until B reaches age eighteen and then will convey Blackacre to B.

  2. Creation of trust

      a. Elements

         (1) Settlor (trustor) with legal capacity

      (a) For inter vivos trusts (transfers between living persons), person must have legal capacity to transfer title of property

      (b) For testamentary trusts (trusts created in wills), person must have legal capacity to make a will

    (2) Settlor intends to create trust

      (a) May be written or oral

        1] If trust is in a will (i.e., testamentary trust) then will must comply with formalities

      (b) No notice to, or acceptance by, beneficiaries required

      (c) No notice to, or acceptance by, trustees required

      (d) No consideration required

        1] Distinguish—a contract to make a future trust does need consideration

      (e) Legality

        1] Purpose of trust must be legal or trust is considered void

    (3) Trustee—one who holds legal title

      (a) May be minor, corporation, or other person

      (b) Death of trustee does not destroy trust—new trustee appointed

    (4) Beneficiary

      (a) Must be identifiable at time trust is created

      (b) May be minor, corporation, or other person

      (c) Class of persons may be beneficiaries

      (d) Settlor may be beneficiary

    (5) Trust property (also called res or corpus)

      (a) Must exist at time of creation of trust

      (b) Must be specifically identified

      (c) Trust must be limited in duration so as to not violate the rule against perpetuities

        1] This rule requires that trust cannot (by its terms) last longer than a life in being plus twenty-one years or it will fail

          EXAMPLE: A forms a trust. The terms of this trust state that the income is to go to his son, B, for life unless B has a child, in which case the property will be distributed to this child at the age of twenty-one.

        2] Purpose is to prevent title to property from being tied up for an unreasonable period of time

        3] This limitation does not apply to charitable trusts

  b. Multiple interests

    (1) Settlor may name him/herself as trustee or cotrustee

    (2) Settlor may name him/herself as beneficiary or one of several beneficiaries

    (3) Same person may not be both sole trustee and sole beneficiary of trust at same time because legal and equitable title are identical

      (a) However, a beneficiary who is one of two or more beneficiaries can also be trustee or co-trustee because legal and equitable title are not identical in this situation

3. Types of Trusts

  a. Inter vivos trust is created by settlor while living

    (1) Transfer in trust is the transferring of property by settlor to trustee for benefit of another

    (2) Declaration of trust is when settlor declares him/herself trustee for beneficiary

      (a) In a declaration of trust, no transfer of property is necessary

  b. A testamentary trust is set up in testator's/testatrix's will to have property transferred in trust after death of settlor

    (1) Requires elements of valid will

   c. Charitable trust—a trust that has as its object some recognized social benefit (e.g., furthering education, religion, relief to poor)

   d. Clifford Trust

      (1) Rules for Clifford Trust started on or before March 1, 1986

         (a) Trust in which its creator retains right to possession of trust property after a stated period of time or upon happening of stated event

         (b) Creator of trust is taxed on trust property unless Internal Revenue Code requirements are met because s/he is still treated as owner

            1] Not treated as owner for tax purposes (i.e., not taxed on) if creator of trust will not obtain possession within ten years from creation of trust

> *EXAMPLE: The Huskies decided they would like to shift some of their income to their children, Herb and Harriet. They decided to create a short-term irrevocable trust for the benefit of the children with Illini Trust Company as trustee. The duration of the trust was ten years plus one day. The trust agreement was dated August 1, 2001. The Huskies then conveyed an apartment building in trust to the trustee on October 10, 2001. The Huskies' trust was not created until October 10, 2001, when title to the building was conveyed to the trustee in writing. Consequently the duration of the trust was less than ten years and it would not qualify as a Clifford Trust. Thus the rental income would be taxed as part of the parents' income and not as part of the children's, which was the Huskies' intent when creating the trust.*

      (2) In general, transfers through a trust made after March 1, 1986, have been changed under the Tax Reform Act of 1986

         (a) Trusts started after the above date do not allow income shifting from the grantor to the beneficiary if the grantor or grantor's spouse retains a reversionary interest in the trust property

         (b) As of this writing, an exception is allowed from the new changes in that Clifford Trusts made under a binding property settlement on or before March 1, 1986, are able to continue to shift income to the beneficiary

            1] However, if the beneficiary is a son or daughter and is under the age of fourteen, the shifted income is taxed at the parent's tax rate

            2] Note that if the beneficiary is either over thirteen years old or is not the son or daughter of the grantor, under the conditions above, the income is taxed at the beneficiary's rate

   e. Spendthrift trusts

      (1) Trusts that prohibit beneficiary from assigning or transferring to another party any unreceived payments

         (a) Protects beneficiary from creditors or from his/her squandering of assets

         (b) However, once beneficiary actually receives income from trust, protection is lost because creditors can seize income or beneficiary is free to use it as s/he chooses

         (c) Generally, beneficiary is restricted to withdrawing only specified amounts during each period of time

      (2) Spendthrift trust may not be terminated by beneficiaries because such action would defeat purpose for which this trust was created

      (3) Furthermore, if trust is irrevocable, it may not be terminated by settlor during term of trust

      (4) Trust is terminated at end of term of trust or when all beneficiaries die

   f. Resulting trusts

      (1) Arise when express trust fails and trustee still has property meant for trust

         (a) Since there is no beneficiary, settlor is presumed to get beneficial interest

> *EXAMPLE: S transfers some real estate to T so that he will pay B, the beneficiary, the rents from the real estate used as rental property. Assume that S did not meet one of the requirements of a valid trust. Since the express trust does not exist, a resulting trust is implied.*

      (2) Arise by fulfillment of trust purpose

> *EXAMPLE: S transfers some assets to T, a trustee, to provide for the care of S's father for his life. Before the assets are all used, S's father dies. T is deemed to hold the assets in a resulting trust for S (or S's heirs.)*

g. Active trust is one wherein trustee has some specific duties to perform

   (1) Passive trust is one requiring no duties of trustee, and trustee is merely holder of legal title of trust property until ownership passes to beneficiaries

h. Totten trusts

   (1) Totten trust pertains to a bank savings account which depositor opens as "John Smith in trust for Sam Smith"
   (2) Revocable by depositor simply by withdrawing money
   (3) Funds may be used during depositor's life in any manner
   (4) Totten trusts become irrevocable at depositor's death

i. Constructive trust arises when person who takes legal interest in property cannot enjoy beneficial interest without violating some established (legal) principle

   (1) Therefore, the court converts legal owner into trustee for the party who is entitled to beneficial enjoyment
   (2) Arises by operation of law as remedial device
   (3) Imposed whenever court determines that one who acquired title to property is under duty to transfer it to another person because acquisition was by fraud, duress, mistake, etc. or because the holder of title would be unjustly enriched if s/he were permitted to retain it

   EXAMPLE: S conveys property to A, but B fraudulently changes conveyance to his own name. Therefore, the court will impose a constructive trust whereby B is deemed to hold the property in trust for A.

D. Administration of Trusts

1. Trustee's duties

   a. Fulfill terms in express trust

      (1) Unless illegal or impossible
      (2) Unless circumstances unanticipated by settlor occur so that fulfillment of trust terms would defeat trust's original purpose
      (3) Unless court decree directs otherwise

   b. Trustee is fiduciary (this concept is very important)

      (1) Owes duty to act in best interests of beneficiary(ies) rather than his/her own

   c. Fiduciary duties owed by trustee to beneficiaries

      (1) Duty of loyalty to beneficiaries (e.g., to not benefit from trust to detriment of beneficiaries and to disclose to them all important information concerning trust)

         (a) Keep trust property separate from own

      (2) Duty of due care to act as a reasonable person in administering trust

         (a) Must act as prudent investor would using modern portfolio theory and diversification

            1] Other strategies such as use of speculative investments are permitted if authorized in trust

         (b) Allocate correctly between principal and income of trust
         (c) Account for all trust property and income to beneficiaries

            1] Keep reasonable records

         (d) Collect claims owed trust
         (e) Defend actions brought against trust

2. Trustee's powers

   a. May be express
   b. May be implied

      (1) Only those powers that are not prohibited under trust and are reasonably necessary to fulfill purpose of trust
      (2) Trustee has right to reimbursement for reasonable expenses incurred on behalf of trust
      (3) May prudently sell and purchase property

(a) Diversification may be used to decrease risk of loss

(4) May lease property if reasonable

(5) If more than one trustee, unanimous consent needed

(6) No implied power to mortgage, pledge, borrow on trust property, or accumulate income

3. Liability of trustee

   a. To beneficiaries based on breach of trust or breach of fiduciary duties

EXAMPLE: The trustee of some income property failed to make proper roof repairs resulting in extensive water damage to the trust property. Evidence shows that there was sufficient warning of needed repairs. The trustee is liable for the loss in value of the property.

EXAMPLE: The trustee sold some shares of stock to himself from the trust property at a price below fair market value. This is a clear breach of the fiduciary duty.

     (1) Beneficiaries can sue to have trustees replaced if they breach their fiduciary duties or exceed their authority in the trust.

EXAMPLE: In the two previous examples, not only can the trustees be liable for damages but can also be removed for breach of their fiduciary duties.

   b. To third parties

     (1) Liable under contract or tort law

       (a) Trustee has right of exoneration (trust property pays for liability) when in performance of trust duties

4. Doctrine of *cy pres*

   a. Applies to charitable trusts when trust purpose becomes impossible or impracticable

     (1) Court directs substitute application that falls within settlor's general intention as nearly as possible

E. Termination of Trusts

1. At end of period stated in trust

2. Revocation by settlor

   a. Can do so only if power of revocation is reserved in trust

   b. If trust is irrevocable, it cannot be terminated for term of trust

     (1) Exceptions

       (a) If settlor is sole beneficiary, may terminate trust when desires to

       (b) By court order

3. Achievement of trust purpose

EXAMPLE: X creates a trust in which his daughter, C, is to receive the income (as beneficiary) to help her become a CPA. She gets her CPA license. Since the purpose of the trust has been achieved, the trust terminates.

EXAMPLE: O conveys some property to T for the benefit of B. The trust terminates when B dies. It does not automatically terminate when the trustee dies because another can be chosen.

4. Failure of trust purpose

EXAMPLE: Same as example above, but unfortunately C dies before her goal is obtained. The trust terminates.

5. Agreement of all beneficiaries

   a. As long as trust purpose not defeated

     (1) Trust may be terminated if settlor joins in to terminate trust

6. By merger

   a. If trustee and beneficiary are ever the same sole person, legal title and equitable title are merged, thus terminating the trust

EXAMPLE: S creates a trust that designates A and B as cotrustees and names B as beneficiary. The trust also states that after six years B has the right to remove A as trustee. If B exercises this right, the trust would terminate because the sole trustee and sole beneficiary would be the same person and legal and equitable title would merge.

EXAMPLE: S creates a trust in which A becomes trustee for A and B as beneficiaries. This trust would not be terminated by merger because B does not hold both legal and equitable title even though A does.

   b.   If sole beneficiary is also a cotrustee, this does not terminate trust

7.   Settlor may revoke (or modify) trust only if terms of trust so state or settlor has reserved that right

   a.   Reason: beneficiary has rights to beneficial interest in trust

8.   Breach of fiduciary duties by trustees does not cause trust to terminate

F.   Allocation between Principal and Income

1.   Typically, interests are divided between an income beneficiary and a remainderman beneficiary

   a.   Income beneficiary receives income from trust property (usually for specified time such as for his/her life)

   b.   Remainderman gets trust property when trust terminates

   EXAMPLE: T puts income property into a trust stating that B will receive the income for life with the remainder going to R when B dies.

2.   It is duty of trustee to distribute income and principal in accordance with terms of trust

   a.   In absence of specific trust provisions, allocation is governed by Uniform Principal and Income Act

      (1)   Provisions of this uniform act are applicable to both estates and trusts

      EXAMPLE: T puts income property and cash into a trust stating that B will receive the income for life with the remainder going to R when B dies. T also provides in the trust that the trustee may pay up to $7,000 out of the principal to B each year. This "sprinkling" provision is enforceable.

3.   Principal includes

   a.   Original trust property, including any income earned up to formation of the trust
   b.   Proceeds and gains from sale of property, including insurance received on destruction of property
   c.   New property purchased with principal or proceeds from principal
   d.   Stock dividends and stock splits (cash dividends are income)
   e.   Liquidating distributions
   f.   Amortization of premium on property bought by trustee

4.   Payable from principal are expenses affecting principal, for example,

   a.   Payment of principal on loans
   b.   Litigation over trust property
   c.   Permanent (capital) improvements
   d.   Costs incurred in purchase or sale of trust property
   e.   Losses on sale or exchange of trust property
   f.   Title insurance
   g.   Environmental expenses
   h.   Inheritance, estate transfer taxes for estate

5.   Income includes profits from trust principal after trust begins, for example,

   a.   Rent (including prepaid rent) less costs of collection
   b.   Interest
   c.   Cash dividends
   d.   Royalties

6.   Payable from income are ordinary and operating expenses, for example,

   a.   Ordinary administrative expenses
   b.   Interest
   c.   Insurance premiums
   d.   Taxes
   e.   Repairs and maintenance
   f.   Depreciation (at trustee's option)

7.   Trust's management expenses, trustee's compensation, and cost of judicial accounting are allocated equally between principal and income

8.   Annuities are allocated between principal and income

9.   Trustee is liable to income beneficiary and remainderman for confusion or commingling of assets

      a.   CPA is often consulted to determine allocation of money to beneficiaries versus amounts to individuals receiving remainder

G. Real Estate Investment Trusts (REIT)

1. Real Estate Investment Trust Act

      a.   Authorized by Congress in 1960
      b.   Permits organization of unincorporated association to invest in real estate
      c.   Association need not pay corporate income taxes

2. Provisions to be met

      a.   100 or more certificate holders during each year
      b.   Must be in writing
      c.   Five or fewer holders must not own more than 50% of certificates
      d.   Trustees must have centralized control
      e.   Owners must have limited liability and free transferability of shares
      f.   Major portion of income must be rents from real property or gains on sale of real property
      g.   Must pay at least 90% of taxable income to certificate holders each year

3. Certificate holders do not have personal liability

      a.   Liability limited to investment in REIT

4. Tax treatment

      a.   Ordinary income and capital gains pass through to investors
      b.   Depreciation and other losses do not pass through

5. Failure to meet provisions, trust taxed as if corporation
6. Trust must comply with applicable SEC securities registration laws

MULTIPLE-CHOICE QUESTIONS (1-27)

1. A decedent's will provided that the estate was to be divided among the decedent's issue, per capita and not per stirpes. If there are two surviving children and three grandchildren who are children of a predeceased child at the time the will is probated, how will the estate be divided?

   a. 1/2 to each surviving child.
   b. 1/3 to each surviving child and 1/9 to each grandchild.
   c. 1/4 to each surviving child and 1/6 to each grandchild.
   d. 1/5 to each surviving child and grandchild.

2. A will provided that an estate was to be distributed per stirpes to the deceased's heirs. The only possible heirs are two daughters, who each have three children, and two children of a predeceased son. What fraction of the estate will each child of the predeceased son receive?

   a. 0
   b. 1/10
   c. 1/6
   d. 1/4

3. Cord's will created a trust to take effect on Cord's death. The will named Cord's spouse as both the trustee and personal representative (executor) of the estate. The will provided that all of Cord's securities were to be transferred to the trust and named Cord's child as the beneficiary of the trust. Under the circumstances,

   a. Cord has created an inter vivos trust.
   b. Cord has created a testamentary trust.
   c. The trust is invalid because it will **not** become effective until Cord's death.
   d. Cord's spouse may **not** serve as both the trustee and personal representative because of the inherent conflict of interest.

4. Which of the following is **not** necessary to create an express trust?

   a. A successor trustee.
   b. A trust corpus.
   c. A beneficiary.
   d. A valid trust purpose.

5. Arno plans to establish a spendthrift trust naming Ford and Sims life income beneficiaries, Trip residuary beneficiary, and Bing as trustee. Arno plans to fund the trust with an office building. Assume an enforceable trust was formed.

Sims has the following personal creditors:

   I. Bank holding a home mortgage note deficiency judgment.
   II. Judgment creditor as a result of an automobile accident.

To which of these creditors can Bing pay Sims' share of trust income?

   a. I only.
   b. II only.
   c. Both I and II.
   d. Neither I nor II.

6. To which of the following trusts would the rule against perpetuities **not** apply?

   a. Charitable.
   b. Spendthrift.
   c. Totten.
   d. Constructive.

7. Which of the following fiduciary duties may be violated by the trustee if the trustee, without express direction in the trust instrument, invests trust assets in unsecured loans to a cotrustee?

   I. Duty to invest prudently.
   II. Duty of loyalty to the trust.

   a. I only.
   b. II only.
   c. Both I and II.
   d. Neither I nor II.

8. Which of the following situations would cause a resulting trust to be created?

   I. Failure of an express trust.
   II. Application of the *cy pres* doctrine.
   III. Fulfillment of the trust purpose.

   a. I and II.
   b. I and III.
   c. II and III.
   d. I, II, and III.

9. If **not** expressly granted, which of the following implied powers would a trustee have?

   I. Power to sell trust property.
   II. Power to borrow from the trust.
   III. Power to pay trust expenses.

   a. I and II.
   b. I and III.
   c. II and III.
   d. I, II, and III.

10. McCoy creates an inter vivos trust by transferring legal title of a rental home to Jansen. The beneficiary of this trust is Jacobs and the current tenant of the home is Lantry. Which of the following statements is true concerning this trust?

   a. Jansen owes a fiduciary duty to both Jacobs and Lantry.
   b. Jansen owes a fiduciary to both McCoy and Jacobs.
   c. If Lantry moves out, Jacobs is obligated to take reasonable steps to find a new tenant.
   d. Jacobs can expect Jansen to act in Jacob's best interest even if it may not always be in Jansen's best interest.

11. In a written trust containing **no** specific powers, the trustee will have all of the following implied powers **except**

   a. Sell trust property.
   b. Pay management expenses.
   c. Accumulate income.
   d. Employ a CPA to prepare trust tax returns.

12. In a typical trust, which of the following is true?

   a. The trustee owes a fiduciary duty to the beneficiaries.
   b. The trustee owes fiduciary duties to the beneficiaries and the trustor.
   c. The trustee and trustor both owe fiduciary duties to the beneficiaries.
   d. The trustee owes a fiduciary duty to the beneficiaries and the beneficiaries owe fiduciary duties to the trustee.

13. Which of the following events will terminate an irrevocable spendthrift trust established for a period of five years?

    a.   Grantor dies.
    b.   Income beneficiaries die.
    c.   Grantor decides to terminate the trust.
    d.   Income beneficiaries agree to the trust's termination.

14. An irrevocable trust that contains **no** provision for change or termination can be changed or terminated only by the

    a.   Courts.
    b.   Income beneficiaries.
    c.   Remaindermen.
    d.   Grantor.

15. On the death of the grantor, which of the following testamentary trusts would fail?

    a.   A trust created to promote the public welfare.
    b.   A trust created to provide for a spouse's health care.
    c.   A trust created to benefit a charity.
    d.   A trust created to benefit a currently childless person's future grandchildren.

16. An irrevocable testamentary trust was created by Park, with Gordon named as trustee. The trust provided that the income will be paid to Hardy for life with the principal then reverting to Park's estate to be paid to King. The trust will automatically end on the death of

    a.   Park.
    b.   Gordon.
    c.   Hardy.
    d.   King.

17. Frost's will created a testamentary trust naming Hill as life income beneficiary, with the principal to Brown when Hill dies. The trust was silent on allocation of principal and income. The trust's sole asset was a commercial office building originally valued at $100,000 and having a current market value of $200,000. If the building was sold, which of the following statements would be correct concerning the allocation of the proceeds?

    a.   The entire proceeds would be allocated to principal and retained.
    b.   The entire proceeds would be allocated to income and distributed to Hill.
    c.   One-half of the proceeds would be allocated to principal and one-half to income.
    d.   One-half of the proceeds would be allocated to principal and one-half distributed to Brown.

18. Absent specific directions, which of the following parties will ordinarily receive the assets of a terminated trust?

    a.   Income beneficiaries.
    b.   Remaindermen.
    c.   Grantor.
    d.   Trustee.

19. Jay properly created an inter vivos trust naming Kroll as trustee. The trust's sole asset is a fully rented office building. Rental receipts exceed expenditures. The trust instrument is silent about the allocation of items between principal and income. Among the items to be allocated by Kroll during the year are insurance proceeds received as a result of fire damage to the building and the mortgage interest payments made during the year. Which of the following items is(are) properly allocable to principal?

	Insurance proceeds on building	Current mortgage interest payments
a.	No	No
b.	No	Yes
c.	Yes	No
d.	Yes	Yes

20. Arno plans to establish a spendthrift trust naming Ford and Sims life income beneficiaries, Trip residuary beneficiary, and Bing as trustee. Arno plans to fund the trust with an office building. Assume an enforceable trust was formed.

Which of the following will be allocated to trust principal?

	Annual property tax	Monthly mortgage principal payment
a.	Yes	Yes
b.	Yes	No
c.	No	Yes
d.	No	No

21. On July 1, Sutter created a living trust by transferring the legal title of 500 shares of Pine Corporation common stock to Ellis as trustee and named Clay as the sole beneficiary. The trust granted Ellis broad powers to sell and repurchase stock as she saw fit. On June 25, a few days before the trust was created, Pine Corporation distributed cash dividends of $1 per share on its common stock. On July 15, Ellis sold the common stock for $105 per share, which was $5 more than the purchase price that Sutter had paid. Ignoring taxes, how much is in the principal of this trust on July 16?

    a. $ 2,500
    b. $50,000
    c. $52,500
    d. $53,000

22. Which of the following expenditures resulting from a trust's ownership of commercial real estate should be allocated to the trust's principal?

    a.   Building management fees.
    b.   Insurance premiums.
    c.   Sidewalk assessments.
    d.   Depreciation.

23. Which of the following would ordinarily be distributed to a trust income beneficiary?

  I.   Royalties.
  II.   Stock received in a stock split.
  III.   Cash dividends.
  IV.   Settlements of claims for damages to trust property.

    a.   I and II.
    b.   I and III.
    c.   II and III.
    d.   II and IV.

24. Farrel's will created a testamentary trust naming Gordon as life income beneficiary, with the principal going to Hall on Gordon's death. The trust's sole asset was a commercial office building valued at $200,000. The trustee sold the building for $250,000. To what amount of the sale price is Gordon entitled?

    a. $0
    b. $ 50,000

c. $200,000
d. $250,000

25. Cox transferred assets into a trust under which Smart is entitled to receive the income for life. After Smart's death, the remaining assets are to be given to Mix. In 2001, the trust received rent of $1,000, stock dividends of $6,000, interest on certificates of deposit of $3,000, municipal bond interest of $4,000, and proceeds of $7,000 from the sale of bonds. Both Smart and Mix are still alive. What amount of the 2001 receipts should be allocated to trust principal?

    a. $ 7,000
    b. $ 8,000
    c. $13,000
    d. $15,000

26. Under the Real Estate Investment Trust Act, which of the following is **not** true of a Real Estate Investment Trust (REIT)?

    a.   A REIT has limited liability for its owners.
    b.   A REIT is taxed as a corporation.
    c.   The owners of a REIT can freely transfer the shares.
    d.   The trust to create a REIT must be in writing.

27. Congress passed the Real Estate Investment Trust Act. Which of the following is true of a Real Estate Investment Trust (REIT) formed under this Act?

    a.   Ordinary income and capital gains earned by the trust pass through to investors for tax purposes.
    b.   Five or fewer certificate holders of the REIT must not own more than half of the certificates.
    c.   The REIT must have at least 100 certificate holders.
    d.   All of the above.

OTHER OBJECTIVE QUESTIONS

Problem 1   (15 to 25 minutes)

In 1999, Park, after consulting a CPA and an attorney, decided to have an inter vivos trust and will prepared. Park wanted to provide for the welfare of three close relatives: Archer, Book, and Cable, during Park's lifetime and after Park's death.

The trust was funded by cash and real estate transfers. The trust contained spendthrift provisions directing the trustees to pay the income to only the trust beneficiaries, Archer, Book, and Cable. Park also provided for $10,000 "sprinkling" provisions allowing for the annual distribution of up to $10,000 of principal to each beneficiary at the trustee's discretion.

Park's will provided for a "pour over" transfer of any residuary estate to the trust.

Young, a CPA, and Zack, a stockbroker, were named trustees of the trust and executors of the will. Young and Zack were directed to perform their duties as "prudent business people" in investing and protecting the assets of the trust and estate.

During 2000, Young and Zack properly allocated income and principal and paid the trust income to Park's relatives as directed. They also made $5,000 principal payments to two of the beneficiaries for a medical emergency and to pay college tuition.

During 2001, Zack, with Young's consent, borrowed $10,000 from the trust. Zack agreed to repay the loan at a higher interest rate than the trust normally received on its investments. Archer, one of the trust beneficiaries, asked for and received a $15,000 principal payment. The money was used to enable Archer to invest in a joint venture with Zack.

In January 2002, Park died and the will was probated. After payment of all taxes, debts, and bequests, the residuary estate was transferred to the trust. Archer, Book, and Cable sued

- To have the court allow distribution of the residuary estate instead of the residuary being transferred to the trust.
- To have the spendthrift trust terminated.
- To remove Young and Zack as trustees for making the $5,000 principal payments.
- To remove Young and Zack as trustees for allowing Zack to borrow money from the trust.
- To remove Young and Zack as trustees for making the $15,000 principal payment to Archer.

Required:

Determine whether each of the following legal conclusions is correct or incorrect.

1. Archer, Book, and Cable will win in their lawsuit to have the court allow distribution of the residuary estate instead of the residuary being transferred to the trust.

2. Archer, Book, and Cable will win in their suit to have the trust terminated.

3. Archer, Book, and Cable owe fiduciary duties to Young and Zack.

4. Young and Zack owe fiduciary duties to the beneficiaries.

5. The beneficiaries may remove Young and Zack as trustees because they made the $5,000 principal payments.

6. The trustees may invade the principal but only for medical needs or education of the beneficiaries.

7. The beneficiaries will win in their suit to remove Zack because he borrowed $10,000 from the trust.

8. The beneficiaries will win their suit to remove Young because of Zack's borrowing the $10,000.

9. It was proper to distribute the $15,000 to Archer because Archer requested it.

10. The beneficiaries will win in their lawsuit to remove the trustees because of the $15,000 payment from principal.

Problem 2   (10 to 15 minutes)

It is the duty of the trustee to distribute income and principal in accordance with the terms of the trust. For the numbered items shown below, indicate how allocations are generally made in absence of specific trust provisions. For each of the numbered items, select one letter from the following List A. Each letter may be used once, more than once, or not at all.

List A
A. Principal includes this.
B. Income includes this.
C. This is payable from principal.
D. This is payable from income.

1. Shares of stock purchased before the trust was formed and placed in the trust.

2. Cash dividends received on the stock **up to** the formation of the trust.

3. Cash dividends received on the stock **after** formation of the trust.

4. Stock dividends after the trust is formed.

5. Stock splits after the trust is formed.

6. Rental property placed in the trust.

7. Payment of principal on mortgage for rental property.

8. Capital improvements on rental property.

9. Repairs and maintenance on rental property.

10. Prepaid rent received from rental property.

11. Payment of interest on the mortgage for the rental property.

12. Fire insurance paid on property.

13. Gain on sale of part of rental property.

14. Insurance received due to fire destruction of the rest of the rental property.

15. Litigation costs over trust property.

Problem 3   (5 to 10 minutes)

Under the provisions of Glenn's testamentary trust, after payment of all administrative expenses and taxes, the entire residuary estate was to be paid to Strong and Lake as trustees. The trustees were authorized to invest the trust assets, and directed to distribute income annually to Glenn's children for their lives, then distribute the principal to Glenn's grandchildren, per capita. The trustees were also authorized to make such principal payments to the income beneficiaries that the trustees determined to be reasonable for the beneficiaries' welfare. Glenn died in 1998. On Glenn's death there were two surviving children, aged twenty-one and thirty, and one two-year-old grandchild.

On June 15, 2001, the trustees made the following distributions from the trust:

• Paid the 1998, 1999, and 2000 trust income to Glenn's children. This amount included the proceeds from the sale of stock received by the trust as a stock dividend.
• Made a $10,000 principal payment for medical school tuition to one of Glenn's children.
• Made a $5,000 principal payment to Glenn's grandchild.

Required:

Items 1 through 5 relate to the above fact pattern. For each item, select from List II whether only statement I is correct, whether only statement II is correct, whether both statements I and II are correct, or whether neither statement I nor II is correct.

List II

A. I only.
B. II only.
C. Both I and II.
D. Neither I nor II.

1. I.   Glenn's trust was valid because it did **not** violate the rule against perpetuities.
   II. Glenn's trust was valid even though it permitted the trustees to make principal payments to income beneficiaries.

2. I.   Glenn's trust would be terminated if both of Glenn's children were to die.
   II. Glenn's trust would be terminated because of the acts of the trustees.

3. I.   Strong and Lake violated their fiduciary duties by making any distributions of principal.
   II. Strong and Lake violated their fiduciary duties by failing to distribute the trust income annually.

4. I.   Generally, stock dividends are considered income and should be distributed.
   II. Generally, stock dividends should be allocated to principal and remain as part of the trust.

5. I.   The $10,000 principal payment was an abuse of the trustees' authority.
   II. The $5,000 principal payment was valid because of its payment to a nonincome beneficiary.

PROBLEM

Problem 1   (15 to 25 minutes)

On January 1, 2001, Stone prepared an inter vivos spendthrift trust. Stone wanted to provide financial security for several close relatives during their lives, with the remainder payable to several charities. Stone funded the trust by transferring stocks, bonds, and a commercial building to the trust. Queen Bank was named as Trustee. The trust was to use the calendar year as its accounting period. The trust instrument contained no provision for the allocation of receipts and disbursements to principal and income.

The following transactions involving trust property occurred in 2001:

- The trust sold stock it owned for $50,000. The cost basis of the stock was $10,000. $40,000 was allocated to income and $10,000 to principal.
- The trust received a stock dividend of 500 shares of $10 par value common stock selling, at the time, for $50 per share. $20,000 was allocated to income and $5,000 to principal.
- The trust received bond interest of $18,000, which was allocated to income. The interest was paid and received semiannually on May 1 and November 1.
- The trust made mortgage amortization payments of $40,000 on the mortgage on the commercial building. The entire amount was allocated to principal.

On December 31, 2001, all the income beneficiaries and the charities joined in a petition to have the court allow the trust to be terminated and all trust funds distributed.

Required:

a. State the requirements to establish a valid inter vivos spendthrift trust and determine whether the Stone trust meets those requirements.

b. State whether the allocations made in the four transactions were correct and, if not, state the proper allocation to be made under the majority rule. Disregard any tax effect of each transaction.

c. State whether the trust will be terminated by the court and give the reasons for your conclusion.

1. d __ __	7. c __ __	13. b __ __	19. c __ __	25. c __ __
2. c __ __	8. b __ __	14. a __ __	20. c __ __	26. b __ __
3. b __ __	9. b __ __	15. d __ __	21. d __ __	27. d __ __
4. a __ __	10. d __ __	16. c __ __	22. c __ __	
5. d __ __	11. c __ __	17. a __ __	23. b __ __	1st: __/27 = __%
6. a __ __	12. a __ __	18. b __ __	24. a __ __	2nd: __/27 = __%

MULTIPLE-CHOICE ANSWER EXPLANATIONS

B. Administration of Estates

1.   (d)   Per capita means that the heirs who stand in the same degree of relationship to the deceased each receive an equal share of the estate. Per stirpes means that the surviving heirs of their parents represent their parents and take their parent's share in the estate by such representation to be divided among themselves. In this example, the decedent had three children but only two survived him/her. Three grandchildren came from the third child who had died before this will was probated. Since there are five to receive a share, each receives 1/5.

2.   (c)   Per stirpes means that each person takes his/her deceased parent's share. Since he was one of three children, the predeceased son's share of the estate would be 1/3. The two children of the predeceased son would equally divide their parent's share. Therefore, each child of the predeceased son would receive 1/6.

C. Trusts

3.   (b)   A testamentary trust is a trust that takes effect on the death of the settlor. A trustee of a testamentary trust may also serve as the executor of the estate from which the trust was formed without causing a conflict of interest. An inter vivos trust is to take effect while the settlor is still living.

4.   (a)   There are several elements needed to create an express trust. There needs to be a trustor who intentionally creates the trust for a valid trust purpose. Trust property, also called the corpus, must exist at the creation of the trust. There must also be a trustee who holds legal title on behalf of at least one beneficiary. A successor trustee is not necessary to create an express trust.

5.   (d)   A spendthrift trust is a trust created so that the beneficiaries are prohibited from assigning or transferring any unreceived payments to any other party (including creditors).

6.   (a)   The rule against perpetuities limits the duration of a trust to a life in being plus twenty-one years. This rule does not typically apply to charitable trusts because they may involve a beneficial interest being given to other than a person or a life in being plus twenty-one years. The rule against perpetuities does apply to spendthrift trusts, totten trusts, and constructive trusts.

D.   Administration of Trusts

7.   (c)   In a trust, the trustees have fiduciary duties to act in the best interests of the beneficiaries. If a trustee, without express authorization or direction in the trust instrument, invests trust assets in unsecured loans to a cotrustee, this violates fiduciary duties. In particular, this vio-

lates the duty of loyalty to the trust and the beneficiaries because the trustees should not benefit from the trust to the detriment of the beneficiaries. It also violates the duty to invest prudently because the unsecured loan to a cotrustee creates a conflict of interest and may not give the best terms that the beneficiaries could receive.

8.   (b)   A resulting trust can arise in different ways. One way is when the express trust fails and the trustee is still holding the property of the trust. Since there is no beneficiary and the beneficial interest of the trust is not intended for the trustee, the settlor is presumed to get the beneficial interest. Thus, a resulting trust is created. Another way a resulting trust is created is when the trust purpose is fulfilled but the trust still has property in it. The settlor again is presumed to get the beneficial interest. Answers (a), (c), and (d) are incorrect because they include the application of the *cy pres* doctrine. This doctrine applies when the particular trust purpose cannot be carried out, so the court orders that the trust purpose be carried out as nearly as possible under the settlor's intentions.

9.   (b)   The trustee has the implied powers to incur and pay expenses of the trust. The trustee may also sell or lease the trust property under reasonable terms. S/he may also settle claims affecting the trust. The trustee, however, may not borrow from the trust because this is a conflict of interest unless specifically provided for in the trust.

10.   (d)   Jansen is the trustee in this inter vivos trust. As the trustee, s/he owes fiduciary duties to the beneficiary, Jacobs. Basically, the fiduciary duties require the trustee, Jansen, to act in the best interests of the beneficiary rather than his/her own. Jansen should find a new tenant.

11.   (c)   The trustee has the power to do what is reasonably necessary to fulfill the trust's purpose. Unless prohibited in the trust, the trustee may incur and pay management expenses and trust tax preparation fees. The trustee may also sell and purchase trust property. The trustee may not normally accumulate income when this should be paid over to the income beneficiaries.

12.   (a)   In a trust, the trustee owes a fiduciary duty to the beneficiaries. The trustor does not owe fiduciary duties to either the trustee or beneficiaries. Furthermore, neither the trustor nor trustee is owed fiduciary duties by the beneficiaries.

E. Termination of Trusts

13.   (b)   The purpose of a spendthrift trust is to protect the beneficiaries from creditors or from his/her squandering of assets. Once the income beneficiaries die, the trust is no longer needed to achieve its purpose. The trust thus terminates. Even if the grantor dies, the purpose of the spendthrift trust continues. The grantor cannot revoke an irrevocable trust once formed. The purpose of a spendthrift trust is to protect the beneficiaries from their own squandering of the assets.

14. **(a)**   An irrevocable trust which contains no provision for change or termination can be terminated only by a court order.

15. **(d)**   A testamentary trust is one that is created in a will and becomes effective when the grantor dies. The trust was created for the benefit of a **currently childless** person's grandchildren. Because the specific beneficiary(ies) are not identifiable at the time of the grantor's death, a valid trust is not created.

16. **(c)**   Once Hardy dies, the purpose of the trust to pay income to Hardy for life is accomplished. Park's estate then gets all interests in the property, and the trust thus terminates.

F. Allocation between Principal and Income

17. **(a)**   Unless the trust provides differently, principal and income are allocated under the Uniform Principal and Income Act. Under this act, principal includes the entire proceeds, including gains, from the sale of the trust property, such as the office building in this question.

18. **(b)**   Often a trust provides that the income will be paid to one or more beneficiaries for their lives, after which the trust property is turned over to one or more remaindermen. The grantor would get the trust property if there were no designated remaindermen. The trustee manages the trust property for the benefit of the beneficiaries. The trustee does not receive the trust assets when the trust terminates.

19. **(c)**   According to the Uniform Principal and Income Act, insurance proceeds received as a result of damage to trust property are to be allocated to principal; whereas, interest paid on a loan owed by the trust is to be allocated to income.

20. **(c)**   The allocation of trust receipts and expenditures is governed by the Uniform Principal and Income Act. Payable from trust principal are expenses affecting principal (e.g., principal payment of loans). Payable from trust income are ordinary and operating expenses (e.g., taxes).

21. **(d)**   The trust principal includes the $500 cash dividend received before the trust was created even though this would have been allocated to income if it had been received after the trust was created. The trust principal was also given the 500 shares of Pine Corporation common stock. When this stock was sold, the trust principal still included all of the proceeds from the sale of the stock including not only the original cost of $50,000 but also the gain of $2,500.

22. **(c)**   Typically, the interests in a trust are divided between the income and the principal. The principal includes the original trust property or the property into whatever form it gets converted. Permanent or capital improvements are payable from principal. Sidewalk assessments are examples of items payable from principal.

23. **(b)**   An income beneficiary typically receives the profits of the trust principal after the trust begins. These would include royalties, rent, cash dividends, and interest on the trust property. Trust principal includes the original trust property, proceeds (including gains) from the sale of the trust property, insurance received on destruction of property, stock dividends, and stock splits.

24. **(a)**   Gordon receives the income under the trust property for his lifetime, but not the principal amount. The principal would include not only the original trust property (i.e., the commercial building), but also the proceeds from the sale of the property. Any gain on the sale is still considered part of the principal. Since Hall is given the principal upon Gordon's death, Gordon, as the income beneficiary, gets none of the $250,000.

25. **(c)**   In the absence of specific trust terms that define income differently, any allocation between income and principal is governed by the Uniform Principal and Income Act. Under this law, the allocation to principal would include the stock dividend of $6,000 and the proceeds from the sale of bonds of $7,000. The rent received, interest on CD's and municipal bond interest is treated as income rather than principal.

G. Real Estate Investment Trusts

26. **(b)**   Under the Real Estate Investment Trust Act, Congress authorized the formation of Real Estate Investments (REIT) as unincorporated association to invest in real estate. As long as the provisions of the Act are met, the trust is not taxed as a corporation but its ordinary income and capital gains are passed through to the investors. The Act provides that the owners must have limited liability and free transferability of shares. A REIT must be in writing.

27. **(d)**   The REIT has to have ownership dispersed quite broadly. It must have 100 or more certificate holders during each year. Furthermore, five or fewer certificate holders may not own more than 50% of the certificates. The REIT is not taxed as a corporation, but instead capital gains and ordinary income are passed through to the investors.

OTHER OBJECTIVE ANSWERS AND ANSWER EXPLANATIONS

Problem 1

1.   **(I)** Park included a "pour over" transfer of any residuary estate to the trust.

2.   **(I)** Usually the beneficiaries can terminate a trust if all agree. However, this trust was created by Park to protect them from their own mismanagement and to provide for their welfare during Park's life. Termination of the trust would defeat this purpose.

3.   **(I)** The trustees owe fiduciary duties to the beneficiaries, not the reverse.

4.   **(C)** Young and Zack, as trustees, do owe fiduciary duties to the beneficiaries.

5.   **(I)** Typically, trustees may not distribute trust principal but the trustor authorized $10,000 of principal to be paid to each beneficiary annually.

6.   **(I)** The trustor provided that the trustees may pay up to $10,000 to each beneficiary each year. There is no requirement that the money be used for medical or educational needs.

7.   **(C)** A trustee does not have the right to borrow money from the trust unless the trust grants this right.

8.   **(C)** By allowing Zack to borrow the money, Young breached his fiduciary duty.

9.   **(I)** The $15,000 payment exceeded the trustees' authority.

10.   **(C)** The trustees breached their duty to fulfill the terms in the trust.

Problem 2

1.   **(A)** Principal includes the original trust property.

2.   **(A)** Principal includes any income or dividends received before the trust was formed because these are then placed in the trust as the original trust property.

3.   **(B)** Cash dividends and income received after the trust is formed are included in income.

4.   **(A)** Stock dividends are included in principal.

5.   **(A)** Stock splits are simply dividing the original shares into more "pieces" and thus remain as principal.

6.   **(A)** This is the trust property and is treated as principal.

7.   **(C)** Payments of the principal on loans or mortgages come out of principal of the trust.

8.   **(C)** Capital improvements improve the original trust property and thus are payable out of principal.

9.   **(D)** Ordinary repairs and maintenance, unlike permanent or capital improvements, come out of income.

10.   **(B)** Income includes rent as well as prepaid rent.

11.   **(D)** Interest payments come from income.

12.   **(D)** Ordinary operating expenses and insurance premiums are payable out of income.

13.   **(A)** The principal includes the original trust property as well as any proceeds and gains on sale of the original trust property.

14.   **(A)** The principal includes insurance proceeds from destruction of trust property.

15.   **(C)** Litigation costs over the trust property are payable from principal.

Problem 3

1.   **(C)** Statement I is correct. The rule against perpetuities requires that the trust cannot, by its own terms, last longer than a life in being plus twenty-one years. In this case, the trust distributes income to Glenn's children for their lives, then distributes the principal to Glenn's grandchildren. The lives in being are Glenn's children. Even though grandchildren can be born at a later date, and thus are not now necessarily lives in being, they receive the principal before twenty-one years after Glenn's children die. Statement II is correct because it is allowed to let trustees make principal payments to the income beneficiaries when provided for in the trust.

2.   **(A)** When both of Glenn's children die, the purpose of the trust is accomplished. Therefore, the principal is paid to the grandchildren and the trust terminates. Therefore, statement I is correct. Statement II, however, is incorrect because even though the trustees violated their fiduciary duties by not paying the income annually (as provided in the trust), this violation does not terminate the trust.

3.   **(B)** Statement I is incorrect because the trust gave the trustees the power to pay the income beneficiaries out of principal as the trustees determine this is reasonable for the welfare of the income beneficiaries. The $10,000 school tuition payment to one of Glenn's children fits within this power. Statement II is correct because the trustees have a fiduciary duty to act in the best interests of the beneficiaries. They violated this duty when the trust directed them to pay the income annually to the beneficiaries and the trustees failed to do so.

4.   **(B)** Statement I is incorrect and statement II is correct for the same reason. Stock dividends, unlike cash dividends, are allocated to principal and thus remain as part of the trust.

5.   **(D)** Statement I is incorrect because the trust allowed the trustees to make principal payments to the income beneficiaries as the trustees determined this to be reasonable for the welfare of the beneficiaries. Statement II is incorrect because principal should be paid to the grandchild only after the children have died.

ANSWER OUTLINE

Problem 1 Creation of Inter Vivos Spendthrift Trust; Allocation of Receipts and Disbursements between Principal and Income Beneficiaries; Termination of Trust

a. Requirements met for creation of valid inter vivos spendthrift trust

Elements necessary:

- Grantor (Stone)
- Trust res (stocks, bonds, and real estate)
- Intent to create a trust
- Lawful purpose (to provide income for life to relatives with remainder left to charity)
- Trustee (Queen Bank) and separate beneficiaries (specified relatives)

b. Allocation of receipts and disbursements between principal and income

- Incorrect
    Stock sales—entire proceeds to principal
- Incorrect
    Stock dividend—entire amount to principal
- Incorrect
    Bond interest received—$3,000 previously accrued interest to principal, $15,000 earned interest to income
- Correct/incorrect
    Mortgage payment—repayment of mortgage debt to principal, payments deemed to be interest to income

c. Petition to terminate spendthrift trust will fail

- Defeats intent of grantor in establishing trust as long as any income beneficiaries are alive

UNOFFICIAL ANSWER

Problem 1 Creation of Inter Vivos Spendthrift Trust; Allocation of Receipts and Disbursements between Principal and Income Beneficiaries; Termination of Trust

a. The requirements to establish a valid inter vivos spendthrift trust are as follows:

- Grantor
- Trust res
- Intent to create a trust
- Lawful purpose
- Trustee and separate beneficiaries

Stone created a valid spendthrift trust. As grantor, Stone transferred stocks, bonds, and real estate (res) to the trust with a present intent to create the trust for the express lawful purpose of providing income for life to close relatives with the remainder left to charity. Stone designated Queen Bank as trustee.

b.

- Incorrect. The entire proceeds from the sale of the stock should be allocated to principal.
- Incorrect. The entire amount of the stock dividend should be allocated to principal.
- Incorrect. One-third of the semiannual payment of bond interest received on May 1 had already accrued when the trust was created on January 1, 2001. Therefore, $3,000 should be allocated to principal and $15,000 to income.
- Correct/Incorrect. All mortgage payments representing a repayment of a mortgage debt should be allocated to principal. However, if any portion of the payment includes interest on the mortgage, that amount should be allocated to income.

c. The petition to have the trust terminated and distributed will fail. Even though all beneficiaries and remaindermen joined in the petition, termination of the trust, while any of the income beneficiaries is alive, would defeat the intent of the grantor in establishing a spendthrift trust.

MINI OUTLINES

To assist candidates in testing their memory of essential legal principles, we have developed a set of **Mini Outlines.** These can be used after studying each module in depth and as a final review immediately prior to the CPA exam. **In no way are these outlines intended to be a complete coverage of the subject matter.** Candidates should use them to jog their minds by recalling as much information as possible and constructing legal examples to test their comprehension of the subject matter. Using the outlines in this fashion will serve as a barometer (or self-diagnostic tool) of your knowledge. Finally, because the outlines contain only the essential legal principles, **the lettering and numbering of the several levels in the Mini Outlines do not correspond to that found in module outlines.** For those points in the Mini Outlines that you have forgotten, use the index to find the page(s) where that principle is discussed. However, if you are confused about a number of the principles, go back to the module and work through it again.

CONTRACTS (7)[1]

A.   Essential elements of contract[2]
1.   Offer and acceptance
    a.   Offer
       (1) Newspaper advertisement
       (2) Termination of offer
           (a) Death
           (b) Insanity
           (c) Illegality
           (d) Destruction of subject matter
           (e) Rejection
           (f) Revocation
    b.   Acceptance
       (1) Mirror image
       (2) Silence
       (3) Time of acceptance
           (a) Reasonable means rule
       (4) Offeree must intend to accept
       (5) Only offeree may accept
2.   Reality of consent
    a.   Duress
    b.   Fraud
    c.   Undue influence
    d.   Mistake
3.   Consideration
    a.   Legal detriment
       (1) Preexisting legal duty
       (2) Illusory promise
    b.   Bargained for element
    c.   Past consideration
    d.   Moral obligation
    e.   Exceptions
       (1) Promissory estoppel
       (2) Promise to pay debt barred by statute of limitations
       (3) UCC—modification of contract for sale of goods
4.   Capacity
    a.   Minors
       (1) Necessaries
       (2) Contracts for personal property
       (3) Contracts for real property
       (4) Ratification may only occur after reaching majority age
    b.   Incompetent persons
    c.   Intoxicated persons
5.   Legality
    a.   Illegal if contract violates public policy
    b.   Illegal if contract violates a statute
6.   Compliance with Statute of Frauds

    a.   Promise to pay debt of another
       (1) Leading object exception
    b.   An agreement made upon consideration of marriage
       (1) Exception—mutual promises of marriage
    c.   Sale of any interest in land
       (1) Exception—part performance
    d.   An agreement not capable of being performed within one year
    e.   Sale of goods $500 or more
       (1) Exceptions
           (a) Written confirmation between merchants
           (b) Substantial start on specially manufactured goods
           (c) Admission in court
           (d) Part or full performance
    f.   The writing must be signed by the party to be charged
       (1) Can combine two documents together to create sufficient writing
B.   Parol evidence rule
C.   Assignment and delegation
1.   Assignee receives no better rights than the assignor had
D.   Third-party beneficiary contracts
1.   Creditor beneficiary
2.   Donee beneficiary
3.   Incidental beneficiary
E.   Discharge of contractual obligation
1.   By performance
    a.   Doctrine of substantial performance
2.   Objective impossibility
3.   Frustration of purpose
4.   Novation
5.   Breach of contract by other party
    a.   Anticipatory breach (repudiation)
6.   Occurrence or nonoccurrence of contractual condition
7.   Tender of performance
    a.   Tender of payment of money merely stops interest running
F.   Remedies
1.   Damages
    a.   Compensatory
       (1) Must be foreseeable
       (2) Mitigation of damages
    b.   Punitive
    c.   Liquidated

---

[1]   *Numbers in parentheses refer to Modules.*

[2]   *The mnemonic "COLLARS" may be useful in remembering the essential elements of a contract (Consideration, Offer, Legality, Legal capacity, Acceptance, Reality of consent, and Statute of Frauds).*

2. Specific performance
   a. Only available when item is unique
3. Rescission and restitution

G. Statute of limitations
   1. Bars suit if not brought within specified period

SALES (8)

A. Formation of sales contract
   1. Firm offer rule
   2. Battle of forms
   3. Modification of preexisting contract for the sale of goods
   4. Sale of goods $500 or more must be in writing
B. Identification of goods
   1. Buyer's special property interest
C. Passage of title
D. Risk of loss rules
   1. Party with title does not necessarily have risk of loss
   2. Parties can allocate through provision in contract
   3. Breaching party has risk of loss
   4. Carriage contracts
      a. FOB point of shipment
      b. FOB point of destination
   5. Merchant seller transfers risk when goods are delivered to buyer
   6. Nonmerchant seller transfers risk when seller tenders goods
   7. Concerning goods evidenced by negotiable document of title, risk transfers upon proper negotiation of document
   8. In sale on approval (goods purchased for use) risk transfers when buyer approves goods
   9. In sale or return (goods purchased for resale) risk transfers when buyer takes possession
E. Sale of goods by nonowner
   1. Thief
   2. Entrusting situation (deceptive bailment)
   3. Seller has voidable title
   4. Seller has void title
F. Product liability
   1. Negligence
   2. Warranty liability
      a. Warranty of title
         (1) Merchant seller warns against infringement of patent or trademark
      b. Express warranties
      c. Implied warranties
         (1) Merchantability—granted by merchant seller
            (a) Fit for ordinary purposes
            (b) Properly packaged
         (2) Fit for particular purpose
         (3) Disclaimers

            (a) Merchantability—can be oral or written but must contain some form of the word "merchantability"
            (b) Fit for particular purpose—must be in writing but no need for specific language
            (c) Goods sold "as is" or "with all faults" excludes both implied warranties but not the warranty of title
            (d) Offer of inspection by seller disclaims implied warranties concerning all patent defects
   3. Strict liability
      a. Defense—product was not used for intended purpose
G. Seller's rights and remedies for breach of contract
   1. Seller's right to cure
   2. Seller's monetary damages
      a. Difference between market value at the time of tender and contract price plus incidental expenses
      b. Lost profits plus incidental expenses
      c. Full contract price
   3. Seller may refuse to deliver goods unless insolvent buyer is willing to pay cash
   4. Seller may stop goods in transit if buyer is insolvent
   5. Seller may demand return of goods received by insolvent buyer if done within ten days of delivery
   6. Both buyer and seller have right to demand written assurances of performance
H. Buyer's rights and remedies for breach of contract
   1. Right to cover
   2. Right to reject nonconforming goods
      a. Merchant must follow seller's reasonable instructions concerning rejected goods
   3. Buyer may accept nonconforming goods
      a. Buyer may revoke acceptance when
         (1) Defect was hidden
         (2) Guaranteed defect was to be cured and is not
   4. Recover damages
      a. Difference between market value at time buyer should have learned of breach and contract price plus incidental expenses plus consequential damages
I. Statute of limitations is four years
   1. Parties may reduce to one year by agreement

COMMERCIAL PAPER (9)

A. Types
   1. Notes
   2. Drafts
      a. Checks—drawn on a bank and payable on demand
   3. Certificates of deposit
   4. Trade acceptances
B. Requirements of negotiability
   1. Written and signed
   2. Unconditional promise or order to pay sum certain
      a. "Subject to" vs. "in accordance with" another agreement
      b. Limiting payment to particular fund
      c. Cost of collection does not destroy sum certain

      d. Variable interest rates allowed
      e. Foreign currency okay
   3. Payment at a definite time or on demand
      a. Payable on death of someone not payable at definite time
   4. Words of negotiability
   5. Contain no other promise except a promise granting security for the instrument
C. Negotiation
   1. Bearer paper—delivery only
   2. Order paper—delivery and endorsement
   3. Endorsement
      a. Blank vs. special
      b. Qualified

      (1) Destroys secondary (contractual) liability and alters warranty liability
    c. Restrictive

D. Holder in due course
  1. Must be a holder
  2. Gives executed value
    a. Discharge of prior debt
    b. Taking as security for existing debt
  3. Takes in good faith
  4. Takes through proper negotiation prior to knowledge that instrument is overdue or that a defense exists concerning it

E. Shelter provision

F. Defenses
  1. Real
    a. Forgery
      (1) Fictitious payee
      (2) Imposter
    b. Material alteration
    c. Fraud in the execution
    d. Minority
    e. Illegality
    f. Discharge in bankruptcy
    g. Extreme duress

  2. Personal
    a. Misdelivery
    b. Unauthorized completion of an incomplete instrument
    c. Fraud in the inducement
    d. Ordinary duress
    e. Undue influence
    f. Breach of contract
    g. Failure or nonpayment of consideration

G. Liability of parties
  1. Primary
    a. Acceptance by drawee
    b. Certification by bank
  2. Secondary
    a. Presentment
    b. Dishonor
    c. Notice of dishonor
  3. Warranties on transfer
  4. Warranties on presentment for payment or acceptance

H. Banks
  1. Relationship between banks and payee-holder
  2. Stop payment orders
  3. Electronic fund transfers

SECURED TRANSACTIONS (10)

A. Types of collateral
  1. Tangible personal property
    a. Consumer goods
    b. Equipment
    c. Inventory
    d. Farm products
  2. Intangible personal property
    a. Accounts
  3. Documentary collateral
    a. Instruments
    b. Documents of title
  4. The use debtor makes of the property determines the type of collateral

B. Attachment of security interest
  1. Three requirements necessary
    a. There is a security agreement
      (1) When collateral possessed by debtor, security agreement must be in writing, signed by debtor, and contain reasonable description of collateral
      (2) When possessed by secured party, security agreement may be oral
    b. Secured party gives value
    c. Debtor has rights in collateral

C. Perfection of security interest (3 methods)
  1. Filing a financing statement
    a. Valid for all collateral except money and negotiable instruments and securities
    b. Must be signed by debtor
  2. Possession
    a. The only method available concerning perfection in money and negotiable instruments
  3. By attachment only (automatic perfection)
    a. Only available for purchase money security interest in consumer goods

    b. Not available against good-faith purchaser for value who purchases from consumer for consumer use

D. Other issues
  1. After acquired property
  2. Field warehousing
    a. Perfection by possession
  3. Consignments
    a. True consignments
      (1) File a financing statement
    b. Other consignments
      (1) Look for secured transactions

E. Priorities
  1. If both parties perfect by filing, then first to file has priority
  2. If both do not perfect by filing, then first to perfect has priority
  3. Perfected over unperfected
  4. If both unperfected, first to attach
  5. Purchase money security interest has priority over all other security interests if perfected within ten days of delivery except when collateral is inventory
  6. Purchaser in ordinary course of business defeats prior perfected security interest

F. Remedies upon default
  1. Secured party has right to take possession of collateral
    a. By self-help
    b. By judicial process
  2. Secured party may sell collateral
    a. Sale may be public or private
    b. Must be handled in commercially reasonable manner
    c. Debtor can require sale under some conditions
  3. If secured party retains collateral, entire obligation is discharged

BANKRUPTCY (11)

A. Alternatives to bankruptcy relief are sometimes available
  1. Legal proceedings, judgment, levy, attachment, execution
    a. Recover fraudulently conveyed property

  2. Assignment for the benefit of creditors—nonconsenting creditor unaffected
  3. Receiverships
  4. Creditors' composition agreements

B.   Voluntary bankruptcy petition
   1.   Order of relief automatically given upon filing of voluntary petition
   2.   Exempt entities
C.   Involuntary petition
   1.   Fewer than twelve creditors—one can file if owed $10,000 in excess of any security
   2.   Twelve or more creditors—three must sign that are owed $10,000 in excess of security
   3.   Exempt entities
   4.   Order of relief automatically granted if debtor does not contest petition
   5.   If debtor contests, then creditors must show
     a.   Debtor not paying debts as they become due, or
     b.   During the 120 days preceding the filing a custodian was appointed or took possession of substantially all of the property of the debtor
D.   Proceedings and parties
   1.   Always a federal proceeding
   2.   All actions by creditors against debtor are stayed by filing petition, at least temporarily
   3.   First creditors' meeting, notice, time, voting, election of trustee
   4.   Debtor's exempt property
     a.   Federal exemptions
       (1)   State may prohibit selection of federal exemptions

E.   Powers of trustee
   1.   Contest improper claims by creditors
   2.   ·Set aside improper transfers by debtor
     a.   Preferences
       (1)   General
         (a)   Occurred within ninety days of filing petition
         (b)   Debtor's insolvency presumed
         (c)   Payment or granting of security interest concerning antecedent debt
       (2)   Insider preference
         (a)   Within one year of filing petition
         (b)   Debtor's insolvency is not presumed
     b.   Fraudulent conveyances
       (1)   Transfer with intent to delay, hinder, or defraud creditors
       (2)   Transfer of property by debtor for less than reasonable value
       (3)   Occurred within one year of filing petition
F.   Priority of claims
G.   Nondischargeable debts
H.   Acts that bar discharge of any debts
I.   Reorganizations—Chapter 11
   1.   Can be voluntary or involuntary proceedings
   2.   Court supervised rehabilitation plan
J.   Debt adjustment plans—Chapter 13
   1.   Only a voluntary proceeding is available

DEBTOR-CREDITOR RELATIONSHIPS (12)

A.   Rights and duties of debtors and creditors
   1.   Mechanic's lien is used to secure payment of debts for services or materials to improve real property
   2.   Artisan's lien is a possessory lien on personal property
     a.   Generally has priority as long as retains possession
   3.   Attachment and garnishment accomplished by creditors to pay off debt
   4.   Court-ordered execution to sell off debtor's assets to pay off debts
   5.   Composition agreement with creditors based on contract law
   6.   Homestead exemption allowed under state laws
   7.   There are various restrictions on creditors, sellers, and lenders under various acts
   8.   Laws enacted that protect rights for credit card holders and to a lessor extent for debit card holders
B.   Guarantor (surety) is party who promises to be answerable for debt or default of another
C.   Formation of guaranty (suretyship) contracts
   1.   Must meet essential elements of a contract
     a.   Consideration
       (1)   If guarantor's promise is contemporaneous with primary contract, separate consideration not needed
     b.   Compliance with Statute of Frauds since promise to answer for debt of another
       (1)   Exception for "main purpose" rule
         (a)   When guarantor's promise is made for own benefit
D.   Creditor's rights
   1.   Against debtor
     a.   Where debtor owes more than one debt, to apply payment to debt of creditor's choice
       (1)   Unless debtor identifies the debt to which payment should apply
   2.   Against surety
     a.   To proceed immediately upon debtor's default
   3.   Against collateral

     a.   If debtor pays, collateral must be returned
     b.   Creditor may resort to collateral (held by surety or creditor) to satisfy debt
       (1)   If insufficient, may proceed against debtor or guarantor (surety) for deficiency
       (2)   If in excess of debt, excess amount must be returned to debtor
     c.   Not required to resort to collateral
       (1)   May instead proceed immediately against guarantor or debtor
E.   Guarantor's and surety's rights
   1.   Before pays creditor
     a.   Exoneration
   2.   After pays creditor
     a.   Right of reimbursement
     b.   Subrogation to creditor's rights
F.   Guarantor's and surety's defenses
   1.   Contractual defenses derived from debtor against creditor
     a.   Except debtor's personal defenses
       (1)   Death or insolvency of debtor
       (2)   Lack of capacity of debtor
   2.   Guarantor's and surety's own contractual defenses such as fraud, duress, setoffs, etc.
   3.   Acts of creditor materially affecting guarantor performance
     a.   Release of debtor
     b.   Release of guarantor
     c.   Release or impairment of collateral held by creditor
       (1)   Guarantor's liability reduced only to extent of collateral released or impaired
     d.   Tender of performance and refusal by creditor
     e.   Binding material alteration or variance of guaranty agreement without consent of guarantor
       (1)   Substitution of debtors
       (2)   Changes in debtor's duties
       (3)   Variance in amount, place, or time of debtor's payment

G. Following are not defenses of guarantor (surety)
   1. Death of debtor
   2. Insolvency of debtor
   3. Lack of notice given to surety
      a. Unless conditional guarantor
   4. Creditor does not resort to collateral
H. Cosureties (coguarantors)
   1. When more than one promises to answer for the debt of another, each one
      a. Is bound to answer for same debt

   b. Shares in burden upon debtor's default
   2. Cosureties (coguarantors) are jointly and severally liable
   3. Each is liable for its proportionate share
   4. Each entitled to share in collateral pledged
      a. In proportion to each's liability
   5. Right of contribution exists among them
   6. Discharge or release of one cosurety (coguarantor)
      a. Releases those remaining to extent of the released party's pro rata share of liability

AGENCY (13)

A. Agent vs. independent contractor
   1. Employee (servant)
   2. Subagent
B. Types of principals
   1. Disclosed
   2. Partially disclosed
   3. Undisclosed
C. Creation
   1. By agreement
   2. Estoppel
   3. Ratification
D. Contractual liability
   1. Principal is liable for contracts agent enters into within agent's scope of authority
      a. Express authority
      b. Implied authority
      c. Apparent authority
   2. Agent's liability on contracts entered into on behalf of principal
      a. If within scope of authority and
         (1) Representing disclosed principal, agent is not liable on contract
         (2) Representing undisclosed principal, agent is liable

   b. If acting outside scope of authority, then agent is only partly liable on contract
E. Tort liability
   1. Principal is liable if agent commits tort within agent's scope of employment
   2. Agent is also liable for commission of torts
F. Termination of relationship
   1. The power vs. the right to terminate
      a. Agency coupled with an interest
   2. By operation of law
      a. Death or insanity of either party
      b. Bankruptcy of principal
      c. Subject of agreement becomes illegal
   3. By acts of the parties
      a. Unilateral action by either agent or principal
      b. By mutual consent
      c. Expiration of agreement
      d. Principal must give notice of the termination
         (1) Notice by publication to all who knew of the relationship but had not dealt with agent
         (2) Actual notice to all who had previously dealt with agent

PARTNERSHIPS AND JOINT VENTURES (14)

A. General partnership
   1. Characteristics
      a. Normally not a separate entity from general partners
      b. Common law allows formation; no need for statutory authorization
      c. Easy to create
      d. Partners have unlimited liability
   2. Creation
      a. By agreement
      b. By estoppel
      c. Is presumed if parties are sharing net profits
   3. Partnership property
      a. Owned by partners as tenants in partnership
         (1) Surviving partners have right to specific partnership property
         (2) Heirs of deceased partner have no claim to specific partnership property
   4. Partner's partnership interest
      a. Is considered personal property
      b. Can be assigned without consent of other partners
         (1) Does not cause dissolution
         (2) Assignee is not a substitute partner
         (3) Assignee receives assigning partner's share of profits
   5. Partner's rights
      a. To share in profits
      b. To equal voice in management
         (1) Ordinary decisions by majority vote

         (2) Unanimous consent needed for certain acts
      c. To inspect books
      d. To return of capital contribution
      e. No right to salary
      f. No right to interest on capital contribution
   6. Liability to third parties
      a. Partners are agents of copartners
         (1) Partners are jointly and severally liable for torts committed by copartners within scope of partnership business
         (2) Partners are jointly liable for contracts entered into within copartners' authority
   7. Termination
      a. Dissolution occurs every time makeup of partnership changes
         (1) Admission of new partners
            (a) New partner only liable to extent of capital contribution concerning existing partnership debts
         (2) Withdrawal of partner
            (a) Withdrawing partner must give notice of withdrawal to terminate further liability
            (b) Priorities upon winding up
         (1) Creditors
         (2) To partners for loans
         (3) To partners for capital contribution
         (4) To partners for share of profits
      b. Marshalling of assets

B. Limited partnerships
1. Need state statutory authority to create
2. Must have at least one general partner
3. Limited partner's liability is limited to capital contribution
4. Limited partner cannot take part in management
5. Limited partner's name may not be used in name of firm
6. Limited partner has right to an accounting
7. Limited partner has right to inspect books
8. Priorities on dissolution
9. Master limited partnership
C. Joint ventures
1. Characteristics

      a. Association of two or more persons for single business undertaking
      b. Unlike partnership which is formed to conduct ongoing business
      c. Corporations can be joint venturers
2. Each joint venturer has limited power to bind others
3. Rights, duties, and liabilities
      a. Fiduciary duty
      b. Right to participate in management
      c. Unlimited liability
      d. Liability for negligence
      e. Tax treatment similar to partnership
D. Limited Liability Companies
E. Limited Liability Partnerships

CORPORATIONS (15)

A. Types
1. De jure
2. De facto
3. Domestic
4. Foreign
      a. Doing business outside state of incorporation requires permission from foreign state
B. Characteristics
1. Separate entity
      a. Shareholders have limited liability
      b. Piercing corporate veil
2. Must have state statutory authorization to create
3. Duration may be perpetual
4. Expensive to create
C. Creation
1. Promoters
      a. Corporations must adopt promoter's contracts before being liable
      b. Promoter remains liable even after adoption of contracts by corporation
2. Preincorporation stock subscriptions
      a. Subscribers unable to revoke for six months
3. Articles of Incorporation
D. Types of shares
1. Treasury stock—may be sold at less than par value
2. Watered stock
E. Directors
1. Must act as a board
2. Unable to vote by proxy
3. No right to salary for services
4. Individual director is not agent of corporation
5. Declaration of dividends within directors' discretion
      a. Declaration of dividends is illegal if impairs capital
         (1) Payable out of surplus only

6. Liable for negligence but not for bad business judgment
7. Directors may contract with corporation
F. Officers
1. Agents of corporation
2. Indemnification of officers for expenses incurred in legal actions arising from officers' representation of corporation
G. Shareholders
1. Right to transfer shares
2. Preemptive rights
3. Right to vote
      a. By proxy
      b. On amendments of Articles of Incorporation but not necessarily amendments of the bylaws
      c. For election of directors
      d. On fundamental changes (mergers, consolidations)
      e. Voting trusts
4. Engage in derivative lawsuit
5. Right to inspect corporate books
6. Right to fair market value of shares from corporation if fundamental change is proposed
H. Corporate powers
1. Corporation may become partner
2. Corporation may lend money to employees but not to directors without shareholder approval
3. Corporation may not act as accommodating endorser
4. Corporation may only act as a surety if engaged in such business
5. Ultra vires contracts
I. Fundamental changes
1. Mergers
2. Consolidations
3. Must have majority shareholder approval
J. Dissolution

FEDERAL SECURITIES ACTS (16)

A. Blue-sky laws—State security laws
B. 1933 Act
1. Registration statement and prospectus must be approved by SEC before offer to sell or sale of a security in interstate commerce
      a. A "Plain English" rule
      b. Security includes:
         (1) Stocks
         (2) Bonds
         (3) Limited partnership interest
         (4) Investment contracts where profits are to come from the efforts of others

         (a) Shares in a citrus growing farm
         (b) Shares in a cattle raising ranch
      c. Applies primarily to original issues of securities
      d. Purpose of Act
         (1) To allow investor to make informed investment decision
         (2) Not to tell investor that security is a good buy
      e. Exempt securities
         (1) Banks
         (2) Railroads

(3) Commercial paper—with a maturity of nine months or less

(4) Charitable organizations

(5) Insurance contracts

(6) Intrastate issues

(7) Small issuances up to 1,500,000

   (a) Notification of filing is required

  f. Exempt transactions

(1) Stock split

(2) Stock dividend

(3) Sales by person other than issuer, underwriter, or dealer

   (a) Controlling person must register sale (e.g., director owning 10% of stock)

(4) Regulation D—private placement of stock

   (a) Purchasers must buy for investment purposes

  g. Registration statement

(1) Signers, directors of issuer, underwriters, and experts are liable for omission or misrepresentation

   (a) Investor does not have to prove reliance on misrepresentation

   (b) CPA has burden of proving due diligence defense

  h. Statute of limitations—one year from the time the misrepresentation should have been discovered but never longer than three years from the sale of the security

C. 1934 Act

  1. Reporting requirements

  2. Proxy solicitations

PROFESSIONAL RESPONSIBILITIES (17)

A. Ethical, consulting and tax responsibilities

  1. Code of professional conduct

    a. Principles and rules (with interpretations and rulings)

    b. Principles and overall

(1) Minimum levels of conduct

(2) All members observe principles of objectivity, independence and due care

   (a) But members not in practice are not independent

   (b) Members in practice must be independent for attest services

    c. Code—rules (with interpretations and rulings)

(1) No direct or material indirect financial interest in a client

(2) Spouse and dependents same as CPA's investment

(3) Confidential relationship with client, not privileged communication

(4) No false, misleading or deceptive advertising

(5) Contingent fees disallowed

  2. Statements on Standards for Consulting Services (SSCS)

  3. Responsibilities of CPAs in business and industry, and in the public sector

B. Common law liability to clients

  1. Liability for breach of contract

    a. Based on accountant's failure to carry out contract terms

(1) Accountant's duty to perform cannot be delegated

(2) Client must not interfere with accountant's performance

(3) If major breach, accountant not entitled to compensation

    b. Accountant not under duty to discover fraud (irregularities)

(1) Unless accountant's negligence prevents discovery

(2) Unless engaged in special purpose defalcation audit and lack of reasonable professional care prevents discovery

  2. Liability for negligence

    a. Based on accountant's failure to exercise due professional care

(1) Following GAAS and GAAP does not conclusively prove absence of negligence

    b. Client is contributorily negligent if client restricted accountant's investigation

(1) May limit accountant's liability

  3. Liability for fraud

    a. Actual fraud

(1) Intentional act or omission designed to deceive

    b. Constructive fraud

(1) Gross negligence with reckless disregard for truth

C. Common law liability to third parties

  1. Accountant is liable to

    a. Third-party primary beneficiary for ordinary negligence

    b. Foreseen third party—courts are split

    c. All third parties for fraud or gross negligence

  2. Third party must prove

    a. Material misstatement or omission on financial statements

    b. Reliance on financial statements

    c. Damages resulted from such reliance

D. Statutory liability to third parties—Securities Act of 1933

  1. Act requires filing of certified financial statements with SEC

  2. Any purchaser of security may sue accountant

  3. Purchaser establishes prima facie case if s/he proves

    a. Material misstatement or omission on financial statements

    b. Damages were incurred

(1) Measured by difference between purchase price and market value at time of suit

    c. Need not prove reliance on financial statements

  4. Accountant may avoid liability by proving

    a. Due diligence

(1) After reasonable investigation accountant had reasonable grounds to believe statements were true

    b. Purchaser knew financial statements were incorrect when s/he bought stock

    c. Loss caused by factor other than misstatement or omission on financial statements

E. Statutory liability to third parties—Securities Exchange Act of 1934

  1. Accountant's liability arises from annual report containing certified financial statements

  2. Any purchaser or seller of registered security may sue accountant

  3. Third party must prove

a. Material misstatement or omission on financial statements
b. Accountant's intent to deceive (scienter)
c. Reliance on financial statements
d. Damages resulted from such reliance
4. Accountant may avoid liability if s/he acted in good faith

F. Criminal liability
1. Guilty of "willful and knowing" violation
a. Federal statutes
(1) Securities Act of 1933
(2) Securities Exchange Act of 1934
(3) Internal Revenue Code
b. State statutes

G. Other potential liability of accountant from
1. Discovery of subsequent events
H. Privileged communications
1. Preserves confidentiality of communications between accountant and client
2. Does not exist at common law
a. Must be created by statute
3. Privilege protects accountant from being required to testify in court
I. Working papers
1. Owned by accountant
2. Must be kept confidential
3. Must relinquish on an enforceable subpoena

REGULATION OF EMPLOYMENT AND ENVIRONMENT (18)

A. Federal Social Security Act
1. Provides financing for several social insurance programs
a. Old-age, survivor's, and disability coverage
b. Hospital insurance coverage (Medicare)
c. Unemployment insurance coverage
2. Coverage under the Act is mandatory
a. Must be an employee
b. Compensation received must be wages
3. Federal Insurance Contributions Act
a. Imposes social security tax on wages
b. Imposes an equal tax rate on both employee and employer
c. Employer's responsibility to withhold, remit, and match employees' tax
4. Self-Employment Contributions Act
a. Imposes social security tax on self-employment income
b. A higher tax rate is imposed than under FICA
5. Unemployment insurance
a. Employer must pay both federal and state unemployment tax
b. Employer entitled to credit against federal tax for state tax paid
c. Benefits available to eligible persons as governed by state law
6. Old age, survivor's, and disability insurance benefits
a. Availability depends upon attainment of insured status
(1) Based on required length of working time
b. Amount of benefits depends upon
(1) Average monthly earnings
(2) Relationship of beneficiary to employee
7. Income tax considerations
a. Benefits received are tax-free
b. Employer's portion of social security tax is deductible from gross income/ Employee receives **no** deduction

B. Workers' Compensation Acts
1. Employer liable for injuries sustained by employee that arise in the course of employment
2. Employer assumes liability in exchange for employee's forfeiture of right to sue employer for damages
3. Removes employer's common law defenses
a. Assumption of risk
b. Fellow servant doctrine
c. Contributory negligence
4. Employee is entitled to benefits without regard to fault
a. Employee's negligence or gross negligence does not bar recovery
b. Employee may sue in common law if employer fails to provide worker's compensation insurance

C. Torts of employee
D. Employee safety—OSHA
E. Employment discrimination
F. Federal Fair Labor Standards Act
G. Environmental Regulation
1. Common Law
2. Federal Statutory Laws
a. EPA
b. National Environmental Policy Act
c. Clean Air Act and amendments
d. Clean Water Act
e. Safe Drinking Water Act
f. Oil Pollution Act
g. Noise Control Act
h. Resource Conservation and Recovery Act
i. Toxic Substances Control Act
j. Federal Insecticide, Fungicide, and Rodenticide Act
k. Federal Environmental Pesticide Control Act
l. CERCLA
m. Ozone layer protection
n. Nuclear Waste Policy Act
o. Endangered Species Act
3. Environmental Compliance Audits

PROPERTY (19)

A. Fixtures
1. Trade fixtures
B. Bailments
C. Intellectual property and computer technology rights
D. Present interest in real property
1. Fee simple
2. Life estate
E. Future interest
1. Remainder
2. Reversion

F. Concurrent ownership interest
1. Joint tenancy—right of survivorship
2. Tenancy in common—deceased tenant's share passes by his/her estate
3. Tenancy by the entirety
G. Nonpossessory interests
H. Sale of land
1. Contract
a. Must be in writing
b. Buyer is entitled to marketable title

    c. Buyer has risk of loss before deed is transferred
    d. Does not transfer title to buyer
    e. Specific performance is possible remedy for breach
  2. Deeds
    a. Warranty—make various guarantees (e.g., title, quiet enjoyment, etc.)
    b. Bargain and sale
    c. Quitclaim
    d. Must be delivered before title passes to buyer
    e. Recording protects buyer against subsequent good-faith purchasers
      (1) Notice type recording statute
      (2) Race-notice type recording statute
  3. Mortgages
    a. Must be in writing
    b. Recording protects mortgagee against subsequent purchasers
    c. Mortgagee's foreclosure rights upon default
    d. Equity of redemption
    e. Buyer who "assumes" mortgage has personal liability
    f. Buyer who purchases "subject to" mortgage has no personal liability
  4. Deeds of trust
    a. Like mortgages, but a judicial proceeding can be avoided upon default
    b. No redemption by mortgagor
  5. Land installment contract sales
    a. Allows seller to keep money paid and property upon default unless inequitable
I. Title Insurance
  1. Insures against loss due to defect of good title
  2. Title insurance company liable for damages due to title defects
J. Adverse possession
  1. Requirements
    a. Open
    b. Notorious
    c. Hostile
    d. Actual
    e. Continuous
K. Easement by prescription
L. Lessor—lessee
  1. Lease may be oral if less than one year
  2. Various types of leaseholds (e.g., period to period, lease for years)
  3. Lessor's rights and duties
  4. Lessee's right to assign sublease

INSURANCE (20)

A. Insurance contract
  1. Offer and acceptance
  2. Representations
    a. Statements of fact not included as part of policy
    b. Only affect policy when material misrepresentation occurs
  3. Warranties
    a. Statements of fact included in the policy
    b. Even immaterial breaches of warranty release insurer from liability
  4. Statute of Frauds does not require writing
B. Property insurance
  1. Insurable interest
    a. Must be present at time of loss
    b. Following have insurable interest in property:
      (1) Owners
      (2) Partners
      (3) Secured creditors
      (4) Lessees
      (5) Mortgagees
      (6) Bailees
      (7) Identification of goods gives buyer insurable interest
  2. Valued or unvalued policy
  3. Can insure against
    a. Own negligence
    b. Other party's negligence
    c. Other party's intentional acts
    d. But not against own intentional acts
    e. Hostile fires
    f. But not friendly fires
  4. Coinsurance clause
    a. Know—usually tested
    b. Does not apply when there is total destruction of property
  5. Pro rata clause
  6. Loss payable clause
  7. Insurer's right of subrogation

TRUSTS AND ESTATES (21)

A. Administration of an estate
  1. Testate—will is present
  2. Intestate—property passes by intestate succession statutes
  3. Executor and administrator
    a. Right to compensation
    b. Duties and liabilities
  4. Spouse's rights under dower and statutory share
  5. Creditors' rights concerning decedent's estate
  6. Tax considerations—particularly marital deduction
B. Trust
  1. Creation
    a. By implication
      (1) Resulting trust
      (2) Constructive trust
    b. By express intent
  2. Parties
    a. Trustee
      (1) Occupies fiduciary relationship
      (2) Has legal title to property
      (3) Duties and liabilities
        (a) Reasonable prudent investor standard applied to performance of the trustee
    b. Beneficiary—has beneficial title
      (1) Income
      (2) Principal
  3. Types of trust
    a. Inter vivos
    b. Testamentary
    c. Charitable
    d. Constructive trust
  4. Allocation of expenses and receipts to income and principal beneficiaries—very important—know
  5. Tax considerations
C. Real Estate Investment Trusts
  1. Must comply with SEC securities registration laws
  2. Tax considerations

EXAMINATION IN BUSINESS LAW AND PROFESSIONAL RESPONSIBILITIES

NOTE TO CANDIDATES: *Information for Uniform CPA Examination Candidates*, published by the AICPA, states that candidates should allocate the total time for each examination section to the questions for that section in proportion to the point value given for the question. Thus, candidates should begin each examination session by calculating the estimated time to be spent on each question.

		Point Value
All questions are required:		
No. 1		60
No. 2		10
No. 3		10
No. 4		10
No. 5		10
Total		100

Number 1

Select the **best** answer for each of the following items.

1. A CPA purchased stock in a client corporation and placed it in a trust as an educational fund for the CPA's minor child. The trust securities were not material to the CPA but were material to the child's personal net worth. Would the independence of the CPA be considered to be impaired with respect to the client?

a. Yes, because the stock would be considered a direct financial interest and, consequently, materiality is **not** a factor.

b. Yes, because the stock would be considered an indirect financial interest that is material to the CPA's child.

c. No, because the CPA would **not** be considered to have a direct financial interest in the client.

d. No, because the CPA would **not** be considered to have a material indirect financial interest in the client.

2. A violation of the profession's ethical standards would most likely have occurred when a CPA

a. Purchased a bookkeeping firm's practice of monthly write-ups for a percentage of fees received over a three-year period.

b. Made arrangements with a bank to collect notes issued by a client in payment of fees due.

c. Named Smith formed a partnership with two other CPAs and uses "Smith & Co." as the firm name.

d. Issued an unqualified opinion on the 2001 financial statements when fees for the 2000 audit were unpaid.

3. One of the elements necessary to hold a CPA liable to a client for conducting an audit negligently is that the CPA

a. Acted with scienter or guilty knowledge.

b. Was a fiduciary of the client.

c. Failed to exercise due care.

d. Executed an engagement letter.

4. Brown & Co., CPAs, issued an unqualified opinion on the financial statements of its client, King Corp. Based on the strength of King's financial statements, Safe Bank loaned King $500,000. Brown was unaware that Safe would receive a copy of the financial statements or that they would be used in obtaining a loan by King. King defaulted on the loan.

If Safe commences an action for negligence against Brown, and Brown is able to prove that it conducted the audit in conformity with GAAS, Brown will

a. Be liable to Safe because Safe relied on the financial statements.

b. Be liable to Safe because the Statute of Frauds has been satisfied.

c. Not be liable to Safe because there is a conclusive presumption that following GAAS is the equivalent of acting reasonably and with due care.

d. Not be liable to Safe because there was a lack of privity of contract.

5. In general, the third party (primary) beneficiary rule as applied to a CPA's legal liability in conducting an audit is relevant to which of the following causes of action against a CPA?

	Fraud	*Constructive fraud*	*Negligence*
a.	Yes	Yes	No
b.	Yes	No	No
c.	No	Yes	Yes
d.	No	No	Yes

6. In a common law action against an accountant, the lack of privity is a viable defense if the plaintiff

a. Is a creditor of the client who sues the accountant for negligence.

b. Can prove the presence of gross negligence that amounts to a reckless disregard for the truth.

c. Is the accountant's client.

d. Bases his action upon fraud.

7. In which of the following statements concerning a CPA firm's action is scienter or its equivalent absent?

a. Actual knowledge of fraud.

b. Performance of substandard auditing procedures.

c. Reckless disregard for the truth.

d. Intent to gain monetarily by concealing fraud.

8. To recover in a common law action based upon fraud against a CPA with regard to an audit of financial statements, the plaintiff must prove among other things

a. Privity of contract.

b. Unavailability of any other cause of action.

c. That there was a sale or purchase of securities within a six-month period that resulted in a loss.

d. Reliance on the financial statements.

9. If a stockholder sues a CPA for common law fraud based upon false statements contained in the financial statements audited by the CPA, which of the following is the CPA's best defense?

    a.   The CPA did **not** financially benefit from the alleged fraud.

    b.   The contributory negligence of the client.

    c.   The stockholder lacks privity to sue.

    d.   The false statements were immaterial.

10. A CPA was engaged by Jackson & Wilcox, a small retail partnership, to examine its financial statements. The CPA discovered that due to other commitments, the engagement could not be completed on time. The CPA, therefore, unilaterally delegated the duty to Vincent, an equally competent CPA. Under these circumstances, which of the following is true?

    a.   The duty to perform the audit engagement is delegable in that it is determined by an objective standard.

    b.   If Jackson & Wilcox refuses to accept Vincent because of a personal dislike of Vincent by one of the partners, Jackson & Wilcox will be liable for breach of contract.

    c.   Jackson & Wilcox must accept the delegation in that Vincent is equally competent.

    d.   The duty to perform the audit engagement is nondelegable and Jackson & Wilcox need not accept Vincent as a substitute if they do not wish to do so.

11. On July 1, 2001, Kent purchased a common stock of Salem Corp. in an offering subject to the Securities Act of 1933. Mane & Co., CPAs, rendered an unqualified opinion on the financial statements of Salem that were included in Salem's registration statement filed with the SEC on March 1, 2001. Kent has commenced an action against Mane based on the Securities Act of 1933 provisions dealing with omissions of facts required to be stated in the registration statement. Which of the following elements of a cause of action under the Securities Act of 1933 must be proved by Kent?

    a.   Kent relied upon Mane's opinion.

    b.   Kent was the initial purchaser of the stock and gave value for it.

    c.   Mane's omission was material.

    d.   Mane acted negligently or fraudulently.

12. Josephs & Paul is a growing medium-sized partnership of CPAs. One of the firm's major clients is considering offering its stock to the public. This will be the firm's first client to go public. Which of the following is true with respect to this engagement?

    a.   If the client is a service corporation, the Securities Act of 1933 will not apply.

    b.   If the client is not going to be listed on an organized exchange, the Securities Exchange Act of 1934 will not apply.

    c.   The Securities Act of 1933 imposes important additional potential liability on Josephs & Paul.

    d.   As long as Josephs & Paul engages exclusively in intrastate business, the federal securities laws will not apply.

13. A requirement of a private action to recover damages for violation of the registration requirements of the Securities Act of 1933 is that

    a.   The securities can be purchased from an underwriter.

    b.   A registration statement has been filed.

    c.   The issuer or other defendants commit either negligence or fraud in the sale of the securities.

    d.   The plaintiff has acquired the securities in question.

14. The accountant-client privilege is recognized

    a.   Only if the action involved is in federal court.

    b.   Where a state statute has been enacted creating such a privilege.

    c.   By virtue of the common law in the majority of states.

    d.   In the majority of states as a result of legislative enactment and court adoption.

15. Where a client accepts the services of an accountant without an agreement concerning payment there is

    a.   An implied in fact contract.

    b.   An implied in law contract.

    c.   An express contract.

    d.   No contract.

16. Red entered into a contract with Maple on behalf of Gem, a disclosed principal. Red exceeded his authority in entering into the contract. In order for Gem to successfully ratify the contract with Maple,

    a.   Gem must expressly communicate his intention to be bound.

    b.   Gem must have knowledge of the relevant material facts concerning the transaction.

    c.   Red must not have been a minor.

    d.   Red must have acted reasonably and in Gem's best interest.

17. Jim, an undisclosed principal, authorized Rick to act as his agent in securing a contract for the purchase of some plain white paper. Rick, without informing Sam that he was acting on behalf of a principal, entered into a contract with Sam to purchase the paper. If Jim repudiates the contract with Sam, which of the following is correct?

    a.   Rick will be released from his contractual obligations to Sam if he disclosed Jim's identity.

    b.   Upon learning that Jim is the principal, Sam may elect to hold either Jim or Rick liable on the contract.

    c.   Rick may not enforce the contract against Sam.

    d.   Sam may obtain specific performance, compelling Jim to perform on the contract.

18. Notice to third parties is **not** required to terminate a disclosed general agent's apparent authority when the

    a.   Principal has died.

    b.   Principal revokes the agent's authority.

    c.   Agent renounces the agency relationship.

    d.   Agency relationship terminates as a result of the fulfillment of its purpose.

19. Unless otherwise provided for in the partnership agreement, the assignment of a partner's interest in a general partnership will

    a.   Result in the termination of the partnership.

    b.   Not affect the assigning partner's liability to third parties for obligations existing at the time of the assignment.

c. Transfer the assigning partner's rights in specific partnership property to the assignee.

d. Transfer the assigning partner's right to bind the partnership to contracts to the assignee.

20. Daniels, Beal, and Wade agreed to form the DBW Partnership to engage in the import-export business. They had been lifelong friends and had engaged in numerous business dealings with each other. It was orally agreed that Daniels would contribute $20,000, Beal $15,000, and Wade $5,000. It was also orally agreed that in the event the venture proved to be a financial disaster all losses above the amounts of capital contributed would be assumed by Daniels and that he would hold his fellow partners harmless from any additional amount lost. The partnership was consummated with a handshake and the contribution of the agreed upon capital by the partners. There were no other express agreements.

Under these circumstances, which of the following is correct?

a. Profits are to be divided in accordance with the relative capital contributions of each partner.

b. Profits are to be divided equally.

c. The partnership is a nullity because the agreement is **not** contained in a signed writing.

d. Profits are to be shared in accordance with the relative time each devotes to partnership business during the year.

21. Which of the following statements is correct regarding a limited partnership?

a. The general partner must make a capital contribution.

b. It can only be created pursuant to a statute providing for the formation of limited partnerships.

c. It can be created with limited liability for all partners.

d. At least one general partner must also be a limited partner.

22. In the absence of specific provision in a general partnership agreement, partnership losses will be allocated

a. Equally among the partners irrespective of the allocation of partnership profits.

b. In the same manner as partnership profits.

c. In proportion to the partners' capital contributions.

d. In proportion to the partners' capital contributions and outstanding loan balances.

23. Which of the following receipts should be allocated by a trustee exclusively to income?

a. A stock dividend.

b. An extraordinary year-end cash dividend.

c. A liquidating dividend whether in complete or partial liquidation.

d. A stock split.

24. Assuming that a given trust indenture is silent on the point, the trustee has certain rights and duties as a matter of law. The trustee

a. Has a fiduciary duty to the trust but **not** to the beneficiaries.

b. Is **not** entitled to commissions unless so provided.

c. Can elect to terminate the trust as long as the beneficiaries unanimously concur.

d. Must act in a competent, nonnegligent manner, or he may face removal.

25. Which of the following is correct regarding foreclosure of a purchase money mortgage by judicial sale of the property?

a. The mortgagor has the right to any remaining sale proceeds after the mortgagee is paid.

b. The purchaser at the sale is liable for any deficiency owed the mortgagee.

c. The court must confirm **any** price received at the sale.

d. The mortgagor can never be liable for a deficiency owed the mortgagee.

26. The Social Security Act provides for the imposition of taxes and disbursement of benefits. Which of the following is a correct statement regarding these taxes and disbursements?

a. Only those who have contributed to Social Security are eligible for benefits.

b. As between an employer and his employee, the tax rates are the same.

c. A deduction for federal income tax purposes is allowed the employee for Social Security taxes paid.

d. Social Security payments are includable in gross income for federal income tax purposes unless they are paid for disability.

27. With respect to federal unemployment taxes and unemployment compensation, which of the following statements is correct?

a. The Federal Unemployment Tax Act requires both the employer and employee to make payments to an approved state unemployment fund.

b. Federal unemployment taxes are offset by a credit equal to the amount the employer contributes to an approved state unemployment fund.

c. Unemployment compensation received in excess of the employer's contributions is, in all cases, fully includable in the recipient's gross income for federal income tax purposes.

d. Payments made by a corporate employer for federal unemployment taxes are deductible as a business expense for federal income tax purposes.

28. Which of the following parties can be held liable under the Comprehensive Environmental Compensation and Liability Act for the clean up costs of dangerous chemicals on land?

I. The current owners who did not contribute to the hazardous substances problem on this land.

II. Past owner of five years ago who did contribute to the hazardous substances problem.

III. Person who transported the hazardous substance to the land six years ago at the request of the past owner.

a. I only.

b. I and II only.

c. II and III only.

d. I, II, and III.

29. Securities available under a private placement made pursuant to Regulation D of the Securities Act of 1933

    a.   Must be sold to less than twenty-five nonaccredited investors.

    b.   **Cannot** be the subject of an immediate reoffering to the public.

    c.   **Cannot** be subject to the payment of commissions.

    d.   Must be sold to accredited institutional investors.

30. One of the clients of Sherman & Pryor, CPAs, plans to form a limited partnership and offer to the public in interstate commerce 2,000 limited partnership units at $5,000 per unit. Which of the following is correct?

    a.   The dollar amount in question is sufficiently small so as to provide absolute exemption from the Securities Act of 1933.

    b.   The Securities Act of 1933 requires a registration despite the fact that the client is **not** selling stock and the purchasers have limited liability.

    c.   Under the Securities Act of 1933, Sherman & Pryor has **no** responsibility for financial statements since the limited partnership is a new entity.

    d.   Sherman & Pryor may disclaim any liability under the federal securities acts by an unambiguous, boldfaced disclaimer of liability on its audit report.

31. Which of the following provisions of the Securities Exchange Act of 1934 applies despite the fact that a corporation's securities are exempt from registration?

    a.   The antifraud provisions.

    b.   The provisions dealing with the filing of periodic and annual reports.

    c.   The proxy provisions.

    d.   The provisions imposing internal controls.

32. The Securities Exchange Act of 1934

    a.   Applies exclusively to issuers whose securities are listed on an organized stock exchange.

    b.   Has **no** application to issuers who are **not** required to register.

    c.   Imposes additional requirements on those issuers who must register and report.

    d.   Requires registration and reporting by all issuers with $2 million or more of assets or which have 1,000 or more shareholders.

33. Which of the following facts will result in an offering of securities being exempt from registration under the Securities Act of 1933?

    a.   The securities are nonvoting preferred stock.

    b.   The sale or offer to sell the securities is made by a person other than an issuer, underwriter, or dealer.

    c.   The securities are AAA-rated debentures that are collateralized by first mortgages on property that has a value of 200% of the offering price.

    d.   The issuing corporation was closely held prior to the offering.

34. Donn & Co. is considering the sale of $11 million of its common stock to the public in interstate commerce. In this connection, Donn has been correctly advised that registration of the securities with the SEC is

    a.   Not required if the states in which the securities are to be sold have securities acts modeled after the federal act and Donn files in those states.

    b.   Required in that it is necessary for the SEC to approve the merits of the securities offered.

    c.   Not required if the securities are to be sold through a registered brokerage firm.

    d.   Required and must include audited financial statements as an integral part of its registration.

35. Regulation D under the Securities Act of 1933

    a.   Eliminates all small offerings made pursuant to Regulation A of the Securities Act of 1933.

    b.   Permits an exempt offering by a corporation even though it is a "reporting" corporation under the Securities Exchange Act of 1934.

    c.   Is limited to offers and sales of common stock which do **not** exceed $5 million.

    d.   Is exclusively available to "small business corporations" as defined by Regulation D.

36. Under the Securities Act of 1933, an initial offering of securities must be registered with the SEC, unless

    a.   The offering is made through the broker-dealer licensed in the states in which the securities are to be sold.

    b.   The offering prospectus makes a fair and full disclosure of all risks associated with purchasing the securities.

    c.   The issuer's financial condition meets certain standards established by the SEC.

    d.   The type of security or the offering involved is exempt from registration.

37. Under the Securities Act of 1933, which of the following securities must be registered?

    a.   Bonds of a railroad corporation.

    b.   Common stock of an insurance corporation.

    c.   Preferred stock of a domestic bank corporation.

    d.   Long-term notes of a charitable corporation.

38. Universal Corp. intends to sell its common stock to the public in an interstate offering that will be registered under the Securities Act of 1933. Under the Act,

    a.   Universal can make offers to sell its stock before filing a registration statement, provided that it does **not** actually issue stock certificates until after the registration is effective.

    b.   Universal's registration statement become effective at the time it is filed, assuming the SEC does **not** object within twenty days thereafter.

    c.   A prospectus must be delivered to each purchaser of Universal's common stock unless the purchaser qualifies as an accredited investor.

    d.   Universal's filing of a registration statement with the SEC does **not** automatically result in compliance with the "blue-sky" laws of the states in which the offering will be made.

39. Taso Limited Partnership intends to offer $400,000 of its limited partnership interests under Rule 504 of Regulation D of the Securities Act of 1933. Which of the following statements is correct?

    a.   The exemption under Rule 504 is **not** available to an issuer of limited partnership interests.

b. The limited partnership interests may be sold only to accredited investors.

c. The total number of nonaccredited investors who purchase the limited partnership interests may **not** exceed 35.

d. The resale of the limited partnership interest by a purchaser generally will be restricted.

40. For an offering to be exempt under Regulation D of the Securities Act of 1933, Rules 504, 505, and 506 each require that

a. There be a maximum of thirty-five unaccredited investors.

b. All purchasers receive the issuer's financial information.

c. The SEC be notified within ten days of the first sale.

d. The offering be made without general advertising.

41. The following instrument has been received by your client:

March 1, 2001

To: Bill Souther
    Rural Route 1
    Waverly, Iowa

Pay to the order of James Olson six hundred dollars.

Robert Smythe

Robert Smythe

Which of the following is correct?

a. The instrument is payable on demand.

b. The instrument is a negotiable note.

c. As Bill Souther is the drawer, he is primarily liable on the instrument.

d. As Bill Souther is the drawee, he is secondarily liable on the instrument.

42. Which of the following provisions contained in an otherwise negotiable instrument will cause it to be nonnegotiable?

a. It is payable in Mexican pesos.

b. It contains an unrestricted acceleration clause.

c. It grants to the holder an option to purchase land.

d. It is limited to payment out of the entire assets of a partnership.

43. To the extent that a holder of a negotiable promissory note is a holder in due course, s/he takes the note free from which of the following defenses?

a. Minority of the maker where it is a defense to enforcement of a contract.

b. Forgery of the maker's signature.

c. Nonperformance of a condition precedent.

d. Discharge of the maker in bankruptcy.

44. The status of a holder in due course as opposed to a mere holder of a negotiable instrument

a. Is of little consequence as a practical matter.

b. Eliminates the necessity of making due presentment or giving notice of dishonor.

c. Allows the holder in due course to overcome certain defenses that **cannot** be overcome by a mere holder.

d. Allows the further negotiation of the instrument.

45. In order to negotiate bearer paper, one must

a. Endorse the paper.

b. Endorse and deliver the paper with consideration.

c. Deliver the paper.

d. Deliver and endorse the paper.

46. Wilson Corporation entered into a contract to sell goods to Margin who has a place of business in the same town as Wilson. The contract was clear with respect to price and quantity, but failed to designate the place of delivery. Which of the following statements is correct?

a. The contract is unenforceable because of indefiniteness.

b. The place for delivery must be designated by the parties within five days or the contact is voidable.

c. The seller's place of business is the proper place for delivery.

d. The buyer's place of business is the proper place for delivery.

47. Wills, engaged in the business of selling appliances, borrowed $5,000 from Hart on January 20, 2001. Wills executed a promissory note for that amount and pledged all of his customer installment receivables as collateral for the loan. Wills executed a security agreement that described the collateral, but Hart did not file a financing statement. With respect to this transaction

a. The UCC Article on Secured Transactions does **not** apply because Hart failed to file a financing statement.

b. Attachment of the security interest did **not** occur because Hart failed to file a financing statement.

c. Attachment of the security interest took place when Wills executed the security agreement.

d. Perfection of the security interest occurred despite Hart's failure to file a financing statement.

48. The UCC establishes the rights of a secured creditor of a merchant in relation to various types of third parties. Regarding these third parties, which of the following is most likely to have an interest superior to that of a secured party who has a prior perfected security interest?

a. Purchasers from the merchant in the ordinary course of business.

b. General creditors of the merchant.

c. Lien creditors of the merchant.

d. Trustee in bankruptcy.

49. On June 3, Muni Finance loaned Page Corp. $20,000 to purchase four computers for use in Page's trucking business. Page contemporaneously executed a promissory note and security agreement. On June 7, Page purchased the computers with the $20,000, obtaining possession that same day. On June 10, Mort, a judgment creditor of Page, levied on the computers.

If Muni files a financing statement on June 11, which of the parties will have a priority security interest in the computers?

a. Mort, since he lacked notice of Muni's security interest.

b. Mort, since Muni failed to file before Mort levied on the computers.

c. Muni, since its security interest was perfected within the permissible time limits.

d. Muni, since its security interest was automatically perfected upon attachment.

50. Which of the following requirements is **not** necessary in order to have a security interest attach?
- a. There must be a proper filing.
- b. Value must be given by the creditor.
- c. Either the creditor must take possession or the debtor must sign a security agreement that describes the collateral.
- d. The debtor must have rights in the collateral.

Items 51 and 52 are based on the following information:

Abel, Boyd, and Cox are relatives who own a parcel of undeveloped land as joint tenants with right of survivorship. Abel sold his interest in the land to Zahn.

51. As a result of the sale from Abel to Zahn
- a. Zahn will acquire a 1/3 interest in the land as a joint tenant.
- b. Zahn will acquire a 1/3 interest in the land as tenant in common.
- c. Boyd and Cox will each own a 1/3 interest in the land as tenants in common.
- d. Boyd and Cox must consent before Zahn will acquire any interest in the land.

52. If both Boyd and Zahn die, which of the following is correct with respect to the ownership of the land?
- a. Cox and Zahn's heirs are tenants in common with ownership interest as follows: Cox 2/3 and Zahn's heirs 1/3.
- b. Cox and Zahn's heirs are joint tenants with ownership interests as follows: Cox 2/3 and Zahn's heirs 1/3.
- c. Cox, Boyd's heirs, and Zahn's heirs each own a 1/3 interest as tenants in common.
- d. Cox owns the entire interest.

53. In general, which of the following statements is correct with respect to a real estate mortgage?
- a. The mortgage must be in writing and signed by both the mortgagor (borrower) and mortgagee (lender).
- b. The mortgagee may assign the mortgage to a third party without the mortgagor's consent.
- c. The mortgagee need **not** contain a description of the real estate covered by the mortgage.
- d. The mortgage must contain the actual amount of the underlying debt and the rate of interest.

54. Golden sold his moving and warehouse business, including all the personal and real property used therein, to Clark Van Lines, Inc. The real property was encumbered by a duly recorded $300,000 first mortgage upon which Golden was personally liable. Clark acquired the property subject to the mortgage but did not assume the mortgage. Two years later, when the outstanding mortgage was $260,000, Clark decided to abandon the business location because it had become unprofitable and the value of the real property was less than the outstanding mortgage. Clark moved to another location and refused to pay the installments due on the mortgage. What is the legal status of the parties in regard to the mortgage?
- a. Clark took the real property free of the mortgage.
- b. Clark breached its contract with Golden when it abandoned the location and defaulted on the mortgage.

- c. Golden must satisfy the mortgage debt in the event that foreclosure yields an amount less than the unpaid balance.
- d. If Golden pays off the mortgage, he will be able to successfully sue Clark because Golden is subrogated to the mortgagee's rights against Clark.

55. Which of the following statements is correct with respect to the real estate mortgage?
- a. It must be signed only by the mortgagor (borrower).
- b. It must be recorded in order to be effective between the mortgagor and mortgagee.
- c. It does **not** have to be recorded to be effective against third parties without notice if it is a purchase money mortgage.
- d. It is effective even if **not** delivered to the mortgagee.

56. Farber sold his house to Ronald. Ronald agreed among other things to pay the existing mortgage on the house. The Safety Bank, which held the mortgage, released Farber from liability on the debt. The above described transactions (relating to the mortgage debt) is
- a. Invalid in that the bank did not receive any additional consideration from Farber.
- b. Not a release of Farber if Ronald defaults, and the proceeds from the sale of the mortgaged house are insufficient to satisfy the debt.
- c. A novation.
- d. A delegation.

57. Mack & Watts, CPAs, wishes to relocate its office. Its existing lease is for four years, with one year remaining. Its landlord is not agreeable to canceling the lease. The lease also prohibits a sublease without the landlord's consent but is silent as to an assignment. Mack & Watts has found a financially responsible and respectable prospective subtenant but is convinced that the landlord will not consent to a sublease. Which of the following statements is correct?
- a. A sublease without the landlord's consent would **not** be a breach of the lease.
- b. As assignment by Mack & Watts would be a breach of the lease.
- c. An assignment by Mack & Watts would **not** relieve it of liability under the lease.
- d. A sublease with the landlord's consent would relieve Mack & Watts of liability under the lease.

58. Vance obtained a twenty-five-year leasehold interest in an office building from the owner, Stanfield.
- a. Vance's interest is nonassignable.
- b. The conveyance of the ownership of the building by Stanfield to Wax will terminate Vance's leasehold interest.
- c. Stanfield's death will not terminate Vance's leasehold interest.
- d. Vance's death will terminate the leasehold interest.

59. The insurable interest requirement with regard to property insurance
- a. May be waived by a writing signed by the insured and insurer.

b. May be satisfied by a person other than the legal owner of the property.

c. Must be satisfied at the time the policy is issued.

d. Must be satisfied by the insured's legal title to the property at the time of loss.

60. Margo, Inc. insured its property against fire with two separate insurance companies, Excelsior and Wilberforce. Each carrier insured the property for its full value, and neither insurer was aware that the other had also insured the property. The policies were the standard fire insurance policies used throughout the United States. If the property is totally destroyed by fire, how much will Margo recover?

a. Nothing because Margo has engaged in an illegal gambling venture.

b. The full amount from both insurers.

c. A ratable or pro rata share from each insurer, not to exceed the value of the property insured.

d. Only 80% of the value of the property from each insurer because of the standard coinsurance clause.

Number 2

The law of sales governs contracts for the sale of goods. **Items 101 through 110** are related to the topic of sales transactions.

Required:

Both of the lettered statements of fact below are followed by numbered sentences that state legal conclusions relating to those facts. Determine whether each legal conclusion is correct or incorrect. If the conclusion is correct, indicate your agreement with the legal conclusion by blackening the corresponding "yes" oval on the Objective Answer Sheet (not provided in this Sample Exam). If the conclusion is incorrect, blacken the corresponding "no" oval on the Objective Answer Sheet.

Part a.

On January 2, 2000, West Electronics unconditionally offered in writing to sell a new stereo to Young for $450. Young replied in writing.

101. If West had referred to a reasonable price, in lieu of $450, the offer would be too indefinite to create a power of acceptance in Young.

102. In lieu of an offer of $450, if West had provided that the price was to be set by a third person, its offer would be too indefinite to create a power of acceptance in Young.

103. If West's offer is effective, Young's reply of "I will pay $350" constitutes an acceptance.

104. If West's offer stated that Young must accept on or before January 20, 2000, West could withdraw the offer prior to that time.

105. If West's offer failed to state the time within which it could be accepted, West could not withdraw the offer before the expiration of a reasonable period of time.

106. If Young paid $10 to West for a written option exercisable for thirty days to purchase the system, West may withdraw the offer only by a written communication to Young.

Part b.

Albert orally ordered a $600 standard model television for his home from Mastercraft Appliances. Mastercraft accepted the order and later sent Albert a purchase memorandum in duplicate with a request that Albert sign and return one copy. Albert did not sign or return the purchase memorandum and he refused to accept the television. Mastercraft sued and Albert asserted the Statute of Frauds as a defense.

107. The purchase memorandum sent by Mastercraft will be sufficient to defeat Albert's reliance on the Statute of Frauds.

108. If Albert admits in court to making the oral contract, the contract will be enforceable.

109. A purchase memorandum will be insufficient to satisfy the Statute of Frauds if it omits any of the terms agreed to by the parties.

110. A writing sufficient to satisfy the Statute of Frauds would not be necessary if Albert had received and accepted the television.

Number 3

A partnership involves an association between two or more persons to carry on a business as co-owners for profit. **Items 111 through 120** relate to partnership arrangements.

Required:

Both of the lettered statements of fact below are followed by numbered sentences that state legal conclusions relating to those facts. Determine whether each legal conclusion is correct or incorrect. If the conclusion is correct, indicate your agreement with the legal conclusion by blackening the corresponding "yes" oval on the Objective Answer Sheet. If the conclusion is incorrect, blacken the corresponding "no" on the Objective Answer Sheet.

Part a.

Adams, Webster, and Coke were partners in the construction business. Coke decided to retire and found Black who agreed to purchase his interest. Black was willing to pay Coke $20,000 and promise to assume Coke's share of all firm obligations.

111. Unless the partners agree to admit Black as a partner, he could not become a member of the firm.

112. The retirement of Coke would cause a dissolution of the firm.

113. The firm creditors are third-party beneficiaries of Black's promise to Coke.

114. Coke would be released from all liability for firm debts if his interest were purchased by Black and Black promised to pay Coke's share of firm debts.

115. If the other partners refused to accept Black as a partner, Coke could retire, thereby causing a dissolution.

Part b.

Carson, Crocket, and Kitt were partners in the importing business. They needed additional capital to expand and located an investor named White who agreed to purchase a one-quarter interest in the Partnership by contributing $50,000 in capital to the Partnership. At the time he became a partner there were several large creditors who had previously loaned money to the Partnership. The Partnership subsequently failed and the creditors are attempting to asset personal liability against White.

116. White is personally liable on all firm debts contracted subsequent to his entry into the firm.

117. Creditors of the first partnership automatically become creditors of the new partnership continuing the business.

118. Creditors of the old firm that existed prior to White's entry can assert rights against his capital contribution.

119. White has personal liability for firm debts existing prior to his entry into the firm.

120. White must remain in the partnership for at least one year.

Number 4

a.   Craig Manufacturing Company needed an additional supply of water for its plant. Consequently, Craig advertised for bids. Shaw Drilling Company submitted the lowest bid and was engaged to drill a well. After a contract had been executed and drilling begun, Shaw discovered that the consistency of the soil was much harder than had been previously encountered in the surrounding countryside. In addition, there was an unexpected layer of bedrock. These facts, unknown to both Craig and Shaw when the contract was signed, significantly increased the cost of performing the contract. Therefore, Shaw announced its intention to abandon performance unless it was assured of recovering its cost. Craig agreed in writing to pay the amount of additional cost if Shaw would continue to drill and complete the contract. Shaw, on the strength of this written promise, completed the job. The additional cost amount to $10,000 which Shaw now seeks to recover. Craig refuses to pay and asserts that the additional burden was a part of the risk assumed and that the only reason it agreed to pay the additional amount was that it needed the additional water supply on time as agreed.

Shaw has commenced legal action to recover the $10,000 in dispute. Craig denies liability.

Required:

Answer the following, setting forth reasons for any conclusions stated.

What is the legal liability of Craig as a result of the facts described above?

b.   Ogilvie is a wealthy, prominent citizen of Clarion County. Most of his activities and his properties are located in Vista City, the county seat. Among his holdings are large tracts of farmland located in the outlying parts of Clarion. He has not personally examined large portions of his holdings due to the distance factor and the time it would take. One of his agents told him that 95% of the land was fertile and could be used for general farming.

Farber, a recent college graduate who inherited a modest amount of money, decided to invest in farmland and raise avocados. He had read certain advertising literature extolling the virtues of avocado farming as an investment. He called upon Ogilvie and discussed the purchase of his land. In the process, Ogilvie praised his land as a great investment for the future. He stated that the land was virtually all splendid farmland and that it would be suitable for avocado growing. Farber entered into a contract of purchase and made a deposit of 10% on the purchase price.

On the eve of the closing, Farber learned of the presence of extensive rock formations at or near the surface of the land. These rock formations make avocado growing virtually impossible but still permit limited use for some other types of farming. These rock formations are partially visible and could have been seen if Farber had examined the property. They cover approximately 25% of the land.

Accordingly, Farber refused to perform the original contract and demanded that the unsuitable 25% of the land be severed from the contract and the price diminished accordingly.

Ogilvie asserted that "a contract is a contract" and that the doctrine of caveat emptor is applicable in the sale of land. Specifically, he stated that he committed no fraud because

1. Nothing he said was a statement of fact. It was opinion or puffing.
2. His statement was not material since most of the land is okay, and the balance can be used for some types of farming.
3. He had not lied since he had no knowledge of the falsity of his statements.
4. Farber could have and should have inspected and by failing to do so he was negligent and cannot recover.

Farber then commenced legal proceedings against Ogilvie based on fraud.

Required:

Answer the following, setting forth reasons for any conclusions stated.

In separate paragraphs, discuss the validity of each of Ogilvie's four assertions that he committed no fraud.

Number 5

Ultra Corporation is engaged in the metal stamping business. On March 2, 2001, it filed a voluntary petition in bankruptcy seeking relief in the form of a liquidation of the business pursuant to Chapter 7 of the Bankruptcy Code. A trustee was appointed on March 10, 2001, and has commenced amassing the debtor's property. Much of Ultra's property was leased from various third parties. One of Ultra's punch presses was rented from Van Equipment Rental and Sales Corporation under a forty-month lease arrangement. The lease was heavily front loaded and provided for purchase of the punch press for $100 upon expiration of the lease. The fair market value of the punch press at the expiration of the lease is estimated at $4,500. Van failed to file a financing statement or its equivalent with respect to this lease. In addition, Ultra has a fifteen-year lease on a warehouse that has thirteen years of its term remaining. Payments on the lease are current. Dann Corp. has offered to assume all obligations under the warehouse lease and to pay Ultra $8,000 for an assignment of that lease. There is no applicable state law affecting such an assignment and the lease itself is silent in this regard. Specifically, the trustee in bankruptcy asserts that

• The punch press lease is in essence a secured installment sale contract for which Van has an unperfected security interest, and therefore, the punch press should be included in the bankruptcy estate.

• As trustee, she has the right to assume and assign to Dann Corp. the warehouse lease and include the $8,000 in the bankruptcy estate.

Required:

Answer the following, setting forth reasons for any conclusions stated.

a. What rights does a trustee in bankruptcy have regarding property leased by a debtor?

b. Are the trustee's assertions concerning the punch press lease and the warehouse lease correct?

ANSWERS TO SAMPLE EXAMINATION
BUSINESS LAW AND PROFESSIONAL RESPONSIBILITIES

Answer 1

1.	a	11.	c	21.	b	31.	a	41.	a	51.	b
2.	d	12.	c	22.	b	32.	c	42.	c	52.	a
3.	c	13.	d	23.	b	33.	b	43.	c	53.	b
4.	d	14.	b	24.	d	34.	d	44.	c	54.	c
5.	d	15.	a	25.	a	35.	b	45.	c	55.	a
6.	a	16.	b	26.	b	36.	d	46.	c	56.	c
7.	b	17.	b	27.	d	37.	b	47.	c	57.	c
8.	d	18.	a	28.	d	38.	d	48.	a	58.	c
9.	d	19.	b	29.	b	39.	d	49.	c	59.	b
10.	d	20.	b	30.	b	40.	d	50.	a	60.	c

Hints for Multiple-Choice Questions

1. A member's dependent child is held to the same standards of independence as the member.

2. In which situation may the client influence or appear to influence the auditor's opinion?

3. Review the definition of negligence.

4. Safe is a foreseeable third party, to whom the accountant is generally not liable.

5. The CPA is generally liable for gross negligence, fraud, and constructive fraud to all third parties who can prove it.

6. Lack of privity is not relevant for actions based on gross negligence or fraud.

7. Review the definition of scienter.

8. Privity of contract is not required for a common law action based on fraud.

9. Contributory negligence of the client is not a defense available to the accountant in cases of fraud, constructive fraud, or gross negligence.

10. A contract for personal services is generally not delegable.

11. The omission must be a fact that would influence the judgment or decision of an average prudent investor.

12. The intrastate business of the client, not the CPA firm, affects security laws applicability.

13. The plaintiff must have incurred damages.

14. The accountant-client privilege is recognized in only a few states.

15. An implied-in-fact contract is formed by conduct implying assent to its terms.

16. Gem must know the terms of the contract to effectively ratify.

17. A third party may hold either the principal or agent liable when the principal is undisclosed or partially disclosed.

18. If the agency relationship is terminated by an operation of law, no notice need be given to third parties. Which is an operation of law?

19. As assignment of a partnership interest conveys only the right to share in profits and return of contribution on dissolution.

20. Unless specified otherwise, partnership profits and losses are divided equally.

21. At least one general partner with unlimited personal liability and at least one limited partner are required for a limited partnership.

22. If partners agree on unequal division of profits but are silent on losses, losses are allocated per profit sharing proportions.

23. Which receipt has no effect on the number of shares owned by a trust?

24. The trustee owes the duty of loyalty to trust beneficiaries and the duty of care in administering the trust.

25. A mortgagor has certain rights and obligations even if a foreclosure of a purchase money mortgage by judicial sale occurs.

26. The employer and employee generally contribute equally to FICA.

27. Only the employer contributes to FUTA.

28. CERCLA is very comprehensive as to which parties are liable.

29. The resale of securities sold under Regulation D must be restricted, or else the exemption is lost.

30. Limited partnership interests are securities subject to the Securities Act of 1933.

31. Exempt securities and transactions are still subject to the anti-fraud provisions of the act.

32. Securities need not be traded on an organized exchange or meet registration requirements to be subject to the Securities Act of 1934.

33. None of these are exempt securities; which one is an exempt transaction?

34. The SEC does not evaluate the merits or value of securities.

35. Rule 506 under Regulation D pertains to the private placement of any **unlimited** amount of securities.

36. The Securities Act of 1933 exempts certain securities and transactions from its registration requirements.

37. Review the securities exempt from the registration requirements of the Securities Act of 1933.

38. A company may **not** sell securities prior to the effective registration date, which is generally twenty days

after the filing, provided the SEC requires no amendments.

39. No requirements concerning the number or accreditation of investors exist under Rule 504.

40. Securities sold pursuant to Regulation D involve smaller amounts of money or are made in a limited manner, and general advertising or solicitation is not permitted.

41. Bill Souther is the drawee, and has no contractual liability on the draft until he accepts it, which would make him primarily liable.

42. A negotiable instrument must state a fixed amount of money, without need to refer to other sources. Which provision is of an indeterminable value?

43. A holder in due course takes a negotiable instrument free of personal defenses. Which of these is a personal defense?

44. An ordinary holder has the same rights as an assignee, who cannot obtain any greater rights than the assigner had to convey.

45. Bearer paper, unlike order paper, does not require endorsement.

46. A contract will not fail for indefiniteness if the place of delivery is left open.

47. In this example, perfection requires filing.

48. Buyers in the ordinary course of business take goods free of **any** security interest, perfected or not, known by the buyer or not.

49. A secured party with a purchase money security has a grace period in which to file, which is ten days after the debtor receives the collateral.

50. One of these is a method of perfection, but not attachment.

51. If rights in joint tenancy property are conveyed without assent of other joint tenants, the new owner becomes a tenant in common.

52. Boyd's interest as a joint tenant would pass to the surviving joint tenant (Cox), and Zahn's interest would pass to Zahn's heirs.

53. A mortgage need only be signed by the party to be bound.

54. If a buyer takes property "subject to" a mortgage, the buyer accepts no liability for the mortgage and the seller is still primarily liable.

55. A mortgage is effective even without recording.

56. Farber is no longer liable; a new contract is in effect.

57. If no novation or release occurs, the assignor (lessee) is still liable to the lessor.

58. The death of the lessor generally does **not** terminate the lease; the death of the lessee **does** terminate the lease except when the lease covers a period of years.

59. Can a party other than the property owner have both the legal interest and the possibility of pecuniary loss required for an insurable interest in property?

60. The coinsurance clause does not apply to totally destroyed insured property.

Answer 2

101. N	103. N	105. N	107. N	109. N
102. N	104. Y	106. N	108. Y	110. Y

Hints for Other Objective Answer Format Questions

101. Open or uncertain terms will not cause a contract to fail for indefiniteness if the parties intended to form a contract and a reasonable basis for supplying a remedy can be found.

102. Open or uncertain terms will not cause a contract to fail for indefiniteness if the parties intended to form a contract and a reasonable basis for supplying a remedy can be found.

103. Young's statement changes the terms of the original offer, forming a counteroffer.

104. This is not a firm offer.

105. This is not a firm offer.

106. An offer under an option contract is irrevocable during the specified time period.

107. A writing subject to the Statute of Frauds must contain the signature of the party to be charged to be effective.

108. An oral contract is enforceable when the party seeking avoidance admits to the contract in court.

109. The Statute of Frauds requires only a writing sufficient to evidence the existence of a contract, signed by the party to be charged, indicating the quantity of goods involved.

110. Delivery and acceptance validated the contract, even if the writing does not satisfy the Statute of Frauds.

Answer 3

111. Y	113. Y	115. Y	117. Y	119. N
112. Y	114. N	116. Y	118. Y	120. N

Hints for Other Objective Answer Format Questions

111. The admission of a new partner requires the consent of all existing partners.

112. The withdrawal of a partner causes the dissolution of the partnership.

113. A third-party beneficiary is not a party to a contract, but is a beneficiary of it.

114. The liability of a withdrawing partner may be limited by an agreement between the partners, but that agreement is not binding on third parties unless they join in on the agreement.

115. A partner may retire at any time if there is no specified term of existence for the partnership.

116. The key word here is subsequent.

117. Continuation of the partnership after dissolution does not release the new partnership from liability for the old partnership's debts.

118. White is liable for firm debts prior to his entry **only** to the extent of his capital contribution.

119. White is liable for firm debts prior to his entry **only** to the extent of his capital contribution.

120. A partner may retire at any time if there is no specified term of existence for the partnership.

Answer 4

a. The described fact situation deals with the sale of services, not the sale of goods. Consequently, the common law, not the Uniform Commercial Code applies. The general rule under common law is that a modification of an existing contract needs new consideration before it is binding. Shaw gave no additional consideration for Craig's promise to bear the additional cost. Thus, normally Craig would not be liable for the additional $10,000 because Shaw is merely promising to complete the well in the modification which he was already obligated to do under the original contract (i.e., a preexisting legal duty).

However, recently, several courts have recognized an exception to this rule, with regard to construction contracts, even under common law. The exception relates to the situation where one party upon beginning performance discovers a substantial difficulty that is unforeseen and not in the contemplation of the parties at the time of contracting. If this situation is present, these courts allow enforcement of the modification even though there is no new consideration. This exception would apply in the given fact situation, since Shaw Drilling Company discovered a substantially harder soil consistency than was expected and initially contemplated by both Shaw and Craig at the time of contracting. Therefore, Craig's promise to pay the additional money to Shaw falls within the exception and would be enforceable in courts that recognize this exception, thusly resulting in Craig's liability for the additional cost of $10,000.

b. Ogilvie's first assertion is valid. Since Ogilvie is the seller of real property, many of his statements could be construed to be opinion and "puffing" in an attempt to promote the sale of his land. But Ogilvie did engage in a statement of fact when he stated that the land was suitable for avocado growing. This is a representation that is definite, objective, and verifiable. Since the land was not suitable for avocado growing, Ogilvie's statement was false. Therefore, the first requirement for establishing fraud, a misstatement of fact, has been met.

Ogilvie's second assertion that his statements were not material is also invalid. In determining the materiality of a representation, courts look to the impression made upon the mind of the party to whom it was made. The representation must relate to something of sufficient substance to induce reliance. Since Farber purchased the land for the exclusive use of growing avocados, Ogilvie's representation that the land was suitable for avocado growing was material in nature.

Ogilvie's third assertion that he had not lied is invalid. Ogilvie had not personally examined the farmland in question, so he apparently had little basis for making the representations he made. But this lack of knowledge of the facts does not excuse Ogilvie. A party has imputed knowledge (thereby satisfying the knowledge requirement necessary to establish fraud) if s/he makes the representations negligently, with a reckless disregard and indifference as to their truthfulness. Many courts have imputed such knowledge to a party, such as Ogilvie, and have held him responsible where the means of his knowledge was such as to make it his duty to know the truth or falsity of his representations. Ogilvie, who represents something as being based on his own knowledge, but who is in fact completely ignorant of the subject, is treated in the law as knowingly making a false statement, thereby satisfying the scienter (knowledge) requirement of establishing fraud.

The final assertion deals with the reliance requirement necessary to establish fraud. Ogilvie asserts that Farber cannot justifiably rely on Ogilvie's representations, since if Farber would have inspected the land he would have discovered the rock formations. Normally, where the accuracy of the seller's statements can be verified, and it would be feasible to do so, justifiable reliance requires such verification. But in this fact situation, the seller was unable to personally examine the land due to the distance factor and the time it would take. Therefore, the buyer cannot be expected to do something that the seller did not do. To allow Ogilvie's assertion to be a valid defense would result in the promotion of engaging in fraud, because a person who makes a misrepresentation with intent to induce action could simply state that the buyer should have looked for him/herself.

Answer 5

a. The legal effect of the filing of a bankruptcy petition on a debtor's leases permits a bankruptcy trustee to

1. Assume and retain the debtor's leases, or
2. Assume and assign such leases, or
3. Reject the debtor's leases.

A trustee's assumption or rejection of a lease is subject to court approval. In a Chapter 7 case, a lease is deemed rejected by operation of law unless it is assumed by the trustee within sixty days after the order for relief.

b. The trustee's first assertion with regard to the punch press lease is correct. Where the agreement entered into between the parties is a true lease and not a disguised secured installment sales contract, the subject matter of the lease will not be included in the bankruptcy estate.

Whether a lease is intended as security and thereby treated as a secured installment sales contract is determined by the facts of each case. The inclusion of an option to purchase does not, of itself, make the lease one intended as security. However, where by the terms of the lease the lessee will become, or has the option to become, the owner of the property for no additional consideration or for a nominal consideration, the lease is likely one intended for security.

Under the facts of our case, the option to purchase the punch press for $100 at the expiration of the lease would be deemed nominal consideration since the fair market value of the punch press at the time is estimated at $4,500. Thus, the lease is one intended as security and a security interest arises. In order for Van to perfect its security interest it must file a financing statement. In this case, Van did not file a financing statement or its equivalent and thus, Van has an unperfected security interest in the punch press.

The UCC Article on Secured Transactions states that an unperfected security interest is subordinate to a person who becomes a lien creditor before the security interest is perfected. It defines, in part, a lien creditor as a trustee in bankruptcy from the date of the filing of the bankruptcy petition. In addition, the Bankruptcy Code gives the trustee in bankruptcy the power to avoid any transfer of property of the debtor that under nonbankruptcy law is voidable as to a creditor who extended credit and obtained a judicial lien on the date of the filing of the bankruptcy petition. Even though the UCC uses the term subordinate instead of voidable, a security interest that would be subordinate to a creditor that obtained a judicial lien on the date of the filing of the bankruptcy petition is voidable by the trustee. Thus, Van's unperfected security interest may be avoided by the trustee in bankruptcy and the punch press should be included in the debtor's estate in bankruptcy.

The trustee's second assertion is correct. Since there is no applicable state law affecting such an assignment and the lease itself is silent in this regard, the trustee may assume and assign the lease. In this case, the warehouse lease has a substantial value to other potential lessees and therefore, due to the favorable circumstances indicated, commands a substantial premium of $8,000. The debtor's estate in bankruptcy will receive this upon assignment (sale) of the lease to Dann.

APPENDIX B

AICPA Summary of Coverage (Last 6 Exams) from
Business Law and Professional Responsibilities (LPR) Section of
Uniform CPA Examination[1]

Summary of Exam Coverage—May 1999 through November 2001 Uniform CPA Examinations

The following summary of coverage provides an analysis of the Content Specification Outline coverage for the May 1999 through November 2001 LPR Sections of the Uniform CPA Examinations. This summary is intended only as a study aid and should not be used to predict the content of future Examinations.

How to Interpret This Table

The percentages on the second line of the table indicate the percentage points allocated to each type of question on these Examinations. For example, on the May 1999 Business Law and Professional Responsibilities section (LPR), 60% of the examination points were allocated to multiple-choice questions, 20% of the points were allocated to other objective answer format (OOAF), and 20% of the points were allocated to the essays.

The AICPA has also provided the **actual number** of multiple-choice questions asked for each area (identified with roman numerals) and topic (identified with an uppercase letter) of the content specification outlines (e.g., for the May 1999 Examination under I., the Professional and Legal Responsibilities area of LPR, there were fifteen multiple-choice questions asked; of those, three dealt with A., the Code of Professional Conduct topic). In addition, the AICPA has also indicated the **percentage** of OOAF and essay questions asked by area and topic.

---

[1] *These Content Specification Outlines were published in **Selected Questions and Unofficial Answers Supplement Indexed to Content Specification Outlines** (2001 Edition); reprinted with permission of the AICPA.*

Business Law & Professional Responsibilities	Multiple-Choice N01	M01	N00	M00	N99	M99	OOAFs N01	M01	N00	M00	N99	M99	Essays N01	M01	N00	M00	N99	M99
	60 (60%)	60 (60%)	60 (60%)	60 (60%)	60 (60%)	60 (60%)	20%	20%	20%	20%	20%	20%	20%	20%	20%	20%	20%	20%
I. Professional and Legal Responsibilities	5	15	15	5	15	15	10%		0%	0%	0%	0%	0%		0%	10%	0%	0%
A. Code of Professional Conduct					3	3												
B. Proficiency, Independence, and Due Care					3	3												
C. Responsibilities in Other Professional Services					3	3												
D. Disciplinary Systems Imposed by the Profession and State Regulatory Bodies					1	0												
E. Common Law Liability to Clients and Third Parties					1	3												
F. Federal Statutory Liability					1	3												
G. Privileged Communications and Confidentiality					1	0												
H. Responsibilities of CPAs in Business and Industry, and in the Public Sector					2	0												
II. Business Organizations	15	10	10	10	10	10	5%	10%	10%	10%	0%	10%	10%	10%	0%	0%	10%	0%
A. Agency					5	5												
B. Partnership, Joint Ventures, and Other Unincorporated Associations					0	0						5%					7%	
C. Corporations					0	0						5%					3%	
D. Estates and Trusts					5	5												
III. Contracts	10	10	0	10	0	0	10%	10%	10%	0%	0%	10%	10%		0%	0%	10%	0%
A. Formation					0	0												
B. Performance					0	0												
C. Third-Party Assignments					0	0												
D. Discharge, Breach, and Remedies					0	0												

Business Law & Professional Responsibilities	Multiple-Choice						OOAFs						Essays					
	N01	M01	N00	M00	N99	M99	N01	M01	N00	M00	N99	M99	N01	M01	N00	M00	N99	M99
IV. Debtor-Creditor Relationships	10	10	10	5	10	10			0%	5%	0%	0%			0%	0%	0%	0%
A. Rights, Duties, and Liabilities of Debtors and Creditors					0	1												
B. Rights, Duties, and Liabilities of Guarantors					4	4												
C. Bankruptcy					6	5												
V. Government Regulation of Business	15	10	5	15	5	15		5%	0%	0%	10%	0%			10%	0%	0%	0%
A. Federal Securities Acts					0	5					10%							
B. Employment Regulation					5	5												
C. Environmental Regulation					0	5												
VI. Uniform Commercial Code	15	10	20	5	20	0	5%		0%	5%	0%	0%		10%	0%	10%	0%	20%
A. Negotiable Instruments					7	0												10%
B. Sales					5	0												10%
C. Secured Transactions					5	0												
D. Documents of Title					3	0												
VII. Property	5	5	0	10	0	10	5%	5%	0%	0%	10%	0%	5%		10%	0%	0%	0%
A. Real Property Including Insurance					0	6					10%							
B. Personal Property Including Bailments and Computer Technology Rights					0	4												
C. Fire Insurance					0	0												